NEW PERSPECTIVES ON

HTML5 and CSS3
7th Edition

INTRODUCTORY

NEW PERSPECTIVES ON

HTML5 and CSS3

7th Edition

INTRODUCTORY

Patrick Carey

CENGAGE
Learning·

Australia • Brazil • Mexico • Singapore • United Kingdom • United States

New Perspectives on HTML5 and CSS3, 7th Edition, Introductory
Patrick Carey

Product Director: Kathleen McMahon

Senior Product Manager: Jim Gish

Senior Content Developer: Kate Mason

Sr. MQA Project Leader: Chris Scriver

Development Editor: Pam Conrad

Product Assistant: Abby Pufpaff

Marketing Managers: Stephanie Albrecht and Kristie Clark

Marketing Coordinator: William Giuliani

Senior Content Project Manager: Jennifer K. Feltri-George

Art Director: Diane Gibbons

Manufacturing Planner: Fola Orekoya

Senior IP Project Manager: Kathy Kucharek

IP Analyst: Amber Hill

Cover image(s): Shutterstock/AGCuesta

Compositor: GEX Publishing Services

Notice to the Reader

Publisher does not warrant or guarantee any of the products described herein or perform any independent analysis in connection with any of the product information contained herein. Publisher does not assume, and expressly disclaims, any obligation to obtain and include information other than that provided to it by the manufacturer. The reader is expressly warned to consider and adopt all safety precautions that might be indicated by the activities described herein and to avoid all potential hazards. By following the instructions contained herein, the reader willingly assumes all risks in connection with such instructions. The publisher makes no representations or warranties of any kind, including but not limited to, the warranties of fitness for particular purpose or merchantability, nor are any such representations implied with respect to the material set forth herein, and the publisher takes no responsibility with respect to such material. The publisher shall not be liable for any special, consequential, or exemplary damages resulting, in whole or part, from the readers' use of, or reliance upon, this material.

Library of Congress Control Number: 2015942192
ISBN: 978-1-305-57820-3

Cengage Learning
20 Channel Center Street
Boston, MA 02210
USA

Cengage Learning is a leading provider of customized learning solutions with office locations around the globe, including Singapore, the United Kingdom, Australia, Mexico, Brazil, and Japan. Locate your local office at: **www.cengage.com/global**

Cengage Learning products are represented in Canada by Nelson Education, Ltd.

For your course and learning solutions, visit **www.cengage.com**

Purchase any of our products at your local college store or at our preferred online store **www.cengagebrain.com**

Printed in the United States of America
Print Number: 01   Print Year: 2015

Preface

The New Perspectives Series' critical-thinking, problem-solving approach is the ideal way to prepare students to transcend point-and-click skills and take advantage of all that HTML5 and CSS3 has to offer.

In developing the New Perspectives Series, our goal was to create books that give students the software concepts and practical skills they need to succeed beyond the classroom. We've updated our proven case-based pedagogy with more practical content to make learning skills more meaningful to students. With the New Perspectives Series, students understand *why* they are learning *what* they are learning, and are fully prepared to apply their skills to real-life situations.

About This Book

This book provides thorough coverage of HTML5 and CSS3, and includes the following:
- Up-to-date coverage of using HTML5 to create structured websites
- Instruction on the most current CSS3 styles to create visually-interesting pages and captivating graphical designs
- Working with browser developer tools to aid in the creation and maintenance of fully-functioning websites

New for this edition!
- Coverage of responsive design techniques to create website designs that can scale to mobile, tablet, and desktop devices.
- Hands-on study of new HTML elements and CSS styles including layouts using flexboxes and grid frameworks.
- Exploration of CSS3 styles for graphic design, including image borders, drop shadows, gradient fills, 2D and 3D transformations, and graphic filters.

System Requirements

This book assumes that students have an Internet connection, a text editor, and a current browser that supports HTML5 and CSS3. The following is a list of the most recent versions of the major browsers at the time this text was published: Internet Explorer 11, Firefox 38.01, Safari 8, Opera 29.0, and Google Chrome 42. More recent versions may have come out since the publication of this book. Students should go to the Web browser home page to download the most current version. All browsers interpret HTML5 and CSS3 code in slightly different ways. It is highly recommended that students have several different browsers installed on their systems for comparison and, if possible, access to a mobile browser or a mobile emulator. Students might also want to run older versions of these browsers to highlight compatibility issues. The screenshots in this book were produced using Google Chrome 42 running on Windows 8.1 (64-bit), unless otherwise noted. If students are using different devices, browsers, or operating systems, their screens might vary from those shown in the book; this should not present any problems in completing the tutorials.

The New Perspectives Approach

Context

Each tutorial begins with a problem presented in a "real-world" case that is meaningful to students. The case sets the scene to help students understand what they will do in the tutorial.

Hands-on Approach

Each tutorial is divided into manageable sessions that combine reading and hands-on, step-by-step work. Colorful screenshots help guide students through the steps. **Trouble?** tips, which anticipate common mistakes or problems, help students stay on track and continue with the tutorial.

VISUAL OVERVIEW

Visual Overviews

Each session begins with a Visual Overview, a two-page spread that includes colorful, enlarged figures with numerous callouts and key term definitions, giving students a comprehensive preview of the topics covered in the session, as well as a handy study guide.

PROSKILLS

ProSkills Boxes

ProSkills boxes provide guidance for applying concepts to real-world, professional situations, involving one or more of the following soft skills: decision making, problem solving, teamwork, verbal communication, and written communication.

KEY STEP

Key Steps

Important steps are highlighted in yellow with attached margin notes to help students pay close attention to completing the steps correctly and avoid time-consuming rework.

INSIGHT

InSight Boxes

InSight boxes offer expert advice and best practices to help students achieve a deeper understanding of the concepts behind the software features and skills.

Margin Tips

Margin Tips provide helpful hints and shortcuts for more efficient use of the software. The Tips appear in the margin at key points throughout each tutorial, giving students extra information when and where they need it.

REVIEW
APPLY
CHALLENGE
CREATE

Assessment

Retention is a key component to learning. At the end of each session, a series of Quick Check questions helps students test their understanding of the material before moving on. Engaging end-of-tutorial Review Assignments and Case Problems have always been a hallmark feature of the New Perspectives Series. Colorful bars and brief descriptions accompany the exercises, making it easy to understand both the goal and level of challenge a particular assignment holds.

REFERENCE
GLOSSARY/INDEX

Reference

Within each tutorial, Reference boxes appear before a set of steps to provide a succinct summary or preview of how to perform a task. In addition, each book includes a combination Glossary/Index to promote easy reference of material.

Our Complete System of Instruction

Coverage To Meet Your Needs

Whether you're looking for just a small amount of coverage or enough to fill a semester-long class, we can provide you with a textbook that meets your needs.

- Introductory books contain an average of 5 to 8 tutorials and include essential skills on the books concepts.
- Comprehensive books, which cover additional concepts and skills in depth, are great for a full-semester class, and contain 9 to 12+ tutorials.

So, if you are looking for just the essential skills or more complete in-depth coverage of a topic, we probably another offering available. Go to our Web site or contact your Cengage Learning sales representative to find out what else we offer.

CourseCasts – Learning on the Go. Always available…always relevant.

Want to keep up with the latest technology trends relevant to you? Visit our site to find a library of podcasts, CourseCasts, featuring a "CourseCast of the Week," and download them to your mp3 player at http://coursecasts.course.com.

Our fast-paced world is driven by technology. You know because you're an active participant—always on the go, always keeping up with technological trends, and always learning new ways to embrace technology to power your life.

Ken Baldauf, host of CourseCasts, is a faculty member of the Florida State University Computer Science Department where he is responsible for teaching technology classes to thousands of FSU students each year. Ken is an expert in the latest technology trends; he gathers and sorts through the most pertinent news and information for CourseCasts so your students can spend their time enjoying technology, rather than trying to figure it out. Open or close your lecture with a discussion based on the latest CourseCast.

Visit us at http://coursecasts.course.com to learn on the go!

Instructor Resources

We offer more than just a book. We have all the tools you need to enhance your lectures, check students' work, and generate exams in a new, easier-to-use and completely revised package. This book's Instructor's Manual, Cognero testbank, PowerPoint presentations, data files, solution files, figure files, and a sample syllabus are all available at login.cengage/sso.

Acknowledgments

I would like to thank the people who worked so hard to make this book possible. Special thanks to my developmental editor, Pam Conrad, for her hard work, attention to detail, and valuable insights, and to Senior Content Developer, Kate Mason, who has worked tirelessly in overseeing this project and made my task so much easier with her enthusiasm and good humor. Other people at Cengage who deserve credit are Jim Gish, Sr. Product Manager; Kathy Finnegan, Sr. Content Developer; Abby Pufpaff, Product Assistant; Jen Feltri-George, Senior Content Project Manager; Diane Gibbons, Art Director; Fola Orekoya, Manufacturing Planner; Eric LaScola, Sr. Marketing Manager; William Giuliani, Marketing Coordinator; Kathryn Kucharek, Senior IP Project Manager; and GEX Publishing Services, Compositor, as well as Chris Scriver - Sr. MQA Project Leader, and the MQA testers Serge Palladino, John Freitas, and Danielle Shaw.

Feedback is an important part of writing any book, and thanks go to the following reviewers for their helpful ideas and comments: Alison Consol, Wake Technical Community College; Dana Hooper, The University of Alabama; Kenneth Kleiner, Fayetteville Technical Community College; and Laurie Crawford, Franklin University.

I want to thank my wife Joan and my six children for their love, encouragement, and patience in putting up with a sometimes distracted husband and father. This book is dedicated to Nicola Willie, who I am proud to welcome into our extended family.
– Patrick Carey

BRIEF CONTENTS

TABLE OF CONTENTS

OBJECTIVES

Session 1.1
- Explore the history of the web
- Create the structure of an HTML document
- Insert HTML elements and attributes
- Insert metadata into a document
- Define a page title

Session 1.2
- Mark page structures with sectioning elements
- Organize page content with grouping elements
- Mark content with text-level elements
- Insert inline images
- Insert symbols based on character codes

Session 1.3
- Mark content using lists
- Create a navigation list
- Link to files within a website with hypertext links
- Link to e-mail addresses and telephone numbers

Getting Started with HTML5

Creating a Website for a Food Vendor

Case | *Curbside Thai*

Sajja Adulet is the owner and master chef of Curbside Thai, a restaurant owner and now food truck vendor in Charlotte, North Carolina that specializes in Thai dishes. Sajja has hired you to develop the company's website. The website will display information about Curbside Thai including the truck's daily locations, menu, catering opportunities, and contact information. Sajja wants the pages to convey the message that customers will get the same great food and service whether they order in the restaurant or from the food truck. Some of the materials for these pages have already been completed by a former employee and Sajja needs you to finish the job by converting that work into a collection of web page documents. To complete this task, you'll learn how to write and edit HTML5 code and how to get your HTML files ready for display on the World Wide Web.

STARTING DATA FILES

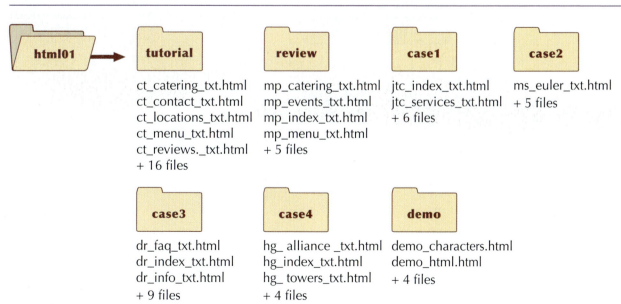

html01

tutorial
ct_catering_txt.html
ct_contact_txt.html
ct_locations_txt.html
ct_menu_txt.html
ct_reviews._txt.html
+ 16 files

review
mp_catering_txt.html
mp_events_txt.html
mp_index_txt.html
mp_menu_txt.html
+ 5 files

case1
jtc_index_txt.html
jtc_services_txt.html
+ 6 files

case2
ms_euler_txt.html
+ 5 files

case3
dr_faq_txt.html
dr_index_txt.html
dr_info_txt.html
+ 9 files

case4
hg_ alliance _txt.html
hg_index_txt.html
hg_ towers_txt.html
+ 4 files

demo
demo_characters.html
demo_html.html
+ 4 files

Session 1.1 Visual Overview:

The **document type declaration** is a processing instruction indicating the markup language used in the document.

The **<html>** tag marks the beginning of the HTML document.

The **<head>** tag marks the **document head** containing information about the document.

An **HTML comment** is a descriptive note added to the HTML file.

The **<meta>** tag marks metadata containing information about the document.

The **<title>** tag marks the page title that appears on the browser title bar or browser tab.

The **<body>** tag marks the **document body** containing all of the content that will appear in the page.

An **opening tag** marks the start of the element content; this tag marks the start of page footer.

A **closing tag** marks the end of the element content; this tag marks the end of the page footer.

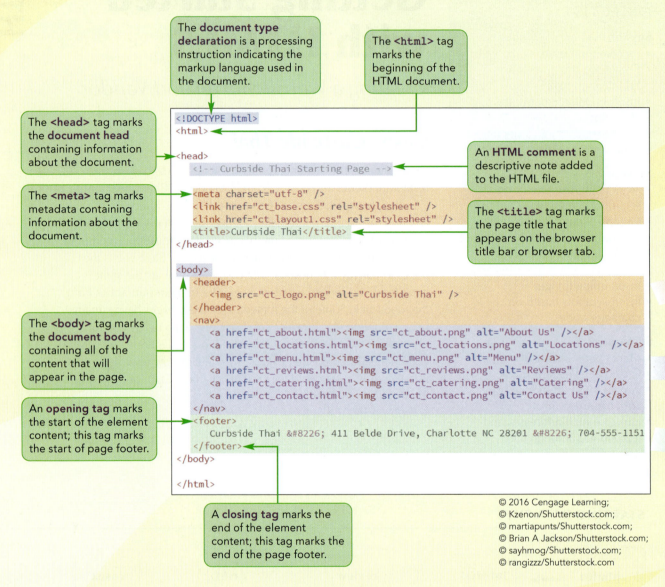

```
<!DOCTYPE html>
<html>

<head>
    <!-- Curbside Thai Starting Page -->

<meta charset="utf-8" />
<link href="ct_base.css" rel="stylesheet" />
<link href="ct_layout1.css" rel="stylesheet" />
<title>Curbside Thai</title>
</head>

<body>
    <header>
        <img src="ct_logo.png" alt="Curbside Thai" />
    </header>
    <nav>
        <a href="ct_about.html"><img src="ct_about.png" alt="About Us" /></a>
        <a href="ct_locations.html"><img src="ct_locations.png" alt="Locations" /></a>
        <a href="ct_menu.html"><img src="ct_menu.png" alt="Menu" /></a>
        <a href="ct_reviews.html"><img src="ct_reviews.png" alt="Reviews" /></a>
        <a href="ct_catering.html"><img src="ct_catering.png" alt="Catering" /></a>
        <a href="ct_contact.html"><img src="ct_contact.png" alt="Contact Us" /></a>
    </nav>
    <footer>
        Curbside Thai &#8226; 411 Belde Drive, Charlotte NC 28201 &#8226; 704-555-1151
    </footer>
</body>

</html>
```

The Structure of an HTML Document

Document as it appears in the browser.

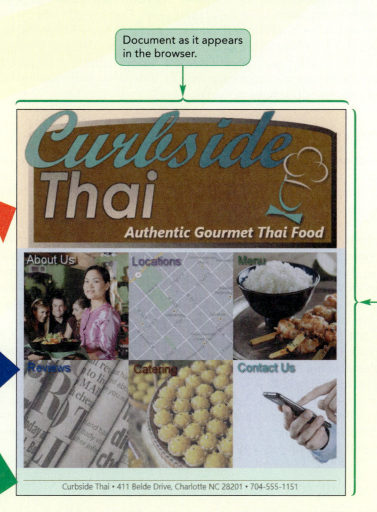

The exact layout of the document elements is determined by a style sheet and not by the document markup.

Exploring the World Wide Web

It is no exaggeration to say that the World Wide Web has had as profound an effect on human communication as the printing press. One key difference is that operation of the printing press was limited to a few select tradesmen but on the web everyone has his or her own printing press; everyone can be a publisher of a website. Before creating your first website, you'll examine a short history of the web because that history impacts the way you write code for your web pages. You'll start by exploring the basic terminology of computer networks.

Networks

A **network** is a structure in which information and services are shared among devices known as **nodes** or **hosts**. A host can be any device that is capable of sending and/or receiving data electronically. The most common hosts that you will work with are desktop computers, laptops, tablets, mobile phones, and printers.

A host that provides information or a service to other devices on the network is called a **server**. For example, a print server is a network host that provides printing services and a file server is a host that provides storage space for saving and retrieving files. The device that receives these services is called a **client**. A common network design is the **client-server network**, in which the clients access information provided by one or more servers. You might be using such a network to access your data files for this tutorial.

Networks are classified based on the range of devices they cover. A network confined to a small geographic area, such as within a building or department, is referred to as a **local area network** or **LAN**. A network that covers a wider area, such as several buildings or cities, is called a **wide area network** or **WAN**. Wide area networks typically consist of two or more interconnected local area networks. The largest WAN in existence is the **Internet**, which incorporates an almost uncountable number of networks and hosts involving computers, mobile devices (such as phones, tablets, and so forth), MP3 players, and gaming systems.

Locating Information on a Network

The biggest obstacle to effectively using the Internet is the network's sheer scope and size. Most of the early Internet tools required users to master a bewildering array of terms, acronyms, and commands. Because network users had to be well versed in computers and network technology, Internet use was largely limited to programmers and computer specialists working for universities, large businesses, and the government.

The solution to this problem was developed in 1989 by Timothy Berners-Lee and other researchers at the CERN nuclear research facility near Geneva, Switzerland. They needed an information system that would make it easy for their researchers to locate and share data on the CERN network. To meet this need, they developed a system of hypertext documents. **Hypertext** is a method of organization in which data sources are interconnected through a series of links or **hyperlinks** that users activate to jump from one data source to another. Hypertext is ideally suited for the Internet because end users don't need to know where a particular document, information source, or service is located—they only need to know how to activate the link. The effectiveness of this technique quickly spread beyond Geneva and was adopted with other networks across the Internet. The totality of these interconnected hypertext documents became known as the **World Wide Web**. The fact that the Internet and the World Wide Web are synonymous in many users' minds is a testament to the success of the hypertext approach.

Web Pages and Web Servers

Documents on the web are stored on **web servers** in the form of **web pages** and accessed through a software program called a **web browser**. The browser retrieves the document from the web server and renders it locally in a form that is readable on a client device. However, because there is a wide selection of client devices ranging from desktop computers to mobile phones to screen readers that relay data aurally, each web page must be written in code that is compatible with every device. How does the same document work with so many different devices? To understand, you need to look at how web pages are created.

Introducing HTML

A web page is a simple text file written in **HTML (Hypertext Markup Language)**. You've already read about hypertext, but what is a markup language? A **markup language** is a language that describes the content and structure of a document by "marking up" or tagging, different document elements. For example, this tutorial contains several document elements such as the tutorial title, main headings, subheadings, paragraphs, figures, figure captions, and so forth. Using a markup language, each of these elements could be tagged as a distinct item within the "tutorial document." Thus, a Hypertext Markup Language is a language that supports both the tagging of distinct document elements and connecting documents through hypertext links.

The History of HTML

In the early years, no single organization defined the rules or **syntax** of HTML. Browser developers were free to define and modify the language in different ways which, of course, led to problems as different browsers supported different "flavors" of HTML and a web page that was written based on one browser's standard might appear totally different when rendered by another browser. Ultimately, a group of web designers and programmers called the **World Wide Web Consortium**, or the **W3C**, settled on a set of standards or specifications for all browser manufacturers to follow. The W3C has no enforcement power, but, because using a uniform language is in everyone's best interest, the W3C's recommendations are usually followed, though not always immediately. Each new version of HTML goes through years of discussion and testing before it is formally adopted as the accepted standard. For more information on the W3C and its services, see its website at *www.w3.org*.

By 1999, HTML had progressed to the fourth version of the language, **HTML 4.01**, which provided support for multimedia, online commerce, and interactive scripts running within the web page. However, there were still many incompatibilities in how HTML was implemented across different browsers and how HTML code was written by web developers. The W3C sought to take control of what had been a haphazard process and enforce a stricter set of standards in a different version of the language called **XHTML (Extensible Hypertext Markup Language)**. By 2002, the W3C had released the specifications for XHTML 1.1. But XHTML 1.1 was intended to be only a minor upgrade on the way to XHTML 2.0, which would correct many of the deficiencies found in HTML 4.01 and become the future language of the web. One problem was that XHTML 2.0 would not be backward compatible with HTML and, as a result, older websites could not be easily brought into the new standard.

Web designers rebelled at this development and, in response, the **Web Hypertext Application Technology Working Group (WHATWG)** was formed in 2004 with the mission to develop a rival version to XHTML 2.0, called **HTML5**. Unlike XHTML 2.0, HTML5 would be compatible with earlier versions of HTML and would not apply the same strict standards that XHTML demanded. For several years, it was unclear which specification would win out; but by 2006, work on XHTML 2.0 had completely stalled and the W3C issued a new charter for WHATWG to develop HTML5 as the de facto standard for the next generation of HTML. Thus today, HTML5 is the current version of the HTML language and it is supported by all current browsers and devices. You can learn more about WHATWG and its current projects at *www.whatwg.org*.

As HTML has evolved, features and code found in earlier versions of the language are often **deprecated**, or phased out, and while deprecated features might not be part of HTML5, that doesn't mean that you won't encounter them in your work—indeed, if you are maintaining older websites, you will often need to interpret code from earlier versions of HTML. Moreover, there are still many older browsers and devices in active use that do not support HTML5. Thus, a major challenge for website designers is writing code that takes advantage of HTML5 but is still accessible to older technology.

Figure 1-1 summarizes some of the different versions of HTML that have been implemented over the years. You can read detailed specifications for these versions at the W3C website.

Figure 1-1 **HTML version history**

Version	Date	Description
HTML 1.0	1989	The first public version of HTML
HTML 2.0	1995	HTML version that added interactive elements including web forms
HTML 3.2	1997	HTML version that provided additional support for web tables and expanded the options for interactive form elements and a scripting language
HTML 4.01	1999	HTML version that added support for style sheets to give web designers greater control over page layout and appearance, and provided support for multimedia elements such as audio and video
XHTML 1.0	2001	A reformulation of HTML 4.01 using the XML markup language in order to provide enforceable standards for HTML content and to allow HTML to interact with other XML languages
XHTML 2.0	discontinued in 2009	The follow-up version to XHTML 1.1 designed to fix some of the problems inherent in HTML 4.01 syntax
HTML 5.0	2012	The current HTML version providing support for mobile design, semantic page elements, column layout, form validation, offline storage, and enhanced multimedia

© 2016 Cengage Learning

This book focuses on HTML5, but you will also review some of the specifications for HTML 4.01 and XHTML 1.1. Note that in the figures that follow, code that was introduced starting with HTML5 will be identified with the label [*HTML5*].

Tools for Working with HTML

Because HTML documents are simple text files, the first tool you will need is a text editor. You can use a basic text editor such as Windows Notepad or TextEdit for the Macintosh, but it is highly recommended that you use one of the many inexpensive editors that provide built-in support for HTML. Some of the more popular HTML editors are Notepad++ (*notepad-plus-plus.org*), UltraEdit (*www.ultraedit.com*), CoffeeCup (*www.coffeecup.com*), BBEdit (*www.barebones.com*) and ConTEXT (*www.contexteditor.org*). These editors include such features as syntax checking to weed out errors, automatic insertion of HTML code, and predesigned templates with the initial code already prepared for you.

These enhanced editors are a good way to start learning HTML and they will be all you need for most basic projects, but professional web developers working on large websites will quickly gravitate toward using a web **IDE (Integrated Development Environment)**, which is a software package providing comprehensive coverage of all phases of the development process from writing HTML code to creating scripts for programs running on web servers. Some of the popular IDEs for web development include Adobe Dreamweaver (*www.adobe.com*), Aptana Studio (*www.aptana.com*), NetBeans IDE (*netbeans.org*) and Komodo IDE (*komodoide.com*). Web IDEs can be very expensive, but most software companies will provide a free evaluation period for you to test their product to see if it meets your needs.

Testing your Code

TIP

You can analyze each browser for its compatibility with HTML5 at the website *www.html5test.com*.

Once you've written your code, you can test whether your HTML code employs proper syntax and structure by validating it at the W3C validation website (*validator.w3.org*). **Validators**, like the one available through the W3C website, are programs that test code to ensure that it contains no syntax errors. The W3C validator will highlight all of the syntax errors in your document with suggestions about how to fix those errors.

Finally, you'll need to test it to ensure that your content is rendered correctly. You should test your code under a variety of screen resolutions, on several different browsers and, if possible, on different versions of the same browser because users are not always quick to upgrade their browsers. What may look good on a widescreen monitor might look horrible on a mobile phone. At a minimum you should test your website using the following popular browsers: Google Chrome, Internet Explorer, Apple Safari, Mozilla Firefox, and Opera.

It is not always possible to load multiple versions of the same browser on one computer, so, in order to test a website against multiple browser versions, professional designers will upload their code to online testing services that report on the website's compatibility across a wide range of browsers, screen resolutions, and devices, including both desktop and mobile devices. Among the popular testing services are BrowserStack (*www.browserstack.com*), CrossBrowserTesting (*www.crossbrowsertesting.com*), and Browsera (*www.browsera.com*). Most of these sites charge a monthly connection fee with a limited number of testing minutes, so you should not upload your code until you are past the initial stages of development.

Supporting the Mobile Web

Currently, the most important factor impacting website design is the increased use of mobile devices to access the Internet. By the end of 2014, the number of mobile Internet users exceeded the number of users accessing the web through laptop or desktop devices. The increased reliance on mobile devices means that web designers must be careful to tailor their websites to accommodate both the desktop and mobile experience. You'll explore the challenge of designing for the mobile web in more detail in Tutorial 5.

Exploring an HTML Document

Now that you have reviewed the history of the web and some of the challenges in developing your own website, you will look at the code of an actual HTML file. To get you started, Sajja Adulet has provided you with the ct_start.html file containing the code for the initial page users see when they access the Curbside Thai website. Open Sajja's file now.

To open the ct_start.html file:

1. Use the editor of your choice to open the **ct_start.html** file from the html01 ▸ tutorial folder.

   Figure 1-2 shows the complete contents of the file as viewed in the Notepad++ editor.

Figure 1-2   Elements and attributes from an HTML document

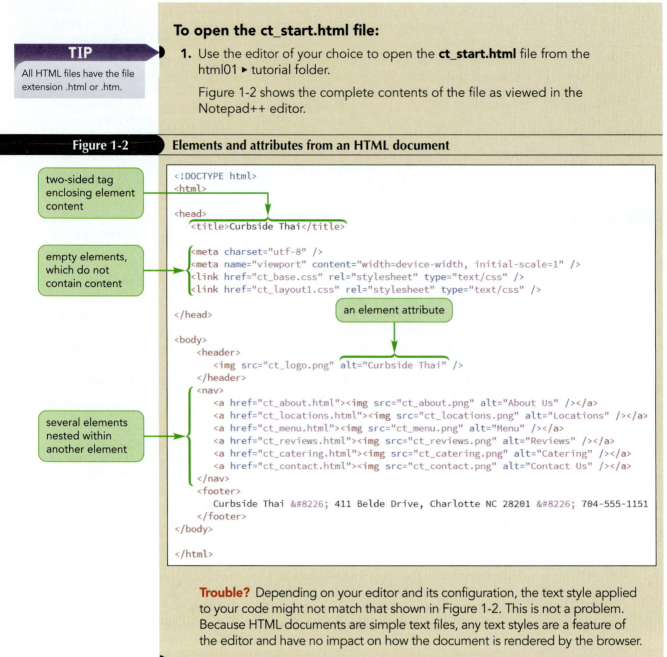

two-sided tag enclosing element content

empty elements, which do not contain content

an element attribute

several elements nested within another element

```
<!DOCTYPE html>
<html>

<head>
    <title>Curbside Thai</title>

    <meta charset="utf-8" />
    <meta name="viewport" content="width=device-width, initial-scale=1" />
    <link href="ct_base.css" rel="stylesheet" type="text/css" />
    <link href="ct_layout1.css" rel="stylesheet" type="text/css" />

</head>

<body>
    <header>
        <img src="ct_logo.png" alt="Curbside Thai" />
    </header>
    <nav>
        <a href="ct_about.html"><img src="ct_about.png" alt="About Us" /></a>
        <a href="ct_locations.html"><img src="ct_locations.png" alt="Locations" /></a>
        <a href="ct_menu.html"><img src="ct_menu.png" alt="Menu" /></a>
        <a href="ct_reviews.html"><img src="ct_reviews.png" alt="Reviews" /></a>
        <a href="ct_catering.html"><img src="ct_catering.png" alt="Catering" /></a>
        <a href="ct_contact.html"><img src="ct_contact.png" alt="Contact Us" /></a>
    </nav>
    <footer>
        Curbside Thai &#8226; 411 Belde Drive, Charlotte NC 28201 &#8226; 704-555-1151
    </footer>
</body>

</html>
```

Trouble? Depending on your editor and its configuration, the text style applied to your code might not match that shown in Figure 1-2. This is not a problem. Because HTML documents are simple text files, any text styles are a feature of the editor and have no impact on how the document is rendered by the browser.

2. Scroll through the document to become familiar with its content but do not make any changes to the text.

The Document Type Declaration

The first line in an HTML file is the document type declaration or doctype, which is a processing instruction indicating the markup language used in the document. The browser uses the document type declaration to know which standard to use to display the content. For HTML5, the doctype is entered as

```
<!DOCTYPE html>
```

You might also see the doctype entered in lowercase letters as

```
<!doctype html>
```

Both are accepted by all browsers. Older versions of HTML had more complicated doctypes. For example, the doctype for HTML 4.01 is the rather foreboding

```
<!DOCTYPE HTML PUBLIC "-//W3C//DTD HTML 4.01//EN"
   "http://www.w3.org/TR/html4/strict.dtd">
```

You might even come across older HTML files that do not have a doctype. Because early versions of HTML did not require a doctype, many browsers interpret the absence of the doctype as a signal that the page should be rendered in **quirks mode**, based on styles and practices from the 1990s and early 2000s. When the doctype is present, browsers will render the page in **standards mode**, employing the most current specifications of HTML. The difference between quirks mode and standards mode can mean the difference between a nicely laid-out page and a confusing mess, so, as a result, you should always put your HTML5 file in standards mode by including the doctype.

Introducing Element Tags

The fundamental building block in every HTML document is the **element tag**, which marks an element in the document. A **starting tag** indicates the beginning of that element, while an **ending tag** indicates the ending. The general syntax of a two-sided element tag is

```
<element>content</element>
```

where *element* is the name of the element, *content* is the element's content, *<element>* is the starting tag, and *</element>* is the ending tag. For example, the following code marks a paragraph element:

```
<p>Welcome to Curbside Thai.</p>
```

Here the <p></p> tags are the starting and ending HTML tags that indicate the presence of a paragraph and the text *Welcome to Curbside Thai.* comprises the paragraph text.

Not every element tag encloses document content. **Empty elements** are elements that are either nontextual (such as images) or contain directives to the browser about how the page should be treated. An empty element is entered using one of the following forms of the **one-sided element tag**:

```
<element />
```

or

```
<element>
```

For example, the following br element, which is used to indicate the presence of a line break in the text, is entered with the one-sided tag:

```
<br />
```

Note that, while this code could also be entered as <br>, the ending slash /> form is the required form in XHTML documents as well as other markup languages. While HTML5 allows for either form, it's a good idea to get accustomed to using the ending slash /> form if you intend to work with other markup languages in the future. We'll follow the /> convention in the code in this book.

Elements can contain other elements, which are called **nested elements**. For example, in the following code, the em element (used to mark emphasized text) is nested within the paragraph element by placing the em markup tag completely within the p markup tag.

Proper syntax:

```
<p>Welcome to <em>Curbside Thai</em>.</p>
```

Note that when nesting one element inside of another, the entire code of the inner element must be contained within the outer element, including opening and closing tags. Thus, it would not be correct syntax to place the closing tag for the em element outside of the p element as in the following code:

Improper syntax:

```
<p>Welcome to <em>Curbside Thai</p>.</em>
```

Now that you've examined the basics of tags, you'll look at how they're used within an HTML file.

The Element Hierarchy

The entire structure of an HTML document can be thought of as a set of nested elements in a hierarchical tree. At the top of the tree is the html element, which marks the entire document. Within the html element is the head element used to mark information about the document itself and the body element used to mark the content that will appear in the web page. Thus, the general structure of an HTML file, like the one shown in Figure 1-2, is

```
<!DOCTYPE html>
<html>
<head>
    head content
</head>

<body>
    body content
</body>
</html>
```

where *head content* and *body content* are nested elements that mark the content of the document head and body. Note that the body element is always placed after the head element.

REFERENCE

Creating the Basic Structure of an HTML File

• To create the basic structure of an HTML file, enter the tags

```
<!DOCTYPE html>
<html>
<head>
    head content
</head>

<body>
    body content
</body>
</html>
```

where *head*, *content*, and *body content* contain nested elements that mark the content of the head and body sections.

Introducing Element Attributes

TIP

Attributes can be listed in any order but they must come after the element name and be separated from each other by a blank space; each attribute value must be enclosed within single or double quotation marks.

Elements will often contain one or more **element attributes**. Each attribute provides additional information to the browser about the purpose of the element or how the element should be handled by the browser. The general syntax of an element attribute within a two-sided tag is

```
<element attr1="value1" attr2="value2" …>
    content
</element>
```

Or, for a one-sided tag

```
<element attr1="value1" attr2="value2" … />
```

where $attr1$, $attr2$, and so forth are attributes associated with $element$ and $value1$, $value2$, and so forth are the corresponding attribute values. For example, the following code adds the id attribute with the value "intro" to the <p> tag in order to identify the paragraph as an introductory paragraph.

```
<p id="intro">Welcome to Curbside Thai.</p>
```

HTML editors will often color-code attributes and their values. The attributes in Figure 1-2 are rendered in a blue font while the corresponding attribute values are rendered in magenta.

Each element has its own set of attributes but, in addition to these element-specific attributes, there is a core set of attributes that can be applied to almost every HTML element. Figure 1-3 lists some of the most commonly used core attributes; others are listed in Appendix B.

Figure 1-3   **Commonly used core HTML attributes**

Attribute	Description
class="text"	Defines the general classification of the element
dir="ltr|rtl|auto"	Defines the text direction of the element content as left-to-right, right-to-left, or determined by the browser
hidden	Indicates that the element should be hidden or is no longer relevant [**HTML5**]
id="text"	Provides a unique identifier for the element
lang="text"	Specifies the language of the element content
style="definition"	Defines the style or appearance of the element content
tabindex="integer"	Specifies the tab order of the element (when the tab button is used to navigate the page)
title="text"	Assigns a title to the element content

© 2016 Cengage Learning

Some attributes do not require a value, so, as a result, HTML supports **attribute minimization** in which no value is shown in the document. For example, the hidden attribute used in the following code does not require a value, its mere presence indicates that the marked paragraph should be hidden in the rendered page.

```
<p hidden>Placeholder Text</p>
```

Attribute minimization is another example of how HTML5 differs from other markup languages such as XHTML in which minimization is not allowed and all attributes must have attribute values.

Adding an Attribute to an Element

- To add an attribute to an element, enter

```
<element attr1="value1" attr2="value2" …>
    content
</element>
```

where *attr1*, *attr2*, and so forth are HTML attributes associated with *element* and *value1*, *value2*, and so forth are the corresponding attribute values.

Handling White Space

Because an HTML file is a text file, it is composed only of text characters and white-space characters. A **white-space character** is any empty or blank character such as a space, tab, or line break. When the browser reads an HTML file, it ignores the presence of white-space characters between element tags and makes no distinction between spaces, tabs, or line breaks. Thus, a browser will treat the following two pieces of code in exactly the same way:

```
<p>Welcome to <em>Curbside Thai</em>.</p>
```

and

```
<p>
    Welcome to <em>Curbside Thai</em>.
</p>
```

The browser will also collapse consecutive occurrences of white-space characters into a single occurrence. This means that the text of the paragraph in the following code is still treated as "Welcome to Curbside Thai" because the extra white spaces between "Curbside" and "Thai" are ignored by the browser.

```
<p>
    Welcome to <em>Curbside        Thai</em>.
</p>
```

The bottom line is that it doesn't matter how you lay out your HTML code because the browser is only interested in the text content and not how that text is entered. This means you can make your file easier to read by indenting lines and by adding extra white-space characters to separate one code block from another. However, this also means that any formatting you do for the page text to make the code more readable, such as tabs or extra white spaces, is *not* transferred to the web page.

Viewing an HTML File in a Browser

The structure of the HTML file shown in Figure 1-2 should now be a little clearer, even if you don't yet know how to interpret the meaning and purpose of each of element and attribute. To see what this page looks like, open it within a web browser.

To open the ct_start.html file in a web browser:

1. Open your web browser. You do not need to be connected to the Internet to view local files stored on your computer.

2. After your browser loads its home page, open the ct_start.html file from the html01 ▸ tutorial folder. Figure 1-4 shows the page as it appears on a mobile phone and on a tablet device. The two devices have different screen widths, which affects how the page is rendered.

Figure 1-4 **The Curbside Thai starting page as rendered by a mobile and tablet device**

mobile device   tablet device

© 2016 Cengage Learning; © Kzenon/Shutterstock.com; © martiapunts/Shutterstock.com; © Brian A Jackson/Shutterstock.com; © sayhmog/Shutterstock.com; © rangizz/Shutterstock.com; BenBois/openclipart; Jmlevick/openclipart

Trouble? If you're not sure how to open a local file with your browser, check for an Open or Open File command under the browser's File menu. You can also open a file by double-clicking the file name from within Windows Explorer or Apple Finder.

3. Reduce the width of your browser window and note that when the width falls below a certain value (in this case 480 pixels), the layout automatically changes to a stacked row of images (as shown in the mobile device image in Figure 1-4) that are better suited to the narrower layout.

4. Increase the width of the browser window and confirm that the layout changes to a 2×3 grid of images (as shown in the tablet device image in Figure 1-4), which is a design more appropriate for the wider window.

Figure 1-4 illustrates an important principle: *HTML does not describe the document's appearance, it only describes the document's content and structure.* The same HTML document can be rendered completely differently between one device and another or between one screen size and another. The actual appearance of the document is determined by style sheets—a topic you'll explore later in this tutorial.

Creating an HTML File

Now that you've studied the structure of an HTML file, you'll start creating your own documents for the Curbside Thai website. Sajja wants you to create a web page containing information about the restaurant. Start by inserting the doctype and the markup tags for the `html`, `head`, and `body` elements.

TIP

HTML filenames should be entered in lowercase letters and have *no* blank spaces.

To begin writing the HTML file:

1. Using the editor of your choice, create a new blank HTML file in the html01 ▸ tutorial folder, saving the file as **ct_about.html**.

2. Enter the following code into the file:

```
<!DOCTYPE html>
<html>

<head>
</head>

<body>
</body>

</html>
```

Figure 1-5 shows the initial elements in the document.

Figure 1-5   **Initial structure of the ct_about.html file**

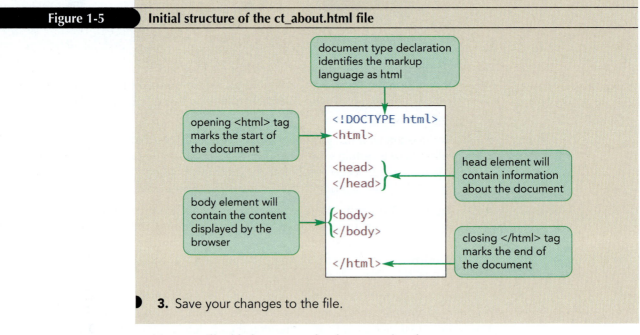

3. Save your changes to the file.

Next, you'll add elements to the document head.

Written Communication: Writing Effective HTML Code

Part of writing good HTML code is being aware of the requirements of various browsers and devices, as well as understanding the different versions of the language. Here are a few guidelines for writing good HTML code:

- Become well versed in the history of HTML and the various versions of HTML and XHTML. Unlike other languages, HTML's history does impact how you write your code.
- Know your market. Do you have to support older browsers, or have your clients standardized on one particular browser or browser version? Will your web pages be viewed on a single device such as a computer, or do you have to support a variety of devices?
- Test your code on several different browsers and browser versions. Don't assume that if your page works in one browser, it will work in other browsers or even in earlier versions of the same browser. Also check on the speed of the connection. A large file that performs well with a high-speed connection might be unusable with a slower connection.
- Read the documentation on the different versions of HTML and XHTML at the W3C website and keep up to date with the latest developments in the language.

To effectively communicate with customers and users, you need to make sure your website content is always readable. Writing good HTML code is a great place to start.

Creating the Document Head

The document head contains **metadata**, which is content that describes the document or provides information about how the document should be processed by the browser. Figure 1-6 describes the different metadata elements found in the document head.

Figure 1-6 | **HTML metadata elements**

Element	Description
head	Contains a collection of metadata elements that describe the document or provide instructions to the browser
base	Specifies the document's location for use with resolving relative hypertext links
link	Specifies an external resource that the document is connected to
meta	Provides a generic list of metadata values such as search keywords, viewport properties, and the file's character encoding
script	Provides programming code for programs to be run within the document
style	Defines the display styles used to render the document content
title	Stores the document's title or name, usually displayed in the browser title bar or on a browser tab

© 2016 Cengage Learning

The first metadata you'll add to the About Curbside Thai web page is the `title` element.

Setting the Page Title

The `title` element is part of the document head because it's not actually displayed as part of the web page, but rather appears externally within the browser title bar or browser tab. Page titles are defined using the following `title` element

```
<title>document title</title>
```

where *document title* is the text of the title. Add a page title to the Curbside Thai page now.

Adding a Document Title

- To define the document title, enter the following tag into the document head:

  ```
  <title>document title</title>
  ```

  where *document title* is the text that will appear on the browser title bar or a browser tab.

To insert the document title:

1. Directly after the opening `<head>` tag, insert the following `title` element, indented to make the code easier to read.

```
<title>About Curbside Thai</title>
```

Figure 1-7 highlights the code for the page title.

Figure 1-7 Entering the document title

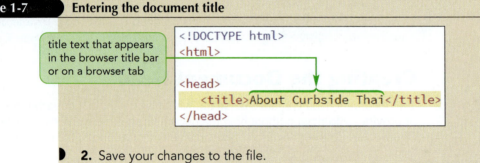

title text that appears in the browser title bar or on a browser tab

```
<!DOCTYPE html>
<html>

<head>
    <title>About Curbside Thai</title>
</head>
```

2. Save your changes to the file.

Adding Metadata to the Document

Another metadata is the `meta` element, which is used for general lists of metadata values. The `meta` element structure is

```
<meta attributes />
```

where *attributes* define the type of metadata that is to be added to a document. Figure 1-8 lists the attributes of the `meta` element.

Figure 1-8 Attributes of the meta element

Attribute	Description
`charset="encoding"`	Specifies the character encoding used in the HTML document [**HTML5**]
`content="text"`	Provides the value associated with the `http-equiv` or `name` attributes
`http-equiv="content-type|default-style|refresh"`	Provides an HTTP header for the document's content, default style, or refresh interval (in seconds)
`name="text"`	Sets the name associated with the metadata

For example, you can use the following `meta` element to provide a collection of keywords for the Curbside Thai website that would aid web search engines, such as Google or Bing search tools, to locate the page for potential customers:

```
<meta name="keywords" content="Thai, restaurant, Charlotte,
food" />
```

In this tag, the `name` attribute defines the type of metadata and the `content` attribute provides the data values. HTML does not specify a set of values for the `name` attribute, but commonly used names include `keywords`, `description`, `author`, and `viewport`.

TIP

The `title` element and the `charset` meta element are both required in a valid HTML5 document.

Another use of the `meta` element is to define the character encoding used in the HTML file. **Character encoding** is the process by which the computer converts text into a sequence of bytes when it stores the text and then converts those bytes back into characters when the text is read. The most common character encoding in use is **UTF-8**, which supports almost all of the characters you will need. To indicate that the document is written using UTF-8, you add the following `meta` element to the document head:

```
<meta charset="utf-8" />
```

The `charset` attribute was introduced in HTML5 and replaces the following more complicated expression used in earlier versions of HTML:

```
<meta http-equiv="Content-Type" content="text/html;
charset=UTF-8" />
```

REFERENCE

Adding Metadata to the Document

- To define the character encoding used in the document, enter

```
<meta charset="encoding" />
```

where *encoding* is the character encoding used in the document.
- To define search keywords associated with the document, enter

```
<meta name="keywords" content="terms" />
```

where *terms* is a comma-separated list of keyword terms.

Add `meta` elements to the document head now, providing the character set and a list of keywords describing the page.

TIP

The `<meta>` tag that defines the character encoding should always be the first `meta` element in the document head.

To insert metadata:

1. Directly after the opening `<head>` tag, insert the following `meta` elements, indented to make the code easier to read:

```
<meta charset="utf-8" />
<meta name="keywords"
 content="Thai, restaurant, Charlotte, food" />
```

Figure 1-9 highlights the newly added `meta` elements used in the document head.

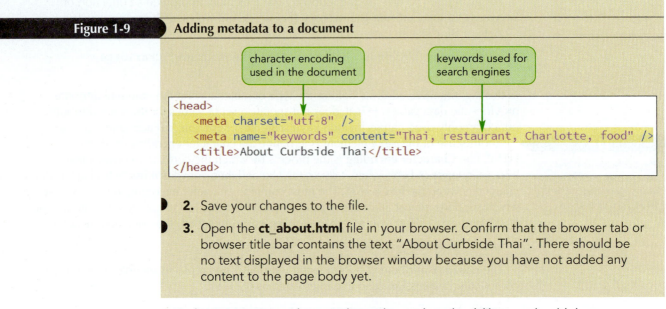

Figure 1-9   Adding metadata to a document

2. Save your changes to the file.

3. Open the **ct_about.html** file in your browser. Confirm that the browser tab or browser title bar contains the text "About Curbside Thai". There should be no text displayed in the browser window because you have not added any content to the page body yet.

Before continuing with your edits to the ct_about.html file, you should document your work. You can do this with a comment.

Adding Comments to your Document

A comment is descriptive text that is added to the HTML file but that does not appear in the browser window when the page is displayed. Comments can include the name of the document's author, the date the document was created, and the purpose for which the document was created. Comments are added with the following markup:

```
<!-- comment -->
```

where *comment* is the text of the comment or note. For example, the following code inserts a comment describing the page you're creating for Curbside Thai:

```
<!-- General Information about Curbside Thai -->
```

TIP

Always include comments when working with a team so that you can document the development process for other team members.

A comment can be spread across several lines as long as the comment text begins with <!-- and ends with -->. Because comments are ignored by the browser, they can be added anywhere within a document, though it's good practice to always include a comment in the document head in order to describe the document content that follows.

REFERENCE

Adding a Comment to an HTML Document

• To insert a comment anywhere within your HTML document, enter

```
<!-- comment -->
```

where *comment* is the text of the HTML comment.

Add comments to the ct_about.html file indicating the document's author, date of creation, and purpose.

To add a comment to the document:

1. Return to the **ct_about.html** file in your HTML editor.

HTML comments must be closed with the --> characters.

2. Directly after the opening `<head>` tag, insert the following comment text, indented to make the code easier to read:

```
<!--
New Perspectives on HTML5 and CSS3, 7th Edition
Tutorial 1
Tutorial Case
General Information about Curbside Thai
Author: your name
Date:    the date

Filename: ct_about.html
-->
```

where **your name** is your name and **the date** is the current date. Figure 1-10 highlights the newly added comment in the file.

Figure 1-10   Adding a comment to the document

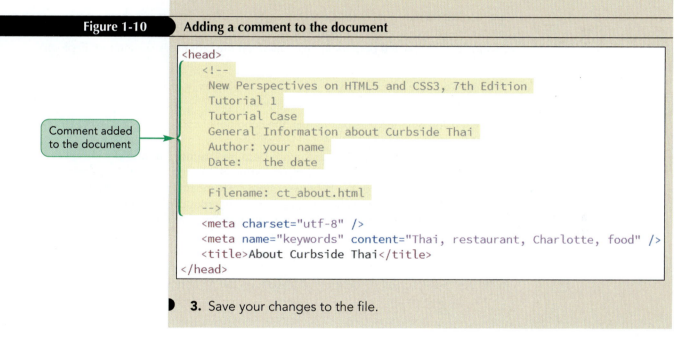

3. Save your changes to the file.

INSIGHT

Conditional Comments and Internet Explorer

Another type of comment you will encounter in many HTML files is a **conditional comment**, which encloses content that should only be run by particular versions of the Internet Explorer browser. The general form of the conditional comment is

```
<!--[if operator IE version]>
   content
<![endif]-->
```

where *operator* is a logical operator (such as less than or greater than), *version* is the version number of an Internet Explorer browser, and *content* is the HTML code that will be run only if the conditional expression is true. The following code uses the lt (less than) logical operator to warn users that they need to upgrade their browser if they are running Internet Explorer prior to version 8.

```
<!--[if lt IE 8]>
   <p>Upgrade your browser to view this page.</p>
<![endif]-->
```

Other logical operators include lte (less than or equal to), gt (greater than), gte (greater than or equal to) and ! (not). For example, the following code uses the logical operator ! to display the paragraph text only when the browser is *not* Internet Explorer:

```
<!--[if !IE]>
   <p>You are not running Internet Explorer.</p>
<![endif]-->
```

Note that if you omit the version number, the conditional comment is applied to all Internet Explorer versions.

The need for conditional comments arose because Internet Explorer significantly differed from other browsers in how it implemented HTML and there was a need to separate the code meant for the IE browser from code meant for other browsers. This is not as much of a problem with recent versions of Internet Explorer, but you may still need to use conditional comments if you are writing code that will be compatible with versions of Internet Explorer earlier than IE 8.

In the next session, you'll continue your work on the ct_about.html file by adding content to the page body.

Session 1.1 Quick Check

1. What is a markup language?

2. What is XHTML? How does XHTML differ from HTML?

3. What is the W3C? What is the WHATWG?

4. What is a doctype? What is the doctype for an HTML5 document?

5. What is incorrect about the following code? Suggest a possible revision of the code to correct the error.

   ```
   <p><strong>Curbside Thai now delivers!</p></strong>
   ```

6. Provide code to mark *Curbside Thai Employment Opportunities* as the document title.

7. Provide code to create metadata adding the keywords *food truck*, *North Carolina*, and *dining* to the document.

8. Provide code to tell the browser that the character encoding UTF-16 is used in the document.

9. Provide code to add the comment *Created by Sajja Adulet* to the document.

Session 1.2 Visual Overview:

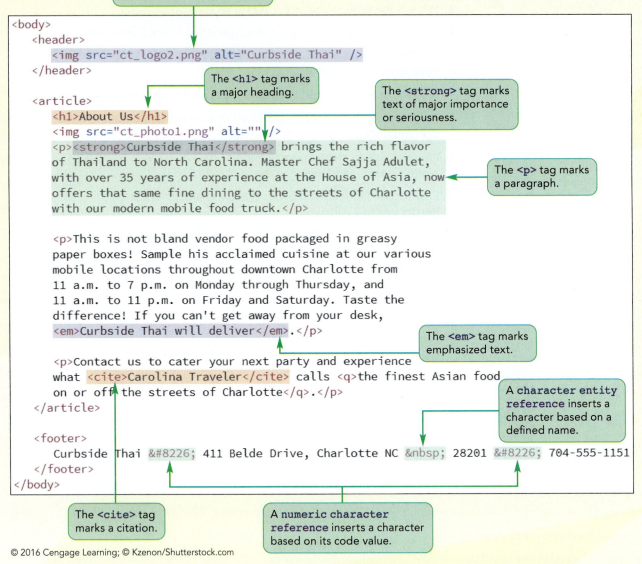

The `<img>` tag marks an image using the file specified in the `src` attribute.

The `<h1>` tag marks a major heading.

The `<strong>` tag marks text of major importance or seriousness.

The `<p>` tag marks a paragraph.

The `<em>` tag marks emphasized text.

A **character entity reference** inserts a character based on a defined name.

The `<cite>` tag marks a citation.

A **numeric character reference** inserts a character based on its code value.

```
<body>
   <header>
      <img src="ct_logo2.png" alt="Curbside Thai" />
   </header>

   <article>
      <h1>About Us</h1>
      <img src="ct_photo1.png" alt="" />
      <p><strong>Curbside Thai</strong> brings the rich flavor
      of Thailand to North Carolina. Master Chef Sajja Adulet,
      with over 35 years of experience at the House of Asia, now
      offers that same fine dining to the streets of Charlotte
      with our modern mobile food truck.</p>

      <p>This is not bland vendor food packaged in greasy
      paper boxes! Sample his acclaimed cuisine at our various
      mobile locations throughout downtown Charlotte from
      11 a.m. to 7 p.m. on Monday through Thursday, and
      11 a.m. to 11 p.m. on Friday and Saturday. Taste the
      difference! If you can't get away from your desk,
      <em>Curbside Thai will deliver</em>.</p>

      <p>Contact us to cater your next party and experience
      what <cite>Carolina Traveler</cite> calls <q>the finest Asian food
      on or off the streets of Charlotte</q>.</p>
   </article>

   <footer>
      Curbside Thai &#8226; 411 Belde Drive, Charlotte NC   28201 &#8226; 704-555-1151
   </footer>
</body>
```

HTML Page Elements

The opening paragraph of the article is marked with the <p> tag.

Images are added to the web page.

Curbside Thai

The main heading of the article is marked with the <h1> tag.

About Us

The restaurant name marked with the <strong> tag to indicate its importance.

Curbside Thai brings the rich flavor of Thailand to North Carolina. Owner and chef Sajja Adulet, with over 35 years of experience as the award-winning master chef at the House of Asia, now offers that same fine dining to the streets of Charlotte through our modern mobile food truck.

This is not bland vendor food packaged in greasy paper boxes! Sample our acclaimed cuisine at our various mobile locations throughout downtown Charlotte from 11 a.m. to 7 p.m. (M-R) and 11 a.m. to 11 p.m. on Friday and Saturday. Taste the difference! If you can't get away from your desk, *Curbside Thai will deliver.*

Nonbreaking space is inserted with the   character entity reference.

Contact us to cater your next party and experience what *Carolina Traveler* calls "the finest Asian food on or off the streets of Charlotte."

A citation to a magazine is marked with the <cite> tag.

Curbside Thai • 411 Belde Drive, Charlotte NC 28201 • 704-555-1151

An example of emphasized text is marked with the <em> tag.

Bullet characters are inserted with the • numeric character reference.

Writing the Page Body

Now that you have created the document head of the About Curbside Thai web page, you'll begin writing the document body. You will start with general markup tags that identify the major sections of the page body and then work inward to more specific content within those sections.

Using Sectioning Elements

The first task in designing the page body is to identify the page's major topics. A page typically has a header, one or more articles that are the chief focus of the page, and a footer that provides contact information for the author or company. HTML marks these major topical areas using the **sectioning elements** described in Figure 1-11.

| Figure 1-11 | HTML sectioning elements |

Element	Description
address	Marks contact information for an individual or group
article	Marks a self-contained composition in the document such as a newspaper story [**HTML5**]
aside	Marks content that is related to a main article [**HTML5**]
body	Contains the entire content of the document
footer	Contains closing content that concludes an article or section [**HTML5**]
h1, h2, h3, h4, h5, h6	Marks major headings with h1 representing the heading with the highest rank, h2 representing next highest-ranked heading, and so forth
header	Contains opening content that introduces an article or section [**HTML5**]
nav	Marks a list of hypertext or navigation links [**HTML5**]
section	Marks content that shares a common theme or purpose on the page [**HTML5**]

© 2016 Cengage Learning

For example, a news blog page might contain several major topics. To identify these areas, the HTML code for the blog might include the following elements to mark off the page's header, navigation list, article, aside, and footer.

```
<body>
   <header>
   </header>
   <nav>
   </nav>
   <article>
   </article>
   <aside>
   </aside>
   <footer>
   </footer>
</body>
```

TIP

Sectioning elements can be nested within each other; for example, an article might contain its own header, footer, and collection of navigation links.

These sectioning elements are also referred to as **semantic elements** because the tag name describes the purpose of the element and the type of content it contains. Even without knowing much about HTML, the page structure defined in the above code is easily understood because of the tag names.

Defining Page Sections

- To mark the page header, use the `header` element.
- To mark self-contained content, use the `article` element.
- To mark a navigation list of hypertext links, use the `nav` element.
- To mark a sidebar, use the `aside` element.
- To mark the page footer, use the `footer` element.
- To group general content, use the `section` element.

The About Curbside Thai page will have a simple structure containing a header, a single article, and a footer. Within the header, there will be an `h1` element providing the page title (not to be confused with the document title, which is displayed on the browser title bar or a browser tab). Add this structure to the document body.

To define the sections in the page body:

1. If you took a break after the previous session, return to the **ct_about.html** file in your HTML editor.

2. Directly after the opening `<body>` tag, insert the following HTML code, indented to make the code easier to read:

```
<header>
    <h1>Curbside Thai</h1>
</header>
<article>
    <h1>About Us</h1>
</article>
<footer>
    Curbside Thai 411 Belde Drive, Charlotte NC 28201 704-555-
1151
</footer>
```

Figure 1-12 highlights the sectioning elements used in the page body.

Figure 1-12	Adding sectioning elements to the page body

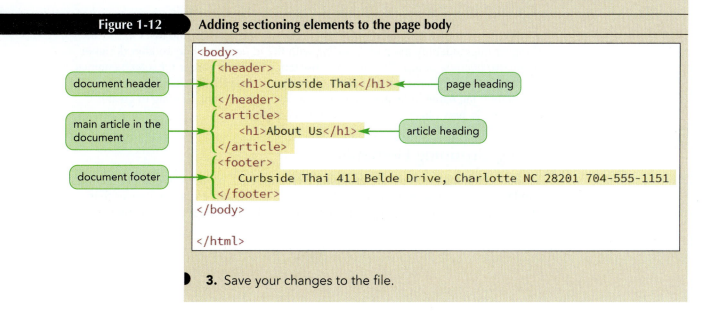

3. Save your changes to the file.

Comparing Sections in HTML4 and HTML5

Many of the sectioning elements described in Figure 1-11 were introduced in HTML5. Prior to HTML5, sections were defined as divisions created using the following `div` element:

```
<div id="id">
    content
</div>
```

where *id* is a name that uniquely identifies the division. Figure 1-13 shows how the same page layout marked up using sectioning elements in HTML5 would have been defined in HTML 4.01 using `div` elements.

Figure 1-13 **Sections in HTML 5.0 vs. divisions in HTML 4.01**

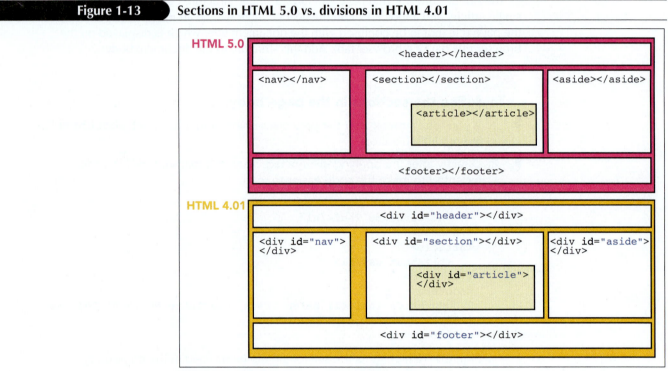

© 2016 Cengage Learning

One problem with `div` elements is that there are no rules for the ids. One web designer might identify the page heading with the id *header* while another designer might use *heading* or *top*. The lack of consistency makes it harder for search engines to identify the page's main topics. The advantage of the HTML5 sectioning elements is that their tag name indicates their purpose in the document, leading to greater uniformity in how pages are designed and interpreted.

Using Grouping Elements

Within sectioning elements are **grouping elements**. Each grouping element organizes similar content into a distinct group, much like a paragraph groups sentences that share a common theme. Figure 1-14 describes all the HTML grouping elements.

| Figure 1-14 | HTML grouping elements |

Element	Description
blockquote	Contains content that is quoted from another source, often with a citation and often indented on the page
div	Contains a generic grouping of elements within the document
dl	Marks a description list containing one or more dt elements with each followed by one or more dd elements
dt	Contains a single term from a description list
dd	Contains the description or definition associated with a term from a description list
figure	Contains an illustration, photo, diagram, or similar object that is cross-referenced elsewhere in the document [**HTML5**]
figcaption	Contains the caption associated with a figure [**HTML5**]
hr	Marks a thematic break such as a scene change or a transition to a new topic (often displayed as a horizontal rule)
main	Marks the main content of the document or application; only one main element should be used in the document [**HTML5**]
ol	Contains an ordered list of items
ul	Contains an unordered list of items
li	Contains a single item from an ordered or unordered list
p	Contains the text of a paragraph
pre	Contains a block of preformatted text in which line breaks and extra spaces in the code are retained (often displayed in a monospace font)

© 2016 Cengage Learning

For example, the following code shows three paragraphs nested within a page article with each paragraph representing a group of similar content:

```
<article>
    <p>Content of 1st paragraph.</p>
    <p>Content of 2nd paragraph.</p>
    <p>Content of 3rd paragraph.</p>
</article>
```

When a browser encounters a sectioning element or a grouping element, the default style is to start the enclosed content on a new line, separating it from any content that appears before it. Thus, each of these paragraphs will be started on a new line as will the article itself. Note that the exact appearance of the paragraphs and the space between them depends on the styles applied by the browser to those elements. You'll learn more about styles later in this tutorial.

REFERENCE

Defining Page Groups

- To mark a paragraph, use the p element.
- To mark an extended quote, use the blockquote element.
- To mark the main content of a page or section, use the main element.
- To mark a figure box, use the figure element.
- To mark a generic division of page content, use the div element.

Sajja has written up the article describing Curbside Thai in a text file. Enter his text into the `article` element in the About Curbside Thai web page and use `p` elements to mark the paragraphs in the article.

To group the page text into paragraphs:

1. Use a text editor to open the **ct_pages.txt** file from the html01 ▶ tutorial folder.

2. Select and copy the three paragraphs of text directly after the About Us title.

3. Close the file, but do not save any changes you may have inadvertently made to the document.

4. Return to the **ct_about.html** file in your HTML editor.

5. Directly after the `<h1>About Us</h1>` line within the page article, insert a new blank line and paste the text you copied.

6. Enclose each of the three paragraphs of pasted content between an opening `<p>` tag and a closing `</p>` tag. Indent the code within the `article` element to make the code easier to read.

   Figure 1-15 highlights the newly added code for the three paragraphs of article text

| Figure 1-15 | Grouping article content by paragraphs |

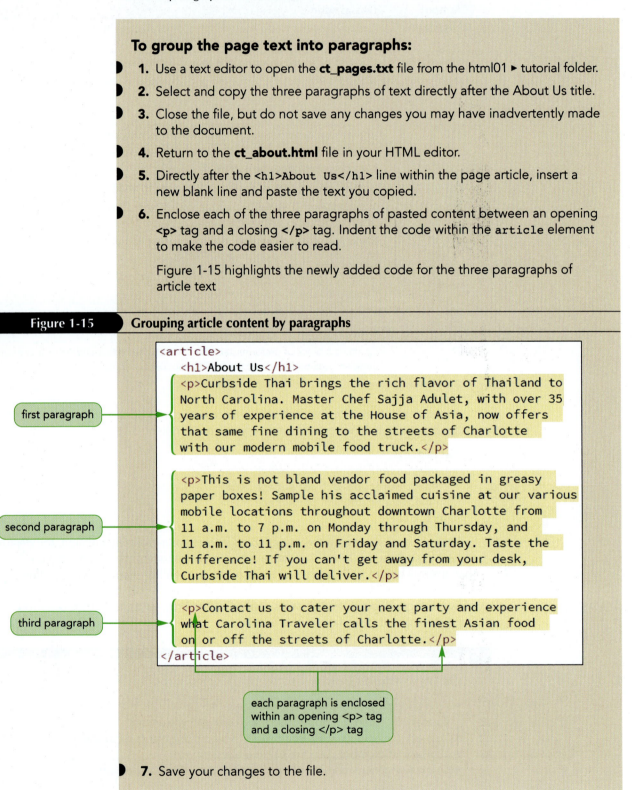

7. Save your changes to the file.

Using Text-Level Elements

Within each grouping element are **text-level elements**, which act like phrases or characters within a paragraph. Unlike sectioning or grouping elements that start content on a new line and mark a self-contained block of content, text-level elements appear in line with the surrounding content and are known as **inline elements**. For example, the *italicized* or **boldface** text in this paragraph is considered inline content because it appears alongside the surrounding text. Figure 1-16 describes some of the many text-level elements in HTML.

Figure 1-16   **HTML text-level elements**

Element	Description
a	Marks content that acts as a hypertext link
abbr	Marks an abbreviation or acronym
b	Indicates a span of text to which attention should be drawn (text usually appears in bold)
br	Represents a line break within the grouping element
cite	Marks a citation to a title or author of a creative work (text usually appears in italics)
code	Marks content that represents computer code (text usually appears in a monospace font)
data	Associates a data value with the marked text with the `value` attribute providing the value [**HTML5**]
dfn	Marks a defined term for which a definition is given elsewhere in the document
em	Indicates content that is emphasized or stressed (text usually appears in italics)
i	Indicates a span of text that expresses an alternate voice or mood (text usually appears in italics)
kbd	Marks text that represents user input, typically from a computer keyboard or a voice command
marks	Contains a row of text that is marked or highlighted for reference purposes [**HTML5**]
q	Marks content that is quoted from another source
s	Marks content that is no longer accurate or relevant (text is usually struck through)
samp	Marks text that represents the sample output from a computer program or application
small	Marks side comments (text usually in small print)
span	Contains a generic run of text within the document
strong	Indicates content of strong importance or seriousness (text usually appears in bold)
sub	Marks text that should be treated as a text subscript
sup	Marks text that should be treated as a text superscript
time	Marks a time value or text string [**HTML5**]
u	Indicates text that appears stylistically different from normal text (text usually appears underlined)
var	Marks text that is treated as a variable in a mathematical expression or computer program
wbr	Represents where a line break should occur, if needed, for a long text string [**HTML5**]

© 2016 Cengage Learning

The following HTML code demonstrates how to employ text-level elements to mark select phrases or characters within a paragraph.

```
<p>
   Contact us to cater your next party and experience what
   <cite>Carolina Traveler</cite> calls <q>the finest
   Asian food on or off the streets of Charlotte.</q>
</p>
```

Two text-level elements are used in this paragraph: the cite element to mark the citation to the *Carolina Traveler* magazine and the q element to mark the direct quote from the magazine's review of Curbside Thai. Both the citation and the quoted material will appear specially formatted within the paragraph alongside the other, unmarked, text.

REFERENCE

Defining Text-Level Content

- To mark emphasized text, use the em element.
- To mark text of great importance, use the strong element.
- To mark a citation, use the cite element.
- To mark a selection of quoted material, use the q element.
- To mark a subscript, use the sub element; to mark a superscript, use the sup element.
- To mark a generic selection of text-level content, use the span element.

Use text-level elements in the About Curbside Thai web page to mark examples of emphasized text, strongly important text, citations, and quoted material.

To apply text-level elements to a page:

1. Go to the first paragraph within the page article and enclose the opening words *Curbside Thai* within a set of opening and closing **<strong>** tags. You use the **<strong>** tags when you want to strongly reinforce the importance of the text, such as the restaurant name, for the reader.

2. In the second paragraph, enclose the phrase, *Curbside Thai will deliver* within a set of opening and closing **<em>** tags to emphasize this text.

3. Go the third paragraph and mark *Carolina Traveler* using the cite element and then mark the extended quote, *the finest Asian food on or off the streets of Charlotte*, using the q element.

Figure 1-17 highlights the application of the four text-level elements to the paragraph text.

Figure 1-17   **Marking text-level content**

strong and important text marked with the <strong> tag

emphasized text marked with the <em> tag

citation marked with the <cite> tag

quoted material marked with the <q> tag

```
<article>
   <h1>About Us</h1>
   <p><strong>Curbside Thai</strong> brings the rich flavor of Thailand to
   North Carolina. Master Chef Sajja Adulet, with over 35
   years of experience at the House of Asia, now offers
   that same fine dining to the streets of Charlotte
   with our modern mobile food truck.</p>

   <p>This is not bland vendor food packaged in greasy
   paper boxes! Sample his acclaimed cuisine at our various
   mobile locations throughout downtown Charlotte from
   11 a.m. to 7 p.m. on Monday through Thursday, and
   11 a.m. to 11 p.m. on Friday and Saturday. Taste the
   difference! If you can't get away from your desk,
   <em>Curbside Thai will deliver</em>.</p>

   <p>Contact us to cater your next party and experience
   what <cite>Carolina Traveler</cite> calls <q>the finest Asian food
   on or off the streets of Charlotte</q>.</p>
</article>
```

4. Save your changes to the file.

5. Open the **ct_about.html** file in your browser to view how your browser renders the page content.

Figure 1-18 shows the current appearance of the page.

Figure 1-18   **The About Curbside Thai page as rendered by the browser**

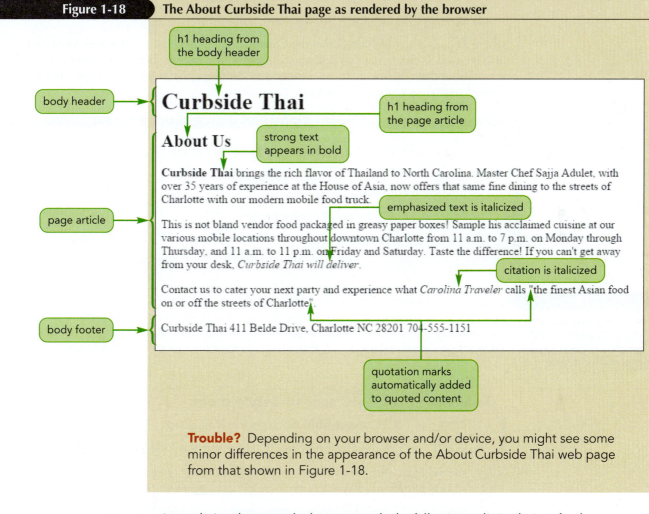

Trouble? Depending on your browser and/or device, you might see some minor differences in the appearance of the About Curbside Thai web page from that shown in Figure 1-18.

In rendering the page, the browser made the following stylistic choices for the different page elements:

- The h1 heading from the body header is assigned the largest font and is displayed in bold to emphasize its importance. The h1 heading from the page article is given a slightly smaller font but is still displayed in bold.
- Strong text is displayed in bold while emphasized text is displayed in italics.
- Citations are displayed in italic while quoted material is automatically surrounded by quotation marks.

It needs to be emphasized again that all of these stylistic choices are not determined by the markup tags; they are default styles used by the browser. Different browsers and different devices might render these page elements differently. To exert more control over your page's appearance, you can apply a style sheet to document contents.

Linking an HTML Document to a Style Sheet

A **style sheet** is a set of rules specifying how page elements are displayed. Style sheets are written in the **Cascading Style Sheets** (**CSS**) language. Like HTML, the CSS language was developed and enhanced as the web grew and changed and, like HTML, CSS specifications are managed by the W3C. To replace the browser's internal style sheet with one of your own, you can link your HTML file to a style sheet file using the following link element:

```
<link href="file" rel="stylesheet" />
```

where `file` is a text file containing the CSS style sheet. Because the link element can also be used to link to data other than style sheets, the `rel` attribute is required to tell the browser that it is linking to style sheet data. Note that older browsers might include `type="text/css"` as part of the `link href` element.

TIP

Because the link element is another example of metadata, it's always added to the document head.

Sajja has supplied you with two CSS files that he wants applied to his website. The ct_base.css file contains styles specifying the appearance of text-level elements. The ct_layout2.css file contains styles that govern the arrangement of sectioning and grouping elements on the page. Link the ct_about.html file to both of these style sheets now.

To link an HTML document to a style sheet:

1. Return to the **ct_about.html** file in your HTML editor.

2. Directly before the closing `</head>` tag, insert the following link elements:

   ```
   <link href="ct_base.css" rel="stylesheet" />
   <link href="ct_layout2.css" rel="stylesheet" />
   ```

   Figure 1-19 highlights the two style sheet links added to the document.

Figure 1-19　Linking to style sheets

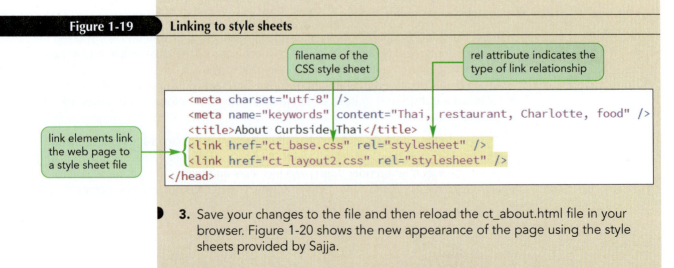

filename of the CSS style sheet

rel attribute indicates the type of link relationship

link elements link the web page to a style sheet file

```
<meta charset="utf-8" />
<meta name="keywords" content="Thai, restaurant, Charlotte, food" />
<title>About Curbside Thai</title>
<link href="ct_base.css" rel="stylesheet" />
<link href="ct_layout2.css" rel="stylesheet" />
</head>
```

3. Save your changes to the file and then reload the ct_about.html file in your browser. Figure 1-20 shows the new appearance of the page using the style sheets provided by Sajja.

Figure 1-20   The About Curbside Thai page rendered under a new style sheet

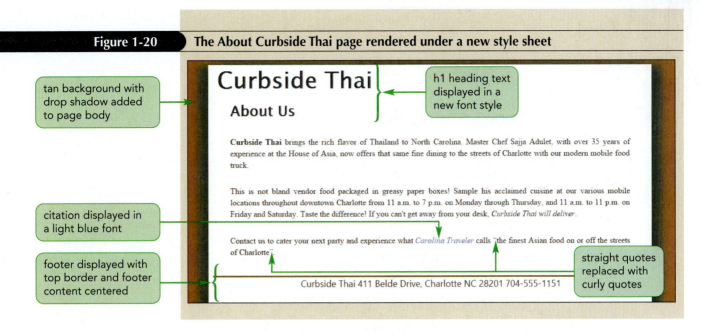

tan background with drop shadow added to page body

h1 heading text displayed in a new font style

Curbside Thai

About Us

Curbside Thai brings the rich flavor of Thailand to North Carolina. Master Chef Sajja Adulet, with over 35 years of experience at the House of Asia, now offers that same fine dining to the streets of Charlotte with our modern mobile food truck.

This is not bland vendor food packaged in greasy paper boxes! Sample his acclaimed cuisine at our various mobile locations throughout downtown Charlotte from 11 a.m. to 7 p.m. on Monday through Thursday, and 11 a.m. to 11 p.m. on Friday and Saturday. Taste the difference! If you can't get away from your desk, *Curbside Thai will deliver*.

citation displayed in a light blue font

Contact us to cater your next party and experience what *Carolina Traveler* calls "the finest Asian food on or off the streets of Charlotte".

footer displayed with top border and footer content centered

Curbside Thai 411 Belde Drive, Charlotte NC 28201 704-555-1151

straight quotes replaced with curly quotes

Applying these style sheets to the HTML code causes the page body to be displayed on a tan background with a drop shadow, the font used in the two h1 headings has changed, a top border has been added to the footer to set it off from the preceding content, and the citation to the *Carolina Traveler* magazine is displayed in a light blue font. The effect makes the page content easier to read and more pleasing to the eye.

Sajja is concerned that the contact information in the page footer is difficult to read. He wants you to add bullet characters (•) separating the name of the restaurant, the street address, and the restaurant phone number. However, this character is not represented by any keys on your keyboard. How then, do you insert this symbol into the web page?

Working with Character Sets and Special Characters

Every character that your browser is capable of rendering belongs to a collection of characters and symbols called a **character set**. The character set used for the English alphabet is the **American Standard Code for Information Interchange** more simply known as **ASCII**. A more extended character set, called **Latin-1** or the **ISO 8859-1** character set, supports 255 characters and can be used by most languages that employ the Latin alphabet, including English, French, Spanish, and Italian. **Unicode**, the most extended character set, supports up to 65,536 symbols and can be used with any of the world's languages.

Character Encoding

TIP

You can explore different character encoding values by opening the demo_characters.html file in the html01 ▶ demo folder.

Each character from a character set is associated with an encoding value that can then be stored and read by a computer program. For example, the copyright symbol © from the Unicode character set is encoded with the number 169. If you know the encoding value, you can insert the corresponding character directly into your web page using the following character encoding reference:

    &#code;

where *code* is the encoding reference number. Thus, to display the © symbol in your web page, you would enter

```
&#169;
```

into your HTML file.

Character Entity References

Another way to insert a special symbol is to use a character entity reference, which is a short memorable name used in place of the encoding reference number. Character entity references are inserted using the syntax

```
&char;
```

where *char* is the character's entity reference. The character entity reference for the copyright symbol is **copy**, so to display the © symbol in your web page, you could insert the following expression into your HTML code:

```
&copy;
```

In the last session, you learned that HTML will collapse consecutive occurrences of white space into a single white-space character. You can force HTML to display extra white space by using the following character entity reference

```
 
```

where **nbsp** stands for *nonbreaking space*. When you want to display extra white space, you need to insert the nonbreaking space character reference in the HTML code for each space you want to display.

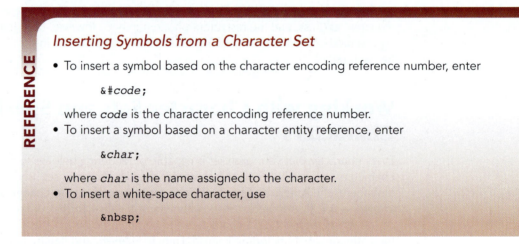

REFERENCE

Inserting Symbols from a Character Set

- To insert a symbol based on the character encoding reference number, enter

  ```
  &#code;
  ```

  where *code* is the character encoding reference number.
- To insert a symbol based on a character entity reference, enter

  ```
  &char;
  ```

  where *char* is the name assigned to the character.
- To insert a white-space character, use

  ```
   
  ```

For the footer in the About Curbside Thai page, use the bullet symbol (•), which has the encoding value 8226, to separate the restaurant name, address, and phone number. Use the ` ` character reference to insert an extra blank space prior to the postal code in the restaurant address.

To insert a character encoding reference number and an entity reference:

1. Return to the **ct_about.html** file in your HTML editor.

2. Go to the `footer` element and insert the character encoding number `&#8226;` directly after the word *Thai* and after the postal code *28201*. Insert the character reference ` ` directly before the postal code.

Figure 1-21 highlights the character codes and references added to the footer.

Character encoding reference numbers must always begin with &# and end with a semicolon, otherwise the code won't be recognized as a code number.

Figure 1-21   Inserting special characters

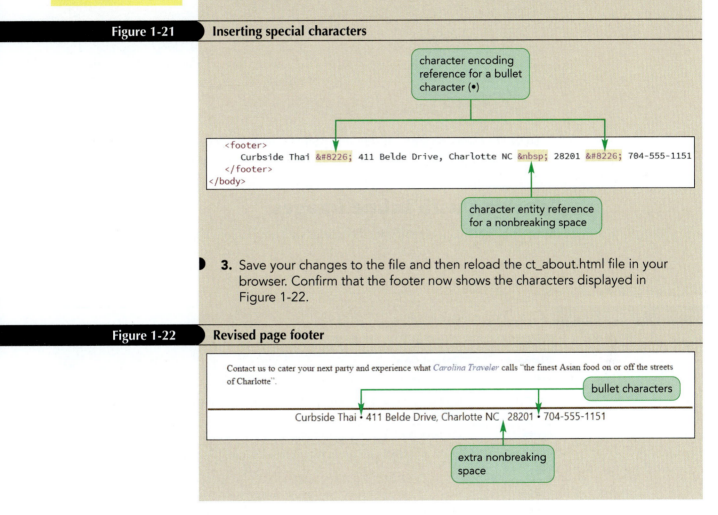

character encoding reference for a bullet character (•)

```
<footer>
    Curbside Thai &#8226; 411 Belde Drive, Charlotte NC   28201 &#8226; 704-555-1151
</footer>
</body>
```

character entity reference for a nonbreaking space

3. Save your changes to the file and then reload the ct_about.html file in your browser. Confirm that the footer now shows the characters displayed in Figure 1-22.

Figure 1-22   Revised page footer

Contact us to cater your next party and experience what *Carolina Traveler* calls "the finest Asian food on or off the streets of Charlotte".

Curbside Thai • 411 Belde Drive, Charlotte NC   28201 • 704-555-1151

bullet characters

extra nonbreaking space

Presentational Attributes

Early versions of HTML supported **presentational elements** and **presentational attributes** designed to describe how each element should be rendered by web browsers. For example, to align text on a page, web authors would use the following `align` attribute

```
<element align="alignment">content</element>
```

where *alignment* is either `left`, `right`, `center`, or `justify`. Thus, to center an h1 heading on a page, they would use the following code:

```
<h1 align="center">Curbside Thai</h1>
```

Almost all presentational elements and attributes are now deprecated in favor of style sheets, but you may still see them in the code from older websites. Using a deprecated attribute like `align` would probably not cause your web page to fail, however, it's still best practice to adhere to a standard in which HTML is used only to describe the content and structure of the document and style sheets are used to format its appearance.

So far your work on the Curbside Thai page has been limited to textual content. Next, you'll explore how to add graphical content to your web page.

Working with Inline Images

Most web pages include **embedded content**, which is content imported from another resource, often nontextual, such as graphic images, audio soundtracks, video clips, or interactive games. To support this type of content, HTML provides the **embedded elements** listed in Figure 1-23.

Figure 1-23 | **HTML embedded elements**

Element	Description
audio	Represents a sound clip or audio stream [**HTML5**]
canvas	Contains programming scripts used to construct bitmap images and graphics [**HTML5**]
embed	Contains general embedded content including application or interactive content
iframe	Contains the contents of an external web page or Internet resource
img	Contains a graphic image retrieved from an image file
object	Contains general embedded content including application or interactive content
video	Represents a video clip or video stream with captions [**HTML5**]

© 2016 Cengage Learning

TIP

Always include the `alt` attribute; it is required in XHTML code and is highly recommended as a way of accommodating users running nonvisual web browsers.

These elements are also known as **interactive elements** because they allow for interaction between the user and the embedded object. For example, embedded audio or video content usually contains player buttons to control the playback.

Images are inserted into a web page using the following `img` element

```
<img src="file" alt="text" />
```

where *file* is the name of the image file. If the browser cannot display images, the text in the `alt` attribute is used in place of the image. As with other one-sided tags, the `img` element can be entered without the closing slash as

```
<img src="file" alt="text">
```

Images are also known as **inline images** because they are placed, like text-level elements, in line with surrounding content.

By default, the image size matches the size of the image in the file but you can specify a different size by adding the following `width` and `height` attributes to the `img` element

```
width="value" height="value"
```

where the `width` and `height` values are expressed in pixels. If you specify only the width, browsers automatically set the height to maintain the proportions of the image; similarly, if you define the height, browsers automatically set the width to maintain the image proportions. Image sizes can also be set within the document's style sheet.

Embedding an Inline Image

- To embed an inline image into the document, use

  ```
  <img src="file" alt="text" />
  ```

  where `file` is the name of the graphic image file and `text` is text displayed by browsers in place of the graphic image.

Sajja has provided you with two images. The image from the ct_logo2.png file displays the restaurant logo, while the ct_photo1.png image provides an image of customers being served by an employee at his brick-and-mortar restaurant. Sajja included this image to emphasize that the food from his food truck is the same quality and great taste as the food at his award winning restaurant. Add both of these images to the ct_about.html file.

To insert inline images into a document:

1. Return to the **ct_about.html** file in your HTML editor.

2. Go to the `header` element and replace the `h1` element with the tag

   ```
   <img src="ct_logo2.png" alt="Curbside Thai" />
   ```

3. Go to the `article` element and, directly after the `h1` element, insert the tag

   ```
   <img src="ct_photo1.png" alt="" />
   ```

   Figure 1-24 highlights the newly added `img` elements in the document.

TIP

Include the `alt` attribute as a blank text string if the image file does not convey any text message to the user.

Figure 1-24   **Inserting inline images**

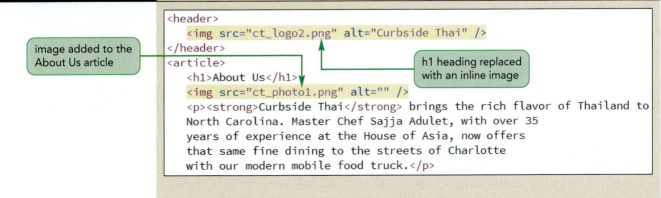

```
<header>
    <img src="ct_logo2.png" alt="Curbside Thai" />
</header>
<article>
    <h1>About Us</h1>
    <img src="ct_photo1.png" alt="" />
    <p><strong>Curbside Thai</strong> brings the rich flavor of Thailand to
    North Carolina. Master Chef Sajja Adulet, with over 35
    years of experience at the House of Asia, now offers
    that same fine dining to the streets of Charlotte
    with our modern mobile food truck.</p>
```

image added to the About Us article

h1 heading replaced with an inline image

> **4.** Save your changes to the file and then reload the ct_about.html file in your browser. Figure 1-25 displays the newly added graphic images in the web page.

| Figure 1-25 | Images on the About Curbside Thai page |

restaurant logo used for the page header

About Us

Curbside Thai brings the rich flavor of Thailand to North Carolina. Master Chef Sajja Adulet, with over 35 years of experience at the House of Asia, now offers that same fine dining to the streets of Charlotte with our modern mobile food truck.

This is not bland vendor food packaged in greasy paper boxes! Sample his acclaimed cuisine at our various mobile locations throughout downtown Charlotte from 11 a.m. to 7 p.m. on Monday through Thursday, and 11 a.m. to 11 p.m. on Friday and Saturday. Taste the difference! If you can't get away from your desk, *Curbside Thai will deliver.*

© 2016 Cengage Learning; © Kzenon/Shutterstock.com

photo floated on the right margin of the article

Trouble? The exact appearance of the text as it flows around the image will vary depending on the width of your browser window.

Note that the photo of the Curbside Thai customers is floated alongside the right margin of the article, with the surrounding paragraphs flowing around the image. This is the result of code in the style sheets. You'll learn about styles used to float images in Tutorial 3.

Line Breaks and Other Empty Elements

The `img` element is inserted using the empty element tag because it does not enclose any page content, but instead links to an external image file. Another important empty element is the following `br` element, which creates a line break

```
<br />
```

Line breaks are placed within grouping elements, such a paragraphs or headings, to force page content to start on a new line within the group. While useful for controlling the flow of text within a group, the `br` element should not be used as a formatting tool. For example, it would not make semantic sense to insert two or more `br` elements in a row if the only reason to do so is to increase the spacing between lines of text. Instead, all such formatting choices belong in a style sheet.

If the text of a line cannot fit within the width of the viewing window, the browser will wrap the text automatically at the point the browser identifies as the most appropriate. To recommend a different line break point, use the `wbr` (word break) element to indicate where a line break should occur if needed. For example, the following HTML code uses the `wbr` element to break a long web address between ".com/" and "general", but this break happens only if the address will not fit on one line.

```
www.curbsidethai.com/<wbr />general/docs/ct_about.html
```

Finally, another oft-used empty element is the following `hr` or horizontal rule element

```
<hr />
```

Today, the purpose of this element is to denote a major topic change within a section. Originally, the `hr` element was used to insert horizontal lines into the page and, although that task is better left to style sheets, you will still see the `hr` element used in that capacity in older web pages.

Working with Block Quotes and Other Elements

Now that you've written the code for the ct_about.html file, you'll work on other pages in the Curbside Thai website. The ct_reviews.html file provides excerpts of reviews from food critics and magazines. Because these excerpts contain extended quotes, you'll place each review in the following `blockquote` element

```
<blockquote>
   content
</blockquote>
```

where `content` is the text of the quote. By default, most browsers render block quotes by indenting the quoted material to separate from it from the website author's words, however, you can substitute your own style with a custom style sheet.

Sajja has created much of the code required for the reviews page. The code is contained in the two style sheets that are already linked to the reviews page. Complete the page by adding the excerpts of the reviews marked as block quotes.

To create the reviews page:

▶ 1. Open the **ct_reviews_txt.html** file from the html01 ▸ tutorial folder in your HTML editor. Enter *your name* and *the date* in the comment section and save the file as **ct_reviews.html**.

▶ 2. Go to the **ct_pages.txt** file in your text editor.

▶ 3. Locate the section containing the restaurant reviews and copy the text of the four reviews and awards.

> 4. Return to the **ct_reviews.html** file in your HTML editor and paste the text of the four reviews directly after the `<h1>Reviews</h1>` line.

> 5. Enclose each review within a set of `<blockquote>` tags. Enclose each paragraph within each review with a set of `<p>` tags. Align and indent your code to make it easier to read.

Figure 1-26 highlights the newly added code in the document.

Figure 1-26	Marking extended text as block quotes

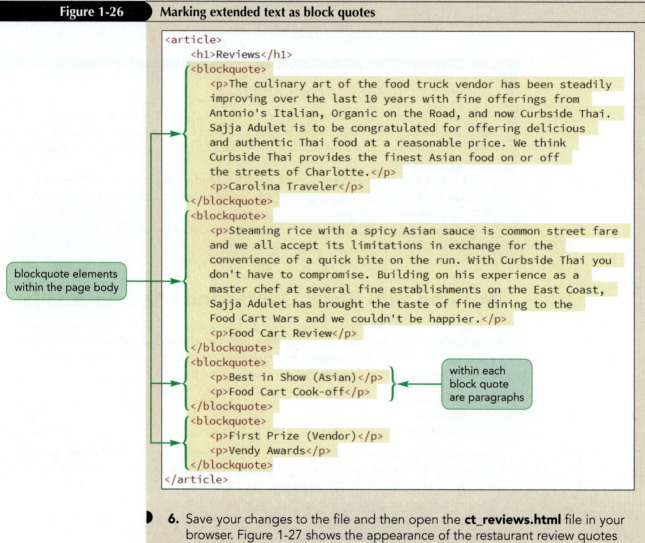

```
<article>
    <h1>Reviews</h1>
    <blockquote>
        <p>The culinary art of the food truck vendor has been steadily
        improving over the last 10 years with fine offerings from
        Antonio's Italian, Organic on the Road, and now Curbside Thai.
        Sajja Adulet is to be congratulated for offering delicious
        and authentic Thai food at a reasonable price. We think
        Curbside Thai provides the finest Asian food on or off
        the streets of Charlotte.</p>
        <p>Carolina Traveler</p>
    </blockquote>
    <blockquote>
        <p>Steaming rice with a spicy Asian sauce is common street fare
        and we all accept its limitations in exchange for the
        convenience of a quick bite on the run. With Curbside Thai you
        don't have to compromise. Building on his experience as a
        master chef at several fine establishments on the East Coast,
        Sajja Adulet has brought the taste of fine dining to the
        Food Cart Wars and we couldn't be happier.</p>
        <p>Food Cart Review</p>
    </blockquote>
    <blockquote>
        <p>Best in Show (Asian)</p>
        <p>Food Cart Cook-off</p>
    </blockquote>
    <blockquote>
        <p>First Prize (Vendor)</p>
        <p>Vendy Awards</p>
    </blockquote>
</article>
```

blockquote elements within the page body

within each block quote are paragraphs

> 6. Save your changes to the file and then open the **ct_reviews.html** file in your browser. Figure 1-27 shows the appearance of the restaurant review quotes using Sajja's style sheet.

Figure 1-27   **Block quotes of restaurant reviews**

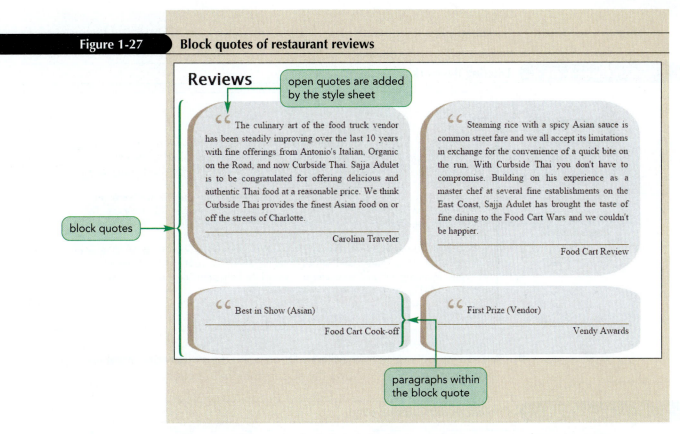

Because of the styles in Sajja's style sheets, each `blockquote` element appears within its own formatted box with an opening quote character added to reinforce the fact that this is quoted material.

The next page you'll create contains information about catering from Curbside Thai. The structure of this page is identical to the structure of the About Curbside Thai page. Sajja has linked the catering page to two style sheets containing the style rules that dictate how the page will look when the page is rendered in a browser.

To create the Catering page:

1. Open the **ct_catering_txt.html** file from the html01 ▸ tutorial folder in your HTML editor. Enter **your name** and **the date** in the comment section and save the file as **ct_catering.html**.

2. Return to the **ct_pages.txt** file in your text editor.

3. Locate the section containing information about Curbside Thai's catering service and copy the four paragraphs of information.

4. Return to the **ct_catering.html** file in your HTML editor and paste the copied text directly after the `<h1>Catering</h1>` line.

5. Mark each paragraph in the article using the `p` element. Align and indent your code to make it easier to read.

6. Directly after the `<h1>Catering</h1>` tag, insert an inline image using **ct_photo2.png** as the source and an empty text string for the `alt` attribute.

Figure 1-28 highlights the newly added paragraphs in the document.

Figure 1-28 Entering the markup for the Catering page

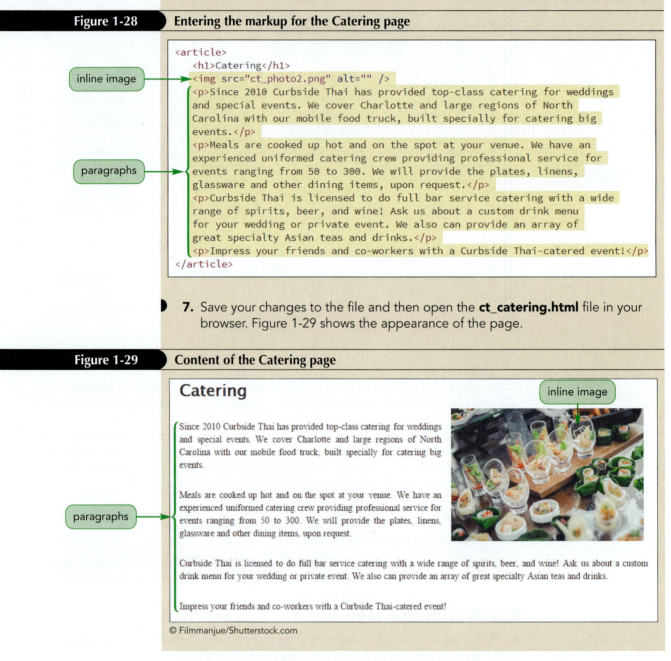

inline image

paragraphs

```
<article>
    <h1>Catering</h1>
    <img src="ct_photo2.png" alt="" />
    <p>Since 2010 Curbside Thai has provided top-class catering for weddings
    and special events. We cover Charlotte and large regions of North
    Carolina with our mobile food truck, built specially for catering big
    events.</p>
    <p>Meals are cooked up hot and on the spot at your venue. We have an
    experienced uniformed catering crew providing professional service for
    events ranging from 50 to 300. We will provide the plates, linens,
    glassware and other dining items, upon request.</p>
    <p>Curbside Thai is licensed to do full bar service catering with a wide
    range of spirits, beer, and wine! Ask us about a custom drink menu
    for your wedding or private event. We also can provide an array of
    great specialty Asian teas and drinks.</p>
    <p>Impress your friends and co-workers with a Curbside Thai-catered event!</p>
</article>
```

7. Save your changes to the file and then open the **ct_catering.html** file in your browser. Figure 1-29 shows the appearance of the page.

Figure 1-29 Content of the Catering page

Catering

inline image

Since 2010 Curbside Thai has provided top-class catering for weddings and special events. We cover Charlotte and large regions of North Carolina with our mobile food truck, built specially for catering big events.

paragraphs

Meals are cooked up hot and on the spot at your venue. We have an experienced uniformed catering crew providing professional service for events ranging from 50 to 300. We will provide the plates, linens, glassware and other dining items, upon request.

Curbside Thai is licensed to do full bar service catering with a wide range of spirits, beer, and wine! Ask us about a custom drink menu for your wedding or private event. We also can provide an array of great specialty Asian teas and drinks.

Impress your friends and co-workers with a Curbside Thai-catered event!

© Filmmanjue/Shutterstock.com

The final page you'll create in this session will contain contact information for Curbside Thai. Mark the content using paragraphs within the main page article.

To create the Contact Us page:

▶ 1. Open the **ct_contact_txt.html** file from the html01 ▶ tutorial folder in your HTML editor. Enter **your name** and **the date** in the comment section and save the file as **ct_contact.html**. Note that this page is linked to two style sheets that Sajja created.

▶ 2. Go to the **ct_pages.txt** file in your text editor.

▶ 3. Copy the Contact Us section in the text file (excluding the title).

▶ 4. Return to the **ct_contact.html** file in your HTML editor and paste the copied text directly after the `<h1>Contact Us</h1>` tag.

▶ 5. Enclose the introductory paragraph within a set of opening and closing `<p>` tags to mark it as a paragraph.

▶ 6. Enclose the three lines containing the street address within a set of opening and closing `<address>` tags to mark that content as an address. Insert the `<br />` tag at the end of the first two lines to create a line break between the name of the restaurant and the street address.

▶ 7. Mark the last two lines as paragraphs using the p element.

Figure 1-30 highlights the marked up code for Curbside Thai's contact information.

Figure 1-30	Entering the markup for the Contact Us page

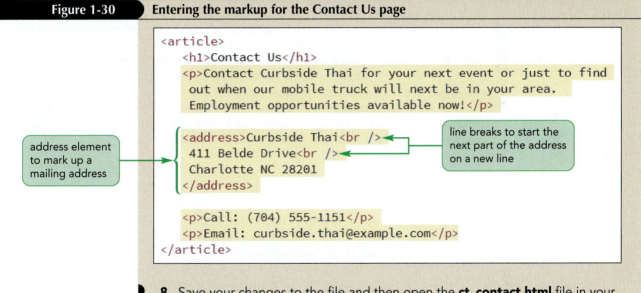

```
<article>
   <h1>Contact Us</h1>
   <p>Contact Curbside Thai for your next event or just to find
   out when our mobile truck will next be in your area.
   Employment opportunities available now!</p>

   <address>Curbside Thai<br />
   411 Belde Drive<br />
   Charlotte NC 28201
   </address>

   <p>Call: (704) 555-1151</p>
   <p>Email: curbside.thai@example.com</p>
</article>
```

address element to mark up a mailing address

line breaks to start the next part of the address on a new line

▶ 8. Save your changes to the file and then open the **ct_contact.html** file in your browser as shown in Figure 1-31.

Figure 1-31   **Content of the Contact Us page**

The Contact Us page only provides the text of the contact information but that text is static. In the next session, you'll learn how to make this content interactive by turning the contact information into hypertext.

PROSKILLS

Problem Solving: Making your Page Accessible with ARIA

The web is for everyone and that presents a special challenge when writing code for the visually impaired who will be accessing your website with a screen reader. One standard to assist screen readers is **Accessible Rich Internet Applications** (**ARIA**), which supplements HTML elements with additional attributes that provide clues as to the element's purpose as well as provide information on the current status of every page element.

One of the cornerstones of ARIA is the `role` attribute, which specifies the purpose of a given element. For example, the following `role` attribute indicates that the `header` element contains a banner, such as a logo that introduces the web page

```
<header role="banner">
    content
</header>
```

ARIA supports a list of approved role names including the following:
- alert   Content with important and usually time-sensitive information
- application   A web application, as opposed to a web document
- definition   A definition term or concept
- dialog   An application window that will require user input
- log   A region of data that is constantly modified and updated
- progress bar   Content that displays the progress status for ongoing tasks
- search   Content that provides search capability to the user
- separator   A divider that separates one region of content from another
- timer   A region that contains a numerical counter reporting on elapsed time

You can view the complete list of role attribute values and how to apply them at *www.w3.org/TR/wai-aria/roles*.

ARIA is a useful tool for enhancing the accessibility of your web page and making the rich resource that is the World Wide Web open to all. A side benefit is that accessibility and usability go hand-in-hand. A website that is highly accessible is also highly usable and that is of value to all users.

In the next session, you'll continue to work on the Curbside Thai website by adding pages describing the restaurant menu and listing the time and locations where the mobile food truck is parked.

Session 1.2 Quick Check

1. Provide code to mark the text *Gourmet Thai Cooking* as a heading with the second level of importance.

2. What element should you use to mark page content as a sidebar?

3. What is the `div` element and why will you often encounter it in pre-HTML5 code?

4. What element would you use to indicate a change of topic within a section?

5. Provide the code to mark the text *Daily Special* as emphasized text.

6. Provide the code to mark the text H_2SO_4 with subscripts.

7. Provide the code to link the web page to the CSS file mystyles.css.

8. Provide the expression to insert an em dash into a web page using the character code 8212.

9. Provide the code to insert an inline image using the source file awlogo.png and the alternate text *Art World*.

Session 1.3 Visual Overview:

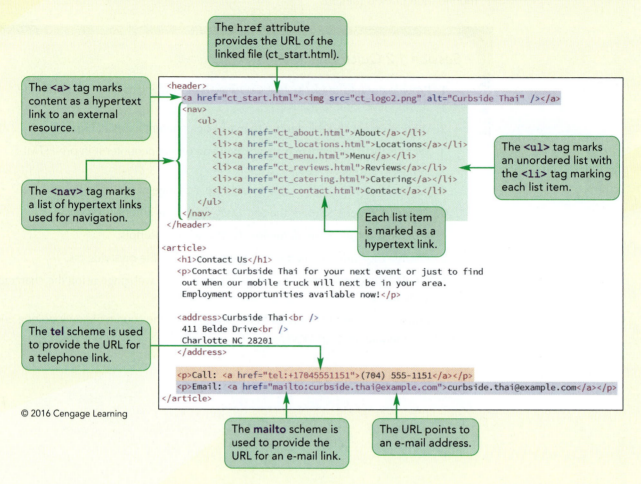

The href attribute provides the URL of the linked file (ct_start.html).

The **<a>** tag marks content as a hypertext link to an external resource.

The **<nav>** tag marks a list of hypertext links used for navigation.

The **<ul>** tag marks an unordered list with the **<li>** tag marking each list item.

Each list item is marked as a hypertext link.

The **tel** scheme is used to provide the URL for a telephone link.

```
<header>
    <a href="ct_start.html"><img src="ct_logo2.png" alt="Curbside Thai" /></a>
    <nav>
        <ul>
            <li><a href="ct_about.html">About</a></li>
            <li><a href="ct_locations.html">Locations</a></li>
            <li><a href="ct_menu.html">Menu</a></li>
            <li><a href="ct_reviews.html">Reviews</a></li>
            <li><a href="ct_catering.html">Catering</a></li>
            <li><a href="ct_contact.html">Contact</a></li>
        </ul>
    </nav>
</header>

<article>
    <h1>Contact Us</h1>
    <p>Contact Curbside Thai for your next event or just to find
    out when our mobile truck will next be in your area.
    Employment opportunities available now!</p>

    <address>Curbside Thai<br />
    411 Belde Drive<br />
    Charlotte NC 28201
    </address>

    <p>Call: <a href="tel:+17045551151">(704) 555-1151</a></p>
    <p>Email: <a href="mailto:curbside.thai@example.com">curbside.thai@example.com</a></p>
</article>
```

© 2016 Cengage Learning

The **mailto** scheme is used to provide the URL for an e-mail link.

The URL points to an e-mail address.

Lists and Hypertext Links

Clicking the logo jumps the user to the ct_start.html file.

About   Locations   Menu   Reviews   Catering   Contact

Contact Us

Contact Curbside Thai for your next event or just to find out when our mobile truck will next be in your area. Employment opportunities available now!

The navigation list encloses links to pages in the Curbside Thai website.

Curbside Thai
411 Belde Drive
Charlotte NC 28201

The telephone link opens a telephony application when clicked.

Call: (704) 555-1151

Email: curbside.thai@example.com

Curbside Thai • 411 Belde Drive, Charlotte NC 28201 • 704-555-1151

The e-mail link opens an e-mail program when clicked.

Working with Lists

In the last session, you worked with some of HTML's sectioning and grouping elements to add order and structure to your web page. Another type of grouping element is a list. HTML supports three types of lists: ordered lists, unordered lists, and description lists.

Ordered Lists

Ordered lists are used for items that follow some defined sequential order, such as items arranged alphabetically or numerically. An ordered list is marked using the `ol` (ordered list) element with each list item marked using the `li` element. The general structure is

```
<ol>
   <li>item1</li>
   <li>item2</li>
   ...
</ol>
```

where *item1*, *item2*, and so forth are the items in the list. For example, the following ordered list ranks the top-three most populated states:

```
<ol>
   <li>California</li>
   <li>Texas</li>
   <li>New York</li>
</ol>
```

By default, browsers will display list items alongside a numeric marker. In the case of ordered lists, this is a numeric value starting with the number 1 and ascending in value. For example, the ordered list of states would be rendered in most browsers as

1. California
2. Texas
3. New York

Note that because both the `ol` and `li` elements are considered grouping elements, each list item will appear, by default, on a new line in the document unless a different style is applied to those elements.

To display different numbering, you use the `start` and `reversed` attributes of the `ol` element. The `start` attribute provides the numeric value for the first item in the list, while the `reversed` attribute specifies that the list numbers should be displayed in descending order. Thus, the following HTML code that lists the most populated states

```
<ol reversed start="50">
   <li>California</li>
   <li>Texas</li>
   <li>New York</li>
</ol>
```

would be rendered as a list in descending order starting from 50

50. California
49. Texas
48. New York

You can explicitly define the item value by adding the `value` attribute to each list item. The list shown previously could also have been generated with the following code:

```
<ol>
   <li value="50">California</li>
   <li value="49">Texas</li>
   <li value="48">New York</li>
</ol>
```

You can use style sheets to display lists using alphabetical markers (A, B, C, …) or Roman Numerals (I, II, III, …) in place of numeric values. You'll explore this technique in Tutorial 2.

Unordered Lists

Unordered lists are used for lists in which the items have no sequential order. The structure for an unordered list is similar to that used with ordered lists except that the list items are grouped within the following `ul` (unordered list) element:

```
<ul>
   <li>item1</li>
   <li>item2</li>
   …
</ul>
```

For example, the following HTML code creates an ordered list of all of the states along the Pacific coast:

```
<ul>
   <li>California</li>
   <li>Oregon</li>
   <li>Washington</li>
</ul>
```

By default, browsers will display items from an unordered list alongside a marker such as a bullet point. Thus, an unordered list of Pacific coast states might be rendered as

- California
- Oregon
- Washington

Once again, the exact appearance of an unordered list will depend on the style sheet that is applied to the element.

Creating a Nested List

Because the li element is itself a grouping element, it can be used to group other lists, which in turn creates a series of **nested lists**. The general structure for a nested collection of unordered list is

```
<ul>
    <li>Item 1</li>
    <li>Item 2
        <ul>
            <li>Sub Item 1</li>
            <li>Sub Item 2</li>
        </ul>
    </li>
</ul>
```

where Sub Item 1, Sub Item 2, and so forth are items contained within the Item 2 list. For example, an unordered list of states and cities within those states could be marked up as

```
<ul>
    <li>California</li>
    <li>Oregon
        <ul>
            <li>Portland</li>
            <li>Salem</li>
        </ul>
    </li>
    <li>Washington</li>
</ul>
```

Most browsers will differentiate the various levels by increasing the indentation and using a different list symbol at each level of nested lists, for example, rendering the HTML code above as

- California
- Oregon
    - Portland
    - Salem
- Washington

The markers used at each level and the amount of indentation applied to each nested list is determined by style sheets, either those built into the browser or those supplied by the page designer. You'll explore this technique in Tutorial 2.

Description Lists

A third type of list is the **description list** containing a list of terms and matching descriptions. The description list is grouped by the dl (description list) element, the terms are marked with the dt (description term) element, and the description(s) associated with each term is marked by the dd element. The general structure is

```
<dl>
    <dt>term1</dt>
    <dd>description1</dd>
    <dt>term2</dt>
    <dd>description2a</dd>
    <dd>description2b</dd>
    ...
</dl>
```

where *term1*, *term2*, and so forth are the terms in the list and *description1*, *description2a*, *description2b*, and so forth are the descriptions associated with the terms. Note that descriptions must always directly follow the term they describe and that more than one description may be provided with each term.

By default, most browsers will indent the descriptions associated with each term. Markers are rarely displayed alongside either the description term or the description.

Sajja wants to use a description list in a page that displays some of the menu items sold by Curbside Thai. He's already started work on the HTML code but needs you to complete it by adding the markup for the description list.

To Complete the Menu Page:

1. Open the **ct_menu_txt.html** file from the html01 ▸ tutorial folder in your HTML editor. Enter *your name* and *the date* in the comment section and save the file as **ct_menu.html**.

2. Open the **ct_pages.txt** file in your text editor if it is not already open and copy the five menu items listed in the Mobile Menu section.

3. Return to the **ct_menu.html** file in your HTML editor and paste the copied text directly after the <h1>Mobile Menu</h1> tag.

4. Enclose the entire menu within an opening and closing <dl> tag.

5. Mark the name of each menu item using the dt element. Mark the corresponding description using the dd element. Indent your code to make it easier to read and interpret.

   Figure 1-32 shows the completed code for the description list of the mobile menu.

Figure 1-32 | **Marking the restaurant menu as a description list**

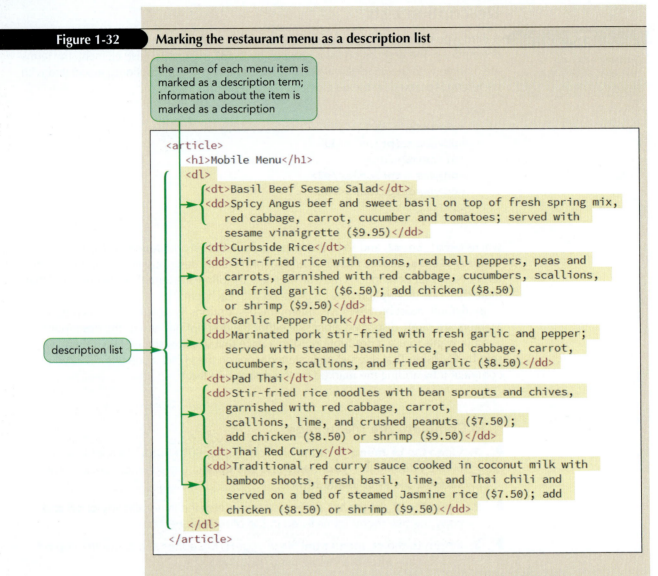

the name of each menu item is marked as a description term; information about the item is marked as a description

description list

```
<article>
    <h1>Mobile Menu</h1>
    <dl>
        <dt>Basil Beef Sesame Salad</dt>
        <dd>Spicy Angus beef and sweet basil on top of fresh spring mix,
            red cabbage, carrot, cucumber and tomatoes; served with
            sesame vinaigrette ($9.95)</dd>
        <dt>Curbside Rice</dt>
        <dd>Stir-fried rice with onions, red bell peppers, peas and
            carrots, garnished with red cabbage, cucumbers, scallions,
            and fried garlic ($6.50); add chicken ($8.50)
            or shrimp ($9.50)</dd>
        <dt>Garlic Pepper Pork</dt>
        <dd>Marinated pork stir-fried with fresh garlic and pepper;
            served with steamed Jasmine rice, red cabbage, carrot,
            cucumbers, scallions, and fried garlic ($8.50)</dd>
        <dt>Pad Thai</dt>
        <dd>Stir-fried rice noodles with bean sprouts and chives,
            garnished with red cabbage, carrot,
            scallions, lime, and crushed peanuts ($7.50);
            add chicken ($8.50) or shrimp ($9.50)</dd>
        <dt>Thai Red Curry</dt>
        <dd>Traditional red curry sauce cooked in coconut milk with
            bamboo shoots, fresh basil, lime, and Thai chili and
            served on a bed of steamed Jasmine rice ($7.50); add
            chicken ($8.50) or shrimp ($9.50)</dd>
    </dl>
</article>
```

6. Save your changes to the file and then open the **ct_menu.html** file in your browser. Figure 1-33 shows the completed menu for Curbside Thai.

Figure 1-33 **Curbside Thai menu as a description list**

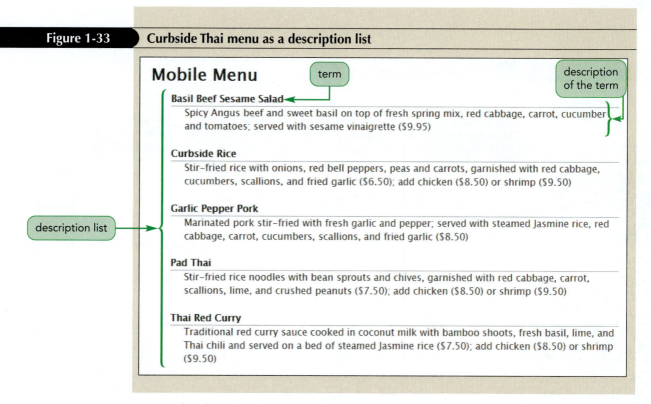

Note that the style sheet that Sajja uses for his website inserts a dividing line between each term and description in the list.

Description lists can also be used with any general list that pairs one list of items with another list that provides additional information about the items in the first list. For example, Sajja has a page that lists the times and locations at which the Curbside Thai will make an appearance. Complete this page by enclosing the content within a description list, marking the times as the list "terms" and the locations as the list "descriptions".

To Create a Page of Times and Locations:

1. Open the **ct_locations_txt.html** file from the html01 ▶ tutorial folder in your HTML editor. Enter **your name** and **the date** in the comment section and save the file as **ct_locations.html**.

2. Return to **the ct_pages.txt** file in your text editor and copy the four locations from the Today's Locations section.

3. Return to the **ct_locations.html** file in your HTML editor and paste the copied text directly after the `<h1>Today's Locations</h1>` tag.

4. Mark the entire list of times and locations using the `dl` element. Mark each time using the `dt` element and each location using the `dd` element. Indent your code to make it easier to read and interpret.

5. In order to distinguish this description list from other description lists in the website, add the attribute `id="ct_locations"` to the opening `<dl>` tag.

6. Sajja has a map that he wants displayed alongside the list of times and locations. Directly after the `h1` element within the `article` element, insert the following inline image:

   ```
   <img src="ct_map.png" alt="" />
   ```

Figure 1-34 highlights the newly added code for the Today's Locations page.

Figure 1-34 Creating a description list

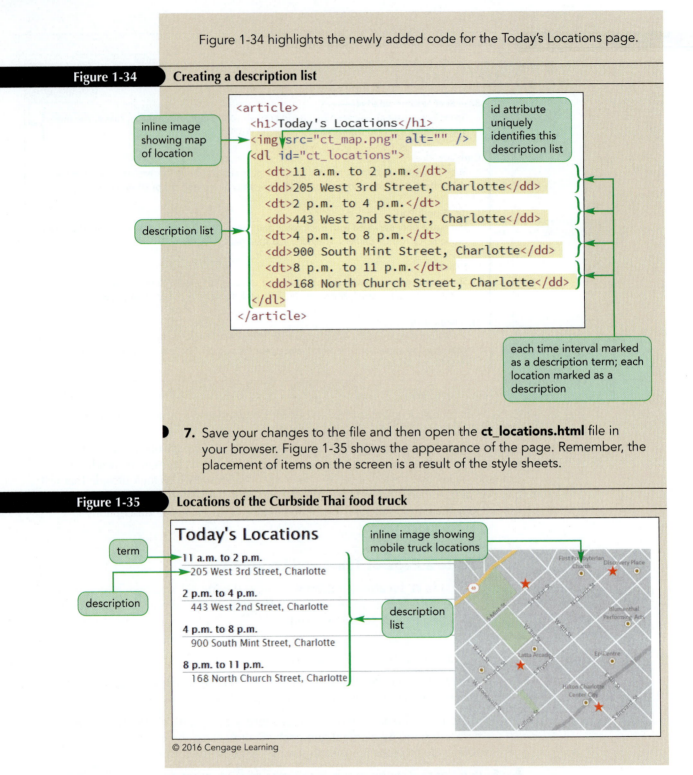

7. Save your changes to the file and then open the **ct_locations.html** file in your browser. Figure 1-35 shows the appearance of the page. Remember, the placement of items on the screen is a result of the style sheets.

Figure 1-35 Locations of the Curbside Thai food truck

© 2016 Cengage Learning

From this page, Curbside Thai customers can quickly find the mobile truck. A page like this will have to be updated, probably daily, as the truck moves around. This is often better accomplished using database programs on the web server that will generate both the HTML and the inline image file.

INSIGHT

Marking Dates and Times

The adage that nothing ever quite disappears on the Internet also means that the web is populated with old articles, documents, and news stories that are no longer relevant or perhaps, even accurate. Any content you publish to the web should be time-stamped to document its history. One way of marking a date-time value is with the following `time` element

```
<time datetime="value">content</time>
```

where *value* is the date and time associated with the enclosed content. Dates should be entered in the *yyyy-mm-dd* format where *yyyy* is the four-digit year value, *mm* is the two-digit month value, and *dd* is the two-digit day value. Times should be entered in the *hh:mm* format for the two-digit hour and minute values entered in 24-hour time. To combine both dates and times, enter the date and time values separated by a space or the letter *T* as in the following code:

```
<footer>Last updated at:
   <time datetime="2017-03-01T14:52">March 1 2017 at 2:52
p.m.</time>
</footer>
```

For international applications, you can base your time values on the common standard of Greenwich Mean Time. For example, the following code includes the information that the time is based on the Eastern time zone, which is 5 hours behind Greenwich Mean Time:

```
<p>Webinar starts at:
   <time datetime="2017-03-10T20:30-05:00">3:30 p.m.
(EST)</time>
</p>
```

While the value of the `datetime` attribute is not visible to users, it is readable by machines such as search engines, which can include the date and time in reporting search results. You can read more about the `time` element on the W3C website, including information on marking a time duration between two events.

You've now created six web pages for the Curbside Thai website. Next, you'll link these pages together so that users can easily navigate between the pages in the website. You'll start by creating a navigation list.

Navigation Lists

A **navigation list** is an unordered list of hypertext links placed within the `nav` element. The general structure is

```
<nav>
   <ul>
      <li>link1</li>
      <li>link2</li>
...
   </ul>
</nav>
```

where *link1*, *link2*, and so forth are hypertext links. While hypertext links can be placed anywhere within the page, having a central list of links makes the website easier to work with and navigate.

Add this structure to the About Curbside Thai web page, creating entries for each of the six web pages you created in this tutorial.

To Create a Navigation List:

1. Open the **ct_about.html** file in your HTML editor if it is not already open.

2. Go to the body header and, directly below the inline image for the Curbside Thai logo, insert the following navigation list:

```
<nav>
    <ul>
        <li>About</li>
        <li>Locations</li>
        <li>Menu</li>
        <li>Reviews</li>
        <li>Catering</li>
        <li>Contact</li>
    </ul>
</nav>
```

Figure 1-36 highlights the structure of the navigation list.

Figure 1-36 **Creating a navigation list**

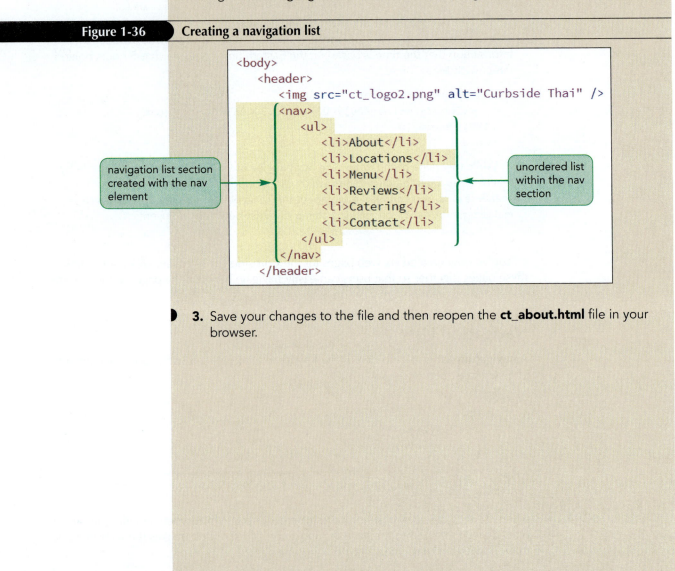

3. Save your changes to the file and then reopen the **ct_about.html** file in your browser.

Figure 1-37 shows appearance of the navigation list.

| Figure 1-37 | Navigation list for the Curbside Thai website |

layout of the navigation list based on Sajja's style sheet

items within the navigation list

Curbside Thai brings the rich flavor of Thailand to North Carolina. Master Chef Sajja Adulet, with over 35 years of experience at the House of Asia, now offers that same fine dining to the streets of Charlotte with our modern mobile food truck.

This is not bland vendor food packaged in greasy paper boxes! Sample his acclaimed cuisine at our various mobile locations throughout downtown Charlotte from 11 a.m. to 7 p.m. on Monday through Thursday, and 11 a.m. to 11 p.m. on Friday and Saturday. Taste the difference! If you can't get away from your desk, *Curbside Thai will deliver.*

© 2016 Cengage Learning; © Kzenon/Shutterstock.com

Note that the appearance of the navigation list in the ct_about.html file is based on styles in Sajja's style sheets. Navigation lists can be displayed in a wide variety of ways depending on the styles being employed and the same navigation list might be arranged one way for desktop devices and another way for mobile devices. You'll learn more about this in Tutorial 5.

Now that you've created the structure of the navigation list, you can mark the items within the list as hypertext links.

Working with Hypertext Links

Hypertext is created by enclosing content within a set of opening and closing <a> tags in the following structure

```
<a href="url">content</a>
```

where *url* is the **Uniform Resource Locator** (**URL**), which is a standard address format used to link to a variety of resources including documents, e-mail addresses, telephone numbers, and text messaging services, and *content* is the document content marked as a link. When linking to another HTML file in the same folder, the URL is simply the name of the file. For example, a hypertext link to the ct_menu.html file would be marked as

```
<a href="ct_menu.html">Menu</a>
```

When the user clicks or touches the word *Menu*, the browser will load the ct_menu.html file in the browser. Note that filenames are case sensitive on some web servers, which means those servers differentiate between files named ct_menu.html and CT_Menu.html. The standard for all web filenames is to always use lowercase letters and to avoid using special characters and blank spaces.

The default style is to underline hypertext links and to display a hypertext link in a different text color if the user has previously visited the page. However, page designers can substitute different hypertext link styles from their own style sheets. We'll explore this technique in Tutorial 2.

Marking a Hypertext Link

- To mark content as a hypertext link, use

  `<a href="url">content</a>`

  where *url* is the address of the linked document and *content* is the document content that is being marked as a link.

Mark the six entries in the navigation list, pointing each entry to the corresponding Curbside Thai page.

To create hypertext links:

1. Return to the **ct_about.html** file in your HTML editor.

2. Mark the first entry as a hypertext link pointing to ct_about.html file by changing the list item to

   `<a href="ct_about.html">About</a>`

3. Change the code of the second list item to

   `<a href="ct_locations.html">Locations</a>`

4. Continuing in the same fashion, change the Menu entry to a link pointing to the **ct_menu.html** file, the Reviews entry to a link pointing to the **ct_reviews.html** file, the Catering entry to a link pointing to the **ct_catering.html** file, and the Contact entry to a link pointing to the **ct_contact.html** file.

   Figure 1-38 highlights the newly added code that changes all of the items in the navigation list to hypertext links.

Figure 1-38 **Marking hypertext links**

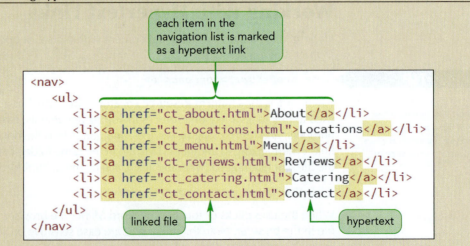

5. Save your changes to the file and then reopen the **ct_about.html** file in your browser.

6. Click each of the six navigation list entries and verify that the browser loads the corresponding web page. Use the Back button on your browser to return to the About Curbside Thai page after you view each document.

Trouble? If the links do not work, be sure your code matches Figure 1-38. For example, check the spelling of each filename in the `href` attribute of each `<a>` tag to ensure it matches the filename of the corresponding Curbside Thai web page and check to be sure you have all needed opening and closing tags.

You may have noticed that when your mouse pointer moved over a hypertext link in the navigation list, the appearance of the link changed to white text on a black background. This is an example of a **rollover effect**, which is used to provide visual clues that the text is hypertext rather than normal text. You'll learn how to create rollover effects in Tutorial 2.

Turning an Inline Image into a Link

Inline images can also be turned into links by enclosing the image within opening and closing `<a>` tags. Turn the Curbside Thai logo into a hyperlink that points to the Startup page you opened in the first session.

To mark an image as a hypertext link:

▶ **1.** Return to the **ct_about.html** file in your HTML editor.

▶ **2.** Mark the image in the body header as a hyperlink by changing the HTML code to

```
<a href="ct_start.html"><img src="ct_logo2.png"
alt="Curbside Thai" /></a>
```

Figure 1-39 highlights the code to change the logo image to a hypertext link.

Figure 1-39   Marking an inline image as a hypertext link

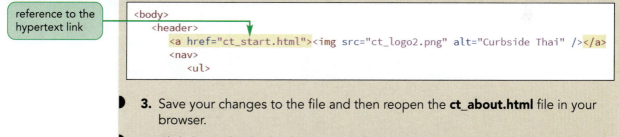

```
<body>
    <header>
        <a href="ct_start.html"><img src="ct_logo2.png" alt="Curbside Thai" /></a>
        <nav>
            <ul>
```

reference to the hypertext link

▶ **3.** Save your changes to the file and then reopen the **ct_about.html** file in your browser.

▶ **4.** Click the Curbside Thai logo and verify that the browser opens the Curbside Thai Startup page. Click the Back button to return to the About Curbside Thai page.

Sajja wants to be able to jump to any document in the Curbside Thai website from any page. He asks you to copy the hypertext links, including the image hyperlink, you just created in the ct_about.html file to the other documents in the website.

To copy and paste the hypertext links:

▶ **1.** Return to the **ct_about.html** file in your HTML editor.

▶ **2.** Copy the entire content of the page header from the opening `<header>` tag through to the closing `</header>` tag, including the revised code for the company logo and navigation list.

3. Go to the **ct_locations.html** file in your HTML editor. Paste the copied HTML code, replacing the previous page header in this document. Save your changes to the file.

4. Repeat the previous step for the **ct_menu.html**, **ct_reviews.html**, **ct_catering.html**, and **ct_contact.html** files, replacing the body header in each of those documents with the revised header from ct_about.html. Save your changes to each file.

5. Reopen the **ct_locations.html** file in your browser and verify that you can jump from one page to another by clicking items in the navigation list at the top of each page. Also verify that you can jump to the Startup page at any time by clicking the Curbside Thai logo.

Specifying the Folder Path

In the links you created, the browser assumed that the linked files were in the same folder as the current page. However, large websites containing hundreds of documents often place documents in separate folders to make them easier to manage.

Figure 1-40 shows a preview of how Sajja might organize his files as the Curbside Thai website increases in size and complexity. In this structure, all folders start from a **root folder** named *thai* that contains the site's home page, which Sajja has stored in the index.html file. Sajja has moved all of his images and CSS style sheet files into their own folders. He has divided the rest of the web pages among three subfolders: the general folder for pages containing general information about the restaurant, the mobile folder for pages with content specifically about the mobile food service, and the catering folder for pages describing Curbside Thai's catering opportunities.

Figure 1-40 A sample folder structure

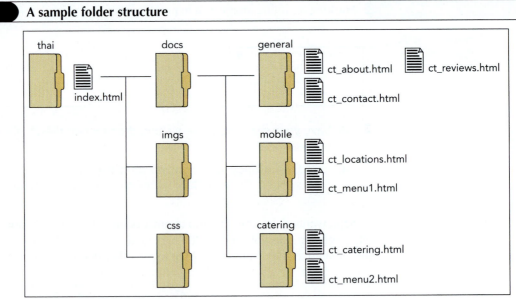

© 2016 Cengage Learning

To create links between files in separate folders, you must provide a path to the linked file. HTML supports two kinds of paths: absolute and relative.

Absolute Paths

An **absolute path** is a path that starts from the root folder and processes down the entire folder structure described with the expression

```
/folder1/folder2/folder3/file
```

where *folder1* is the root folder, followed by the subfolders *folder2*, *folder3*, and so forth, down to the linked file. For example, based on the structure shown previously in Figure 1-40, an absolute path pointing to the ct_catering.html file would have the expression

```
/thai/docs/catering/ct_catering.html
```

If files are located on different drives as well as in different folders, you must include the drive letter in the path with the expression

```
/drive|/folder1/folder2/folder3/file
```

where *drive* is the letter assigned to the drive. Note that the drive letter must be followed by the | character. Thus, if the ct_catering.html file were located on drive E, the absolute path that includes the drive would have the expression

```
/E|/thai/docs/catering/ct_catering.html
```

Note that you don't have to include a drive letter if the linked document is located on the same drive as the current file.

Relative Paths

When many folders and subfolders are involved, absolute path expression can quickly become long and cumbersome to work with. For this reason, most web designers prefer **relative paths** in which the path is expressed relative to the location of the current document. If the current document and linked file are in the same folder, there is no path and you need only include the filename. If the linked file is in a subfolder of the current document, the path includes all of the subfolder names starting from the location of the current page using the expression

```
folder1/folder2/folder3/file
```

where *folder1*, *folder2*, *folder3*, and so forth are subfolders of the current document. For example, the relative path to the ct_about.html file starting from the index.html file is

```
docs/general/ct_about.html
```

Note that relative paths are often expressed in terms of familial relationships such as parent, child, descendant, sibling, and so forth in order to indicate the hierarchical nature of the folder structure. Relative paths can also go up the hierarchy to parent folders by including the symbol (**..**), which means "go up one level." Thus, to go from ct_about.html in the general folder up two levels to the index.html file, you would enter the expression

```
../../index.html
```

TIP

You can reference the current folder using a single period (.) character.

Finally, to go sideways in the folder structure by going to a file in a different folder but on the same level, you go up to the parent folder and then back down to a different child folder. For example, to go from the ct_about.html file in the general folder to the ct_locations.html file in the mobile folder, you would use the relative path expression

```
../mobile/ct_locations.html
```

In this expression, the link goes up to the parent folder docs through the use of the `..` reference and then back down through the mobile folder to ct_locations.html.

You should almost always use relative paths in your links. If you have to move your files to a different computer or server, you can move the entire folder structure without having to edit the relative paths you've created. If you use absolute paths, you will have to revise each link to reflect the new location of the folder tree on the new device.

Setting the Base Path

As you've just seen, a browser resolves relative paths based on the location of the current document. You define a different starting point for relative paths by adding the following base element to the document head

```
<base href="url" />
```

where `url` is the location that you want the browser to use when resolving relative paths in the current document. The `base` element is useful when a single document from the website is moved to a new folder. Rather than rewriting all of the relative paths to reflect the document's new location, the `base` element can point to the document's old location allowing relative paths to work as before.

PROSKILLS

Decision Making: Managing Your Website

Websites can quickly grow to dozens or hundreds of pages. As the size of a site increases, it becomes more difficult to get a clear picture of the site's structure and content. Imagine deleting or moving a file in a website that contains dozens of folders and hundreds of files. Could you easily project the effect of this change? Would all of your hypertext links still work after you moved or deleted the file?

To effectively manage a website, you should implement clear decision making skills by following a few important rules. The first is to be consistent in how you structure the site. If you decide to collect all image files in one folder, you should continue that practice as you add more pages and images. Websites are more likely to break down if files and folders are scattered throughout the server without a consistent rule or pattern. Decide on a structure early and stick with it.

A second rule is to decide on and then create a folder structure that matches the structure of the website itself. If the pages can be easily categorized into different groups, those groupings should also be reflected in the groupings of the subfolders. The names you assign to your files and folders should also reflect their uses on the website. This makes it easier for you to predict how modifying a file or folder might impact other pages on the website.

Finally, you should document your work by adding comments to each new web page. Comments are useful not only for colleagues who may be working on the site but also for the author who must revisit those files months or even years after creating them. The comments should include

- The page's filename and location
- The page's author and the date the page was initially created
- A list of any supporting files used in the document, such as image and audio files
- A list of the files that link to the page and their locations
- A list of the files that the page links to and their locations

By following these rules, you can reduce a lot of the headaches associated with maintaining a large and complex website.

Linking to a Location within a Document

Hypertext can point to locations within a document. For example, you could link a specific definition within a long glossary page to save users the trouble of scrolling through the document. Websites containing the text of novels or plays can contain links to key passages or phrases within those works. When a link is established to a location within a document, the browser will jump to that location automatically scrolling the page to the linked location.

Marking Locations with the `id` Attribute

In order to enable users to jump to a specific location within a document, you need to identify that location by adding the following `id` attribute to an element tag at that location

```
id="text"
```

where *text* is the name assigned to the ID. Imagine that Sajja writes a long page describing the full menu offered by Curbside Thai. He could mark the location in the page where the lunch menu is displayed by adding the following `id` attribute to the h2 heading that marks the start of the Lunch Menu section.

```
<h2 id="lunch">Lunch Menu</h2>
```

Note that IDs must be unique. If you assign the same ID to more than one element, the browser will jump to the first occurrence of that ID value.

Linking to an `id`

Once you've marked the location with an ID, you link to that element using the following hypertext link:

```
<a href="file#id">content</a>
```

where *file* points to the location and filename of the linked document and *id* is the value of an `id` attribute within that document. For example the following hypertext link points to the element with the ID "lunch" within the ct_fullmenus.html file.

```
<a href="ct_fullmenus.html#lunch">View our Lunch Menu</a>
```

To link to a location within the current page, include only the ID value along with the # symbol. Thus, the following hypertext link points to the lunch ID within the current web page:

```
<a href="#lunch">View our Lunch Menu</a>
```

In both cases, clicking or touching the link will cause the browser to automatically scroll to the location within the page.

Anchors and the `name` Attribute

Early web pages did not support the use of the `id` attribute as a way of marking locations within a document. Instead, they used the <a> tag as an anchor to mark that page location (hence the "a" in <a> tag). The general form of the anchor was

```
<a name="anchor">content</a>
```

where *anchor* is the name given to the anchored text. Inserting content within the <a> tag was optional because the primary purpose of the tag was to mark a document location, not to mark up content. For example, the following code would establish an anchor at the start of the lunch section in the Curbside Thai full menu:

```
<h2><a name="lunch"></a>Lunch Menu</h2>
```

Once an anchor had been set, you would link to the anchor using the same syntax you would use with the `id` attribute. The use of anchors is a deprecated feature of HTML and is not supported in strict applications of XHTML, but you will still see anchors used in older code.

REFERENCE

Linking to a Location Within a Document

- To mark a location, add a unique ID to an element at that document location using the following `id` attribute

  `id="text"`

  where *text* is the value of the ID.
- To link to that location from a different document, use the hypertext reference

  `<a href="file#text">content</a>`

  where *file* is the name and path location (if necessary) of the external file and *text* is the value of the ID.
- To link to that location from within the same document, use the hypertext reference

  `<a href="#text">content</a>`

Linking to the Internet and Other Resources

The type of resource that a hypertext link points to is indicated by the link's URL. All URLs share the general structure

  `scheme:location`

where *scheme* indicates the resource type and *location* provides the resource location. The name of the scheme is taken from the network protocol used to access the resource where a **protocol** is a set of rules defining how information is passed between two devices. Pages on the web use the **Hypertext Transfer Protocol** (**HTTP**) protocol and therefore the URL for many web pages start with the `http` scheme. Other schemes that can be included within a URL are described in Figure 1-41.

Figure 1-41 **Commonly used URL schemes**

Scheme	Description
`fax`	A FAX phone number
`file`	A document stored locally on a user's computer
`ftp`	A document stored on an FTP server
`geo`	A geophysical coordinate
`http`	A resource on the World Wide Web
`https`	A resource on the World Wide Web accessed over a secure encrypted connection
`mailto`	An e-mail address
`tel`	A telephone number
`sms`	A mobile text message sent via the Short Message Service

© 2016 Cengage Learning

Linking to a Web Resource

If you have ever accessed the web, you should be very familiar with website URLs, which have the general structure

```
http://server/path/filename#id
```

or for secure connections

```
https://server/path/filename#id
```

where *server* is the name of the web server hosting the resource, *path* is the path to the file on that server, *filename* is the name of the file, and if necessary, *id* is the name of an id or anchor within the file. For example, the following URL uses the HTTP protocol to access the web server at *www.curbsidethai.com*, linking to the document location named *lunch* within the ct_menus.html file in the /thai/docs folder:

```
http://www.curbsidethai.com/thai/docs/ct_menus.html#lunch
```

URLs are often entered in a more abbreviated form, *http://www.curbsidethai.com* for example, with no path or filename. Those URLs point to the default home page located in the top folder in the server's folder tree. Many servers use index.html as the filename for the default home page, so the URL *http://www.curbsidethai.com* would be equivalent to *http://www.curbsidethai.com/index.html*.

INSIGHT

Understanding Domain Names

The server name portion of a URL is also called the **domain name**. By studying a domain name, you learn about the server hosting the website. Each domain name contains a hierarchy of names separated by periods (.), with the top level appearing at the far right end. The top level, called an **extension**, indicates the general audience supported by the web server. For example, *.edu* is the extension reserved for educational institutions, *.gov* is used for agencies of the United States government, and *.com* is used for commercial sites or general-use sites.

The next lower level appearing to the immediate left of the extension displays the name of the individual or organization hosting the site. The domain name *curbsidethai.com* indicates a commercial or general-use site owned by Curbside Thai. To avoid duplicating domain names, the top two levels of the domain must be registered with the **Internet Assigned Numbers Authority** (**IANA**) before they can be used. You can usually register your domain name through your web hosting company. Note: You must pay an annual fee to keep a domain name.

The lowest levels of the domain, which appear farthest to the left in the domain name, are assigned by the individual or company hosting the site. Large websites involving hundreds of pages typically divide their domain names into several levels. For example, a large company like Microsoft might have one domain name for file downloads—*downloads.microsoft.com*—and another domain name for customer service—*service.microsoft.com*. Finally, the first part of the domain name displays the name of the hard drive or resource storing the website files. Many companies have standardized on www as the initial part of their domain names.

Linking to an E-Mail Address

Many websites use e-mail to allow users to communicate with a site's owner, sales representative, or technical support staff. You can turn an e-mail address into a hypertext link using the URL:

```
mailto:address
```

where *address* is the e-mail address. Activating the link opens the user's e-mail program with the e-mail address automatically inserted into the To field of a new outgoing message. To create a hypertext link to the e-mail address *s.adulet@example.com*, you could use the following URL:

```
mailto:s.adulet@example.com
```

TIP

To link to more than one e-mail address, add the addresses to the mailto link in a comma-separated list.

The mailto protocol also allows you to insert additional fields into the e-mail message using the URL:

```
mailto:address?field1=value1&field2=value2&...
```

where *field1*, *field2*, and so forth are different e-mail fields and *value1*, *value2*, and so forth are the field values. Fields include `subject` for the subject line of the e-mail message and `body` for the message body. To create a link to an e-mail message with the following content

```
TO: s.adulet@example.com
SUBJECT: Test
BODY: Test Message
```

you would use the URL

```
mailto:s.adulet@example.com?subject=Test&body=Test%20Message
```

Notice that the body text uses `%20` character code to represent a blank space since URLs cannot contain blank spaces.

On the Contact Us page, Sajja has inserted the Curbside Thai's e-mail address. Convert this e-mail address into a hypertext link.

To link to an e-mail address:

1. Go to the **ct_contact.html** file in your HTML editor.

2. Change the Curbside Thai e-mail address into the following mailto hypertext link:

A mailto hypertext link to an external resource must include the mailto scheme name in order to be recognized by the browser.

```
<a href="mailto:curbside.thai@example.com">
    curbside.thai@example.com
</a>
```

Note that this is a fictional e-mail address. If you want to test this link, change the URL to a link pointing to your own e-mail address. Figure 1-42 highlights the hypertext code to the linked e-mail address.

Figure 1-42 **Linking to an e-mail address**

e-mail address

e-mail address marked as a hyperlink

mailto scheme indicates that this is an e-mail link

```
<p>Call: (704) 555-1151</p>
<p>Email: <a href="mailto:curbside.thai@example.com">curbside.thai@example.com</a></p>
</article>
```

3. Save your changes to the file and then reopen the **ct_contact.html** file in your browser.

> **4.** Click the e-mail address link and verify that your device opens your e-mail program with the Curbside Thai address already entered. Close the e-mail program without sending a message.
>
> **Trouble?** Depending on your device, you may have to set up your e-mail program to accept hypertext links.

E-Mail Links and Spam

Use caution when adding e-mail links to your website. While it may make it more convenient for users to contact you, it also might make you more vulnerable to spam. **Spam** is unsolicited e-mail sent to large numbers of people, promoting products, services, and in some cases inappropriate websites. Spammers create their e-mail lists by scanning discussion groups, stealing Internet mailing lists, and using programs called **e-mail harvesters** to scan HTML code for the e-mail addresses contained in mailto URLs. Many developers have removed e-mail links from their websites in order to foil these harvesters, replacing the links with web forms that submit e-mail requests to a secure server.

There is no quick and easy solution to this problem. Fighting spammers is an ongoing battle, and they have proved very resourceful in overcoming some of the defenses people have created. As you develop your website, you should carefully consider how to handle e-mail addresses and review the most current methods for safeguarding that information.

Linking to a Phone Number

With the increased use of mobile phones to access the web, many developers now include links to phone numbers for their company's customer service or help line. Activating the link brings up the user's phone app with the number already entered, making it easier and more convenient to call the business or organization. The URL for a phone link is

```
tel:phone
```

where *phone* are the digits of the linked number. For example, the following code creates a telephone link to the Curbside Thai number:

```
Call: <a href="tel:+17045551151">(704) 555-1151</a>
```

> **TIP**
>
> Currently, Skype on the desktop uses `callto:` in place of the `tel:` scheme for telephone links. There are program scripts available on the web that you can use in order to work with both protocols.

Because websites are international, any telephone link should include the international dialing prefix (+1 for the United States) and the area code. Spaces or dashes between digits are optional with the exception of the + symbol before the international calling code. However, you can insert pauses in the phone number (used when accessing an extension) by inserting the p symbol, as in the following telephone link:

```
<a href="tel:+17045551151p22">Call: 555-1151 ext. 22</a>
```

Sajja asks you to change the telephone number from the Contact Us page into a telephone link.

To link to a phone number:

1. Return to the **ct_contact.html** file in your HTML editor.

2. Change the Curbside Thai phone number into the following hypertext link:

   ```
   <a href="tel:+17045551151">
       (704) 555-1151
   </a>
   ```

   Once again this number is fictional; you can change the URL to a link pointing to your own phone number if you want to test the link on a mobile device. Figure 1-43 highlights the hypertext code of the telephone link.

Figure 1-43   **Marking a telephone link**

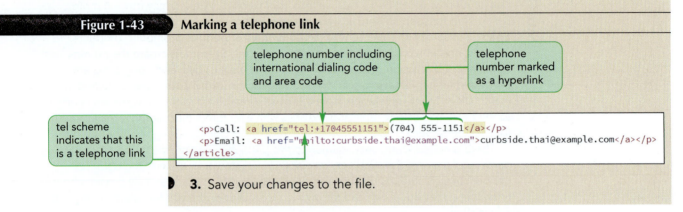

3. Save your changes to the file.

HTML supports links to other types of telephony devices. For example, you can create a link to a fax machine using the `fax:` scheme and a link to your text messaging app by using the `sms:` scheme.

Working with Hypertext Attributes

HTML provides several attributes to the a element that control the behavior and appearance of hypertext links. Figure 1-44 describes these attributes.

Figure 1-44   **Attributes of the a element**

Attribute	Description
`href="url"`	Provides the *url* of the hypertext link
`target=(_blank|_parent|_self|_top)`	Specifies where to open the linked document
`download="filename"`	Indicates that the link should be downloaded as a file, where *filename* is the name given to the downloaded file [**HTML5**]
`rel="type"`	Provides the relationship between the linked document and the current page
`hreflang="lang"`	Indicates the language of the linked document
`type="mime-type"`	Indicates the media type of the linked document

© 2016 Cengage Learning

Using the `target` attribute, you can control how a page is opened. By default the target of a link replaces the contents of the current page in the browser window. In some websites, you will want to open a link in a new browser window or tab so that you can keep the current page and the linked page in view. To force a document to appear in a new window or tab, add the following `target` attribute to the `<a>` tag:

```
<a href="url" target="window">content</a>
```

where `window` is a name assigned to the browser window or browser tab in which the linked page will appear. You can choose any name you wish for the browser window or you can use one of the following target names:

- `_self` opens the page in the current window or tab (the default)
- `_blank` opens the page in a new unnamed window or tab, depending on how the browser is configured
- `_parent` opens the page in the parent of the current frame (for framed websites)
- `_top` opens the page in the top frame (for framed websites)

You should use the `target` attribute sparingly in your website. Creating secondary windows can clutter up a user's desktop. Also, because the page is placed in a new window, users cannot use the Back button to return to the previous page in that window; they must click the browser's program button or the tab for the original website. This confuses some users and annoys others. Many designers now advocate not using the `target` attribute at all, but instead provide the user with the choice of opening a link in a new tab or window.

PROSKILLS

Written Communication: Creating Effective Hypertext Links

To make it easier for users to navigate your website, the text of your hypertext links should tell readers exactly what type of document the link points to. For example, the link text

Click <u>here</u> for more information.

doesn't tell the user what type of document will appear when <u>here</u> is clicked. In place of phrases like "click here", you should use descriptive link text such as

For more information, view our list of <u>frequently asked questions</u>.

If the link points to a non-HTML file, such as a PDF document, include that information in the link text. If the linked document is extremely large and will take a while to download to the user's computer, include that information in your link text so that users can decide whether or not to initiate the transfer. For example, the following link text informs users of both the type of document and its size so users have this information before they initiate the link:

Download our <u>complete manual (PDF 2 MB)</u>.

Finally, when designing the style of your website, make your links easy to recognize. Users should never be confused about a link. Also, if you apply a color to your text, do not choose colors that make your hyperlinks harder to pick out against the web page background.

You've completed your work on the Curbside Thai website. Sajja will study your work and get back to you with future projects for his restaurant. For now, you can close any open files or applications.

REVIEW

Session 1.3 Quick Check

1. Provide the code to mark the unordered list containing the items: Packers, Vikings, Bears, Lions.
2. Provide the code to mark the following list of the top-five most popular movies ranked in descending order according to IMDB:

   5. Pulp Fiction
   4. The Dark Knight
   3. The Godfather: Part II
   2. The Godfather
   1. The Shawshank Redemption

3. Describe the three HTML elements used in a description list.
4. Provide the code to create a navigation list for the following list items: Home, FAQ, Contact Us and pointing to the index.html, faq.html, and contacts.html files respectively.
5. Using the folder structure shown in Figure 1-40, provide the relative path going from the ct_about.html file to the ct_catering.html file.
6. Provide the URL pointing to the element in the glossary.html file with the ID c_terms. Assume that the glossary.html file is in the same folder as the current page.
7. Provide the URL to access the website at the address www.example.com/curbside over a secure connection.
8. Provide the URL for an e-mail link to the address sajja@curbside.com with the subject line FYI.
9. Provide the URL for a telephone link to the U.S. phone number 970-555-0002.

Review Assignments

Data Files needed for the Review Assignments: mp_index_txt.html, mp_menu_txt.html, mp_events_txt.html, mp_catering_txt.html, 2 CSS files, 2 PNG files, 1 TXT file

Curbside Thai has partnered with another food truck vendor Mobile Panini. Sajja asks you to create a website for the company similar to what you did for his restaurant. The site will have a home page, an online menu, a description of catering opportunities, and a calendar of upcoming events that Mobile Panini will host. A preview of the home page is shown in Figure 1-45.

| Figure 1-45 | Mobile Panini home page |

© 2016 Cengage Learning; © Glenn Price/Shuttertock.com

The page text has already been written for you and style sheets and graphic files have been created. Your job will be to complete this project by writing the HTML markup.

Complete the following:

1. Use your HTML editor to open the **mp_index_txt.html**, **mp_menu.txt.html**, **mp_events_txt.html**, and **mp_catering_txt.html** files from the html01 ▸ review folder. Enter *your name* and *the date* in the comment section of each file, and save them as **mp_index.html**, **mp_menu.html**, **mp_events.html**, and **mp_catering.html** respectively.

2. Go to the **mp_index.html** file in your HTML editor. Within the document head, do the following:

    a. Use the `meta` element to set the character encoding of the file to **utf-8**.

    b. Add the following search keywords to the document: **Italian**, **Mobile**, **food**, and **Charlotte**.

    c. Set the title of the document to **Mobile Panini**.

    d. Link the document to the mp_base.css and mp_layout.css style sheet files.

3. Go to the document body and insert a `header` element containing the following:

   a. An inline image from the mp_logo.png file with the alternate text **Mobile Panini**. Mark the image as a hypertext link pointing to the mp_index.html file.

   b. A navigation list containing an unordered list with the following list items: **Home**, **Menu**, **Events**, and **Catering**. Link the items to the mp_index.html, mp_menu.html, mp_events.html, and mp_catering.html files respectively.

4. Below the `header` element insert an `article` element. Below the `article` element, insert a `footer` element containing the following text:

   Mobile Panini ♨ 31 West Avenue, Charlotte NC 28204 ♨ 704-555-2188

   where ♨ is inserted using the **9832** character code and an extra space is added between NC and **28204** using the `nbsp` character name.

5. Go to the **mp_pages.txt** file in your text editor. This file contains the text content of the four pages in the Mobile Panini website. Copy the text of the Welcome section, which will be used in the home page of the website. Return to **mp_index.html** in your HTML editor and paste the copied text into the `article` element.

6. Within the `article` element, do the following:

   a. Mark the Welcome line as an h1 heading.

   b. Below the `h1` element, insert an inline image containing the mp_photo1.png file with an empty text string for the alternate text.

   c. Mark the next five paragraphs as paragraphs using the `p` element. Within the first paragraph, mark the text *Mobile Panini* as strong text. Within the third paragraph mark the text *Curbside Thai* as emphasized text.

   d. The fourth paragraph contains Mobile Panini's phone number. Mark the phone number as a telephone link and be sure to include the international code in the URL. Note that this number is fictional, so, if you have access to a mobile browser and want to test the link, you might want to replace this number with your phone number.

   e. The fifth paragraph contains Mobile Panini's e-mail address. Mark the e-mail address as a hypertext link. Once again, note that this e-mail address is fictional, so, if you want to test this link, you will need to replace the Mobile Panini e-mail address with your e-mail address.

7. Save your changes to the file and then open the **mp_index.html** file in your browser. Verify that the layout and appearance of the page resemble that shown in Figure 1-45. If possible, test the telephone links and e-mail links to verify that they open the correct application.

8. Go to the **mp_index.html** file in your HTML editor, and copy the `header` and `footer` elements. Then go to the **mp_menu.html** file in your HTML editor and paste the `header` and `footer` elements into the `body` element so that this page has the same logo and navigation list and footer used in the home page. Insert an `article` element between the header and footer.

9. Return to the **mp_pages.txt** file in your text editor and copy the contents of the Mobile Panini menu. Then, go to the **mp_menu.html** file in your HTML editor and paste the copied text into the `article` element.

10. Within the article element of the mp_menu.htm file, do the following:

    a. Mark the text title *Our Menu* as an h1 heading.

    b. Enclose the menu items in a description list with the name of each menu item marked with the `dt` element and each menu description marked with the `dd` element.

11. Save your changes to mp_menu.html file. Open the page in your browser and verify that each menu item name appears in a bold font and is separated from the indented item description by a horizontal line.

12. Go to the **mp_index.html** file in your HTML editor and copy the `header` and `footer` elements. Then, go to the **mp_events.html** file in your HTML editor and paste the `header` and `footer` elements into the `body` element. Insert an `article` element between the header and footer.

13. Return to the **mp_pages.txt** file in your text editor and copy the list of upcoming events under the Calendar section heading. Then, go to the **mp_events.html** file in your HTML editor and paste the copied text into the `article` element.

14. Within the `article` element, do the following:
    a. Mark the text *Where Are We This Week?* as an h1 heading.
    b. Enclose each day's worth of events within a separate `div` (or division) element.
    c. Within each of the seven day divisions, enclose the day and date as an h1 heading. Enclose the location within a paragraph element. Insert a line break element, `<br />`, directly before the time of the event so that each time interval is displayed on a new line within the paragraph.

15. Save your changes to mp_events.html file. Open the page in your browser and verify that each calendar event appears in its own box with the day and date rendered as a heading.

16. Go to the **mp_index.html** file in your HTML editor and copy the `header` and `footer` elements. Then, go to the **mp_catering.html** file in your HTML editor and paste the `header` and `footer` elements into the `body` element. Insert an `article` element between the header and footer and then insert an `aside` element within the article.

17. Directly after the opening `<article>` tag, insert an `h1` element containing the text **Catering**.

18. Return to the **mp_pages.txt** file in your text editor and copy the text about the mobile kitchen, including the heading. Then, go to the **mp_catering.html** file in your HTML editor and paste the copied text into the `aside` element.

19. Within the `article` element, do the following:
    a. Mark the text *About the Mobile Kitchen* as an h1 heading.
    b. Mark the next two paragraphs as paragraphs.

20. Return to the **mp_pages.txt** file in your text editor and copy the text describing Mobile Panini's catering opportunities; do not copy the Catering head. Then, go to the **mp_catering.html** file in your HTML editor and paste the copied text directly after the `aside` element.

21. Make the following edits to the pasted text:
    a. Mark the first two paragraphs as paragraphs.
    b. Enclose the list of the six catering possibilities within an unordered list with each item marked as a list item.
    c. Mark the concluding paragraph as a paragraph.

22. Save your changes to mp_catering.html file. Open the page in your browser and verify that the information about the mobile kitchen appears as a sidebar on the right edge of the article.

23. Return to the **mp_index.html** file in your browser and verify that you can jump from one page to another by clicking the entries in the navigation list at the top of each page.

Case Problem 1

Data Files needed for this Case Problem: jtc_index_txt.html, jtc_services_txt.html, 2 CSS files, 3 PNG files, 1 TXT file

Jedds Tree Care Carol Jedds is the owner and operator of Jedds Tree Care and tree removal and land-scaping company in Lansing, Michigan. She has asked for your help in developing her company's website. She has already written some of the text for a few sample pages and wants you to write the HTML code. Figure 1-46 shows a preview of the company's home page that you'll create.

Figure 1-46	Jedds Tree Care home page

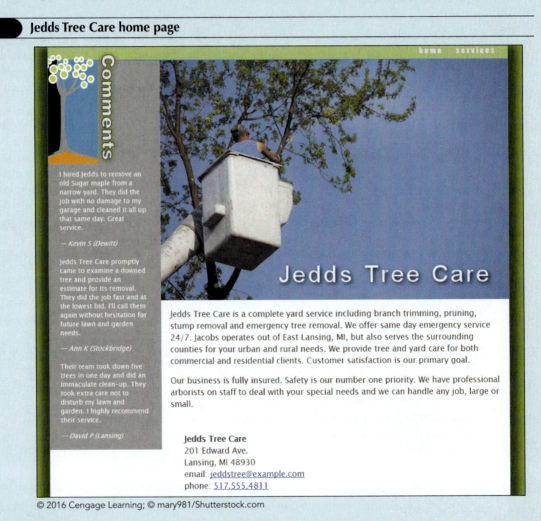

© 2016 Cengage Learning; © mary981/Shutterstock.com

The style sheets and graphic files have already been created for you. Your job is to write the HTML markup.

Complete the following:

1. Using your editor, open the **jtc_index_txt.html** and **jtc_services_txt.html** files from the html01 ▸ case1 folder. Enter ***your name*** and ***the date*** in the comment section of each file, and save them as **jtc_index.html** and **jtc_services.html** respectively.

2. Go to the **jtc_index.html** file in your HTML editor. Within the document head, do the following:

   a. Use the `meta` element to set the character encoding of the file to **utf-8**.

   b. Set the document title to **Jedds Tree Care**.

   c. Link the document to the jtc_base.css and jtc_layout.css style sheet files.

3. Within the document body, insert a `header` element, an `aside` element, and an `article` element.

4. Within the `header` element, insert a navigation list with links to jtc_index.html and jtc_services.html file. The text of the links should be **home** and **services** respectively.

5. Go to the **jtc_pages.txt** file in your text editor. The first section in the file contains comments made by Jedds Tree Care customers. Copy the text of the three reviews including the reviewer names. Then, go to the **jtc_index.html** file in your HTML editor and paste the copied text within the `aside` element.

6. Within the `aside` element, add the following content and markup:

   a. Directly after the opening `<aside>` tag, insert an inline image for the jtc_comments.png file. Specify **Comments** as the alternate text.

   b. Enclose each of the three reviewer comments within a `blockquote` element, including both the text of the quote and the name of the review.

   c. Within each of the three `blockquote` elements,

      i. mark the review as a paragraph.

      ii. mark the line containing the reviewer name as a `cite` element.

      iii. replace the "---" text with the em dash character (—) using the character reference name `mdash`.

7. Go to the `article` element and insert a `header` element containing the inline image file jtc_photo1.png with the alternate text *Jedds Tree Care*.

8. Return to the **jtc_pages.txt** file in your text editor and copy the second section of text containing the description of the company and its contact information. Then, go to the **jtc_index.html** file in your HTML editor and paste the copied text in the `article` element, directly below the article header.

9. Mark up the content of the page article as follows:

   a. Mark the first two paragraphs using the `<p>` tag.

   b. Enclose the five lines of the contact information within an `address` element. Insert a line break element at the end of the first four lines so that each part of the address appears on a new line in the rendered page.

   c. Mark the text *Jedds Tree Care* in the first line of the address as a `strong` element.

   d. Mark the e-mail address as a hypertext link. Make the telephone number a telephone link, including the international access code.

10. Save your changes to the jtc_index.html file. Open the page in your browser and verify that the layout and contents of the page resemble that shown in Figure 1-46. Note that under the smaller screen widths associated with mobile devices, the text of the reviewer comments is not displayed.

11. Go to the **jtc_services.html** file in your HTML editor. Insert the same metadata in the document head to match what you did for the jtc_index.html file *except* name the page title **Jedds Tree Care Services**.

12. Go to the **jtc_index.html** file in your HTML editor and copy the body header. Then, go to the **jtc_services.html** file and paste the copied header into the document body so that both files share a common header design.

13. Return to the **jtc_pages.txt** file in your text editor and copy the content of the third section, which contains information on the services offered by Jedds Tree Care. Be sure to copy the heading as well. Then, go to the **jtc_services.html** file in your HTML editor and paste the copied text directly after the header.

14. Mark the content describing Jedds Tree Care services as follows:

   a. Mark the heading *Jedds Tree Care Services* as an h1 heading.

   b. Directly after the `h1` element, insert an inline image file for the **jtc_photo2.png** with the alternate text set to empty.

   c. Mark each of the headings associated with individual services as h2 headings.

   d. Mark each service description as a paragraph.

15. Directly after the text of the last service, insert a `footer` element containing the following text:

   Jedds Tree Care ◆ 201 Edward Ave. ◆ Lansing, MI 48930

   where the ◆ symbol is inserted using the character code **9830**.

16. Save your changes to the file and open the **jtc_services.html** file in your browser. Verify that the page title is displayed as a major heading and the name of each service is displayed as a second level heading.

APPLY

Case Problem 2

Data Files needed for this Case Problem: ms_euler_txt.html, 2 CSS files, 2 PNG files, 1 TXT file

Math Strings Professor Lauren Coe of the Mathematics Department of Coastal University in Anderson, South Carolina, is one of the founders of *Math Strings*, a website containing articles and course materials for high school and college math instructors. She has written a series of biographies of famous mathematicians for the website and would like you to use that content in a web page. You'll create the first one in this exercise. Figure 1-47 shows a preview of the page you'll create, which profiles the mathematician Leonhard Euler.

Figure 1-47   **Math Strings Leonhard Euler page**

Leonhard Euler (1707-1783)

The greatest mathematician of the eighteenth century, **Leonhard Euler** was born in Basel, Switzerland. There, he studied under another giant of mathematics, **Jean Bernoulli**. In 1731 Euler became a professor of physics and mathematics at St. Petersburg Academy of Sciences. Euler was the most prolific mathematician of all time, publishing over *800 different books and papers*. His influence was felt in physics and astronomy as well.

He is perhaps best known for his research into mathematical analysis. Euler's work, *Introductio in analysin infinitorum (1748)*, remained a standard textbook in the field for well over a century. For the princess of Anhalt-Dessau, he wrote *Lettres à une princesse d'Allemagne (1768-1772)*, giving a clear non-technical outline of the main physical theories of the time.

One can hardly write a mathematical equation without copying Euler. Notations still in use today, such as e and π, were introduced in Euler's writings. Leonhard Euler died in 1783, leaving behind a legacy perhaps unmatched, and certainly unsurpassed, in the annals of mathematics.

The Most Beautiful Equation in Math?

Perhaps the most elegant equation in the history of math is:

$$\cos(x) + i\sin(x) = e^{xi}$$

which demonstrates the relationship between algebra, complex analysis, and trigonometry. From this equation, it's easy to derive the identity:

$$e^{\pi i} + 1 = 0$$

which relates the fundamental constants: 0, 1, π, e, and i in a single beautiful and elegant statement. A poll of readers conducted by *The Mathematical Intelligencer* magazine named Euler's Identity as the most beautiful theorem in the history of mathematics.

Learn more about Euler

Euler at Wikipedia

The Euler Archive

Euler at Biography.com

Euler at Famous Scientists

The style sheet and graphics are provided for you. Your job is to write the HTML markup.

Complete the following:

1. Using your editor, open the **ms_euler_txt.html** file from the html01 ▸ case2 folder. Enter *your name* and *the date* in the comment section of the file, and save it as **ms_euler.html**.

2. Add the following to the document head:
   a. Set the character encoding of the file to **utf-8**.
   b. Add the following search keywords: **math**, **Euler**, **pi**, and **geometry**.
   c. Set the title of the document to **Leonhard Euler (1707-1783)**.
   d. Link the document to the ms_base.css and ms_layout.css style sheet files.

3. Add a `header`, `article`, `aside`, `nav`, and `footer` element to the document body.

4. Within the body header, insert an inline image for the ms_logo.png file with the alternate text **Math Strings**.

5. Go to the **ms_pages.txt** file in your text editor and copy the text of the main article (located in the first section of the file), including the title. Then, go to the **ms_euler.html** file in your HTML editor and paste the copied text into the `article` element.

6. Within the `article` element, make the following markup changes:
   a. Mark the text *Leonhard Euler (1707-1783)* as an h1 heading.
   b. Mark the three paragraphs of the article content using the `p` element.
   c. In the first paragraph, mark the names *Leonhard Euler* and *Jean Bernoulli* as strong text. Mark the phrase *800 different books and papers* as emphasized text.
   d. In the second paragraph mark the works *Introductio in analysin infinitorum (1748)* and *Lettres à une princesse d'Allemagne (1768-1772)* as citations. Insert the à character using the character reference `&agrave;`.
   e. In the third paragraph, mark the mathematical symbols *e* and π using the `var` (variable) element. Insert the π character by replacing [pi] with the `&pi;` character reference.

7. Return to the **ms_pages.txt** in your text editor and copy the text of the second section containing information about Euler's Equation, the most beautiful equation in math. Then, go to the ms_euler.html file in your HTML editor and paste the copied text into the `aside` element.

8. Within the `aside` element, add the following markup:
   a. Mark the title *The Most Beautiful Equation in Math?* as an h1 heading.
   b. Mark the two equations in the pasted text using the `code` element. Mark the three other text groups as paragraphs.
   c. Throughout the text of the `aside` element, mark *x*, *i*, *e*, *xi*, and *pi* using the `var` element, replacing [pi] from the pasted text with the character reference `&pi;`.
   d. Use the `sup` element in the following equations to mark *xi* and πi as superscripts:
   $$\cos(x) + i\sin(x) = e^{xi}$$
   $$e^{\pi i} + 1 = 0$$
   e. Mark the text *The Mathematical Intelligencer* as a citation.

9. Return to the **ms_pages.txt** file in your text editor and copy the text of the third section listing more ways to learn about Euler. Then, go to the **ms_euler.html** file in your HTML editor and paste the copied text into the `nav` element.

10. Within the `nav` element, add the following markup:
    a. Mark the title *Learn more about Euler* as an h1 heading.
    b. Mark the four Euler websites as an unordered list.
    c. Change the text of the Euler websites to hypertext links pointing to the following URLs:
    Euler at Wikipedia linked to *http://en.wikipedia.org/wiki/Leonhard_Euler*
    The Euler Archive linked to *http://eulerarchive.maa.org/*
    Euler at Biography.com linked to *http://www.biography.com/people/leonhard-euler-21342391*
    Euler at Famous Scientists linked to *http://www.famousscientists.org/leonhard-euler*

11. Within the `footer` element, insert the text **Math Strings: A Site for Educators and Researchers**.

12. Save your changes to the file and open the **ms_euler.html file** in your browser. Verify that the equations in the sidebar match the ones shown in Figure 1-47 and that all occurrences of the [pi] character have been replaced with π. Click the four links in the navigation list and verify that your browser opens the websites.

CHALLENGE

Case Problem 3

Data Files needed for this Case Problem: dr_index_txt.html, dr_info_txt.htm, dr_faq_txt.html, 4 CSS files, 2 PNG files, 3 TXT files

Diane's Run   *Diane's Run* is a charity run to raise money for breast cancer awareness and research funding. Peter Wheaton is the charity run's organizer and he has asked you to help modify the run's website. He has revised text that he wants added to the current site. A preview of the page you'll create is shown in Figure 1-48.

| Figure 1-48 | Diane's Run home page |

FAQ   Race Info   Home

What Your Support Does

Every 10 minutes a woman is diagnosed with breast cancer. Her first reaction is fear and confusion. Support is just a phone call or mouse click away. Our free services offer a friendly ear and expert guidance to anyone dealing with this life-threatening illness.

By running or walking with us, you can ensure that we are there when people need us. Here is how your contribution can help:

- **$15** pays for a headscarf set, boosting the confidence of women who have lost their hair from their breast cancer treatment.

- **$50** trains a member of our support network for a year to help improve the care of women with breast cancer.

- **$125** covers the cost of counselling sessions to help women cope with the distress of their cancer treatment.

- **$250** funds a hospital information station for a year so that people affected by breast cancer have easy access to the latest resources and help.

Diane's Run - September 9, 2017

Join over 2000 athletes in Cheyenne, Wyoming, for **Diane's Run** to raise money for breast cancer awareness and research. The 5K and 10K races are challenging, yet attainable. You can aim for a personal best while taking part to raise money for this important charity. If you can't run, consider walking; joining young and old in the fight by participating in the 1-Mile Walk for Hope.

How to Join

You can guarantee a spot by filling out the entry form and mailing it to dianesrun@example.com. The $35 entry fee is tax deductible and goes directly to important research and women in need. We keep our overhead very low so every dollar counts. More than 75% of the net proceeds fund screening and treatment programs in your communities. We welcome out-of-town visitors. We will help you find accommodations during your visit.

History

Since its inception in 2004, Diane's Run has grown from a purely local event involving 100 runners to a signature Wyoming event with more than 2000 participants annually. The event is enormously effective in spreading the message that breast cancer need not be fatal if caught early enough with mammography and breast self-exam. As well as a top-flight athletic event, Diane's Run is an emotionally moving event attracting many first timers and recreational runners. This event provides all of us with the opportunity to spread a hopeful message about breast cancer to our families and our communities.

Remembering Diane

Diane's Run is named in remembrance of Diane Wheaton, mother of 2 and wife of Peter, who passed away in May, 2003. Diane was an outspoken advocate of physical fitness and healthy living. She was an inspiration to all who knew her and continues to be an inspiration to the thousands of runners who have participated in this event.

We hope you can join us this year and become part of the Diane's Run family.

Diane's Run ♥ 45 Mountain Drive ♥ Cheyenne, WY 82001

Peter has supplied you with the text content, the graphic images, and style sheets you need for the project. Your job will be to write HTML code for three pages: the site's home page, a page containing race information, and finally a page containing a list of frequently asked questions (FAQ's).

Complete the following:

1. Using your editor, open the **dr_index_txt.html**, **dr_info_txt.html**, and **dr_faq_txt.html** files from the html01 ▶ case3 folder. Enter *your name* and *the date* in the comment section of each file, and save them as **dr_index.html**, **dr_info.html**, and **dr_faq.html** respectively.

2. Go to the **dr_index.html** file in your HTML editor. Within the document head, add the following metadata:
   a. Set the character encoding of the file to **utf-8**.
   b. Insert the search keywords: **breast cancer**, **run**, **race**, and **charity**.
   c. Set the title of the document to **Diane's Run**.
   d. Link the document to the dr_base.css and dr_layout.css style sheet files.

3. Within the document body, insert a `header` element, two `section` elements, and a `footer` element.

4. In the `header` element, insert a navigation list containing an unordered list with the items: **Home**, **Race Info**, and **FAQ**. Link the items to the dr_index.html, dr_info.html, and dr_faq.html files respectively.

5. The file dr_index.txt contains the text to be inserted into the Diane's Run home page. Go to the **dr_index.txt** file in your text editor and copy the text from the first section of the file. Then, go to the **dr_index.html** file in your HTML editor and paste it into the first `section` element.

6. Add the following markup to the content of the first `section` element:
   a. Mark the line *What Your Support Does* as an h1 heading.
   b. Mark the next two paragraphs as paragraphs using the `p` element.
   c. Mark the four ways a contribution can help as an unordered list. Mark the dollar amounts of each list item using the `strong` element.

7. Return to the **dr_index.txt** file in your text editor, copy the text from the second section, then close the dr_index.txt file. Go to the **dr_index.html** file in your HTML editor and paste the copied text within the second `section` element.

8. Within the second `section` element in the dr_index.html file, add the following:
   a. Enclose the opening heading *Diane's Run - September 9, 2017* within a `header` element and marked as an h1 heading. Directly above this heading, insert the inline image file dr_photo1.png with **Diane's Run** as the alternate text of the image.
   b. Mark the first paragraph after the header as a paragraph. Mark the text *Diane's Run* in this opening paragraph using the `strong` element.
   c. Mark the minor headings *How to Join*, *History*, and *Remembering Diane* as h2 headings. Mark the other blocks of text as paragraphs.

9. Within the `footer` element, insert the following text:
   Diane's Run ♥ 45 Mountain Drive ♥ Cheyenne, WY 82001
   where the ♥ character is inserted using the character code **9829**.

10. Save your changes to the file and then open **dr_index.html** in your browser. Verify that the content and the layout of the page resemble that shown in Figure 1-48.

11. Go to the **dr_info.html** file in your HTML editor. Within the document head, link the page to the dr_base.css and dr_layout2.css style sheets.

12. Go to the **dr_index.html** file in your HTML editor and copy the body header content. Then, go to the **dr_info.html** file in your HTML editor and paste the copied content into the document body. Repeat for the body footer so that the Racing Information page has the same navigation list and footer as the home page. Between the `header` and `footer` element, insert a `section` element.

✦ **Explore**   13. Within the `section` element, insert a `header` element with the following content:
   a. Insert a paragraph with the text **Page last updated: Tuesday, August 29, 2017.** Mark the date using the `time` element with the `datetime` attribute equal to **2017-08-29**.
   b. Add the text **Race Information** as an h1 heading.
   c. Insert the inline image file dr_logo.png with **Diane's Run** as the alternate text.

14. Go to the **dr_info.txt** file in your text editor. This file contains the text describing the race. Copy the content describing the race from the file, then close the dr_info.txt file. Go to the dr_info.html file in your HTML editor and paste the copied text into the `section` element, directly after the section header.

15. Mark the content of the `section` element as follows:
   a. Mark the opening block of text directly after the section header as a paragraph.
   b. Mark the headings *Race Times*, *Goodies and Stuff*, and *Notes* as h2 headings.
   c. Below each of the h2 elements, mark the list of items that follows as an unordered list.

16. Save your changes to the file and then load **dr_info.html** in your browser to verify that the layout and content are readable.

17. Go to the **dr_faq.html** file in your HTML editor. Within the document head, link the page to the dr_base.css and dr_layout3.css style sheets.

18. Go to the **dr_index.html** file in your HTML editor and copy the body header content. Then, go to the **dr_faq.html** file in your HTML editor and paste the copied content into the document body. Repeat with the body footer so that the FAQ page has the same navigation list and footer as was used in the home page. Between the `header` and `footer` element, insert a `section` element.

19. Within the `section` element, insert a `header` element with the `id` attribute **pagetop**. Within the header, insert the inline image file dr_logo.png with the alternate text **Diane's Run** followed by the `h1` element with the text **Frequently Asked Questions**.

20. Go to the **dr_faq.txt** file in your text editor. This file contains a list of frequently asked questions followed by the question answers. Copy the text and then close the dr_faq.txt file. Then, go to the dr_faq.html file in your HTML editor and paste the copied text into the `section` element, directly after the section header.

✦ **Explore**   21. Next, you'll create a series of hypertext links between the list of questions and their answers within the same document. Make the following changes to the `section` element in the dr_faq.html file:
   a. Mark the 13 questions at the top of the section as an ordered list.
   b. Notice that below the ordered list you just created, the questions are repeated and each question is followed by its answer. Mark the text of those questions as an h2 heading and the answer as a paragraph. Add an `id` attribute to each of the 13 h2 headings with the first heading given the id **faq1**, the second heading **faq2**, and so forth down to **faq13** for the last h2 heading.
   c. After the last answer, insert a paragraph with the text **Return to the Top** and mark the text as a hypertext link pointing to the `header` element with the id **pagetop**.
   d. Return to the ordered list at the top of the section that you created in Step a. Change each item in the ordered list to a hypertext link pointing to the h2 heading containing the question's answer that you created in Step b. For example, the first question *How do I sign up?* should be linked to the h2 heading with the faq1 id.

22. Save your changes to the file and then open **dr_faq.html** in your browser. Verify that by clicking a question within the ordered list, the browser jumps to that question's answer. Further, verify that clicking the Return to the Top link at the bottom of the page causes the browser to return to the top of the page.

⊕ **Explore** 23. Return to the **dr_index.html** file in your HTML editor. Add the following two hypertext links to the *How to Join* paragraph in the second `section` element:

    a. Change the e-mail address *dianesrun@example.com* to an e-mail link with the subject heading Entry Form.

    b. Change the word *accommodations* to a hypertext link pointing to the element with the id faq13 in the dr_faq.html file.

24. Save your changes to the file and reload dr_index.html in your browser. Verify that clicking the e-mail link brings up your e-mail program with the e-mail address and the subject heading already filled in.

25. Click the accommodations hypertext link and verify that the browser goes to the last answer on the FAQ page.

26. Verify that you can jump between all three pages by clicking the navigation links at the top of the page.

CREATE

Case Problem 4

Data Files needed for this Case Problem: hg_index_txt.html, hg_towers_txt.html, hg_alliance_txt.html, 3 PNG files, 1 TXT file

Harpe Gaming Sean Greer is the owner of *Harpe Gaming*, a small board game store in Morgantown, West Virginia. You've been asked to work on the store's new website. Sean wants you to write the HTML code for the store's home page. Sean also publishes reviews of new games as a service to his loyal customers. He would also like you to write the HTML code for two new reviews that Sean has written for the *Towers and Temples* game and the *Alliance* game. Sean has already written all of the content for the three pages and only requires your help to turn them into HTML documents.

Complete the following:

1. Using your editor, open the **hg_index_txt.html**, **hg_towers_txt.html**, and **hg_alliance_txt.html** files from the html01 ▸ case4 folder. Save them as **hg_index.html**, **hg_towers.html**, and **hg_alliance.html** respectively.

2. Content for each of the three pages is contained in the hg_text.txt file. Take some time to review the content of this file. The Harpe Gaming home page will have a short introduction to the store and its philosophy and includes contact information for the interested customer. The Towers and Temples page and the Alliance page have an overview of each game with the Harpe Gaming's rating and reviews from popular gaming magazines and websites. Sean has also supplied you with the hg_logo.png, hg_towers.png, and hg_alliance.png files as images to be used in the files. You are free to supplement Sean's material with appropriate material of your own.

3. Once you are familiar with the content that needs to be inserted into the web pages, start creating the HTML code for each page. For each file, insert the structure of an HTML document including the opening doctype, `html` element, document head, and document body.

4. For the document head of each file, do the following (there are no style sheets for this project, so you do *not* have to include links to any style sheet files):

    a. Insert a comment that includes ***your name*** and ***the date*** and the purpose of the page.

    b. Insert metadata that sets the character encoding used in the file.

    c. Insert metadata that specifies the page title.

    d. Insert a list of search keywords appropriate to the content of each file.

5. Within the document body, insert a navigation list within a body header that has hypertext links to all three pages in this sample website.

6. Use the content from the hg_text.txt file to populate the content of the three pages. The markup used in the three pages is up to you. In your website there should be at least one example of the following:

   a. Sectioning elements, including the `header`, `article`, `aside`, `section`, and `footer` elements

   b. Grouping elements, including paragraphs, block quotes, and lists

   c. Text-level elements used to mark single words or phrases from within a grouping element. Include at least one example of the `strong` element and the `em` element.

   d. An inline image, including appropriate alternate text for the image

   e. A character symbol inserted using its character name or encoding number

   f. A hypertext link to an individual's e-mail address

   g. A hypertext link to a phone number

   h. A hypertext link to a website URL

7. Save your changes to the files and then open them in your browser. Verify that the links work as expected when moving between the pages in the website, when accessing your e-mail program, and when accessing external links on the web. If you have a telephony application on your computer, test that clicking the phone link opens that application.

Getting Started with CSS

Designing a Website for a Fitness Club

OBJECTIVES

Session 2.1
- Explore the history of CSS
- Study different types of style sheets
- Explore style precedence and inheritance
- Apply colors in CSS

Session 2.2
- Use contextual selectors
- Work with attribute selectors
- Apply text and font styles
- Use a web font

Session 2.3
- Define list styles
- Work with margins and padding space
- Use pseudo-classes and pseudo-elements
- Insert page content with CSS

Case | *Tri and Succeed Sports*

Alison Palmer runs Tri and Succeed Sports, an athletic club in Austin, Texas that specializes in coaching men and women aspiring to compete in triathlons and other endurance sports. The center provides year-round instruction in running, swimming, cycling, and general fitness with one-on-one and group training classes. Alison has asked you to work on the company's new website.

Alison designed the original Tri and Succeed Sports website several years ago but she now feels that the site needs a makeover. She wants a new design that uses color and interesting typography to create visual interest and impact. She wants you to use CSS to help give the website a new look.

STARTING DATA FILES

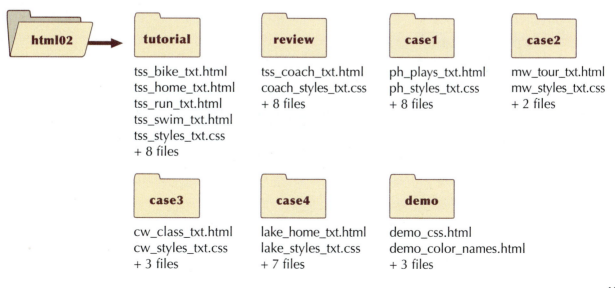

html02 →

tutorial
tss_bike_txt.html
tss_home_txt.html
tss_run_txt.html
tss_swim_txt.html
tss_styles_txt.css
+ 8 files

review
tss_coach_txt.html
coach_styles_txt.css
+ 8 files

case1
ph_plays_txt.html
ph_styles_txt.css
+ 8 files

case2
mw_tour_txt.html
mw_styles_txt.css
+ 2 files

case3
cw_class_txt.html
cw_styles_txt.css
+ 3 files

case4
lake_home_txt.html
lake_styles_txt.css
+ 7 files

demo
demo_css.html
demo_color_names.html
+ 3 files

Session 2.1 Visual Overview:

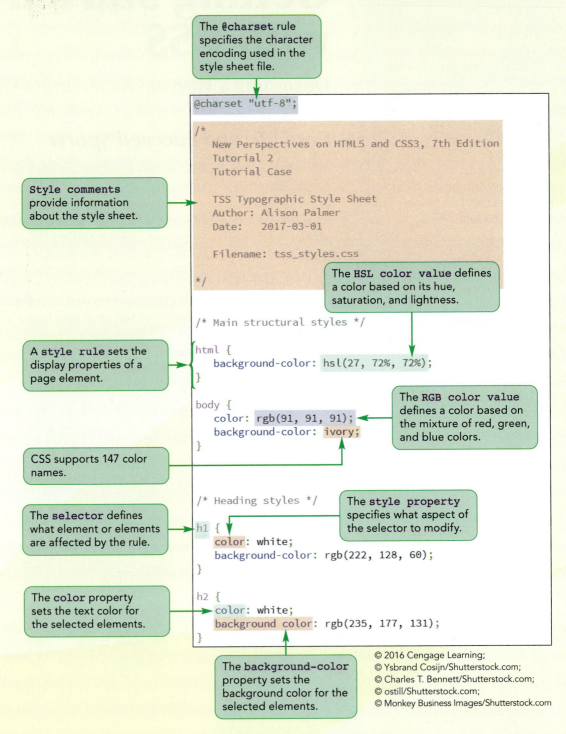

The **@charset** rule specifies the character encoding used in the style sheet file.

```
@charset "utf-8";

/*
    New Perspectives on HTML5 and CSS3, 7th Edition
    Tutorial 2
    Tutorial Case

    TSS Typographic Style Sheet
    Author: Alison Palmer
    Date:    2017-03-01

    Filename: tss_styles.css

*/
```

Style comments provide information about the style sheet.

The **HSL color value** defines a color based on its hue, saturation, and lightness.

```
/* Main structural styles */

html {
    background-color: hsl(27, 72%, 72%);
}
```

A **style rule** sets the display properties of a page element.

```
body {
    color: rgb(91, 91, 91);
    background-color: ivory;
}
```

The **RGB color value** defines a color based on the mixture of red, green, and blue colors.

CSS supports 147 color names.

```
/* Heading styles */

h1 {
    color: white;
    background-color: rgb(222, 128, 60);
}
```

The **style property** specifies what aspect of the selector to modify.

The **selector** defines what element or elements are affected by the rule.

The **color** property sets the text color for the selected elements.

```
h2 {
    color: white;
    background color: rgb(235, 177, 131);
}
```

The **background-color** property sets the background color for the selected elements.

CSS Styles and Colors

The browser window background color is set to the color value hsl(27, 73%, 72%) using the `html` style rule.

The h1 headings appear in white on a dark orange background as specified by the h1 style rule.

Links

- Home
- Running
- Cycling
- Swimming
- Active.com
- Runner's World
- endomondo.com
- Strava
- Bicycling Magazine
- VeloNews
- Bicycle Tutor
- Swim Smooth
- Swimming World
- USA Swimming
- triathlon.org
- usatriathlon.org
- Texas Triathlons
- CapTex Triathlon
- Triathlon Calendar
- Triathlete.com
- Trifuel.com

About TSS

Since 2002, **Tri and Succeed Sports** has provided Austin with a first class training center for athletes of all abilities and goals. We specialize in helping you reach your full potential. You tell us what you want to do; we work to fulfill your needs.

Want to swim? Great! Interested in improving your cycling? Fantastic! Want to tackle a triathlon? We're there for you: before, during, and after the race. Or do you just want to get more fit? We are on it. We customize our instruction to match your goals. And you will finish what you start.

Classes

Winter instruction starts soon. Get a jump on your summer goals by joining us for individual or group instruction in:

- **Running**: We start with the basics to help you run faster and farther than you ever thought possible without aches and pains.
- **Cycling**: The indoor bike trainers at TSS include everything you need to refine your technique, stamina, and power for improved results on the road.
- **Swimming**: The open water swim can be one of the most frightening sports to master. Our classes begin with basic techniques so that your swim can be very enjoyable, and not a chore.

Contact us to set up individual instruction and assessment.

Our Philosophy

Athletes are the foundation of every successful training program. The best coach is an experienced guide who begins with each athlete's hopes, dreams and desires and then tailors a training plan based on that individuals's current fitness and lifestyle. Since 2002, TSS has helped hundreds of individuals achieve success in many fitness areas. The winner is not the one who finishes first but anyone who starts the race and perseveres. Join us and begin exploring the possible.

Comments

Thank you for all that you have done. I am amazed at my progress. I realize that I have l lofty goals but you have me well on my way.

Alison kept me focused working toward my dreams. She fosters a supportive and caring environment for growth as an athlete and as a person. Thank you!

You do it right! Your track record proves it. Proud to be a TSS athlete and I'm honored to have you all as my coaches and support team.

The coaches at TSS treat you with the highest respect: whether you're an individual getting off the couch for the first time or an elite athlete training for the Iron Man. They know their stuff.

The h2 headings appear in white on a light orange background as specified by the h2 style rule.

Page body background color is set to ivory using the body style rule.

Page text is set to the color value rgb(91, 91, 91).

Introducing CSS

One of the important principles discussed in the previous tutorial was that HTML does not define how a document should be displayed; it only defines the document's structure and content. The appearance of the page is determined by one or more style sheets written in the Cascading Style Sheets (CSS) language. Starting with this tutorial, you'll learn how to write your own CSS style sheets.

The CSS specifications are maintained by the same World Wide Web Consortium (W3C) that defines the standards for HTML. As with HTML, the CSS language has gone through several versions, the latest of which is CSS Version 3, more commonly known as **CSS3**. CSS3 is not based on a single specification but rather is built upon several **modules**, where each module is focused on a separate design topic. At the time of this writing, there were over 50 CSS3 modules with each module experiencing a different level of browser support. The W3C continues to expand the scope of the language, which means that many new design features are still at the stage where few, if any, browsers support them.

In these tutorials, you'll focus mostly on CSS features that have near-universal support among current browsers. However, you'll also examine workarounds to support older browsers and study ways to accommodate the difference between browsers in how they implement CSS designs.

TIP

You can research the support for CSS by browser version at *www.caniuse.com*.

Types of Style Sheets

A website's design is usually not the product of a single style sheet; rather, it is a combination of styles starting from the browser style sheet and then superseded by the user-defined style sheet, external style sheets, embedded style sheets, and concluding with inline styles (see Figure 2-1.) Let's examine each of these style sources in more detail.

| Figure 2-1 | Hierarchy of styles |

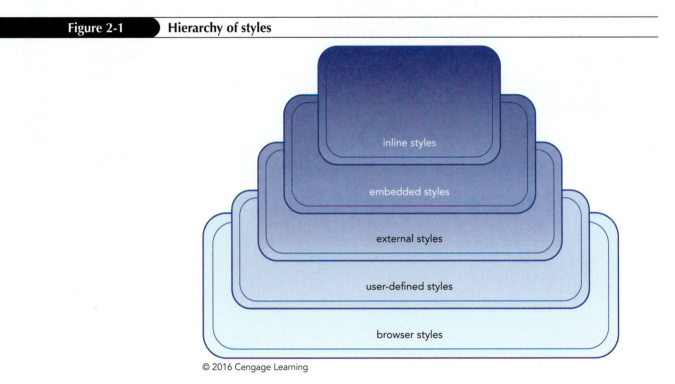

© 2016 Cengage Learning

The first styles to be processed are the **browser styles** or **user agent styles**, which are the styles built into the browser itself. In the absence of competing styles from other style sheets, a browser style is the one applied to the web page.

The next styles to be processed are the **user-defined styles**, which are styles defined by the user based on the settings he or she makes in configuring the browser. For example, a user with a visual impairment could alter the browser's default settings to display text with highly contrasting colors and a large font size for improved readability. Any user-defined style has precedence over its browser style counterpart.

User-defined styles can be superseded by **external styles**, which are the styles that the website author creates and places within a CSS file and links to the page. You used external style sheets in the last tutorial when you linked the Curbside Thai website to a collection of CSS files. As you saw in that tutorial, multiple documents can access the same style sheet, which makes it easy to apply a common design to an entire website.

Above the external styles in the hierarchy of style sheets are **embedded styles**, which are the styles added to the head of an HTML document. Embedded styles only apply to the HTML document in which they are created and they are not accessible to other documents in the website, but they do override any styles in an external style sheet.

Finally, at the highest order of precedence are **inline styles**, which are added as element attributes within an HTML document and thus apply to that element alone. Embedded styles and inline styles are not considered best practice and their use should be avoided because they violate the basic tenets of HTML, which is that HTML should only describe the content and structure of the document and that design styles should be placed outside of the HTML code.

The overall design of a web page is based on a combination of the styles from these different sources. Some of the styles might originate from the browser style sheet while others will be defined in an external style sheet or an embedded style sheet. Part of the challenge of CSS is determining how styles from these different style sheets interact to determine the page's final appearance.

Viewing a Page Using Different Style Sheets

You'll start your work on the Tri and Succeed Sports website by viewing how the home page appears when it is rendered in the default styles of the style sheet built into your browser.

To view the Tri and Succeed Sports home page:

1. Use your editor to open the **tss_home_txt.html** file from the html02 ▶ tutorial folder. Enter *your name* and *the date* in the comment section of the file and save the document as **tss_home.html**.

2. Take some time to scroll through the document to become familiar with its content and structure.

3. Open the **tss_home.html** page in your browser. Part of the appearance of the page is shown in Figure 2-2.

Figure 2-2   **The TSS home page rendered using only the browser style sheet**

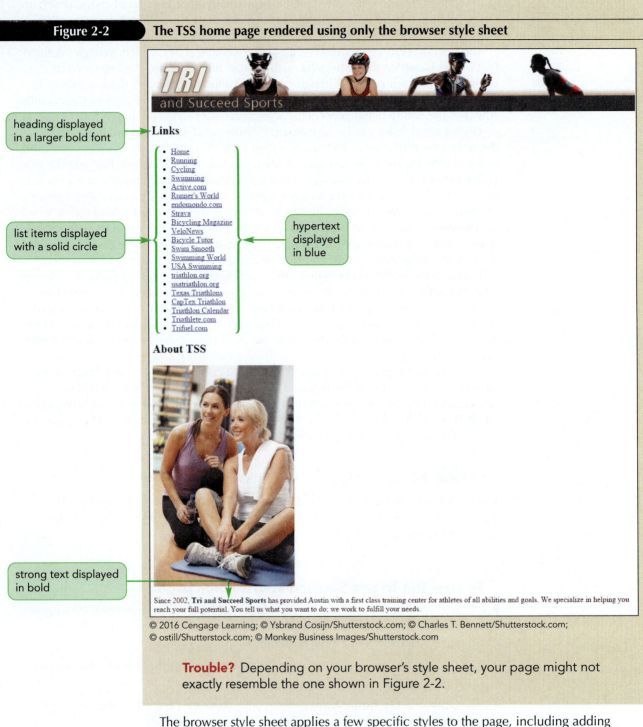

heading displayed in a larger bold font

list items displayed with a solid circle

hypertext displayed in blue

strong text displayed in bold

Trouble? Depending on your browser's style sheet, your page might not exactly resemble the one shown in Figure 2-2.

The browser style sheet applies a few specific styles to the page, including adding solid circles to the navigation list items, as well as displaying hypertext in blue, headings in a large bold font, and strong text in a bold font.

However the page layout is difficult to read. Alison has an external style sheet containing styles that will present this page in a more pleasing three-column layout. Link this page now to her style sheet file and then reload the document in your browser to view the impact on the page's appearance.

To change the layout of the TSS home page:

1. Return to the **tss_home.html** file in your HTML editor and add the following link element to the head section directly after the title element:

   ```
   <link href="tss_layout.css" rel="stylesheet" />
   ```

   Figure 2-3 highlights the newly added code in the document.

Figure 2-3	Linking to the tss_layout.css file

rel attribute indicates that the file is a style sheet

```
<meta charset="utf-8" />
<meta name="keywords" content="triathlon, running, swimming, cycling" />
<title>Tri and Succeed Sports</title>
<link href="tss_layout.css" rel="stylesheet" />
</head>
```

filename of style sheet

2. Save your changes to the file and then reopen the **tss_home.html** file in your browser. Figure 2-4 shows the appearance of the page using the layout styles defined in the tss_layout.css file.

Figure 2-4	The TSS home page using the tss_layout.css style sheet

© 2016 Cengage Learning; © Ysbrand Cosijn/Shutterstock.com; © Charles T. Bennett/Shutterstock.com; © ostill/Shutterstock.com; © Monkey Business Images/Shutterstock.com

The tss_layout.css file controls the placement of the page elements but not their appearance. The colors, fonts, and other design styles are still based on the browser style sheet.

Exploring Style Rules

If the element tag is the building block of the HTML file, then the **style rule**, which defines the styles applied to an element or group of elements, is the building block of the CSS style sheet. Style rules have the general form

```
selector {
    property1: value1;
    property2: value2;
    ...
}
```

where *selector* identifies an element or a group of elements within the document and the *property: value* pairs specify the style properties and their values applied to that element or elements. For example, the following style rule has a selector of `h1` to match all `h1` elements in the document and it has *property: value* pairs of `color: red` and `text-align: center` that tell the browser to display all h1 headings in red and centered on the page:

```
h1 {
    color: red;
    text-align: center;
}
```

Selectors can also be entered as comma-separated lists as in the following style rule that displays both h1 and h2 headings in red:

```
h1, h2 {
    color: red;
}
```

Like HTML, CSS ignores the use of white space, so you can also enter this style more compactly as follows:

```
h1, h2 {color: red;}
```

Writing a style rule on a single line saves space, but entering each style property on a separate line often makes your code easier to read and edit. You will see both approaches used in the CSS files you encounter on the web.

Browser Extensions

In addition to the W3C-supported style properties, most browsers supply their own extended library of style properties, known as **browser extensions**. Many of the styles that become part of the W3C specifications start as browser extensions and for older browser versions, sometimes the only way to support a particular CSS feature is through a browser extension tailored to a particular browser.

Browser extensions are identified through the use of a **vendor prefix**, which indicates the browser vendor that created and supports the property. Figure 2-5 lists the browser extensions you'll encounter in your work on web design.

Figure 2-5	Vendor prefixes for browser extensions

Vendor Prefix	Rendering Engine	Browsers
-khtml-	KHTML	Konqueror
-moz-	Mozilla	Firefox, Camino
-ms-	Trident	Internet Explorer
-o-	Presto	Opera, Nintendo Wii browser
-webkit-	WebKit	Android browser, Chrome, Safari

For example, one of the more recent style features added to CSS3 is the layout style to display content in separate columns. The number of columns is indicated using the `column-count` property. To apply this style in a way that supports both older and current browsers, you would include the browser extensions first followed by the most current CSS specification:

```
article {
    -webkit-column-count: 3;
    -moz-column-count: 3;
    column-count: 3;
}
```

In general, browsers process style properties in the order they're listed, ignoring those properties they don't recognize or support, so you always want the most current specifications listed last.

Embedded Style Sheets

The style rule structure is also used in embedded style sheets and inline styles. Embedded styles are inserted directly into the HTML file as metadata by adding the following `style` element to the document head

```
<style>
    style rules
</style>
```

where *style rules* are the different rules you want to embed in the HTML page. For example, the following embedded style applies the same style rules described previously to make all h1 headings in the current document appear in red and centered:

```
<style>
    h1 {
        color: red;
        text-align: center;
    }
</style>
```

Remember that, when all else is equal, the style that is loaded last has precedence over styles defined earlier. In the following code, the browser will load the embedded style sheet last, giving it precedence over the style rules in the tss_styles.css file.

```
<link href="tss_styles.css" rel="stylesheet" />
<style>
    style rules
</style>
```

TIP

To avoid confusion, always place your embedded styles after any links to external style sheet files so that the embedded styles always have precedence.

If the order of the `link` and `style` elements is reversed, the styles from the tss_styles.css file are loaded last and given precedence.

Inline Styles

The very last styles to be interpreted by the browser are inline styles, which are styles applied directly to specific elements using the following `style` attribute

```
<element style="property1: value1;property2: value2; …">
    content
</element>
```

where the `property: value` pairs define the styles, which are applied directly to that element. Thus, the following inline style sets the appearance of the h1 heading to red text centered on the page:

```
<h1 style="color: red; text-align: center;">
    Tri and Succeed Sports
</h1>
```

This style applies only to this particular h1 heading and not to any other h1 heading on the page or in the website. The advantage of inline styles is that it is clear exactly what page element is being formatted; however, inline styles are not recommended in most cases because they make changing designs tedious and inefficient. For example, if you used inline styles to format all of your headings, you would have to locate all of the `h1` through `h6` elements in all of the pages within the entire website and add `style` attributes to each tag. This would be no small task on a large website containing hundreds of headings spread out among dozens of pages. Likewise, it would be a nightmare if you had to modify the design of those headings at a later date. Thus, the recommended practice is to always use external style sheets that can be applied across pages and page elements.

Style Specificity and Precedence

With so many different style rules to be applied to the same document, there has to be an orderly method by which conflicts between those different rules are resolved. You've already learned that the style that is defined last has precedence, but that is not the whole story. Another important principle is that *the more specific style rule has precedence over the more general style rule*. Thus, a rule applied to a specific paragraph takes precedence over a rule applied to the entire page, and a rule applied to a section of text within that paragraph takes precedence over the rule for the paragraph. For example, in the following style rules, the color of the text in all paragraphs is set to red, taking precedence over the color black applied to the rest of the text in the page:

```
p {color: red;}
body {color: black;}
```

Note that specificity is only an issue when two or more styles conflict, as in the example above. When the style rules involve different properties (such as color and size), there is no conflict and both rules are applied. If two rules have equal specificity and thus, equal importance, then the one that is defined last has precedence.

Style Inheritance

TIP

Not all properties are inherited; for example, a style property that defines text color has no meaning for an inline image.

An additional factor in how an element is rendered is that properties are passed from a parent element to its children in a process known as **style inheritance**. Thus, the following style rule sets the color of article text to blue and that rule is passed to any paragraph, header, footer, or other element nested within that article. In addition, the text in a paragraph within that article is centered:

```
article {color: blue;}
p {text-align: center;}
```

Thus, the final rendering of any page element is the result of styles drawn from rules across multiple style sheets and from properties passed down from one element to another within the hierarchy of page elements. These style sheets and style rules form the "cascade" of styles in Cascading Style Sheets.

Browser Developer Tools

TIP

In most browsers, you can quickly access information about a specific page element by right-clicking the element in the browser window and choosing Inspect Element from the pop-up menu.

If the idea of multiple style sheets and multiple style rules is intimidating, there are tools available to help you manage your styles. Most browsers include developer tools allowing the designer to view HTML code, CSS styles, and other parts of the web page. These developer tools make it easier for the designer to locate the source of a style that has been applied to a specific page element.

Each browser's developer tools are different and are constantly being updated and improved with every new browser version. However, to give you the flavor of the tools you have at your disposal, you'll examine both the HTML code and the CSS style sheet under the developer tools built into your desktop browser. Note that the figures in the steps that follow use the desktop version of the Google Chrome browser.

Accessing the Browser Developer Tools:

1. Return to the **tss_home.html** file in your browser.

2. Press **F12** to open the developer tools window.

   Trouble? If pressing F12 doesn't open the developer tools, your browser might need a different keyboard combination. In Safari for the Macintosh, you can view the developer tools by pressing ctrl+shift+I or command+option+I.

3. From the hierarchical list of elements in the web page, click the <body> tag if it is not already selected.

   Figure 2-6 shows the layout of panes using the developer tools under Google Chrome for the desktop.

Figure 2-6	Developer tools in Google Chrome

hierarchical list of elements on the web page

styles applied to the body element from tss_layout.css style sheet

the margin style in the browser style sheet has been superseded by the margin style in the tss_layout.css style sheet

diagram of the layout of the body element

styles applied to the body element from the browser style sheet

layout styles applied to the body element

© 2016 Cengage Learning; © Ysbrand Cosijn/Shutterstock.com; © Charles T. Bennett/Shutterstock.com; © ostill/Shutterstock.com; © Monkey Business Images/Shutterstock.com

As shown in Figure 2-6, the styles pane lists the styles that have been applied to the body element. Note that the margin property from the browser style sheet has been crossed out, indicating that this browser style has been superseded by a style defined in the external style sheet.

Trouble? Every browser has a different set of developer tools and configurations. Your tools might not resemble those shown in Figure 2-6.

4. Take some time to explore the content and styles used in the other page elements by selecting the elements tags from the hierarchical list of elements.

5. Press **F12** again to close the developer tools window.

Trouble? In Safari, you can close the developer tools by pressing ctrl+shift+I or by command+option+I.

In this and future tutorials, you may find that your browser's developer tools are a great aid to working through your website designs. Most developer tools allow the user to insert new style rules in order to view their immediate impact on the page's appearance; however, these modifications are only applied during the current session and are not saved permanently. So, once you find a setting that you want to use, you must enter it in the appropriate style sheet for it to take effect permanently.

INSIGHT

Defining an !important Style

You can override the style cascade by marking a particular property with the following `!important` keyword:

```
property: value !important;
```

The following style rule sets the color of all h1 headings to orange; and because this property is marked as important, it takes precedence over any conflicting styles found in other style sheets.

```
h1 {color: orange !important;}
```

The `!important` keyword is most often used in user-defined style sheets in which the user needs to substitute his or her own styles in place of the designer's. For example, a visually impaired user might need to have text displayed in a large font with highly contrasting colors. In general, designers should not use the `!important` keyword because it interferes with the cascade order built into the CSS language.

Creating a Style Sheet

Now that you've reviewed some history and concepts behind style sheets, you'll start creating your own. You should usually begin your style sheets with comments that document the purpose of the style sheet and provide information about who created the document and when.

Writing Style Comments

Style sheet comments are entered as

```
/*
 comment
*/
```

where `comment` is the text of the comment. Because CSS ignores the presence of white space, you can insert your comments on a single line to save space as:

```
/* comment */
```

Create a style sheet file now, placing a comment with your name and the current date at the top of the file.

Writing a Style Comment:

1. Use your editor to open the **tss_styles_txt.css** file from the html02 ▸ tutorial folder.

2. Within the comment section at the top of the file, enter **your name** following the Author: comment and **the date** following the Date: comment.

3. Save the file as **tss_styles.css**.

4. Return to the **tss_home.html** file in your HTML editor and add the following `link` element directly before the closing `</head>` tag.

   ```
   <link href="tss_styles.css" rel="stylesheet" />
   ```

5. Close the tss_home.html file, saving your changes.

Defining the Character Encoding

As with HTML files, it is a good idea in every CSS document to define the character encoding used in the file. In CSS, you accomplish this using the following @charset rule

    @charset "encoding";

where *encoding* defines the character encoding used in the file. Add the @charset rule to the tss_styles.css style sheet file now, specifying that the UTF-8 character set is used in the CSS code.

To indicate the character encoding:

▶ **1.** Return to the **tss_styles.css** file in your editor.

▶ **2.** Directly above the initial comment section, insert the line: **@charset "utf-8";**.

   Figure 2-7 highlights the new code in the style sheet.

Figure 2-7   **Adding the @charset rule and style comments**

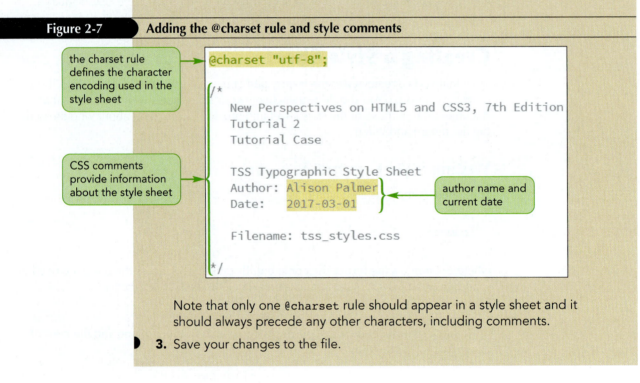

Note that only one @charset rule should appear in a style sheet and it should always precede any other characters, including comments.

▶ **3.** Save your changes to the file.

Importing Style Sheets

The @charset rule is an example of a **CSS at-rule**, which is a rule used to send directives to the browser indicating how the contents of the CSS file should be interpreted and parsed. Another at-rule is the following @import used to import the contents of a style sheet file

    @import url(url);

where *url* is the URL of an external style sheet file.

   The @import is used to combine style rules from several style sheets into a single file. For example, an online store might have one style sheet named basic.css containing all of the basic styles used in every web page and another style sheet named sales.css containing styles used with merchandise-related pages. The following code imports styles from both files:

```
@import url(company.css);
@import url(support.css);
```

Using multiple `@import` rules in a CSS file has the same impact as adding multiple `link` elements to the HTML file. One advantage of the `@import` rule is that it simplifies your HTML code by placing the decision about which style sheets to include and exclude in the CSS file rather than in the HTML file.

Working with Color in CSS

The first part of your style sheet for the Tri and Succeed Sports website will focus on color. If you've worked with graphics software, you've probably made your color selections using a graphical interface where you can see your color options. Specifying color with CSS is somewhat less intuitive because CSS is a text-based language and requires colors to be defined in textual terms. This is done through either a color name or a color value.

Color Names

TIP

You can view the complete list of CSS color names by opening the demo_color_names.html file in the html02 ▶ demo folder.

You've already seen from previous code examples that you can set the color of page text using the `color` property along with a color name such as red, blue, or black. CSS supports 147 color names covering common names such as red, green, and yellow to more exotic colors such as ivory, orange, crimson, khaki, and brown.

PROSKILLS

Written Communication: Communicating in Color

Humans are born to respond to color. Studies have shown that infants as young as two months prefer bright colors with strong contrast to drab colors with little contrast, and market research for clothing often focuses on what colors are "in" and what colors are passé.

Your color choices can impact the way your website is received so you want to choose a color scheme that is tailored to the personality and interests of your target audience. Color can evoke an emotional response and is associated with particular feelings or concepts, such as

- *red*—assertive, powerful, sexy, dangerous
- *pink*—innocent, romantic, feminine
- *black*—strong, classic, stylish
- *gray*—business-like, detached
- *yellow*—warm, cheerful, optimistic
- *blue*—consoling, serene, quiet
- *orange*—friendly, vigorous, inviting
- *white*—clean, pure, straightforward, innocent

If your website will be used internationally, you need to be aware of how cultural differences can affect your audience's response to color. For instance, white, which is associated with innocence in Western cultures, is the color of mourning in China; yellow, which is considered a bright, cheerful color in the West, represents spirituality in Buddhist countries.

RGB Color Values

Because a palette of 147 color names is extremely limited for graphic design and color names can be constricting (how do you name a color that is slightly redder than ivory with a tinge of blue?), CSS also supports **color values**, in which the color is given by an exact numeric representation. CSS3 supports two types of color values: RGB values and HSL values.

RGB color values are based on classical color theory in which all colors are determined by adding three primary colors—red, green, and blue—at different levels of intensity. For example, adding all three primary colors at maximum intensity produces the color white, while adding any two of the three primary colors at maximum intensity produces the trio of complementary colors—yellow, magenta, and cyan (see Figure 2-8).

Figure 2-8   **Color addition in the RGB color model**

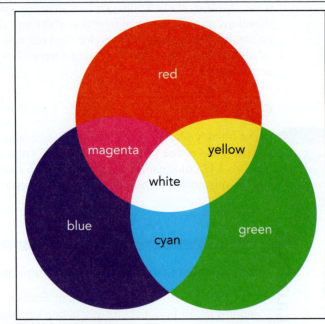

© 2016 Cengage Learning

Varying the intensity of the three primary colors extends the palette to other colors. Orange, for example, is created from a high intensity of red, a moderate intensity of green, and a total absence of blue. CSS represents these intensities mathematically as a set of numbers called an **RGB triplet**, which has the format

```
rgb(red, green, blue)
```

where *red*, *green*, and *blue* are the intensities of the red, green, and blue components of the color. Intensities range from 0 (absence of color) to 255 (maximum intensity); thus, the color white has the value rgb(255, 255, 255), indicating that red, green, and blue are mixed equally at the highest intensity, and orange is represented by rgb(255, 165, 0). RGB triplets can describe 256^3 (16.7 million) possible colors, which is a greater number of colors than the human eye can distinguish.

RGB values are sometimes expressed as hexadecimal numbers where a **hexadecimal number** is a number expressed in the base 16 numbering system rather than in the commonly used base 10 system. In base 10 counting, numeric values are expressed using combinations of 10 characters (0 through 9). Hexadecimal numbering includes these ten numeric characters and six extra characters: A (for 10), B (for 11), C (for 12), D (for 13), E (for 14), and F (for 15). For values above 15, you use a combination of those 16 characters. For example, the number 16 has a hexadecimal representation of 10, and a value of 255 has a hexadecimal representation of FF. The style value for color represented as a hexadecimal number has the form

```
#redgreenblue
```

where *red*, *green*, and *blue* are the hexadecimal values of the red, green, and blue components. Therefore, the color yellow could be represented either by the RGB triplet

```
rgb(255,255,0)
```

or more compactly as the hexadecimal

```
#FFFF00
```

Most HTML editors and graphic programs provide color picking tools that allow the user to choose a color and then copy and paste the RGB or hexadecimal color value. Hexadecimal color values have the advantage of creating smaller style sheets, which can be loaded faster—an important consideration for mobile devices. However, for others viewing and studying your style sheet code, they are more difficult to interpret than RGB values.

Finally you can enter each component value as a percentage, with 100% representing the highest intensity. In this form, you would specify the color orange with the following values

```
rgb(100%, 65%, 0%)
```

which is equivalent to the rgb(255, 165, 0) value described above.

HSL Color Values

HSL color values were introduced in CSS3 and are based on a color model in which each color is determined by its hue, saturation, and lightness. **Hue** is the tint of the color and is usually represented by a direction on a color wheel. Hue values range from 0° up to 360°, where 0° matches the location of red on the color wheel, 120° matches green, and 240° matches blue. **Saturation** measures the intensity of the chosen color and ranges from 0% (no color) up to 100% (full color). Finally, **lightness** measures the brightness of the color and ranges from 0% (black) up to 100% (white). Figure 2-9 shows how setting the hue to 38°, the saturation to 90%, and the lightness to 60% results in a medium shade of orange.

Defining the color orange under the HSL color model

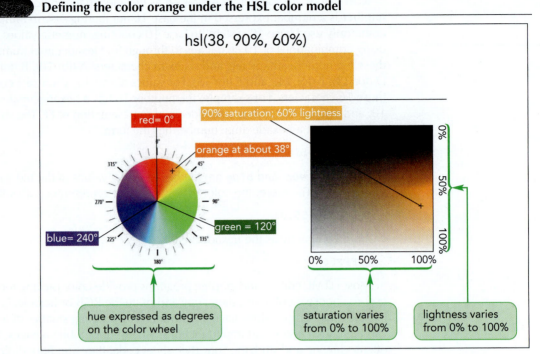

© 2016 Cengage Learning

Color values using the HSL model are described in CSS3 using

```
hsl(hue, saturation, lightness)
```

where *hue* is the tint of the color in degrees, *saturation* is the intensity in percent, and *lightness* is the brightness in percent of the color. Thus, a medium orange color would be represented as

```
hsl(38, 90%, 60%)
```

Graphic designers consider HSL easier to use because it allows them to set the initial color based on hue and then fine-tune the saturation and lightness values. This is more difficult in the RGB model because you have to balance three completely different colors to achieve the right mix. For example, the RGB equivalent to the color orange in Figure 2-9 would be the color value rgb(245, 177, 61); however, it's not immediately apparent why that mixture of red, green, and blue would result in that particular shade of orange.

Defining Semi-Opaque Colors

CSS3 introduced opacity to the CSS color models where **opacity** defines how solid the color appears. The color's opacity can be specified using either of the following rgba and hsla properties

```
rgba(red, green, blue, opacity)
hsla(hue, saturation, lightness, opacity)
```

where *opacity* sets the opacity of the color ranging from 0 (completely transparent) up to 1.0 (completely opaque). For example, the following style property uses the HSL color model to define a medium orange color with an opacity of 0.7:

```
hsla(38, 90%, 60%, 0.7)
```

The final appearance of a semi-opaque color is influenced by the background color. Displayed against a white background, a medium orange color would appear in a lighter shade of orange because the orange will appear mixed with the background white.

On the other hand, the same orange color displayed on a black background would appear as a darker shade of orange. The advantage of using semi-transparent colors is that it makes it easier to create a color theme in which similarly tinted colors are blended with other colors on the page.

Setting Text and Background Colors

Now that you've studied how CSS works with colors, you can start applying color to some of the elements displayed on the Tri and Succeed Sports website. CSS supports the following styles to define both the text and background color for each element on your page

```
color: color;
background-color: color;
```

where *color* is either a color value or a color name.

Alison wants to use an HSL color value (27, 72%, 72%) to set the background of the document to orange and she would like the text of the home page to appear in a medium gray color on an ivory background. The style rules to modify the appearance of these document elements are

```
html {
    background-color: hsl(27, 72%, 72%);
}
body {
    color: rgb(91, 91, 91);
    background-color: ivory;
}
```

The `html` selector in this code selects the entire HTML document so that any part of the browser window background that is not within the page body will be displayed using the HSL color (27, 72%, 72%).

Within the page body, Alison wants the h1 and h2 headings to be displayed in white text on dark and lighter orange colors using the RGB color values (222, 128, 60) and (235, 177, 131) respectively. The style rules are

```
h1 {
    color: white;
    background-color: rgb(222, 128, 60);
}

h2 {
    color: white;
    background-color: rgb(235, 177, 131);
}
```

Setting Text and Background Color

- To set the text color of an element, use the following property

```
color: color;
```

- To set the background color of an element, use the following property

```
background-color: color;
```

where *color* is a color name or a color value.

Next, add style rules for text and background colors to the tss_styles.css file.

To define background and text colors:

Saturation and lightness values in an hsl color value must be expressed as percentages.

1. Add the following code within the HTML and Body Styles section:

```
html {
    background-color: hsl(27, 72%, 72%);
}

body {
    color: rgb(91, 91, 91);
    background-color: ivory;
}
```

TIP

Almost 8% of all men and 0.5% of all women have some sort of color blindness. Because red-green color blindness is the most common type of color impairment, you should avoid using red text on a green background and vice-versa.

2. Add the following style rules within the Heading Styles section:

```
h1 {
    color: white;
    background-color: rgb(222, 128, 60);
}

h2 {
    color: white;
    background-color: rgb(235, 177, 131);
}
```

Figure 2-10 highlights the new style rules.

| Figure 2-10 | Adding text and background colors |

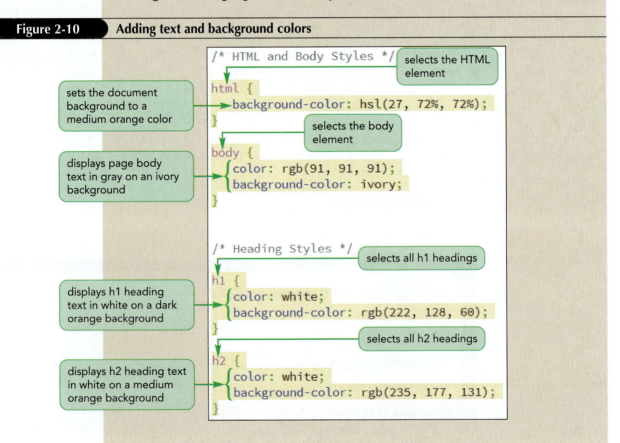

```
/* HTML and Body Styles */          selects the HTML
                                    element
html {
    background-color: hsl(27, 72%, 72%);
}
                          selects the body
                          element
body {
    color: rgb(91, 91, 91);
    background-color: ivory;
}


/* Heading Styles */            selects all h1 headings

h1 {
    color: white;
    background-color: rgb(222, 128, 60);
}
                                selects all h2 headings
h2 {
    color: white;
    background-color: rgb(235, 177, 131);
}
```

sets the document background to a medium orange color

displays page body text in gray on an ivory background

displays h1 heading text in white on a dark orange background

displays h2 heading text in white on a medium orange background

3. Save your changes to the file and then reload the **tss_home.html** file in your browser. Figure 2-11 shows the appearance of the page under the new styles.

| Figure 2-11 | Text and background colors in the web page |

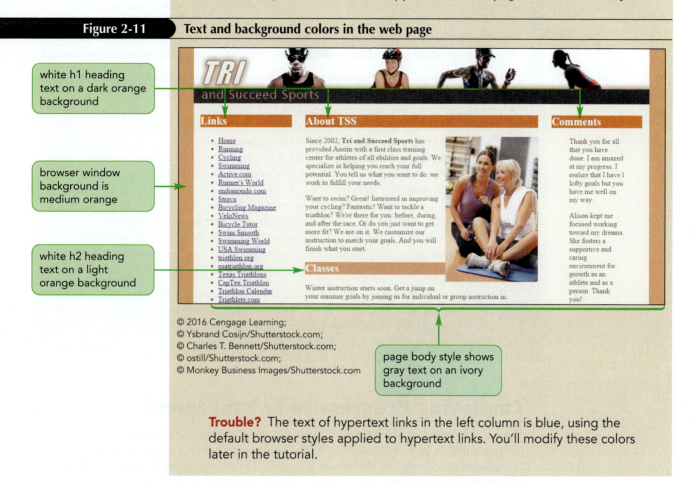

white h1 heading text on a dark orange background

browser window background is medium orange

white h2 heading text on a light orange background

© 2016 Cengage Learning;
© Ysbrand Cosijn/Shutterstock.com;
© Charles T. Bennett/Shutterstock.com;
© ostill/Shutterstock.com;
© Monkey Business Images/Shutterstock.com

page body style shows gray text on an ivory background

Trouble? The text of hypertext links in the left column is blue, using the default browser styles applied to hypertext links. You'll modify these colors later in the tutorial.

PROSKILLS

Problem Solving: Choosing a Color Scheme

One of the worst things you can do to your website is to associate interesting and useful content with jarring and disagreeable color. Many designers prefer the HSL color system because it makes it easier to select visually pleasing color schemes. The following are some basic color schemes you may want to apply to websites you design:

- *monochrome*—a single hue with varying values for saturation and lightness; this color scheme is easy to manage but is not as vibrant as other designs
- *complementary*—two hues separated by 180° on the color wheel; this color scheme is the most vibrant and offers the highest contrast and visual interest, but it can be misused and might distract users from the page content
- *triad*—three hues separated by 120° on the color wheel; this color scheme provides the same opportunity for pleasing color contrasts as a complementary design, but it might not be as visibly striking
- *tetrad*—four hues separated by 90° on the color wheel; perhaps the richest of all color schemes, it is also the hardest one in which to achieve color balance
- *analogic*—two hues close to one another on the color wheel in which one color is the dominant color and the other is a supporting color used only for highlights and nuance; this scheme lacks color contrasts and is not as vibrant as other color schemes

Once you have selected a color design and the main hues, you then vary those colors by altering the saturation and lightness. One of the great advantages of style sheets is that you can quickly modify your color design choices and view the impact of those changes on your page content.

Employing Progressive Enhancement

The HSL color you used for the html selector was introduced with CSS3 and thus it is not supported in very old browsers. If this is a concern, you can insert the older style properties first followed by the newer standards. For example, the following style rule sets the background color of the `html` element to a lighter orange using the RGB value first, and then the equivalent HSL value.

```
html {
    background-color: rgb(235, 177, 131);
    background-color: hsl(27, 72%, 72%);
}
```

Old browsers that don't recognize the HSL color value will ignore it and use the RGB value, while browsers that recognize both values will use the one that is defined last, which in this case is the HSL value. This is an example of a technique known as **progressive enhancement**, which places code conforming to older standards before newer properties, providing support for old browsers but still allowing newer standards and techniques to be used by the browsers that support them.

You show Alison the work you've done on colors. She's pleased with the ease of using CSS to modify the design and appearance of elements on the Tri and Succeed Sports website. In the next session, you'll continue to explore CSS styles, focusing on text styles.

REVIEW

Session 2.1 Quick Check

1. What are inline styles, embedded styles, and external style sheets? Which would you use to define a design for an entire web site?
2. What keyword do you add to a style property to override style precedence and style inheritance?
3. Provide the code to enter the style comment "Tri and Succeed Sports Color Styles".
4. Provide the style rule to display block quote text in red using an RGB triplet.
5. The color chartreuse is located at 90° on the color wheel with 100% saturation and 50% lightness. Provide a style rule to display address text in black with chartreuse as the background color.
6. What is progressive enhancement?
7. Based on the following style rule for paragraph text, which style property will be used by an older browser that supports only CSS2?

```
p {
    color: rgb(232, 121, 50);
    color: hsla(23, 80%, 55%, 0.75);
}
```

8. Provide a style rule to display h1 and h2 headings with a background color of yellow (an equal mixture of red and green at highest intensity with no blue) at 70% opacity.

Session 2.2 Visual Overview:

The `@font-face` rule imports a web font into the style sheet.

```
@font-face {
    font-family: Quicksand;
    src: url('Quicksand-Regular.woff') format('woff'),
         url('Quicksand-Regular.ttf') format('truetype');
}

body {
    color: rgb(91, 91, 91);
    background-color: ivory;
    font-family: Verdana, Geneva, sans-serif;
}

h1 {font-size: 2.2em;}
h2 {font-size: 1.5em;}

h1, h2 {
    font-family: Quicksand, Verdana, Geneva, sans-serif;
    letter-spacing: 0.1em;
}

aside blockquote {
    color: rgb(232, 165, 116);
}

nav > ul {
    line-height: 2em;
}

body > footer address {
    background-color: rgb(222,128,60);
    color: rgba(255, 255, 255, 0.7);
    font: normal small-caps bold 0.9em/3em
          Quicksand, Verdana, Geneva, sans-serif;
    text-align: center;
}
```

The `font-family` property lists the possible fonts used for the element text.

The `font-size` property sets the text size in absolute or relative units.

The `em unit` is a relative unit of length that expresses a size relative to the font size of the containing element.

The `letter-spacing` property sets the **kerning** or space between letters.

The `aside blockquote` selector selects blockquote elements that are descendants of the aside element.

The `nav > ul` selector selects `ul` elements that are direct children of the nav element.

The `line-height` property sets the height of the lines of text in the element.

The `text-align` property sets the horizontal alignment of the text.

CSS Typography

The h1 heading is displayed in the Quicksand font with a font size of 2.2em and letter spacing of 0.1em.

Links

- Home
- Running
- Cycling
- Swimming
- Active.com
- Runner's World
- endomondo.com
- Strava
- Bicycling Magazine
- VeloNews
- Bicycle Tutor
- Swim Smooth
- Swimming World
- USA Swimming
- triathlon.org
- usatriathlon.org
- Texas Triathlons
- CapTex Triathlon
- Triathlon Calendar
- Triathlete.com
- Trifuel.com

Navigation list is double-spaced with a line height of 2em.

About TSS

Since 2002, **Tri and Succeed Sports** has provided Austin with a first class training center for athletes of all abilities and goals. We specialize in helping you reach your full potential. You tell us what you want to do; we work to fulfill your needs.

Want to swim? Great! Interested in improving your cycling? Fantastic! Want to tackle a triathlon? We're there for you: before, during, and after the race. Or do you just want to get more fit? We are on it. We customize our instruction to match your goals. And you will finish what you start.

Body text is displayed in a Verdana font.

Classes

Winter instruction starts soon. Get a jump on your summer goals by joining us for individual or group instruction in:

- **Running**: We start with the basics to help you run faster and farther than you ever thought possible without aches and pains.
- **Cycling**: The indoor bike trainers at TSS include everything you need to refine your technique, stamina, and power for improved results on the road.
- **Swimming**: The open water swim can be one of the most frightening sports to master. Our classes begin with basic techniques so that your swim can be very enjoyable, and not a chore.

Contact us to set up individual instruction and assessment.

Our Philosophy

Athletes are the foundation of every successful training program. The best coach is an experienced guide who begins with each athlete's hopes, dreams and desires and then tailors a training plan based on that individuals's current fitness and lifestyle. Since 2002, TSS has helped hundreds of individuals achieve success in many fitness areas. The winner is not the one who finishes first but anyone who starts the race and perseveres. Join us and begin exploring the possible.

TRI AND SUCCEED SPORTS • 41 VENTURE DR. • AUSTIN, TX 78711 • 512.555.9917

Comments

Thank you for all that you have done. I am amazed at my progress. I realize that I have l lofty goals but you have me well on my way.

Alison kept me focused working toward my dreams. She fosters a supportive and caring environment for growth as an athlete and as a person. Thank you!

You do it right! Your track record proves it. Proud to be a TSS athlete and I'm honored to have you all as my coaches and support team.

The coaches at TSS treat you with the highest respect: whether you're an individual getting off the couch for the first time or an elite athlete training for the Iron Man. They know their stuff.

I just completed my first marathon, following your fitness schedule to the letter. Never once did I come close to bonking and two days later I felt ready for another race!

Page footer is centered and displayed in small caps as specified by the body > footer address style rule.

The h2 headings are displayed in the Quicksand font with a font size of 1.5em and letter spacing of 0.1em.

Exploring Selector Patterns

The following style rule matches every h1 element in the HTML document, regardless of the location of the h1 heading:

```
h1 {
    color: red;
}
```

This style rule will match an h1 heading located within a page article in the same way it matches an h1 heading nested within an aside element or the body header or the body footer. Often, however, you will want your style rules to apply to specific elements, such as h1 headings found within articles but not anywhere else. To direct a style rule to specific elements, you'll use **selector patterns** to match only those page elements that correspond to a specified pattern.

Contextual Selectors

The first selector pattern you'll examine is a **contextual selector**, which specifies the context under which a particular page element is matched. Context is based on the hierarchical structure of the document, which involves the relationships between a **parent element** containing one or more **child elements** and within those child elements several levels of **descendant elements**. A contextual selector relating a parent element to its descendants has the following pattern

```
parent descendant { styles }
```

where *parent* is a parent element, *descendant* is a descendant of that parent and *styles* are styles applied to the descendant element. For example, the following style rule sets the text color of h1 headings to red but only when those headings are nested within the header element:

```
header h1 {
    color: red;
}
```

As shown in the code that follows, the descendant element does not have to be a direct child of the parent; in fact, it can appear several levels below the parent in the hierarchy. This means that the above style rule matches the h1 element in the following HTML code:

```
<header>
    <div>
        <h1>Tri and Succeed Sports</h1>
    </div>
</header>
```

In this example, the h1 element is a direct child of the div element; but, because it is still a descendant of the header element, the style rule still applies.

Contextual selectors follow the general rule discussed in the last session; that is, the more specific style is applied in preference to the more general rule. For instance, the following style rules would result in h1 headings within the section element being displayed in red while all other h1 headings would appear in blue:

```
section h1 {color: red;}
h1          {color: blue;}
```

Figure 2-12 describes some of the other contextual selectors supported by CSS.

Figure 2-12   Contextual selectors

Selector	Description
*	Matches any element
elem	Matches the element *elem* located anywhere in the document
elem1, elem2, …	Matches any of the elements *elem1*, *elem2*, etc.
parent descendant	Matches the *descendant* element that is nested within the *parent* element at some level
parent > child	Matches the *child* element that is a child of the *parent* element
elem1 + elem2	Matches *elem2* that is immediately preceded by the sibling element *elem1*
elem1 ~ elem2	Matches *elem2* that follows the sibling element *elem1*

To match any element, use the **wildcard selector** with the * character. For example, the following style rule matches every child of the `article` element, setting the text color to blue:

```
article > * {color: blue;}
```

Sibling selectors are used to select elements based on elements that are adjacent to them in the document hierarchy. The following style rule uses the + symbol to select the `h2` element, but only if it is immediately preceded by an `h1` element:

```
h1+h2 {color: blue;}
```

On the other hand, the following style rule uses the ~ symbol to select any `h2` element that is preceded (but, not necessarily immediately) by an `h1` element:

```
h1 ~ h2 {color: blue;}
```

Figure 2-13 provides additional examples of selectors and highlights in red those elements in the document that would be selected by the specified selector.

Figure 2-13   Contextual selector patterns

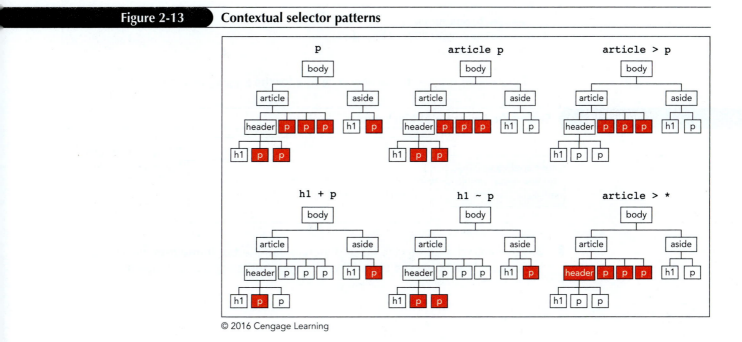

© 2016 Cengage Learning

Remember that, because of style inheritance, any style applied to an element is passed down the document tree. Thus, a style applied to a `header` element is automatically passed down to elements contained within that header unless that style conflicts with a more specific style.

Using Contextual Selectors

- To select all elements, use the * selector.
- To select a single element, use the *elem* selector, where *elem* is the name of the element.
- To select a descendant element, use the *parent descendant* selector where *parent* is a parent element and *descendant* is an element nested within the parent at some lower level.
- To select a child element, use the *parent > child* selector.
- To select a sibling element, *elem2*, that directly follows *elem1*, use the *elem1 + elem2* selector.
- To select a sibling element, *elem2*, that follows, but not necessarily directly *elem1*, use the *elem1 ~ elem2* selector.

Now, you'll create a style rule to change the text color of the customer testimonials on the Tri and Succeed Sports home page to a dark orange using the RGB color value rgb(232, 165, 116). You'll use a contextual selector to apply the style rule only to block quotes that are descendants of the `aside` element.

To create style rule with a contextual selector:

1. If you took a break after the previous session, make sure the **tss_styles.css** file is open in your editor.

2. Within the Aside and Blockquote Styles section, insert the following style rule:

```
aside blockquote {
    color: rgb(232, 165, 116);
}
```

Figure 2-14 highlights the new style rule for the `blockquote` element.

Figure 2-14   **Setting the text color of block quotes**

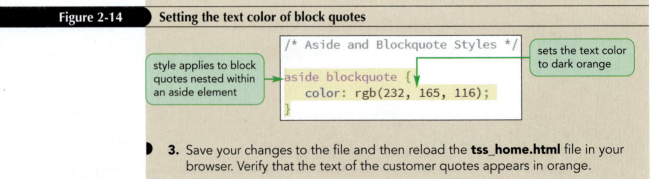

3. Save your changes to the file and then reload the **tss_home.html** file in your browser. Verify that the text of the customer quotes appears in orange.

Attribute Selectors

Selectors also can be defined based on attributes and attribute values within elements. Two attributes, `id` and `class`, are often key in targeting styles to specific elements. Recall that the `id` attribute is used to identify specific elements within the document. To apply a style to an element based on its id, you use either the selector

`#id`

or the selector

`elem#id`

where `id` is the value of the `id` attribute and `elem` is the name of the element. Because ids are supposed to be unique, either form is acceptable but including the element name removes any confusion about the location of the selector. For example, the selector for the following h1 heading from the HTML file

`<h1 id="title">Tri and Succeed Sports</h1>`

can be entered as either `#title` or `h1#title` in your CSS style sheet.

Because no two elements can share the same ID, HTML uses the `class` attribute to identify groups of elements that share a similar characteristic or property. For example, the following `h1` element and paragraph element both belong to the intro class of elements:

```
<h1 class="intro">Tri and Succeed Sports</h1>
<p class="intro"> … </p>
```

To select an element based on its `class` value, use the selector

`elem.class`

where `class` is the value of the `class` attribute. Thus the following style rule displays the text of h1 headings from the intro class in blue:

`h1.intro {color: blue;}`

> **TIP**
>
> An element can belong to several classes by including the class names in a space-separated list in the `class` attribute.

To apply the same style rule to all elements of a particular class, omit the element name. The following style rule displays the text of all elements from the intro class in blue:

`.intro {color: blue;}`

While `id` and `class` are the most common attributes to use with selectors, any attribute or attribute value can be the basis for a selector. Figure 2-15 lists all of the CSS attribute selector patterns based on attributes and attribute values.

Figure 2-15 **Attribute selectors**

Selector	Selects	Example	Selects
elem#id	Element *elem* with the ID value *id*	h1#intro	The h1 heading with the id *intro*
#id	Any element with the ID value *id*	#intro	Any element with the id *intro*
elem.class	All *elem* elements with the class attribute value *class*	p.main	All paragraphs belonging to the *main* class
.class	All elements with the class value *class*	.main	All elements belonging to the *main* class
elem[att]	All *elem* elements containing the *att* attribute	a[href]	All hypertext elements containing the href attribute
elem[att="text"]	All *elem* elements whose *att* attribute equals *text*	a[href="top.html"]	All hypertext elements whose href attribute equals *top.html*
elem[att~="text"]	All *elem* elements whose *att* attribute contains the word *text*	a[rel~="glossary"]	All hypertext elements whose rel attribute contains the word *glossary*
elem[att|="text"]	All *elem* elements whose *att* attribute value is a hyphen-separated list of words beginning with *text*	p[id|="first"]	All paragraphs whose id attribute starts with the word *first* in a hyphen-separated list of words
elem[att^="text"]	All *elem* elements whose *att* attribute begins with *text* [**CSS3**]	a[rel^="prev"]	All hypertext elements whose rel attribute begins with *prev*
elem[att$="text"]	All *elem* elements whose *att* attribute ends with *text* [**CSS3**]	a[href$="org"]	All hypertext elements whose href attribute ends with *org*
elem[att*="text"]	All *elem* elements whose *att* attribute contains the value *text* [**CSS3**]	a[href*="faq"]	All hypertext elements whose href attribute contains the text string faq

Note that some of the attribute selectors listed in Figure 2-15 were first introduced in CSS3 and, thus, might not be supported in older browsers.

REFERENCE

Using Attribute Selectors

- To select an element based on its ID, use the *elem#id* or *#id* selector, where *elem* is the name of the element and *id* is the value of the id attribute.
- To select an element based on its class value, use the *.class* or the *elem.class* selectors, where *class* is the value of the class attribute.
- To select an element that contains an *att* attribute, use *elem[att]*.
- To select an element based on whether its attribute value equals a specified value, *val*, use *elem[att="val"]*.

In the Tri and Succeed Sports home page, the main content is enclosed within an `article` element with the ID *about_tss*. Alison wants the h1 and h2 heading styles you entered in the last session to be applied only to `h1` and `h2` elements within articles that have this particular ID. Revise the style sheet now.

To apply an id selector:

▶ **1.** Return to the **tss_styles.css** file in your editor.

▶ **2.** Change the selectors for the `h1` and `h2` elements in the Heading Styles section to `article#about_tss h1` and `article#about_tss h2` respectively.

   Figure 2-16 highlights the revised selectors in the style sheet.

| Figure 2-16 | Using an id selector |

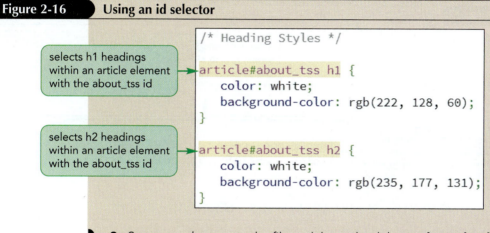

selects h1 headings within an article element with the about_tss id

selects h2 headings within an article element with the about_tss id

```
/* Heading Styles */

article#about_tss h1 {
    color: white;
    background-color: rgb(222, 128, 60);
}

article#about_tss h2 {
    color: white;
    background-color: rgb(235, 177, 131);
}
```

▶ **3.** Save your changes to the file and then reload the **tss_home.html** file in your browser. Verify that the design of the h1 and h2 headings is only applied to the headings in the about_tss article but not to the other headings on the page.

The `article` element will be used in other pages in the Tri and Succeed Sports website. Alison has provided you with three additional HTML files containing descriptions of the instruction her company offers for runners, cyclists, and swimmers. On those pages the `article` elements have the `class` attribute with the value *syllabus*. Create style rules for the `h1` and `h2` elements within the articles on those pages.

To apply a class selector:

▶ **1.** Use your editor to open the **tss_run_txt.html**, **tss_bike_txt.html**, and **tss_swim_txt.html** files from the html02 ▶ tutorial folder. Enter **your name** and **the date** in the comment section of each file and save them as **tss_run.html**, **tss_bike.html**, and **tss_swim.html** respectively.

▶ **2.** Within each of the three files insert the following `link` elements before the closing `</head>` tag to link these files to the tss_layout.css and tss_styles.css files, respectively:

```
<link href="tss_layout.css" rel="stylesheet" />
<link href="tss_styles.css" rel="stylesheet" />
```

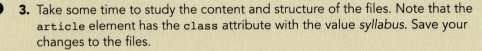

3. Take some time to study the content and structure of the files. Note that the `article` element has the `class` attribute with the value *syllabus*. Save your changes to the files.

4. Return to the **tss_style.css** file in your editor.

5. Within the Heading Styles section, add the following style rule to display the text of h1 and h2 headings in medium gray on a light purple background:

```
article.syllabus h1, article.syllabus h2 {
    background-color: rgb(255, 185, 255);
    color: rgb(101, 101, 101);
}
```

Figure 2-17 highlights the new style rule in the file.

Figure 2-17 Using a class selector

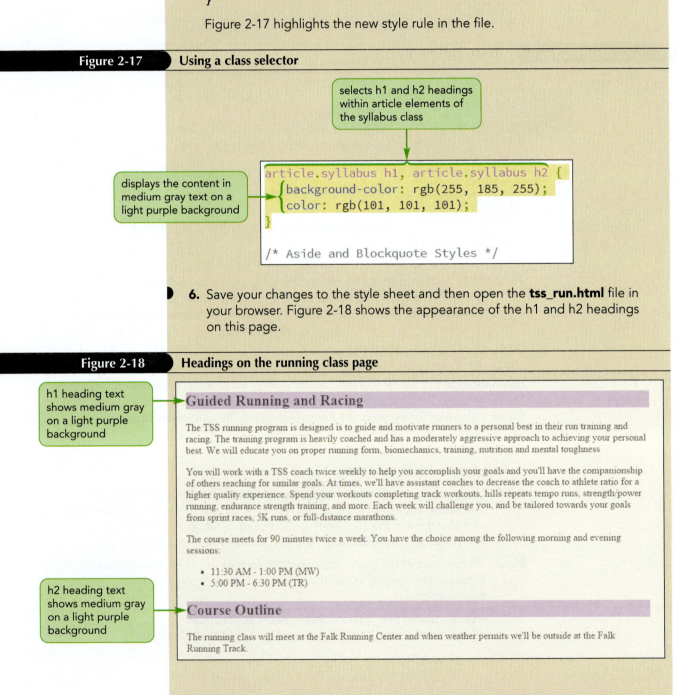

selects h1 and h2 headings within article elements of the syllabus class

displays the content in medium gray text on a light purple background

```
article.syllabus h1, article.syllabus h2 {
    background-color: rgb(255, 185, 255);
    color: rgb(101, 101, 101);
}

/* Aside and Blockquote Styles */
```

6. Save your changes to the style sheet and then open the **tss_run.html** file in your browser. Figure 2-18 shows the appearance of the h1 and h2 headings on this page.

Figure 2-18 Headings on the running class page

h1 heading text shows medium gray on a light purple background

Guided Running and Racing

The TSS running program is designed is to guide and motivate runners to a personal best in their run training and racing. The training program is heavily coached and has a moderately aggressive approach to achieving your personal best. We will educate you on proper running form, biomechanics, training, nutrition and mental toughness

You will work with a TSS coach twice weekly to help you accomplish your goals and you'll have the companionship of others reaching for similar goals. At times, we'll have assistant coaches to decrease the coach to athlete ratio for a higher quality experience. Spend your workouts completing track workouts, hills repeats tempo runs, strength/power running, endurance strength training, and more. Each week will challenge you, and be tailored towards your goals from sprint races, 5K runs, or full-distance marathons.

The course meets for 90 minutes twice a week. You have the choice among the following morning and evening sessions:

- 11:30 AM - 1:00 PM (MW)
- 5:00 PM - 6:30 PM (TR)

h2 heading text shows medium gray on a light purple background

Course Outline

The running class will meet at the Falk Running Center and when weather permits we'll be outside at the Falk Running Track.

7. Use the navigation links on the page to view the content and design of the cycling and the swimming pages, and then confirm that the h1 and h2 headings on these pages have similar formats.

Calculating Selector Specificity

The general rule in CSS is that the more specific selector takes precedence over the more general selector, but the application of this rule is not always clear. For example, which of the following selectors is the more specific?

```
header h1.top
```

vs.

```
#main h1
```

To answer that question, CSS assigns a numeric value to the specificity of the selector using the formula

```
(inline, ids, classes, elements)
```

where *inline* is 1 for an inline style and 0 otherwise, *ids* is 1 for every id in the selector, *classes* is 1 for every class or attribute in the selector, and *elements* is 1 for every element in the selector. For example, the selector `ul#links li.first` would have a value of (0, 1, 1, 2) because it references one id value (`#links`), 1 class value (`.first`) and two elements (`ul` and `li`). Specificity values are read from left to right with a larger number considered more specific than a smaller number.

To answer our earlier question: the selector `header h1.top` has a value of (0, 0, 1, 2) but `#main h1` has a value of (0, 1, 0, 1) and, thus, is considered more specific because 0101 is larger than 0012.

By the way, every inline style has the value (1, 0, 0, 0) and thus will always be more specific than any style set in an embedded or external style sheet.

Working with Fonts

Typography is the art of designing the appearance of characters and letters on a page. So far, the only typographic style you've used is the `color` property to set the text color. For the rest of this session, you'll explore other properties in the CSS family of typographical styles, starting with choosing the text font.

Choosing a Font

Text characters are based on **fonts** that define the style and appearance of each character in the alphabet. The default font used by most browsers for displaying text is Times New Roman, but you can specify a different font for any page element using the following `font-family` property

```
font-family: fonts;
```

where *fonts* is a comma-separated list, also known as a **font stack**, of specific or generic font names. A **specific font** is a font that is identified by name, such as Times New Roman or Helvetica, and based on a font definition file that is stored on the user's computer or accessible on the web. A **generic font** describes the general appearance of the characters in the text but does not specify any particular font definition file. Instead, the font definition file is selected by the browser to match the general characteristics of the generic font. CSS supports the following generic font groups:

- **serif**—a typeface in which a small ornamentation appears at the tail end of each character
- **sans-serif**—a typeface without any serif ornamentation
- **monospace**—a typeface in which each character has the same width; often used to display programming code
- **cursive**—a typeface that mimics handwriting with highly stylized elements and flourishes; best used in small doses for decorative page elements
- **fantasy**—a highly ornamental typeface used for page decoration; should never be used as body text

Because you have no control over which font definition file the browser will choose for a generic font, the common practice is to list specific fonts first, in order of preference, and end the font stack with a generic font. If the browser cannot find any of the specific fonts listed, it uses a generic font of its own choosing. For example, the style

```
font-family: 'Arial Black', Gadget, sans-serif;
```

tells a browser to use the Arial Black font if available; if not, to look for the Gadget font; and if neither of those fonts are available, to use its generic sans-serif font. Note that font names containing one or more blank spaces (such as Arial Black) must be enclosed within single or double quotes.

Because the available fonts vary by operating system and device, the challenge is to choose a font stack limited to **web safe fonts**, which are fonts that will be displayed in mostly the same way in all operating systems and on all devices. Figure 2-19 lists several commonly used web safe font stacks.

Figure 2-19	Web safe font stacks

Arial
abcdefghijklmnopqrstuvwxyz/1234567890
font-family: Arial, Helvetica, sans-serif;

Arial Black
abcdefghijklmnopqrstuvwxyz/1234567890
font-family: 'Arial Black', Gadget, sans-serif;

Century Gothic
abcdefghijklmnopqrstuvwxyz/1234567890
font-family: 'Century Gothic', sans-serif;

Comic Sans MS
abcdefghijklmnopqrstuvwxyz/1234567890
font-family: 'Comic Sans MS', cursive;

Courier New
abcdefghijklmnopqrstuvwxyz/1234567890
font-family: 'Courier New', Courier, monospace;

Georgia
abcdefghijklmnopqrstuvwxyz/1234567890
font-family: Georgia, serif;

Impact
abcdefghijklmnopqrstuvwxyz/1234567890
font-family: Impact, Charcoal, sans-serif;

Lucida Console
abcdefghijklmnopqrstuvwxyz/1234567890
font-family: 'Lucida Console', Monaco, monospace;

Lucida Sans Unicode
abcdefghijklmnopqrstuvwxyz/1234567890
font-family: 'Lucida Sans Unicode', 'Lucida Grande', sans-serif;

Palatino Linotype
abcdefghijklmnopqrstuvwxyz/1234567890
font-family: 'Palatino Linotype', 'Book Antiqua', Palatino, serif;

Tahoma
abcdefghijklmnopqrstuvwxyz/1234567890
font-family: Tahoma, Geneva, sans-serif;

Times New Roman
abcdefghijklmnopqrstuvwxyz/1234567890
font-family: 'Times New Roman', Times, serif;

Trebuchet MS
abcdefghijklmnopqrstuvwxyz/1234567890
font-family: 'Trebuchet MS', Helvetica, sans-serif;

Verdana
abcdefghijklmnopqrstuvwxyz/1234567890
font-family: Verdana, Geneva, sans-serif;

TIP

Including too many fonts can make your page difficult to read. Don't use more than two or three typefaces within a single page.

A general rule for printing is to use sans-serif fonts for headlines and serif fonts for body text. For computer monitors, which have lower resolutions than printed material, the general rule is to use sans-serif fonts for headlines and body text, leaving serif fonts for special effects and large text.

Currently, the body text for the Tri and Succeed Sports website is based on a serif font applied by the browser. You'll add the following font stack for sans-serif fonts, which will take precedence over the browser font style rule:

```
font-family: Verdana, Geneva, sans-serif;
```

As a result of this style rule, the browser will first try to load the Verdana font, followed by the Geneva font. If both of these fonts are unavailable, the browser will load a generic sans-serif font of its own choosing. Add this font family to the style rule for the page body.

To specify a font family for the page body:

1. Return to the **tss_styles.css** file in your editor.

2. Add the following style to the style rule for the body element:

   ```
   font-family: Verdana, Geneva, sans-serif;
   ```

   Figure 2-20 highlights the new style for the body element.

> Font stacks should be listed in a comma-separated list with the most desired fonts listed first.

Figure 2-20	Specifying a font stack

> browser attempts to use the Verdana font first, followed by Geneva, and finally any generic sans-serif font

```
body {
    color: rgb(91, 91, 91);
    background-color: ivory;
    font-family: Verdana, Geneva, sans-serif;
}
```

3. Save your changes to the file and then reload the **tss_home.html** file in your browser. Figure 2-21 shows the revised appearance of the body text using the sans-serif font.

Figure 2-21	Sans-serif font applied to the home page

Links

- Home
- Running
- Cycling
- Swimming
- Active.com
- Runner's World
- endomondo.com
- Strava
- Bicycling Magazine
- VeloNews
- Bicycle Tutor
- Swim Smooth
- Swimming World
- USA Swimming
- triathlon.org
- usatriathlon.org
- Texas Triathlons
- CapTex Triathlon
- Triathlon Calendar
- Triathlete.com
- Trifuel.com

About TSS

Since 2002, **Tri and Succeed Sports** has provided Austin with a first class training center for athletes of all abilities and goals. We specialize in helping you reach your full potential. You tell us what you want to do; we work to fulfill your needs.

Want to swim? Great! Interested in improving your cycling? Fantastic! Want to tackle a triathlon? We're there for you: before, during, and after the race. Or do you just want to get more fit? We are on it. We customize our instruction to match your goals. And you will finish what you start.

Classes

Winter instruction starts soon. Get a jump on your summer goals by joining us for individual or group instruction in:

Comments

Thank you for all that you have done. I am amazed at my progress. I realize that I have I lofty goals but you have me well on my way.

Alison kept me focused working toward my dreams. She fosters a supportive and caring environment for growth as an athlete and as a person. Thank you!

© 2016 Cengage Learning; © Monkey Business Images/Shutterstock.com

4. View the other three pages in the website to verify that the sans-serif font is also applied to the body text on those pages.

Exploring Web Fonts

Because web safe fonts limit your choices to a select number of fonts that have universal support, another approach is to supply a **web font** in which the definition font is supplied to the browser in an external file. Figure 2-22 describes the different web font file formats and their current levels of browser support. The format most universally accepted in almost all current browsers and on almost all devices is the Web Open Font Format (WOFF).

Figure 2-22 **Web font formats**

Format	Description	Browser
Embedded OpenType (EOT)	A compact form of OpenType fonts designed for use as embedded fonts in style sheets	IE
TrueType (TTF)	Font standard used on the Mac OS and Microsoft Windows operating systems	IE, Firefox, Chrome, Safari, Opera
OpenType (OTF)	Font format built on the TrueType format developed by Microsoft	IE, Firefox, Chrome, Safari, Opera
Scalable Vector Graphics (SVG)	Font format based on an XML vocabulary designed to describe resizable graphics and vector images	Chrome, Safari
Web Open Font Format (WOFF)	The W3C recommendation font format based on OpenType and TrueType with compression and additional metadata	IE, Firefox, Chrome, Safari, Opera

Web font files can be downloaded from several sites on the Internet. In many cases, you must pay for their use; in some cases, the fonts are free but are licensed only for non-commercial use. You should always check the EULA (End User License Agreement) before downloading and using a web font to make sure you are in compliance with the license. Finally, many web fonts are available through Web Font Service Bureaus that supply web fonts on their servers, which page designers can link to for a fee.

The great advantage of a web font is that it gives the author more control over the fonts used in the document; the disadvantage is that it becomes another file for the browser to download, adding to the time required to render the page. This can be a huge issue with mobile devices in which you want to limit the number and size of files downloaded by the browser.

The @font-face Rule

To access and load a web font, you add the following `@font-face` rule to the style sheet

```
@font-face {
   font-family: name;
   src: url('url1') format('text1'),
        url('url2') format('text2'),
   …;
   descriptor1: value1;
   descriptor2: value2;
   …
}
```

where *name* is the name of the font, *url* is the location of the font definition file, *text* is an optional text description of the font format, and the *descriptor*: *value* pairs are optional style properties that describe when the font should be used. Note several font definition files can be placed in a comma-separated list, allowing the browser to pick the file format it supports. For example, the following `@font-face` rule defines a font named Gentium installed from either the Gentium.woff file or if that fails, the Gentium.ttf file:

```
@font-face {
    font-family: Gentium;
    src: url('Gentium.woff') format('woff'),
        url('Gentium.ttf') format('truetype');
}
```

If the style sheet includes instructions to display a web font in italics, boldface, or other variants, the browser will modify the font, which sometimes results in poorly rendered text. However if the manufacturer has supplied its own version of the font variant, you can direct the browser to use that font file. For example the following `@font-face` rule directs the browser to use the GentiumBold.woff or GentiumBold.ttf file when it needs to display Gentium in bold.

```
@font-face {
    font-family: Gentium;
    src: url('GentiumBold.woff') format('woff'),
        url('GentiumBold.ttf') format('truetype');
    font-weight: bold;
}
```

Note that the web font is given the same font-family name Gentium, which is the font name you use in a font stack. The added *descriptor*: *value* pair and `font-weight:` `bold` declarations tell the browser that these font files should be used with boldface Gentium.

Once you've defined a web font using the `@font-face` rule, you can include it in a font stack. For example, the following style will attempt to load the Gentium font first, followed by Arial Black, Gadget, and then a sans-serif font of the browser's choosing:

```
font-family: Gentium, 'Arial Black', Gadget, sans-serif;
```

Alison decides that the rendering of the Verdana font in the h1 and h2 heading text is too thick and heavy. She has located a web font named Quicksand that she is free to use under the End User License Agreement and she thinks it would work better for the page headings. She asks you to add this font to the style sheet and apply it to all `h1` and `h2` elements.

To install and use a web font:

1. Return to the **tss_styles.css** file in your editor.

2. Directly after the `@charset` rule at the top of the file, insert the following `@font-face` rule:

```
@font-face {
    font-family: Quicksand;
    src: url('Quicksand-Regular.woff') format('woff'),
        url('Quicksand-Regular.ttf') format('truetype');
}
```

3. At the top of the section for Heading Styles, insert the style rule:

```
h1, h2 {
    font-family: Quicksand, Verdana, Geneva, sans-serif;
}
```

Figure 2-23 highlights the code to create and use the Quicksand web font.

| Figure 2-23 | Accessing a web font |

```
@charset "utf-8";

@font-face {
    font-family: Quicksand;
    src: url(Quicksand-Regular.woff) format('woff'),
         url(Quicksand-Regular.ttf) format('truetype');
}
```

@font-face rule defines the web font

name given to the web font

WOFF font file

TTF font file

```
/* Heading Styles */

h1, h2 {
    font-family: Quicksand, Verdana, Geneva, sans-serif;
}
```

adds the web font to the list of available fonts

style rule for all h1 and h2 headings

4. Save your changes to the file and reload the **tss_home.html** file in your browser. Figure 2-24 shows the revised appearance of the h1 and h2 headings using the Quicksand web font.

| Figure 2-24 | Quicksand font used for all h1 and h2 headings |

h1 and h2 text rendered in the Quicksand font

TRI and Succeed Sports

Links
- Home
- Running
- Cycling
- Swimming
- Active.com
- Runner's World
- endomondo.com
- Strava
- Bicycling Magazine
- VeloNews
- Bicycle Tutor
- Swim Smooth
- Swimming World
- USA Swimming
- triathlon.org
- usatriathlon.org
- Texas Triathlons
- CapTex Triathlon
- Triathlon Calendar
- Triathlete.com
- Trifuel.com

About TSS

Since 2002, **Tri and Succeed Sports** has provided Austin with a first class training center for athletes of all abilities and goals. We specialize in helping you reach your full potential. You tell us what you want to do; we work to fulfill your needs.

Want to swim? Great! Interested in improving your cycling? Fantastic! Want to tackle a triathlon? We're there for you: before, during, and after the race. Or do you just want to get more fit? We are on it. We customize our instruction to match your goals. And you will finish what you start.

Classes

Winter instruction starts soon. Get a jump on your summer goals by joining us for individual or group instruction in:

Comments

Thank you for all that you have done. I am amazed at my progress. I realize that I have l lofty goals but you have me well on my way.

Alison kept me focused working toward my dreams. She fosters a supportive and caring environment for growth as an athlete and as a person. Thank you!

INSIGHT

Using Google Fonts

Google Fonts (*google.com/fonts*) hosts a library of free web fonts. Once you have selected fonts from the Google Font catalog, you will receive the code for the `link` element to access the font files. For example, the following `link` element accesses a style sheet for a Google font named Monoton:

```
<link href="http://fonts.googleapis.com/css?family=Monoton"
 rel="stylesheet" />
```

To use the Monoton font, include the following `font-family` property in the CSS style sheet:

```
font-family: Monoton, fantasy;
```

Google fonts, like all web fonts, need to be used in moderation because they can greatly increase the load times for your website. To help you know when you have exceeded a reasonable limit, the Google Fonts page shows a timer estimating the load times for all of the fonts you have selected. You can also limit the size of the font file by using the `&text` parameter to specify only those characters you want to download. For example, the following `link` element limits the Monoton font file to only the characters found in "TSS Sports":

```
<link href="http://fonts.googleapis.com/css?family=Monoton
 &text=TSS%20Sports" rel="stylesheet" />
```

Note that blank spaces are indicated using the `%20` character. If you have a longer text string, you can shorten the value of the `href` attribute by removing duplicate characters, as the order of characters doesn't matter.

Setting the Font Size

Another important consideration in typography is the text size, which is defined using the following `font-size` property

```
font-size: size;
```

where *size* is a length in a CSS unit of measurement. Size values for any of these measurements can be whole numbers (0, 1, 2 ...) or decimals (0.5, 1.6, 3.9 ...). Lengths (and widths) in CSS are expressed in either absolute units or relative units.

Absolute Units

Absolute units are units that are fixed in size regardless of the output device and are usually used only with printed media. They are specified in one of five standard units of measurement: `mm` (millimeters), `cm` (centimeters), `in` (inches), `pt` (points), and `pc` (picas). For example, to set the font size of your page body text to a 12pt font, you would apply the following style rule:

```
body {font-size: 12pt;}
```

Note that you should not insert a space between the size value and the unit abbreviation.

Relative Units

Absolute units are of limited use because, in most cases, the page designer does not know the exact properties of the device rendering the page. In place of absolute units, designers use **relative units**, which are expressed relative to the size of other objects within the web page or relative to the display properties of the device itself.

The basic unit for most devices is the **pixel (px)**, which represents a single dot on the output device. A pixel is a relative unit because the actual pixel size depends on the resolution and density of the output device. A desktop monitor might have a pixel density of about 96ppi (pixels per inch), laptops are about 100 to 135ppi, while mobile phones have dense displays at 200 to 300ppi or more. Typically, most browsers will apply a base font size of 16px to body text with slightly larger font sizes applied to h1, h2, and h3 headings. You can override these default sizes with your own style sheet. For example, the following style rules set the font size of the text on the page body to 10px and the font size of all `h1` headings text to 14px:

```
body {font-size: 10px;}
h1 {font-size: 14px;}
```

TIP

You explore typography styles using the demo_css.html file from the html02 ▶ demo folder.

The exact appearance of the text depends greatly on the device's pixel density. While a 10px font might be fine on a desktop monitor, that same font size could be unreadable on a mobile device.

Scaling Fonts with ems and rems

Because the page designer doesn't know the exact properties of the user's device, the common practice is to make the text **scalable** with all font sizes expressed relative to a default font size. There are three relative measurements used to provide scalability: percentages, ems, and rems.

A percentage sets the font size as a percent of the font size used by the containing element. For example, the following style rule sets the font size of an h1 heading to 200% or twice the font size of the h1 heading's parent element:

```
h1 {font-size: 200%;}
```

The em unit acts the same way as a percentage, expressing the font size relative to the font size of the parent element. Thus, to set the font size of h1 headings to twice the font size used in their parent elements, you can also use the style rule:

```
h1 {font-size: 2em;}
```

The em unit is the preferred style unit for web page text because it makes it easy to develop pages in which different page elements have consistent relative font sizes under any device.

Context is very important with relative units. For example, if this `h1` element is placed within a `body` element where the font size is 16px, the h1 heading will have a font size twice that size or 32px. On the other hand, an h1 heading nested within an `article` element where the font size is 9px will have a font size of 18px. In general, you can think of font sizes based on percentages and em units as relative to the size of immediately adjacent text.

The fact that relative units cascade through the style sheet can lead to confusing outcomes. For example, consider the following set of style rules for an `h1` element nested within an `article` element in the page body:

```
body {font-size: 16px;}
body > article {font-size: 0.75em;}
body > article > h1 {font-size: 1em;}
```

Glancing at the style rules, you might conclude that the font size of the `h1` element is larger than the font size used in the `article` element (since 1em > 0.75em). However, this is not the case: both font sizes are the same. Remember, em unit expresses the text size relative to font size used in the parent element and since the h1 heading is contained within the `article` element its font size of 1em indicates that it will have the same size used in the `article` element. In this case, the font size in the article element is 75% of 16px or 12 pixels as is the size of h1 headings in the article.

Because of this confusion, some designers advocate using the **rem** or **root em unit** in which all font sizes are always expressed relative to the font size used in the `html` element. Using rems, the following style rule sets the font size of article text to 75% of 16 pixels or 12 pixels while the h1 heading size is set to 16 pixels:

```
html {font-size: 16px;}
article {font-size: 0.75rem;}
article > h1 {font-size: 1rem;}
```

The rem unit has become increasingly popular with designers as browser support grows and its use might possibly replace the use of the em unit as the font size unit of choice in upcoming years.

Using Viewport Units

Another relative unit is the **viewport unit** in which lengths are expressed as a percentage of the width or height of the browser window. As the browser window is resized, the size of text based on a viewport unit changes to match. CSS3 introduced four viewport units: `vw`, `vh`, `vmin`, and `vmax` where

- 1vw = 1% of the browser window width
- 1vh = 1% of the browser window height
- 1vmin = 1vw or 1vh (whichever is smaller)
- 1vmax = 1vw or 1vh (whichever is larger)

For example, if the browser window is 1366 pixels wide, a length of 1vw would be equal to 13.66px. If the width of the window is reduced to 780 pixels, 1vw is automatically rescaled to 7.8 pixels. Auto-rescaling has the advantage that font sizes set with a viewport unit will be sized to match the browser window, maintaining a consistent page layout. The disadvantage is that page text can quickly become unreadable if the browser window becomes too small.

Sizing Keywords

Finally, you also can express font sizes using the following keywords: `xx-small`, `x-small`, `small`, `medium`, `large`, `x-large`, `xx-large`, `larger`, or `smaller`. The font size corresponding to each of these keywords is determined by the browser. Note that the `larger` and `smaller` keywords are relative sizes, making the font size of the element one size larger or smaller than the font size of the `container` element. For example, the following style rules set the sidebar to be displayed in a small font, while an `h1` element nested within that `aside` element is displayed in a font one size larger (medium):

```
aside {font-size: small;}
aside > h1 {font-size: larger;}
```

Use em units now to set the font size for the h1 and h2 headings, as well as the text within the navigation list and the `aside` element.

To set font sizes of the page elements:

1. Return to the **tss_styles.css** file in your editor.

2. Add the following style rules directly below the Heading Styles comment to define the font sizes for h1 and h2 headings throughout the website:

```
h1 {
    font-size: 2.2em;
}

h2 {
    font-size: 1.5em;
}
```

3. Go to the Aside and Blockquote Styles section and add the following style rule to set the default font size of text in the `aside` element to 0.8em:

```
aside {
    font-size: 0.8em;
}
```

4. Go to the Navigation Styles section and add the following style rule to set the default font size of text in the navigation list to 0.8em:

```
nav {
    font-size: 0.8em;
}
```

Figure 2-25 highlights the new font sizes for the website.

Figure 2-25 **Setting font sizes for the website**

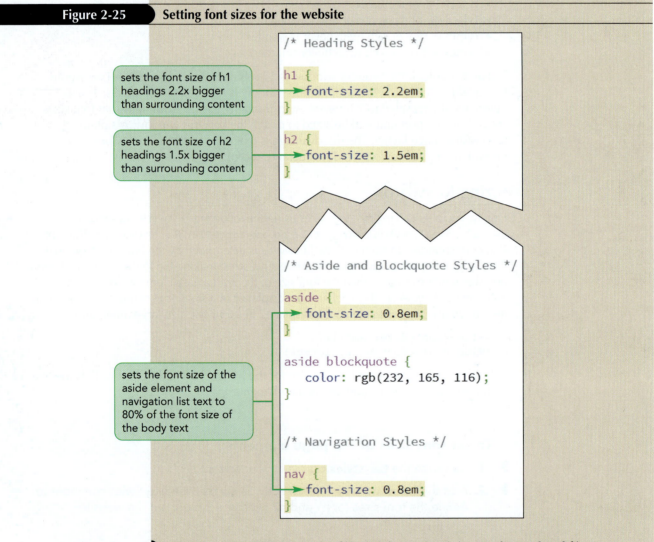

sets the font size of h1 headings 2.2x bigger than surrounding content

sets the font size of h2 headings 1.5x bigger than surrounding content

sets the font size of the aside element and navigation list text to 80% of the font size of the body text

```
/* Heading Styles */

h1 {
    font-size: 2.2em;
}

h2 {
    font-size: 1.5em;
}
```

```
/* Aside and Blockquote Styles */

aside {
    font-size: 0.8em;
}

aside blockquote {
    color: rgb(232, 165, 116);
}

/* Navigation Styles */

nav {
    font-size: 0.8em;
}
```

5. Save your changes to the file and then reload the **tss_home.html** file in your browser. Figure 2-26 shows the revised font sizes of the headings, navigation list, and aside element.

Figure 2-26   **Revised font sizes in the About TSS page**

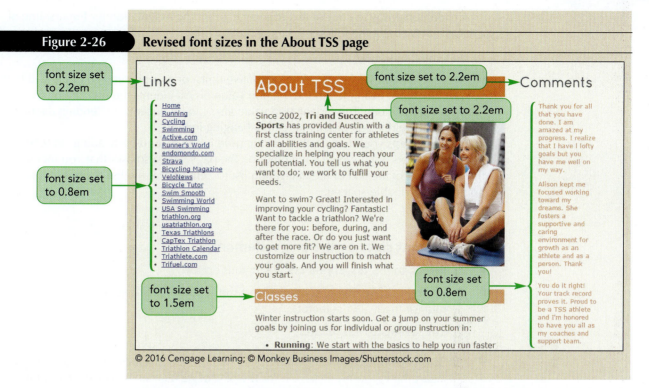

© 2016 Cengage Learning; © Monkey Business Images/Shutterstock.com

Note that the text of the h1 heading in the page article is larger than the text in the h1 headings from the navigation list and the aside element even though all headings have a font size of 2.2em. This is because you reduced the default font size of the text in the navigation list and aside elements by 80% and thus the h1 headings in those elements are also reduced by the same proportion.

Controlling Spacing and Indentation

CSS supports styles to control some basic typographic attributes, such as kerning, tracking, and leading. Kerning measures the amount of space between characters, while **tracking** measures the amount of space between words. The properties to control an element's kerning and tracking are

```
letter-spacing: value;
word-spacing:   value;
```

where `value` is the size of space between individual letters or words. You specify these sizes with the same units that you use for font sizing. The default value for both kerning and tracking is 0 pixels. A positive value increases the letter and word spacing, while a negative value reduces the space between letters and words. If you choose to make your text scalable under a variety of devices and resolutions, you can express kerning and tracking values as percentages or em units.

Leading measures the amount of space between lines of text and is set using the following `line-height` property

```
line-height: size;
```

where `size` is a value or a percentage of the font size of the text on the affected lines. If no unit is specified, the size value represents the ratio of the line height to the font size. The default value is 1.2 or 1.2em so that the line height is 20% larger than the font size. By contrast, the following style sets the line height to twice the font size, making the text appear double-spaced:

```
line-height: 2em;
```

TIP

You can give multi-line titles more impact by tightening the space between the lines using a large font-size along with a small line-height.

An additional way to control text spacing is to set the indentation for the first line of a text block by using the following text-indent property

```
text-indent: size;
```

where *size* is expressed in absolute or relative units, or as a percentage of the width of the text block. For example, an indentation value of 5% indents the first line by 5% of the width of the block. The indentation value also can be negative, extending the first line to the left of the text block to create a **hanging indent**.

Alison suggests you increase the kerning used in the h1 and h2 headings to 0.1em so that the letters don't crowd each other on the page. She also asks that you increase the line height of the text of the navigation list to 2em so that the list of links on the home page is double-spaced.

To set font sizes of the page elements:

1. Return to the **tss_styles.css** file in your editor.

2. In the Heading Styles section, insert the following style as part of the style rule for the h1, h2 selector:

```
letter-spacing: 0.1em;
```

3. Scroll down to the Navigation Styles section near the bottom of the file and insert the following style rule for the text of ul elements nested within the nav element:

```
nav > ul {
    line-height: 2em;
}
```

Figure 2-27 highlights the letter-spacing and line-height styles for the website.

Figure 2-27	Controlling letter spacing and line height

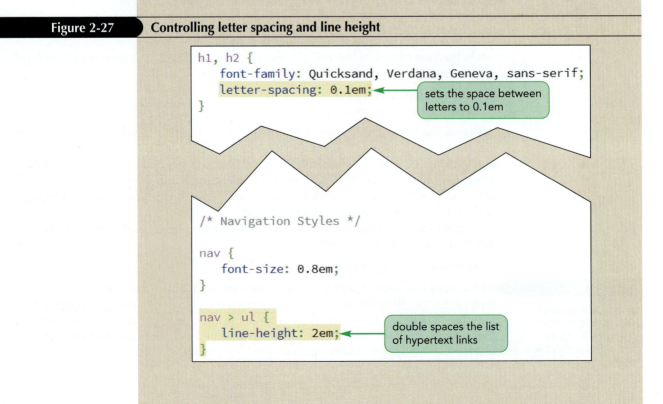

```
h1, h2 {
    font-family: Quicksand, Verdana, Geneva, sans-serif;
    letter-spacing: 0.1em;                    ← sets the space between
}                                                 letters to 0.1em



/* Navigation Styles */

nav {
    font-size: 0.8em;
}

nav > ul {
    line-height: 2em;                         ← double spaces the list
}                                                 of hypertext links
```

> **4.** Save your changes to the file and then reload the **tss_home.html** file in your browser. Verify that the space between letters in the h1 and h2 headings has been increased and the list of links is now double-spaced.

By increasing the kerning in the headings, you've made the text appear less crowded, making it easier to read.

Working with Font Styles

The style sheet built into your browser applies specific styles to key page elements; for instance, `address` elements are often displayed in italic, headings are often displayed in boldface. You can specify a different font style using the following `font-style` property

```
font-style: type;
```

where `type` is `normal`, `italic`, or `oblique`. The italic and oblique styles are similar in appearance, but might differ subtly depending on the font in use.

To change the weight of the text, use the following `font-weight` property

```
font-weight: weight;
```

where `weight` is the level of bold formatting applied to the text. CSS uses the keyword `bold` for boldfaced text and `normal` for non-boldfaced text. You also can use the keywords `bolder` or `lighter` to express the weight of the text relative to its surrounding content. Finally for precise weights, CSS supports weight values ranging from 100 (extremely light) up to 900 (extremely heavy) in increments of 100. In practice, however, it's difficult to distinguish font weights at that level of precision.

You can apply decorative features to text through the following `text-decoration` property

```
text-decoration: type;
```

where `type` equals `none` (for no decoration), `underline`, `overline`, or `line-through`. The `text-decoration` property supports multiple types so that the following style places a line under and over the element text:

```
text-decoration: underline overline;
```

Note that the `text-decoration` style has no effect on non-textual elements, such as inline images.

To control the case of the text within an element, use the following `text-transform` property

```
text-transform: type;
```

where `type` is `capitalize`, `uppercase`, `lowercase`, or `none` (to make no changes to the text case). For example, to capitalize the first letter of each word in an element, apply the style:

```
text-transform: capitalize;
```

Finally, CSS supports variations of the text using the `font-variant` property

```
font-variant: type;
```

where `type` is `normal` (for no variation) or `small-caps` (small capital letters). Small caps are often used in legal documents, such as software agreements, in which the capital letters indicate the importance of a phrase or point, but the text is made small so as not to detract from other elements in the document.

Aligning Text Horizontally and Vertically

Text can be aligned horizontally or vertically within an element. To align the text horizontally, use the following `text-align` property

```
text-align: alignment;
```

where `alignment` is `left`, `right`, `center`, or `justify` (align the text with both the left and the right margins).

To vertically align the text within each line, use the `vertical-align` property

```
vertical-align: alignment;
```

where `alignment` is one of the keywords described in Figure 2-28.

Figure 2-28 | **Values of the vertical-align property**

Value	Description
`baseline`	Aligns the baseline of the element with the baseline of the parent element
`bottom`	Aligns the bottom of the element with the bottom of the lowest element in the line
`middle`	Aligns the middle of the element with the middle of the surrounding content in the line
`sub`	Subscripts the element
`super`	Superscripts the element
`text-bottom`	Aligns the bottom of the element with the bottom of the text in the line
`text-top`	Aligns the top of the element with the top of the text in the line
`top`	Aligns the top of the element with the top of the tallest object in the line

TIP

The subscript and superscript styles lower or raise text vertically, but do not resize it. To create true subscripts and superscripts, you also must reduce the font size.

Instead of using keywords, you can specify a length or a percentage for an element to be vertically aligned relative to the surrounding content. A positive value moves the element up as in the following style that raises the element by half the line height of the surrounding content:

```
vertical-align: 50%;
```

A negative value drops the content. For example the following style drops the element an entire line height below the baseline of the current line:

```
vertical-align: -100%;
```

Combining All Text Formatting in a Single Style

You can combine most of the text and font style properties into the following shorthand `font` property

```
font: style variant weight size/height family;
```

where `style` is the font's style, `variant` is the font variant, `weight` is the font weight, `size` is the font size, `height` is the height of each line, and `family` is the font stack. For example, the following style rule displays the element text in italic, bold, and small capital letters using Arial or another sans-serif font, with a font size of 1.5em and a line height of 2em:

```
font: italic small-caps bold 1.5em/2em Arial, sans-serif;
```

You do not have to include all of the values in the shorthand `font` property; the only required values are the `size` and `family` values. A browser assumes the default value for any omitted property; however, you must place any properties that you do include in the order indicated above.

At the bottom of each page in the Tri and Succeed Sports website, Alison has nested an `address` element within the body footer. The default browser style sheet displays address text in italics. Alison suggests that you display the text in a semi-transparent bold white font on a dark orange background and centered on the page. She also suggests that you use the small-cap font variant to add visual interest, and she wants you to increase the height of the address line to 3em. To make your CSS code more compact, you'll set all of the font values using the shorthand `font` property.

To apply the font property:

1. Return to the **tss_styles.css** file in your editor.

2. Go down to the Footer Styles section and add the following style rule:

```
body > footer address {
    background-color: rgb(222,128,60);
    color: white;
    color: rgba(255, 255, 255, 0.7);
    font: normal small-caps bold 0.9em/3em
          Quicksand, Verdana, Geneva, sans-serif;
    text-align: center;
}
```

Note that this style rule uses progressive enhancement by placing each color rule on its own line so that browsers that do not support semi-transparent colors will display the address text in white. Figure 2-29 highlights the style rule for the footer.

Figure 2-29   **Style rule for the body footer**

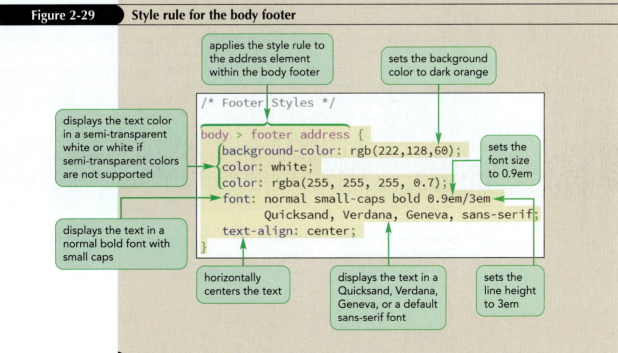

3. Save your changes to the file and then reload the **tss_home.html** file in your browser. Figure 2-30 shows the revised appearance of the body footer.

Figure 2-30	Formatted body footer

PROSKILLS

Decision Making: Selecting a Font

HTML and CSS provide a lot of typographic design options. Your main goal, however, is always to make your text easily readable. When designing your page, keep in mind the following principles:

- *Keep it plain*—Avoid large blocks of italicized text and boldfaced text. Those styles are designed for emphasis, not readability.
- *Sans-serif vs. serif*—Sans-serif fonts are more readable on a computer monitor and should be used for body text. Reserve the use of serif, cursive, and fantasy fonts for page headings and special decorative elements.
- *Relative vs. absolute*—Font sizes can be expressed in relative or absolute units. A relative unit like the em unit is more flexible and will be sized to match the screen resolution of the user's device, but you have more control over your page's appearance with an absolute unit. Generally, you want to use an absolute unit only when you know the configuration of the device the reader is using to view your page.
- *Size matters*—Almost all fonts are readable at a size of 14 pixels or greater; however, for smaller sizes, you should choose fonts that were designed for screen display, such as Verdana and Georgia. If you have to go really small (at a size of only a few pixels), you should either use a web font that is specially designed for that purpose or replace the text with an inline image.
- *Avoid long lines*—In general, try to keep the length of your lines to 60 characters or fewer. Anything longer is difficult to read.

When choosing any typeface and font style, the key is to test your selection on a variety of browsers, devices, screen resolutions, and densities. Don't assume that text that is readable and pleasing to the eye on your computer screen will work as well on another device.

Alison likes the typographic changes you made to her website. In the next session, you'll explore how to design styles for hypertext links and lists, and you'll learn how to use CSS to add special visual effects to your web pages.

Session 2.2 Quick Check

1. Provide a selector to match all `address` elements that are direct children of the `footer` element.
2. The initial h1 heading in a document has the ID *top*. Provide a style rule to display the text of this h1 heading in Century Gothic, Helvetica, or a sans-serif font.
3. For the following style rules, what is the font size of the h1 heading in pixels?

```
body {font-size: 16px;}
body > article {font-size: 0.75em;}
body > article > h1 {font-size: 1.5em;}
```

4. Provide a style rule to set the size of body text to 2% of the viewport width.
5. Provide a style rule to remove underlining from the hypertext links marked with the <a> tag and nested within a navigation list.
6. Provide the `@font-face` rule to create a web font named Cantarell based on the font files cantarell.woff and cantarell.ttf.
7. Provide a style rule to display all `blockquote` elements belonging to the Reviews class in italic and indented 3em.
8. Provide a style rule to horizontally center all h1 through h6 headings and to display their text with normal weight.

Session 2.3 Visual Overview:

The `list-style-type` property defines the appearance of the list marker.

The `visited` pseudo-class selects previously-visited links; the `link` pseudo-class selects unvisited links.

The `margin-top` property sets the margin space above the element.

The `hover` pseudo-class selects links that are hovered over; the `active` pseudo-class selects actively-clicked links.

The `first-of-type` pseudo-class selects the first element type of the parent element.

The `list-style-image` property is used to insert an image for the list marker.

The `quotes` property defines characters for quotation marks.

The `content` property is used to insert content into a page element.

The `nth-of-type` pseudo-class selects the nth element type of the parent.

The `last-of-type` pseudo-class selects the last element type of the parent element.

The `before` and `after` pseudo-elements are used to select page space before and after a page element.

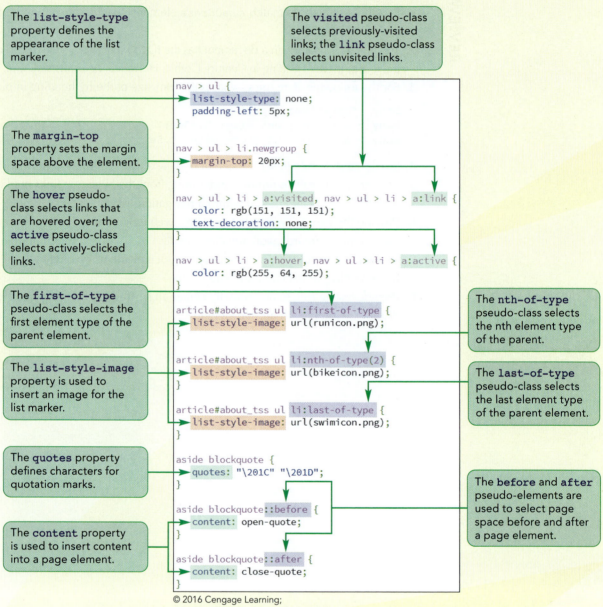

```css
nav > ul {
    list-style-type: none;
    padding-left: 5px;
}

nav > ul > li.newgroup {
    margin-top: 20px;
}

nav > ul > li > a:visited, nav > ul > li > a:link {
    color: rgb(151, 151, 151);
    text-decoration: none;
}

nav > ul > li > a:hover, nav > ul > li > a:active {
    color: rgb(255, 64, 255);
}

article#about_tss ul li:first-of-type {
    list-style-image: url(runicon.png);
}

article#about_tss ul li:nth-of-type(2) {
    list-style-image: url(bikeicon.png);
}

article#about_tss ul li:last-of-type {
    list-style-image: url(swimicon.png);
}

aside blockquote {
    quotes: "\201C" "\201D";
}

aside blockquote::before {
    content: open-quote;
}

aside blockquote::after {
    content: close-quote;
}
```

© 2016 Cengage Learning;
© Monkey Business Images/Shutterstock.com;
© Courtesy Patrick Carey

Pseudo Elements and Classes

Style of the link changes when the mouse pointer hovers over it.

Open quote character is inserted using the content property.

Close quote character is inserted using the content property.

Links

Home

Running

Cycling

Swimming

Active.com

Runner's World

endomondo.com

Strava

Bicycling Magazine

VeloNews

Bicycle Tutor

Swim Smooth

Swimming World

USA Swimming

triathlon.org

usatriathlon.org

Texas Triathlons

CapTex Triathlon

Triathlon Calendar

Triathlete.com

Trifuel.com

Top margins at each newgroup class are set to 20 pixels.

About TSS

Since 2002, **Tri and Succeed Sports** has provided Austin with a first class training center for athletes of all abilities and goals. We specialize in helping you reach your full potential. You tell us what you want to do; we work to fulfill your needs.

Want to swim? Great! Interested in improving your cycling? Fantastic! Want to tackle a triathlon? We're there for you: before, during, and after the race. Or do you just want to get more fit? We are on it. We customize our instruction to match your goals. And you will finish what you start.

Classes

Winter instruction starts soon. Get a jump on your summer goals by joining us for individual or group instruction in:

- **Running**: We start with the basics to help you run faster and farther than you ever thought possible without aches and pains.
- **Cycling**: The indoor bike trainers at TSS include everything you need to refine your technique, stamina, and power for improved results on the road.
- **Swimming**: The open water swim can be one of the most frightening sports to master. Our classes begin with basic techniques so that your swim can be very enjoyable, and not a chore.

This is the first li element.

An image is used to mark each of the three list markers.

This is the last li element.

This is the second li element.

Comments

" Thank you for all that you have done. I am amazed at my progress. I realize that I have l lofty goals but you have me well on my way."

" Alison kept me focused working toward my dreams. She fosters a supportive and caring environment for growth as an athlete and as a person. Thank you!"

" You do it right! Your track record proves it. Proud to be a TSS athlete and I'm honored to have you all as my coaches and support team."

" The coaches at TSS treat you with the highest respect: whether you're an individual getting off the couch for the first time or an elite athlete training for the Iron Man. They know their stuff."

" I just completed my first marathon, following your fitness schedule to the letter. Never once did I come close to bonking and two days later I felt ready for another race!"

Formatting Lists

In this session, you'll explore how to use CSS to create styles for different types of lists that you learned about in Tutorial 1. You'll start by examining how to create styles for the list marker.

Choosing a List Style Type

The default browser style for unordered and ordered lists is to display each list item alongside a symbol known as a **list marker**. By default, unordered lists are displayed with a solid disc while ordered lists are displayed with numerals. To change the type of list marker or to prevent any display of a list marker, apply the following `list-style-type` property

```
list-style-type: type;
```

where `type` is one of the markers described in Figure 2-31.

Figure 2-31	Values of the list-style-type property

list-style-type	Marker(s)
disc	●
circle	○
square	■
decimal	1, 2, 3, 4, …
decimal-leading-zero	01, 02, 03, 04, …
lower-roman	i, ii, iii, iv, …
upper-roman	I, II, III, IV, …
lower-alpha	a, b, c, d, …
upper-alpha	A, B, C, D, …
lower-greek	α, β, γ, δ, …
upper-greek	A, B, Γ, Δ, …
none	no marker displayed

TIP

List style properties can be applied to individual items in a list, through the `li` element.

For example, the following style rule marks each item from an ordered list with an uppercase Roman numeral:

```
ol {list-style-type: upper-roman;}
```

Creating an Outline Style

Nested lists can be displayed in an outline style through the use of contextual selectors. For example, the following style rules create an outline style for a nested ordered list:

```
ol {list-style-type: upper-roman;}
ol ol {list-style-type: upper-alpha;}
ol ol ol {list-style-type: decimal;}
```

In this style, the `ol` selector selects the top level of the list, displaying the list items with a Roman numeral. The `ol ol` selector selects the second level, marking the items with capital letters. The third level indicated by the `ol ol ol` selector is marked with decimal values.

To see how these style rules are rendered on a page, you'll apply them to the three pages that Alison has set up describing the running, cycling, and swimming programs offered by Tri and Succeed sports. Each page contains a syllabus outlining the course of study for the next several weeks.

To apply an outline style:

▶ 1. If you took a break after the previous session, make sure the **tss_styles.css** file is open in your editor.

▶ 2. Scroll down to the List Styles section and insert the following style rules to format nested ordered lists within the syllabus article:

```
article.syllabus ol {
    list-style-type: upper-roman;
}

article.syllabus ol ol {
    list-style-type: upper-alpha;
}

article.syllabus ol ol ol {
    list-style-type: decimal;

}
```

Figure 2-32 highlights the style rule for the nested lists.

Figure 2-32	Creating an outline style for a nested list

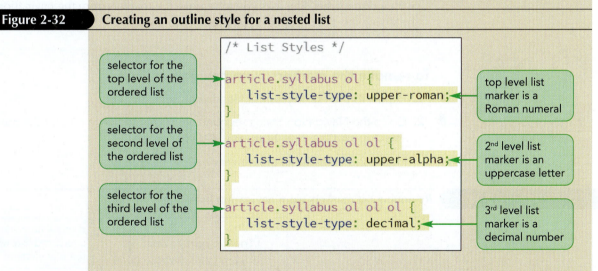

▶ 3. Save your changes to the file and then open the **tss_run.html** file in your browser. As shown in Figure 2-33, the syllabus for the class should now be displayed in an outline style.

Figure 2-33 **Class outline**

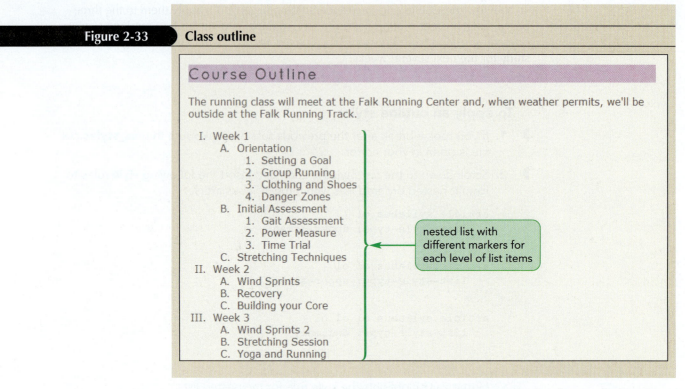

Alison points out that the hypertext links from the navigation list are displayed with a disc marker. She asks you to remove the markers from the navigation list by setting the `list-style-type` property to `none`.

To remove the markers from navigation lists:

1. Return to the **tss_styles.css** file in your editor.

2. Go to the Navigation Styles section and, within the style rule for the `nav > ul` selector, add the style `list-style-type: none;`

Figure 2-34 highlights the new style.

Figure 2-34 **Removing list markers from navigation lists**

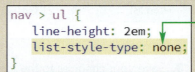

```
nav > ul {
    line-height: 2em;
    list-style-type: none;
}
```

displays no markers for unordered lists within the nav element

3. Save your changes to the file and then open the **tss_home.html** file in your browser. Verify that there are no markers next to the navigation list items in the left column.

4. Go to the other three pages in the website and verify that navigation lists in these pages also do not have list markers.

Designing a List

- To define the appearance of the list marker, use the property

  ```
  list-style-type: type;
  ```

  where *type* is disc, circle, square, decimal, decimal-leading-zero, lower-roman, upper-roman, lower-alpha, upper-alpha, lower-greek, upper-greek, or none.
- To insert a graphic image as a list marker, use the property

  ```
  list-style-image: url(url);
  ```

  where *url* is the URL of the graphic image file.
- To set the position of list markers, use the property

  ```
  list-style-position: position;
  ```

  where *position* is inside or outside.
- To define all of the list style properties in a single style, use the property

  ```
  list-style: type url(url) position;
  ```

Using Images for List Markers

You can supply your own graphic image for the list marker using the following list-style-image property

```
list-style-image: url(url);
```

where *url* is the URL of a graphic file containing the marker image. Marker images are only used with unordered lists in which the list marker is the same for every list item. For example, the following style rule displays items from unordered lists marked with the graphic image in the redball.png file:

```
ul {list-style-image: url(redball.png);}
```

Alison has an icon image in a file named runicon.png that she wants to use for the classes listed on the Tri and Succeed Sports home page in the About TSS article. Apply her image file to the list now.

To use an image for a list marker:

1. Return to the **tss_styles.css** file in your editor.
2. At the top of the List Styles section, insert the following style rule:

   ```
   article#about_tss ul {
       list-style-image: url(runicon.png);
   }
   ```

   Figure 2-35 highlights the style rule to use the runicon.png file as the list marker image.

Figure 2-35   **Displaying an image in place of a list marker**

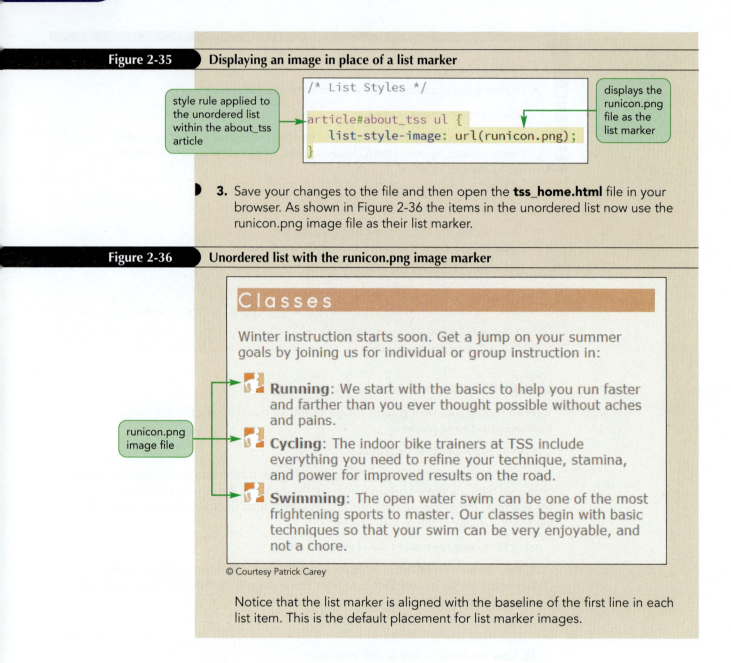

style rule applied to the unordered list within the about_tss article

```
/* List Styles */

article#about_tss ul {
    list-style-image: url(runicon.png);
}
```

displays the runicon.png file as the list marker

> **3.** Save your changes to the file and then open the **tss_home.html** file in your browser. As shown in Figure 2-36 the items in the unordered list now use the runicon.png image file as their list marker.

Figure 2-36   **Unordered list with the runicon.png image marker**

Classes

Winter instruction starts soon. Get a jump on your summer goals by joining us for individual or group instruction in:

runicon.png image file

Running: We start with the basics to help you run faster and farther than you ever thought possible without aches and pains.

Cycling: The indoor bike trainers at TSS include everything you need to refine your technique, stamina, and power for improved results on the road.

Swimming: The open water swim can be one of the most frightening sports to master. Our classes begin with basic techniques so that your swim can be very enjoyable, and not a chore.

© Courtesy Patrick Carey

Notice that the list marker is aligned with the baseline of the first line in each list item. This is the default placement for list marker images.

Setting the List Marker Position

CSS treats each list item as a block-level element, placed within a virtual box in which the list marker is placed outside of the list text. You can change this default behavior using the following list-style-position property

```
list-style-position: position;
```

where *position* is either outside (the default) or inside. Placing the marker inside the virtual box causes the list text to flow around the marker. Figure 2-37 shows how the list-style-position property affects the flow of the text around the bullet marker.

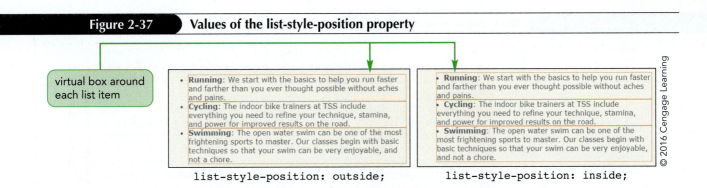

Figure 2-37   **Values of the list-style-position property**

`list-style-position: outside;`   `list-style-position: inside;`

All three of the list styles just discussed can be combined within the following shorthand `list-style` property

`list-style: type image position;`

where `type` is the marker type, `image` is an image to be displayed in place of the marker, and `position` is the location of the marker. For example, the following style rule displays unordered lists using the marker found in the bullet.png image placed inside the containing block:

`ul {list-style: circle url(bullet.png) inside;}`

If a browser is unable to display the bullet.png image, it uses a default circle marker instead. You do not need to include all three style properties with the list style. Browsers will set any property you omit to the default value.

Allison notes that there is a lot of unused space to the left of the items in the navigation list now that the list markers have been removed. She wants you to move the navigation list into that empty space. To do this, you'll work with the CSS styles for margin and padding space.

Working with Margins and Padding

Block-level elements like paragraphs or headings or lists follow the structure of the **box model** in which the content is enclosed within the following series of concentric boxes:

- the content of the element itself
- the **padding space**, which extends from the element's content to a border
- the **border** surrounding the padding space
- the **margin space** comprised of the space beyond the border up to the next page element

Figure 2-38 shows a schematic diagram of the box model for a sample paragraph discussing athletes at Tri and Succeed Sports.

Figure 2-38	The CSS box model

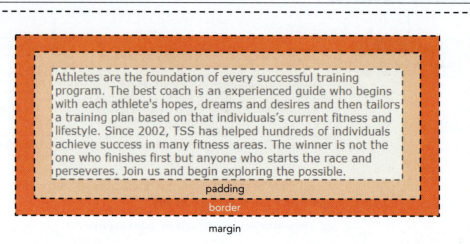

Athletes are the foundation of every successful training program. The best coach is an experienced guide who begins with each athlete's hopes, dreams and desires and then tailors a training plan based on that individuals's current fitness and lifestyle. Since 2002, TSS has helped hundreds of individuals achieve success in many fitness areas. The winner is not the one who finishes first but anyone who starts the race and perseveres. Join us and begin exploring the possible.

padding

border

margin

© 2016 Cengage Learning

TIP

Your browser's developer tools will display a schematic diagram of the box model for each element on your page so that you can determine the size of the padding, border, and margin spaces.

The browser's internal style sheet sets the size of the padding, border, and margin spaces but you can specify different sizes in your style sheet.

Setting the Padding Space

To set the width of the padding space, use the following `padding` property

```
padding: size;
```

where *size* is expressed in one of the CSS units of length or the keyword `auto` to let the browser automatically choose the padding. For example, the following style rule sets the padding space around every paragraph to 20 pixels:

```
p {padding: 20px;}
```

The padding space can also be defined for each of the four sides of the virtual box by writing the padding property as follows

```
padding: top right bottom left;
```

where *top* is the size of the padding space along the top edge of the content, *right* is padding along the right edge, *bottom* is the size of the bottom padding, and *left* is the size of the padding along the left edge. Thus, the following style rule creates a padding space that is 10 pixels on top, 0 pixels to the right, 15 pixels on the bottom and 5 pixels to the left:

```
p {padding: 10px 0px 15px 5px;}
```

To help remember this order, think of moving clockwise around the box, starting with the top edge. While you don't have to supply values for all of the edges, the values you supply are interpreted based on how many values you supply. So, if you specify a single value, it's applied to all four sides equally. Likewise, two values set the padding spaces for the top/bottom edges and then the right/left edges. For example, the following style rule sets the top and bottom padding spaces at 10 pixels and the right and left padding spaces at 5 pixels:

```
p {padding: 10px 5px;}
```

If you insert three values, the padding spaces are set for the top, right/left, and bottom edges. Thus, the following rule sets the size of the top padding space to 10 pixels, the left/right spaces to 5 pixels, and the bottom space to 0 pixels:

```
p {padding: 10px 5px 0px;}
```

If you want to define the padding space for one edge but not for the others, you can apply the following style properties:

```
padding-top: size;
padding-right: size;
padding-bottom: size;
padding-left: size;
```

The following style rule sets the top padding of every paragraph to 10 pixels but it does not specify a padding size for any of the other three remaining edges:

```
p {padding-top: 10px;}
```

With ordered and unordered lists, the default style used by most browsers is to set the left padding space to 40 pixels in order to provide the extra space needed for the list markers. Removing the list markers doesn't remove this padding space. Allison suggests you recover this unused space by reducing the size of the left padding space in the navigation list to 5 pixels.

To change the left padding used in the navigation list:

> Include the unit in any style involving padding or margin spaces.

1. Return to the **tss_styles.css** file in your editor.

2. Locate the `nav > ul` style rule in the Navigation Styles section and insert the style `padding-left: 5px;`.

   Figure 2-39 highlights the new style for all navigation lists.

Figure 2-39 | **Setting the size of the left padding space**

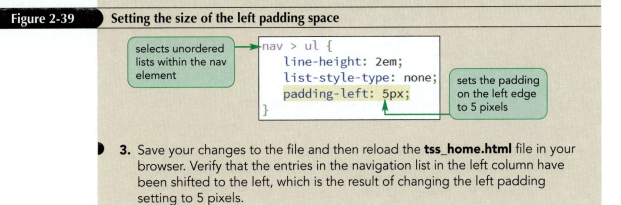

3. Save your changes to the file and then reload the **tss_home.html** file in your browser. Verify that the entries in the navigation list in the left column have been shifted to the left, which is the result of changing the left padding setting to 5 pixels.

Now that you've worked with the padding space, you'll examine how to work with margins.

REFERENCE

Setting Padding and Margin Space

- To set the padding space around all sides of the element, use

  ```
  padding: size;
  ```

  where *size* is the size of the padding using one of the CSS units of length.
- To set the margin space around all sides of the element, use

  ```
  margin: size;
  ```

- To set padding or margin on only one side (top, right, bottom, or left) include the name of the side in the property as

  ```
  padding-side: size;
  margin-side: size;
  ```

  where *side* is top, right, bottom, or left.
- To set different padding or margins on each side of the element, enter the sides as

  ```
  padding: top right bottom left;
  margin: top right bottom left;
  ```

  where *top*, *right*, *bottom*, and *left* are individual sizes for the associated side.

Setting the Margin and the Border Spaces

Styles to set the margin space have the same form as styles to set the padding space. To set the size of the margin around your block-level elements, use either of the following properties:

```
margin: size;
```

or

```
margin: top right bottom left;
```

The margins of individual sides are set using the style properties

```
margin-top: size;
margin-right: size;
margin-bottom: size;
margin-left: size;
```

where once again *size* is expressed in one of the CSS units of length or using the keyword `auto` to have the browser automatically set the margin.

The size of the border space is set using the following `border-width` property

```
border-width: size;
```

or

```
border-width: top right bottom left;
```

or with the properties `border-top-width`, `border-right-width`, `border-bottom-width`, and `border-left-width` used to specify the size of individual borders. You'll explore borders in more detail in Tutorial 4.

The navigation list that Alison created for the home page groups the list into those links for pages within the Tri and Succeed Sports website and those links to external websites. The list item at the start of each group is marked with the `class` value *newgroup*. Alison suggests you increase the top margin above each group of links to 20 pixels in order to offset it from the preceding group. The groups will be easier to recognize after the top margin for each group has been increased.

To increase the top margin:

1. Return to the **tss_styles.css** file in your editor.

2. Directly below the style rule for the `nav > ul` selector in the Navigation Styles section, insert the following rule:

```
nav > ul > li.newgroup {
    margin-top: 20px;
}
```

Figure 2-40 highlights the style rule setting the top margin value.

Figure 2-40   Setting the size of the top margin

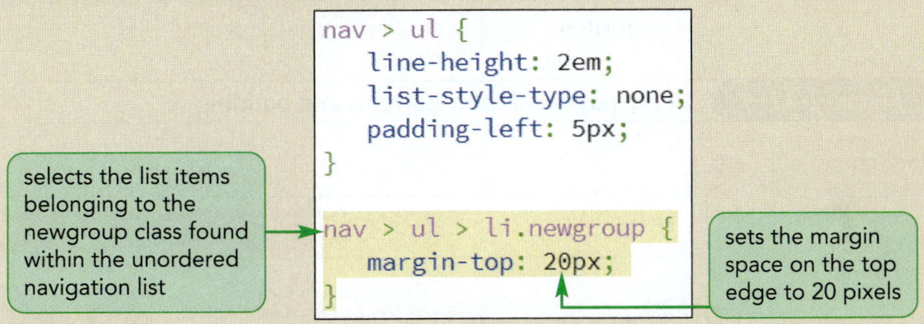

selects the list items belonging to the newgroup class found within the unordered navigation list

```
nav > ul {
    line-height: 2em;
    list-style-type: none;
    padding-left: 5px;
}

nav > ul > li.newgroup {
    margin-top: 20px;
}
```

sets the margin space on the top edge to 20 pixels

3. Save your changes to the file and then reload the **tss_home.html** file in your browser. Verify that the entries in the navigation list are now split into three groups: the first group containing the links from the Tri and Succeed Sports website; the second group containing links to websites on running, cycling, and swimming; and the third group containing links to triathlon websites.

Alison has also noticed that the block quotes in the right column of the home page have unused space to the left, leaving less space for the customer quotes. The default browser style for the `blockquote` element offsets block quotes from the surrounding text by setting the left and right margins to 40 pixels. To adjust this spacing and to make the block quotes more readable, you'll reduce the left/right margins to 5 pixels. You'll also increase the top/bottom margins to 20 pixels to better separate one customer quote from another.

To change the margin space around block quotes:

1. Return to the **tss_styles.css** file in your editor.

2. Locate the style rule for the `aside blockquote` selector in the Aside and Blockquote Styles section and insert the **margin: 20px 5px;** style into the style rule.

Figure 2-41 displays the style to change the margin space around the `blockquote` element.

Figure 2-41 | **Setting the margin size for block quotes**

selects block quotes within the aside element

```
aside blockquote {
    color: rgb(232, 165, 116);
    margin: 20px 5px;
}
```

sets the size of the top and bottom margins to 20 pixels

sets the size of the left and right margins to 5 pixels

> **3.** Save your changes to the file and then reload the **tss_home.html** file in your browser. Figure 2-42 displays the revised appearance of the page with the new padding and margin sizes applied to the navigation list and the block quotes.

Figure 2-42 | **Home page with new margins and padding**

each block quote surrounded by a 20 pixel top/bottom margin and a 5 pixel left/right margin

left padding set to 5 pixels

each new group offset by a 20 pixel top margin

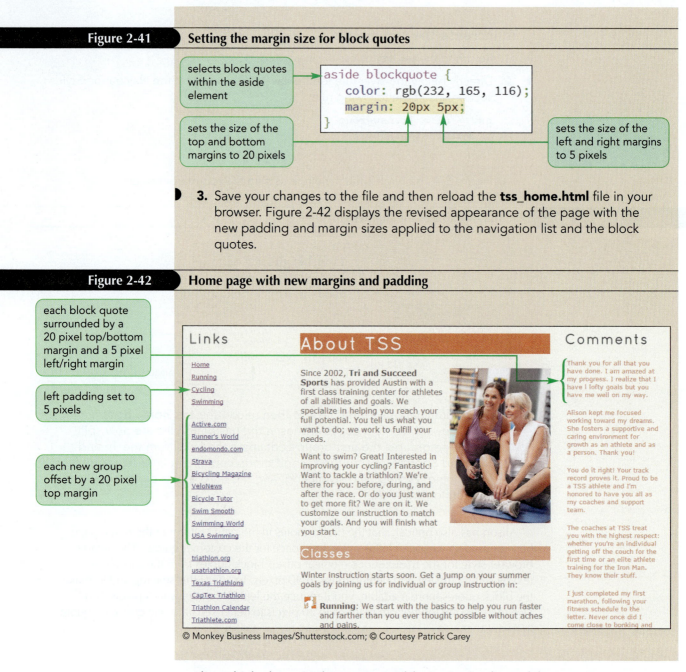

© Monkey Business Images/Shutterstock.com; © Courtesy Patrick Carey

Alison thinks the revised appearance of the navigation list and the customer quotes is a big improvement. However, she doesn't like the underlining in the navigation list. She would like the underlining to appear only when the user hovers the mouse pointer over the link. She would also like a different list marker to appear next to each list item in the classes section. You can make these changes using pseudo-classes and pseudo-elements.

Using Pseudo-Classes and Pseudo-Elements

Not everything that appears in the rendered page is marked up in the HTML file. For example, a paragraph has a first letter or a first line but those are not marked up as distinct elements. Similarly, an element can be classified based on a particular property without having a `class` attribute. The initial entry from an ordered list has the property of being the first item, but no `class` attribute in the HTML file identifies it as such. These elements and `class` attributes that exist only within the rendered page but not within the HTML document are known as pseudo-elements and pseudo-classes. Despite not being part of the HTML document, you can still write style rules for them.

Pseudo-Classes

A **pseudo-class** is a classification of an element based on its current status, position, or use in the document. The style rule for a pseudo-class is entered using the selector

```
element:pseudo-class
```

where *element* is an element from the document and *pseudo-class* is the name of a CSS pseudo-class. Pseudo-classes are organized into structural and dynamic classes. A **structural pseudo-class** classifies an element based on its location within the structure of the HTML document. Figure 2-43 lists the structural pseudo-classes supported in CSS.

Figure 2-43   **Structural pseudo-classes**

Pseudo-Class	Matches
`:root`	The top element in the document hierarchy (the `html` element)
`:empty`	An element with no content
`:only-child`	An element with no siblings
`:first-child`	The first child of the parent element
`:last-child`	The last child of the parent element
`:first-of-type`	The first descendant of the parent that matches the specified type
`:last-of-type`	The last descendant of the parent that matches the specified type
`:nth-of-type(n)`	The nth element of the parent of the specified type
`:nth-last-of-type(n)`	The nth from the last element of the parent of the specified type
`:only-of-type`	An element that has no siblings of the same type
`:lang(code)`	The element that has the specified language indicated by *code*
`:not(selector)`	An element not matching the specified *selector*

For example, the `first-of-type` pseudo-class identifies the first element of a particular type. The following selector uses this `first-of-type` pseudo-class to select the first list item found within an unordered list:

```
ul > li:first-of-type
```

This selector will not select any other list item and it will not select the first list item if it is not part of an unordered list.

Alison would like to modify the marker images used with the list of classes on the home page. Currently the runicon.png image file is used as the marker for all three list items. Instead, she would like to use the runicon.png image only for the first item, the bikeicon.png image as the marker for the second list item, and the swimicon.png as the third and last item's maker. You can use the `first-of-type`, `nth-of-type`, and `last-of-type` pseudo-classes to match the appropriate png file with each item.

To apply pseudo-classes to an unordered list:

1. Return to the **tss_styles.css** file in your editor.

2. Go to the List Styles section at the bottom of the style sheet, delete the `article#about_tss ul` style rule that sets the list style image marker and replace it with the following three style rules:

```
article#about_tss ul li:first-of-type {
    list-style-image: url(runicon.png);
}

article#about_tss ul li:nth-of-type(2) {
    list-style-image: url(bikeicon.png);
}

article#about_tss ul li:last-of-type {
    list-style-image: url(swimicon.png);
}
```

Figure 2-44 highlights the three selectors and their associated style rules using pseudo-classes with the unordered list items.

Figure 2-44 **Applying pseudo-classes to list items**

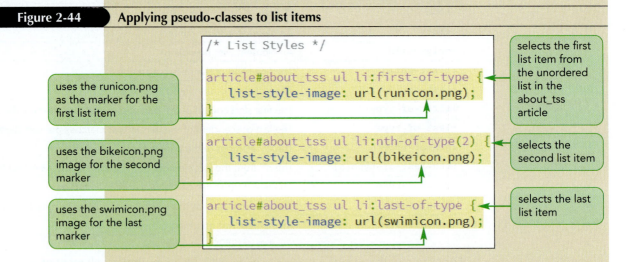

uses the runicon.png as the marker for the first list item

uses the bikeicon.png image for the second marker

uses the swimicon.png image for the last marker

selects the first list item from the unordered list in the about_tss article

selects the second list item

selects the last list item

3. Save your changes to the file and then reload the **tss_home.html** file in your browser. Figure 2-45 shows the new format of the unordered list with different image markers used with each of the list items.

Figure 2-45   **List marker images for each item**

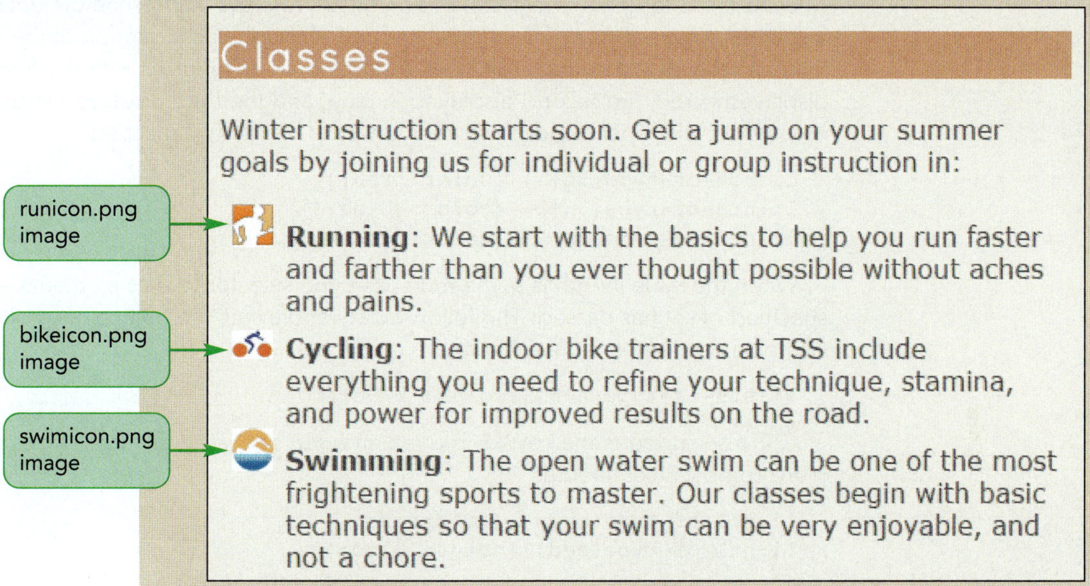

runicon.png image

bikeicon.png image

swimicon.png image

Classes

Winter instruction starts soon. Get a jump on your summer goals by joining us for individual or group instruction in:

Running: We start with the basics to help you run faster and farther than you ever thought possible without aches and pains.

Cycling: The indoor bike trainers at TSS include everything you need to refine your technique, stamina, and power for improved results on the road.

Swimming: The open water swim can be one of the most frightening sports to master. Our classes begin with basic techniques so that your swim can be very enjoyable, and not a chore.

© Courtesy Patrick Carey

Exploring the nth-of-type Pseudo-class

The `nth-of-type` pseudo-class is a powerful tool for formatting groups of elements in cyclical order. Cycles are created using the selector

```
nth-of-type(an+b)
```

where a is the length of the cycle, b is an offset from the start of the cycle, and n is a counter, which starts at 0 and increases by 1 through each iteration of the cycle. For example, the following style rules create a cycle of length 3 with the first list item displayed in red, the second displayed in blue, and the third displayed in green, after which the cycle repeats red-blue-green until the last item is reached:

```
li:nth-of-type(3n+1) {color: red;}
li:nth-of-type(3n+2) {color: blue;}
li:nth-of-type(3n+3) {color: green;}
```

When the cycle length is 1, the `nth-of-type` selector selects elements after the specified offset has passed. The following style rule sets the text color to blue for all list items starting from the 5th item

```
li:nth-of-type(n+5) {color: blue;}
```

CSS also supports the keywords `even` and `odd` so that two-length cycles can be more compactly entered as

```
li:nth-of-type(even) {color: red;}
li:nth-of-type(odd) {color: blue;}
```

with a red font applied to the even-numbered list items and a blue font applied to the odd-numbered items.

The same cyclical methods described above can be applied to the `nth-child` selector with the important difference that the `nth-child` selector selects any child element of the parent while the `nth-of-type` selector only selects elements of a specified type.

Pseudo-classes for Hypertext

Another type of pseudo-class is a **dynamic pseudo-class** in which the class can change state based on the actions of the user. Dynamic pseudo-classes are used with hypertext links such as the `visited` class, which indicates whether the target of the link has already been visited by the user. Figure 2-46 describes the dynamic pseudo-classes.

Figure 2-46   **Dynamic pseudo-classes**

Pseudo-Class	Description
:link	The link has not yet been visited by the user.
:visited	The link has been visited by the user.
:active	The element is in the process of being activated or clicked by the user.
:hover	The mouse pointer is hovering over the element.
:focus	The element is receiving the focus of the keyboard or mouse pointer.

For example, to display all previously visited links in a red font, you could apply the following style rule to the a element:

```
a:visited {color: red;}
```

To change the text color to blue when the mouse pointer is hovered over the link, apply the following rule:

```
a:hover {color: blue;}
```

TIP

The hover, active, and focus pseudo-classes also can be applied to non-hypertext elements to create dynamic page elements that change their appearance in response to user actions.

In some cases, two or more pseudo-classes can apply to the same element. For example, a hypertext link can be both visited previously and hovered over. In such situations, the standard cascading rules apply with the pseudo-class listed last applied to the element. As a result, you should enter the hypertext pseudo-classes in the following order—link, visited, hover, and active. The link pseudo-class comes first because it represents a hypertext link that has not been visited yet. The visited pseudo-class comes next, for links that have been previously visited. The hover pseudo-class follows, for the situation in which a user has moved the mouse pointer over a hypertext link prior to clicking the link. The active pseudo-class is last, representing the exact instant in which a link is activated.

Users with disabilities might interact with hypertext links through their keyboard rather than through a mouse pointer. Most browsers allow users to press the Tab key to navigate through the list of hypertext links on the page and to activate those links by pressing the Enter key. A link reached through the keyboard has the focus of the page and most browsers will indicate this focus by displaying an outline around the linked text. You can substitute your own style by using the focus pseudo-class in the same way that you used the hover pseudo-class.

REFERENCE

Using Dynamic Pseudo-Class to Create Hypertext

• To create a rollover for a hypertext link, use the pseudo-classes

```
a:link
a:visited
a:hover
a:active
```

where the link pseudo-element matches unvisited link, visited matches previously visited links, hover matches links that have the mouse pointer hovering over them, and active matches links that are in the action of being clicked.

The default browser style is to underline all hypertext links; displaying the links in a blue font with previously visited links in purple. Alison wants the links in the navigation list to appear in a medium gray font with no distinction between unvisited and previously visited links. She does not want the hypertext underlined in the navigation list except when the link is hovered over or active. She also wants hovered or active links to appear in purple. Add these style rules to the style sheet now.

To apply pseudo-classes to a hypertext links:

1. Return to the **tss_styles.css** file in your editor.

2. Go to the Navigation Styles section and insert the following style rules for hypertext links that have been visited or not visited.

   ```
   nav > ul > li > a:link, nav > ul > li > a:visited {
       color: rgb(151, 151, 151);
       text-decoration: none;
   }
   ```

3. Add the following new style rules for links that are being hovered over or are active:

   ```
   nav > ul > li > a:hover, nav > ul > li > a:active {
       color: rgb(255, 64, 255);
       text-decoration: underline;
   }
   ```

   Figure 2-47 highlights the style rules for hypertext links in the navigation list.

Figure 2-47   **Using pseudo-classes with hypertext links**

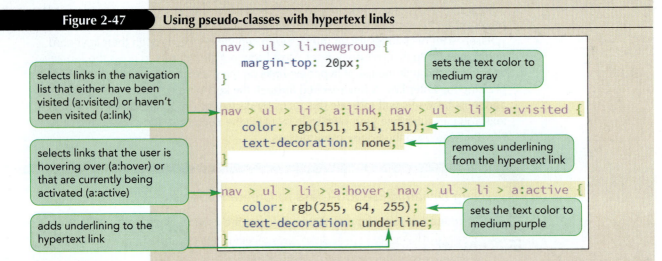

selects links in the navigation list that either have been visited (a:visited) or haven't been visited (a:link)

selects links that the user is hovering over (a:hover) or that are currently being activated (a:active)

adds underlining to the hypertext link

sets the text color to medium gray

removes underlining from the hypertext link

sets the text color to medium purple

```
nav > ul > li.newgroup {
    margin-top: 20px;
}

nav > ul > li > a:link, nav > ul > li > a:visited {
    color: rgb(151, 151, 151);
    text-decoration: none;
}

nav > ul > li > a:hover, nav > ul > li > a:active {
    color: rgb(255, 64, 255);
    text-decoration: underline;
}
```

4. Save your changes to the file and then reload the **tss_home.html** file in your browser and hover your mouse pointer over the links in the navigation list. Figure 2-48 shows the hover effect applied to the link to the TSS swimming class.

Figure 2-48   **Style applied to a hovered link**

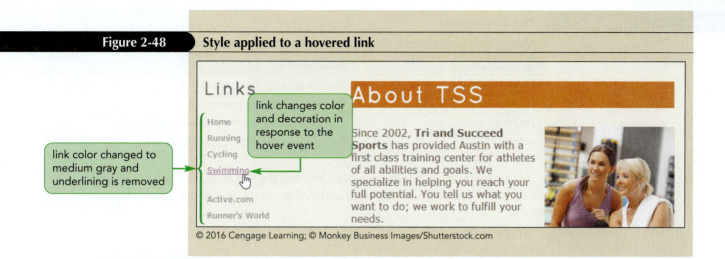

© 2016 Cengage Learning; © Monkey Business Images/Shutterstock.com

PROSKILLS

Problem Solving: Hover with Touch Devices

The `hover` pseudo-class was written to apply only to user interfaces that support mice or similar pointing devices. Technically, there is no hover event with touch devices, such as mobile phones and tablets. However, most mobile devices will still respond to a hover style by briefly applying the style when the user initially touches a hypertext link.

Many mobile devices also apply a "double tap" response so that initially touching a page element invokes the hover style and then immediately tapping the page element a second time invokes the click event. This technique is most often used for web pages that use the hover event to reveal hidden menus and page objects. You'll explore how to work with this technique to create hidden menus on mobile devices in Tutorial 5.

With the increasing importance of touch devices, a good guiding principle is that you should avoid making support for the hover style a necessary condition for the end-user. Hover effects should be limited to enhancing the user experience but they should not be a critical component of that experience.

Pseudo-Elements

Another type of pseudo selector is a **pseudo-element**, which is an object that exists only in the rendered page. For example, a paragraph is an element that is marked in the HTML file, but the first line of that paragraph is not. Similarly, the first letter of that paragraph is also not a document element, but it certainly can be identified as an object in the web page. Pseudo-elements can be selected using the following CSS selector

```
element::pseudo-element
```

where `element` is an element from the HTML file and `pseudo-element` is the name of a CSS pseudo-element. Figure 2-49 describes the pseudo-elements supported in CSS.

Figure 2-49 **Pseudo-elements**

Pseudo-Element	Description
`::first-letter`	The first letter of the element text
`::first-line`	The first line of the element text
`::before`	Content inserted directly before the element
`::after`	Content inserted directly after the element

For example, the following style rule matches the first displayed line of every paragraph in the rendered web page and transforms the text of that line to uppercase letters:

```
p::first-line {text-transform: uppercase;}
```

The following style rule matches the first letter of every paragraph within a block quote and displays the character in a Times New Roman font that is 250% larger than the surrounding text:

```
blockquote p::first-letter {
    font-family: 'Times New Roman', Times, serif;
    font-size: 250%;
}
```

Note that the double colon separator ":::" was introduced in CSS3 to differentiate pseudo-elements from pseudo-classes. Older browsers use the singe colon ":" for both pseudo-elements and pseudo-classes.

Generating Content with CSS

Another type of pseudo-element is used to generate content for the web page. New content can be added either before or after an element using the following `before` and `after` pseudo-elements

```
element::before {content: text;}
element::after {content: text;}
```

where `text` is the content to be inserted into the rendered web page. The `content` property supports several types of text content as described in Figure 2-50.

Figure 2-50 **Values of the content property**

Value	Description
`none`	Sets the content to an empty text string
`counter`	Displays a counter value
`attr(attribute)`	Displays the value of the selector's `attribute`
`text`	Displays the specified `text`
`open-quote`	Displays an opening quotation mark
`close-quote`	Displays a closing quotation mark
`no-open-quote`	Removes an opening quotation mark, if previously specified
`no-close-quote`	Removes a closing quotation mark, if previously specified
`url(url)`	Displays the content of the media (image, video, etc.) from the file located at `url`

For example, the following style rules combine the `before` and `after` pseudo-elements with the `hover` pseudo-class to insert the "<" and ">" characters around every hypertext link in a navigation list:

```
nav a:hover::before {content: "<";}
nav a:hover::after {content: ">";}
```

TIP

You cannot use CSS to insert HTML markup tags, character references, or entity references. Those can only be done within the HTML file.

Note that these style rules use both the `hover` pseudo-class and the `before`/`after` pseudo-elements so that the content is only inserted in response to the hover event.

If you want to insert a special symbol, you have to insert the code number for that symbol using text string "`\code`" where *code* is the code number. For example, if instead of single angled brackets as indicated above, you wanted to show double angled brackets, « and », you would need to use the Unicode character code for these characters, `00ab` and `00bb` respectively. To insert these characters before and after a navigation list hypertext link, you would apply the following style rules:

```
nav a:hover::before {content: "\00ab";}
nav a:hover::after {content: "\00bb";}
```

In addition to adding content to an element as just discussed, you can also insert content that is a media file, such as an image or video clip, by using the following `content` property

```
content: url(url);
```

where *url* is the location of the media file. For example, the following style rule appends the image file uparrow.png to any hypertext link in the document when it is hovered over:

```
a:hover::after {content: url(uparrow.png);}
```

An image file or any content generated by the style sheet should not consist of material that is crucial to understanding your page. Instead, generated content should only consist of material that supplements the page for artistic or design-related reasons. If the generated content is crucial to interpreting the page, it should be placed in the HTML file in the first place.

Displaying Attribute Values

The content property can also be used to insert an attribute value into the rendered web page through the use of the following `attr()` function

```
content: attr(attribute);
```

where *attribute* is an attribute of the selected element. One application of the `attr()` function is to add the URL of any hypertext link to the link text. In the following code, the value of the `href` attribute is appended to every occurrence of text marked with the `a` element:

```
a::after {
   content: "( " attr(href) ")";
}
```

Notice that URL is enclosed within opening and closing parentheses. Thus, a hypertext link in an HTML document, such as

```
<a href="http://www.triathlon.org">Triathlons</a>
```

will be displayed in the rendered web page as:

Triathlons (http://www.triathlon.org)

This technique is particularly useful for printed output in which the author wants to have the URLs of all links displayed on the printed page for users to read and have as references. You'll explore this issue further in Tutorial 5.

Inserting Content using CSS

- To insert content directly before a page element, use the style rule

  ```
  element::before {content: text;}
  ```

  where *element* is the page element and *text* is the content to be inserted before the element.
- To insert content directly after a page element, use the style rule

  ```
  element::after {content: text;}
  ```

Inserting Quotation Marks

The `blockquote` and `q` elements are used for quoted material. The content of these elements is usually placed in quotation marks and, while you can insert these quotation marks within the HTML file, you can also insert decorative opening and closing quotation marks using the `content` property with the following values:

```
content: open-quote;
content: close-quote;
```

The actual characters used for the open and closing quotation marks are defined for the selector with the following `quotes` property

```
quotes: "open1" "close1" "open2" "close2" …;
```

where *open1* is the character used for the opening quotation mark and *close1* is character used for the closing quotation mark. The text strings *open2*, *close2*, and so on are used for nested quotation marks. In the example that follows, character codes are used to define the curly quotes for opening and closing quotation marks

```
quotes: "\201C" "\201D" "\2018" "\2019";
```

TIP

Quotations marks generated by CSS are often used with international pages in which different languages require different quotation mark symbols.

where the character code 201C returns the opening curly double quote ", the code 201D returns the closing curly double quote ", the code 2018 returns the nested opening single quote ', and 2019 provides the closing single quote '.

Alison suggests that you use decorative quotes for the customer comments on the Tri and Succeed Sports home page. You display curly quotes in a bold Times New Roman font with a font size of 1.6em (which is slightly bigger than the font size of the block quote text.)

To insert quotes into block quotes:

1. Return to the **tss_styles.css** file in your editor.

2. Go to the Aside and Blockquote Styles section and, within the style rule for the `aside blockquote` selector, insert the following `quotes` property to use curly quotes for the quotation marks:

   ```
   quotes: "\201C" "\201D";
   ```

3. Add the following style rules to insert quotation marks before and after each block quote in the `aside` element:

   ```
   aside blockquote::before {
       content: open-quote;
       font-family: 'Times New Roman', Times, serif;
       font-size: 1.6em;
       font-weight: bold;
   }
   ```

```
aside blockquote::after {
    content: close-quote;
    font-family: 'Times New Roman', Times, serif;
    font-size: 1.6em;
    font-weight: bold;
}
```

Figure 2-51 highlights the styles to add curly quotes before and after each block quote.

Figure 2-51   Adding quotation marks to block quotes

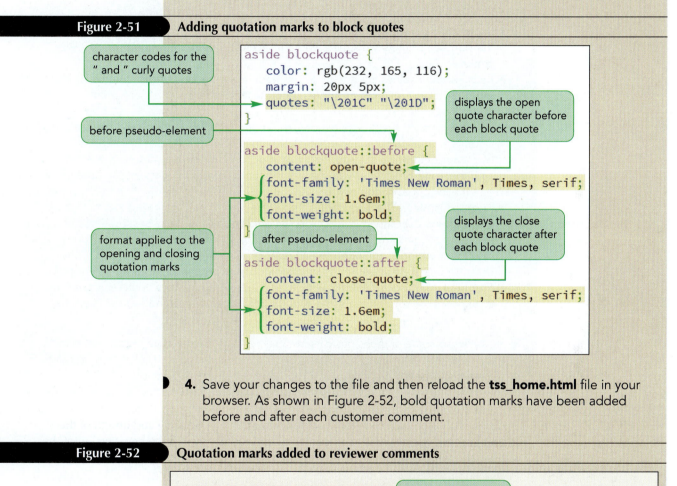

character codes for the
" and " curly quotes

```
aside blockquote {
    color: rgb(232, 165, 116);
    margin: 20px 5px;
    quotes: "\201C" "\201D";
}
```

before pseudo-element

displays the open
quote character before
each block quote

```
aside blockquote::before {
    content: open-quote;
    font-family: 'Times New Roman', Times, serif;
    font-size: 1.6em;
    font-weight: bold;
}
```

after pseudo-element

format applied to the
opening and closing
quotation marks

displays the close
quote character after
each block quote

```
aside blockquote::after {
    content: close-quote;
    font-family: 'Times New Roman', Times, serif;
    font-size: 1.6em;
    font-weight: bold;
}
```

4. Save your changes to the file and then reload the **tss_home.html** file in your browser. As shown in Figure 2-52, bold quotation marks have been added before and after each customer comment.

Figure 2-52   Quotation marks added to reviewer comments

About TSS

opening and closing
quotes enclose each
comment

Comments

Since 2002, **Tri and Succeed Sports** has provided Austin with a first class training center for athletes of all abilities and goals. We specialize in helping you reach your full potential. You tell us what you want to do; we work to fulfill your needs.

Want to swim? Great! Interested in improving your cycling? Fantastic!

" Thank you for all that you have done. I am amazed at my progress. I realize that I have l lofty goals but you have me well on my way. "

" Alison kept me focused working toward my dreams. She fosters a supportive and caring environment for growth as an athlete and as a person. Thank you! "

Teamwork: Managing a Style Sheet

Your style sheets often will be as long and as complex as your website content. As the size of a style sheet increases, you might find yourself overwhelmed by multiple style rules and definitions. This can be an especially critical problem in a workplace where several people need to interpret and sometimes edit the same style sheet. Good management skills are as crucial to good design as a well-chosen color or typeface are. As you create your own style sheets, here are some techniques to help you manage your creations:

- Use style comments throughout, especially at the top of the file. Clearly describe the purpose of the style sheet, where it's used, who created it, and when it was created.
- Because color values are not always immediately obvious, include comments that describe your colors. For example, annotate a color value with a comment such as "body text is tan".
- Divide your style sheet into sections, with comments marking the section headings.
- Choose an organizing scheme and stick with it. You may want to organize style rules by the order in which they appear in your documents, or you may want to insert them alphabetically. Whichever you choose, be consistent and document the organizing scheme in your style comments.
- Keep your style sheets as small as possible, and break them into separate files if necessary. Use one style sheet for layout, another for text design, and perhaps another for color and graphics. Combine the style sheets using the @import rule, or combine them using the link element within each page. Also, consider creating one style sheet for basic pages on your website, and another for pages that deal with special content. For example, an online store could use one style sheet (or set of sheets) for product information and another for customer information.

By following some of these basic techniques, you'll find your style sheets easier to manage and develop, and it will be easier for your colleagues to collaborate with you to create an eye-catching website.

Alison is pleased with the work you've done on the typography and design of the Tri and Succeed Sports website. Alison will continue to develop the new version of the website and will get back to you with future changes and design ideas.

Session 2.3 Quick Check

1. Provide a style rule to display all unordered lists with lowercase letters as the list marker.

2. Provide a style rule to display all unordered lists using the star.png image file, placed inside the virtual box.

3. Provide a style rule to display the text of all previously visited hypertext links in gray.

4. Provide the style rule to set the padding around every h1 heading in a `section` element to 1em on top, 0.5em on the left and right, and 2em on the bottom.

5. Provide the style rule to change the left margin of the `figure` element to 20 pixels.

6. Describe the item selected by the following selector:

   `#top > p:first-of-type:first-line`

7. Describe the items selected by the following selector:

   `div.Links img[usemap]`

8. Provide a style rule to insert the text string "***" before every paragraph belonging to the Review class.

9. Provide the style property to set the opening quotation mark and closing quotation marks to curly quotes with Unicode values of 2018 and 2019 respectively.

PRACTICE

Review Assignments

Data Files needed for the Review Assignments: coach_styles_txt.css, tss_coach_txt.html, 1 CSS file, 5 PNG files, 1 TTF file, 1 WOFF file

Alison has created another page for the Tri and Succeed Sports website providing biographies of the coaches at the club. She has already written the page content, acquired image files, and created a style sheet for the page layout. She wants you to finish the design of the page by developing a style sheet for the page's color scheme and typography. A preview of the page you'll design is shown in Figure 2-53.

Figure 2-53 **TSS coaches profile page**

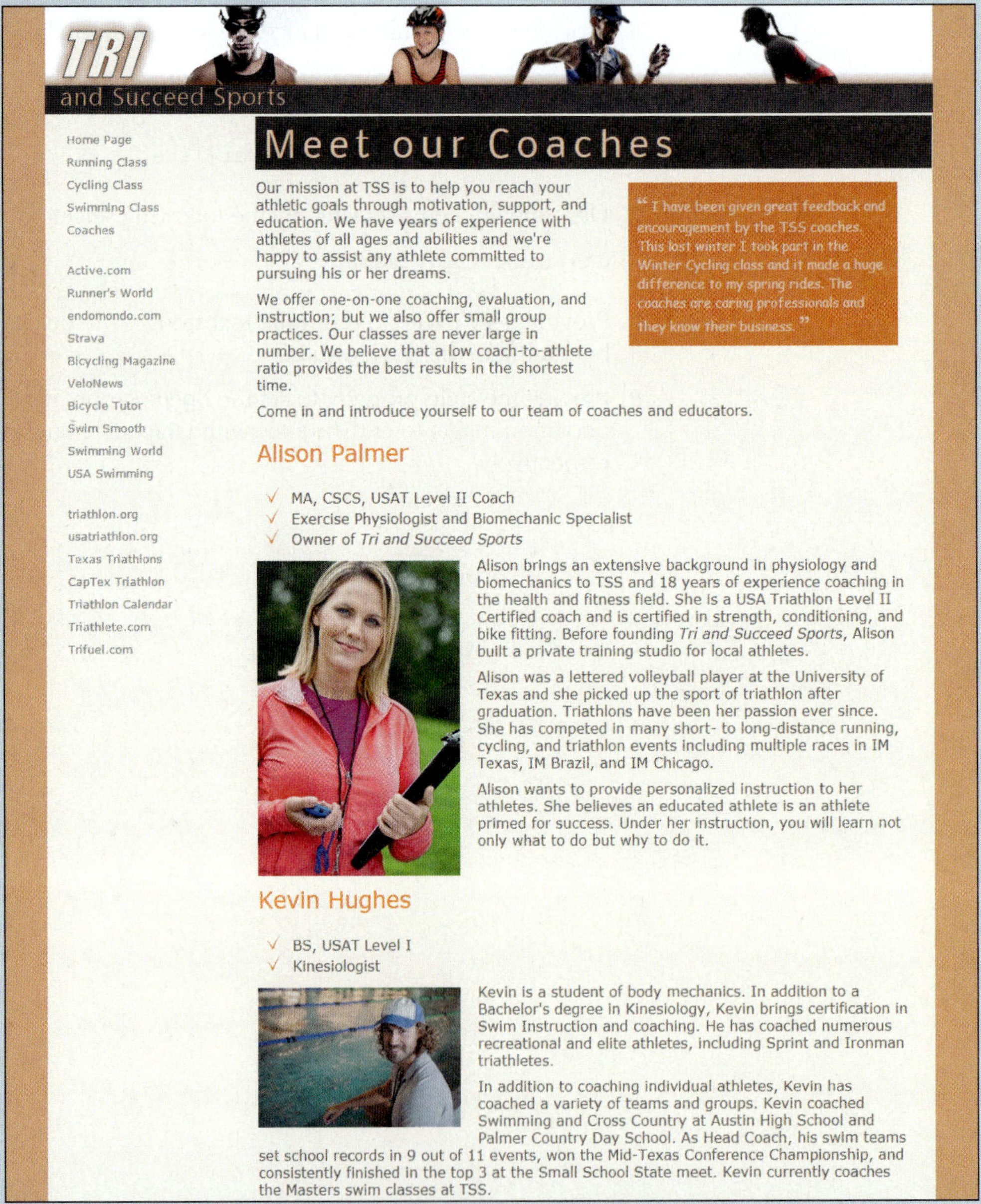

Complete the following:

1. Use your HTML editor to open the **tss_coach_txt.html** and **coach_styles_txt.css** files from the html02 ▸ review folder. Enter *your name* and *the date* in the comment section of each file, and save them as **tss_coach.html** and **coach_styles.css** respectively.

2. Go to the **tss_coach.html** file in your editor and then within the document head, create links to the **coach_layout.css** and **coach_styles.css** style sheets.

3. Take some time to study the content and structure of the file and then close the document, saving your changes.

4. Go to the **coach_styles.css** file in your editor. At the top of the file and before the comment section do the following:

   a. Insert an `@charset` rule to set the character encoding for the file to utf-8.

   b. Use the `@font-face` rule to define a web font named Nobile, which is based on the nobile-webfont.woff file and, if that format is not supported, on the nobile-webfont.ttf file.

5. Go to the Main Structural Styles section and do the following:

   a. Change the background color of the browser window by creating a style rule for the `html` element that sets the background color to the value hsl(27, 72%, 72%).

   b. For the `body` element, create a style rule to set the text color to the value rgb(91, 91, 91), the background color to ivory, and body text to the font stack: Verdana, Geneva, sans-serif.

6. Create a style rule for the `body > footer address` selector containing the following styles:

   a. The background color set to the value rgb(222, 128, 60)

   b. The font color to white and then to the semitransparent value rgba(255, 255, 255, 0.6)

   c. The font style to normal displayed in bold small capital letters with a font size of 0.9em and a line height of 3em using the font stack Nobile, Verdana, Geneva, sans-serif

   d. The text horizontally centered on the page

7. Go to the Heading Styles section and create a style rule for every h1 heading that displays the text with a normal font weight from the font stack: Nobile, Verdana, Geneva, sans-serif. Set the letter spacing to 0.2em and the margin to 0 pixels.

8. Alison wants you to format the main h1 heading at the top of the page. Create a style rule for the `section#tss_coaches h1` selector that sets the font size to 2.5em with a color value of hsl(27, 82%, 85%) and background color of hsl(27, 6%, 21%). Set the left padding space to 10 pixels.

9. Alison also wants you to format the h2 headings for each coach. Create a style rule for the `article.coach_bio h2` selector that sets the font size to 1.6em with normal weight and the font color to rgb(240, 125, 0).

10. Alison has inserted a comment from an athlete about the coaches. Format this comment by going to the Blockquote Styles section and creating a style rule for the `aside blockquote` selector to do the following:

    a. Set the font size to 0.95em using the font stack 'Comic Sans MS', cursive.

    b. Set the font color to rgb(222, 128, 60) and use a semi-transparent background color with the value rgba(255, 2555, 255, 0.75).

    c. Set the padding space to 10 pixels.

    d. Define opening and closing quotes for the element using the Unicode character 201C and 201D respectively.

11. Format the appearance of the opening quotes by creating a style rule for the `aside blockquote::before` selector to write a boldfaced open quote before the block quote with the font size set to 1.6em from the font stack 'Times New Roman', Times, serif.

12. Format the appearance of the closing quotes by creating a style rule for the `aside blockquote::after` selector to write a boldfaced open quote after the block quote with the font size once again set to 1.6em from the font stack 'Times New Roman', Times, serif.

13. Next, you'll format the appearance of the navigation list by going to the Navigation Styles section and creating a style rule for `body > nav` selector that sets the text of the navigation list in a 0.8em font size with a line height of 2em.

14. Create a style rule for the `nav > ul` selector that removes the list marker and sets the left padding to 5 pixels.

15. Alison wants to break up the long list of links in the navigation list. Create style rules for the 6th and 16th `li` elements within the `nav > ul` selector that sets the size of the top margin of those items to 20 pixels.

16. For every previously visited or unvisited hypertext link within the `nav > ul > li` selector, set the text to the RGB color value rgb(151, 151, 151) and remove the underlining from the text link.

17. For every hovered or active hypertext link within the `nav > ul > li` selector, set the text color to RGB value rgb(222, 128, 60) and underline the hypertext link.

18. Go to the Paragraph Styles section and insert a style rule that sets the top margin and bottom margin to 10 pixels, the right margin to 30 pixels, and the left margin to 0 pixels for every paragraph in the document.

19. Every coach has a list of accomplishments. Go to the List Styles section and insert a style rule for the `article.coach_bio > header > ul` selector that displays the check.png file as the list marker and sets the margin space to 0 pixels, except for the bottom margin, which should be set to 10 pixels.

20. Save your changes to the style sheet and then open the **tss_coach.html** file in your browser. Verify that the color and typography match that shown in Figure 2-53. Verify that when you hover the mouse pointer over the links in the navigation list the text is displayed in an underlined orange font.

Case Problem 1

APPLY

Data Files needed for this Case Problem: ph_plays_txt.html, ph_styles_txt.css, 1 CSS file, 1 PNG file, 3 TTF files, 3 WOFF files

Philip Henslowe Classic Theatre   Randall Chen is the media director for the *Philip Henslowe Classic Theatre*, a regional classical theatre in Coeur d'Alene, Idaho. You've been asked to work on the website design for the company. The first page you'll manage lists the plays for next summer's repertoire. A preview of the page is shown in Figure 2-54.

Figure 2-54   List of Plays at the Philip Henslowe Classic Theatre

© 2016 Cengage Learning; © Christian Bertrand/Shutterstock.com

The content and layout of the page has already been created for you. Your job will be to create a style sheet for the typography of the page.

Complete the following:

1. Using your editor, open the **ph_plays_txt.html** and **ph_styles_txt.css** files from the html02 ▸ case1 folder. Enter *your name* and *the date* in the comment section of each file, and save them as **ph_plays.html** and **ph_styles.css** respectively.

2. Go to the **ph_plays.html** file in your HTML editor, and within the document head create links to the **ph_layout.css** and **ph_styles.css** style sheet files. Take some time to study the content and structure of the document and then close the file, saving your changes.

3. Go to the **ph_styles.css** file in your editor, and at the top of the file before the comment section, define the character encoding used in the document as utf-8.

4. Randall has several web fonts that he wants used for the titles of the plays produced by the company. Add the following web fonts to the style sheet, using `@font-face` rules before the comment section:

    a. The Champagne font using the cac_champagne.woff and cac_champagne.ttf files

    b. The Grunge font using the 1942.woff and 1942.ttf files

    c. The Dobkin font using the DobkinPlain.woff and DobkinPlain.ttf files

5. Go to the Structural Styles section, creating a style rule that sets the background color of the `html` element to the value hsl(91, 8%, 56%).

6. Add a style rule for the `body` element to set the background color to the value hsl(58, 31%, 84%) and the font of the body text to the font stack: 'Palatino Linotype', 'Book Antiqua', Palatino, serif.

7. Create a style rule for the `header` element that sets the background color to black.

8. Create a style rule for every paragraph that sets the margin space to 0 pixels and the padding space to 5 pixels on top and 25 pixels on the right, bottom, and left.

9. For paragraphs that are direct children of the body element, create a style rule that sets the font size to 1.1em and horizontally centers the paragraph text.

10. Create a style rule for the address element that sets the font style to normal with a font size of 0.9em, horizontally centered on the page. Set the top and bottom padding to 10 pixels.

11. Next, you'll format the appearance of navigation lists on the page. Go to the Navigation Styles section and create a style rule for the `nav a` selector that displays the hypertext links using the font stack 'Trebuchet MS', Helvetica, sans-serif, and sets the top and bottom padding to 10 pixels.

12. For every unvisited and previously visited hypertext link within a `nav` element, set the text color to white, remove underlining from the link text, and set the background color to the semi-transparent value hsla(0, 0%, 42%, 0.4).

13. For every active or hovered link in a `nav` element, set the text color to the semi-transparent value hsla(0, 0%, 100%, 0.7) and set the background color to the semi-transparent value hsl(0, 0%, 42%, 0.7).

14. Go to the Section Styles section of the style sheet. In this section, you'll define the appearance of the four playbills. You'll start with the h1 headings from the sections. Create a style rule for the `section.playbill h1` selector that sets the font size to 3em and the font weight to normal. Set the margin space around the h1 headings to 0 pixels. Set the padding space to 20 pixels on top, 0 pixels on the right, 10 pixels on the bottom, and 20 pixels on the left.

15. Each playbill section is identified by a different ID value ranging from play1 to play4. Create style rules that set a different background color for each playbill using the following background colors:

    ID: play1 set to hsl(240, 100%, 88%)

    ID: play2 set to hsl(25, 88%, 73%)

    ID: play3 set to hsl(0, 100%, 75%)

    ID: play4 set to hsl(296, 86%, 86%)

16. Each playbill section heading will also have a different font. For the h1 headings within the four different playbills, create style rules to apply the following font stacks:

    ID: play1 set to Champagne, cursive

    ID: play2 set to Grunge, 'Times New Roman', Times, serif

    ID: play3 set to Impact, Charcoal, sans-serif

    ID: play4 set to Dobkin, cursive

17. Randall has put the author and the director of each play within a definition list. Format these definition lists now by going to the Definition List Styles section and creating a style rule for the dt element that sets the font size to 1.3em, the font weight to bold, and the font color to the semi-transparent value hsla(0, 0%, 0%, 0.4).

18. Create a style rule for every dd element to set the font size to 1.3em, the left margin space to 0 pixels, and the bottom margin space to 10 pixels.

19. Save your changes to the file and then open the **ph_plays.html** file in your browser. Verify that the typography and colors used in the document match those shown in Figure 2-54. Also, verify that, when you hover the mouse pointer over an item in the navigation lists for the entire page and for each play, the background color of the link becomes more opaque.

Case Problem 2

CHALLENGE

Data Files needed for this Case Problem: mw_styles_txt.css, mw_tour_txt.html, 1 CSS file, 1 PNG file

Mountain Wheels   Adriana and Ivan Turchenko are the co-owners of Mountain Wheels, a bike shop and touring company in Littleton, Colorado. One of their most popular tours is the Bike the Mountains Tour, a six-day excursion over some of the highest roads in Colorado. Adriana wants to update the company's website to provide more information about the tour. She already has had a colleague design a three-column layout with a list of links in the first column and descriptive text in the second and third columns. She has asked for your help in completing the design by formatting the text and colors in the page. Figure 2-55 shows a preview of the design used in the final page.

| Figure 2-55 | Description of the Bike the Mountains tour |

© 2016 Cengage Learning; © visuall2/Shutterstock.com

Complete the following:

1. Using your editor, open the **mw_tour_txt.html** and **mw_styles_txt.css** files from the html02 ▸ case2 folder. Enter *your name* and *the date* in the comment section of each file, and save them as **mw_tour.html** and **mw_styles.css** respectively.

2. Go to the **mw_tour.html** file in your HTML editor. Within the document head, create links to the **mw_layout.css** and **mw_styles.css** style sheet files. Study the content and structure of the document and then close the file, saving your changes.

3. Go to the **mw_styles.css** file in your editor. At the top of the file, insert the `@charset` rule to set the encoding for this style sheet to utf-8.

4. Go to the Structural Styles section and create a style rule that sets the background color of the browser window to rgb(173, 189, 227).

5. Create a style rule for the `body` element that sets the background color to rgb(227, 210, 173) and sets the body font to the font stack: 'Century Gothic', sans-serif.

6. Create a style rule to display the body footer with a background color of rgb(208, 184, 109) and set the top and bottom padding space to 5 pixels.

7. Create a style rule for the `address` element to display the text in a normal font with a font size of 0.9em, horizontally center the text, and set the top and bottom padding to 10 pixels.

8. Go to the Heading Styles section and create a style rule to set the font weight of all h1 and h2 headings to normal.

9. Go to the Navigation Styles section and create a style rule for the `nav > ul` selector that removes all list markers, sets the line height to 2em, and sets the font size to 0.9em.

10. For every previously visited or unvisited hypertext link within the navigation list, create a style rule to remove the underlining from the hypertext link and to set the text color to rgb(43, 59, 125).

11. For every hovered or active link within the navigation list, create a style rule to set the text color to rgb(212, 35, 35).

12. Adriana has put information about the tour in an article with the ID "tour_summary". Format this article, starting with the heading. Go to the Article Styles section and create a style rule for `h1` elements nested within the tour_summary article that sets the font size to 2.2em and the letter spacing to 0.2em.

13. Create a style rule for paragraphs within the tour_summary article that sets the font size to 1.1em.

➕ **Explore** 14. Adriana wants the first line in the tour_summary article to appear in small capital letters. Use the `first-of-type` pseudo-class and the `first-line` pseudo-element to create a style rule that displays the first line of the first paragraph within the tour_summary article at a font size of 1.2em and in small caps.

15. The tour itinerary is displayed within an `aside` element with the ID *tour_itinerary*. Go to the Aside Styles section and for every `h1` element nested within the tour_itinerary `aside` element, create a style rule that sets the font size to 1.2em.

16. For every h2 element within the tour_itinerary `aside` element, set the font size to 0.9em.

17. Set the font size of paragraphs within the tour_itinerary `aside` element to 0.8em.

➕ **Explore** 18. Adriana wants the text color of each day's schedule to alternate between gray and blue. Create the following style rules:

   a. For odd-numbered h2 headings and paragraphs that set the font color to rgb(79, 91, 40). (*Hint*: Use the `nth-of-type(odd)` pseudo-class.)

   b. For even-numbered h2 headings and paragraphs that set the font color to rgb(81, 95, 175). (*Hint*: Use the `nth-of-type(even)` pseudo-class.)

19. The page contains a review within a block quote. Go to the Blockquote Styles section and create a style rule for the `blockquote` element that sets the background color to rgb(173, 189, 227) and the text color to the rgb(255, 255, 255) with an opacity of 0.65.

20. For every paragraph within the `blockquote` element create a style rule that sets the top/bottom padding space to 2.5 pixels and the left/right padding space to 10 pixels.

21. Save your changes to the file and then open the **mw_tour.html** file in your browser. Verify that your design matches that shown in Figure 2-55 including the format applied to the first paragraph of the tour_itinerary article and the alternating colors used in the listing of the itinerary days.

Case Problem 3

Data Files needed for this Case Problem: cw_class_txt.html, cw_styles_txt.css, 1 CSS file, 2PNG files

The Civil War and Reconstruction   Peter Craft is a professor of military history at Mountain Crossing University. The university is offering a series of online courses, one of which is "The Civil War and Reconstruction" taught by Professor Craft. He has developed the online content and has had a colleague help with the page layout. You've been asked to complete the project by creating text and color styles. A preview of the sample page is shown in Figure 2-56.

CHALLENGE

| Figure 2-56 | Civil War History home page |

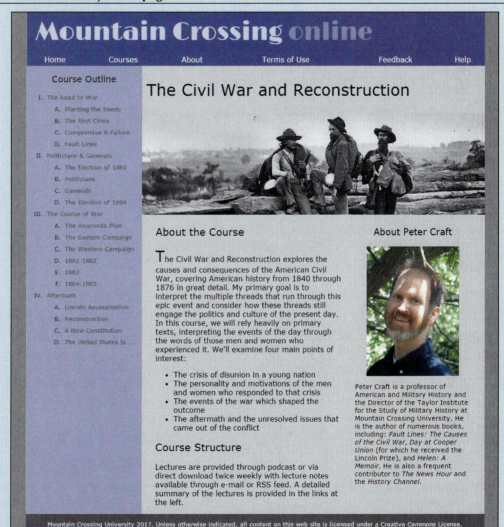

Complete the following:

1. Using your editor, open the **cw_class_txt.html** and **cw_styles_txt.css** files from the html02 ▶ case3 folder. Enter *your name* and *the date* in the comment section of each file, and save them as **cw_class.html** and **cw_styles.css** respectively.

2. Go to the **cw_class.html** file in your HTML editor. Within the document head, create a link to the **cw_styles.css** style sheet file.

✪ **Explore** 3. Using the Google Fonts website, locate the Limelight font. Copy the code for the `link` element to use this font and paste the copied code to the document head in the cw_class.html file.

4. Study the content and structure of the cw_class.html file and then close the file, saving your changes.

5. Go to the **cw_styles.css** file in your editor. At the top of the file, define the character encoding as utf-8.

✪ **Explore** 6. On the next line, use the `@import` rule to import the contents of the cw_layout.css file into the style sheet.

7. Go to the Structural Styles section. Within that section create a style rule to set the background color of the browser window to rgb(151, 151, 151).

8. Create a style rule to set the background color of the page body to rgb(180, 180, 223) and set the body text to the font stack: Verdana, Geneva, sans-serif.

9. Display all h1 and h2 headings with normal weight.

10. Create a style rule for every hypertext link nested within a navigation list that removes underlining from the text.

11. Create a style rule for the `footer` element that sets the text color to white and the background color to rgb(101, 101, 101). Set the font size to 0.8em. Horizontally center the footer text, and set the top/bottom padding space to 1 pixel.

12. Next, you'll format the body header that displays the name of the university. Go to the Body Header Styles section and, for the `body > header` selector, create a style rule that sets the background color to rgb(97, 97, 211).

13. The university name is stored in an h1 heading. Create a style rule for the h1 heading that is a direct child of the body header that sets the font size to 4vw with the color value rgba(255, 255, 255, 0.8). Display the text with the font stack: Limelight, cursive. Set the margin space to 0 pixels.

14. The last word of the h1 heading text is enclosed within a `span` element. Create a style rule for the `span` element nested within the h1 heading that is nested within the body header, setting the text color to rgba(255, 255, 255, 0.4).

15. Go the Navigation Styles section. In this section, you format the navigation list that has the ID *mainLinks*. For hypertext links within this navigation list, set the top and bottom padding space to 5 pixels.

16. For previously visited and unvisited links within the mainLinks navigation list, create a style rule that displays the hypertext links in a white font.

17. For hovered or active links within the mainLinks navigation list, create a style rule that displays the hypertext links in white with an opacity of 0.8 and set the background color to the value rgba(51, 51, 51, 0.5).

18. Go to the Outline Styles section. In this section, you'll format the course outline that appears on the page's left column. The navigation list in this outline has the ID *outline*. Create a style rule for this navigation list that sets the text color to rgb(51, 51, 51) and the font size to 0.8em.

19. Horizontally center the h1 headings within the outline navigation list.

20. For the first level `ol` elements that are a direct child of the outline navigation list, create a style rule that sets the line height to 2em, the top/bottom margin to 0 pixels and the left/right margin to 5 pixels. Display the list marker as an upper-case Roman numeral.

21. Display the second level of `ol` elements nested within the outline navigation list with an upper-case letter as the list marker.

22. Display all previously visited and unvisited links in the outline navigation list using the color value rgb(101, 101, 101).

23. Display hovered and active links in the outline navigation list using the color value rgb(97, 97, 211) with the text underlined.

24. Go to the Section Styles section. In this section, format the description of the course. Create a style rule that sets the background color of the `section` element to rgb(220, 220, 220).

25. Format the heading of this section by creating a style rule for the `section header h1` selector that sets the font size of 2.2em and the left padding space to 10 pixels.

26. Go to the Article Styles section and create a style rule for h2 headings within the `article` element that sets the font size to 1.4em.

✦ **Explore** 27. Display the first letter of the first paragraph within the `article` element with a font size of 2em and vertically aligned with the baseline of the surrounding text. (*Hint*: Use the `first-of-type` pseudo-class and the `first-letter` pseudo-element.)

28. Information about Peter Craft has been placed in an `aside` element. Go to the Aside Styles section and create a style rule that sets the font size of text in the `aside` element to 0.9em.

29. For h1 headings nested within the `aside` element, create a style rule that sets the font size to 1.4em and horizontally centers the text.

30. Save your changes to the file and then open the `cw_class.html` file in your browser. Verify that the appearance of the page resembles that shown in Figure 2-56. Confirm that when you change the width of the browser window, the size of the page heading text changes in response to setting the heading text using the vw unit.

CREATE

Case Problem 4

Data Files needed for this Case Problem: lake_home_txt.html, lake_styles_txt.css, 1 CSS file, 2 PNG files, 2 TTF files, 2 WOFF files

The Great Lakescape Lodge Ron Nelson is the owner of The Great Lakescape Lodge in Baileys Harbor, Wisconsin. He has hired you to work on the redesign of the lodge's website. You'll start by working on the site's home page. Ron has already written the text of the page, gathered all of the graphic files, and had a colleague design the page layout. He wants you to work on the page's color scheme and typography. A possible solution is shown in Figure 2-57.

Figure 2-57   **Home page of the Great Lakescape Lodge**

© 2016 Cengage Learning; © Courtesy Patrick Carey; © Dmitry Kalinovsky/Shutterstock.com

Complete the following:

1. Using your editor, open the **lake_home_txt.html** and **lake_styles_txt.css** files from the html02 ▸ case4 folder. Save them as **lake_home.html** and **lake_styles.css** respectively.

2. Go to the **lake_home.html** file in your editor and link it to the **lake_layout.css** and **lake_styles.css** style sheet file. Take some time to study the content and structure of the document and then save your changes to the file.

3. Go to the **lake_styles.css** file in your editor and begin creating the color scheme and typographic styles for the lodge's home page. The final design is up to you but it should include the following features:

   • Definition of the character encoding used in the style sheet file
   • Application of a web font (Two fonts are supplied for you in the html02 ▸ case4 folder.)
   • Setting background and text colors using both color values and color names
   • An application of a semi-transparent color
   • Selectors showing style rules applied to nested elements, child elements, and elements based on the id attribute
   • Styles that modify the appearance of list and list markers
   • Use of pseudo-elements and pseudo-classes as selectors
   • Styles that modify the padding space and margin space around an element
   • A style rule to generate content in the rendered page

4. Include informative style comments throughout the style sheet.

5. Save your completed style sheet.

TUTORIAL **3**

Designing a Page Layout

Creating a Website for a Chocolatier

<block>**OBJECTIVES**

Session 3.1
- Create a reset style sheet
- Explore page layout designs
- Center a block element
- Create a floating element
- Clear a floating layout
- Prevent container collapse

Session 3.2
- Explore grid-based layouts
- Create a layout grid
- Format a grid
- Explore the CSS grid styles

Session 3.3
- Explore positioning styles
- Work with relative positioning
- Work with absolute positioning
- Work with overflow content</block>

Case | *Pandaisia Chocolates*

Anne Ambrose is the owner and head chocolatier of *Pandaisia Chocolates*, a chocolate shop located in Essex, Vermont. You have been asked to assist on the redesign of the company's website. Anne has provided you with three pages from the website to start your work. She has written all of the content, compiled the necessary images and graphics, and written some of the text and color styles. She needs you to complete the project by designing the page layout using the CSS layout properties.

STARTING DATA FILES

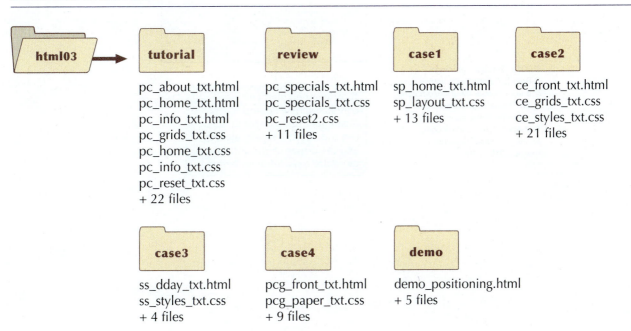

html03 → **tutorial**
pc_about_txt.html
pc_home_txt.html
pc_info_txt.html
pc_grids_txt.css
pc_home_txt.css
pc_info_txt.css
pc_reset_txt.css
+ 22 files

review
pc_specials_txt.html
pc_specials_txt.css
pc_reset2.css
+ 11 files

case1
sp_home_txt.html
sp_layout_txt.css
+ 13 files

case2
ce_front_txt.html
ce_grids_txt.css
ce_styles_txt.css
+ 21 files

case3
ss_dday_txt.html
ss_styles_txt.css
+ 4 files

case4
pcg_front_txt.html
pcg_paper_txt.css
+ 9 files

demo
demo_positioning.html
+ 5 files

Session 3.1 Visual Overview:

To horizontally center a block element, set the left and right margins to auto.

The **width** property defines the width of an element, the **max-width** property sets its maximum possible width, the **min-width** property sets its minimum width.

All horizontal list items are floated on the left to create columns.

The **display** property defines how an element should be laid out.

The **float** property takes an object out of normal document flow and floats it on the left or right margin of its container element.

The **clear** property displays the element only when the left, right, or both floated objects have been cleared.

The left and right column section are floated with widths of 33% and 67% respectively.

The vertical navigation list and Contact Info section are floated as separate columns.

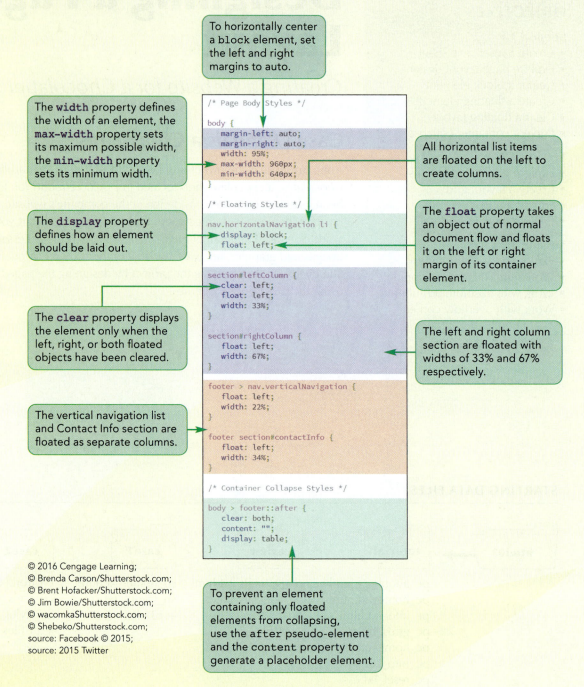

```
/* Page Body Styles */

body {
    margin-left: auto;
    margin-right: auto;
    width: 95%;
    max-width: 960px;
    min-width: 640px;
}

/* Floating Styles */

nav.horizontalNavigation li {
    display: block;
    float: left;
}

section#leftColumn {
    clear: left;
    float: left;
    width: 33%;
}

section#rightColumn {
    float: left;
    width: 67%;
}

footer > nav.verticalNavigation {
    float: left;
    width: 22%;
}

footer section#contactInfo {
    float: left;
    width: 34%;
}

/* Container Collapse Styles */

body > footer::after {
    clear: both;
    content: "";
    display: table;
}
```

To prevent an element containing only floated elements from collapsing, use the **after** pseudo-element and the **content** property to generate a placeholder element.

Page Layout with Floating Elements

Page body is horizontally centered within the browser window.

Horizontal list items are floated into separate columns.

Left and right sections are floated into separate columns.

The contents of the page footer are floated into separate columns.

Pandaisia Chocolates

414 Tree Lane • Essex, VT 05452

Home   Online Store   My Account   Specials   Contact Us

Pandaisia Chocolates has been creating gourmet chocolates and sweets for happy customers since 1993. Our hand-dipped truffles, savory chocolates, and mouth-watering toffees are made from the finest organic cacao. We use only natural ingredients with wildflower honey replacing corn syrup and cream that comes fresh from local dairy farms. Chocolate is an art: come tour our gallery.

Chocolates   Fudges   Toffees   Truffles

The Store
About Us
Facebook
Twitter
Reviews
Infographic

Products
Online Store
Gift Boxes
Collections
Weddings
Specials

Services
My Account
Order History
Tracking
Privacy Policy
Contact Us

Location & Hours
414 Tree Lane
Essex, Vermont 05452
(802) 555-0414

Mon - Thu: 9 a.m. - 8 p.m.
Sat - Sun: 9 a.m. - 5 p.m.

Toll Free: 1-800-555-0414

Introducing the `display` Style

The study of page layout starts with defining how an individual element is presented on the page. In the first tutorial, you learned that HTML elements are classified into block elements such as paragraphs or headings, or into inline elements, such as emphasized text or inline images. However, whether an element is displayed as a block or as inline depends on the style sheet. You can define the display style for any page element with the following `display` property

```
display: type;
```

where *type* defines the display type. A few of the many *type* values are shown in Figure 3-1.

Figure 3-1 **Some values of the display property**

Display Value	Appearance
`block`	Displayed as a block
`table`	Displayed as a web table
`inline`	Displayed in-line within a block
`inline-block`	Treated as a block placed in-line within another block
`run-in`	Displayed as a block unless its next sibling is also a block, in which case, it is displayed in-line, essentially combining the two blocks into one
`inherit`	Inherits the display property of the parent element
`list-item`	Displayed as a list item along with a bullet marker
`none`	Prevented from displaying, removing it from the rendered page

© 2016 Cengage Learning

For example, to supersede the usual browser style that displays images inline, you can apply the following style rule to display all of your images as blocks:

```
img {display: block;}
```

If you want to display all block quotes as list items, complete with list markers, you can add the following style rule to your style sheet:

```
blockquote {display: list-item;}
```

> **TIP**
>
> You also can hide elements by applying the style `visibility: hidden;`, which hides the element content but leaves the element still occupying the same space in the page.

You can even prevent browsers from displaying an element by setting its `display` property to `none`. In that case, the element is still part of the document structure but it is not shown to users and does not occupy space in the displayed page. This is useful for elements that include content that users shouldn't see or have no need to see.

You'll use the `display` property in creating a reset style sheet.

Creating a Reset Style Sheet

You learned in the last tutorial that your browser applies its own styles to your page elements unless those styles are superseded by your own style sheet. Many designers prefer to work with a "clean slate" and not have any browser style rules creep into the final design of their website. This can be accomplished with a **reset style sheet** that supersedes the browser's default styles and provides a consistent starting point for page design.

You'll create a reset style sheet for the Pandaisia Chocolates website. The first style rules in your sheet will use the `display` property to display all of the HTML5 structural elements in your web page as blocks. While current browsers already do this, there are some older browsers that do not recognize or have predefined display styles for elements as such `header`, `article`, or `footer`. By including the `display` property in a reset style sheet, you add a little insurance that these structural elements will be rendered correctly.

To create a reset style sheet:

1. Use the text editor or HTML editor of your choice to open the **pc_reset_txt.css** file from the html03 ▸ tutorial folder. Enter **your name** and **the date** in the comment section of the file and save the document as **pc_reset.css**.

2. Within the Structural Styles section, insert the following style rule to define the display properties of several HTML5 structural elements.

```
article, aside, figcaption, figure,
footer, header, main, nav, section {
    display: block;
}
```

Figure 3-2 highlights the new style rule in the document.

Figure 3-2   Displaying HTML5 structural elements as blocks

```
/* Structural Styles */

article, aside, figcaption, figure,
footer, header, main, nav, section {
    display: block;
}
```

You will complete the reset style sheet by adding other style rules that set default padding and margins around commonly used page elements, define some basic typographic properties, and remove underlining from hypertext links found within navigation lists.

To complete the reset style sheet:

1. Within the Typographic Styles section, insert the following style rule to define the typographic styles for several page elements:

```
address, article, aside, blockquote, body, cite,
div, dl, dt, dd, em, figcaption, figure, footer,
h1, h2, h3, h4, h5, h6, header, html, img,
li, main, nav, ol, p, section, span, ul {

    background: transparent;
    font-size: 100%;
    margin: 0;
    padding: 0;
    vertical-align: baseline;
}
```

2. Add the following style rules to remove list markers from list items found within navigation lists:

```
nav ul {
    list-style: none;
    list-style-image: none;
}


nav a {
    text-decoration: none;
}
```

3. Set the default line height to 1 (single-spaced) by applying the following style rule to the page body:

```
body {
    line-height: 1;
}
```

Figure 3-3 describes the new style rules in the document.

Figure 3-3   **Completing the reset style sheet**

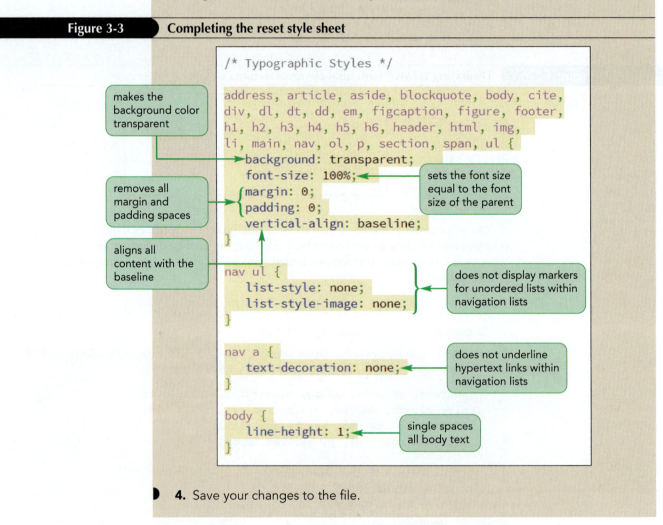

```
/* Typographic Styles */

address, article, aside, blockquote, body, cite,
div, dl, dt, dd, em, figcaption, figure, footer,
h1, h2, h3, h4, h5, h6, header, html, img,
li, main, nav, ol, p, section, span, ul {
    background: transparent;
    font-size: 100%;
    margin: 0;
    padding: 0;
    vertical-align: baseline;
}

nav ul {
    list-style: none;
    list-style-image: none;
}

nav a {
    text-decoration: none;
}

body {
    line-height: 1;
}
```

makes the background color transparent

removes all margin and padding spaces

aligns all content with the baseline

sets the font size equal to the font size of the parent

does not display markers for unordered lists within navigation lists

does not underline hypertext links within navigation lists

single spaces all body text

4. Save your changes to the file.

This is a very basic reset style sheet. There are premade reset style sheets freely available on the web that contain more style rules used to reconcile the various differences between browsers and devices. Before using any of these reset style sheets, you should study the CSS code and make sure that it meets the needs of your website. Be aware that some reset style sheets may contain more style rules than you actually need and you can speed up your website by paring down the reset sheet to use only the elements you need for your website.

The first page you will work on for Pandaisia Chocolates is the site's home page. Anne has already created a typographical style sheet in the pc_styles1.css file. Link to the style sheet file now as well as the pc_reset.css style sheet you just created and the pc_home.css style sheet that you will work on for the remainder of this session to design the page layout.

To get started on the Pandaisia Chocolates home page:

1. Use your editor to open the **pc_home_txt.css** file from the html03 ▸ tutorial folder. Enter **your name** and **the date** in the comment section of the file and save the document as **pc_home.css**.

2. Use your editor to open the **pc_home_txt.html** file from the same folder. Enter **your name** and **the date** in the comment section and save the file as **pc_home.html**.

3. Within the document head, directly after the `title` element, insert the following `link` elements to link the home page to the pc_reset.css, pc_styles1.css, and pc_home.css style sheets.

   ```
   <link href="pc_reset.css" rel="stylesheet" />
   <link href="pc_styles1.css" rel="stylesheet" />
   <link href="pc_home.css" rel="stylesheet" />
   ```

4. Take some time to study the content and structure of the pc_home.html document. Pay particular attention to the use of ID and class names throughout the document.

5. Save your changes to the file. You might want to keep this file open as you work with the pc_home.css style sheet so that you can refer to its content and structure.

TIP

The reset style sheet should *always* be the first style sheet listed before any other style sheets to ensure that your default styles are applied first.

Anne has sketched the general layout she wants for the home page, shown in Figure 3-4. Compare the pc_home.html file content to the sketch shown in Figure 3-4 to get a better understanding of how the page content relates to Anne's proposed layout.

Figure 3-4   **Proposed home page layout**

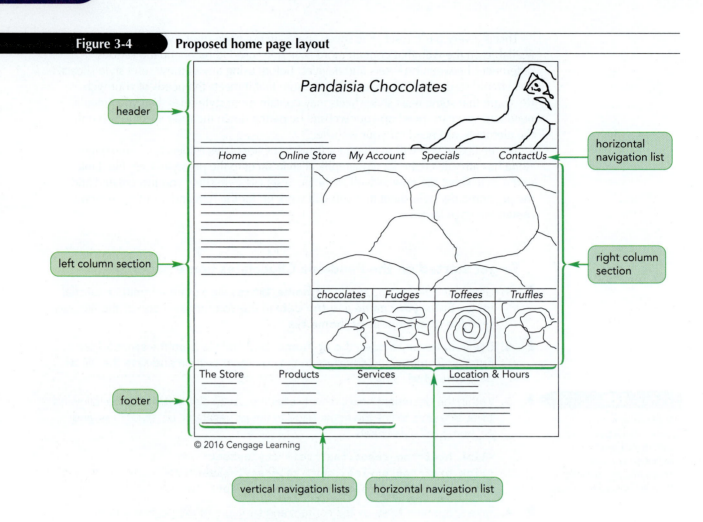

© 2016 Cengage Learning

Before creating the page layout that Anne has sketched out for you, you'll examine different types of layout designs.

Exploring Page Layout Designs

One challenge of layout is that your document will be viewed on many different devices with different screen resolutions. When designing for the web, you're usually more concerned about the available screen width than screen height because users can scroll vertically down the length of the page, but it is considered bad design to make them scroll horizontally.

A page designer needs to cope with a wide range of possible screen widths ranging from wide screen monitors with widths of 1680 pixels or more, down to mobile devices with screen widths of 320 pixels and even less. Complicating matters even more is that a screen width represents the maximum space available to the user, but some space is always taken up by toolbars, sidebar panes and other browser features. In addition, the user might not even have the browser window maximized to fill the entire screen. Thus, you need a layout plan that will accommodate a myriad of screen resolutions and browser configurations.

Fixed, Fluid, and Elastic Layouts

Web page layouts fall into three general categories: fixed, fluid, and elastic. A **fixed layout** is one in which the size of the page and the size of the page elements are fixed, usually using pixels as the unit of measure. The page width might be set at 960 pixels and the width of the company logo set to 780 pixels. These widths are set regardless of the screen resolution of the user's device and this can result in the page not fitting into the browser window if the device's screen is not wide enough.

By contrast, a **fluid layout** sets the width of page elements as a percent of the available screen width. For example, the width of the page body might be set to fill 90% of the screen and the width of the company logo might be set to fill 80% of that page body. Under a fluid layout, the page resizes automatically to match the screen resolution of the user's device. Figure 3-5 shows how a three-column layout might appear in both a fixed and a fluid design.

Figure 3-5   **Fixed layouts vs. fluid layouts**

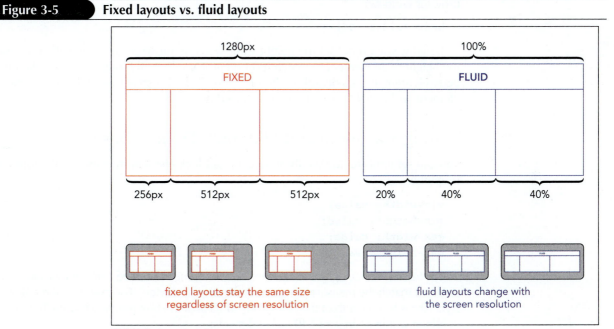

© 2016 Cengage Learning

With different devices accessing your website, it's usually best to work with a fluid layout that is more adaptable to a range of screen resolutions. Fixed layouts should only be used when you have more control over the devices that will display your page, such as a web page created specifically for a digital kiosk at a conference.

Another layout design is an **elastic layout** in which all measurements are expressed in em units and based on the default font size used in the page. If a user or the designer increases the font size, then the width, height, and location of all of the other page elements, including images, change to match. Thus, images and text are always sized in proportion to each other and the layout never changes with different font sizes. The disadvantage to this approach is that, because sizing is based on the font size and not on the screen resolution, there is a danger that if a user sets the default font size large enough, the page will extend beyond the boundaries of the browser window.

Finally, the web is moving quickly toward the principles of **responsive design** in which the layout and design of the page changes in response to the device that is rendering it. The page will have one set of styles for mobile devices, another for tablets, and yet another for laptops or desktop computers. You'll explore how to implement responsive design in Tutorial 5.

Because width is such an integral part of layout, you will start designing the Pandaisia Chocolates home page by defining the width of the page body and elements within the page.

Working with Width and Height

The width and height of an element are set using the following `width` and `height` properties

```
width: value;
height: value;
```

where `value` is the width or height using one of the CSS units of measurement or as a percentage of the width or height of the parent element. For example, the following style rule sets the width of the page body to 95% of the width of its parent element (the browser window):

```
body {width: 95%;}
```

Usually, you do not set the height value because browsers automatically increase the height of an element to match its content. Note that all block elements, like the `body` element, have a default width of 100%. Thus, this style rule makes the `body` element width slightly smaller than it would be by default.

Setting Maximum and Minimum Dimensions

You can set limits on the width or height of a block element by applying the following properties

```
min-width: value;
min-height: value;
max-width: value;
max-height: value;
```

where `value` is once again a length expressed in one of the CSS units of measure (usually pixels to match the measurement unit of the display device). For example, the following style rule sets the width of the page body to 95% of the browser window width but confined within a range of 640 to 1680 pixels:

```
body {
    width: 95%;
    min-width: 640px;
    max-width: 1680px;
}
```

Maximum and minimum widths are often used to make page text easier to read. Studies have shown that lines of text that are too wide are difficult to read because the eye has to scan across a long section of content and that lines of text that are too narrow with too many line returns, break the flow of the material.

REFERENCE

Setting Widths and Heights

- To set the width and height of an element, use the styles

```
width: value;
height: value;
```

where *value* is the width or height in one of the CSS units of measurement or a percentage of the width or height of the parent element.
- To set the minimum possible width or height, use the styles

```
min-width: value;
min-height: value;
```

- To set the maximum possible width or height, use the styles

```
max-width: value;
max-height: value;
```

Set the width of the page body for the Pandaisia Chocolates home page to 95% of the browser window ranging from 640 pixels to 960 pixels. Also display the company logo image as a block with its width set to 100% so that it extends across the page body. You do not have to set the height of the logo because the browser will automatically scale the height to keep the original proportions of the image.

To set the initial dimensions of the page:

1. Return to the **pc_home.css** file in your editor and add the following style rule to the Body Styles section:

```
body {
    max-width: 960px;
    min-width: 640px;
    width: 95%;
}
```

2. Within the Body Header Styles section insert the following style rule to set the display type and width of the logo image:

```
body > header > img {
    display: block;
    width: 100%;
}
```

Figure 3-6 highlights the newly added style rules in the style sheet.

Figure 3-6 Setting the width of the page body and logo

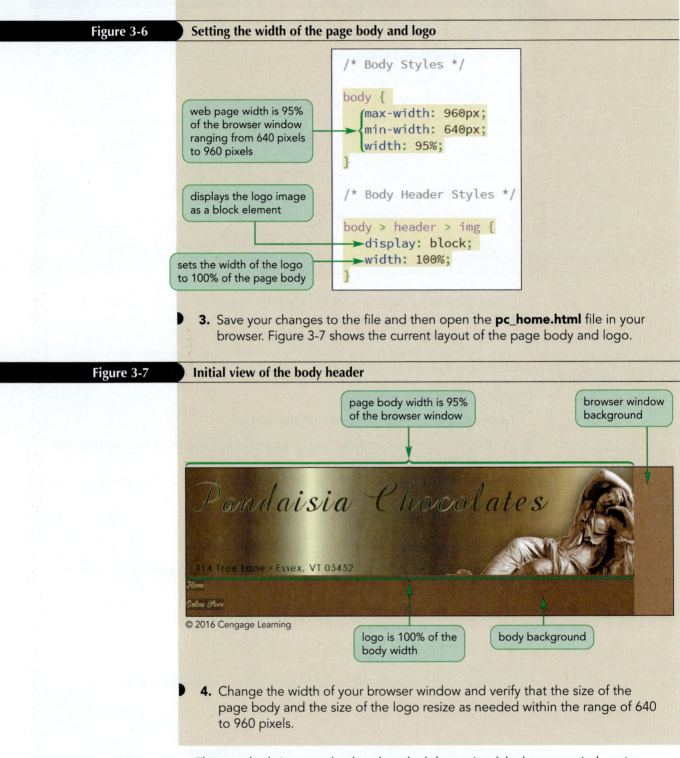

web page width is 95% of the browser window ranging from 640 pixels to 960 pixels

displays the logo image as a block element

sets the width of the logo to 100% of the page body

```
/* Body Styles */

body {
    max-width: 960px;
    min-width: 640px;
    width: 95%;
}

/* Body Header Styles */

body > header > img {
    display: block;
    width: 100%;
}
```

3. Save your changes to the file and then open the **pc_home.html** file in your browser. Figure 3-7 shows the current layout of the page body and logo.

Figure 3-7 Initial view of the body header

page body width is 95% of the browser window

browser window background

Pandaisia Chocolates

414 Tree Lane • Essex, VT 05452

Home

Online Store

© 2016 Cengage Learning

logo is 100% of the body width

body background

4. Change the width of your browser window and verify that the size of the page body and the size of the logo resize as needed within the range of 640 to 960 pixels.

The page body is currently placed on the left margin of the browser window. Anne would like it centered horizontally within the browser window.

Centering a Block Element

Block elements can be centered horizontally within their parent element by setting both the left and right margins to auto. Thus, you can center the page body within the browser window using the style rule:

```
body {
    margin-left: auto;
    margin-right: auto;
}
```

Modify the style rule for the page body to center the Pandaisia Chocolates home page horizontally by setting the left and right margins to auto.

To center the page body horizontally:

1. Return to the **pc_home.css** file in your editor and, within the style rule for the body selector, insert the properties:

```
margin-left: auto;
margin-right: auto;
```

Figure 3-8 highlights the newly added styles.

Figure 3-8   Centering the page body

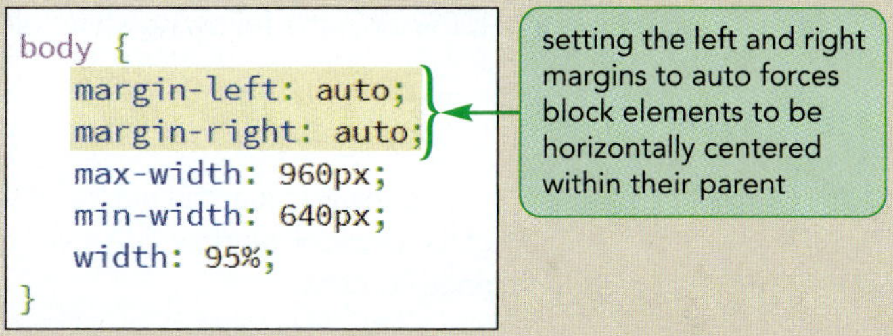

```
body {
    margin-left: auto;
    margin-right: auto;
    max-width: 960px;
    min-width: 640px;
    width: 95%;
}
```

setting the left and right margins to auto forces block elements to be horizontally centered within their parent

2. Save your changes to the file and then reload the **pc_home.html** file in your browser. Verify that the page body is now centered within the browser window.

Working with Element Heights

The fact that an element's height is based on its content can cause some confusion. For example, the following style rule appears to set the height of the header to 50% of the height of the page body:

```
body > header {height: 50%;}
```

However, because the total height of the page body depends on the height of its individual elements, including the body header, there is circular reasoning in this style rule. You can't set the page body height without knowing the height of the body header and you can't set the body header height unless you know the height of the page body. Most browsers deal with this circularity by leaving the body header height undefined, resulting in no change in the layout.

Heights need to be based on known values, as in the following style rules where the body height is set to 1200 pixels and thus the body header is set to half of that or 600 pixels.

```
body {height: 1200px;}
body > header {height: 50%;}
```

It is common in page layout design to extend the page body to the height of the browser window. To accomplish this, you set the height of the `html` element to 100% so that it matches the browser window height (a known value defined by the physical properties of the screen) and then you set the minimum height of the page body to 100% as in the following style rules:

```
html {height: 100%;}
body {min-height: 100%;}
```

The result is that the height of the page body will always be at least equal to the height of the browser window, but it will extend beyond that if necessary to accommodate extra page content.

Vertical Centering

Centering an element vertically within its parent element is not easily accomplished because the height of the parent element is usually determined by its content, which might not be a defined value. One solution is to display the parent element as a table cell with a defined height and then set the `vertical-align` property set to `middle`. For example, to vertically center the following h1 heading within the `div` element

```
<div>
    <h1>Pandaisia Chocolates</h1>
</div>
```

you would apply the style rule:

```
div {
    height: 40px;
    display: table-cell;
    vertical-align: middle;
}
```

Using this style rule, the h1 heading will be vertically centered.

To vertically center a single line of text within its parent element, set the line height of the text larger than the text's font size. The following style rule will result in an h1 heading with vertically centered heading text.

```
h1 {
    font-size: 1.4em;
    line-height: 2em;
}
```

Note that this approach will only work for a single line of text. If the text wraps to a second line, it will no longer be vertically centered. Vertical centering is a common design challenge and there are several other workarounds that have been devised over the years. You can do a search on the web for other solutions to vertical centering.

Next, you will lay out the links in the navigation list. Anne wants the links displayed horizontally rather than vertically. You can accomplish this using CSS floats.

Floating Page Content

By default, content is displayed in the page in the order it appears within the HTML file as part of the normal document flow. **Floating** an element takes it out of position and places it along the left or right edge of its parent element. Subsequent content that is not floated occupies the space previously taken up by the floated element. Figure 3-9 shows a diagram of an element that is floated along the right margin of its container and its effect on the placement of subsequent content.

 Figure 3-9   Floating an element

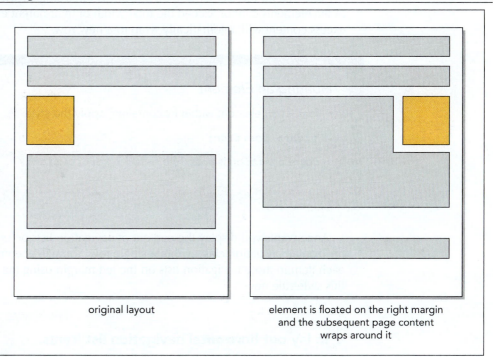

original layout

element is floated on the right margin and the subsequent page content wraps around it

© 2016 Cengage Learning

To float an element, apply the following `float` property

```
float: position;
```

where *position* is none (the default), `left` to float the object on the left margin, or `right` to float the object on the right margin. If sibling elements are floated along the same margin, they are placed alongside each other within a row as shown in Figure 3-10.

Figure 3-10 Floating multiple elements in a row

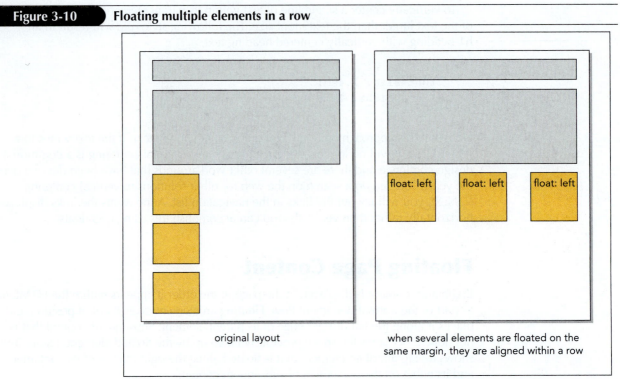

original layout

when several elements are floated on the same margin, they are aligned within a row

© 2016 Cengage Learning

Note that for the elements to be placed within a single row, the combined width of the elements cannot exceed the total width of their parent element, otherwise any excess content will automatically wrap to a new row.

Floating an Element

- To float an element within its container, apply the style

  ```
  float: position;
  ```

  where *position* is none (the default), `left`, or `right`.

Anne wants you display the content of navigation lists belonging to the horizontalNavigation class within a single row. You will accomplish this by floating each item in those navigation lists on the left margin using the `float` property. Create this style rule now.

To lay out horizontal navigation list items:

1. Return to the **pc_home.css** file in your editor and go to the Body Header Styles section.

2. Because there are five links in the navigation list, you'll make each list item 20% of the width of the navigation list by adding the following style rule:

```
body > header > nav.horizontalNavigation li {
    width: 20%;
}
```

To be confined to a single row, the total width of floated elements cannot exceed the width of the container.

3. Insert the following style rule within the Horizontal Navigation Styles section to display every list item within a horizontal navigation list as a block floated on the left.

```
nav.horizontalNavigation li {
    display: block;
    float: left;
}
```

Figure 3-11 highlights the styles used with list items.

Figure 3-11   **Floating items in the navigation list**

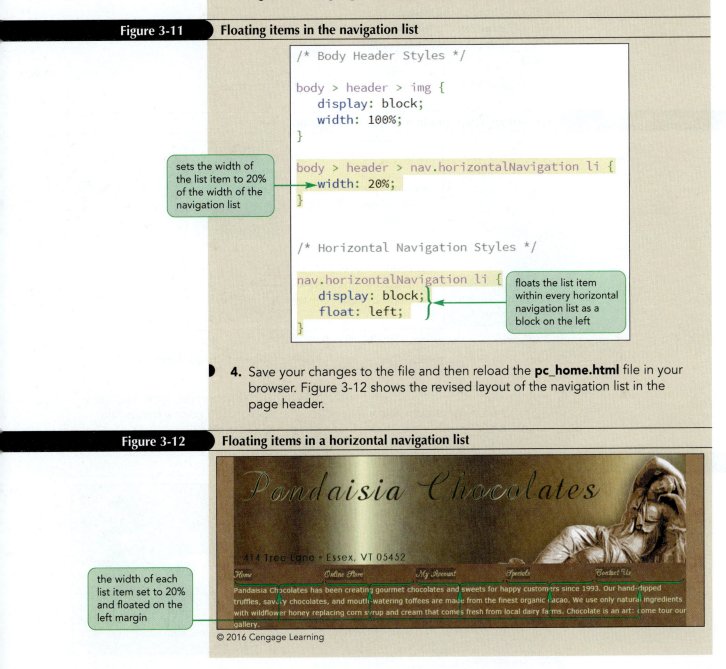

```
/* Body Header Styles */

body > header > img {
    display: block;
    width: 100%;
}

body > header > nav.horizontalNavigation li {
    width: 20%;
}


/* Horizontal Navigation Styles */

nav.horizontalNavigation li {
    display: block;
    float: left;
}
```

sets the width of the list item to 20% of the width of the navigation list

floats the list item within every horizontal navigation list as a block on the left

4. Save your changes to the file and then reload the **pc_home.html** file in your browser. Figure 3-12 shows the revised layout of the navigation list in the page header.

Figure 3-12   **Floating items in a horizontal navigation list**

Pandaisia Chocolates

414 Tree Lane • Essex, VT 05452

Home   Online Store   My Account   Specials   Contact Us

Pandaisia Chocolates has been creating gourmet chocolates and sweets for happy customers since 1993. Our hand-dipped truffles, savory chocolates, and mouth-watering toffees are made from the finest organic cacao. We use only natural ingredients with wildflower honey replacing corn syrup and cream that comes fresh from local dairy farms. Chocolate is an art: come tour our gallery.

the width of each list item set to 20% and floated on the left margin

© 2016 Cengage Learning

Anne doesn't like the appearance of the hypertext links in the navigation list. Because the links are inline elements, the background color extends only as far as the link text. She suggests you change the links to block elements and center the link text within each block.

To change the display of the hypertext links:

1. Return to the **pc_home.css** file in your editor.

2. Within the Horizontal Navigation Styles section, insert the following style rule to format the appearance of the hypertext links within the horizontal navigation lists.

```
nav.horizontalNavigation a {
    display: block;
    text-align: center;
}
```

Figure 3-13 highlights the style rule for the hypertext links.

Figure 3-13	Formatting hyperlinks in horizontal navigation lists

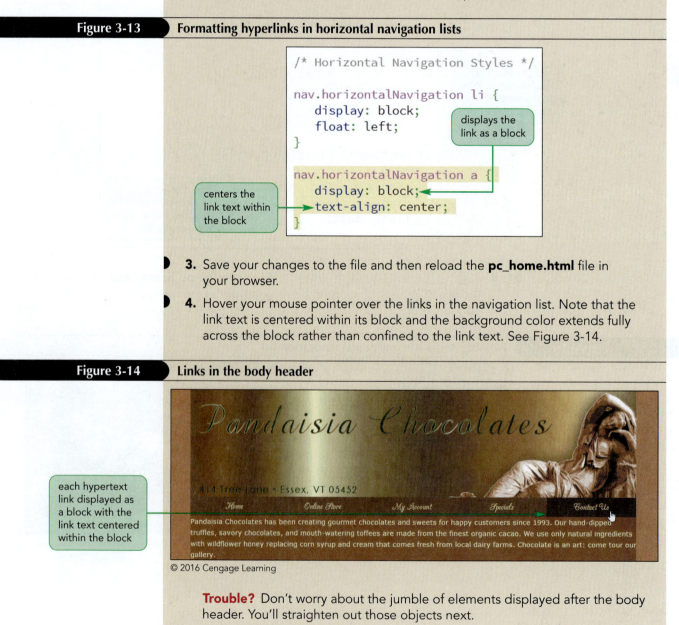

3. Save your changes to the file and then reload the **pc_home.html** file in your browser.

4. Hover your mouse pointer over the links in the navigation list. Note that the link text is centered within its block and the background color extends fully across the block rather than confined to the link text. See Figure 3-14.

Figure 3-14	Links in the body header

© 2016 Cengage Learning

Trouble? Don't worry about the jumble of elements displayed after the body header. You'll straighten out those objects next.

You have completed the design of the body header. Next, you will lay out the middle section of the home page.

Clearing a Float

In some layouts, you will want an element to be displayed on a new row, clear of previously floated objects. To ensure that an element is always displayed below your floated elements, apply the following `clear` property:

    clear: *position*;

where *position* is `left`, `right`, `both`, or `none`. A value of `left` displays the element only when the left margin is clear of floating objects. A value of `right` displays the element only when the right margin is clear. A value of `both` displays the element only when both margins are clear of floats. The default clear value is `none`, which allows the element to be displayed alongside any floated objects.

Figure 3-15 shows how use of the `clear` property prevents an element from being displayed until the right margin is clear of floats. The effect on the page layout is that the element is shifted down and is free to use the entire page width since it is no longer displayed alongside a floating object.

Figure 3-15	Clearing a float

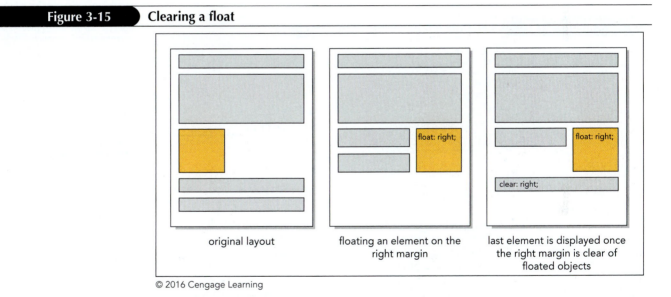

original layout

floating an element on the right margin

last element is displayed once the right margin is clear of floated objects

© 2016 Cengage Learning

The next part of the Pandaisia Chocolates home page contains two `section` elements named "leftColumn" and "rightColumn". Set the width of the left column to 33% of the body width and set the width of the right column to 67%. Float the sections side-by-side on the left margin, but only when the left margin is clear of all previously floated objects.

To float the left and right column sections:

1. Return to the **pc_home.css** file in your editor. Go to the Left Column Styles section and insert the style rule:

```
section#leftColumn {
    clear: left;
    float: left;
    width: 33%;
}
```

2. Within the Right Column Styles section, insert:

```
section#rightColumn {
    float: left;
    width: 67%;
}
```

Note that you do not apply the `clear` property to the right column because you want it to be displayed in the same row alongside the left column. Figure 3-16 highlights the style rules for the left and right columns.

Figure 3-16 **Float the left and right column sections**

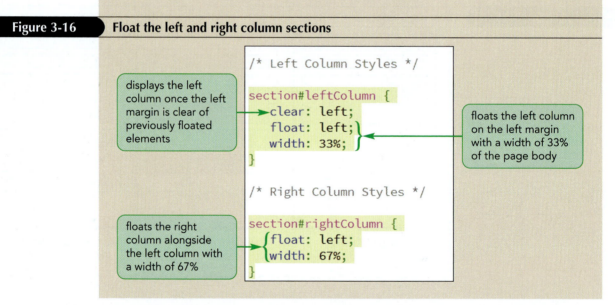

The right column contains a horizontal navigation list containing four items, each consisting of an image and a label above the image. Anne wants the four items placed side-by-side with their widths set to 25% of the width of the navigation list. Anne also wants the images in the right column displayed as blocks with their widths set to 100% of their parent element.

To complete the right column section:

1. Within the Right Column Styles section, insert the following style rules to format the inline images and list items:

```
section#rightColumn img {
   display: block;
   width: 100%;
}


section#rightColumn > nav.horizontalNavigation li {
   width: 25%;
}
```

Note that you do not have to include a style rule to float the items in the horizontal navigation list because you have already created that style rule in Figure 3-11. Figure 3-17 describes the new style rules in the style sheet.

Figure 3-17   **Formatting the right column section**

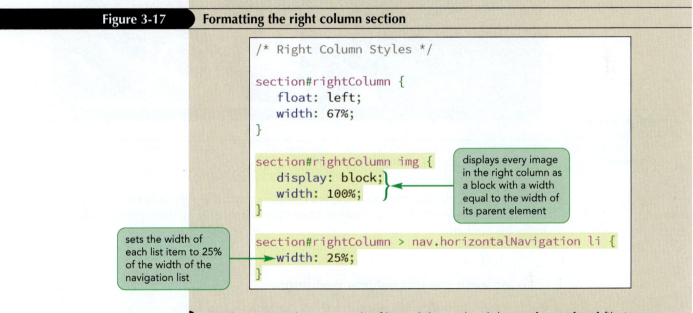

```
/* Right Column Styles */

section#rightColumn {
   float: left;
   width: 67%;
}

section#rightColumn img {
   display: block;
   width: 100%;
}

section#rightColumn > nav.horizontalNavigation li {
   width: 25%;
}
```

displays every image in the right column as a block with a width equal to the width of its parent element

sets the width of each list item to 25% of the width of the navigation list

2. Save your changes to the file and then reload the **pc_home.html** file in your browser. Figure 3-18 shows the layout of the left and right column sections.

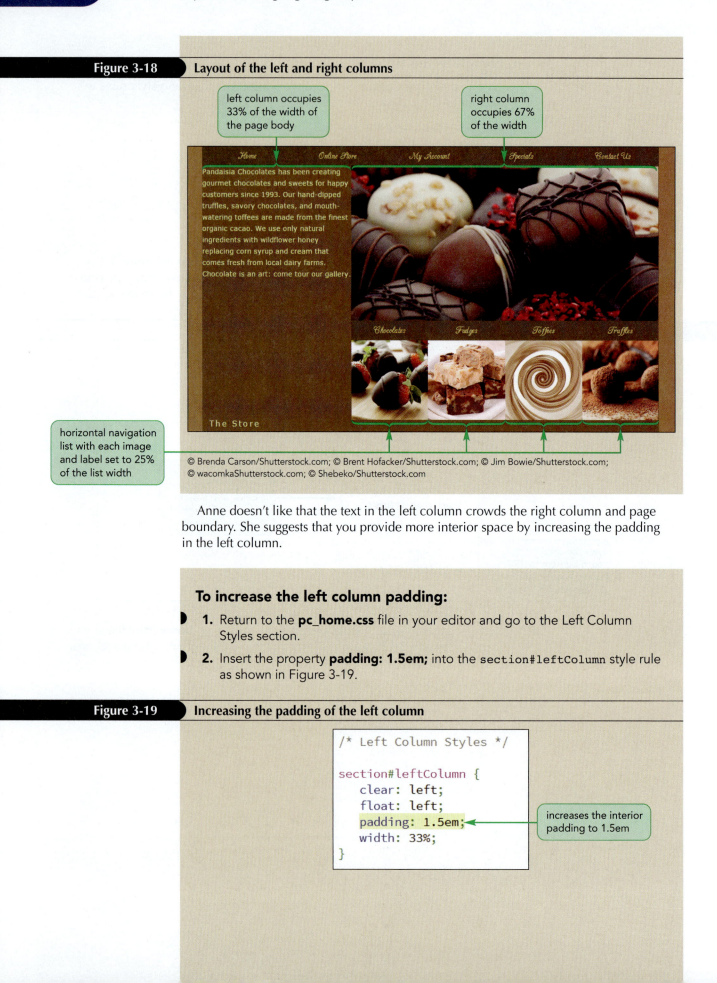

Figure 3-18 Layout of the left and right columns

left column occupies 33% of the width of the page body

right column occupies 67% of the width

horizontal navigation list with each image and label set to 25% of the list width

© Brenda Carson/Shutterstock.com; © Brent Hofacker/Shutterstock.com; © Jim Bowie/Shutterstock.com; © wacomkaShutterstock.com; © Shebeko/Shutterstock.com

Anne doesn't like that the text in the left column crowds the right column and page boundary. She suggests that you provide more interior space by increasing the padding in the left column.

To increase the left column padding:

1. Return to the **pc_home.css** file in your editor and go to the Left Column Styles section.

2. Insert the property **padding: 1.5em;** into the `section#leftColumn` style rule as shown in Figure 3-19.

Figure 3-19 Increasing the padding of the left column

```
/* Left Column Styles */

section#leftColumn {
    clear: left;
    float: left;
    padding: 1.5em;
    width: 33%;
}
```

increases the interior padding to 1.5em

3. Save your changes to the style sheet and then reload the **pc_home.html** file in your browser. Figure 3-20 shows the result of your change.

Figure 3-20   **Page layout crashes with increased padding**

increased padding increases the width of the left column, making it bigger than 33% of the page body width

the right column is forced to wrap to a new row, ruining the page layout

© Brenda Carson/Shutterstock.com; source: Facebook © 2015; source: 2015 Twitter

This simple change has caused the layout to crash. What went wrong?

Refining a Floated Layout

When the total width of floated objects exceeds the width of their parent, excess content is automatically wrapped to a new row. The reason the layout for the Pandaisia Chocolates home page crashed is that increasing the padding in the left column, increased the column's width beyond its set value of 33%. Even this small increase caused the total width of the two columns to exceed 100% and, as a result, the right column moved to a new row.

To keep floats within the same row, you have to understand how CSS handles widths. Recall that block elements are laid out according to the box model, as illustrated previously in Figure 2-38, in which the content is surrounded by the padding space, the border space, and finally the margin space. By default, browsers measure widths using the **content box model** in which the width property only refers to the width of the element content and any padding or borders constitute added space.

CSS also supports the **border box model**, in which the width property is based on the sum of the content, padding, and border spaces and any space taken up by the padding and border is subtracted from space given to the content. Figure 3-21 shows how the two different models interpret the same width, padding, and border values.

Figure 3-21 **Comparing the Content Box and Border Box models**

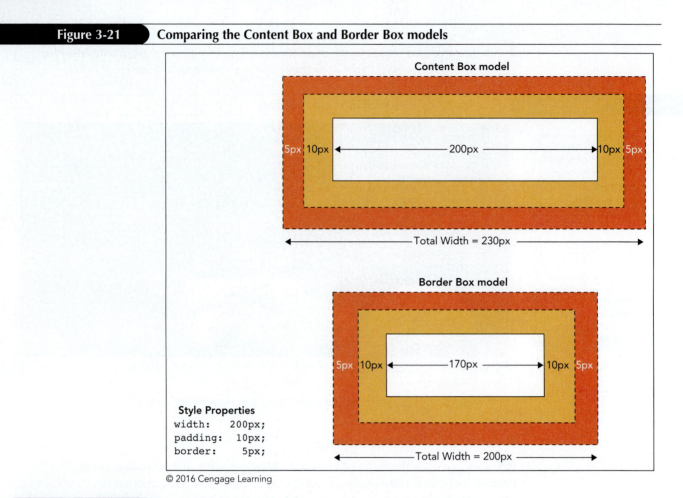

© 2016 Cengage Learning

You can choose the layout model using the following `box-sizing` property

```
box-sizing: type;
```

where `type` is `content-box` (the default), `border-box`, or `inherit` (to inherit the property defined for the element's container). This CSS3 `box-sizing` property was initially introduced as a browser extension, so, in order to support older browsers, it is commonly entered using progressive enhancement with the following extensions

```
-webkit-box-sizing: type;
-moz-box-sizing: type;
box-sizing: type;
```

where `type` has the same values as before. Many designers prefer to use the border box model in page layout so that there is no confusion about the total width of each element.

REFERENCE

Defining How Widths Are Interpreted

• To define what the `width` property measures, use the style:

```
box-sizing: type;
```

where `type` is `content-box` (the default), `border-box`, or `inherit` (to inherit the property defined for the element's container).

Add the `box-sizing` property to the reset style sheet and apply it to all block elements.

To set the block layout model:

1. Return to the **pc_reset.css** file in your editor.

2. Add the following style properties to the style rule for the list of block elements

   ```
   -webkit-box-sizing: border-box;
   -moz-box-sizing: border-box;
   box-sizing: border-box;
   ```

   Figure 3-22 highlights the revised style rule.

Figure 3-22   Adding the border-box style to the reset style sheet

```
address, article, aside, blockquote, body, cite,
div, dl, dt, dd, em, figcaption, figure, footer,
h1, h2, h3, h4, h5, h6, header, html, img,
li, main, nav, ol, p, section, span, ul {
    background: transparent;
    font-size: 100%;
    margin: 0;
    padding: 0;
    vertical-align: baseline;
    -webkit-box-sizing: border-box;
    -moz-box-sizing: border-box;
    box-sizing: border-box;
}
```

applies border box sizing to all of the listed block elements

3. Save your changes to the style sheet and then reload the **pc_home.html** file in your browser. Verify that the layout of the left and right columns has been restored and additional padding has been added within the left column.

The final part of the Pandaisia Chocolates home page is the footer, which contains three vertical navigation lists and a `section` element with contact information for the store. Once the left margin is clear of previously floated objects, float these four elements on the left margin with the widths of the three navigation lists each set to 22% of the body width and the `section` element occupying the remaining 34%.

To lay out the page footer:

1. Return to the **pc_home.css** file in your editor and scroll down to the Footer Styles section.

2. Insert the following style rules:

   ```
   footer {
       clear: left;
   }

   footer > nav.verticalNavigation {
       float: left;
       width: 22%;
   }
   ```

```
footer > section#contactInfo {
    float: left;
    width: 34%;
}
```

Figure 3-23 highlights the layout style rules for the page footer.

Figure 3-23   **Setting the layout of the page footer**

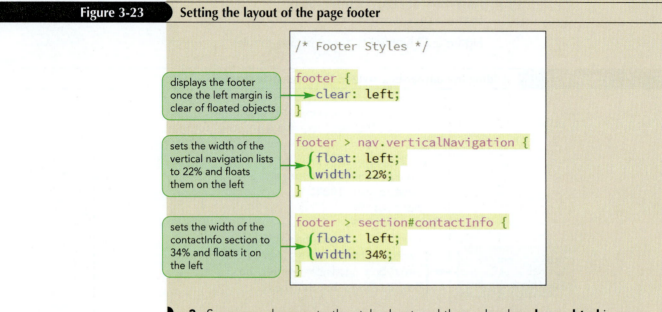

```
/* Footer Styles */

footer {
    clear: left;
}
```
displays the footer once the left margin is clear of floated objects

```
footer > nav.verticalNavigation {
    float: left;
    width: 22%;
}
```
sets the width of the vertical navigation lists to 22% and floats them on the left

```
footer > section#contactInfo {
    float: left;
    width: 34%;
}
```
sets the width of the contactInfo section to 34% and floats it on the left

3. Save your changes to the style sheet and then reload **pc_home.html** in your browser. Figure 3-24 shows the new layout of the footer.

Figure 3-24   **Page footer layout**

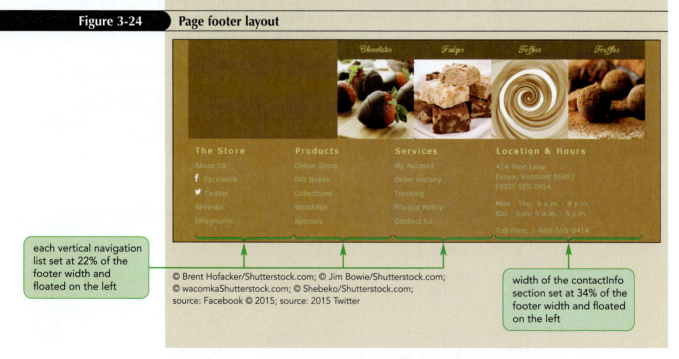

each vertical navigation list set at 22% of the footer width and floated on the left

width of the contactInfo section set at 34% of the footer width and floated on the left

© Brent Hofacker/Shutterstock.com; © Jim Bowie/Shutterstock.com;
© wacomkaShutterstock.com; © Shebeko/Shutterstock.com;
source: Facebook © 2015; source: 2015 Twitter

Anne asks you to change the background color of the footer to a dark brown to better show the text content.

To set the footer background color:

▶ **1.** Return to the **pc_home.css** file in your editor and go to the Footer Styles section.

▶ **2.** Insert the following property for the `footer` selector:

```
background-color: rgb(71, 52, 29);
```

Figure 3-25 highlights the footer background color style.

Figure 3-25 **Setting the footer background color**

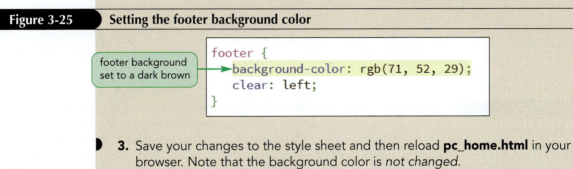

footer background set to a dark brown

```
footer {
    background-color: rgb(71, 52, 29);
    clear: left;
}
```

▶ **3.** Save your changes to the style sheet and then reload **pc_home.html** in your browser. Note that the background color is *not changed*.

Why didn't the change to the background color take effect? To help you understand why, you'll look once again at the nature of floated elements.

Working with Container Collapse

Recall that a floated element is taken out of the document flow so that it is no longer "part" of the element that contains it. Literally it is floating free of its container. When every element in a container is floated, there is no content left. As far as the browser is concerned, the container is empty and thus has no height and no background to color, a situation known as **container collapse**. Figure 3-26 demonstrates container collapse for a container that has three floating objects that exceed the boundaries of their container.

Figure 3-26 **Container collapse**

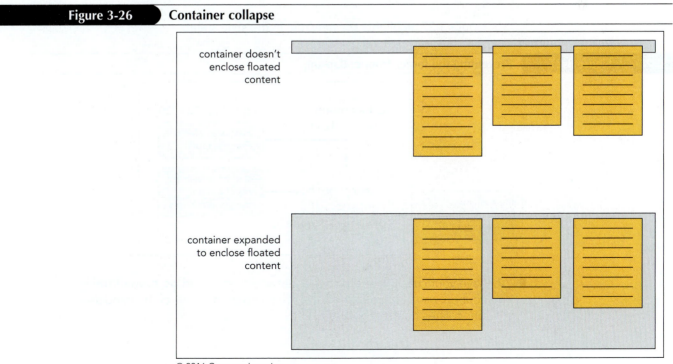

container doesn't enclose floated content

container expanded to enclose floated content

© 2016 Cengage Learning

What you usually want in your layout is to have the container expand to surround all of its floating content. One way this can occur is if the container is followed by another element that is displayed only when the margins are clear of floats. In that situation, the container's height will expand up to that trailing element and in the process surround its floating content.

The problem with the footer in the Pandaisia home page is that there is no trailing element—the footer is the last element in the page body. One way to fix that problem is to use the `after` pseudo-element to add a placeholder element after the footer. The general style rule is

```
container::after {
    clear: both;
    content: "";
    display: table;
}
```

TIP

To find other ways to prevent container collapse, search the web using the keywords *CSS clearfix*.

where `container` is the selector for the element containing floating objects. The `clear` property keeps this placeholder element from being inserted until both margins are clear of floats. The element itself is a web table but contains only an empty text string so that no actual content is written to the web page. That's okay because the mere presence of this placeholder element is enough to keep the container from collapsing.

Add a style rule now to create a placeholder element that keeps the footer from collapsing around its floating content.

To keep the footer from collapsing:

1. Return to Footer Styles section in the **pc_home.css** file and, after the style rule for the footer element, insert the following rule:

```
footer::after {
    clear: both;
    content: "";
    display: table;
}
```

Figure 3-27 highlights the new rule in the style sheet.

Figure 3-27 **Preventing the footer from collapsing**

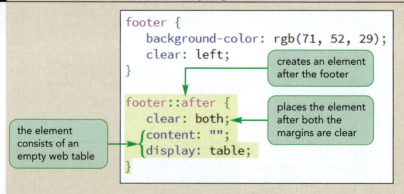

2. Save your changes to the style sheet and then reload **pc_home.html** in your browser. Figure 3-28 shows the completed layout of the Pandaisia Chocolates home page.

| Figure 3-28 | Final layout of the Pandaisia Chocolates home page |

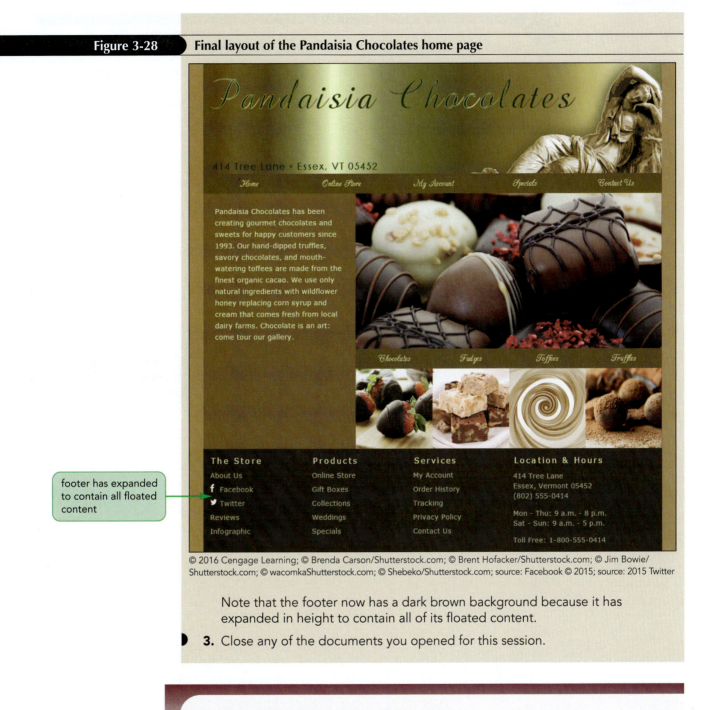

footer has expanded to contain all floated content

Note that the footer now has a dark brown background because it has expanded in height to contain all of its floated content.

3. Close any of the documents you opened for this session.

REFERENCE

Keeping a Container from Collapsing

- To prevent a container from collapsing around its floating content, add the following style rule to the container

```
container::after {
   clear: both;
   content: "";
   display: table;
}
```

where *container* is the selector for the element containing the floating content.

PROSKILLS

Problem Solving: The Virtue of Being Negative

It's common to think of layout in terms of placing content, but good layout also must be concerned with placing emptiness. In art and page design, this is known as working with positive and negative space. Positive space is the part of the page occupied by text, graphics, borders, icons, and other page elements. Negative space, or white space, is the unoccupied area, and provides balance and contrast to elements contained in positive space.

A page that is packed with content leaves the eye with no place to rest; which also means that the eye has no place to focus and maybe even no clear indication about where to start reading. Negative space is used to direct users to resting stops before moving on to the next piece of page content. This can be done by providing a generous margin between page elements and by increasing the padding within an element. Even increasing the spacing between letters within an article heading can alleviate eye strain and make the text easier to read.

White space also has an emotional aspect. In the early days of print advertising, white space was seen as wasted space, and thus, smaller magazines and direct mail advertisements would tend to crowd content together in order to reduce waste. By contrast, upscale magazines and papers could distinguish themselves from those publications with an excess of empty space. This difference carries over to the web, where a page with less content and more white space often feels more classy and polished, while a page crammed with a lot of content feels more commercial. Both can be effective; you should decide which approach to use based on your customer profile.

You've completed your work on the Pandaisia Chocolates home page. In the next session, you'll work on page layout using the technique of grids.

Session 3.1 Quick Check

1. Provide the style rule to display all hypertext links within a navigation list as block elements with a gray background.
2. Briefly describe the three types of page layouts.
3. Provide a style rule to set the width of the page body to 90% of the browser window ranging from 320 pixels up to 960 pixels.
4. Provide a style rule to horizontally center the `header` element within the `body` element. Assume that the header is a direct child of the page body.
5. Provide a style rule to set the width of the `aside` element to 240 pixels and to float on the right margin of its container.
6. Provide a style rule to display the `footer` element only after all floated elements have cleared.
7. Your layout has four floated elements in a row but unfortunately the last element has wrapped to a new line. What is the source of the layout mistake?
8. Provide a style rule to change the `width` property for the `header` element so that it measures the total width of the header content, padding, and border spaces. Include web extensions for older browsers.
9. Provide a style rule to prevent the `header` element from collapsing around its floating content.

Session 3.2 Visual Overview:

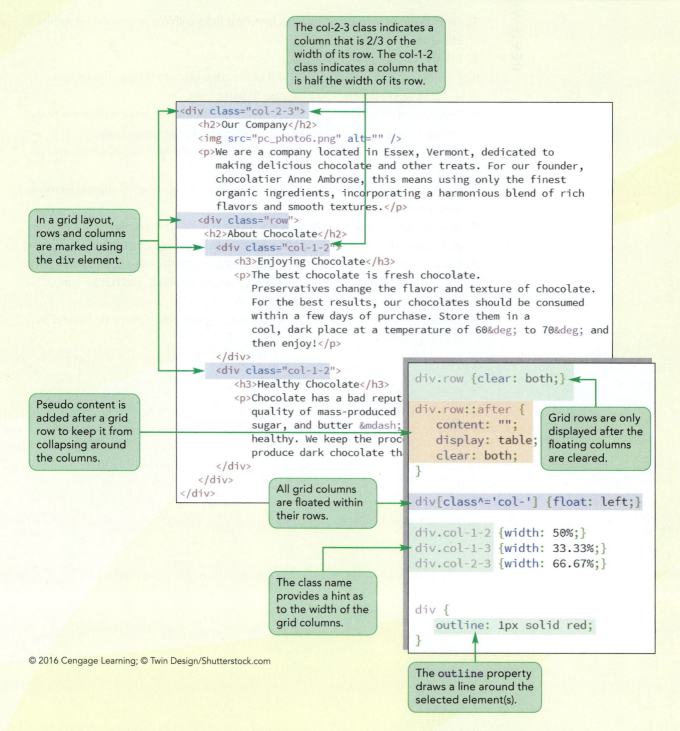

The col-2-3 class indicates a column that is 2/3 of the width of its row. The col-1-2 class indicates a column that is half the width of its row.

In a grid layout, rows and columns are marked using the div element.

Pseudo content is added after a grid row to keep it from collapsing around the columns.

```
<div class="col-2-3">
    <h2>Our Company</h2>
    <img src="pc_photo6.png" alt="" />
    <p>We are a company located in Essex, Vermont, dedicated to
       making delicious chocolate and other treats. For our founder,
       chocolatier Anne Ambrose, this means using only the finest
       organic ingredients, incorporating a harmonious blend of rich
       flavors and smooth textures.</p>
<div class="row">
    <h2>About Chocolate</h2>
    <div class="col-1-2">
        <h3>Enjoying Chocolate</h3>
        <p>The best chocolate is fresh chocolate.
           Preservatives change the flavor and texture of chocolate.
           For the best results, our chocolates should be consumed
           within a few days of purchase. Store them in a
           cool, dark place at a temperature of 60&deg; to 70&deg; and
           then enjoy!</p>
    </div>
    <div class="col-1-2">
        <h3>Healthy Chocolate</h3>
        <p>Chocolate has a bad reput
           quality of mass-produced
           sugar, and butter &mdash;
           healthy. We keep the proc
           produce dark chocolate th
    </div>
</div>
</div>
```

```
div.row {clear: both;}

div.row::after {
    content: "";
    display: table;
    clear: both;
}

div[class^='col-'] {float: left;}

div.col-1-2 {width: 50%;}
div.col-1-3 {width: 33.33%;}
div.col-2-3 {width: 66.67%;}

div {
    outline: 1px solid red;
}
```

Grid rows are only displayed after the floating columns are cleared.

All grid columns are floated within their rows.

The class name provides a hint as to the width of the grid columns.

The outline property draws a line around the selected element(s).

Page Layout Grids

A **grid layout** arranges the page content within **grid rows** with **grid columns** floated inside those rows.

Red outline indicates the location of grid rows and columns.

Grid rows are displayed starting on a new line.

The grid columns are floated with their rows.

Introducing Grid Layouts

In the previous session, you used the `float` property to lay out a page in sections that floated alongside each other like columns. In this session, you'll explore how to generalize this technique by creating a page layout based on a grid.

Overview of Grid-Based Layouts

Grids are a classic layout technique that has been used in publishing for hundreds of years and, like many other publishing techniques, can be applied to web design. The basic approach is to imagine that the page is comprised of a system of intersecting rows and columns that form a grid. The rows are based on the page content. A long page with several articles might span several rows, or it could be a home page with introductory content that fits within a single row. The number of columns is based on the number that provides the most flexibility in laying out the page content. Many grid systems are based on 12 columns because 12 is evenly divisible by 2, 3, 4, and 6, but other sizes are also used. Figure 3-29 shows a 12-column grid layout.

Figure 3-29 Page grid

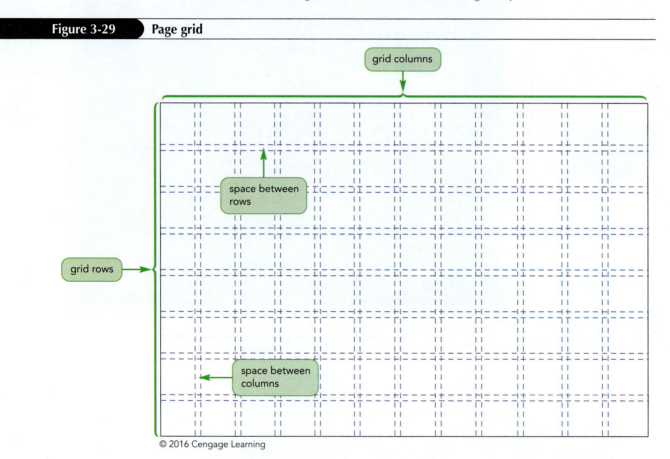

© 2016 Cengage Learning

The page designer then arranges the page elements within the chosen grid. Figure 3-30 shows one possible layout comprised of a main header element (the tan area), three major sections (the lavender, light green, and blue areas), as well as a navigation bar and a footer (the dark green areas). Some sections (like the dark green and blue areas) are further divided into small subsections.

Figure 3-30   **Layout based on a grid**

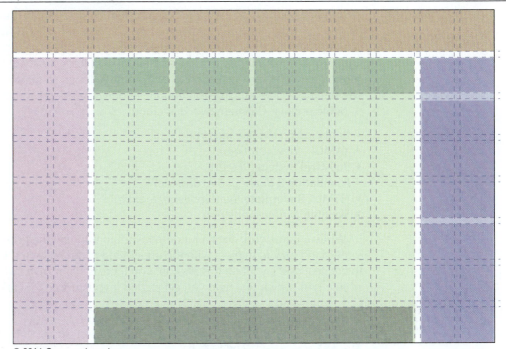

© 2016 Cengage Learning

It should be stressed that the grid is not part of the web page content. Instead, it's a systematic approach to visualizing how to best fit content onto the page. Working from a grid has several aesthetic and practical advantages, including

- Grids add order to the presentation of page content, adding visual rhythm, which is pleasing to the eye.
- A consistent logical design gives readers the confidence to find the information they seek.
- New content can be easily placed within a grid in a way that is consistent with previously entered information.
- A well designed grid is more easily accessible for users with disabilities and special needs.
- Grids speed up the development process by establishing a systematic framework for the page layout.

There are two basic types of grid layouts: fixed grids and fluid grids.

Fixed and Fluid Grids

In a **fixed grid**, the widths of the columns and margins are specified in pixels, where every column has a fixed position. Many fixed grid layouts are based on a page width of 960 pixels because most desktop screen widths are at 1024 pixels (or higher) and a 960-pixel width leaves room for browser scrollbars and other features. The 960-pixel width is also easily divisible into halves, thirds, quarters, and so forth, making it easier to create evenly spaced columns.

The problem of course with a fixed grid layout is that it does not account for other screen sizes and thus, a **fluid grid**, in which column widths are expressed in percentages rather than pixels, is often used to provide more support across different devices. In the examples to follow, you'll base your layouts on a fluid grid system.

Grids are often used with responsive design in which one grid layout is used with mobile devices, another grid layout is used with tablets, and yet another layout is used with desktop computers. A layout for a mobile device is typically based on a 1-column grid, tablet layouts are based on grids of 4 to 12 columns, and desktop layouts are often based on layouts with 12 or more columns.

CSS Frameworks

Designing your own grids can be time-consuming. To simplify the process, you can choose from the many CSS frameworks available on the web. A **framework** is a software package that provides a library of tools to design your website, including style sheets for grid layouts and built-in scripts to provide support for a variety of browsers and devices. Most frameworks include support for responsive design so that you can easily scale your website for devices ranging from mobile phones to desktop computers.

Some popular CSS frameworks include

- **Bootstrap** (*getbootstrap.com*)
- **YAML4** (*www.yaml.de*)
- **960 Grid System** (*960.gs*)
- **Foundation 3** (*foundation.zurb.com*)
- **HTML5 Boilerplate** (*html5boilerplate.com*)
- **Skeleton** (*getskeleton.com*)

While a framework does a lot of the work in building the grid, you still need to understand how to interact with the underlying code, including the style sheets used to create a grid layout. In this session, you'll create your own style sheet based on a simple grid, which will help you get started if you choose to work with commercial CSS frameworks.

Setting up a Grid

A grid layout is based on rows of floating elements, much as you did in the layout of the Pandaisia home page in the last session. Each floating element constitutes a column. The set of elements floating side-by-side establishes a row. To give a consistent structure to these floating objects, many grid layouts use the `div` (or division) element to mark distinct rows and columns of the grid. Let's examine the following simple example of a grid consisting of a single row with two columns:

```
<div class="row">
   <div class="column1"></div>
   <div class="column2"></div>
</div>
```

Within these `div` elements, you place your page content, but you don't need to worry about that yet. For more elaborate layouts, a column can contain its own grid of rows and columns. The following code expands the previous grid layout by placing a grid of two rows and two columns within each row `div` within the column1 `div` element:

```
<div class="row">
   <div class="column1">
      <div class="row">
         <div class="column1a"></div>
         <div class="column1b"></div>
      </div>
      <div class="row">
         <div class="column1c"></div>
         <div class="column1d"></div>
      </div>
   </div>
   <div class="column2"></div>
</div>
```

It's common in grid layouts to give the columns class names indicating their width. For example, use a class name of "col-1-4" to indicate a column with a width of 1/4 or 25% or use a class name of "col-2-3" to indicate a column with a width of 2/3 or 67%. Using this class name system, the following HTML markup

```
<div class="row">
  <div class="col-2-3">
    <div class="row">
      <div class="col-1-4"></div>
      <div class="col-1-4"></div>
      <div class="col-1-2"></div>
    </div>
    <div class="row">
      <div class="col-1-1"></div>
    </div>
  </div>
  <div class="col-1-3"></div>
</div>
```

results in the grid layout shown in Figure 3-31. Note that this layout consists of a single row with two columns with the first column itself containing three columns arranged across two rows. Remember though that the actual column widths are not set by the class names, instead they are defined in the style sheet. The class names are just aids for us to interpret the grid layout in the HTML file.

Figure 3-31 **Sample grid layout**

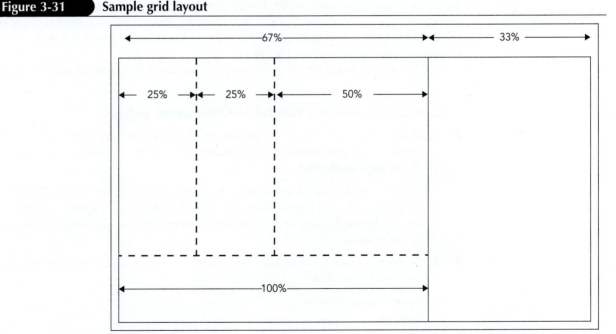

© 2016 Cengage Learning

Now that you've seen the general structure for the HTML code in a layout grid, you'll create one for a new page in the Pandaisia Chocolates website that provides information about chocolate and the company. Anne has laid out a grid for the page's content shown in Figure 3-32.

Figure 3-32 **Proposed grid layout for the About Pandaisia Chocolates page**

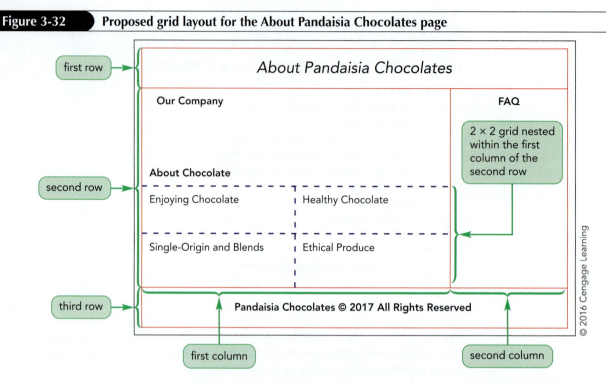

Anne's layout consists of three main rows. The first row contains the page title and the third row contains the page footer. The second row consists of two columns: the first column displaying information about the company and the second column displaying a list of frequently asked questions. Within the first row is a nested 2 × 2 grid containing short articles about chocolate.

Add the `div` elements for this grid layout to the About Pandaisia Chocolates page.

To create the About Pandaisia Chocolates page:

1. Use your editor to open the **pc_about_txt.html** file from the html03 ▸ tutorial folder. Enter **your name** and **the date** in the comment section and save the file as **pc_about.html**.

   Anne has already added the same header used for the Pandaisia Chocolates home page to this page. Using the same header tags keeps a consistent header for each page and, therefore, a consistent look and feel across pages in the website.

2. Below the closing `</header>` tag, insert the following `div` elements for the first row in the grid.

   ```
   <div class="row">
   </div>
   ```

3. Next, insert the following `div` elements for the second row containing two columns within the nested 2 × 2 grid in the first column.

   ```
   <div class="row">
      <div class="col-2-3">
         <div class="row">
            <div class="col-1-2">
            </div>
            <div class="col-1-2">
            </div>
         </div>
   ```

```
            <div class="row">
                <div class="col-1-2">
                </div>
                <div class="col-1-2">
                </div>
            </div>
        </div>
        <div class="col-1-3">
        </div>
    </div>
```

4. Finally, insert the following `div` elements for the third row of the grid:

```
<div class="row">
</div>
```

Figure 3-33 highlights the complete code for the grid you've created.

Figure 3-33 div elements in the About Pandaisia Chocolates page

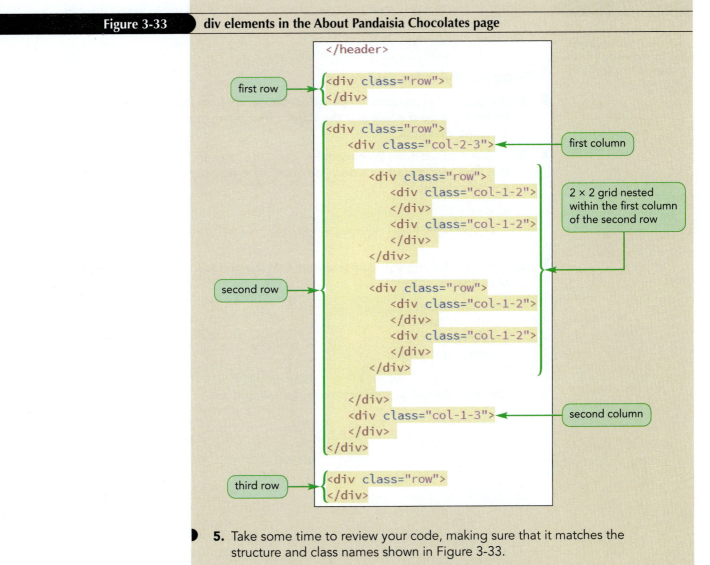

5. Take some time to review your code, making sure that it matches the structure and class names shown in Figure 3-33.

6. Save your changes to the file but do not close it.

Now that you've established the grid for the page content, you'll set up the styles for the grid, starting with the grid row.

Designing the Grid Rows

Grid rows contain floating columns. Since a grid row starts a new line within the page, it should only be displayed when both margins are clear of previously floated columns. Since it contains its own set of floating columns, it has to be able to expand in height to cover those objects (or else the floating columns run the risk of bleeding into the next row.) As with the page footer from the last session, you can establish these rules for grid rows using the following style rule:

```
div.row::after {
    clear: both;
    content: "";
    display: table;
}
```

Add this style rule to a new style sheet, pc_grids.css, that you will use to format the grid layout used in the pc_about.html file.

TIP

The class name *row* for grid rows is not mandatory; you can choose a different class name for your own grid rows.

To create styles for grid rows:

1. Use your editor to open the **pc_grids_txt.css** file from the html03 ▸ tutorial folder. Enter **your name** and **the date** in the comment section and save the file as **pc_grids.css**.

2. Within the Grid Rows Styles section, insert the following style rules to ensure that rows always start on a new line once the margins are clear of previously floated columns.

```
div.row {
    clear: both;
}
```

3. Add the following style rule to ensure that the grid row expands to cover all of its floating columns:

```
div.row::after {
    clear: both;
    content: "";
    display: table;
}
```

Figure 3-34 highlights the style rules for the grid rows.

Figure 3-34 **Styles for row div elements**

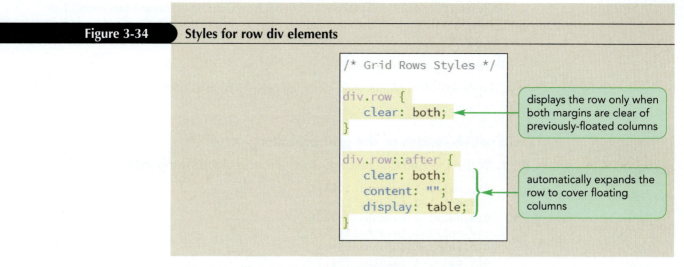

Next, you'll create style rules for the grid columns.

Designing the Grid Columns

Every grid column needs to be floated within its row. In the grid you set up for the About Pandaisia Chocolates page, grid columns are placed within a `div` element having the general class name

```
class="col-numerator-denominator"
```

where *numerator-denominator* provides the fractional width of the column. For example, the col-1-3 class indicates that the column is one-third the total row width. To float all grid columns, you can use the following attribute selector, which matches all `div` elements whose `class` attribute begins with the text string "col-":

```css
div[class^="col-"] {
    float: left;
}
```

Add this style rule to the pc_grids.css style sheet file now.

To float the grid columns:

1. Within the Grid Columns Styles section, insert the following style rule:

```css
div[class^="col-"] {
    float: left;
}
```

Figure 3-35 highlights the style rule for the grid columns.

Figure 3-35 **Style for column div elements**

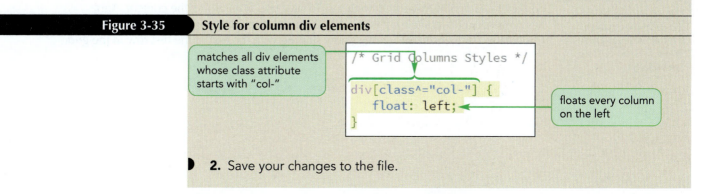

2. Save your changes to the file.

Finally, you have to establish the width of each column based on its class name. For example `div` elements with the class name col-1-3 will use the following style rule to set their width to 1/3 or 33.33% of the width of the parent element—the grid row.

```
div.col-1-3 {width: 33.33%;}
```

Add style rules for column widths ranging from 25% up to 100%.

To set the width of the grid columns:

The class name associated with each column provides a clue to the column's width.

1. Within the Grid Columns Styles section, add the following style rules:

```
div.col-1-1 {width: 100%;}
div.col-1-2 {width: 50%;}
div.col-1-3 {width: 33.33%;}
div.col-2-3 {width: 66.67%;}
div.col-1-4 {width: 25%;}
div.col-3-4 {width: 75%;}
```

Figure 3-36 highlights the width values assigned to `div` elements of different classes.

Figure 3-36 | **Setting the column widths**

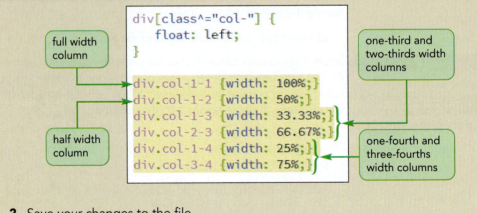

2. Save your changes to the file.

Continuing in this same fashion, you could have included styles for other column widths based on percentages. For example, a one-sixth column would have a width of 16.66%, a one-twelfth column would have a width of 8.33%, and so forth.

Adding the Page Content

TIP

Choose percent values for the column widths so that the total width of all of the columns in the row does not exceed 100%.

Now that you have established the basic framework for your grid you can add the page content to each of its rows and columns. To save you from typing the content, Anne has prepared a file containing the text of the articles to appear in the About Pandaisia Chocolates page. Insert this content now starting with the text of the first row in the grid.

To insert page content into the grid:

1. Return to the **pc_about.html** file in your editor.

2. Directly after the opening `<div class="row">` tag, insert the following h1 heading:

   ```
   <h1>About Pandaisia Chocolates</h1>
   ```

   Figure 3-37 shows the placement of the h1 heading in the first grid row.

Figure 3-37   **Adding the heading to the first row of the grid**

```
</header>

<div class="row">
    <h1>About Pandaisia Chocolates</h1>
</div>
```

Next, you'll insert the text for the left column of the second row of the grid.

3. Open the **pc_text.txt** file using your text editor and copy the HTML code from the About the Company section, which includes the h2 heading, an `img` element, and two paragraphs.

4. Paste the copied code directly after the first `<div class="col-2-3">` tag near the top of the grid.

   Figure 3-38 shows the placement of the left column text.

Figure 3-38   **Adding information about the company**

```
<div class="row">
    <h1>About Pandaisia Chocolates</h1>
</div>

<div class="row">
    <div class="col-2-3">
        <h2>Our Company</h2>
        <img src="pc_photo6.png" alt="" />
        <p>We are a company located in Essex, Vermont, dedicated to
            making delicious chocolate and other treats. For our founder,
            chocolatier Anne Ambrose, this means using only the finest
            organic ingredients, incorporating a harmonious blend of rich
            flavors and smooth textures.</p>
        <p>Anne learned her trade as part of a three-year apprenticeship
            program in Switzerland. Her introduction into the world of
            confectioneries was a springboard to working with leaders in
            the field. Early in 1993 she brought that expertise back to
            Vermont and Pandaisia Chocolates was born.</p>
        <div class="row">
```

content pasted into the left column

Within the left column are two nested rows containing short articles about chocolate. You will add this content to the grid now.

5. Directly after the nested `<div class="row">` tag, insert the heading tag
   `<h2>About Chocolate</h2>`

6. Return to the **pc_text.txt** file in your editor and copy the HTML code from the first of four Enjoying Chocolates sections, which includes the h3 heading and a paragraph. Paste the copied text into the first of the four nested half-width columns, as shown in Figure 3-39.

Figure 3-39 **Adding content about chocolate**

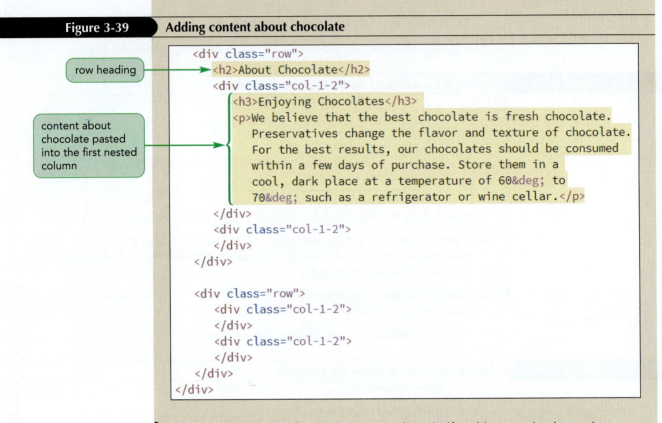

7. Add the content for the remaining three half-width nested columns by returning to the **pc_text.txt** file in your editor and copying the HTML code from the last three Enjoying Chocolate sections: Healthy Chocolate, Single-Origin and Blends, and Ethical Produce. Each section includes an h3 heading and a paragraph. Paste the copied code from each section into one of the three remaining nested half-width columns. Figure 3-40 shows the placement of the copied HTML code for the last three half-width nested columns.

| Figure 3-40 | Adding content to the rest of the nested columns |

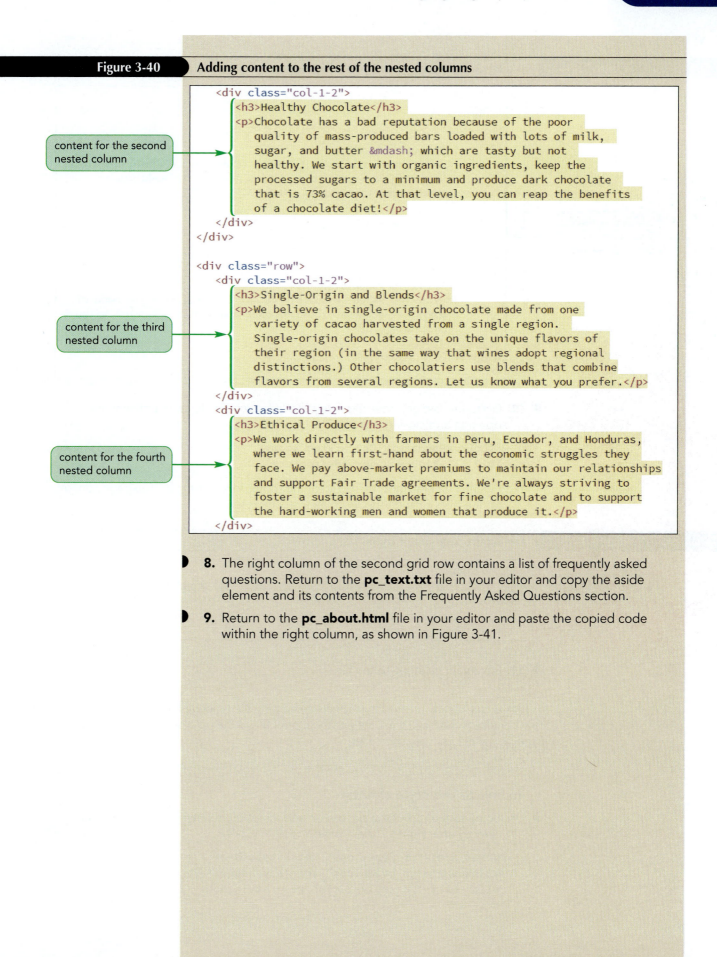

content for the second nested column

```
<div class="col-1-2">
   <h3>Healthy Chocolate</h3>
   <p>Chocolate has a bad reputation because of the poor
      quality of mass-produced bars loaded with lots of milk,
      sugar, and butter &mdash; which are tasty but not
      healthy. We start with organic ingredients, keep the
      processed sugars to a minimum and produce dark chocolate
      that is 73% cacao. At that level, you can reap the benefits
      of a chocolate diet!</p>
</div>
</div>

<div class="row">
   <div class="col-1-2">
      <h3>Single-Origin and Blends</h3>
      <p>We believe in single-origin chocolate made from one
         variety of cacao harvested from a single region.
         Single-origin chocolates take on the unique flavors of
         their region (in the same way that wines adopt regional
         distinctions.) Other chocolatiers use blends that combine
         flavors from several regions. Let us know what you prefer.</p>
   </div>
   <div class="col-1-2">
      <h3>Ethical Produce</h3>
      <p>We work directly with farmers in Peru, Ecuador, and Honduras,
         where we learn first-hand about the economic struggles they
         face. We pay above-market premiums to maintain our relationships
         and support Fair Trade agreements. We're always striving to
         foster a sustainable market for fine chocolate and to support
         the hard-working men and women that produce it.</p>
   </div>
```

content for the third nested column

content for the fourth nested column

8. The right column of the second grid row contains a list of frequently asked questions. Return to the **pc_text.txt** file in your editor and copy the aside element and its contents from the Frequently Asked Questions section.

9. Return to the **pc_about.html** file in your editor and paste the copied code within the right column, as shown in Figure 3-41.

Figure 3-41   **Adding content for frequently asked questions**

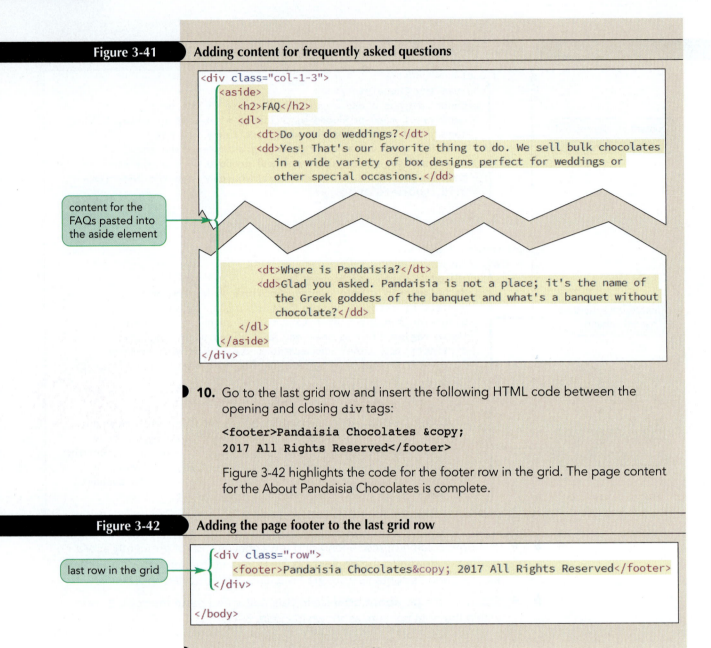

content for the FAQs pasted into the aside element

```
<div class="col-1-3">
    <aside>
        <h2>FAQ</h2>
        <dl>
            <dt>Do you do weddings?</dt>
            <dd>Yes! That's our favorite thing to do. We sell bulk chocolates
                in a wide variety of box designs perfect for weddings or
                other special occasions.</dd>



            <dt>Where is Pandaisia?</dt>
            <dd>Glad you asked. Pandaisia is not a place; it's the name of
                the Greek goddess of the banquet and what's a banquet without
                chocolate?</dd>
        </dl>
    </aside>
</div>
```

10. Go to the last grid row and insert the following HTML code between the opening and closing `div` tags:

    ```
    <footer>Pandaisia Chocolates &copy;
    2017 All Rights Reserved</footer>
    ```

    Figure 3-42 highlights the code for the footer row in the grid. The page content for the About Pandaisia Chocolates is complete.

Figure 3-42   **Adding the page footer to the last grid row**

last row in the grid

```
<div class="row">
    <footer>Pandaisia Chocolates&copy; 2017 All Rights Reserved</footer>
</div>

</body>
```

11. Save your changes to the file.

Anne has already created style sheets containing the typographic and color styles for the content of this page. Link the pc_about.html file to the pc_reset.css, pc_grids.css and pc_styles2.css style sheet files.

To link to the style sheets:

1. Scroll to the top of the document and insert the following `link` elements directly after the `title` element:

    ```
    <link href="pc_reset.css" rel="stylesheet" />
    <link href="pc_grids.css" rel="stylesheet" />
    <link href="pc_styles2.css" rel="stylesheet" />
    ```

2. Save your changes to the file and then reload the **pc_about.html** file in your browser. Figure 3-43 shows the final layout of the page content.

Figure 3-43   Format of the content in the About Pandaisia Chocolates page

first row

second row

third row

2 × 2 grid nested within the first column of the second row

© Twin Design/Shutterstock.com

first column

second column

Compare the appearance of the page content with the schematic diagram shown earlier in Figure 3-32 to see how using a grid provided a unified layout for the page. As you become more experienced with setting up and applying grids, you can move to more intricate and interesting page layouts.

Generating Content with Lorem Ipsum

Lorem ipsum dolor sit amet, consectetur adipiscing elit. Integer nec odio. Praesent libero. Sed cursus ante dapibus diam. Sed nisi. Nulla quis sem at nibh elementum imperdiet. Duis sagittis ipsum. Vestibulum lacinia arcu eget nulla. Sed dignissim lacinia nunc.

That previous paragraph is an example of **lorem ipsum**, which is nonsensical, improper Latin commonly used in page design as filler text. Rather than creating large portions of sample text before you can view your layout, lorem ipsum is used to quickly generate sentences, lines, and paragraphs that resemble the structure and appearance of real text. Lorem ipsum is a particularly useful tool for web designers because they can begin working on page design without waiting for their clients to supply all of the page content.

Many popular web editors include tools to generate lorem ipsum text strings in a wide variety of formats and styles. There are also lorem ipsum generators freely available on the web, which will supplement the lorem ipsum text with HTML markup tags.

Once you've established a grid layout, you might want to be able to view the grid structure to confirm that the content has been placed properly. One way to do this is by using the outline style.

Outlining a Grid

Outlines are simply lines drawn around an element, enclosing the element content, padding, and border spaces. Unlike borders, which you'll study in the next tutorial, an outline doesn't add anything to the width or height of the object, it only indicates the extent of the element on the rendered page.

The width of the line used in the outline is defined by the following `outline-width` property

```
outline-width: value;
```

where `value` is expressed in one of the CSS units of length, or with the keywords `thin`, `medium`, or `thick`.

The line color is set using the `outline-color` property

```
outline-color: color;
```

where `color` is a CSS color name or value.

Finally, the design of the line can be set using the following `outline-style` property

```
outline-style: style;
```

where `style` is `none` (to display no outline), `solid` (for a single line), `double`, `dotted`, `dashed`, `groove`, `inset`, `ridge`, or `outset`.

All of the outline styles properties can be combined into the `outline` shorthand property

```
outline: width style color;
```

where `width`, `style`, and `color` are the values for the line's width, design, and color. For example, the following style rule uses the wildcard selector along with the `outline` shorthand property to draw a 1px dotted green line around every element on the web page:

```
* {
   outline: 1px dotted green;
}
```

Note that there are no separate outline styles for the left, right, top, or bottom edge of the object. The outline always surrounds an entire element.

REFERENCE

Adding an Outline

- To add an outline around an element, use the property

  outline: *width style color*;

  where *width*, *style*, and *color* are the outline width, outline design, and outline color respectively. These attributes can be listed in any order.

Use the outline property now to outline every div element in your grid so that you can see how the page content is related to the grid you created.

To outline the grid:

1. Return to the **pc_grids.css** file in your editor.

2. Go to the Grid Outline Styles section and insert the following style rule:

   ```
   div {
       outline: 1px solid red;
   }
   ```

   Figure 3-44 describes the use of the outline shorthand property.

Figure 3-44   **Add outlines to grid rows and columns**

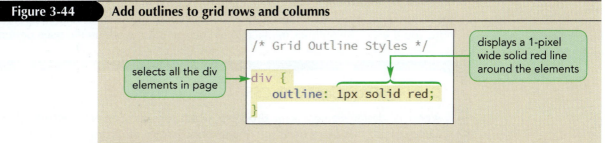

```
/* Grid Outline Styles */

div {
    outline: 1px solid red;
}
```

selects all the div elements in page

displays a 1-pixel wide solid red line around the elements

3. Save your changes to the style sheet.

4. Reload the **pc_about.html** file in your browser. Figure 3-45 shows the appearance of the part of the page with the grid lines superimposed on the page layout.

Figure 3-45   Outlines added to every div element

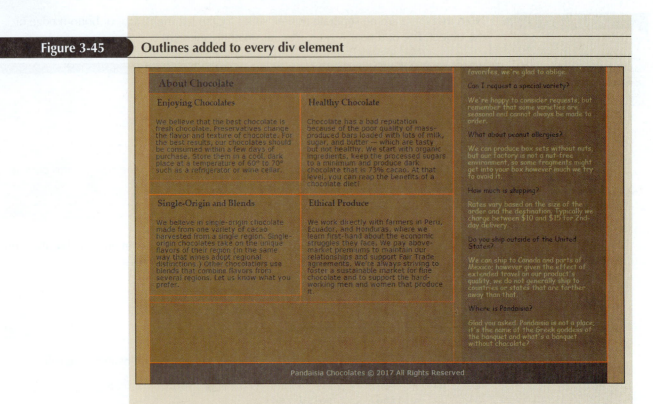

5. Close any of your open files now.

Anne appreciates the work you've done on the About Pandaisia Chocolates page. She thinks that the outlines around the grid rows and columns make it easier to view the layout style, which will make it easier to make modifications in future pages. For now, you'll leave the outlines in place to aid her in future work on the page design.

Creating Drop Caps with CSS

A popular design element is the **drop cap**, which consists of an enlarged initial letter in a body of text that drops down into the text body. To create a drop cap, you increase the font size of an element's first letter and float it on the left margin. Drop caps also generally look better if you decrease the line height of the first letter, enabling the surrounding content to better wrap around the letter. Finding the best combination of font size and line height is a matter of trial and error; and unfortunately, what looks best in one browser might not look as good in another. The following style rule works well in applying a drop cap to the first paragraph element:

```
p:first-of-type::first-letter {
    font-size: 4em;
    float: left;
    line-height: 0.8;
}
```

For additional design effects, you can change the font face of the drop cap to a cursive or decorative font.

Introducing CSS Grids

Grids are a fast and flexible way of creating a layout, but they are not without their problems. The most obvious problem is that setting up the grid increases the size and complexity of the HTML code by adding another level of markup. Another equally serious problem is that grids undermine the fundamental rule that the HTML file should consist solely of informational content while all instructions regarding presentation should be placed within an external style sheet. However, under the HTML grid system, the `div` elements have no purpose other than for defining how the page should be rendered. And if the designer wants to change the layout, the HTML file and the style sheet will both have to be modified, adding another layer of complexity to the site design.

Defining a CSS Grid

Since grids are an important and useful design tool, the W3C is working toward adding grid styles to CSS. To create a grid display without the use of `div` elements, CSS is now adding the following grid-based properties:

```
selector {
   display: grid;
   grid-template-rows: track-list;
   grid-template-columns: track-list;
}
```

The `grid` keyword for the `display` property establishes that the selected element(s) will be displayed as a grid. The number of rows and columns in the grid are set by the `grid-template-rows` and `grid-template-columns` properties where `track-list` is a space-separated list of row heights or column widths. Heights and widths can be expressed in any of the CSS units of measurement, including the keyword `auto` where the row or column will be automatically sized according to its content.

For example, the following style rule establishes a grid for the section element. The grid consists of three rows with the height of the first and last rows set to 100 pixels and the middle row automatically sized to match its content The grid also consists of three columns with the first and last column widths set to 25% and the middle column occupying half of each grid row.

```
section {
   display: grid;
   grid-template-rows: 100px auto 100px;
   grid-template-columns: 25% 50% 25%;
}
```

The CSS grid styles also introduce the **fr unit**, which represents the fraction of available space left on the grid after all other rows or columns have attained their maximum allowable size. For example, the following style creates four columns: two columns that are 200 and 250 pixels wide respectively and then two columns that are 1fr and 2fr respectively:

```
grid-template-columns: 200px 250px 1fr 2fr;
```

The `fr` unit can be thought of as a "share" of the available space so that, in this example, after 450 pixels have been given to the first two columns, whatever space remains is divided between the last two columns with 1`fr` or one-third allotted to the third column and 2`fr` or two-thirds to the fourth column.

Assigning Content to Grid Cells

Once you've established a CSS grid, you place a specific element within a **grid cell** at the intersection of a specified row and column. By default, all of the specified elements are placed in the grid cell located at the intersection of the first row and first column. To place the element in a different cell, use the following properties

```
grid-row-start: integer;
grid-row-end: integer;
grid-column-start: integer;
grid-column-end: integer;
```

where *integer* defines the starting and ending row or column that contains the content. For example, the following style rule places the aside element to cover the second and third rows and the first and second columns of the grid.

```
aside {
    grid-row-start: 2;
    grid-row-end: 3;
    grid-column-start: 1;
    grid-column-end: 2;
}
```

These coordinates can also be written in a more compact form as

```
grid-row: start/end;
grid-column: start/end;
```

where *start* and *end* are the starting and ending coordinates of the row and columns containing the element. Thus, you can place the aside element in the same location described above using the equivalent style rule, which follows:

```
aside {
    grid-row: 2/3;
    grid-column: 1/2;
}
```

If you specify a single number, the content is placed within a single grid cell. The following style rule places the aside element in the second row and first column of the grid:

```
aside {
    grid-row: 2;
    grid-column: 1;
}
```

Defining Grids with CSS

- To assign a CSS grid to an element, use the property

  ```
  display: grid;
  ```

- To define the number of rows and columns within the grid, use the properties

  ```
  grid-template-rows: track-list;
  grid-template-columns: track-list;
  ```

  where *track-list* is a space-separated list of row heights or column widths.

- To place an element within a specific intersection of grid rows and columns, use the properties

  ```
  grid-row-start: integer;
  grid-row-end: integer;
  grid-column-start: integer;
  grid-column-end: integer;
  ```

  where *integer* defines the starting and ending row or column that contains the content.

- To more compactly set the location of the element within the grid, use the properties

  ```
  grid-row: start/end;
  grid-column: start/end;
  ```

  where *start* and *end* are the starting and ending coordinates of the row and columns containing the element.

You have only just scratched the surface of the future of grid design using CSS. Other properties in the current draft include styles for creating nested grids, collapsing and expanding rows and columns, and creating named grid areas. You can view the most current draft specifications at the W3C website. The CSS grid styles are not well-supported by current browsers at the time of this writing. Internet Explorer supports grid styles using the `-ms-` browser prefix. Other browsers are starting to provide support through experimental extensions. Eventually, CSS-based grids will supplant grid designs created via `div` elements, once again separating layout from content. Until that time, you should continue to either create your own grids using the techniques described in this session or use one of the many CSS frameworks available on the web.

PROSKILLS

Written Communication: Getting to the Point with Layout

Page layout is one of the most important aspects of web design. A well-constructed page layout naturally guides a reader's eyes to the most important information in the page. You should use the following principles to help your readers quickly get to the point:

- *Guide the eye.* Usability studies have shown that a reader's eye first lands in the top center of the page, then scans to the left, and then to the right and down. Arrange your page content so that the most important items are the first items a user sees.
- *Avoid clutter.* If a graphic or an icon is not conveying information or making the content easier to read, remove it.
- *Avoid overcrowding.* Focus on a few key items that will be easy for readers to locate while scanning the page, and separate these key areas from one another with ample white space. Don't be afraid to move a topic to a different page if it makes the current page easier to scan.
- *Make your information manageable.* It's easier for the brain to process information when it's presented in smaller chunks. Break up long extended paragraphs into smaller paragraphs or bulleted lists.
- *Use a grid.* Users find it easier to scan content when page elements are aligned vertically and horizontally. Use a grid to help you line up your elements in a clear and consistent way.
- *Cut down on the noise.* If you're thinking about using blinking text or a cute animated icon, don't. The novelty of such features wears off very quickly and distracts users from the valuable content in your page.

Always remember that your goal is to convey information to readers, and that an important tool in achieving that is to make it as easy as possible for readers to find that information. A thoughtfully constructed layout is a great aid to effective communication.

In the next session, you'll explore how to create page layouts that are not based on grids but instead allow objects to be placed anywhere within the rendered page.

Session 3.2 Quick Check

1. What is the difference between a fixed grid and a fluid grid?
2. What is a CSS framework?
3. In a proposed grid, all of the grid rows have the class name *container*. Create a style rule to expand those grid rows around their floating columns.
4. In a proposed grid, the columns all have the class names "span-*integer*" where *integer* indicates the size of the column. Create a style rule to float every grid column on the left margin.
5. Create a style rule to set the width of columns belonging to the span-4 class to 25% of the row width.
6. What is lorem ipsum?
7. Create a style rule for the grid rows described in question 3 above so that their sizes are measured using the Border Box model.
8. Create a style that adds a 2 pixel green dotted outline around all block quotes in the document.
9. Using the proposed specifications for CSS-based grids, create a grid for the `body` element that has three rows with heights automatically defined by the page content and five columns with widths of 25%, 2.5%, 50%, 2.5%, and 20%. Place the `nav` element in the first column, the `article` element in the third column, and the `aside` element in the fifth column.

Session 3.3 Visual Overview:

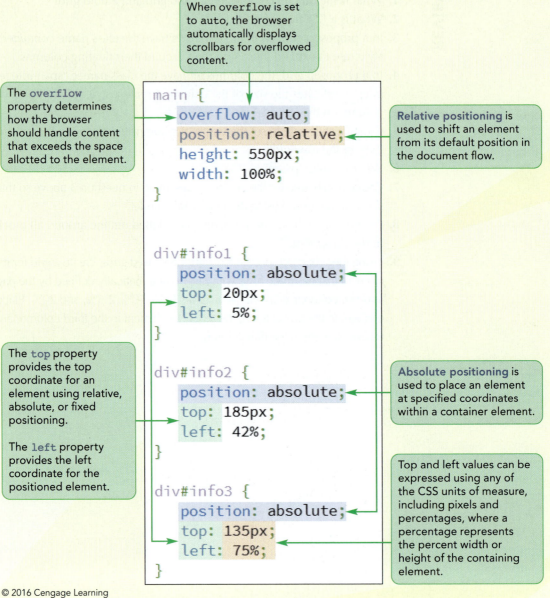

When overflow is set to auto, the browser automatically displays scrollbars for overflowed content.

The overflow property determines how the browser should handle content that exceeds the space allotted to the element.

Relative positioning is used to shift an element from its default position in the document flow.

```
main {
    overflow: auto;
    position: relative;
    height: 550px;
    width: 100%;
}


div#info1 {
    position: absolute;
    top: 20px;
    left: 5%;
}


div#info2 {
    position: absolute;
    top: 185px;
    left: 42%;
}


div#info3 {
    position: absolute;
    top: 135px;
    left: 75%;
}
```

The top property provides the top coordinate for an element using relative, absolute, or fixed positioning.

The left property provides the left coordinate for the positioned element.

Absolute positioning is used to place an element at specified coordinates within a container element.

Top and left values can be expressed using any of the CSS units of measure, including pixels and percentages, where a percentage represents the percent width or height of the containing element.

© 2016 Cengage Learning

Layout with Positioning Styles

info1 is placed 20 pixels from the top of the main element and 5% from the left edge.

info2 is placed 185 pixels from the top and 42% from the left edge of the main element.

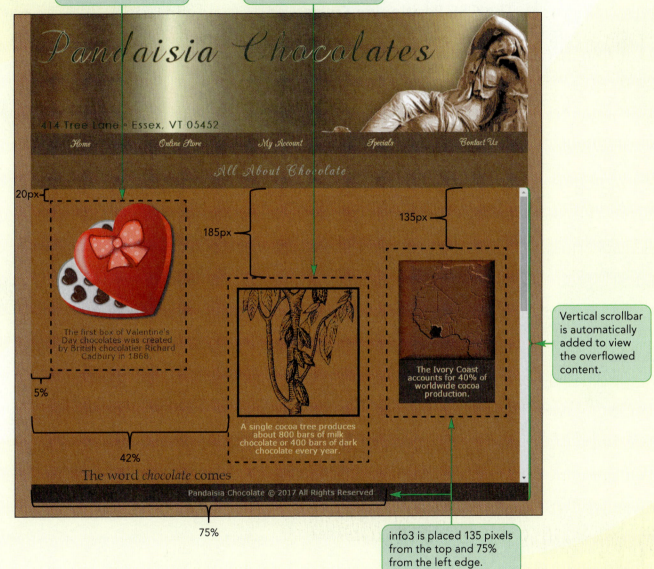

20px

185px

135px

5%

42%

75%

Vertical scrollbar is automatically added to view the overflowed content.

info3 is placed 135 pixels from the top and 75% from the left edge.

Positioning Objects

In the last session, you developed a layout in which page objects were strictly aligned according to the rows and columns of a grid. While a grid layout gives a page a feeling of uniformity and structure, it does limit your freedom to place objects at different locations within the page. In this session, you'll explore how to "break out" of the grid using the CSS positioning styles.

The CSS Positioning Styles

CSS supports several properties to place objects at specific coordinates within the page or within their container. To place an element at a specific position within its container, you use the following style properties

```
position: type;
top: value;
right: value;
bottom: value;
left: value;
```

where *type* indicates the kind of positioning applied to the element, and the `top`, `right`, `bottom`, and `left` properties indicate the coordinates of the top, right, bottom, and left edges of the element, respectively. The coordinates can be expressed in any of the CSS measuring units or as a percentage of the container's width or height.

CSS supports five kinds of positioning: `static` (the default), `relative`, `absolute`, `fixed`, and `inherit`. In **static positioning**, the element is placed where it would have fallen naturally within the flow of the document. This is essentially the same as not using any CSS positioning at all. Browsers ignore any values specified for the `top`, `left`, `bottom`, or `right` properties under static positioning.

Relative Positioning

Relative positioning is used to nudge an element out of its normal position in the document flow. Under relative positioning, the `top`, `right`, `bottom`, and `left` properties indicate the extra space that is placed alongside the element as it is shifted into a new position. For example, the following style rule adds 250 pixels of space to the top of the element and 450 pixels to the left of the element, resulting in the element being shifted down and to the right (see Figure 3-46):

```
div {
    position: relative;
    top: 250px;
    left: 450px;
}
```

Figure 3-46   **Moving an object using relative positioning**

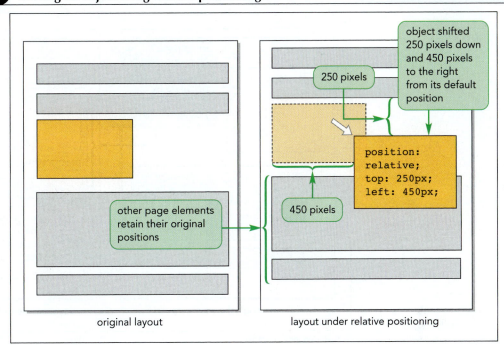

position:
relative;
top: 250px;
left: 450px;

object shifted
250 pixels down
and 450 pixels
to the right
from its default
position

250 pixels

other page elements
retain their original
positions

450 pixels

original layout   layout under relative positioning

© 2016 Cengage Learning

Note that the layout of the other page elements are not affected by relative positioning; they will still occupy their original positions on the rendered page, just as if the object had never been moved at all.

Relative positioning is sometimes used when the designer wants to "tweak" the page layout by slightly moving an object from its default location to a new location that fits the overall page design better. If no top, right, bottom, or left values are specified with relative positioning, their assumed values are 0 and the element will not be shifted at all.

Absolute Positioning

Absolute positioning places an element at specific coordinates within a container where the `top` property indicates the position of the element's top edge, the `right` property sets the position of the right edge, the `bottom` property sets the bottom edge position, and the `left` property sets the position of the left edge.

For example, the following style rule places the `header` element 620 pixels from the top edge of its container and 30 pixels from the left edge (see Figure 3-47).

```
header {
    position: absolute;
    top: 620px;
    left: 30px;
}
```

TIP

To place an element at the bottom right corner of its container, use absolute positioning with the right and bottom values set to 0 pixels.

Figure 3-47   **Moving an object using absolute positioning**

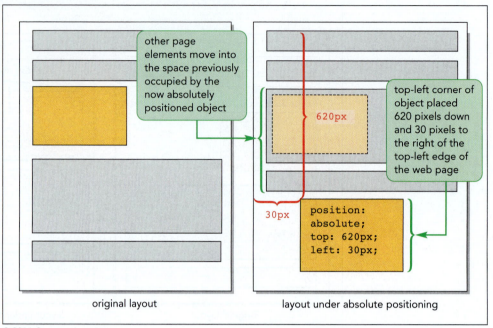

© 2016 Cengage Learning

To place an object with absolute positioning, you use either the top/left coordinates or the bottom/right coordinates, but you don't use all four coordinates at the same time because that would confuse the browser. For example an object cannot be positioned along both the left and right edge of its container simultaneously.

As with floating an element, absolute positioning takes an element out of normal document flow with subsequent elements moving into the space previously occupied by the element. This can result in an absolutely positioned object overlapping other page elements.

TIP

You can work with an interactive demo of positioning styles using the demo_positioning.html file from the demo folder.

The interpretation of the coordinates of an absolutely positioned object are all based on the edges of the element's container. Thus the browser needs to "know" where the object's container is before it can absolutely position objects within it. If the container has been placed using a `position` property set to `relative` or `absolute`, the container's location is known and the coordinate values are based on the edges of the container. For example the following style rules place the `article` element at a coordinate that is 50 pixels from the top edge of the section element and 20 pixels from the left edge.

```
section {
    position: relative;
}
section > article {
    position: absolute;
    top: 50px;
    left: 20px;
}
```

Note that you don't have to define coordinates for the `section` element as long as you've set its position to relative.

The difficulty starts when the container has not been set using relative or absolute positioning. In that case, the browser has no context for placing an object within the container using absolute positioning. As a result, the browser must go up a level in the hierarchy of page elements, that is, to the container's container. If that container has been placed with absolute or relative positioning, then any object nested within it can be placed with absolute positioning. For example, in the following style rule, the position of the `article` element is measured from the edges of the `body` element, not the `section` element:

```
body {position: absolute;}

body > section {position: static;}

body > section > article {
    position: absolute;
    top: 50px;
    left: 20px;
}
```

TIP

If all of the objects within a container are placed using absolute positioning, the container will have no content and will collapse.

Proceeding in this fashion the browser will continue to go up the hierarchy of elements until it finds a container that has been placed with absolute or relative positioning or it reaches the root `html` element. If it reaches the `html` element, the coordinates of any absolutely positioned object are measured from the edges of the browser window itself. Figure 3-48 shows how the placement of the same object can differ based on which container supplies the context for the top and left values.

Figure 3-48	Context of the top and left coordinates

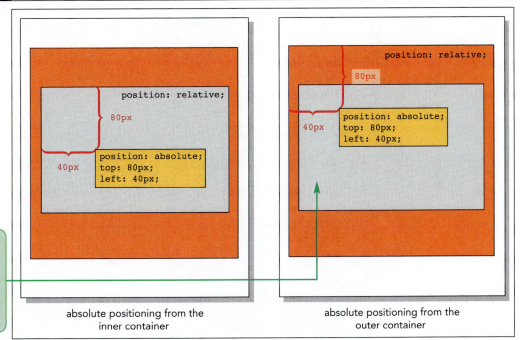

because the inner container has not been placed using relative or absolute positioning, the context shifts up the hierarchy to the outer container

© 2016 Cengage Learning

Coordinates can be expressed in percentages as well as pixels. Percentages are used for flexible layouts in which the object should be positioned in relation to the width or height of its container. Thus, the following style rule places the `article` element halfway down and 30% to the right of the top-left corner of its container.

```
article {
    position: absolute;
    top: 50%;
    left: 30%;
}
```

As the container of the article changes in width or height, the article's position will automatically change to match.

Fixed and Inherited Positioning

When you scroll through a document in the browser window, the page content scrolls along. If you want to fix an object within the browser window so that it doesn't scroll, you can set its `position` property to `fixed`. For example, the following style rule keeps the `footer` element at a fixed location, 10 pixels up from the bottom of the browser window:

```
footer {
    position: fixed;
    bottom: 10px;
}
```

Note that a fixed object might cover up other page content, so you should use it with care in your page design.

Finally, you can set the `position` property to `inherit` so that an element inherits the position value of its parent element.

Positioning Objects with CSS

- To shift an object from its default position, use the properties

```
position: relative;
top: value;
left: value;
bottom: value;
right: value;
```

where *value* is the distance in one of the CSS units of measure that the object should be shifted from the corresponding edge of its container.
- To place an object at a specified coordinate within its container, use the properties

```
position: absolute;
top: value;
left: value;
bottom: value;
right: value;
```

where *value* is a distance in one of the CSS units of measure or a percentage of the container's width or height.
- To fix an object within the browser window so that it does not scroll with the rest of the document content, use the property

```
position: fixed;
```

Using the Positioning Styles

Anne wants you to work on the layout for a page that contains an infographic on chocolate. She sketched the layout of the infographic page, as shown in Figure 3-49.

Figure 3-49 Proposed layout of the chocolate infographic

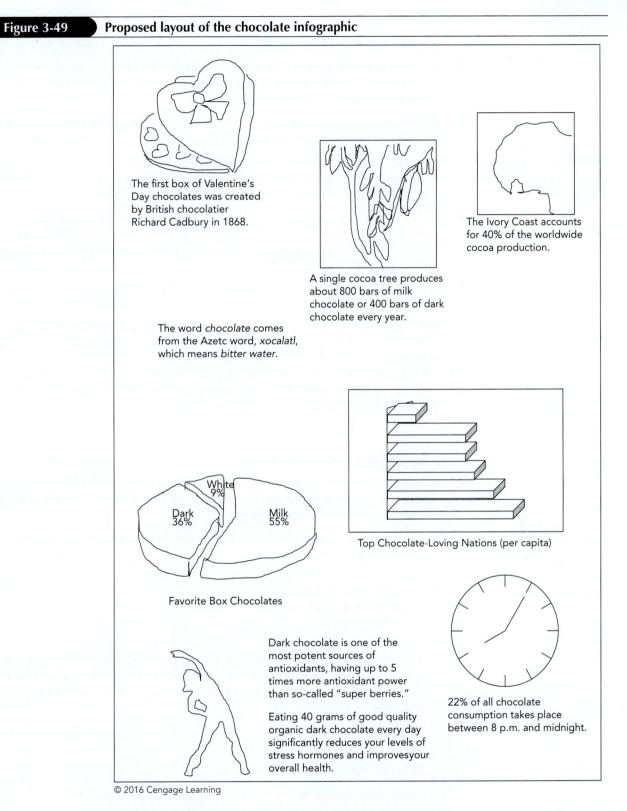

The first box of Valentine's Day chocolates was created by British chocolatier Richard Cadbury in 1868.

A single cocoa tree produces about 800 bars of milk chocolate or 400 bars of dark chocolate every year.

The Ivory Coast accounts for 40% of the worldwide cocoa production.

The word *chocolate* comes from the Azetc word, *xocalatl*, which means *bitter water*.

White 9%
Dark 36%
Milk 55%

Top Chocolate-Loving Nations (per capita)

Favorite Box Chocolates

Dark chocolate is one of the most potent sources of antioxidants, having up to 5 times more antioxidant power than so-called "super berries."

Eating 40 grams of good quality organic dark chocolate every day significantly reduces your levels of stress hormones and improvesyour overall health.

22% of all chocolate consumption takes place between 8 p.m. and midnight.

© 2016 Cengage Learning

Because the placement of the text and figures do not line up nicely within a grid, you'll position each graphic and text box using the CSS positioning styles. Anne has already created the content for this page and written the style sheets to format the appearance of the infographic. You will write the style sheet to layout the infographic contents using the CSS positioning styles.

To open the infographic file:

▶ **1.** Use your editor to open the **pc_info_txt.html** file from the html03 ▶ tutorial folder. Enter **your name** and **the date** in the comment section of the file and save the document as **pc_info.html**.

▶ **2.** Directly after the `title` element, insert the following `link` elements to attach the file to the pc_reset.css, pc_styles3.css, and pc_info.css style sheets.

```
<link href="pc_reset.css" rel="stylesheet" />
<link href="pc_styles3.css" rel="stylesheet" />
<link href="pc_info.css" rel="stylesheet" />
```

▶ **3.** Take some time to study the structure and content of the pc_info.html document. Note that Anne has placed eight information graphics, each within a separate `div` element with a class name of infobox and an id name ranging from info1 to info8.

▶ **4.** Close the file, saving your changes.

Next, you'll start working on the pc_info.css file, which will contain the positioning and other design styles for the objects in the infographic. You will begin by formatting the `main` element, which contains the infographics. Because you'll want the position of each infographic to be measured from the top-left corner of this container, you will place the `main` element with relative positioning and extend the height of the container to 1400 pixels so that it can contain all eight of the graphic elements.

To format the main element:

▶ **1.** Use your editor to open the **pc_info_txt.css** file from the html03 ▶ tutorial folder. Enter **your name** and **the date** in the comment section of the file and save the document as **pc_info.css**.

> When you want to position objects in an exact or absolute position within a container, set the `position` property of the container to `relative`.

▶ **2.** Go to the Main Styles section and insert the following style rule to format the appearance of the `main` element:

```
main {
    position: relative;
    height: 1400px;
    width: 100%;
}
```

It will be easier to see the effect of placing the different `div` elements if they are not displayed until you are ready to position them. Add a rule to hide the `div` elements, then as you position each element, you can add a style rule to redisplay it.

▶ **3.** Directly before the Main Styles section, insert the following style rule to hide all of the infoboxes:

```
div.infobox {display:none;}
```

Figure 3-50 highlights the newly added code in the style sheet.

Figure 3-50   Setting the display styles of the main element

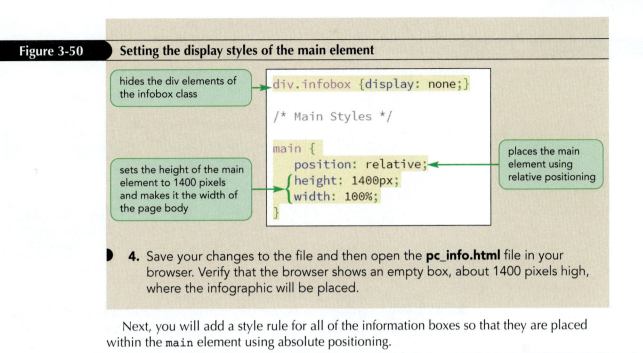

hides the div elements of the infobox class

```
div.infobox {display: none;}

/* Main Styles */

main {
    position: relative;
    height: 1400px;
    width: 100%;
}
```

sets the height of the main element to 1400 pixels and makes it the width of the page body

places the main element using relative positioning

4. Save your changes to the file and then open the **pc_info.html** file in your browser. Verify that the browser shows an empty box, about 1400 pixels high, where the infographic will be placed.

Next, you will add a style rule for all of the information boxes so that they are placed within the main element using absolute positioning.

To position the information boxes:

1. Return to the **pc_info.css** file in your editor and scroll down to the Infographic Styles section.

2. Add the following style rule to set the position type of all of the information boxes.

```
div.infobox {
    position: absolute;
}
```

3. Position the first information box 20 pixels from the top edge of its container and 5% from the left edge.

```
div#info1 {
    display: block;
    top: 20px;
    left: 5%;
}
```

Note that we set the `display` property to `block` so that the first information box is no longer hidden on the page. Figure 3-51 highlights the style rules for all of the information boxes and the placement of the first information box.

Figure 3-51 **Placing the first information box**

```
/* Infographic Styles */

div.infobox {
    position: absolute;
}

/* First Infographic */

div#info1 {
    display: block;
    top: 20px;
    left: 5%;
}
```

places every information box using absolute positioning

places the first box 20 pixels from the top edge of the main element and 5% from the left

4. Save your changes to the file and then reload the **pc_info.html** file in your browser. Figure 3-52 shows the placement of the first information box.

Figure 3-52 **Appearance of the first information box**

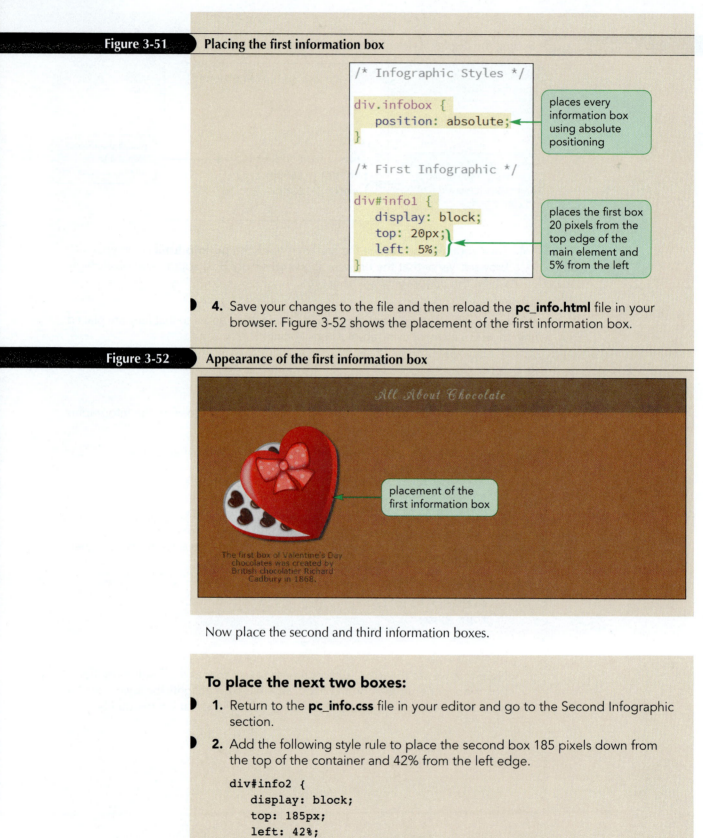

All About Chocolate

placement of the first information box

The first box of Valentine's Day chocolates was created by British chocolatier Richard Cadbury in 1868.

Now place the second and third information boxes.

To place the next two boxes:

1. Return to the **pc_info.css** file in your editor and go to the Second Infographic section.

2. Add the following style rule to place the second box 185 pixels down from the top of the container and 42% from the left edge.

```
div#info2 {
    display: block;
    top: 185px;
    left: 42%;
}
```

3. Within the Third Infographic section insert the following style rule to place the third box 135 pixels from the top edge and 75% of the width of its container from the left edge.

```
div#info3 {
    display: block;
    top: 135px;
    left: 75%;
}
```

Figure 3-53 highlights the style rules to position the second and third information boxes.

Figure 3-53   **Positions of the second and third boxes**

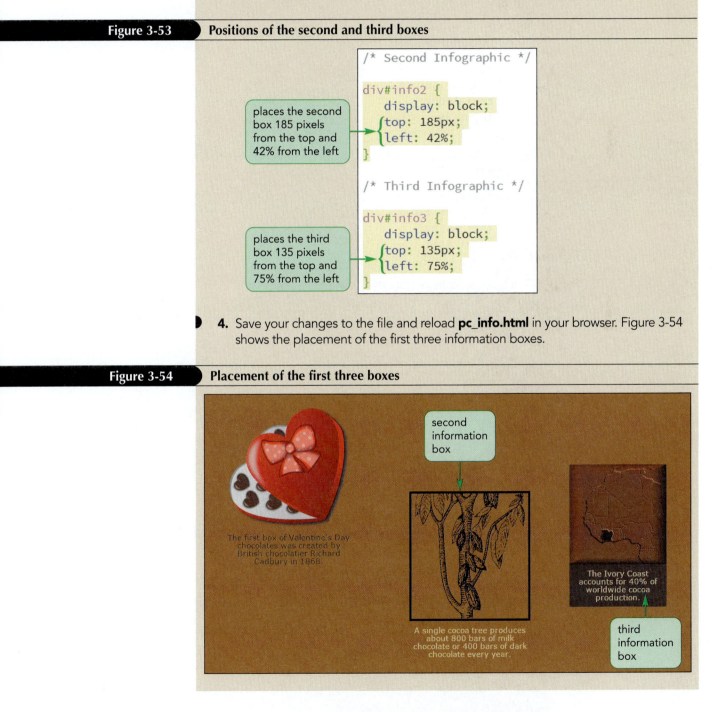

places the second box 185 pixels from the top and 42% from the left

```
/* Second Infographic */

div#info2 {
    display: block;
    top: 185px;
    left: 42%;
}
```

places the third box 135 pixels from the top and 75% from the left

```
/* Third Infographic */

div#info3 {
    display: block;
    top: 135px;
    left: 75%;
}
```

4. Save your changes to the file and reload **pc_info.html** in your browser. Figure 3-54 shows the placement of the first three information boxes.

Figure 3-54   **Placement of the first three boxes**

second information box

The first box of Valentine's Day chocolates was created by British chocolatier Richard Cadbury in 1868.

A single cocoa tree produces about 800 bars of milk chocolate or 400 bars of dark chocolate every year.

The Ivory Coast accounts for 40% of worldwide cocoa production.

third information box

Place the next three information boxes.

To place the next three boxes:

1. Return to the **pc_info.css** file in your editor, go to the Fourth Infographic section and place the fourth box 510 pixels from the top edge and 8% from the left edge.

```
div#info4 {
    display: block;
    top: 510px;
    left: 8%;
}
```

2. Add the following style rule to the Fifth Infographic section to position the fifth box:

```
div#info5 {
    display: block;
    top: 800px;
    left: 3%;
}
```

3. Add the following style rule to the Sixth Infographic section to position the sixth box:

```
div#info6 {
    display: block;
    top: 600px;
    left: 48%;
}
```

Figure 3-55 highlights the positioning styles for the fourth, fifth, and sixth information boxes.

Figure 3-55   **Positions of the fourth, fifth, and sixth boxes**

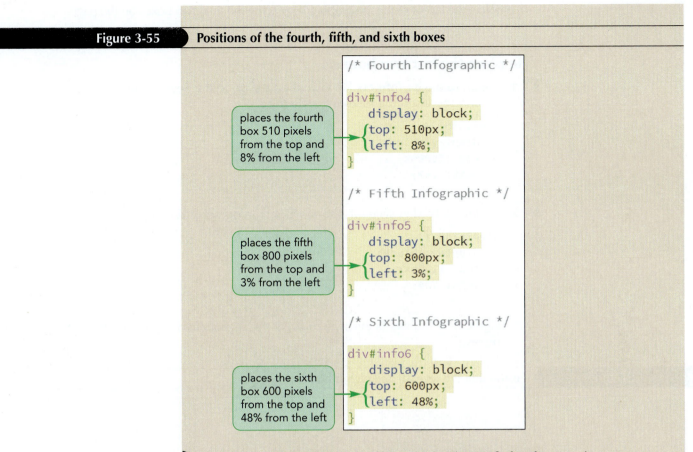

places the fourth box 510 pixels from the top and 8% from the left

```
/* Fourth Infographic */

div#info4 {
     display: block;
     top: 510px;
     left: 8%;
}
```

places the fifth box 800 pixels from the top and 3% from the left

```
/* Fifth Infographic */

div#info5 {
     display: block;
     top: 800px;
     left: 3%;
}
```

places the sixth box 600 pixels from the top and 48% from the left

```
/* Sixth Infographic */

div#info6 {
     display: block;
     top: 600px;
     left: 48%;
}
```

4. Save your changes to the file and reload **pc_info.html** in your browser. Figure 3-56 shows the revised layout of the infographic.

Figure 3-56   **Placement of the next three boxes**

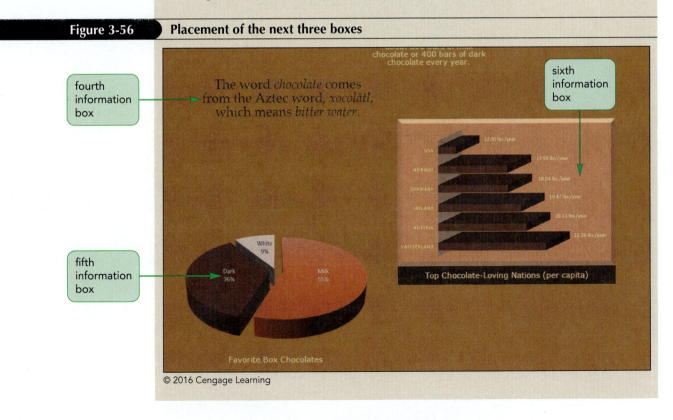

fourth information box

fifth information box

sixth information box

Complete the layout of the infographic by placing the final two boxes on the page.

To place the last two boxes:

1. Return to the **pc_info.css** file in your editor, go to the Seventh Infographic section and insert the following style rules:

```
div#info7 {
    display: block;
    top: 1000px;
    left: 68%;
}
```

2. Add the following style rules to the Eighth Infographic section:

```
div#info8 {
    display: block;
    top: 1100px;
    left: 12%;
}
```

Figure 3-57 highlights the style rules for the seventh and eighth information boxes.

Figure 3-57   **Positioning the seventh and eighth boxes**

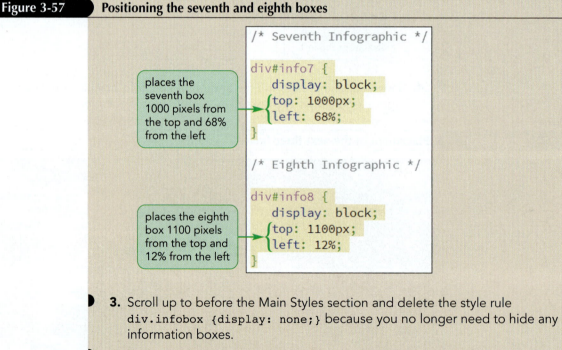

3. Scroll up to before the Main Styles section and delete the style rule `div.infobox {display: none;}` because you no longer need to hide any information boxes.

4. Save your changes to the file and reload **pc_info.html** in your browser. Figure 3-58 show the complete layout of the eight boxes in the infographic.

Figure 3-58   **Final layout of the infographic**

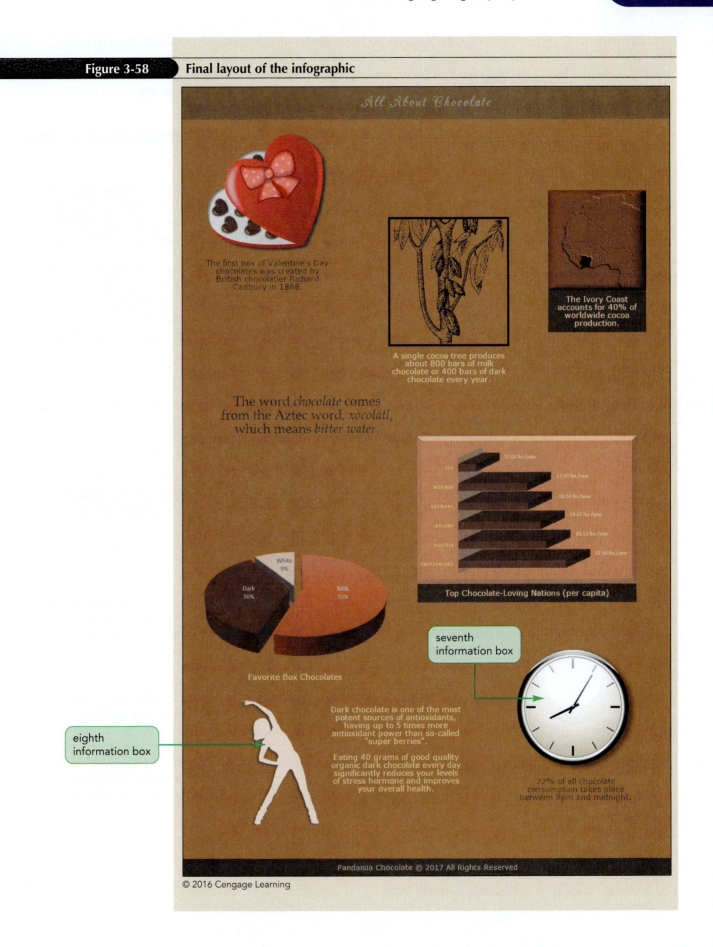

Anne likes the appearance of the infographic, but she is concerned about its length. She would like you to reduce the height of the infographic so that it appears within the boundaries of the browser window. This change will create overflow because the content is longer than the new height. You will read more about overflow and how to handle it now.

Creating an Irregular Line Wrap

Many desktop publishing and word-processing programs allow designers to create irregular line wraps in which the text appears to flow tightly around an image. This is not easily done in a web page layout because all images appear as rectangles rather than as irregularly shaped objects. However, with the aid of a graphics package, you can simulate an irregularly shaped image.

The trick is to use your graphics package to slice the image horizontally into several pieces and then crop the individual slices to match the edge of the image you want to display. Once you've edited all of the slices, you can use CSS to stack the separate slices by floating them on the left or right margin, displaying each slice only after the previous slice has been cleared. For example, the following style rule stacks all inline images that belong to the "slice" class on the right margin:

```
img.slice {
    clear: right;
    float: right;
    margin-top: 0px;
    margin-bottom: 0px;
}
```

Now any text surrounding the stack of images will tightly match the image's boundary, creating the illusion of an irregular line wrap. Note that you should always set the top and bottom margins to 0 pixels so that the slices join together seamlessly.

Handling Overflow

The infographic is long because it displays several information boxes. If you reduce the height of the infographic you run the risk of cutting off several of the boxes that will no longer fit within the reduced infographic. However you can control how your browser handles this excess content using the following overflow property

```
overflow: type;
```

where *type* is visible (the default), hidden, scroll, or auto. A value of visible instructs browsers to increase the height of an element to fit the overflow content. The hidden value keeps the element at the specified height and width, but cuts off excess content. The scroll value keeps the element at the specified dimensions, but adds horizontal and vertical scroll bars to allow users to scroll through the overflowed content. Finally, the auto value keeps the element at the specified size, adding scroll bars only as they are needed. Figure 3-59 shows examples of the effects of each overflow value on content that is too large for its space.

Figure 3-59   **Values of the overflow property**

overflow: visible;	overflow: hidden;	overflow: scroll;	overflow: auto;
We are a company located in Essex, Vermont, dedicated to making delicious chocolate and other treats. For our founder, chocolatier Anne Ambrose, this means using only the finest organic ingredients, incorporating a harmonious blend of rich flavors and smooth textures. Anne learned her trade as part of a three-year apprenticeship program in Switzerland. Her introduction into the world of confectioneries was a springboard to working with leaders in the field. Early in 1993 she brought that expertise back to Vermont and Pandaisia Chocolates was born.	We are a company located in Essex, Vermont, dedicated to making delicious chocolate and other treats. For our founder, chocolatier Anne Ambrose, this means using only the finest organic ingredients, incorporating a harmonious blend of rich flavors and smooth textures. Anne learned her trade as part of a three-year apprenticeship program in Switzerland. Her introduction into the world of confectioneries was a springboard to working with leaders in the field. Early in 1993 she brought that expertise back to	We are a company located in Essex, Vermont, dedicated to making delicious chocolate and other treats. For our founder, chocolatier Anne Ambrose, this means using only the finest organic ingredients, incorporating a harmonious blend of rich flavors and smooth textures. Anne learned her trade as part of a three-year apprenticeship program in Switzerland. Her introduction into the world of confectioneries was a	We are a company located in Essex, Vermont, dedicated to making delicious chocolate and other treats. For our founder, chocolatier Anne Ambrose, this means using only the finest organic ingredients, incorporating a harmonious blend of rich flavors and smooth textures. Anne learned her trade as part of a three-year apprenticeship program in Switzerland. Her introduction into the world of confectioneries was a springboard to working with
box extends to make all of the content visible	overflowed content is hidden from the reader	horizontal and vertical scrollbars are added to the box	scrollbars are added only where needed

CSS3 also provides the `overflow-x` and `overflow-y` properties to handle overflow specifically in the horizontal and vertical directions.

Working with Overflow

- To specify how the browser should handle content that overflows the element's boundaries, use the property

  `overflow: type;`

  where *type* is `visible` (the default), `hidden`, `scroll`, or `auto`.

You decide to limit the height of the infographic to 450 pixels and to set the `overflow` property to `auto` so that browsers displays scroll bars as needed for the excess content.

To apply the `overflow` property:

1. Return to the **pc_info.css** file in your editor and go to the Main Styles section.

2. Within the style rule for the `main` selector, insert the property **overflow: auto;**.

3. Reduce the height of the element from 1400px to **450px**.

   Figure 3-60 highlights the revised code in the style rule.

Figure 3-60   Setting the overflow property

```
/* Main Styles */

main {
    overflow: auto;
    position: relative;
    height: 450px;
    width: 100%;
}
```

displays scrollbars if the content overflows the allotted height

sets the height of the infographic to 450 pixels

4. Close the file, saving your changes.

5. Reload the **pc_info.html** file in your browser. As shown in Figure 3-61, the height of the infographic has been reduced to 450 pixels and scrollbars have been added that you can use to view the entire infographic.

Figure 3-61   Final layout of the infographic page

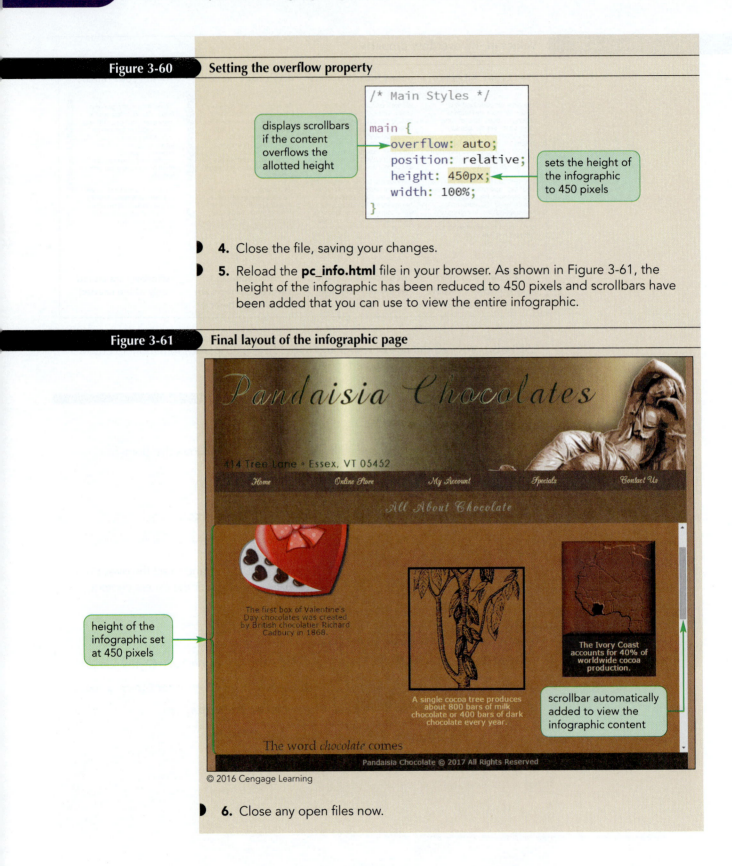

height of the infographic set at 450 pixels

scrollbar automatically added to view the infographic content

© 2016 Cengage Learning

6. Close any open files now.

Managing White Space with CSS

Scroll bars for overflow content are usually placed vertically so that you scroll down to view the extra content. In some page layouts, however, you may want to view content in a horizontal rather than a vertical direction. You can accomplish this by adding the following style properties to the element:

```
overflow: auto;
white-space: nowrap;
```

The white-space property defines how browsers should handle white space in the rendered document. The default is to collapse consecutive occurrences of white space into a single blank space and to automatically wrap text to a new line if it extends beyond the width of the container. However, you can set the white-space property of the element to nowrap to keep inline content on a single line, preventing line wrapping. With the content thus confined to a single line, browsers will display only horizontal scroll bars for the overflow content. Other values of the white-space property include normal (for default handling of white space), pre (to preserve all white space from the HTML file), and pre-wrap (to preserve white space but to wrap excess content to a new line).

Clipping an Element

Closely related to the overflow property is the clip property, which defines a rectangular region through which an element's content can be viewed. Anything that lies outside the boundary of the rectangle is hidden. The syntax of the clip property is

```
clip: rect(top, right, bottom, left);
```

where top, right, bottom, and left define the coordinates of the clipping rectangle. For example, a clip value of rect(100px, 270px, 260px, 65px) defines a clip region whose top and bottom boundaries are 100 and 260 pixels from the top edge of the element, and whose right and left boundaries are 270 and 65 pixels from the element's left edge. See Figure 3-62.

Figure 3-62   **Clipping an image**

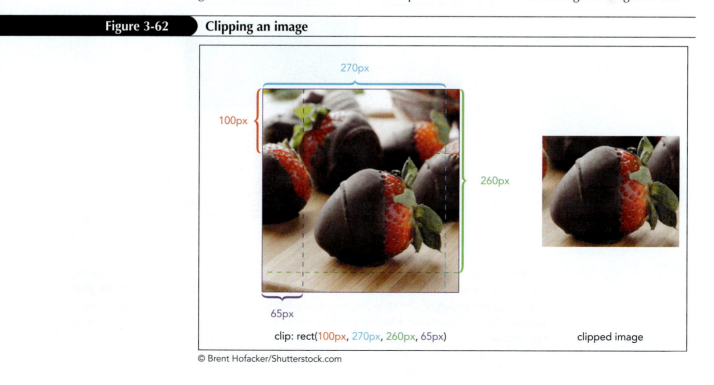

clip: rect(100px, 270px, 260px, 65px)   clipped image

The top, right, bottom, and left values also can be set to `auto`, which matches the specified edge of the clipping region to the edge of the parent element. A clip value of rect(10, auto, 125, 75) creates a clipping rectangle whose right edge matches the right edge of the parent element. To remove clipping completely, apply the style `clip: auto`. Clipping can only be applied when the object is placed using absolute positioning.

Clipping Content

- To clip an element's content, use the property

  `clip: rect(top, right, bottom, left);`

  where *top*, *right*, *bottom*, and *left* define the coordinates of the clipping rectangle.
- To remove clipping for a clipped object, use

  `clip: auto;`

Stacking Elements

Positioning elements can sometimes lead to objects that overlap each other. By default, elements that are loaded later by the browser are displayed on top of elements that are loaded earlier. In addition, elements placed using CSS positioning are stacked on top of elements that are not. To specify a different stacking order, use the following `z-index` property:

`z-index: value;`

where *value* is a positive or negative integer, or the keyword `auto`. As shown in Figure 3-63, objects with the highest z-index values are placed on top of other page objects. A value of `auto` stacks the object using the default rules.

Figure 3-63   **Using the z-index property to stack elements**

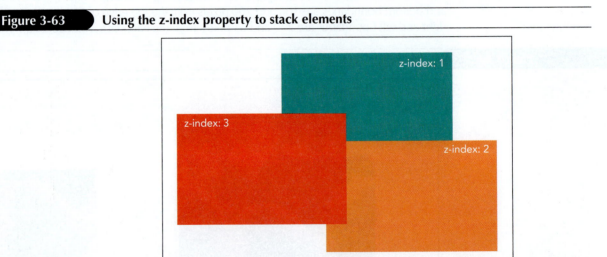

© 2016 Cengage Learning

The `z-index` property works only for elements that are placed with absolute positioning. Also, an element's z-index value determines its position relative only to other elements that share a common parent; the style has no impact when applied to elements with different parents. Figure 3-64 shows a layout in which the object with a high z-index value of 4 is still covered because it is nested within another object that has a low z-index value of 1.

Figure 3-64   Stacking nested objects

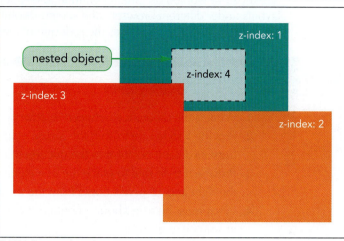

© 2016 Cengage Learning

You do not need to include the `z-index` property in your style sheet because none of the elements in the infographic page are stacked upon another.

Problem Solving: Principles of Design

Good web page design is based on the same common principles found in other areas of art, which include balance, unity, contrast, rhythm, and emphasis. A pleasing layout involves the application of most, if not all, of these principles, which are detailed below:

- **Balance** involves the distribution of elements. It's common to think of balance in terms of **symmetrical balance**, in which similar objects offset each other like items on a balance scale; but you often can achieve more interesting layouts through asymmetrical balance, in which one large page object is balanced against two or more smaller objects.
- **Unity** is the ability to combine different design elements into a cohesive whole. This is accomplished by having different elements share common colors, font styles, and sizes. One way to achieve unity in a layout is to place different objects close to each other, forcing your viewers' eyes to see these items as belonging to a single unified object.
- **Contrast** consists of the differences among all of the page elements. To create an effective design, you need to vary the placement, size, color, and general appearance of the objects in the page so that your viewers' eyes aren't bored by the constant repetition of a single theme.
- **Rhythm** is the repetition or alteration of a design element in order to provide a sense of movement, flow, and progress. You can create rhythm by tiling the same image horizontally or vertically across the page, by repeating a series of elements that progressively increase or decrease in size or spacing, or by using elements with background colors of the same hue but that gradually vary in saturation or lightness.
- **Emphasis** involves working with the focal point of a design. Your readers need a few key areas to focus on. It's a common design mistake to assign equal emphasis to all page elements. Without a focal point, there is nothing for your viewers' eyes to latch onto. You can give a page element emphasis by increasing its size, by giving it a contrasting color, or by assigning it a prominent position in the page.

Designers usually have an intuitive sense of what works and what doesn't in page design, though often they can't say why. These design principles are important because they provide a context in which to discuss and compare designs. If your page design doesn't feel like it's working, evaluate it in light of these principles to identify where it might be lacking.

PROSKILLS

Anne is pleased with the final design of the infographic page and all of the other pages you've worked on. She'll continue to develop the website and test her page layouts under different browsers and screen resolutions. She'll get back to you with future projects as she continues the redesign of the Pandaisia Chocolates website.

REVIEW

Session 3.3 Quick Check

1. What is the difference between relative positioning and absolute positioning?
2. Provide a style rule to shift the `aside` element 5% to the right and 10% down from its default position in the document flow.
3. Provide a style rule to place the `div` element with the id *graph1* 50 pixels to the right and 15 pixels down from the top-left corner of its container element.
4. What must be true about a container element to have objects positioned absolutely within it?
5. Provide a style rule to set the height of a navigation list with the id *nav1* to 300 pixels but to be displayed with a scrollbar if there are too many entries to fit within the navigation list's boundaries.
6. An inline image with the id *logo_img* is 400 pixels wide by 300 pixels high. Provide a style rule to clip this image by 10 pixels on each edge.
7. One element has a `z-index` value of 1; a second element has a `z-index` value of 5. Will the second element always be displayed on top of the first? Explain why or why not.

Review Assignments

Data Files needed for the Review Assignments: pc_specials_txt.html, pc_specials_txt.css, 2 CSS files, 8 PNG files, 1 TTF file, 1 WOFF file

Anne wants you to work on another page for the Pandaisia Chocolates website. This page will contain information on some of the specials offered by the company in March; it will also display a list of some awards that the company has won. As you work on the page, you will use clip art images as placeholders until photographs of the awards are available. A preview of the completed page is shown in Figure 3-65.

Figure 3-65	March Specials web page

Anne has already created the page content and some of the design styles to be used in the page. Your job will be to come up with the CSS style sheet to set the page layout.

Complete the following:

1. Use your editor to open the **pc_specials_txt.html** and **pc_specials_txt.css** files from the html03 ▸ review folder. Enter *your name* and *the date* in the comment section of each file, and save them as **pc_specials.html** and **pc_specials.css** respectively.

2. Go to the **pc_specials.html** file in your editor. Within the document head, create links to the pc_reset2.css, pc_styles4.css, and pc_specials.css style sheets.

3. Take some time to study the content and structure of the document, paying careful attention to the use of ids and class names in the file. Save your changes to the file.

4. Go to the **pc_specials.css** file in your editor. Within the Page Body Styles section, add a style rule for the `body` element that sets the width of the page body to 95% of the browser window width within the range 640 pixels to 960 pixels. Horizontally center the page body within the window by setting the left and right margins to `auto`.

5. Go to the Image Styles section and create a style rule that displays all `img` elements as blocks with a width of 100%.

6. Anne wants the navigation list to be displayed horizontally on the page. Go to the Horizontal Navigation Styles section and create a style rule for every list item within a horizontal navigation list that displays the list item as a block floated on the left margin with a width of 16.66%.

7. Display every hypertext link nested within a navigation list item as a block.

8. Next, you'll create the style rules for the grid section of the March Specials page. Go to the Row Styles section. For every `div` element of the newRow class, create a style rule that displays the element with a width of 100% and only when all floated elements have been cleared. Using the technique from this tutorial, add another style rule that uses the `after` pseudo-element to expand each newRow class of the `div` element around its floating columns.

9. Next, you'll format the grid columns. Go to the Column Styles section. Create a style rule to float all `div` elements whose class value starts with "col-" on the left margin. Set the padding around all such elements to 2%. Finally, apply the Border Box Sizing model to the content of those elements. (*Note*: Remember to use web extensions to provide support for older browsers.)

10. In the same section, create style rules for `div` elements with class names col-1-1, col-1-2, col-1-3, col-2-3, col-1-4, and col-3-4 to set their widths to 100%, 50%, 33.33%, 66.67%, 25%, and 75% respectively.

11. Go to the Specials Styles section. In this section, you will create styles for the monthly specials advertised by the company. Create a style rule for all `div` elements of the specials class that sets the minimum height to 400 pixels and adds a 1 pixel dashed outline around the element with a color value of rgb(71, 52, 29).

12. Go to the Award Styles section. In this section, you will create styles for the list of awards won by Pandaisia Chocolates. Information boxes for the awards are placed within the `div` element with id *awardList*. Create a style rule for this element that places it using relative positioning, sets its height to 650 pixels, and automatically displays scrollbars for any overflow content.

13. Every information box in the awardList element is stored in a `div` element belonging to the awards class. Create a style rule that places these elements with absolute positioning and sets their width to 30%.

14. Position the individual awards within the awardList box by creating style rules for the `div` elements with id values ranging from award1 to award5 at the following (*top, left*) coordinates: award1 (80px, 5%), award2 (280px, 60%), award3 (400px, 20%), award4 (630px, 45%), and award5 (750px, 5%). (Hint: In the pc_specials.html file, the five awards have been placed in a `div` element belonging to the awards class with id values ranging from award1 to award5.)

15. Go to the Footer Styles section and create a style rule for the body footer that displays the footer once both margins are clear of previously floated elements.

16. Save your changes to the style sheet and then open the **pc_specials.html** file in your browser. Verify that the layout and design styles resemble the page shown in Figure 3-65.

Case Problem 1

Data Files needed for this Case Problem: sp_home_txt.html, sp_layout_txt.cst, 2 CSS files, 11 PNG files

Slate & Pencil Tutoring Karen Cooke manages the website for *Slate & Pencil Tutoring*, an online tutoring service for high school and college students. Karen is overseeing the redesign of the website and has hired you to work on the layout of the site's home page. Figure 3-66 shows a preview of the page you'll create for Karen.

Figure 3-66 Slate & Pencil Tutoring home page

© 2016 Cengage Learning; © Monkey Business Images/Shutterstock.com;
© Courtesy Patrick Carey

Karen has supplied you with the HTML file and the graphic files. She has also given you a base style sheet to initiate your web design and a style sheet containing several typographic styles. Your job will be to write up a layout style sheet according to Karen's specifications.

Complete the following:

1. Using your editor, open the **sp_home_txt.html** and **sp_layout_txt.css** files from the html03 ▸ case1 folder. Enter ***your name*** and ***the date*** in the comment section of each file, and save them as **sp_home.html** and **sp_layout.css** respectively.

2. Go to the **sp_home.html** file in your editor. Within the document head, create links to the **sp_base.css**, **sp_styles.css**, and **sp_layout.css** style sheet files. Study the content and structure of the file and then save your changes to the document.

3. Go to the **sp_layout.css** file in your editor. Go to the Window and Body Styles section. Create a style rule for the `html` element that sets the height of the browser window at 100%.

4. Create a style rule for the page body that sets the width to 95% of the browser window ranging from 640 pixels up to 960 pixels. Horizontally center the page body within the browser window. Finally, Karen wants to ensure that the height of the page body is always at least as high as the browser window itself. Set the minimum height of the browser window to 100%.

5. Create a style rule to apply the Border Box model to all `header`, `ul`, `nav`, `li`, and `a` elements in the document.

6. Go to the Row Styles section. Karen has placed all elements that should be treated as grid rows in the row class. For every element of the row class, create a style rule that expands the element to cover any floating content within the element. (Hint: Use the technique shown in the tutorial that employs the `after` pseudo-element.)

7. Go to the Page Header Styles section. In this section, you will create styles for the content of the body header. Create a style rule for the logo image within the body header that displays the image as a block with a width of 70% of the header, floated on the left margin.

8. The header also contains a navigation list that Karen wants to display vertically. Create a style rule for the `nav` element within the body header that: a) floats the navigation list on the left, b) sets the size of the left and right padding to 2%, and c) sets the width of the navigation list to 30% of the width of the header.

9. The hypertext links in the navigation list should be displayed as blocks. Create a style rule for every `a` element in the header navigation list that displays the element as a block with a width of 100%.

10. Go to the Horizontal Navigation List Styles section. Karen has added a second navigation list that she wants to display horizontally. For all list items within the horizontal navigation list, create a style rule that displays the items as blocks with a width of 12.5% floated on the left margin.

11. Go to the Topics Styles section. This section sets the styles for a list of four topics describing what the company is offering. Karen wants this list to also be displayed horizontally on the page. For list items within the `ul` element with the id *topics*, create a style rule to: a) display the items as blocks with a width of 20%, b) float the items on the left margin, and c) set the size of the left margin space to 0% and the right margin space to 1.5%.

12. Karen wants the topics list to be well away from the left and right edges of the page body. In the same section, create a rule that sets the size of the left margin of the first item in the topics list to 7.75% and sets the right margin of the last item to 7.75%.

13. In the same section, create a rule that displays the image within each list item in the topics list as a block with a width of 50% and centered within the list item block. (Hint: Set the left and right margins to auto.)

14. Go to the HR Styles section. The `hr` element is used to display a horizontal divider between sections of the page. Add a style rule that sets the width of the `hr` element to 50%.

15. Go to the Customer Comment Styles section. In this section, you will create style rules for the customer comments displayed near the bottom of the page. For the `ul` element with the id *comments*, create a style rule that sets the width to 75% and centers the element by setting the top/bottom margin to 40 pixels and the left/right margin to auto.

16. Karen wants the list items to appear in two columns on the page. In the same section, create a style rule for every list item in the comments list that: a) displays the item as a block with a width of 50% floated on the left and b) sets the size of the bottom margin to 30 pixels.

17. Every customer comment is accompanied by an image of the student. Karen wants these images displayed to the left of the comment. Create a style rule to display the image within each comment list item as a block with a width of 20%, floated on the left, and with a left/right margin of 5%.

18. Create a style rule for every paragraph nested within a customer list item that floats the paragraph on the left margin with a width of 70%.

19. Go to the Footer Styles section and create a style rule that displays the footer only when both margins are clear of floating objects.

20. Save your changes to the file and then open the **sp_home.html** file in your browser. Verify that the layout and appearance of the page elements resemble that shown in Figure 3-66.

Case Problem 2

Data Files needed for this Case Problem: ce_front_txt.html, ce_grids_txt.css, ce_styles_txt.css, 21 PNG files

Costume Expressions   Richard Privette is the owner of *Costume Expressions*, a small but growing costume and party business located in Rockville, Maryland. He has asked you to work on the website for the company. Richard envisions a front page that resembles the jumbled advertising pages often found in the back pages of the comic books from his youth. Figure 3-67 shows a preview of the grid-based layout he has in mind.

Figure 3-67   Costume Expressions front page

© 2016 Cengage Learning; © Oleg Gekman/Shutterstock.com;
© Pavel L Photo and Video/Shutterstock.com; © Courtesy Patrick Carey;
© Robles Designery/Shutterstock.com

Richard has supplied you with the HTML code and all of the image files required for this page. You'll supply him with style sheets based on a grid layout that he can use to render his page's content.

Complete the following:

1. Using your editor, open the **ce_front_txt.html**, **ce_styles_txt.css**, and **ce_grids_txt.css** files from the html03 ▸ case2 folder. Enter *your name* and *the date* in the comment section of each file, and save them as **ce_front.html**, **ce_styles.css**, and **ce_grids.css** respectively.

2. Go to the **ce_front.html** file in your editor. Within the document head, create links to the **ce_styles.css** and **ce_grids.css** style sheet files. Take some time to study the structure of the document. Note that Richard has placed much of the document content within a `div` element with the name container and that grid rows are marked with the row class and grid columns are marked with the column *size* class where *size* indicates the width of the column. The content of the page consists almost entirely of images that Richard will link to pages in the Costume Expressions website later.

3. Save your changes to the file and then go to the **ce_grids.css** file in your editor.

4. Within the Grid Rows Styles section, create a style rule to set the width of each `div` element of the row class to 100% of its container, displaying the row only when it's clear of floated content on both margins.

5. Create a style rule to allow grid rows to expand around all of their floated content.

6. Go to the Grid Columns Style section. Create a style rule to float every `div` element whose class name begins with *column* on the left.

7. Create style rules for `div` elements belonging to the following classes: column100, column50, column33, column67, column25, column75, column20, column40, column60, and column80 so that the width of each column is a percent equal to the size value. For example, `div` elements belonging to the column100 class should have widths of 100%, column50 should have widths of 50%, and so forth.

8. Go to the Grid Spacing Styles section. Create a style rule to apply the Border Box model to the `div` elements belonging to the following classes: container, row, classes that begin with *column*, cell, and a elements nested within `div` elements belonging to the cell class.

9. Save your changes to the **ce_grids.css** file and then go to the **ce_styles.css** file in your editor.

10. Go to the Window and Body Styles section and create a style rule to set the background color of the browser window to rgb(101, 101, 101).

11. Create a style rule for the `body` element that: a) sets the background color to white, b) sets the default font to the stack: Verdana, Geneva, Arial, sans-serif, c) centers the page by setting the top/bottom margins to 20 pixels and the left/right margins to auto, and d) sets the width of the page body to 95% ranging from 320 pixels up to 960 pixels.

12. Insert style rules to display all images in the document as blocks with widths of 100%.

13. Insert a style rule to remove all underlining from hypertext links within navigation lists.

14. Go to the Body Header Styles section. Richard wants you to format the links that are displayed in the header at the top of the web page. To format the links, create a style rule that sets the background color of the body header to rgb(191, 68, 70) and sets the height to 40 pixels.

15. Create a style that displays all list items within the navigation unordered list in the body header as blocks, floated on the left, with a right margin of 20 pixels and top/bottom padding of 10 pixels with left/right padding of 0 pixels.

16. Create a style rule to set the font size of hypertext links within the body header navigation list to 0.9em with a color value of rgb(51, 51, 51) for both visited and non-visited links. Change the text color to rgb(255, 211, 211) when the user hovers over or activates those links.

17. Go to the DIV Container Styles section. Richard wants you to add some additional spacing between the images and the edge of the page body. To add this spacing, create a style rule that sets the right and bottom padding of the `div` element with the id *container* to 8 pixels.

18. For every `a` element within a `div` element belonging to the cell class, create a style rule to: a) display the hypertext link as a block with a width of 100% and b) set the left and top padding to 8 pixels.

19. Richard wants the page footer to be displayed in the bottom right corner of the web page. To place the footer in this position, go to the Windows and Body Styles section and set the `position` property of the `body` element to relative, then go to the Footer Styles section and create a style rule for the `footer` element to do the following: a) set the `position` property of the footer to absolute with a right coordinate and bottom coordinate of 8 pixels, b) set the text of the footer to rgb(143, 33, 36), c) right-align the footer text, and d) set the font size to 2vmin so that the text resizes automatically with the width and/or height of the browser window.

20. Save your changes to the **ce_styles.css** file and then open the **ce_front.html** file in your browser. Verify that the layout resembles that shown in Figure 3-67.

CHALLENGE

Case Problem 3

Data Files needed for this Case Problem: ss_dday_txt.html, ss_layout_txt.css, 1 CSS file, 3 PNG files

A Soldier's Scrapbook   Jakob Bauer is a curator at the Veteran's Museum in Raleigh, North Carolina. Currently he is working on an exhibit called *A Soldier's Scrapbook* containing mementos, artifacts, journals, and other historic items from the Second World War. You've been asked to work on a page for an interactive kiosk used by visitors to the exhibit. Jakob has already supplied much of the text and graphics for the kiosk pages but he wants you to complete the job by working on the page layout.

The page you will work on provides an overview of the Normandy beach landings on June 6th, 1944. Since this page will be displayed only on the kiosk monitor, whose screen dimensions are known, you'll employ a fixed layout based on a screen width of 1152 pixels.

Jakob also wants you to include an interactive map of the Normandy coast where the user can hover a mouse pointer over location markers to view information associated with each map point. To create this effect, you'll mark each map point as a hypertext link so that you can apply the `hover` pseudo-class to the location. In addition to the interactive map, Jakob wants you to create a drop cap for the first letter of the first paragraph in the article describing the Normandy invasion. Figure 3-68 shows a preview of the page you'll create.

Figure 3-68 Normandy Invasion kiosk page

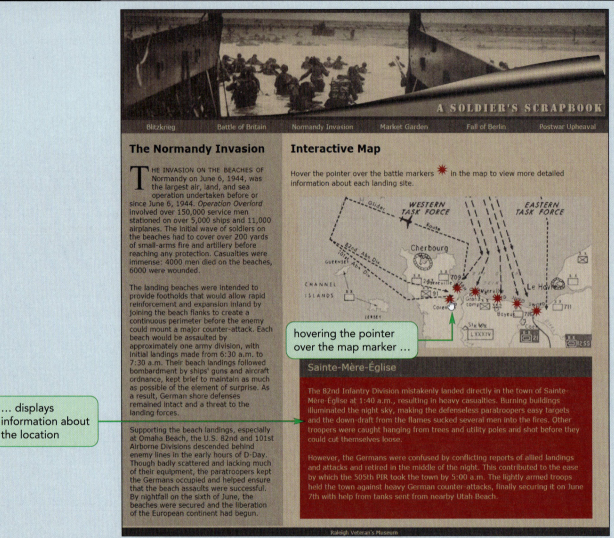

© 2016 Cengage Learning; source: Chief Photographer's Mate (CPHOM) Robert F. Sargent, U.S. Coast Guard; source: U.S Department of Defense; © Patrick Carey

Complete the following:

1. Using your editor, open the **ss_dday_txt.html** and **ss_layout_txt.css** files from the html03 ▶ case3 folder. Enter **your name** and **the date** in the comment section of each file, and save them as **ss_dday.html** and **ss_layout.css** respectively.

2. Go to the **ss_dday.html** file in your editor. Within the document head, create links to the **ss_styles.css** and **ss_layout.css** style sheet files. Study the content and structure of the document. Note that within the `aside` element is an image for the battle map with the id *mapImage*. Also note that there are six marker images enclosed within hypertext links with ids ranging from marker1 to maker6. After each marker image are `div` elements of the mapInfo class with IDs ranging from info1 to info6. Part of your style sheet will include style rules to display these `div` elements in response to the mouse pointer hovering over each of the six marker images.

3. Save your changes to the file and then go to the **ss_layout.css** file in your editor.

4. Go to the Article Styles section. Within this section, you'll lay out the article describing the Normandy Invasion. Create a style rule to float the `article` element on the left margin and set its width to 384 pixels.

⊕ **Explore** 5. Jakob wants the first line from the article to be displayed in small capital letters. Go to the First Line and Drop Cap Styles section and create a style rule for the first paragraph of the article element and the first line of that paragraph, setting the font size to 1.25em and the font variant to small-caps. (Hint: Use the `first-of-type` pseudo-class for the paragraph and the `first-line` pseudo-element for the first line of that paragraph.)

⊕ **Explore** 6. Jakob also wants the first letter of the first line in the article's opening paragraph to be displayed as a drop cap. Create a style rule for the article's first paragraph and first letter that applies the following styles: a) sets the size of the first letter to 4em in a serif font and floats it on the left, b) sets the line height to 0.8em, and c) sets the right and bottom margins to 5 pixels. (Hint: Use the `first-letter` pseudo-element for the first letter of that paragraph.)

7. The interactive map is placed within an `aside` element that Jakob wants displayed alongside the Normandy Invasion article. Go the Aside Styles section and create a style rule that sets the width of the aside element to 768 pixels and floats it on the left margin.

8. Next, you will lay out the interactive map. The interactive map is placed within a `div` element with the ID *battleMap*. Go to the Map Styles section and create a style rule for this element that sets its width to 688 pixels. Center the map by setting its top/bottom margins to 20 pixels and its left/right margins to `auto`. Place the map using relative positioning.

9. The actual map image is placed within an `img` element with the ID *mapImage*. Create a style rule for this element that displays it as a block with a width of 100%.

10. Go to the Interactive Map Styles section. Within this section, you'll create style rules that position each of the six map markers onto the battle map. The markers are placed within hypertext links. Create a style rule for every `a` element of the battleMarkers class that places the hypertext link using absolute positioning.

11. Create style rules for the six `a` elements with IDs ranging from marker1 to marker6, placing them at the following (*top, left*) coordinates:

    marker1   (220, 340)
    marker2   (194, 358)
    marker3   (202, 400)
    marker4   (217, 452)
    marker5   (229, 498)
    marker6   (246, 544)

12. The information associated with each map marker has been placed in `div` elements belonging to the mapInfo class. Go to the Map Information Styles section and create a style rule that hides this class of elements so that this information is not initially visible on the page.

⊕ **Explore** 13. To display the information associated with each map maker, you need to create a style rule that changes the map information's `display` property in response to the mouse pointer hovering over the corresponding map marker. Since the map information follows the map marker in the HTML file, use the following selector (see Figure 2-12) to select the map information corresponding to the hovered map marker: `a.battleMarkers:hover + div.mapInfo`. Write a style rule for this selector that sets its `display` property to `block`.

14. Save your changes to the style sheet and then load **ss_dday.html** in your browser. Verify that a drop cap appears for the first letter of the Normandy Invasion article and the first line of the first paragraph is displayed in small caps. Test the interactive map by first verifying that none of the information about the six battle locations appears on the page unless you hover your mouse pointer over the marker on the battle map. Further verify that when you are not hovering over the battle marker, the information is once again not visible on the page.

Case Problem 4

Data Files needed for this Case Problem: pcg_front_txt.html, pcg_paper_txt.css, 2 JPG files, 7 TXT files

The Park City Gazette Estes Park, Colorado, is a rural mountain community next to Rocky Mountain National Park. Kevin Webber is the editor of the weekly *Park City Gazette*. The paper recently redesigned its printed layout, and Kevin wants you to do the same thing for the online version. He's prepared several files containing sample text from recent articles and a few lists of links that usually appear in the front page of the newspaper's website. He's also provided you with image files that can be used for the paper's logo and background. Your job will be to use all of these pieces to create a sample web page for him to evaluate.

Complete the following:

1. Using your editor, open the **pcg_front_txt.html** and **pcg_paper_txt.css** files from the html03 ▸ case4 folder. Save them as **pcg_front.html** and **pcg_paper.css** respectively.

2. Using the content of the address, two links, and four story text files, create the content and structure of the pcg_front.html file. You are free to supplement the material in these text files with additional content of your own if appropriate. Use the # symbol for the value of the `href` attribute in your hypertext links because you will be linking to pages that don't actually exist.

3. Link the pcg_front.html file to the pcg_paper.css style sheet file and then save your changes.

4. Go to the **pcg_paper.css** style sheet file in your editor and create a layout for your Park City Gazette sample page. The layout should be based on a fluid design ranging from 640 pixels up to 960 pixels.

5. The specifics of the page design are up to your imagination and skill but must include the following features:
   - Use of the `display` property
   - Application of `width` and `height` style properties
   - Floated elements and cleared elements
   - A container element with a style rule so that it expands around its floated content
   - Defined margin and padding spaces as well as maximum and minimum widths
   - An example of relative or absolute positioning

6. Test your layout and design on a variety of devices, browsers, and screen resolutions to ensure that your sample page is readable under different conditions.

Graphic Design with CSS

Creating a Graphic Design for a Genealogy Website

Case | *Tree and Book*

Kevin Whitmore is the founder of *Tree and Book*, a social networking website for people interested in documenting their family histories, creating online photo albums, and posting stories and information about members of their extended families. He has come to you for help in upgrading the site's design. Kevin wants to take advantage of some of the CSS styles that can be used to add interesting visual effects to his site in order to give his website more impact and visual interest.

STARTING DATA FILES

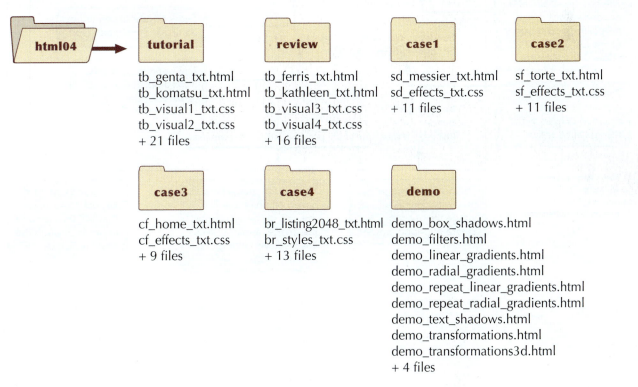

html04 → tutorial
tb_genta_txt.html
tb_komatsu_txt.html
tb_visual1_txt.css
tb_visual2_txt.css
+ 21 files

review
tb_ferris_txt.html
tb_kathleen_txt.html
tb_visual3_txt.css
tb_visual4_txt.css
+ 16 files

case1
sd_messier_txt.html
sd_effects_txt.css
+ 11 files

case2
sf_torte_txt.html
sf_effects_txt.css
+ 11 files

case3
cf_home_txt.html
cf_effects_txt.css
+ 9 files

case4
br_listing2048_txt.html
br_styles_txt.css
+ 13 files

demo
demo_box_shadows.html
demo_filters.html
demo_linear_gradients.html
demo_radial_gradients.html
demo_repeat_linear_gradients.html
demo_repeat_radial_gradients.html
demo_text_shadows.html
demo_transformations.html
demo_transformations3d.html
+ 4 files

Session 4.1 Visual Overview:

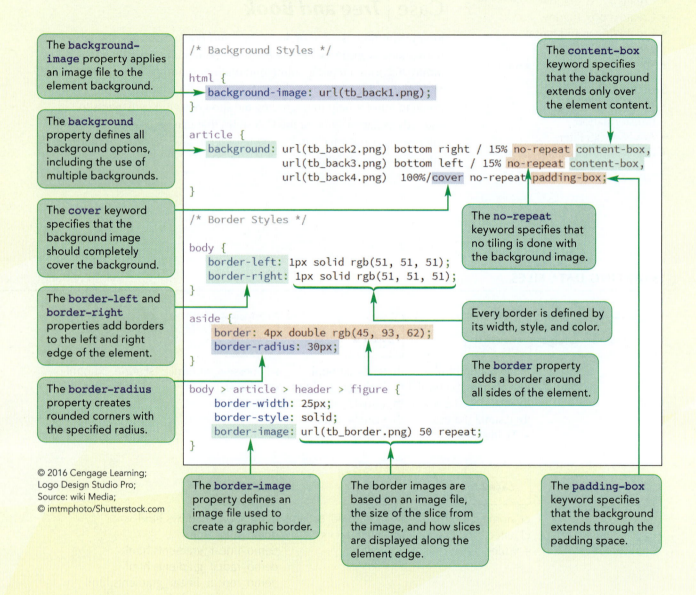

The **background-image** property applies an image file to the element background.

The **background** property defines all background options, including the use of multiple backgrounds.

The **cover** keyword specifies that the background image should completely cover the background.

The **border-left** and **border-right** properties add borders to the left and right edge of the element.

The **border-radius** property creates rounded corners with the specified radius.

The **content-box** keyword specifies that the background extends only over the element content.

The **no-repeat** keyword specifies that no tiling is done with the background image.

Every border is defined by its width, style, and color.

The **border** property adds a border around all sides of the element.

The **border-image** property defines an image file used to create a graphic border.

The border images are based on an image file, the size of the slice from the image, and how slices are displayed along the element edge.

The **padding-box** keyword specifies that the background extends through the padding space.

```
/* Background Styles */

html {
    background-image: url(tb_back1.png);
}

article {
    background: url(tb_back2.png) bottom right / 15% no-repeat content-box,
                url(tb_back3.png) bottom left / 15% no-repeat content-box,
                url(tb_back4.png)  100%/cover no-repeat padding-box;
}

/* Border Styles */

body {
    border-left: 1px solid rgb(51, 51, 51);
    border-right: 1px solid rgb(51, 51, 51);
}

aside {
    border: 4px double rgb(45, 93, 62);
    border-radius: 30px;
}

body > article > header > figure {
    border-width: 25px;
    border-style: solid;
    border-image: url(tb_border.png) 50 repeat;
}
```

Backgrounds and Borders

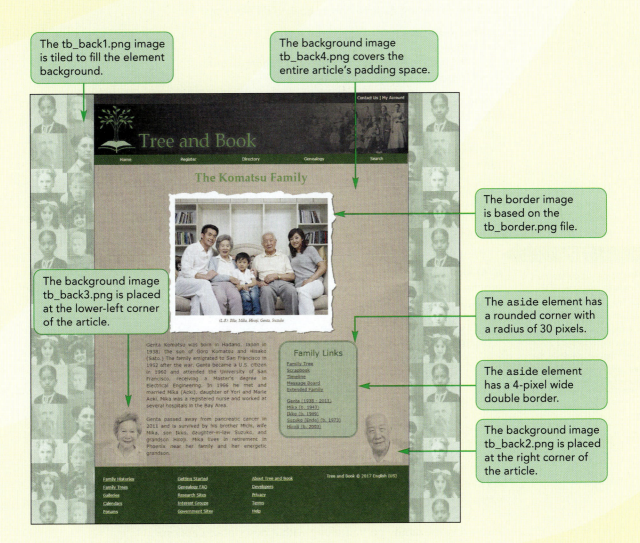

The tb_back1.png image is tiled to fill the element background.

The background image tb_back4.png covers the entire article's padding space.

The border image is based on the tb_border.png file.

The background image tb_back3.png is placed at the lower-left corner of the article.

The aside element has a rounded corner with a radius of 30 pixels.

The aside element has a 4-pixel wide double border.

The background image tb_back2.png is placed at the right corner of the article.

Creating Figure Boxes

So far your work with CSS visual design styles has been limited to typographical styles and styles that modify the page's color scheme. In this tutorial, you'll explore other CSS styles that allow you to add figure boxes, background textures, background images, and three dimensional effects to your web pages.

You'll start by examining how to work with figure boxes. In books and magazines, figures and figure captions are often placed within a separate box that stands apart from the main content of the article. HTML5 introduced a similar structural element with the following `figure` and `figcaption` elements:

```
<figure>
   content
   <figcaption>caption text</figcaption>
</figure>
```

where *content* is the content that will appear within the figure box and *caption text* is the description text that accompanies the figure. The `figcaption` element is optional and can be placed either directly before or directly after the figure box content. For example, the following code marks a figure box containing the tb_komatsu.png image file with the caption *(L-R): Ikko, Mika, Hiroji, Genta, Suzuko.*

```
<figure>
   <img src="tb_komatsu.png" alt="family portrait" />
   <figcaption>(L-R): Ikko, Mika, Hiroji, Genta, Suzuko</figcaption>
</figure>
```

While the `figure` element is used to contain an image file, it can also be used to mark any page content that you want to stand apart from the main content of an article. For instance, the `figure` element could contain a text excerpt, as the following code demonstrates:

```
<figure>
   <p>'Twas brillig, and the slithy toves<br />
      Did gyre and gimble in the wabe;<br />
      All mimsy were the borogoves,<br />
      And the mome raths outgrabe.</p>
   <figcaption>
      <cite>Jabberwocky, Lewis Carroll, 1832-98</cite>
   </figcaption>
</figure>
```

Kevin plans on using figure boxes throughout the Tree and Book website to mark up family and individual photos along with descriptive captions. He's created a set of sample pages for the Komatsu family that you will work on to learn about HTML and CSS visual elements and styles. Open the family's home page and create a figure box displaying the family portrait along with a descriptive caption.

To create a figure box:

1. Use your editor to open the **tb_komatsu_txt.html** file from the html04 ▸ tutorial folder. Enter *your name* and *the date* in the comment section of the file and save it as **tb_komatsu.html**.

   For this web page, you'll work with a new style sheet named tb_visual1.css. Kevin has already created a reset style sheet and a typographical style sheet in the tb_reset.css and tb_styles1.css files respectively.

2. Within the document head, insert the following `link` elements to link the page to the tb_reset.css, tb_styles1.css, and tb_visual1.css style sheet files.

```
<link href="tb_reset.css" rel="stylesheet" />
<link href="tb_styles1.css" rel="stylesheet" />
<link href="tb_visual1.css" rel="stylesheet" />
```

3. Scroll down to the `article` element and, directly after the `h1` element, insert the following code for the figure box displaying the Komatsu family portrait.

```
<figure>
    <img src="tb_komatsu.png" alt="family portrait" />
    <figcaption>(L-R): Ikko, Mika, Hiroji,
                Genta, Suzuko
    </figcaption>
</figure>
```

Figure 4-1 highlights the code for the family portrait figure box.

Figure 4-1   **Inserting a figure box**

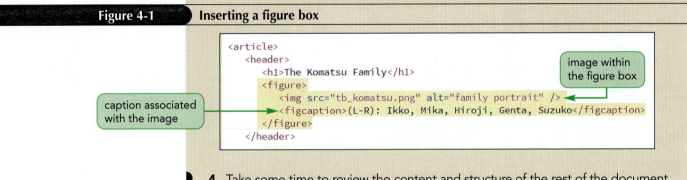

4. Take some time to review the content and structure of the rest of the document and then save your changes to the file.

Format the appearance of the figure box by adding new style rules to the tb_visual1.css style sheet file.

To format and view the figure box:

1. Use your editor to open the **tb_visual1_txt.css** files from the html04 ▸ tutorial folder. Enter **your name** and **the date** in the comment section of the file and save it as **tb_visual1.css**.

2. Scroll down to the Figure Box Styles section at the bottom the document and insert the following style rule for the `figure` element:

```
figure {
    margin: 20px auto 0px;
    width: 80%;
}
```

3. Add the following style to format the appearance of the image within the figure box:

```
figure img {
    display: block;
    width: 100%;
}
```

4. Finally, insert the following rule for the figure caption:

```
figure figcaption {
    background-color: white;
    font-family: 'Palatino Linotype', Palatino,
                 'Times New Roman', serif;
    font-style: italic;
    padding: 10px 0;
    text-align: center;
}
```

Figure 4-2 highlights the style rules for the figure box, image, and caption.

Figure 4-2 | **Formatting the figure box and caption**

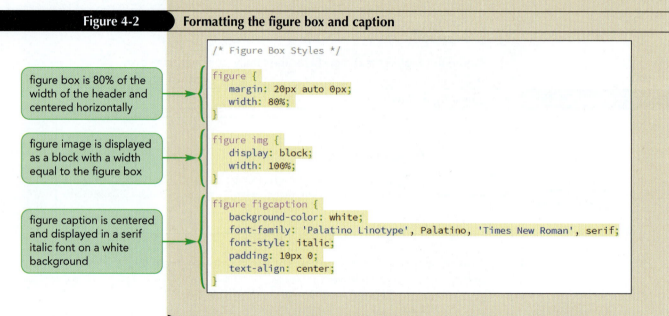

figure box is 80% of the width of the header and centered horizontally

figure image is displayed as a block with a width equal to the figure box

figure caption is centered and displayed in a serif italic font on a white background

```
/* Figure Box Styles */

figure {
    margin: 20px auto 0px;
    width: 80%;
}

figure img {
    display: block;
    width: 100%;
}

figure figcaption {
    background-color: white;
    font-family: 'Palatino Linotype', Palatino, 'Times New Roman', serif;
    font-style: italic;
    padding: 10px 0;
    text-align: center;
}
```

5. Save your changes to the file and then open the **tb_komatsu.html** file in your browser. Figure 4-3 shows the initial appearance of the page.

Figure 4-3   **Initial design of the Komatsu family page**

© 2016 Cengage Learning; Logo Design Studio Pro; Source: wiki Media; © imtmphoto/Shutterstock.com

With all of the content for the Komatsu Family page now added, you will start working on enhancing the page's appearance, starting with the CSS background styles.

Choosing your Graphic File Format

Graphic files on the web fall into two basic categories: vector images and bitmap images. A **vector image** is an image comprised of lines and curves that are based on mathematical functions. The great advantage of vector images is that they can be easily resized without losing their clarity and vector files tend to be compact in size. The most common vector format for the web is **SVG (Scalable Vector Graphics)**, which is an XML markup language that can be created using a basic text editor and knowledge of the SVG language.

A **bitmap image** is an image that is comprised of pixels in which every pixel is marked with a different color. Because a graphic file can be comprised of thousands of pixels, the file size of a bitmap image is considerably larger than the file size of a vector image. The most common bitmap formats on the web are GIF, JPEG, and PNG.

GIF (Graphic Interchange Format) is the oldest standard with a palette limited to 256 colors. GIF files, which tend to be large, have two advantages: first, GIFs support transparent colors and second, GIFs can be used to create animated images. Because GIFs have a limited color palette, they are unsuitable for photos. The most popular photo format is **JPEG (Joint Photographic Experts Group)**, which supports a palette of over 16 million colors. JPEGs also support file compression, allowing a bitmap image to be stored at a smaller file size than would be possible with other bitmap formats. JPEGs do not support transparent colors or animations.

The **PNG (Portable Network Graphics)** format was designed to replace GIFs with its support for several levels of transparent colors and palette of millions of colors. A PNG file can also be compressed, creating a file that is considerably smaller and, therefore, takes up considerably less space than its equivalent GIF file. PNG files also contain color correction information so that PNGs can be accurately rendered across a variety of display devices.

In choosing a graphic format for your website, the most important consideration is often file size; you want to choose the smallest size that still gives you an acceptable image. This combination means that users will view a quality image but they will not have to wait for the graphic file to download. In addition to file size, you want to choose a format that supports a large color palette. For these reasons, most graphics on the web are now in either JPEG or PNG format, though GIFs are still often found on legacy sites.

Exploring Background Styles

Thus far, your design choices for backgrounds have been limited to color using either the RGB or HSL color models. CSS also supports the use of images for backgrounds through the following `background-image` style:

```
background-image: url(url);
```

where `url` specifies the name and location of the background image. For example, the following style rule uses the trees.png file as the background of the page body.

```
body {
    background-image: url(trees.png);
}
```

This code assumes that the trees.png file is in the same folder as the style sheet; if the figure is not in the same folder, then you will have to include path information pointing to the folder location in which the image file resides.

Tiling a Background Image

The default browser behavior is to place the background image at the top-left corner of the element and repeat the image in both the vertical and horizontal direction until the background is filled. This process is known as **tiling** because of its similarity to the process of filling up a floor or other surface with tiles.

You can specify the type of tiling to be applied to the background image, or even turn off tiling, by applying the following background-repeat style:

```
background-repeat: type;
```

where *type* is repeat (the default), repeat-x, repeat-y, no-repeat, round, or space. Figure 4-4 displays the effect of each background-repeat type.

| Figure 4-4 | Examples of background-repeat types |

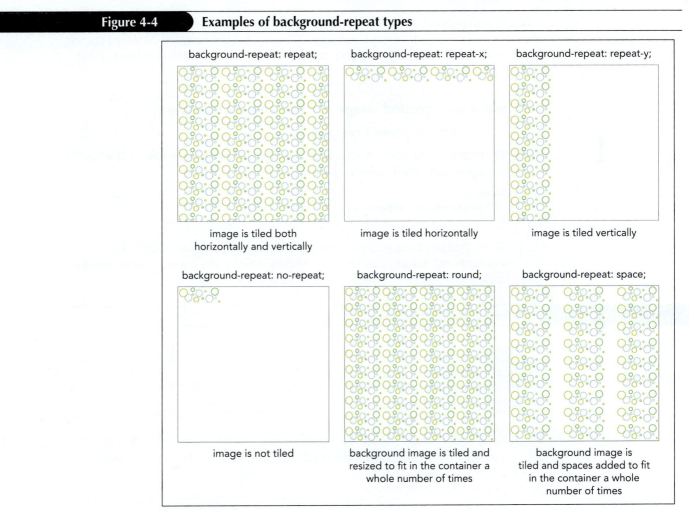

background-repeat: repeat;

image is tiled both horizontally and vertically

background-repeat: repeat-x;

image is tiled horizontally

background-repeat: repeat-y;

image is tiled vertically

background-repeat: no-repeat;

image is not tiled

background-repeat: round;

background image is tiled and resized to fit in the container a whole number of times

background-repeat: space;

background image is tiled and spaces added to fit in the container a whole number of times

© 2016 Cengage Learning

Adding a Background Image

- To add an image to the background, use the CSS style

  ```
  background-image: url(url);
  ```

  where *url* specifies the name and location of the background image.
- To specify how the image should be tiled, use

  ```
  background-repeat: type;
  ```

  where *type* is `repeat` (the default), `repeat-x`, `repeat-y`, `no-repeat`, `round`, or `space`.

Kevin has supplied you with an image file, tb_back1.png to fill the background of the browser window. Use the default option for tiling so that the image is displayed starting from the top-left corner of the window and repeating until the entire window is filled.

To add a background image to the browser window:

1. Return to the **tb_visual1.css** file in your editor.

2. Go to the HTML Styles section and add the following style rule to change the background of the browser window:

   ```
   html {
       background-image: url(tb_back1.png);
   }
   ```

   Note that because you are using the default setting for tiling the background image, you do not need to include the `background-repeat` style rule. Figure 4-5 highlights the new style rule.

Figure 4-5	Defining a background image

tiles the tb_back1.png image file across the browser window background

```
/* HTML Styles */

html {
    background-image: url(tb_back1.png);
}
```

3. Save your changes to the file and then reload tb_komatsu.html in your browser. Figure 4-6 shows the tiled background in the browser window.

Figure 4-6   **Tiled background image in the browser window**

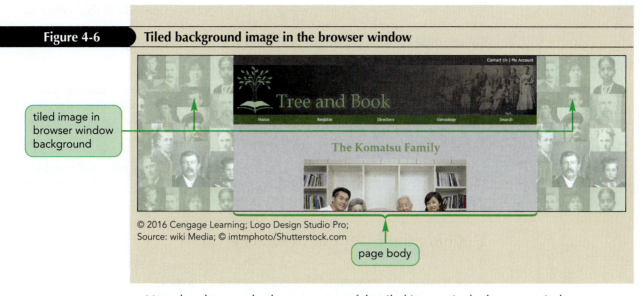

tiled image in browser window background

The Komatsu Family

page body

© 2016 Cengage Learning; Logo Design Studio Pro;
Source: wiki Media; © imtmphoto/Shutterstock.com

Note that the page body covers part of the tiled images in the browser window. However, even though the background images are hidden, the tiling still continues behind the page body.

Attaching the Background Image

A background image is attached to its element so that as you scroll through the element content, the background image scrolls with it. You can change the attachment using the following `background-attachment` property

```
background-attachment: type;
```

where *type* is `scroll` (the default), `fixed`, or `local`. The `scroll` type sets the background to scroll with the element content. The `fixed` type creates a background that stays in place even as the element content is scrolled horizontally or vertically. Fixed backgrounds are sometimes used to create **watermarks**, which are translucent graphics displayed behind the content with a message that the content material is copyrighted or in draft form or some other message directed to the reader. The `local` type is similar to `scroll` except that it is used for elements, such as scroll boxes, to allow the element background to scroll along with the content within the box.

Setting the Background Image Position

By default, browsers place the background image in the element's top-left corner. You can place the background image at a different position using the following `background-position` property:

```
background-position: horizontal vertical;
```

TIP

Background coordinates are measured from the top-left corner of the background to the top-left corner of the image.

where *horizontal* and *vertical* provide the coordinates of the image within the element background expressed using one of the CSS units of measure or as a percentage of the element's width and height. For example, the following style places the image 10% of the width of the element from the left edge of the background and 20% of the element's height from the background's top edge.

```
background-position: 10% 20%;
```

If you specify a single value, the browser applies that value to both the horizontal and vertical position. Thus, the following style places the background image 30 pixels from the element's left edge and 30 pixels down from the top edge.

```
background-position: 30px;
```

You can also place the background image using the keywords `left`, `center`, and `right` for the horizontal position and `top`, `center`, and `bottom` for the vertical position. The following style places the background image in the bottom-right corner of the element.

```
background-position: right bottom;
```

Typically, the `background-position` property is only useful for non-tiled images because, if the image is tiled, the tiled image fills the background and it usually doesn't matter where the tiling starts.

Defining the Extent of the Background

You learned in Tutorial 2 that every block element follows the Box Model in which the element content is surrounded by a padding space and beyond that a border space (see Figure 2-38). However, the element's background is defined, by default, to extend only through the padding space and not to include the border space. You can change this definition using the following `background-clip` property:

```
background-clip: type;
```

where *type* is `content-box` (to extend the background only through the element content), `padding-box` (to extend the background through the padding space), or `border-box` (to extend the background through the border space). For example, the following style rule defines the background for the page body to extend only as far as the page content. The padding and border spaces would not be considered part of the background and thus would not show any background image.

```
body {
    background-clip: content-box;
}
```

Because the background extends through the padding space by default, all coordinates for the background image position are measured from the top-left corner of that padding space. You can choose a different context by applying the following `background-origin` property:

```
background-origin: type;
```

where *type* is once again `content-box`, `padding-box`, or `border-box`. Thus, the following style rule places the background image at the bottom-left corner of the page body content and not the bottom-left corner of the padding space (which would be the default).

```
body {
    background-position: left bottom;
    background-origin: content-box;
}
```

Based on this style rule, the padding space of page body would not have any background image or color, other than what would be defined for the browser window itself.

Sizing and Clipping an Image

The size of the background image is equal to the size stored in the image file. To specify a different size, apply the following `background-size` property:

```
background-size: width height;
```

where `width` and `height` are the width and height of the image in one of the CSS units of length or as a percentage of the element's width and height. The following style sets the size of the background image to 300 pixels wide by 200 pixels high.

```
background-size: 300px 200px;
```

CSS also supports the sizing keywords `auto`, `cover`, and `contain`. The `auto` keyword tells the browser to automatically set the width or height value based on the dimensions of the original image. The following style sets the height of the image to 200 pixels and automatically scales the width to keep the original proportions of the image:

```
background-size: auto 200px;
```

> **TIP**
>
> If you specify only one size value, the browser applies it to the image width and scales the height proportionally.

The `cover` keyword tells the browser to resize the image to cover all of the element background while still retaining the image proportions. Depending on the size of the element, this could result in some of the background image being cropped. The `contain` keyword scales the image so that it's completely contained within the element, even if that means that not all of the element background is covered. Figure 4-7 displays examples of a background set to a specific size, as well as resized to either cover the background or to have the image completely contained within the background.

| Figure 4-7 | Examples of background-size types |

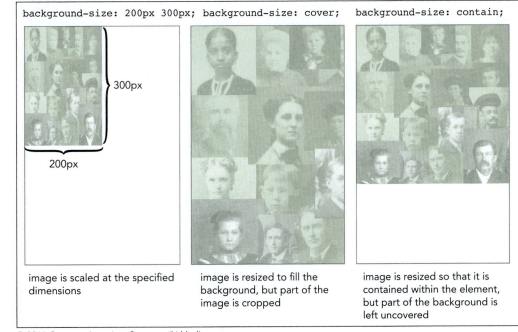

© 2016 Cengage Learning; Source: wiki Media

Setting Background Image Options

- To specify how the image is attached to the background, use

  ```
  background-attachment: type;
  ```

  where *type* is `scroll` (the default), `fixed`, or `local`.
- To set the position of the background image, use

  ```
  background-position: horizontal vertical;
  ```

  where *horizontal* and *vertical* provide the coordinates of the image within the element background.
- To define the extent of the background, use

  ```
  background-clip: type;
  ```

  where *type* is `content-box`, `padding-box` (the default), or `border-box`.
- To define how position coordinates are measured, use

  ```
  background-origin: type;
  ```

  where *type* is `content-box`, `padding-box` (the default), or `border-box`.

The background Property

All of these different background options can be organized in the following `background` property:

```
background: color url(url) position / size repeat attachment
origin clip;
```

where *color* is the background color, *url* is the source of the background image, *position* is the image's position, *size* sets the image size, *repeat* sets the tiling of the image, *attachment* specifies whether the image scrolls with the content or is fixed, *origin* defines how positions are measured on the background, and *clip* specifies the extent over which the background is spread. For example, the following style rule sets the background color to ivory and then uses the draft.png file as the background image fixed at the horizontal and vertical center of the page body and sized at 10% of the body's width and height:

```
body {
   background: ivory url(draft.png)
               center center / 10% 10%
               no-repeat fixed content-box content-box;
}
```

The rest of the property sets the image not to repeat and to use the content box for defining the background origin and clipping. Note that the page body will have an ivory background color at any location where the draft.png image is not displayed. If you don't specify all of the option values, the browser will assume the default values for the missing options. Thus, the following style rule places the draft.png at the horizontal and vertical center of the page body without tiling:

```
body {
   background: ivory url(draft.png) center center no-repeat;
}
```

TIP

The background property includes the "/" character only when you need to separate the image position value from the image size value.

Since no *size*, *attachment*, *origin*, and *clip* values are specified, the size of the image will be based on the dimensions from the image file, the image will scroll with the body content, and the background origin and clipping will extend through the page body's padding space.

Kevin wants you to include a semi-transparent image of the family patriarch, Genta Komatsu, as a background image placed in the lower-right corner of the article on the Komatsu family. Add a style rule to the tb_visual1.css file to display the tb_back2.png image within that element without tiling.

To add a background image to the page article:

1. Return to the **tb_visual1.css** file in your editor and scroll down to the Article Styles section.

2. Add the following style rule:

```
article {
    background: url(tb_back2.png) bottom right / 15%
                no-repeat content-box;
}
```

Figure 4-8 highlights the style rule applied to the page article.

Figure 4-8   Adding a background to the page article

places the image at the lower-right corner

does not tile the image

```
/* Article Styles */

article {
    background: url(tb_back2.png) bottom right / 15% no-repeat content-box;
}
```

image file

sets the width of the image to 15% of the article width

positions the image with respect to the article content

3. Save your changes and then reload tb_komatsu.html in your browser. Figure 4-9 shows the placement of the background image.

Figure 4-9   Placement of the background image

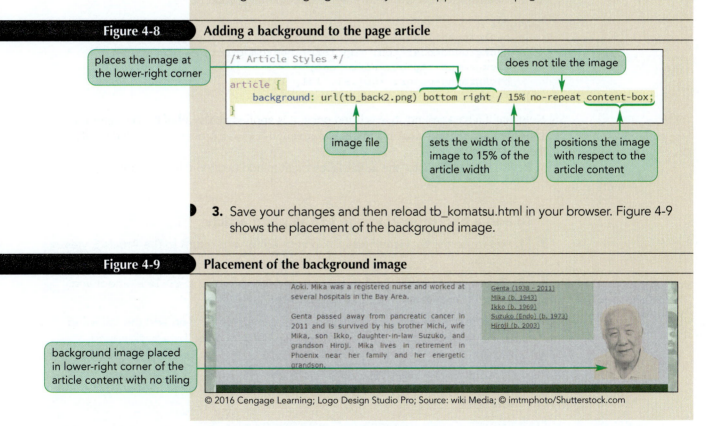

background image placed in lower-right corner of the article content with no tiling

© 2016 Cengage Learning; Logo Design Studio Pro; Source: wiki Media; © imtmphoto/Shutterstock.com

Kevin likes the addition of the image of Genta Komatsu and would like you to add another background image showing the family matriarch, Mika Komatsu, and a third image giving the article a paper-textured background.

Adding Multiple Backgrounds

To add multiple backgrounds to the same element, you list the backgrounds in the following comma-separated list:

```
background: background1, background2, …;
```

where *background1*, *background2*, and so on are the properties for each background. For example the following style rule applies three different backgrounds to the `header` element:

```
header {
    background: url(back2.png) top left no-repeat,
                url(back1.png) bottom right no-repeat,
                rgb(191, 191, 191);
}
```

Backgrounds are added in the reverse order in which they're listed in the style rule. In this style rule, the background color is applied first, the back1.png background image is placed on top of that, and finally the back2.png background image is placed on top of those two backgrounds.

Individual background properties can also contain multiple options placed in a comma-separated list. The following style rule creates the same multiple backgrounds for the `header` element without using the `background` property:

```
header {
    background-image: url(back2.png), url(back1.png);
    background-position: top left, bottom right;
    background-repeat: no-repeat;
    background-color: rgb(191, 191, 191);
}
```

Note that if a background style is listed once, it is applied across all of the backgrounds. Thus the `background-color` and the `background-repeat` properties are used in all the backgrounds.

Revise the style rule for the `article` element to add two more backgrounds.

To add a background image to the page article:

1. Return to the **tb_visual1.css** file in your editor and return to the Article Styles section.

2. Type a comma after the first background listed for the `article` element and before the semicolon (;), then press **Enter**.

3. Be sure the insertion point is before the semicolon (;), then add the following code to display two more background images followed by a background color:

```
url(tb_back3.png) bottom left / 15% no-repeat content-box,
url(tb_back4.png) 100%/cover no-repeat,
rgb(211, 211, 211)
```

The background color acts as a fallback design element and will not be displayed except for browsers that are incapable of displaying background images. Figure 4-10 displays the code for the multiple backgrounds applied to the page article.

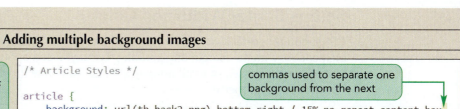

Figure 4-10   **Adding multiple background images**

places the second background image at the lower-left corner of the article content with no tiling and a width of 15%

commas used to separate one background from the next

places the third background image, scaled to cover all of the padding box of the article without repeating

uses a gray color as the background if the browser doesn't support background images

```
/* Article Styles */

article {
    background: url(tb_back2.png) bottom right / 15% no-repeat content-box,
               url(tb_back3.png) bottom left / 15% no-repeat content-box,
               url(tb_back4.png) 100% / cover no-repeat,
               rgb(211, 211, 211);
}
```

Trouble? Be sure your code matches the code in Figure 4-10, including the commas used to separate the components in the list and the ending semicolon.

4. Save your changes and then reload tb_komatsu.html in your browser. Figure 4-11 shows the three background images displayed with the article.

Figure 4-11   **Revised background for the page article**

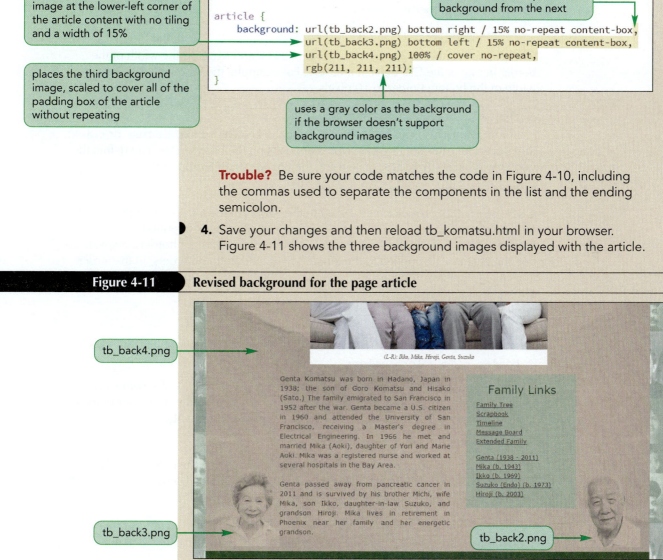

tb_back4.png

tb_back3.png

tb_back2.png

© 2016 Cengage Learning; Logo Design Studio Pro; Source: wiki Media; © imtmphoto/Shutterstock.com

Kevin is pleased with the revised backgrounds for the browser window and the page article. Next, you will explore how to work with CSS border properties.

Working with Borders

So far, you have only worked with the content, padding, and margin spaces from the CSS Box model. Now, you will examine the border space that separates the element's content and padding from its margins and essentially marks the extent of the element as it is rendered on the page.

Setting Border Width and Color

CSS supports several style properties that are used to format the border around each element. As with the margin and padding styles, you can apply a style to the top, right, bottom, or left border, or to all borders at once. To define the thickness of a specific border, use the property

```
border-side-width: width;
```

where *side* is either `top`, `right`, `bottom`, or `left` and *width* is the width of the border in one of the CSS units of measure. For example, the following style sets the width of the bottom border to 10 pixels.

```
border-bottom-width: 10px;
```

Border widths also can be expressed using the keywords `thin`, `medium`, or `thick`; the exact application of these keywords depends on the browser. You can define the border widths for all sides at once using the `border-width` property

```
border-width: top right bottom left;
```

where *top*, *right*, *bottom*, and *left* are the widths of the matching border. As with the `margin` and `padding` properties, if you enter one value, it's applied to all four borders; two values set the width of the top/bottom and left/right borders, respectively; and three values are applied to the top, left/right, and bottom borders, in that order. Thus, the following property sets the widths of the top/bottom borders to 10 pixels and the left/right borders to 20 pixels:

```
border-width: 10px 20px;
```

The color of each individual border is set using the property

```
border-side-color: color;
```

where *side* once again specifies the border side and *color* is a color name, color value, or the keyword `transparent` to create an invisible border. The color of the four sides can be specified using the following `border-color` property

```
border-color: top right bottom left;
```

where *top right bottom left* specifies the side to which the color should be applied. Thus, the following style uses gray for the top and left borders and black for the right and bottom borders:

```
border-color: gray black black gray;
```

If no border color is specified, the border will use the text color assigned to the element.

Setting the Border Design

CSS allows you to further define the appearance of borders using the following border styles:

```
border-side-style: style;
```

where *side* once again indicates the border side and *style* specifies one of the nine border styles displayed in Figure 4-12.

Figure 4-12  **Examples of border styles**

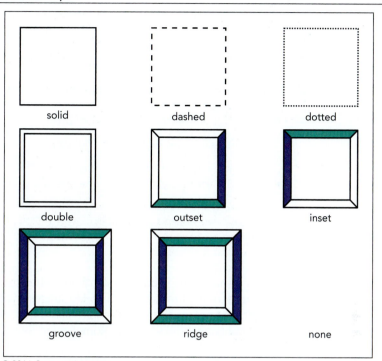

© 2016 Cengage Learning

Or to specify styles for all four borders use the property:

    border-style: *top right bottom left*;

As with the other border rules, you can modify the style of all borders or combinations of the borders. For example, the following style uses a double line for the top/bottom borders and a single solid line for the left/right borders.

    border-style: double solid;

All of the border styles discussed above can be combined into the following property that formats the width, style, and color of all of the borders

    border: *width style color*;

where *width* is the thickness of the border, *style* is the style of the border, and *color* is the border color. The following style rule inserts a 2-pixel-wide solid blue border around every side of each h1 heading in the document:

    h1 {border: 2px solid blue;}

To modify the width, style, and color of a single border, use the property

    border-*side*: *width style color*;

where *side* is either top, right, bottom, or left.

REFERENCE

Adding a Border

- To add a border around every side of an element, use the CSS property

  ```
  border: width style color;
  ```

  where *width* is the width of the border, *style* is the design style, and *color* is the border color.
- To apply a border to a specific side, use

  ```
  border-side: width style color;
  ```

  where *side* is top, right, bottom, or left for the top, right, bottom, and left borders.
- To set the width, style, or color of a specific side, use the properties

  ```
  border-side-width: width;
  border-side-style: style;
  border-side-color: color;
  ```

Kevin wants the page body to stand out better against the tiled images used as the background for the browser window. He suggests you add solid borders to the left and right edges of the page body and that you add a double border around the `aside` element containing links to other Komatsu family pages.

To add borders to the page elements:

1. Return to the **tb_visual1.css** file in your editor and go to the Page Body Styles section.

2. Add the following style rule for the page body:

   ```
   body {
       border-left: 1px solid rgb(51, 51, 51);
       border-right: 1px solid rgb(51, 51, 51);
   }
   ```

3. Go to the Aside Styles section and add the following style rule for the `aside` element:

   ```
   aside {
       border: 4px double rgb(45, 93, 62);
   }
   ```

   Figure 4-13 highlights the style rules that create borders for the page body and `aside` element.

Figure 4-13   **Adding borders to the page body and aside element**

```
/* Page Body Styles */

body {
   border-left: 1px solid rgb(51, 51, 51);
   border-right: 1px solid rgb(51, 51, 51);
}


/* Aside Styles */

aside {
   border: 4px double rgb(45, 93, 62);
}
```

adds a 1-pixel solid gray border to the left and right edges of the page body

adds a 4-pixel double medium green border to the aside element

▶ **4.** Save your changes to the file and then reload tb_komatsu.html in your browser. Figure 4-14 shows the appearance of the page with the newly added borders. Note that the background color and other styles associated with the `aside` element are in the tb_styles1.css file.

Figure 4-14   **Page design with borders**

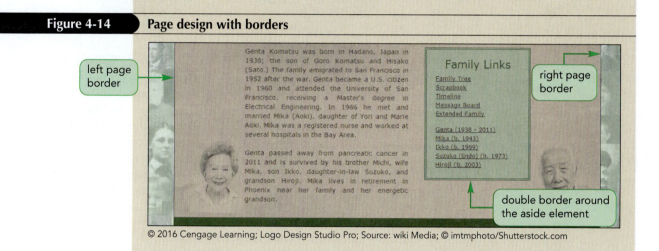

left page border

right page border

Family Links

Family Tree
Scrapbook
Timeline
Message Board
Extended Family

Genta (1938 - 2011)
Mika (b. 1943)
Ikko (b. 1969)
Suzuko (Endo) (b. 1973)
Hiroji (b. 2003)

Genta Komatsu was born in Hadano, Japan in 1938; the son of Goro Komatsu and Hisako (Sato.) The family emigrated to San Francisco in 1952 after the war. Genta became a U.S. citizen in 1960 and attended the University of San Francisco, receiving a Master's degree in Electrical Engineering. In 1966 he met and married Mika (Aoki), daughter of Yori and Marie Aoki. Mika was a registered nurse and worked at several hospitals in the Bay Area.

Genta passed away from pancreatic cancer in 2011 and is survived by his brother Michi, wife Mika, son Ikko, daughter-in-law Suzuko, and grandson Hiroji. Mika lives in retirement in Phoenix near her family and her energetic grandson.

double border around the aside element

Kevin is concerned that the design of the page is too boxy and he wants you to soften the design by adding curves to some of the page elements. You can create this effect using rounded corners.

Creating Rounded Corners

To round off any of the four corners of a border, apply the following `border-radius` property:

```
border-radius: top-left top-right bottom-right bottom-left;
```

where *top-left*, *top-right*, *bottom-right*, and *bottom-left* are the radii of the individual corners. The radii are equal to the radii of hypothetical circles placed at the corners of the box with the arcs of the circles defining the rounded corners (see Figure 4-15).

Figure 4-15   Setting rounded corners based on corner radii

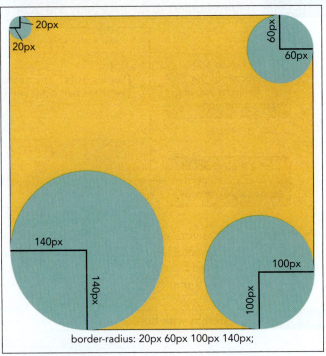

border-radius: 20px 60px 100px 140px;

© 2016 Cengage Learning

If you enter only one radius value, it is applied to all four corners; if you enter two values, the first is applied to the top-left and bottom-right corners, and the second is applied to the top-right and bottom-left corners. If you specify three radii, they are applied to the top-left, top-right/bottom-left, and bottom-right corners, in that order. For example, the following style rule creates rounded corners for the `aside` element in which the radii of the top-left and bottom-right corners is 50 pixels and the radii of the top-right and bottom-left corners is 20 pixels.

```
aside {border-radius: 50px 20px;}
```

To set the curvature for only one corner, use the property:

```
border-corner-radius: radius;
```

where *corner* is either `top-left`, `top-right`, `bottom-right`, or `bottom-left`.

The corners do not need to be circular. Elongated or elliptical corners are created by specifying the ratio of the horizontal radius to the vertical radius using the style:

```
border-radius: horizontal/vertical;
```

where *horizontal* is the horizontal radius of the corner and *vertical* is the vertical radius of the same corner (see Figure 4-16).

Figure 4-16 **Creating an elongated corner**

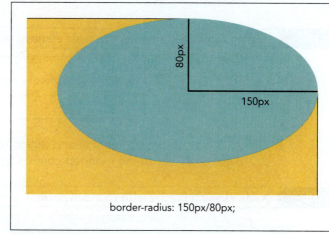

border-radius: 150px/80px;

© 2016 Cengage Learning

Thus, the following style rule creates elongated corners in which the ratio of the horizontal to vertical radius is 50 pixels to 20 pixels.

```
border-radius: 50px/20px;
```

Note that using percentages for the radius value can result in elongated corners if the element is not perfectly square. The following style rule sets the horizontal radius to 15% of element width and 15% of the element height. If the element is twice as wide as it is high for example, the corners will not be rounded but elongated.

```
border-radius: 15%;
```

TIP

To create a circular border, use a square element with an equal width and height and the corner radii set to 50%.

When applied to a single corner, the format to create an elongated corner is slightly different. You remove the slash between the horizontal and vertical values and use the following syntax:

```
border-corner-radius: horizontal vertical;
```

For example, the following style creates an elongated bottom-left corner with a horizontal radius of 50 pixels and a vertical radius of 20 pixels.

```
border-bottom-left-radius: 50px 20px;
```

Rounded and elongated corners do not clip element content. If the content of the element extends into the corner, it will still be displayed as part of the background. Because this is often unsightly, you should avoid heavily rounded or elongated corners unless you can be sure they will not obscure or distract from the element content.

Add rounded corners with a radius of 30 pixels to the `aside` element.

To add rounded corners to an element:

▶ 1. Return to the **tb_visual1.css** file in your editor and go to the Aside Styles section.

▶ 2. Add the following style to the style rule for the `aside` element:

```
border-radius: 30px;
```

Figure 4-17 highlights the style to create the rounded corners for the aside border.

Figure 4-17   **Adding rounded corners to the aside element border**

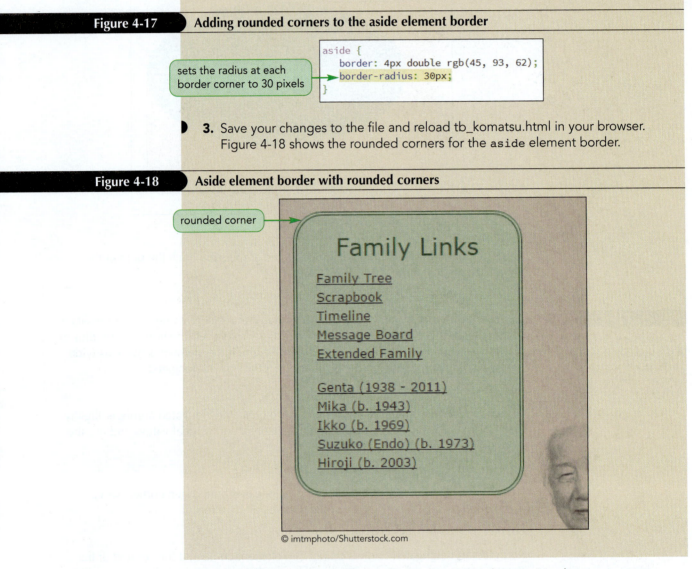

sets the radius at each border corner to 30 pixels

```
aside {
    border: 4px double rgb(45, 93, 62);
    border-radius: 30px;
}
```

▶ 3. Save your changes to the file and reload tb_komatsu.html in your browser. Figure 4-18 shows the rounded corners for the `aside` element border.

Figure 4-18   **Aside element border with rounded corners**

rounded corner

Family Links

Family Tree
Scrapbook
Timeline
Message Board
Extended Family

Genta (1938 - 2011)
Mika (b. 1943)
Ikko (b. 1969)
Suzuko (Endo) (b. 1973)
Hiroji (b. 2003)

© imtmphoto/Shutterstock.com

Kevin likes the revision to the border for the `aside` element. He also wants you to add a border to the family portrait on the Komatsu Family page. However, rather than using one of the styles shown in Figure 4-12, Kevin wants you to use a graphic border that makes it appear as if the figure box came from a torn piece of paper. You can create this effect using border images.

Applying a Border Image

A border image is a border that it is based on a graphic image. The graphic image is sliced into nine sections representing the four corners, the four sides, and the interior piece. The interior piece is discarded because that is where the content of the object will appear; the four corners become the corners of the border and the four sides are either stretched or tiled to fill in the border's top, right, bottom, and left sides. Figure 4-19 shows an example of an image file, frame.png, sliced into nine sections to create a border image.

Figure 4-19   **Slicing a graphic image to create a border**

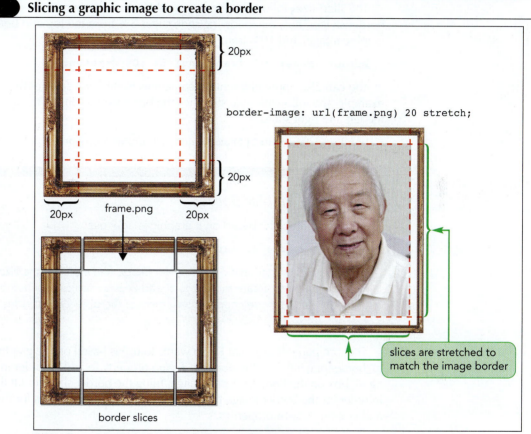

`border-image: url(frame.png) 20 stretch;`

frame.png

border slices

slices are stretched to match the image border

© 2016 Cengage Learning; © imtmphoto/Shutterstock.com

To apply a border image, use the following property

`border-image: url(url) slice repeat;`

where *url* is the source of the graphic image, *slice* is the width or height of the slices used to create the sides and corners, and *repeat* indicates whether the side slices should be stretched or tiled to cover the border's four sides. The *repeat* option supports the following values:

- `stretch`: The slices are stretched to fill each side.
- `repeat`: The slices are tiled to fill each side.
- `round`: The slices are tiled to fill each side; if they don't fill the sides with an integer number of tiles, the slices are rescaled until they do.
- `space`: The slices are tiled to fill each side; if they don't fill the sides with an integer number of tiles, extra space is distributed around the tiles.

For example, the following style cuts 10-pixel-wide slices from the frame.png image file with the four side slices stretched to cover the length of the four sides of the object's border:

`border-image: url(frame.png) 10 stretch;`

The size of the slices is measured either in pixels or as a percentage of the image file width and height. A quirk of this property is that you should *not* specify the pixel unit if you want the slices measured in pixels but you must include the % symbol when slices are measured in percentages.

You can create slices of different widths or heights by entering the size values in a space-separated list. For instance, the following style slices the graphic image 5 pixels on the top, 10 pixels on the right, 15 pixels on the bottom, and 25 pixels on the left:

```
border-image: url(frame.png) 5 10 15 25 stretch;
```

The slice sizes follow the same top/right/bottom/left syntax used with all of the CSS border styles. Thus, the following style slices 5% from the top and bottom sides of the graphic image, and 10% from the left and right sides:

```
border-image: url(frame.png) 5% 10% stretch;
```

You can also apply different repeat values to different sides of the border. For example, the following style stretches the border slices on the top and bottom but tiles the left and right slices:

```
border-image: url(frame.png) 10 stretch repeat;
```

Creating a Graphic Border

- To create a border based on a graphic image, use

  ```
  border-image: url(url) slice repeat;
  ```

  where *url* is the source of the border image file, *slice* is the size of the border image cut off to create the borders, and *repeat* indicates whether the side borders should be either stretched or tiled to cover the object's four sides.

The torn paper image that Kevin wants to use is based on the graphic image file tp_border.png file. Use the `border-image` property to add a border image around the figure box on the Komatsu Family page, tiling the border slices to fill the sides. Note that in order for the border image to appear you must include values for the `border-width` and `border-style` properties.

To create a graphic border:

1. Return to the **tb_visual1.css** file in your editor and scroll to the Figure Box Styles at the top of the file.

2. Add the following style to the style rule for the figure box:

   ```
   border-style: solid;
   border-width: 25px;
   border-image: url(tb_border.png) 50 repeat;
   ```

   Figure 4-20 displays the styles used to create the graphic border.

Figure 4-20 | Adding a border image

border width and style values are required for the border image

```
figure {
   border-style: solid;
   border-width: 25px;
   border-image: url(tb_border.png) 50 repeat;
   margin: 20px auto 0px;
   width: 80%;
}
```

uses the tb_border.png file for the graphical border

slices 50 pixels from each side of the border image

tiles the side slices to fill the border sides

3. Save your changes and reload tb_komatsu.html in your browser. Figure 4-21 shows the appearance of the border image.

Figure 4-21 | Figure box with border image

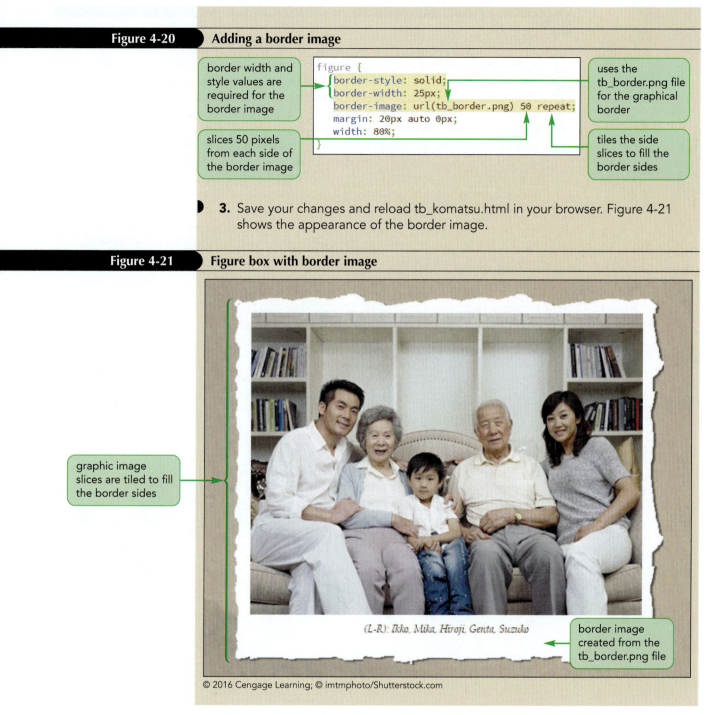

graphic image slices are tiled to fill the border sides

(L-R): Ikko, Mika, Hiroji, Genta, Suzuko

border image created from the tb_border.png file

© 2016 Cengage Learning; © imtmphoto/Shutterstock.com

Kevin appreciates the effect you created, making it appear as if the family portrait was torn from an album and laid on top of the web page.

PROSKILLS

Problem Solving: Graphic Design and Legacy Browsers

Adding snazzy graphics to your page can be fun, but you must keep in mind that the fundamental test of your design is not how cool it looks but how usable it is. Any design you create needs to be compatible across several browser versions if you want to reach the widest user base. To support older browsers, your style sheet should use progressive enhancement in which the older properties are listed first, followed by browser extensions, and then by the most current CSS properties. As each property supersedes the previous properties, the browser will end up using the most current property that it supports.

For example, the following style rule starts with a basic 5-pixel blue border that will be recognized by every browser. It is followed by browser extensions for Opera, Mozilla, and WebKit to support older browsers that predate adoption of the CSS3 `border-image` property. Finally, the style list ends with the CSS3 `border-image` property, recognized by every current browser. In this way, every browser that opens the page will show some type of border.

```
border: 5px solid blue;
-o-border-image: url(paper.png) 30 repeat;
-moz-border-image: url(paper.png) 30 repeat;
-webkit-border-image: url(paper.png) 30 repeat;
border-image: url(paper.png) 30 repeat;
```

Be aware, however, that the syntax for an extension may not match the syntax for the final CSS3 specification. For example, the following list of styles creates a rounded top-right corner that is compatible across a wide range of browser versions:

```
-moz-border-radius-top-right: 15px;
-webkit-border-top-right-radius: 15px;
border-top-right-radius: 15px;
```

Note that the syntax for the Mozilla extension does not match the syntax for the WebKit extension or for the final CSS3 specification. As always, you need to do your homework to learn exactly how different browser versions handle these CSS design styles.

In the next session, you'll continue to work with the CSS graphic styles to add three-dimensional effects through the use of drop shadows and color gradients. If you want to take a break, you can close your open files and documents now.

Session 4.1 Quick Check

1. Provide code to create a figure box containing the logo.png image file, no alt text, and a caption with the text *Tree and Book*.

2. What is the difference between a vector image and a bitmap image?

3. Provide the code to use the sidebar.png file as the background image for the page body. Have the image placed in the top-left corner of the page and tiled only in the horizontal direction.

4. Create a style rule for the `header` element that fills the header background with tiled images of the back.png, but only over the element content.

5. Provide a style rule to display the logo.png and side.png image files in the top-left corner of the page body's background. Do not tile the logo.png image, but tile the side.png image vertically. Design your style rule so that logo.png appears on top of the side.png. For the rest of the page body, set the background color to ivory.

6. Provide a style rule to add a 5-pixel dotted brown border around the `aside` element.

7. Provide a style rule to add a 3-pixel solid blue border around the `header` element with rounded corners of 15 pixels.

8. Provide a style rule to add elongated corners with a 5-pixel gray inset border around the `aside` element and with a horizontal radius of 10 pixels and vertical radius of 5 pixels.

9. Provide a style rule to use the graphic image file border.png as a solid border for the `article` element. Set the size of the image slice to 30 pixels and stretch the sides to match the sides of the element. Assume a border width of 10 pixels.

Session 4.2 Visual Overview:

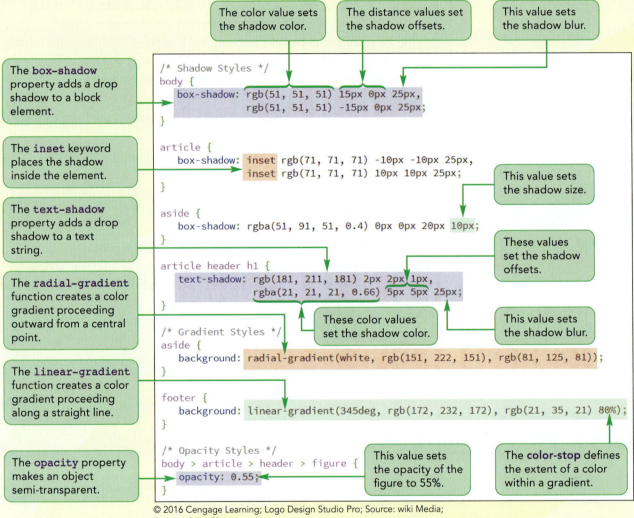

The color value sets the shadow color.

The distance values set the shadow offsets.

This value sets the shadow blur.

The **box-shadow** property adds a drop shadow to a block element.

The **inset** keyword places the shadow inside the element.

The **text-shadow** property adds a drop shadow to a text string.

The **radial-gradient** function creates a color gradient proceeding outward from a central point.

The **linear-gradient** function creates a color gradient proceeding along a straight line.

The **opacity** property makes an object semi-transparent.

This value sets the shadow size.

These values set the shadow offsets.

These color values set the shadow color.

This value sets the shadow blur.

This value sets the opacity of the figure to 55%.

The **color-stop** defines the extent of a color within a gradient.

```
/* Shadow Styles */
body {
    box-shadow: rgb(51, 51, 51) 15px 0px 25px,
                rgb(51, 51, 51) -15px 0px 25px;
}

article {
    box-shadow: inset rgb(71, 71, 71) -10px -10px 25px,
                inset rgb(71, 71, 71) 10px 10px 25px;
}

aside {
    box-shadow: rgba(51, 91, 51, 0.4) 0px 0px 20px 10px;
}

article header h1 {
    text-shadow: rgb(181, 211, 181) 2px 2px 1px,
                 rgba(21, 21, 21, 0.66) 5px 5px 25px;
}

/* Gradient Styles */
aside {
    background: radial-gradient(white, rgb(151, 222, 151), rgb(81, 125, 81));
}

footer {
    background: linear-gradient(345deg, rgb(172, 232, 172), rgb(21, 35, 21) 80%);
}

/* Opacity Styles */
body > article > header > figure {
    opacity: 0.55;
}
```

© 2016 Cengage Learning; Logo Design Studio Pro; Source: wiki Media;
© imtmphoto/Shutterstock.com

Shadows and Gradients

This shows a box shadow on the left edge of the page body.

This shows a box shadow inside the page article.

This shows the figure box is displayed as 55% opaque.

There is a box shadow on the right edge of the page body.

The heading text has a text shadow.

The box shadow creates a halo around the aside element.

The radial gradient proceeds from white in the center to medium green on the edges.

The linear gradient proceeds at an angle of 15° counter-clockwise from light green to dark green.

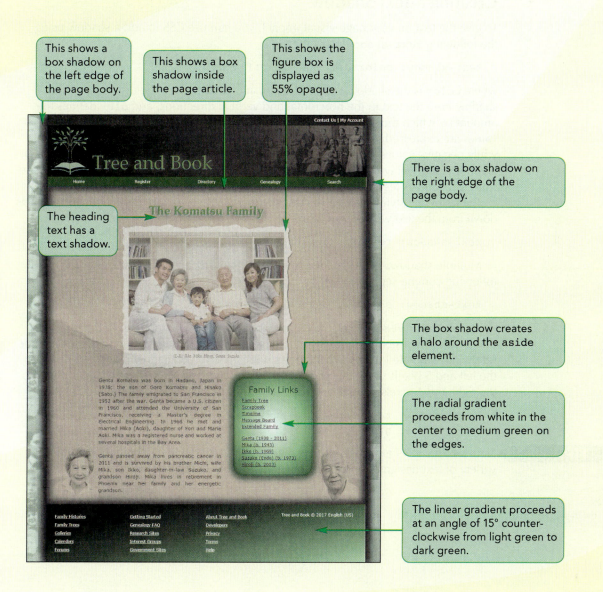

Creating Drop Shadows

In this session, you will examine some design styles that create 3D effects, making the page content appear to jump out of the browser window. The first styles you'll explore are used to create drop shadows around text strings and element boxes.

Creating a Text Shadow

To give the text on your page visual impact, you can use CSS to add a shadow using the following `text-shadow` property

```
text-shadow: color offsetX offsetY blur;
```

where *color* is the shadow color, *offsetX* and *offsetY* are the distances of the shadow from the text in the horizontal and vertical directions, and *blur* defines the amount by which the shadow spreads out, creating a blurred effect. The shadow offset values are expressed so that positive values push the shadow to the right and down while negative values move the shadow to the left and up. The default *blur* value is 0, creating a shadow with distinct hard edges; as the blur value increases, the edge of the shadow becomes less distinct and blends more in the text background.

The following style creates a red text shadow that is 10 pixels to the right and 5 pixels down from the text with blur of 8 pixels:

```
text-shadow: red 10px 5px 8px;
```

Multiple shadows can be added to text by including each shadow definition in the following comma-separated list.

```
text-shadow: shadow1, shadow2, shadow3, …;
```

where *shadow1*, *shadow2*, *shadow3*, and so on are shadows applied to the text with the first shadow listed displayed on top of subsequent shadows when they overlap. The following style rule creates two shadows with the first red shadow placed 10 pixels to the left and 5 pixels up from the text and the second gray shadow is placed 3 pixels to the right and 4 pixels down from the text. Both shadows have a blur of 6 pixels:

```
text-shadow: red -10px -5px 6px,
             gray 3px 4px 6px;
```

Figure 4-22 shows examples of how the `text-shadow` style can be used to achieve a variety of text designs involving single and multiple shadows.

TIP

You can explore more text shadows using the demo_text_shadows.html file from the demo folder.

Figure 4-22   Examples of text shadows

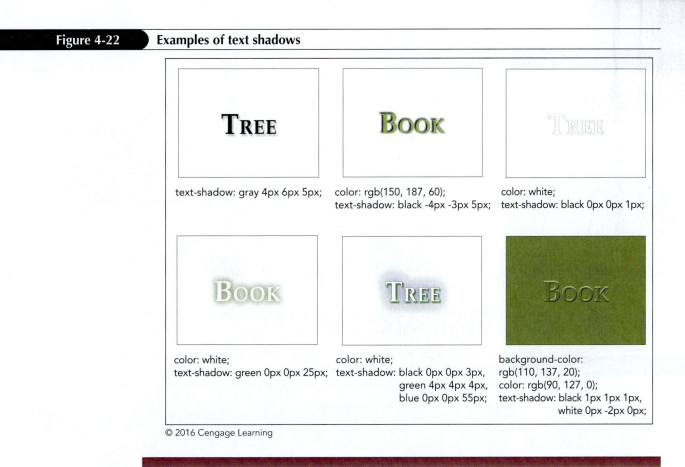

text-shadow: gray 4px 6px 5px;

color: rgb(150, 187, 60);
text-shadow: black -4px -3px 5px;

color: white;
text-shadow: black 0px 0px 1px;

color: white;
text-shadow: green 0px 0px 25px;

color: white;
text-shadow: black 0px 0px 3px,
            green 4px 4px 4px,
            blue 0px 0px 55px;

background-color:
rgb(110, 137, 20);
color: rgb(90, 127, 0);
text-shadow: black 1px 1px 1px,
            white 0px -2px 0px;

© 2016 Cengage Learning

Creating a Text Shadow

- To add a shadow to a text string, use the property

  text-shadow: *color offsetX offsetY blur*;

  where *color* is the shadow color, *offsetX* and *offsetY* are the distances of the shadow from the text in the horizontal and vertical directions, and *blur* defines the amount by which the shadow is stretched.

Kevin wants you to add two text shadows to the h1 heading *The Komatsu Family*. The first text shadow will be a light-green highlight with hard edges and the second shadow will be semi-transparent gray and blurred.

To add a text shadow:

1. If you took a break after the previous session, reopen or return to the **tb_visual1.css** file in your editor and scroll to the Article Styles section.

2. Add the following style for the h1 heading in the article header:

```
article header h1 {
    text-shadow: rgb(181, 211, 181) 2px 2px 1px,
                rgba(21, 21, 21, 0.66) 5px 5px 25px;
}
```

Figure 4-23 highlights the style to add text shadows to the h1 heading.

Figure 4-23 Adding text shadows

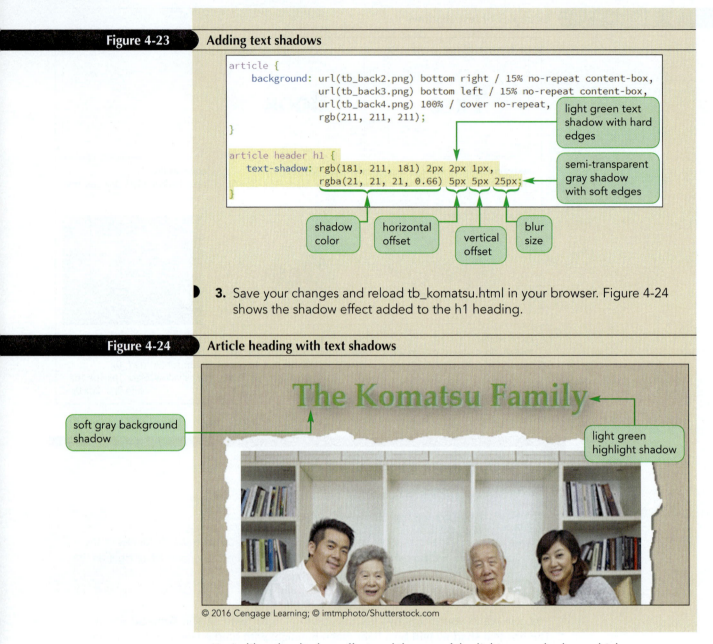

```
article {
    background: url(tb_back2.png) bottom right / 15% no-repeat content-box,
               url(tb_back3.png) bottom left / 15% no-repeat content-box,
               url(tb_back4.png) 100% / cover no-repeat,
               rgb(211, 211, 211);
}

article header h1 {
    text-shadow: rgb(181, 211, 181) 2px 2px 1px,
                 rgba(21, 21, 21, 0.66) 5px 5px 25px;
}
```

light green text shadow with hard edges

semi-transparent gray shadow with soft edges

shadow color

horizontal offset

vertical offset

blur size

3. Save your changes and reload tb_komatsu.html in your browser. Figure 4-24 shows the shadow effect added to the h1 heading.

Figure 4-24 Article heading with text shadows

The Komatsu Family

soft gray background shadow

light green highlight shadow

© 2016 Cengage Learning; © imtmphoto/Shutterstock.com

Kevin likes the shadow effect and the use of the light green shadow, which appears to give a highlight to the heading text. Next, he wants you to add shadows to other page objects.

Creating a Box Shadow

Shadows can be added to any block element in the web page by using the box-shadow property

```
box-shadow: color offsetX offsetY blur;
```

where *color*, *offsetX*, *offsetY*, and *blur* have the same meanings for box shadows as they do for text shadows. As with text shadows, you can add multiple shadows by including them in the following comma-separated list

```
box-shadow: shadow1, shadow2 …;
```

where once again the first shadow listed is displayed on top of subsequent shadows.

In the last session, you used left and right borders to set off the page body from the browser window background. Kevin would like you to increase this visual distinction by adding drop shadows to the left and right sides of the page body.

To add a box shadow:

1. Return to the **tb_visual1.css** file in your editor and go to the Page Body Styles section.

2. Within the style rule for the `body` element, insert the following styles:

   ```
   box-shadow: rgb(51, 51, 51) 15px 0px 25px,
               rgb(51, 51, 51) -15px 0px 25px;
   ```

   Figure 4-25 highlights the style to add box shadows to the page body.

| Figure 4-25 | Adding box shadows |

drop shadow on the page body's right edge

drop shadow on the page body's left edge

gray shadow color

```
body {
    border-left: 1px solid rgb(51, 51, 51);
    border-right: 1px solid rgb(51, 51, 51);
    box-shadow: rgb(51, 51, 51) 15px 0px 25px,
                rgb(51, 51, 51) -15px 0px 25px;
}
```

3. Save your changes and reload tb_komatsu.html in your browser. Figure 4-26 shows the drop shadows added to the page body.

| Figure 4-26 | Page body with drop shadows |

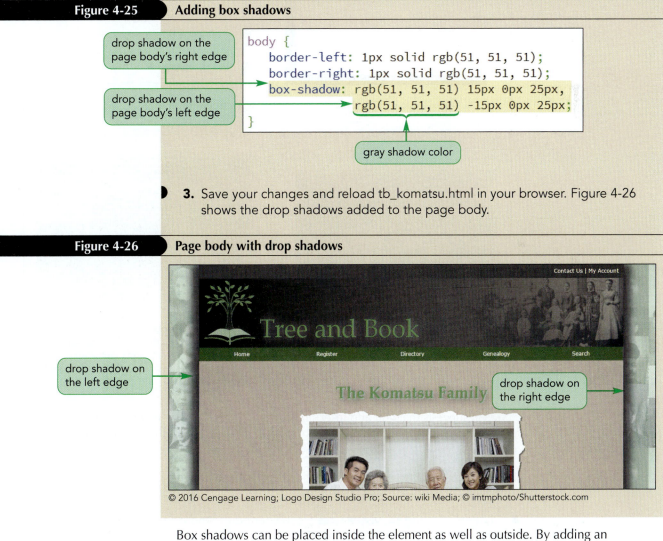

drop shadow on the left edge

drop shadow on the right edge

© 2016 Cengage Learning; Logo Design Studio Pro; Source: wiki Media; © imtmphoto/Shutterstock.com

Box shadows can be placed inside the element as well as outside. By adding an interior shadow you can create the illusion of a beveled edge in which the object appears to rise out of its background. To create an interior shadow, add the `inset` keyword to the `box-shadow` property

```
box-shadow: inset color offsetX offsetY blur;
```

TIP

You can learn more about box shadows using the demo_box_shadows.html file from the demo folder.

where the meanings of the *offsetX* and *offsetY* values are switched when applied to interior shadowing so that positive *offsetX* and *offsetY* values move the shadow to the left and up within the box, while negative *offsetX* and *offsetY* values move the shadow to the right and down.

An object can contain a mixture of exterior and interior shadows. Figure 4-27 shows examples of box shadows, including one example that mixes both interior and exterior shadows.

Figure 4-27   **Examples of box shadows**

box-shadow: 15px 15px;   box-shadow: rgb(127, 90, 0) -10px -10px 15px;

background-color: rgb(90, 141, 191);   background-color: rgb(101, 191, 101);
box-shadow: inset rgb(0, 51, 101) -10px -15px 15px,   box-shadow: inset rgb(0, 101, 51) 10px 15px 15px,
inset white 5px 5px 5px;   inset white -5px -5px 25px,
                                                      rgb(51, 51, 51) -10px -10px 20px;

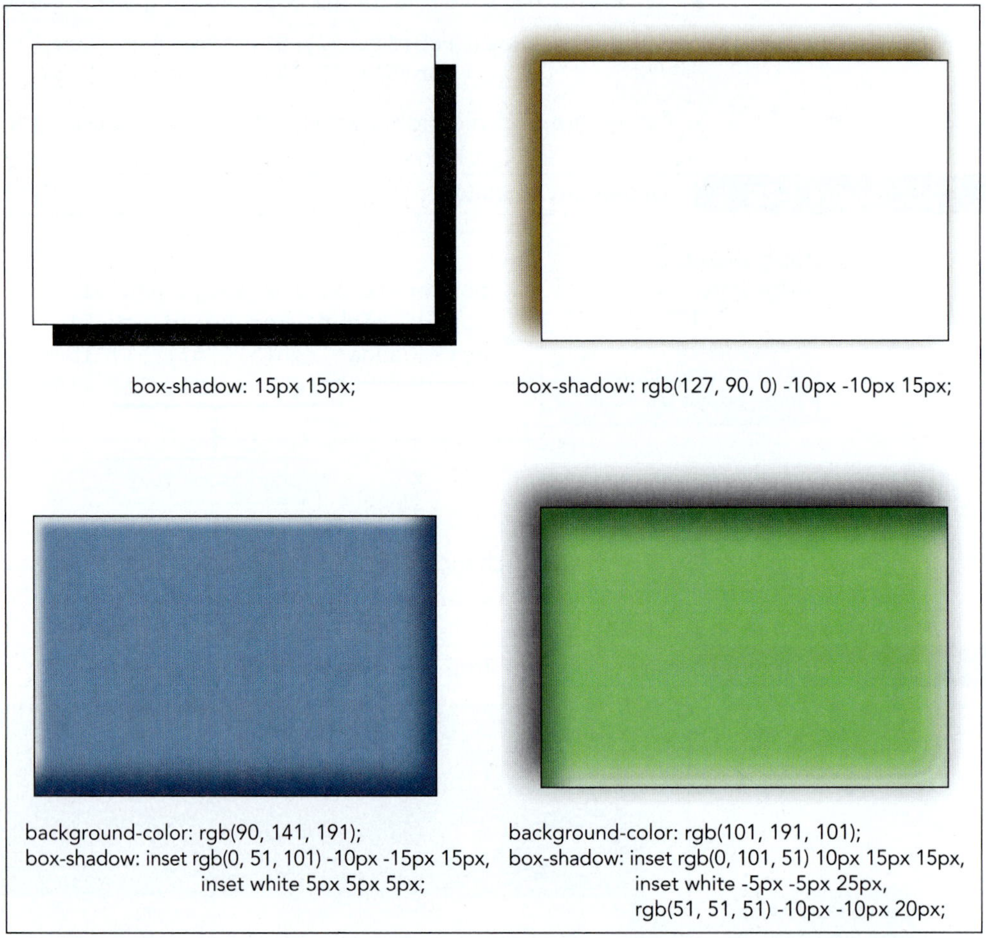

© 2016 Cengage Learning

Kevin suggests that you add inset shadows to the `article` element, placing medium gray shadows within the article to make it appear raised up from the surrounding page content.

To add inset shadows:

1. Return to the **tb_visual1.css** file in your editor and go to the Article Styles section.

2. Within the style rule for the `article` element, insert the following `box-shadow` style:

```
box-shadow: inset rgb(71, 71, 71) -10px -10px 25px,
            inset rgb(71, 71, 71) 10px 10px 25px;
```

Figure 4-28 highlights the newly added code for the inset box shadow.

Positive and negative offset values for interior shadows have the opposite meaning from positive and negative offset values for exterior shadows.

Figure 4-28   **Adding an inset shadow**

places a medium-gray shadow in the lower-right interior corner

inset keyword places shadow inside the object

```
article {
    background: url(tb_back2.png) bottom right / 15% no-repeat content-box,
               url(tb_back3.png) bottom left / 15% no-repeat content-box,
               url(tb_back4.png) 100% / cover no-repeat,
               rgb(211, 211, 211);
    box-shadow: inset rgb(71, 71, 71) -10px -10px 25px,
                inset rgb(71, 71, 71) 10px 10px 25px;
}
```

places a medium-gray shadow in the upper-left interior corner

3. Save your changes and reload tb_komatsu.html in your browser. The inset shadow for the page body element is shown in Figure 4-29.

Figure 4-29   **Page article with interior shadowing**

interior shadow placed on the left and up based on positive offset values

interior shadow placed on the right and down based on negative offset values

© 2016 Cengage Learning; Logo Design Studio Pro; Source: wiki Media; © imtmphoto/Shutterstock.com

By default, a box shadow has the same size and dimensions as its page object offset in the horizontal and vertical direction. To change the shadow size, add the *spread* parameter to the box-shadow property, specifying the size of the shadow relative to the size of the page object. A positive value increases the size of the shadow, while a negative value decreases it. For example, the following style creates a gray shadow that is offset from the page object by 5 pixels in both the vertical and horizontal direction with no blurring but with a shadow that is 15 pixels larger in the horizontal and vertical directions than the object:

```
box-shadow: gray 5px 5px 0px 15px;
```

On the other hand, the following style creates a shadow that is 15 pixels smaller than the page object:

```
box-shadow: gray 5px 5px 0px -15px;
```

REFERENCE

Creating a Box Shadow

- To add a shadow to a block element, use

  box-shadow: *color offsetX offsetY blur spread*;

  where *color* is the shadow color, *offsetX* and *offsetY* are the distances of the shadow from the element in the horizontal and vertical directions, *blur* defines the amount by which the shadow is stretched and *spread* sets the size of the shadow relative to the size of the block element. If no *spread* is specified, the shadow has the same size as the block element.
- To create an interior shadow, include the `inset` keyword

  box-shadow: inset *color offsetX offsetY blur spread*;

- To create multiple shadows place them in a comma-separated list:

  box-shadow: *shadow1, shadow2, …*;

  where *shadow1*, *shadow2*, and so on are definitions for individual shadows with the first shadows listed displayed on top of subsequent shadows.

One application of the *spread* parameter is to create a visual effect in which the object appears to be surrounded by a halo. This is achieved by setting the shadow offsets to 0 pixels while making the shadow larger than the page object itself. Kevin suggests that you use this technique to add a green halo to the `aside` element.

To increase the shadow size:

1. Return to the **tb_visual1.css** file in your editor and go to the Asides Styles section.

2. Within the style rule for the `aside` element, insert the following style:

   ```
   box-shadow: rgba(51, 91, 51, 0.4) 0px 0px 20px 10px;
   ```

   Figure 4-30 highlights the style to add a halo to the `aside` element.

Figure 4-30   **Creating a spreading shadow**

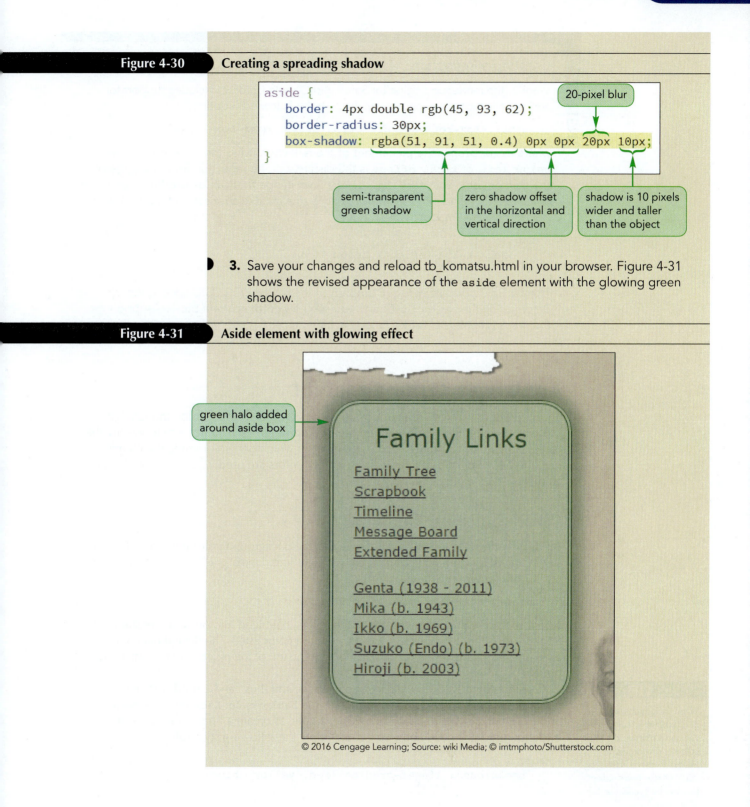

```
aside {
    border: 4px double rgb(45, 93, 62);
    border-radius: 30px;
    box-shadow: rgba(51, 91, 51, 0.4) 0px 0px 20px 10px;
}
```

20-pixel blur

semi-transparent green shadow

zero shadow offset in the horizontal and vertical direction

shadow is 10 pixels wider and taller than the object

3. Save your changes and reload tb_komatsu.html in your browser. Figure 4-31 shows the revised appearance of the `aside` element with the glowing green shadow.

Figure 4-31   **Aside element with glowing effect**

green halo added around aside box

Family Links

Family Tree
Scrapbook
Timeline
Message Board
Extended Family

Genta (1938 - 2011)
Mika (b. 1943)
Ikko (b. 1969)
Suzuko (Endo) (b. 1973)
Hiroji (b. 2003)

Creating a Reflection

WebKit, the rendering engine for Safari and Google Chrome, includes support for adding reflections to page objects through the following property

```
-webkit-box-reflect: direction offset mask-box-image;
```

where *direction* is the placement of the reflection using the keywords **above**, **below**, **left**, or **right**; *offset* is the distance of the reflection from the edge of the element box, and *mask-box-image* is an image that can be used to overlay the reflection. For example, the following style rule creates a reflection that is 10 pixels below the inline image:

```
img {
    -webkit-box-reflect: below 10px;
}
```

There is no equivalent **reflect** property in the official W3C CSS3 specifications. Before using the **reflect** property, you should view the current browser support for the **-webkit-box-reflect** property at *caniuse.com*.

Applying a Color Gradient

So far you have worked with backgrounds consisting of a single color, though that color can be augmented through the use of drop shadows. Another way to modify the background color is through a **color gradient** in which one color gradually blends into another color or fades away if transparent colors are used. CSS3 supports linear gradients and radial gradients.

Creating a Linear Gradient

A linear gradient is a color gradient in which the background color transitions from a starting color to an ending color along a straight line. Linear gradients are created using the **linear-gradient** function

```
linear-gradient(color1, color2, …)
```

where *color1*, *color2*, and so on are the colors that blend into one another starting from *color1*, through *color2*, and onto the last color listed. The default direction for a linear color gradient is vertical, starting from the top of the object and moving to the bottom.

Gradients are treated like background images and thus can be used with any CSS property that accepts an image such as the **background**, **background-image**, and **list-style-image** properties. For example, to create a linear gradient as a background for the page body, you could apply the following style rule:

```
body {
    background: linear-gradient(red, yellow, blue);
}
```

Figure 4-32 shows the appearance of this vertical gradient as the background color transitions gradually from red down to yellow and then from yellow down to blue.

| Figure 4-32 | **Linear gradient with three colors** |

linear-gradient(red, yellow, blue)

© 2016 Cengage Learning

To change from the default vertical direction, you add a *direction* value to the `linear-gradient` function

```
linear-gradient(direction, color1, color2, …)
```

where *direction* is the direction of the gradient using keywords or angles. Direction keywords are written in the form `to` *position* where *position* is either a side of the object or a corner. For example the following linear gradient moves in a straight line to the left edge of the object blending from red to yellow to blue:

```
background: linear-gradient(to left, red, yellow, blue);
```

To move toward the corner, include both corner edges. The following style moves the gradient in the direction of the object's bottom right corner:

```
background: linear-gradient(to bottom right, red, yellow, blue);
```

To move in a direction other than a side or corner, you can express the direction using an angle value. Angles are measured in degrees with 0deg equal to `to top`, 90deg equal to `to right`, 180deg equal to `to bottom`, and 270deg equal to `to left` (see Figure 4-33.)

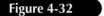

TIP

For square objects, a direction of `45deg` is equivalent to a direction of `to right top`.

Figure 4-33   **Linear gradient directions**

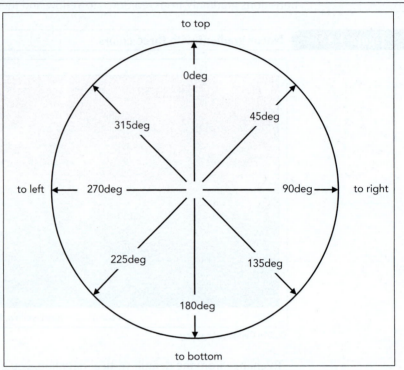

© 2016 Cengage Learning

For example, the following gradient points at a 60 degree angle:

```
background: linear-gradient(60deg, red, yellow, blue);
```

Figure 4-34 shows other examples of linear gradients moving in different directions using both syntaxes.

INSIGHT

Transparency and Gradients

Interesting gradient effects can be achieved using transparent colors so that the background color gradually fades away as it moves in the direction of the gradient. For example, the following style creates a linear gradient that gradually fades away from its initial solid red color:

```
linear-gradient(rgba(255, 0, 0, 1), rgba(255, 0, 0, 0))
```

Note that since the final color is completely transparent it will adopt the background color of the parent element.

You can also use gradients to create background images that appear to fade by using multiple backgrounds in which the gradient appears on top of an image. For example, the following background style creates a fading background using the back.png image file:

```
background: linear-gradient(rgb(255, 255, 255, 0), rgb(255,
255, 255, 1)),url(back.png));
```

When rendered by the browser, the background image will start as solid but gradually fade to white as the linear gradient proceeds through the element background.

Figure 4-34   Directions of linear gradients

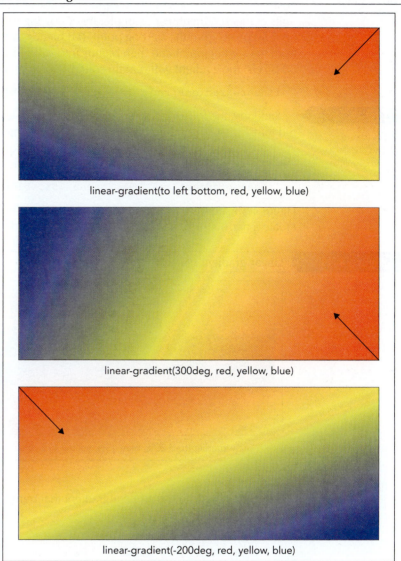

© 2016 Cengage Learning

Note that the degree values can be negative in which case the direction is pointed counter-clockwise around the circle shown in Figure 4-33. A negative angle of –45deg for example would be equivalent to a positive angle of 315deg, an angle of –200deg would be equal to 160deg, and so forth.

Gradients and Color Stops

The colors specified in a gradient are evenly distributed so that the following gradient starts with a solid red, solid green appears halfway through the gradient, and finishes with solid blue:

```
background: linear-gradient(red, green, blue);
```

To change how the colors are distributed, you define color stops, which represent the point at which the specified color stops and the transition to the next color begins. The linear-gradient function using color stops has the general form

```
linear-gradient(direction, color-stop1, color-stop2, …)
```

where *color-stop1*, *color-stop2*, and so on are the colors and their stopping positions within the gradient. Stopping positions can be entered using any of the CSS units of measurement. For example, the following gradient starts with solid red up until 50 pixels from the starting point, red blends to solid green stopping at 60 pixels from the starting point and then blends into solid blue 80 pixels from the start. After 80 pixels, the gradient will remain solid blue to the end of the background.

```
linear-gradient(red 50px, green 60px, blue 80px)
```

TIP

You can test your own gradients using the demo_linear_gradients.html file from the demo folder.

Similarly, the following style rule sets the color stops using percentages with solid red for the first 25% of the background, transitioning to solid green from 25% to 75% of the background, and then transitioning to solid blue from 75% to 95% of the background size. From that point to the end, the background remains solid blue.

```
linear-gradient(red 25%, green 75%, blue 95%)
```

Figure 4-35 shows an example of a linear gradient in which color stops are used to create a narrow strip of yellow within a background of red blended into blue.

Figure 4-35 **Linear gradient color stops**

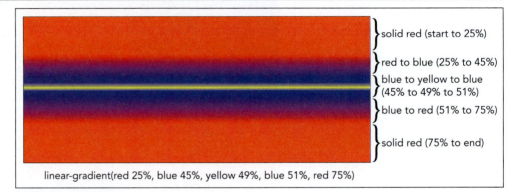

solid red (start to 25%)

red to blue (25% to 45%)

blue to yellow to blue (45% to 49% to 51%)

blue to red (51% to 75%)

solid red (75% to end)

linear-gradient(red 25%, blue 45%, yellow 49%, blue 51%, red 75%)

© 2016 Cengage Learning

Kevin suggests you use a linear gradient that transitions from light green to dark green as the background for the page footer.

To apply a linear gradient:

1. Return to the **tb_visual1.css** file in your editor and go to the Footer Styles section.

2. Insert the following style rule for the `footer` element:

```
footer {
    background: linear-gradient(345deg, rgb(172, 232, 172),
                                rgb(21, 35, 21) 80%);
}
```

Figure 4-36 highlights the style to create the linear gradient.

Figure 4-36   **Applying a linear gradient**

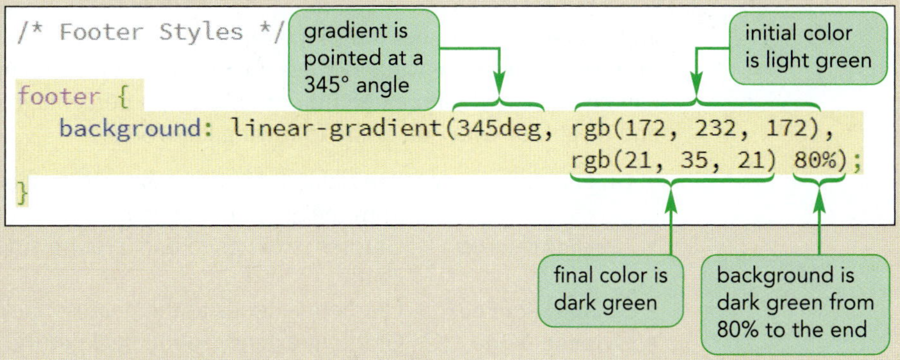

```
/* Footer Styles */

footer {
    background: linear-gradient(345deg, rgb(172, 232, 172),
                                rgb(21, 35, 21) 80%);
}
```

gradient is pointed at a 345° angle

initial color is light green

final color is dark green

background is dark green from 80% to the end

3. Save your changes and reload tb_komatsu.html in your browser. Figure 4-37 shows the revised appearance of the page footer with a linear gradient.

Figure 4-37   **Page footer with linear gradient background**

end of gradient

Family Histories	Getting Started	About Tree and Book	Tree and Book © 2017 English (US)
Family Trees	Genealogy FAQ	Developers	
Galleries	Research Sites	Privacy	
Calendars	Interest Groups	Terms	
Forums	Government Sites	Help	

start of gradient

The other color gradient supported in CSS3 is a radial gradient. You will explore how to create radial gradients now.

Creating a Radial Gradient

A **radial gradient** is a color gradient that starts from a central point and proceeds outward in a series of concentric circles or ellipses. Figure 4-38 shows an example of a radial gradient consisting of a series of concentric ellipses radiating from a central red color to an ending blue color.

Figure 4-38   **A radial gradient of three colors**

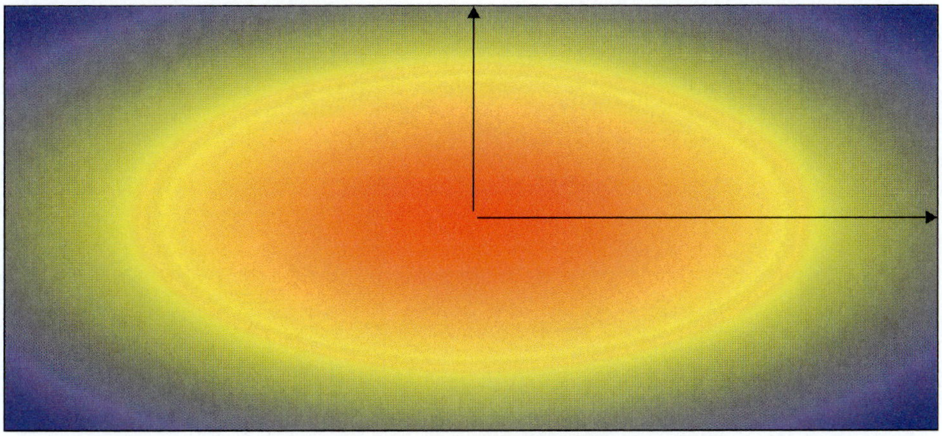

radial-gradient(red, yellow, blue)

Radial gradients are created using the following `radial-gradient` function.

```
radial-gradient(shape size at position, color-stop1,
color-stop2, …)
```

The *shape* value defines the shape of the gradient and is either `ellipse` (the default) or `circle`. The *size* value defines the extent of the gradient as it radiates outward and can be expressed with a CSS unit of measure, a percentage of the background's width and height, or with one of the following keywords:

- `farthest-corner`   (the default) Gradient extends to the background corner farthest from the gradient's center.
- `farthest-side`   Gradient extends to background side farthest from the gradient's center.
- `closest-corner`   Gradient extends to the nearest background corner.
- `closest-side`   Gradient extends to the background side closest to the gradient's center.

The `position` defines where the gradient radiates from and can be expressed in coordinates using pixels, percentages of the element's width and height, or with the keywords: `left`, `center`, `right`, `top`, and `bottom`. The default is to place the gradient within the center of the background.

Finally the *color-stop1, color-stop2* … values are the colors and their stopping positions within the gradient and have the same interpretation used for linear gradients except they mark stopping points as the gradient radiates outward. Note that the color stops are optional, just as they are in linear gradients. For example the following function defines a circular gradient radiating from the horizontal and vertical center of the background through the colors red, yellow, and blue:

```
radial-gradient(circle closest-corner at center center,
                red, yellow, blue)
```

The gradient ends when it reaches the closest background corner. Anything outside of the gradient will be a solid blue.

Figure 4-39 shows other examples of the different effects that can be accomplished using the `radial-gradient` function. Note that when parameters of the radial-gradient function are omitted they take their default values.

TIP

You can explore how to work with the parameters of the `radial-gradient` function using the demo_radial_gradients.html file from the demo folder.

Figure 4-39   **Examples of radial gradients**

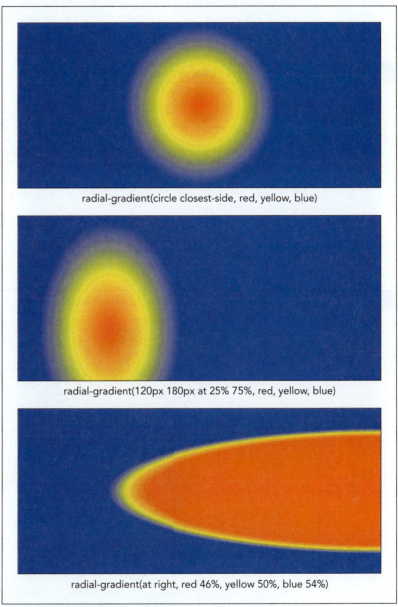

radial-gradient(circle closest-side, red, yellow, blue)

radial-gradient(120px 180px at 25% 75%, red, yellow, blue)

radial-gradient(at right, red 46%, yellow 50%, blue 54%)

© 2016 Cengage Learning

Kevin would like you to apply a radial gradient to the background of the `aside` element. The gradient will start from a white center blending into to a medium green and then into a darker shade of green.

To apply a radial gradient:

1. Return to the **tb_visual1.css** file in your editor and go to the Aside Styles section.

2. Add the following style to the style rule for the `aside` element:

```
background:
radial-gradient(white, rgb(151, 222, 151),
               rgb(81, 125, 81));
```

Note that this style supersedes the previous background style created in the tb_styles1.css style sheet. Figure 4-40 highlights the code to create the radial gradient.

Figure 4-40 Applying a radial gradient

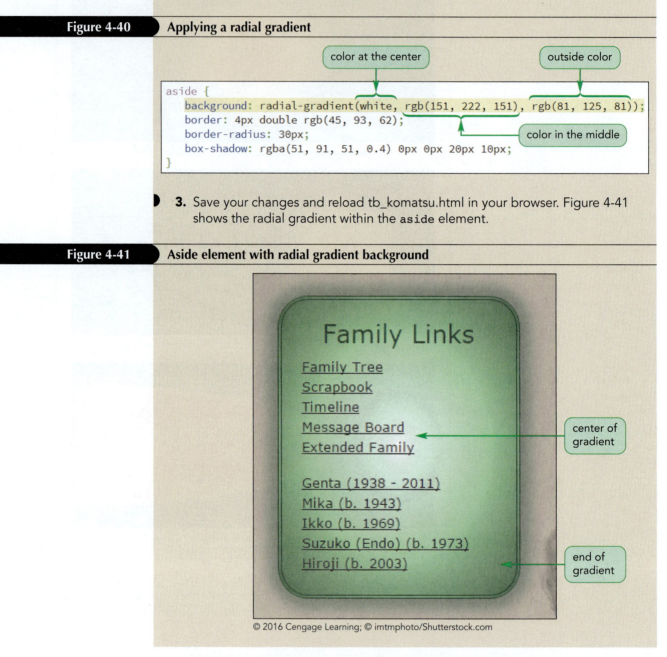

```
aside {
    background: radial-gradient(white, rgb(151, 222, 151), rgb(81, 125, 81));
    border: 4px double rgb(45, 93, 62);
    border-radius: 30px;
    box-shadow: rgba(51, 91, 51, 0.4) 0px 0px 20px 10px;
}
```

color at the center — outside color — color in the middle

3. Save your changes and reload tb_komatsu.html in your browser. Figure 4-41 shows the radial gradient within the aside element.

Figure 4-41 Aside element with radial gradient background

Family Links

Family Tree
Scrapbook
Timeline
Message Board — center of gradient
Extended Family

Genta (1938 - 2011)
Mika (b. 1943)
Ikko (b. 1969)
Suzuko (Endo) (b. 1973)
Hiroji (b. 2003) — end of gradient

© 2016 Cengage Learning; © imtmphoto/Shutterstock.com

Kevin likes the effect of the radial gradient on the aside element and feels that it works well with the glowing effect you added earlier.

INSIGHT

Gradients and Browser Extensions

The gradient functions were heavily revised as they went from being browser-specific properties to the final syntax approved by the W3C. If you work with older browsers, you may need to accommodate their versions of these gradient functions. For example, the following linear gradient that blends red to blue going in the direction to the right edge of the background

```
linear-gradient(to right, red, blue)
```

would be expressed using the old WebKit gradient function as:

```
-webkit-gradient(linear, left, right, from(red), to(blue))
```

Other older versions of browsers such as Mozilla, Internet Explorer, and Opera have their own gradient functions with different syntax. You can study these functions using the online support at the browser websites or doing a search on the Web for CSS gradient functions.

Note that not all browser extensions support the same types of gradients, which means that it is difficult and sometimes impossible to duplicate a particular gradient background for every browser. Thus, you should not make gradients an essential feature of your design if you want to be compatible with older browsers.

Repeating a Gradient

As you add more color stops, the gradient function can become unwieldy and overly complicated. One alternative is to repeat the gradient design. You can repeat linear and radial gradients using the functions

```
repeating-linear-gradient(params)
repeating-radial-gradient(params)
```

TIP

You can create your own repeating gradients using the demo_repeat_linear_gradients.html and demo_repeat_radial_gradients.html files from the demo folder.

where *params* are the parameters of the `linear-gradient` or the `radial-gradient` functions already discussed. The only requirement for a repeating gradient is that a stopping position is required for the last color in the list that is less than the size of the object background. Once the last color in the color list is reached, the gradient starts over again. For example, the following function repeats a vertical gradient starting with white transitioning to black, transitioning back to white at 10% of the height of the object, and then repeating that pattern each time it reaches the next 10% of the height of the object:

```
repeating-linear-gradient(white, black 10%)
```

Figure 4-42 shows some other examples of repeating linear and radial gradients.

Figure 4-42	**Repeating a gradient**

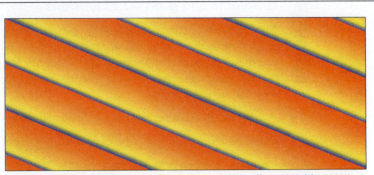

repeating-linear-gradient(to left bottom, red 5%, yellow 18%, blue 20%)

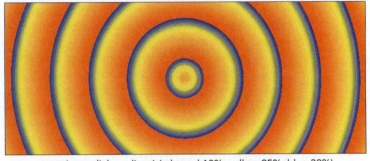

repeating-radial-gradient(circle, red 10%, yellow 25%, blue 30%)

© 2016 Cengage Learning

Creating a Gradient

- To create a linear gradient, use the function

  `linear-gradient(direction, color-stop1, color-stop2, …)`

  where *direction* is the direction of the gradient and *color-stop1*, *color-stop2*, and so on are the colors and their stopping positions within the gradient.
- To create a radial gradient, use the function

  `radial-gradient(shape size at position, color-stop1, color-stop2, …)`

  where *shape* defines the shape of the gradient, *size* sets the gradient size, *position* places the center of the gradient, and *color-stop1*, *color-stop2*, and so on are the colors and their stopping positions within the gradient.
- To repeat a gradient, use the functions

  `repeating-linear-gradient(params)`
  `repeating-radial-gradient(params)`

  where *params* are the parameters of the `linear-gradient` or the `radial-gradient` functions.

The last visual effect that Kevin wants you to add to the Komatsu Family page is to make the figure box semi-transparent so that it blends in better with its background.

Creating Semi-Transparent Objects

In Tutorial 2, you learned that you could create semi-transparent colors that blend with the background color. You can also create whole page objects that are semi-transparent using the following opacity property:

```
opacity: value;
```

where *value* ranges from 0 (completely transparent) up to 1 (completely opaque.) For example, the following style rule makes the page body 70% opaque, allowing a bit of the browser window background to filter through

```
body {
    opacity: 0.7;
}
```

REFERENCE

Making a Semi-transparent Object

- To make a page object semi-transparent, use the property

  ```
  opacity: value;
  ```

  where *value* ranges from 0 (completely transparent) up to 1 (completely opaque).

Kevin suggests that you set the opacity of the figure box to 55% in order to blend the figure box with the paper texture background you added to the article element.

To create a semi-transparent object:

1. Return to the **tb_visual1.css** file in your editor and scroll up to the Figure Box Styles section.

2. Within the style rule for the figure element, insert the following style:

   ```
   opacity: 0.55;
   ```

   Figure 4-43 highlights the code to make the figure box semi-transparent.

| Figure 4-43 | Creating a semi-transparent object |

sets the opacity of the figure box to 55%

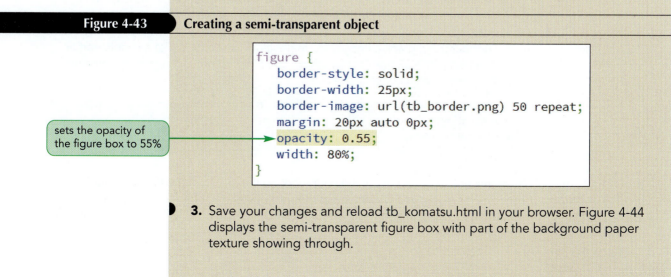

```
figure {
    border-style: solid;
    border-width: 25px;
    border-image: url(tb_border.png) 50 repeat;
    margin: 20px auto 0px;
    opacity: 0.55;
    width: 80%;
}
```

3. Save your changes and reload tb_komatsu.html in your browser. Figure 4-44 displays the semi-transparent figure box with part of the background paper texture showing through.

Figure 4-44 | **Changing the opacity of the figure box**

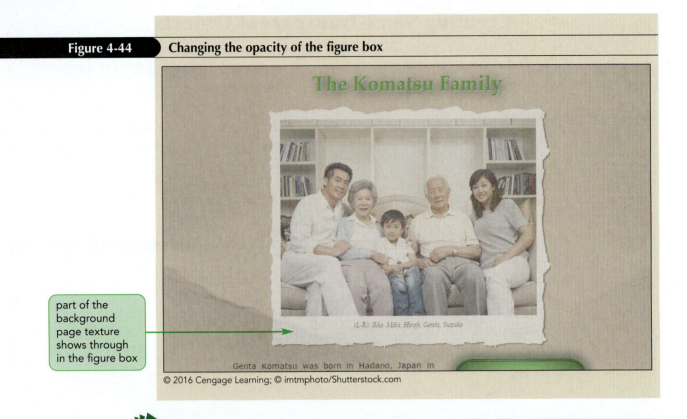

part of the
background
page texture
shows through
in the figure box

© 2016 Cengage Learning; © imtmphoto/Shutterstock.com

Written Communication: How to Use Visual Effects

The CSS visual styles can add striking effects to your website, but they might not be supported by older browsers. This leaves you with the dilemma of when and how to use these styles. Here are some tips to keep in mind when applying visual effects to your website:

- Because not every user will be able to see a particular visual effect, design your page so that it is still readable to users with or without the effect.
- Be aware that some visual effects that flicker or produce strobe-like effects can cause discomfort and even photo-epileptic seizures in susceptible individuals. Avoid clashing color combinations and optical illusions that can cause these conditions.
- If you need to create a cross-browser solution, use browser extensions and be aware that the browser extension syntax might not match the syntax of the CSS3 standard.
- Consider using graphic images to create your visual effects. For example, rather than using the CSS gradient functions, create a background image file containing the gradient effect of your choice.

No matter how you employ visual effects on your website, remember that the most important part of your site is its content. Do not let visual effects distract from your content and message.

At this point you've completed your work on the design of the Komatsu Family page. In the next session, you will learn how to use CSS to apply transformations and filters. You will also learn how to work with image maps to create linkable images. Close any open files now.

Session 4.2 Quick Check

1. Provide code to add a red text shadow to all h1 headings; the shadow should be offset 5 pixels to the left and 10 pixels down with a blur of 7 pixels.

2. Add a gray box shadow to all `aside` elements; the shadow should be placed 2 pixels to the left and 5 pixels above the element with a blur of 10 pixels.

3. Add an inset gray shadow to all footers; the shadow should be offset by 10 pixels to the left and 15 pixels down with a blur of 5 pixels.

4. Create a red halo effect around the `main` element with no shadow offset, a blur of 15 pixels and a shadow size that is 10 pixels larger than the element.

5. Provide code for a linear gradient that moves in the direction of the lower-left corner of the element through the colors: orange, yellow, and green.

6. Create a linear gradient that moves at a 15 degree angle with the color orange stopping at 10% of the background, yellow stopping at 50%, and green stopping at 55%.

7. Create a radial gradient that extends to the farthest background corner, going through the colors orange, yellow, and green.

8. Create a repeating circular gradient of orange, yellow, and green bands centered at the right edge of the element with the colors stopped at 10%, 20%, and 30% respectively.

9. Create a style rule to set the opacity of all inline images to 75%.

Session 4.3 Visual Overview:

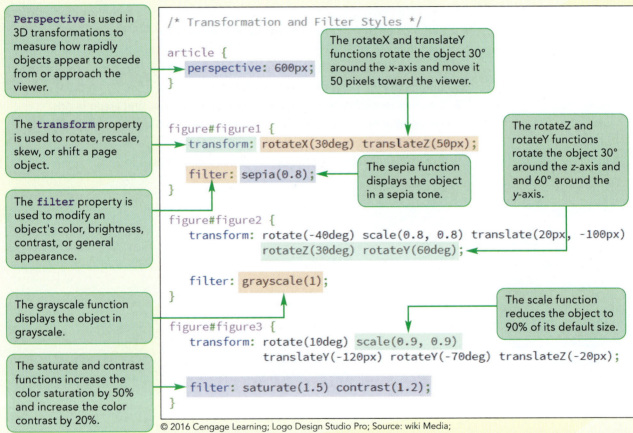

Perspective is used in 3D transformations to measure how rapidly objects appear to recede from or approach the viewer.

The **transform** property is used to rotate, rescale, skew, or shift a page object.

The **filter** property is used to modify an object's color, brightness, contrast, or general appearance.

The grayscale function displays the object in grayscale.

The saturate and contrast functions increase the color saturation by 50% and increase the color contrast by 20%.

```
/* Transformation and Filter Styles */

article {
    perspective: 600px;
}


figure#figure1 {
    transform: rotateX(30deg) translateZ(50px);

    filter: sepia(0.8);
}

figure#figure2 {
    transform: rotate(-40deg) scale(0.8, 0.8) translate(20px, -100px)
               rotateZ(30deg) rotateY(60deg);

    filter: grayscale(1);
}

figure#figure3 {
    transform: rotate(10deg) scale(0.9, 0.9)
               translateY(-120px) rotateY(-70deg) translateZ(-20px);

    filter: saturate(1.5) contrast(1.2);
}
```

The rotateX and translateY functions rotate the object 30° around the x-axis and move it 50 pixels toward the viewer.

The rotateZ and rotateY functions rotate the object 30° around the z-axis and and 60° around the y-axis.

The sepia function displays the object in a sepia tone.

The scale function reduces the object to 90% of its default size.

Transformations and Filters

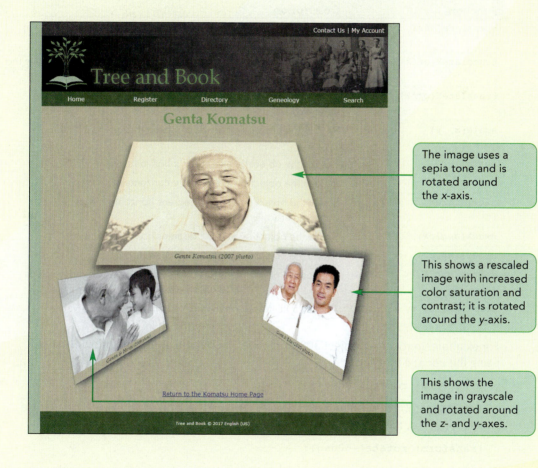

The image uses a sepia tone and is rotated around the x-axis.

This shows a rescaled image with increased color saturation and contrast; it is rotated around the y-axis.

This shows the image in grayscale and rotated around the z- and y-axes.

Transforming Page Objects

In this session, you will examine some CSS3 styles that can be used to transform the appearance of page objects through rotation, rescaling, and translation in space. To accomplish these transformations, you'll use the following `transform` property:

```
transform: effect(params);
```

where *effect* is a transformation function that will be applied to the page object and *params* are any parameters required by the function. Figure 4-45 describes some of the CSS3 transformation functions.

| Figure 4-45 | CSS3 2D transformation functions |

Function	Description
translate(*offX*, *offY*)	Moves the object *offX* pixels to the right and *offY* pixels down; negative values move the object to the left and up
translateX(*offX*)	Moves the object *offX* pixels to the right; negative values move the object to the left
translateY(*offY*)	Moves the object *offY* pixels down; negative values move the object up
scale(*x*, *y*)	Resizes the object by a factor of *x* horizontally and a factor of *y* vertically
scaleX(*x*)	Resizes the object by a factor of *x* horizontally
scaleY(*y*)	Resizes the object by a factor of *y* horizontally
skew(*angleX*, *angleY*)	Skews the object by *angleX* degrees horizontally and *angleY* degrees vertically
skewX(*angleX*)	Skews the object by *angleX* degrees horizontally
skewY(*angleY*)	Skews the object by *angleY* degrees vertically
rotate(*angle*)	Rotates the object by *angle* degrees clockwise; negative values rotate the object counter-clockwise
matrix(*n*, *n*, *n*, *n*, *n*, *n*)	Applies a 2D transformation based on a matrix of six values

For example, to rotate an object 30° clockwise, you would apply the following style using the `rotate` function:

```
transform: rotate(30deg);
```

To rotate an object counter-clockwise, you would use a negative value for the angle of rotation. Thus, the following style rotates an object 60° counter-clockwise:

```
transform: rotate(-60deg);
```

Figure 4-46 displays the effects of other transformation functions on a sample page image.

Figure 4-46	Examples of CSS3 Transformations

transform: translate(40px, -35px);   transform: scale(0.8, 0.5);

transform: skew(30deg, 20deg);   transform: rotate(-90deg);

© imtmphoto/Shutterstock.com

Transforming an object has no impact on the page layout. All of the other page objects will retain their original positions.

You can apply multiple transformations by placing the effect functions in a space-separated list. In this situation, transformations are applied in the order listed. For example, the following style first rotates the object 30° clockwise and then shifts it 20 pixels to the right.

```
transform: rotate(30deg) translateX(20px);
```

REFERENCE

Applying a CSS Transformation

- To apply a transformation to a page object, use the property

  ```
  transform: effect(params);
  ```

  where *effect* is a transformation function that will be applied to the page object and *params* are any parameters required by the function.

The website has pages with photos for each individual in the Komatsu family. Kevin wants you to work on transforming the photos on Genta Komatsu's page. Kevin has already created the page content and a layout and typographical style sheet but wants you to work on the style sheet containing the visual effects. Open the Genta Komatsu page now.

To open the Genta Komatsu page:

1. Use your editor to open the **tb_genta_txt.html** and **tb_visual2_txt.css** files from the html04 ▸ tutorial folder. Enter *your name* and *the date* in the comment section of both files and save them as **tb_genta.html** and **tb_visual2.css** respectively.

2. Return to the **tb_genta.html** file in your editor. Within the document head, insert the following link elements to link the page to the tb_reset.css, tb_styles2.css, and tb_visual2.css style sheet files.

   ```
   <link href="tb_reset.css" rel="stylesheet" />
   <link href="tb_styles2.css" rel="stylesheet" />
   <link href="tb_visual2.css" rel="stylesheet" />
   ```

3. Take some time to scroll through the contents of the file. Note that the document content consists mainly of three figure boxes each containing a different photo of Genta Komatsu.

4. Close the file, saving your changes.

5. Open the **tb_genta.html** file in your browser. Figure 4-47 shows the initial layout and design of the page content.

Figure 4-47 **Initial design of the Genta Komatsu page**

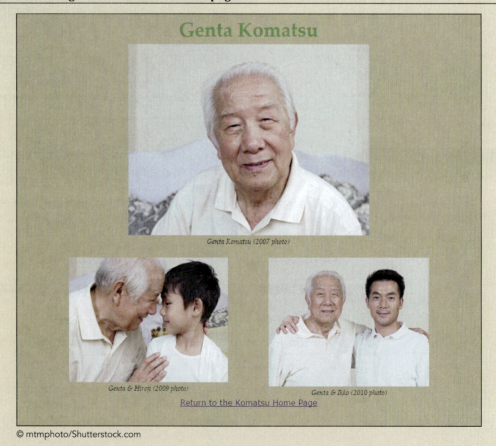

Genta Komatsu (2007 photo)

Genta & Hiroji (2009 photo)

Genta & Ikko (2010 photo)

Return to the Komatsu Home Page

© mtmphoto/Shutterstock.com

Kevin feels that the page lacks visual interest. He suggests you transform the bottom row of photos by rotating them and shifting them upward to partially cover the main photo, creating a collage-style layout. Apply the `transform` property now to make these changes.

To apply the transform style:

1. Go to the **tb_visual2.css** file in your editor and scroll as needed to the Transformation Styles section.

2. Insert the following style rule to rotate the figure2 figure box 40° counter-clockwise, reduce it to 80% of its former size, and shift it 20 pixels to the right and 100 pixels up. Also, add a style to create a drop shadow using the code that follows:

```
figure#figure2 {
    transform: rotate(-40deg) scale(0.8, 0.8)
               translate(20px, -100px);
    box-shadow: rgb(101, 101, 101) 10px 10px 25px;
}
```

3. Add the following style rule to rotate the figure3 figure box 10° clockwise, resize it to 90% of its current size, and shift it 120 pixels upward. Also add a drop shadow to the figure box using the following style rule:

```
figure#figure3 {
    transform: rotate(10deg) scale(0.9, 0.9)
               translateY(-120px);
    box-shadow: rgb(101, 101, 101) 10px -10px 25px;
}
```

Figure 4-48 describes the newly added style rules.

Figure 4-48	Transforming the figure boxes

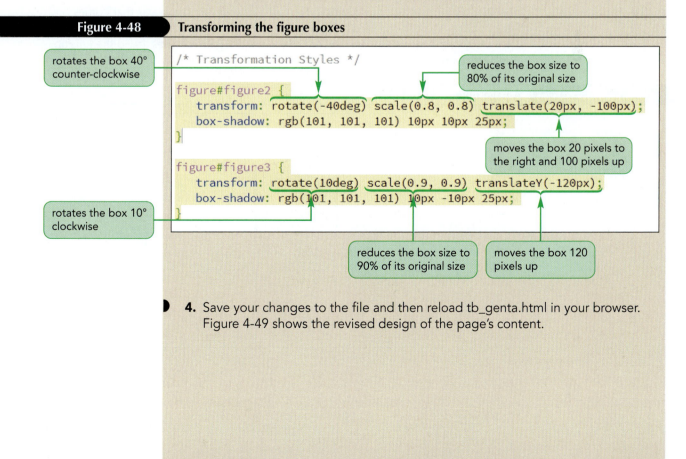

4. Save your changes to the file and then reload tb_genta.html in your browser. Figure 4-49 shows the revised design of the page's content.

Figure 4-49   **Viewing the transformed figure boxes**

box rotated 40° counter-clockwise, rescaled and shifted up and to the right

box rotated 10° clockwise, rescaled and shifted up

©imtmphoto/Shutterstock.com

The transformations you applied rotated the figure boxes along a two-dimensional or 2D space that consisted of a horizontal and vertical axis. CSS also supports transformations that operate in a three-dimensional or 3D space.

Transformations in Three Dimensions

A **3D transformation** is a change that involves three spatial axes: an *x*-axis that runs horizontally across the page, a *y*-axis that runs vertically, and a *z*-axis that comes straight out of the page toward and away from the viewer. Positive values along the axes are to the right, down, and toward the reader; negative values are to the left, up, and away from the reader (see Figure 4-50.)

Figure 4-50   **A page object viewed in 3D**

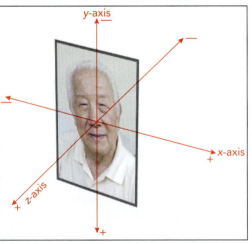

© 2016 Cengage Learning; © imtmphoto/Shutterstock.com

With the addition of a third spatial axis, you can create effects in which an object appears to zoom toward and away from users, or to rotate in three dimensional space. Figure 4-51 describes the 3D transformations supported by CSS.

Figure 4-51   **CSS3 3D transformation functions**

Function	Description
translate3d(*offX*, *offY*, *offZ*)	Shifts the object *offX* pixels horizontally, *offY* pixels vertically, and *offZ* pixels along the z-axis
translateX(*offX*) translateY(*offY*) translateZ(*offZ*)	Shifts the object *offX*, *offY*, or *offZ* pixels along the specified axis
rotate3d(*x*, *y*, *z*, *angle*)	Rotates the object around the three-dimensional vector (*x*, *y*, *z*) at a direction of *angle*
rotateX(*angle*) rotateY(*angle*) rotateZ(*angle*)	Rotates the object around the specified axis at a direction of *angle*
scale3d(*x*, *y*, *z*)	Resizes the object by a factor of *x* horizontally, a factor of *y* vertically, and a factor of *z* along the z-axis
scaleX(*x*) scaleY(*y*) scaleZ(*z*)	Resizes the object by a factor of *x*, *y*, or *z* along the specified axis
perspective(*p*)	Sets the size of the perspective effect to *p*
matrix3d(*n*, *n*, …, *n*)	Applies a 3D transformation based on a matrix of 16 values

For example the following style rotates the object 60° around the x-axis, making it appear as if the top of the object is farther from the viewer and the bottom is closer to the viewer.

```
transform: rotateX(60deg);
```

To truly create the illusion of 3D space however, you also need to set the perspective of that space.

Understanding Perspective

TIP

The default for 3D transformations is to assume no perspective effect so that tracks never appear to converge but are always parallel.

Perspective is a measure of how rapidly objects appear to recede from the viewer in a 3D space. You can think of perspective in terms of a pair of railroad tracks that appear to converge at a point, known as the **vanishing point**. A smaller perspective value causes the tracks to converge over an apparently shorter distance while a larger perspective value causes the tracks to appear to go farther before converging.

You define the perspective of a 3D space using the **perspective** property

```
perspective: value;
```

where *value* is a positive value that measures the strength of the perspective effect with lower values resulting in more extreme distortion. For example, the following style rule sets the perspective of the space within the div element to 400 pixels.

```
div {
   perspective: 400px;
}
```

Any 3D transformations applied to children of that div element will assume a perspective value of 400 pixels. Perspective can also be set for individual transformations using the following perspective function:

```
transform: perspective(value);
```

Thus, the following style rule sets the perspective only for the figure1 figure box within the div element as the figure box is rotated 60° around the x-axis.

```
div figure#figure1 {
   transform: perspective(400px) rotateX(60deg);
}
```

You use the `perspective` property when you have several transformed objects within a container that all need to appear within the same 3D space with a common perspective. You use the `perspective` function when you have only one object that needs to be transformed in the 3D space. Figure 4-52 compares two different perspective values for an object rotated 60° around the *x*-axis in 3D space.

| Figure 4-52 | Transformations in three dimensions |

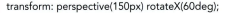

transform: perspective(150px) rotateX(60deg);   transform: perspective(300px) rotateX(60deg);

© imtmphoto/Shutterstock.com

TIP

You can test other 3D transformations using the demo_transformations3d. html file from the demo folder.

Note that the smaller perspective value results in a more extreme distortion as the top of the object appears to more quickly recede from the viewer while the bottom appears to approach the viewer more rapidly.

REFERENCE

Setting Perspective in 3D

- To set the perspective for a container and the objects it contains, use the property

  `perspective: value;`

  where `value` is a positive value that measures the strength of the perspective effect with lower values resulting in more extreme distortion.
- To set the perspective of a single object or to set the perspective individually of objects within a group of objects, use the `perspective` function

  `transform: perspective(value);`

Add a 3D transformation to each of the three figure boxes in the Genta Komatsu page, making it appear that they have been rotated in three dimensional space along the *x*-, *y*-, and *z*-axes, setting the perspective value to 600 pixels for all of the objects in the page article.

To apply the 3D transformations:

1. Return to the **tb_visual2.css** file in your editor.

2. Directly after the Transformation Styles comment, insert the following style rule to set the perspective of the 3D space of the `article` element.

   ```
   article {
       perspective: 600px;
   }
   ```

3. Next, insert the following style rule for the figure1 figure box to rotate it 30° around the *x*-axis, shift it 50 pixels along the *z*-axis, and add a drop shadow.

```
figure#figure1 {
    transform: rotateX(30deg) translateZ(50px);
    box-shadow: rgb(51, 51, 51) 0px 10px 25px;
}
```

4. Add the following functions to the transform property for the figure2 figure box to rotate the box 30° around the *z*-axis and 60° around the *y*-axis:

```
rotateZ(30deg) rotateY(60deg)
```

5. Add the following functions to the transform property for the figure3 figure box to rotate the box counter-clockwise 70° around the *y*-axis and shift it 20 pixels away from the user along the *z*-axis:

```
rotateY(-70deg) translateZ(-20px)
```

Figure 4-53 highlights the 3D transformations styles in the style sheet.

Figure 4-53   **Applying 3D transformations**

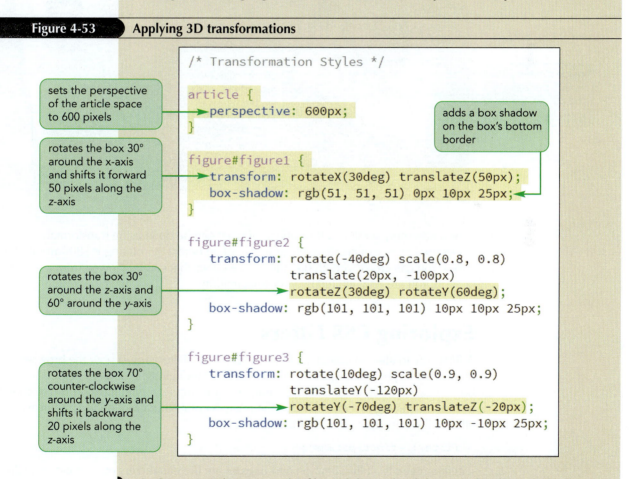

6. Save your changes to the file and then reload tb_genta.html in your browser. Figure 4-54 shows the result of applying 3D transformations to each of the figure boxes on the page.

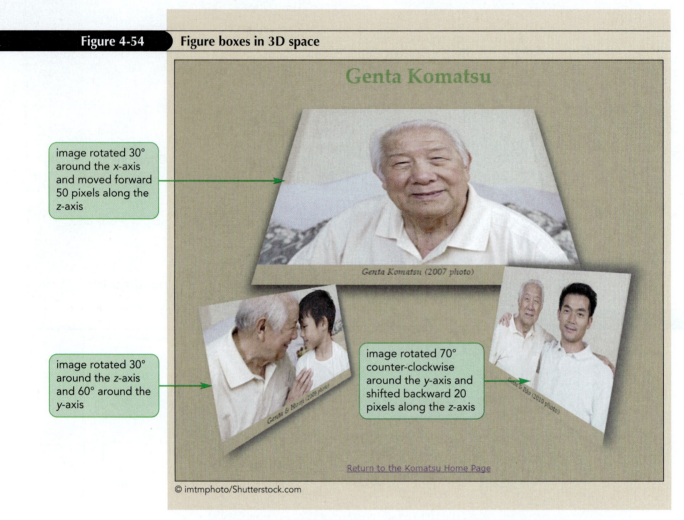

Figure 4-54 | **Figure boxes in 3D space**

image rotated 30° around the x-axis and moved forward 50 pixels along the z-axis

image rotated 30° around the z-axis and 60° around the y-axis

image rotated 70° counter-clockwise around the y-axis and shifted backward 20 pixels along the z-axis

© imtmphoto/Shutterstock.com

You have only scratched the surface of what can be done using transformations. For example you can create a mirror image of an object by rotating it 180° around the y-axis. You can create virtual 3D objects like cubes that can be viewed from any angle or spun. You are only limited by your imagination.

Exploring CSS Filters

A final way to alter an object is through a CSS filter. Filters adjust how the browser renders an image, a background, or a border by modifying the object's color, brightness, contrast, or general appearance. For example, a filter can be used to change a color image to grayscale, increase the image's color saturation, or add a blurring effect. Filters are applied using the `filter` property

```
filter: effect(params);
```

where *effect* is a filter function and *params* are the parameters of the function. Filters were originally introduced as a WebKit browser extension; it is still the best practice to include the following browser extension whenever filters are used:

```
-webkit-filter: effect(params);
filter: effect(params);
```

Figure 4-55 describes the different filter functions supported by WebKit and most current browsers.

Figure 4-55   **CSS3 filter functions**

Function	Description
blur(*length*)	Applies a blur to the image where *length* defines the size of blur in pixels
brightness(*value*)	Adjusts the brightness where values from 0 to 1 decrease the brightness and values greater than 1 increase the brightness
contrast(*value*)	Adjusts the contrast where values from 0 to 1 decrease the contrast and values greater than 1 increase the contrast
drop-shadow(*offsetX offsetY blur color*)	Adds a drop shadow to the image where *offsetX* and *offsetY* are horizontal and vertical distances of the shadow, *blur* is the shadow blurring, and *color* is the shadow color
grayscale(*value*)	Displays the image in grayscale from 0, leaving the image unchanged, up to 1, displaying the image in complete grayscale
hue-rotate(*angle*)	Adjusts the hue by *angle* in the color wheel where 0deg leaves the hue unchanged, 180deg displays the complimentary colors and 360deg again leaves the hue unchanged
invert(*value*)	Inverts the color from 0 (leaving the image unchanged), up to 1 (completely inverting the colors)
opacity(*value*)	Applies transparency to the image from 0 (making the image transparent), up to 1 (leaving the image opaque)
saturate(*value*)	Adjusts the color saturation where values from 0 to 1 decrease the saturation and values greater than 1 increase the saturation
sepia(*value*)	Displays the color in a sepia tone from 0 (leaving the image unchanged), up to 1 (image completely in sepia)
url(*url*)	Loads an SVG filter file from *url*

Figure 4-56 shows the impact of some of the filter functions on a sample image.

Figure 4-56   **CSS filter examples**

filter: none;   filter: sepia(0.8);   filter: saturate(2.5);
filter: blur(3px);   filter: hue-rotate(60deg);   filter: invert(0.9);

Filter functions can be combined in a space-separated list to create new effects. For example, the following style reduces the object's color contrast and applies a sepia tone.

```
filter: contrast(75%) sepia(100%);
```

TIP

You can view other CSS filters using the demo_filters.html file from the demo folder.

With multiple filter effects, the effects are applied in the order they are listed. Thus, a style in which the sepia effect is applied first followed by the contrast effect will result in a different image than if the order is reversed.

REFERENCE

Applying a CSS Filter

- To apply a CSS filter to a page object, use the property

  ```
  filter: effect(params);
  ```

  where *effect* is a filter function and *params* are the parameters of the function.

Kevin wants you to apply filters to the photos in the Genta Komatsu page. He wants a sepia tone applied to the first photo, a grayscale filter applied to the second photo, and a color enhancement applied to the third photo.

To apply the CSS filters:

1. Return the **tb_visual2.css** file in your editor and go down to the Filter Styles section.

To provide the most cross-browser support, use browser extensions with progressive enhancement.

2. Change the figure1 figure box to a sepia tone by adding the following style rule:

   ```
   figure#figure1 {
       -webkit-filter: sepia(0.8);
       filter: sepia(0.8)
   }
   ```

3. Change the figure2 figure box to grayscale by adding the style rule:

   ```
   figure#figure2  {
       -webkit-filter: grayscale(1);
       filter: grayscale(1);
   }
   ```

4. Increase the saturation and contrast for the figure3 figure box with the style rule:

   ```
   figure#figure3  {
       -webkit-filter: saturate(1.5) contrast(1.2);
       filter: saturate(1.5) contrast(1.2);
   }
   ```

   Figure 4-57 highlights the CSS filters added to the style sheet.

Figure 4-57	Applying the filter property

```
/* Filter Styles */

figure#figure1 {
    -webkit-filter: sepia(0.8);
    filter: sepia(0.8)
}

figure#figure2 {
    -webkit-filter: grayscale(1);
    filter: grayscale(1);
}

figure#figure3 {
    -webkit-filter: saturate(1.5) contrast(1.2);
    filter: saturate(1.5) contrast(1.2);
}
```

provides more cross-browser support by adding the WebKit browser extension

displays the figure1 figure box in sepia

displays the figure2 figure box in grayscale

increases the color saturation and contrast in the figure3 figure box

5. Save your changes to the file and then reload tb_genta.html in your browser. Figure 4-58 shows the final design of the Genta Komatsu page.

Figure 4-58	Filters applied to the web page photos

sepia tone

grayscale

color saturation and contrast increased

© imtmphoto/Shutterstock.com

Trouble? CSS filters are not supported by all browsers. Depending on your browser, you might not see any effect from the filters. In particular, Internet Explorer does not support these filter styles at the time of this writing.

INSIGHT

Box Shadows and Drop Shadows

You may wonder why you need a drop-shadow filter if you already have the box-shadow property. While they both can be used to add shadowing to a page object, one important difference is that the drop-shadow filter creates a shadow that traces the shape of the object, while the box-shadow property always applies a rectangular shadow. Another important difference is that you can only change the size of a shadow using the box-shadow property. Thus, if you want to apply a drop shadow around objects such as text or a circular shape, use the drop-shadow filter. However, if you need to create an internal shadow or change the size of the drop shadow shadow, use the box-shadow property.

You've completed your redesign of the Genta Komatsu page by adding transformation and filter effects to make a more visually striking page. Kevin now wants to return to the page for the Komatsu family. He wants you to edit the family portrait on the page so that individual pages like the Genta Komatsu page can be accessed by clicking the person's face on the family portrait. You can create this effect using an image map.

Working with Image Maps

When you mark an inline image as a hyperlink, the entire image is linked to the same file; however, HTML also allows you to divide an image into different zones, or **hotspots**, which can then be linked to different URLs through information provided in an **image map**. HTML supports two kinds of image maps: client-side image maps and server-side image maps. A **client-side image map** is an image map that is defined within the web page and handled entirely by the web browser, while a **server-side image map** relies on a program running on the web server to create and administer the map. Generally client-side maps are easier to create and do not rely on a connection to the server in order to run.

Defining a Client-Side Image Map

Client-side image maps are defined with the following map element

```
<map name="text">
   hotspots
</map>
```

where *text* is the name of the image map and *hotspots* are defined regions within an image that are linked to different URLs. Client-side image maps can be placed anywhere within the body of a web page because they are not actually displayed by browsers but are simply used as references for mapping the locations of the hotspots within the image. The most common practice is to place a map element below the corresponding inline image.

Each hotspot within the map element is defined using the following area element:

```
<area shape="shape" coords="coordinates"
      href="url" alt="text" />
```

where *shape* is the shape of the hotspot region, *coordinates* are the list of points that define the boundaries of that region, *url* is the URL of the hypertext link, and *text* is alternate text displayed for non-graphical browsers.

TIP

Do not overlap the hotspots to avoid confusing the user about which hotspot is associated with which URL.

Hotspots can be created as rectangles, circles, or polygons (multisided figures) using *shape* values of `rect`, `circle`, and `poly` respectively. A fourth possible *shape* value, `default`, represents the remaining area of the inline image not covered by any hotspots. There is no limit to the number of hotspots you can add to an image map.

For rectangular hotspots, the `shape` and `coords` attributes have the general form:

```
shape="rect" coords="left,top,right,bottom"
```

where *left*, *top* are the coordinates of the top-left corner of the rectangle and *right*, *bottom* are the coordinates of the bottom-right corner. Coordinates for hotspot shapes are measured in pixels and thus, the following attributes define a rectangular hotspot with the left-top corner at the coordinates (100, 20) and the right-bottom corner at (230, 220):

```
shape="rect" coords="100,20,230,220"
```

To determine the coordinates of a hotspot, you can use either a graphics program such as Adobe Photoshop or image map software that automatically generates the HTML code for the hotspots you define. Note that coordinates are always expressed relative to the top-left corner of the image, regardless of the position of the image on the page. For example, in Figure 4-59, the top-left corner of this rectangular hotspot is 100 pixels right of the image's left border and 20 pixels down from the top border.

Figure 4-59   Defining a rectangular hotspot

(100, 20)

(230, 220)

```
shape="rect" coords="100,20,230,220"
```

©imtmphoto/Shutterstock.com

Circular hotspots are defined using the attributes

```
shape="circle" coords="x,y,radius"
```

where *x* and *y* are the coordinates of the center of the circle and *radius* is the circle's radius. Figure 4-60 shows the coordinates for a circular hotspot where the center of the circle is located at the coordinates (160, 130) with a radius of 105 pixels.

Figure 4-60 **Defining a circular hotspot**

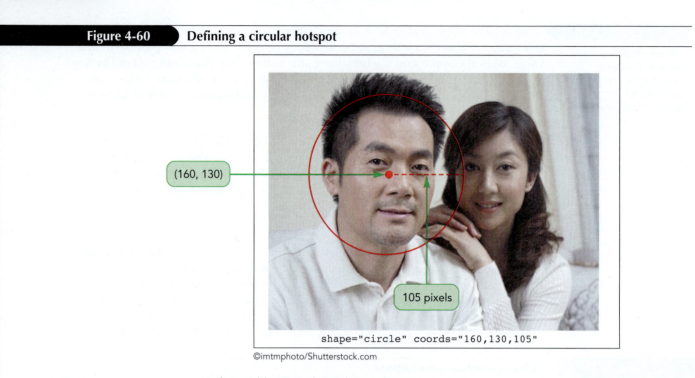

```
shape="circle" coords="160,130,105"
```

©imtmphoto/Shutterstock.com

Polygonal hotspots have the attributes

```
shape="poly" coords="x1,y1,x2,y2,…"
```

where (*x1*, *y1*), (*x2*, *y2*), … set the coordinates of each vertex in the shape. Figure 4-61 shows the coordinates for a 5-sided polygon.

Figure 4-61 **Defining a polygonal hotspot**

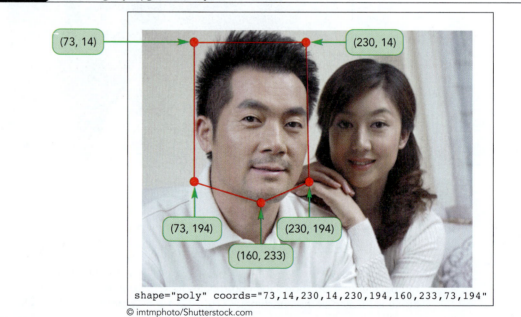

```
shape="poly" coords="73,14,230,14,230,194,160,233,73,194"
```

© imtmphoto/Shutterstock.com

To define the default hotspot for an image, create the following hotspot:

```
shape="default" coords="0,0,width,height"
```

where *width* is the width of the image in pixels and *height* is the image's height. Any region in the image that is not covered by another hotspot activates the default hotspot link.

REFERENCE

Creating an Image Map

- To create an image map, use

```
<map name="text">
    hotspots
</map>
```

where *text* is the name of the image map and *hotspots* are the hotspots within the image.

- To define each hotspot, use

```
<area shape="shape" coords="coordinates" href="url" alt="text" />
```

where *shape* is the shape of the hotspot region, *coordinates* list the points defining the boundaries of the region, *url* is the URL of the hypertext link, and *text* is alternate text that is displayed for non-graphical browsers.

- To define a rectangular hotspot, use the `shape` and `attribute` values

```
shape="rect" coords="left,top,right,bottom"
```

where *left*, *top* are the coordinates of the top-left corner of the rectangle and *right*, *bottom* are the coordinates of the bottom-right corner.

- To define a circular hotspot, use

```
shape="circle" coords="x,y,radius"
```

where *x* and *y* are the coordinates of the center of the circle and *radius* is the circle's radius.

- To define a polygonal hotspot, use

```
shape="poly" coords="x1,y1,x2,y2,…"
```

where (*x1*, *y1*), (*x2*, *y2*), and so on provide the coordinates of each vertex in the multisided shape.

- To define the default hotspot link, use

```
shape="default" coords="0,0,width,height"
```

where *width* and *height* is the width and height of the image.

Kevin has provided you with the coordinates for five rectangular hotspots to cover the five faces on the Komatsu family portrait. Add an image map named "family_map" to the tb_komatsu.html page with rectangular hotspots for each of the faces in the family portrait.

To create an image map:

1. Open or return to the **tb_komatsu.html** file in your editor.

2. Directly below the figure box, insert the following HTML code:

```
<map name="family_map">
   <area shape="rect" coords="74,74,123,141"
    href="tb_ikko.html" alt="Ikko Komatsu" />
   <area shape="rect" coords="126,109,177,172"
    href="tb_mika.html" alt="Mika Komatsu" />
   <area shape="rect" coords="180,157,230,214"
    href="tb_hiroji.html" alt="Hiroji Komatsu" />
```

```
          <area shape="rect" coords="258,96,312,165"
            href="tb_genta.html" alt="Genta Komatsu" />
          <area shape="rect" coords="342,86,398,162"
            href="tb_suzuko.html" alt="Suzuko Komatsu" />
        </map>
```

Figure 4-62 highlights the HTML code for the image map and hotspots.

Figure 4-62	**Inserting an image map**

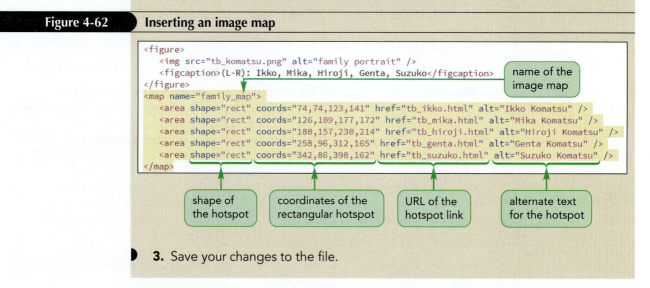

3. Save your changes to the file.

With the image map defined, your next task is to apply that map to the image in the figure box.

Applying an Image Map

To apply an image map to an image, you add the following `usemap` attribute to the `img` element

```
<img src="url" alt="text" usemap="#map" />
```

where *map* is the name assigned to the image map within the current HTML file.

Apply the family_map image map to the figure box and then test it in your web browser.

To apply an image map:

1. Add the attribute `usemap="#family_map"` to the img element for the family portrait.

   Figure 4-63 highlights the code to apply the image map.

Figure 4-63 | **Applying an image map**

> Applies the family_map image map to the image

```
<figure>
   <img src="tb_komatsu.png" alt="family portrait" usemap="#family_map" />
   <figcaption>(L-R): Ikko, Mika, Hiroji, Genta, Suzuko</figcaption>
</figure>
```

2. Save your changes to the file and then reload tb_komatsu.html in your browser.

3. Click the five faces in the family portrait and verify each face is linked to a separate HTML file devoted to that individual. Use the link under the image of each individual to return to the home page.

Kevin likes the addition of the image map and plans to use it on other photos in the website.

PROSKILLS

Problem Solving: Image Maps with Flexible Layouts

Image maps are not easily applied to flexible layouts in which the size of the image can change based on the size of the browser window. The problem is that, because hotspot coordinates are expressed in pixels, they don't resize and will not point to the correct region of the image if the image is resized.

One way to deal with flexible layouts is to create hotspots using hypertext links that are sized and positioned using relative units. The image and the hypertext links would then be nested within a `figure` element as follows:

```
<figure class="map">
   <img src="image" alt="" />
   <a href="url" id="hotspot1"></a>
   <a href="url" id="hotspot2"></a>
   …
</figure>
```

The figure box itself needs to be placed using relative or absolute positioning and the image should occupy the entire figure box. Each hypertext link should be displayed as a block with width and height defined using percentages instead of pixels and positioned absolutely within the figure box, also using percentages for the coordinates. As the figure box is resized under the flexible layout, the hotspots marked with the hypertext links will automatically be resized and moved to match. The opacity of the hotspot links should be set to 0 so that the links do not obscure the underlying image file. Even though the hotspots will be transparent to the user, they will still act as hypertext links.

This approach is limited to rectangular hotspots. To create a flexible layout for other shapes, you need to use a third-party add-in that automatically resizes the shape based on the current size of the image.

You've completed your work on the Komatsu Family pages for *Tree and Book*. Kevin will incorporate your work and ideas with other family pages as he continues on the site redesign. He'll get back to you with more projects in the future. For now you can close any open files or applications.

REVIEW

Session 4.3 Quick Check

1. Provide the transformation to shift a page object 5 pixels to the right and 10 pixels up.

2. Provide the transformation to reduce the horizontal and vertical size of an object by 50%.

3. Provide the transformation to rotate an object 30° counter-clockwise around the *x*-axis.

4. What is the difference between using the `perspective` property and using the `perspective` function?

5. Provide the filter to increase the brightness of an object by 20%.

6. Provide the filter to decrease the contrast of an object to 70% of its default value and to change the hue by 180°.

7. Provide code to create a circular hotspot centered at the coordinates (150, 220) with a radius of 60 pixels, linked to the help.html file.

8. Provide the code to create a triangular hotspot with vertices at (200, 5), (300, 125), and (100, 125), linked to the info.html file.

9. Revise the following `img` element to attach it to the mapsites image map:

```
<img src="logo.png" alt="" />
```

PRACTICE

Review Assignments

Data Files needed for the Review Assignments: tb_ferris_txt.html, tb_kathleen_txt.html, tb_visual3_txt.css, tb_visual4_txt.css, 3 CSS files, 1 HTML file, 10 PNG files, 1 TTF file, 1 WOFF file

Kevin wants you to work on another family page for the Tree and Book website. The page was created for the Ferris family with content provided by Linda Ferris-White. Kevin is examining a new color scheme and design style for the page. A preview of the design you'll create is shown in Figure 4-64.

Figure 4-64   Ferris Family page

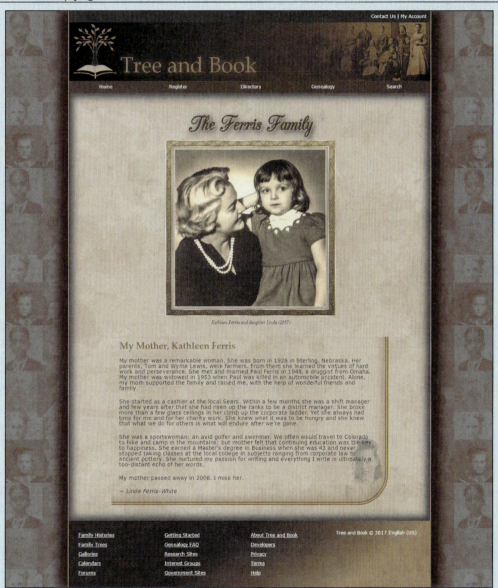

© 2016 Cengage Learning; Logo Design Studio Pro;
Source: wiki Media; © Elzbieta Sekowska/Shutterstock.com

All of the HTML content and the typographical and layout styles have already been created for you. Your task will be to complete the work by writing the visual style sheet to incorporate Kevin's suggestions.

Complete the following:

1. Use your HTML editor to open the **tb_visual3_txt.css**, **tb_visual4_txt.css**, **tb_ferris_txt.html** and **tb_kathleen_txt.html** files from the html04 ▸ review folder. Enter *your name* and *the date* in the comment section of each file, and save them as **tb_visual3.css**, **tb_visual4.css**, **tb_ferris.html**, and **tb_kathleen.html** respectively.

2. Go to the **tb_ferris.html** file in your editor. Add links to the tb_base.css, tb_styles3.css, and tb_visual3.css style sheets in the order listed.

3. Scroll down and, within the `main` element header and after the h1 heading, insert a figure box containing: a) the tb_ferris.png inline image with the alternate text *Ferris Family* using the image map named *portrait_map* and b) a figure caption with the text *Kathleen Ferris and daughter Linda (1957)*.

4. Directly below the figure box, create the portrait_map image map containing the following hotspots: a) a rectangular hotspot pointing to the tb_kathleen.html file with the left-top coordinate (10, 50) and the right-bottom coordinate (192, 223) and alternate text, "Kathleen Ferris" and b) a circular hotspot pointing to the tb_linda.html file with a center point at (264, 108) and a radius of 80 pixels and the alternate text, *Linda Ferris-White*.

5. Take some time to study the rest of the page content and structure and then save your changes to the file.

6. Go to the **tb_visual3.css** file in your editor. In this file, you'll create the graphic design styles for the page.

7. Go to the HTML Styles section and create a style rule for the `html` element to use the image file tb_back5.png as the background.

8. Go to the Page Body Styles section and create a style rule for the `body` element that: a) adds a left and right 3-pixel solid border with color value rgb(169, 130, 88), b) adds a box shadow to the right border with a horizontal offset of 25 pixels, a vertical offset of 0 pixels and a 35-pixel blur and a color value of rgb(53, 21, 0), and then adds the mirror images of this shadow to the left border.

9. Go to the Main Styles section. Create a style rule for the `main` element that: a) applies the tb_back7.png file as a background image with a size of 100% covering the entire background with no tiling and positioned with respect to the padding box and b) adds two inset box shadows, each with a 25-pixel blur and a color value of rgb(71, 71, 71), and then one with offsets of −10 pixels in the horizontal and vertical direction and the other with horizontal and vertical offsets of 10 pixels.

10. Create a style rule for the h1 heading within the main header that adds the following two text shadows: a) a shadow with the color value rgb(221, 221, 221) and offsets of 1 pixels and no blurring and b) a shadow with the color value rgba(41, 41, 41, 0.9) and offsets of 5 pixels and a 20-pixel blur.

11. Go to the Figure Box Styles section. Create a style rule for the figure element that sets the top/bottom margin to 10 pixels and the left/right margin to `auto`. Set the width of the element to 70%.

12. Next, you'll modify the appearance of the figure box image. Create a style rule for the image within the figure box that: a) sets the border width to 25 pixels, b) sets the border style to solid, c) applies the tb_frame.png file as a border image with a slice size of 60 pixels stretched across the sides, d) displays the image as a block with a width of 100%, and e) applies a sepia tone to the image with a value of 80% (include the WebKit browser extension in your style sheet).

13. Create a style rule for the figure caption that: a) displays the text using the font stack 'Palatino Linotype', Palatino, 'Times New Roman', serif, b) sets the style to italic, c) sets the top/bottom padding to 10 pixels and the left/right padding to 0 pixels, and d) centers the text.

14. Go to the Article Styles section. Here you'll create borders and backgrounds for the article that Linda Ferris-White wrote about her mother. Create a style rule for the `article` element that: a) displays the background image file tb_back6.png placed at the bottom-right corner of the element with a size of 15% and no tiling, b) adds an 8-pixel double border with color value rgb(147, 116, 68) to

the right and bottom sides of the `article` element, c) creates a curved bottom-right corner with a radius of 80 pixels, and d) adds an interior shadow with horizontal and vertical offsets of –10 pixels, a 25-pixel blur, and a color value of rgba(184, 154, 112, 0.7).

15. Kevin wants a gradient background for the page footer. Go to the Footer Styles section and create a style rule for the footer that adds a linear gradient background with an angle of 325°, going from the color value rgb(180, 148, 104) with a color stop at 20% of the gradient length to the value rgb(40, 33, 23) with a color stop at 60%.

16. Save your changes to the style sheet and then open **tb_ferris.html** in your browser. Verify that the colors and designs resemble that shown in Figure 4-64.

Next, you will create the design styles for individual pages about Kathleen Ferris and Linda Ferris-White. A preview of the content of the Kathleen Ferris page is shown in Figure 4-65.

Figure 4-65   Kathleen Ferris page

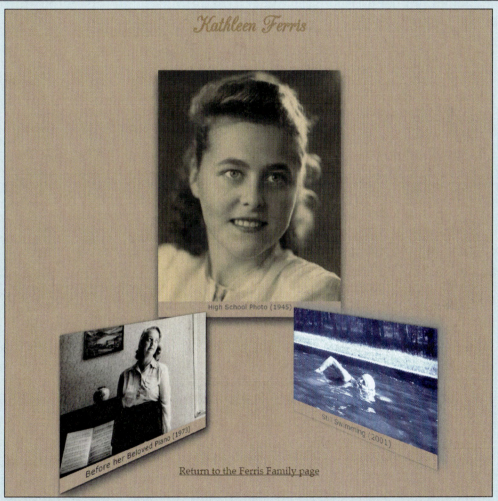

© Elzbieta Sekowska/Shutterstock.com

17. Go to the **tb_kathleen.html** file in your editor and create links to the tb_base.css, tb_styles4.css, and tb_visual4.css files. Study the contents of the file and then close it, saving your changes.

18. Go to the **tb_visual4.css** file in your editor. Scroll down to the Transformation Styles section and add a style rule for the `article` element to set the size of the perspective space to 800 pixels.

19. Create a style rule for the figure1 figure box to translate it –120 pixels along the z-axis.

20. Create a style rule for the figure2 figure box to translate it –20 pixels along the y-axis and rotate it 50° around the y-axis.

21. Create a style rule for the figure3 figure box to translate it –30 pixels along the y-axis and rotate it –50° around the y-axis.

22. Go to the Filter Styles section to apply CSS filters to the page elements. Make sure that you include the WebKit browser extension in your style. Create a style rule for the figure1 figure box that applies a saturation filter with a value of 1.3.

23. Create a style rule for the figure2 figure box that sets the brightness to 0.8 and the contrast to 1.5.

24. Create a style rule for the figure3 figure box that sets the hue rotation to 170°, the saturation to 3, and the brightness to 1.5.

25. Save your changes to the file and then return to the **tb_ferris.html** file in your browser. Verify that you can display the individual pages for Kathleen Ferris and Linda Ferris-White by clicking on their faces in the family portrait. Further verify that the appearance of the Kathleen Ferris page resembles that shown in Figure 4-65. (Note: Use the link under the pictures to return to the home page.)

APPLY

Case Problem 1

Data Files needed for this Case Problem: sd_messier_txt.html, sd_effects_txt.css, 2 CSS files, 9 PNG files

Sky Dust Stories   Dr. Andrew Weiss of Thomson & Lee College maintains an astronomy site called *Sky Dust Stories* for the students in his class. On his website, he discusses many aspects of astronomy and star-gazing and shares interesting stories from the history of stargazing. He wants your help with one page that involves the Messier catalog, which lists the deep sky objects of particular interest to professional and amateur astronomers.

Dr. Weiss has already created the page content and layout but wants you to add some CSS graphic design styles to complete the page. A preview of the page you'll create is shown in Figure 4-66.

Figure 4-66   **The Messier Objects web page**

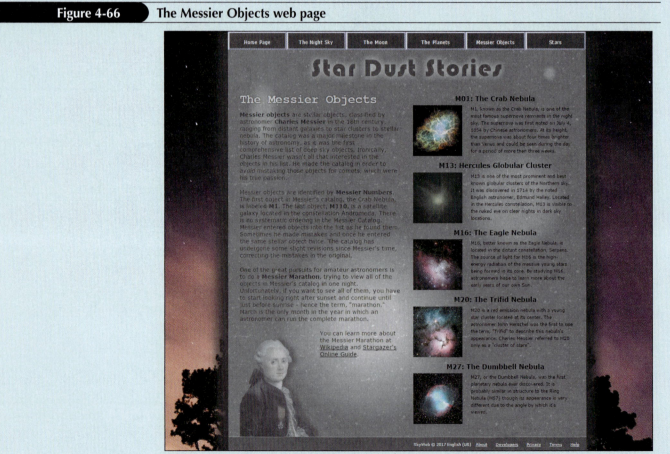

© 2016 Cengage Learning; Source: WikiImages; Source: Étienne Léopold Trouvelot; Source: Fryns; Source: public domain images/Summer woods; Source:PublicDomainArchive; Source: Ansiaume (1729—1786)

Complete the following:

1. Using your editor, open the **sd_messier_txt.html** and **sd_effects_txt.css** files from the html04 ▶ case1 folder. Enter *your name* and *the date* in the comment section of each file, and save them as **sd_messier.html** and **sd_effects.css** respectively.

2. Go to the **sd_messier.html** file in your HTML editor. Within the document head, create links to the sd_base.css, sd_layout.css, and sd_effects.css style sheet files in the order listed. Study the content and structure of the web page and then save your changes to the document.

3. Go to the **sd_effects.css** file in your editor. Andrew wants you to create a fixed background for the browser window. Within the HTML Styles section, insert a style rule for the `html` element to display the sd_back1.png file as the background image with a width of 100% covering the entire browser window. Have the background image fixed so that it does not scroll with the browser window.

4. Andrew wants the web page body background to combine several images and effects. Go to the Body Styles section and create a style rule for the `body` element that adds the following backgrounds in the order listed:

   a. A background containing the night sky image, sd_back2.png

   b. A radial gradient circle with a size extending to the closest corner and placed at the coordinates (40%, 70%) containing the color white stopping at 15% of the gradient and the color value rgba(151, 151, 151, 0.5) stopping at 50%

   c. A radial gradient circle also extending to the closest corner and placed at (80%, 40%) containing the color white stopping at 15% and followed by the color rgba(0, 0, 0, 0) at 30%

   d. A radial gradient extending to the closest side and placed at (10%, 20%) containing the color white stopping at 20% and followed by the color rgba(0, 0, 0, 0) stopping at 45%

   e. A radial gradient with a size of 5% in the horizontal and vertical directions placed at (90%, 10%) with the color white stopping at 15% and followed by the color rgba(0, 0, 0, 0) stopping at 40%

   f. The background color rgb(151, 151, 151) set as a base for the preceding background image and radial gradients

5. Within the style rule for the page body, add styles to place box shadows on the left and right borders. Set the color of the first shadow to rgb(31, 31, 31) with horizontal and vertical offsets of 30 pixels and 0 pixels and a blur of 45 pixels. Set the second shadow equal to the first except that the horizontal offset should be –30 pixels.

6. Go to the Navigation List Styles section. Format the hypertext links in the body header by adding a style rule for the `body > header a` that adds a 5-pixel outset border with color value rgb(211, 211, 255).

7. Next, format the appearance of the article title. Go to the Section Left Styles section and create a style rule for the h1 heading in the left section article that changes the text color to rgb(211, 211, 211) and adds a black text shadow with 0-pixel offsets and a blur size of 5 pixels.

8. Andrew has included an image of Charles Messier, the originator of the Messier catalog of stellar objects. The image is marked with the id "mportrait". In the Section Left Styles section, create a style rule for this object that modifies the appearance of this image by applying the following filters: a) the drop-shadow filter with a horizontal offset of –15 pixels, a blur of 5 pixels, and a color of rgba(51, 51, 51, 0.9); b) a grayscale filter with a value of 0.7; and c) an opacity filter with a value of 0.6.

9. Andrew wants the Charles Messier image flipped horizontally. Add a style to transform the image by rotating it 180° around the *y*-axis.

10. Go to the Footer Styles section and create a style rule for the `footer` element that adds a 2-pixel solid border to the top edge of the footer with a color value of rgb(171, 171, 171).

11. Save your changes to the style sheet file and then open **sd_messier.html** in your browser. Verify that the design of the page resembles that shown in Figure 4-66. Verify that when you scroll through the web page, the browser window background stays fixed. (Note: Some versions of Internet Explorer do not support the `filter` style, which means that you will not see modifications to the Charles Messier image.)

Case Problem 2

Data Files needed for this Case Problem: sf_torte_txt.html, sf_effects_txt.css, 2 CSS files, 9 PNG files

APPLY

Save your Fork   Amy Wu has asked for your help in redesigning her website, *Save your Fork*, a baking site for people who want to share dessert recipes and learn about baking in general. She has prepared a page containing a sample dessert recipe and links to other pages on the website. A preview of the page you'll create is shown in Figure 4-67.

Figure 4-67   **Save your Fork sample recipe page**

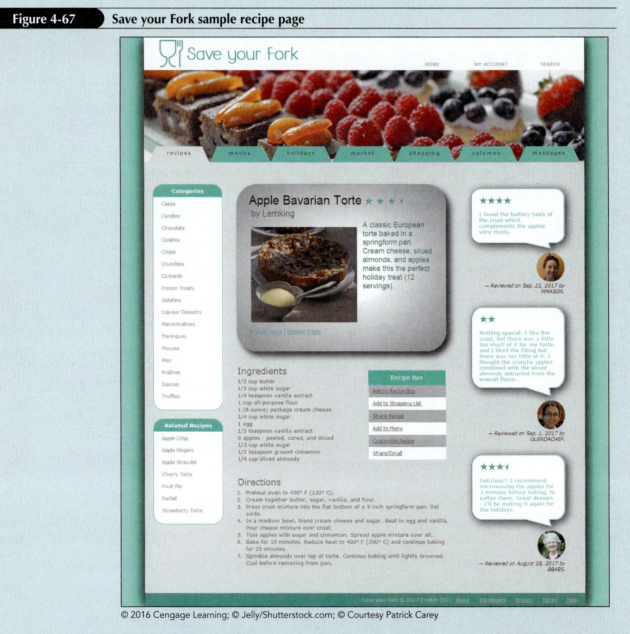

© 2016 Cengage Learning; © Jelly/Shutterstock.com; © Courtesy Patrick Carey

Amy has already created a style sheet for the page layout and typography, so your work will be focused on enhancing the page with graphic design styles.

Complete the following:

1. Using your editor, open the **sf_torte_txt.html** and **sf_effects_txt.css** files from the html04 ▶ case2 folder. Enter *your name* and *the date* in the comment section of each file, and save them as **sf_torte.html** and **sf_effects.css** respectively.

2. Go to the **sf_torte.html** file in your editor. Within the document head create links to the sf_base.css, sf_layout.css, and sf_effects.css style sheet files in that order. Take some time to study the structure of the document and then close the document, saving your changes.

3. Go to the **sf_effects.css** file in your editor. Within the Body Header Styles section, create a style rule for the `body` element to add drop shadows to the left and right border of the page body with an offset of 10 pixels, a blur of 50 pixels, and the color rgb(51, 51, 51). Note that the right border is a mirror image of the left border.

4. Go to the Navigation Tabs List Styles section. Amy has created a navigation list with the class name `tabs` that appears at the top of the page with the body header. Create a style rule for the `body > header nav.tabs` selector that changes the background to the image file sf_back1.png with no tiling, centered horizontally and vertically within the element and sized to cover the entire navigation list.

5. Amy wants the individual list items in the tabs navigation list to appear as tabs in a recipe box. She wants each of these "tabs" to be trapezoidal in shape. To create this effect, you'll create a style rule for the `body > header nav.tabs li` selector that transforms the list item by setting the perspective of its 3D space to 50 pixels and rotating it 20° around the x-axis.

6. As users hover the mouse pointer over the navigation tabs, Amy wants a rollover effect in which the tabs appear to come to the front. Create a style rule for the `body > header nav.tabs li` selector that uses the pseudo-element `hover` that changes the background color to rgb(231, 231, 231).

7. Go to the Left Section Styles section. Referring to Figure 4-67, notice that in the left section of the page, Amy has placed two vertical navigation lists. She wants these navigation lists to have rounded borders. For the vertical navigation lists in the left section, create a style rule for the `section#left nav.vertical` selector that adds a 1-pixel solid border with color value rgb(20, 167, 170) and has a radius of 25 pixels at each corner.

8. The rounded corner also has to apply to the h1 heading within each navigation list. Create a style rule for `h1` elements nested within the left section vertical navigation list that sets the top-left and top-right corner radii to 25 pixels.

9. Go to the Center Article Styles section. The `article` element contains an image and brief description of the Apple Bavarian Torte, which is the subject of this sample page. Create a style rule for the `section#center article` selector that adds the following: a) a radial gradient to the background with a white center with a color stop of 30% transitioning to rgb(151, 151, 151), b) a 1-pixel solid border with color value rgb(151, 151, 151) and a radius of 50 pixels, and c) a box shadow with horizontal and vertical offsets of 10 pixels with a 20-pixel blur and a color of rgb(51, 51, 51).

10. Go to the Blockquote Styles section. Amy has included three sample reviews from users of the Save your Fork website. Amy wants the text of these reviews to appear within the image of a speech bubble. For every `blockquote` element, create a style rule that does the following: a) sets the background image to the sf_speech.png with no tiling and a horizontal and vertical size of 100% to cover the entire block quote, and b) uses the `drop-shadow` filter to add a drop shadow around the speech bubble with horizontal and vertical offsets of 5 pixels, a blur of 10 pixels and the color rgb(51, 51, 51).

11. Amy has included the photo of each reviewer registered on the site within the citation for each review. She wants these images to appear as circles rather than squares. To do this, create a style rule for the selector `cite img` that sets the border radius to 50%.

12. Save your changes to the style sheet file and then open **sf_torte.html** in your browser. Verify that the design of your page matches that shown in Figure 4-67. Confirm that when you hover the mouse over the navigation tabs the background color changes to match the page color. (Note: Some versions of Internet Explorer do not support the `filter` style, which means that you will not see drop shadows around the speech bubbles.)

CHALLENGE

Case Problem 3

Data Files needed for this Case Problem: cf_home_txt.html, cf_effects_txt.css, 2 CSS files, 7 PNG files

Chupacabra Music Festival   Debra Kelly is the director of the website for the *Chupacabra Music Festival*, which takes place every summer in San Antonio, Texas. Work is already underway on the website design for the 15th annual festival and Debra has approached you to work on the design of the home page.

Debra envisions a page that uses semi-transparent colors and 3D transformations to make an attractive and eye-catching page. A preview of her completed design proposal is shown in Figure 4-68.

Figure 4-68   Chupacabra 15 home page

© 2016 Cengage Learning; © Memo Angeles/Shutterstock.com; © Ivan Galashchuk/Shutterstock.com;
© Andrey Armyagov/Shutterstock.com; © Away/Shutterstock.com

Debra has provided you with the HTML code and the layout and reset style sheets. Your job will be to finish her work by inserting the graphic design styles.

Complete the following:

1. Using your editor, open the **cf_home_txt.html** and **cf_effects_txt.css** files from the html04 ▶ case3 folder. Enter *your name* and *the date* in the comment section of each file, and save them as **cf_home.html** and **cf_effects.css** respectively.

2. Go to the **cf_home.html** file in your HTML editor. Within the document head, create a link to the cf_reset.css, cf_layout.css, and cf_effects.css style sheets. Take some time to study the content and structure of the document. Pay special note to the nested `div` elements in the center section of the page; you will use these to create a 3D cube design. Close the file, saving your changes.

3. Return to the **cf_effects.css** file in your editor and go to the HTML Styles section. Debra wants a background displaying a scene from last year's festival. Add a style rule for the `html` element that displays the cf_back1.png as a fixed background, centered horizontally and vertically in the browser window and covering the entire window.

4. Go to the Body Styles section and set the background color of the page body to rgba(255, 255, 255, 0.3).

5. Go to the Body Header Styles section and change the background color of the body header to rgba(51, 51, 51, 0.5).

6. Debra has placed useful information for the festival in `aside` elements placed within the left and right `section` elements. Go to the Aside Styles section and create a style rule for the `section aside` selector that adds a 10-pixel double border with color rgba(92, 42, 8, 0.3) and a border radius of 30 pixels.

7. Debra wants a curved border for every h1 heading within an `aside` element. For the selector `section aside h1`, create a style rule that sets the border radius of the top-left and top-right corners to 30 pixels.

8. Define the perspective of the 3D space for the left and right sections by creating a style rule for those two sections that sets their perspective value to 450 pixels.

9. Create a style rule that rotates the `aside` elements within the left section 25° around the y-axis. Create another style rule that rotates the `aside` elements within the right section –25° around the y-axis.

⊕ **Explore** 10. Go to the Cube Styles section. Here you'll create the receding cube effect that appears in the center of the page. The cube has been constructed by creating a `div` element with the id `cube` containing five `div` elements belonging to the `cube_face` class with the ids `cube_bottom`, `cube_top`, `cube_left`, `cube_right`, and `cube_front`. (There will be no back face for this cube.) Currently the five faces are superimposed upon each other. To create the cube you have to shift and rotate each face in 3D space so that they form the five faces of the cube. First, position the cube on the page by creating a style rule for the `div#cube` selector containing the following styles:

   a. Place the element using relative positioning.
   b. Set the top margin to 180 pixels, the bottom margin to 150 pixels, and the left/right margins to `auto`.
   c. Set the width and height to 400 pixels.
   d. Set the perspective of the space to 450 pixels.

11. For each `div` element of the `cube_face` class, create a style rule that places the faces with absolute positioning and sets their width and height to 400 pixels.

⊕ **Explore** 12. Finally, you'll construct the cube by positioning each of the five faces in 3D space so that they form the shape of a cube. Add the following style rules for each of the five faces to transform their appearance.

   a. Translate the cube_front `div` element –50 pixels along the z-axis.
   b. Translate the cube_left `div` element –200 pixels along the x-axis and rotate it 90° around the y-axis.
   c. Translate the cube_right `div` element 200 pixels along the x-axis and rotate it 90° counter-clockwise around the y-axis.
   d. Translate the cube_top `div` element –200 pixels along the y-axis and rotate it 90° counter-clockwise around the x-axis.
   e. Translate the cube_bottom `div` element 200 pixels along the y-axis and rotate it 90° around the x-axis.

13. Save your changes to style sheet file and open **cf_home.html** in your browser. Verify that the layout of your page matches Figure 4-68 including the center cube with the five faces of photos and text.

Case Problem 4

Data Files needed for this Case Problem: br_listing2048_txt.html, br_styles_txt.css, 1 CSS file, 11 PNG files, 1 TXT file

Browyer Realty   Linda Browyer is the owner of *Browyer Realty*, a real estate company operating in Owatonna, Minnesota. She's asked you to help create a style design for the pages on her site that describe residential listings. Linda has already written up sample content for a listing and collected images of the property. She needs you to create the HTML file and write up the style sheets.

Complete the following:

1. Using your editor, open the **br_listing2048_txt.html** and **br_styles_txt.css** files from the html04 ▸ case4 folder. Enter *your name* and *the date* in the comment section of each file and save them as **br_listing2048.html** and **br_styles.css** respectively.

2. Using the content of the br_listing2048.txt file, create the content and structure of the br_listing2048.html page. You are free to supplement the material in these text files with additional content of your own if appropriate. Use the # symbol for the value of the `href` attribute in your hypertext links because you will be linking to pages that don't actually exist.

3. Link your home page to the br_reset.css and br_styles.css style sheets. Save your changes to the file.

4. Go to the **br_styles.css** file in your editor and create the layout and design styles to be used in your page. The page design is up to you, but must include at least one example of the following graphic design features:
   - A background image
   - A border around a page element, including an example of a curved border
   - A box shadow around a page element
   - A text shadow around a section of element text
   - A background featuring a linear gradient and a radial gradient
   - Changing the appearance of an element using the `transform` property
   - Changing the appearance of an element using the `filter` property

5. Include comments in your style sheet to make it easy for other users to interpret.

6. Test your layout and design on a variety of devices, browsers, and screen resolutions to ensure that your sample page is readable under different conditions.

OBJECTIVES

Session 5.1
- Create a media query
- Work with the browser viewport
- Apply a responsive design
- Create a pulldown menu with CSS

Session 5.2
- Create a flexbox
- Work with flex sizes
- Explore flexbox layouts

Session 5.3
- Create a print style sheet
- Work with page sizes
- Add and remove page breaks

Designing for the Mobile Web

Creating a Mobile Website for a Daycare Center

Case | *Trusted Friends Daycare*

Marjorie Kostas is the owner of *Trusted Friends Daycare*, an early childhood education and care center located in Carmel, Indiana. You've been hired to help work on the redesign of the company's website. Because many of her clients access the website from their mobile phones, Marjorie is interested in improving the site's appearance on mobile devices. However, your design still has to be compatible with tablet devices and desktop computers. Finally, the site contains several pages that her clients will want to print, so your design needs to meet the needs of printed media.

STARTING DATA FILES

tutorial

tf_articles_txt.html
tf_home_txt.html
tf_prek_txt.html
tf_flex_txt.css
tf_navicon_txt.css
tf_print_txt.css
tf_styles1_txt.css
+ 9 files

review

tf_tips_txt.html
tf_print2_txt.css
tf_styles4_txt.css
+ 6 files

case1

gp_cover_txt.html
gp_page1_txt.html
gp_page2_txt.html
gp_page3_txt.html
gp_layout_txt.css
gp_print_txt.css
+ 23 files

case2

wc_styles_txt.css
+ 40 files

case3

cw_home_txt.html
cw_styles_txt.css
+ 12 files

case4

jb_home_txt.html
jb_styles_txt.css
+ 11 files

Session 5.1 Visual Overview:

The viewport meta tag is used to set the properties of the layout viewport.

This sets the width of the layout viewport equal to the width of the visual viewport.

This sets the initial scale of the viewport to 1.0.

```
<meta name="viewport" content="width=device-width, initial-scale=1" />
```

Responsive designs should start with base styles that apply to all devices, followed by mobile styles, tablet styles, and then desktop styles.

A **media query** is used to apply specified style rules to a device based on the device type and the device features.

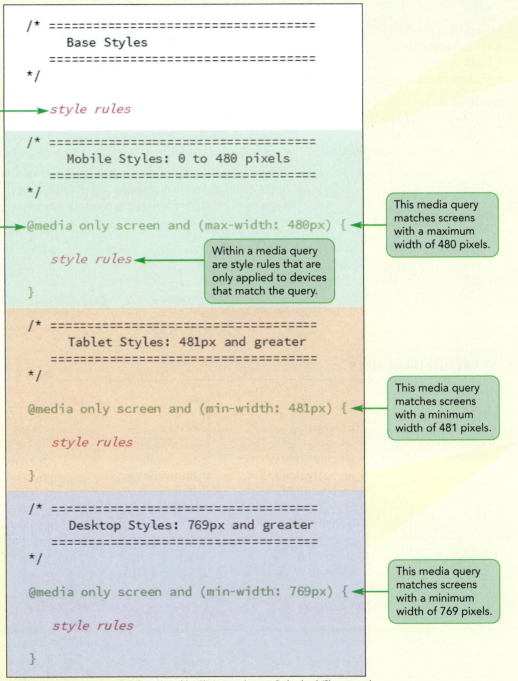

```
/* ======================================
     Base Styles
   ====================================== 
*/

  style rules

/* ======================================
     Mobile Styles: 0 to 480 pixels
   ====================================== 
*/

@media only screen and (max-width: 480px) {

  style rules

}

/* ======================================
     Tablet Styles: 481px and greater
   ====================================== 
*/

@media only screen and (min-width: 481px) {

  style rules

}

/* ======================================
     Desktop Styles: 769px and greater
   ====================================== 
*/

@media only screen and (min-width: 769px) {

  style rules

}
```

This media query matches screens with a maximum width of 480 pixels.

Within a media query are style rules that are only applied to devices that match the query.

This media query matches screens with a minimum width of 481 pixels.

This media query matches screens with a minimum width of 769 pixels.

Media Queries

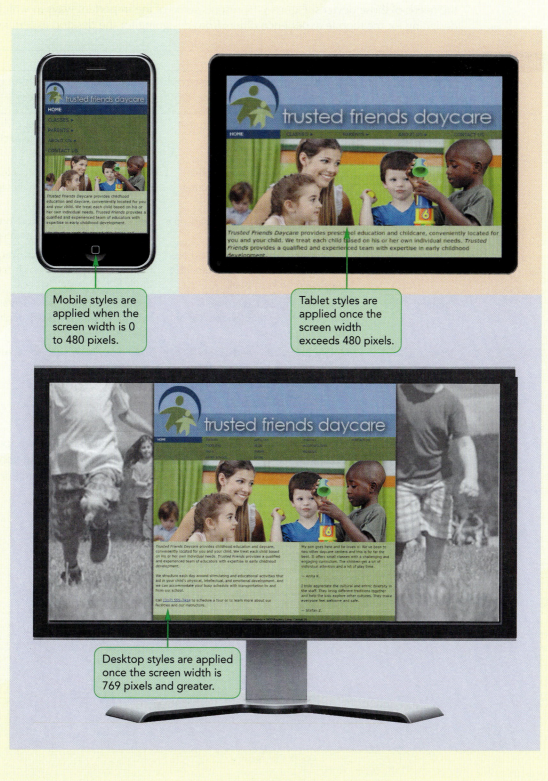

Mobile styles are applied when the screen width is 0 to 480 pixels.

Tablet styles are applied once the screen width exceeds 480 pixels.

Desktop styles are applied once the screen width is 769 pixels and greater.

Introducing Responsive Design

In the first four tutorials, you created a single set of layout and design styles for your websites without considering what type of device would be rendering the site. However, this is not always a practical approach and with many users increasingly accessing the web through mobile devices, a web designer must take into consideration the needs of those devices. Figure 5-1 presents some of the important ways in which designing for the mobile experience differs from designing for the desktop experience.

| Figure 5-1 | Designing for mobile and desktop devices |

User Experience	Mobile	Desktop
Page Content	Content should be short and to the point.	Content can be extensive, giving readers the opportunity to explore all facets of the topic.
Page Layout	Content should be laid out within a single column with no horizontal scrolling.	With a wider screen size, content can be more easily laid out in multiple columns.
Hypertext Links	Links need to be easily accessed via a touch interface.	Links can be activated more precisely using a cursor or mouse pointer.
Network Bandwidth	Sites tend to take longer to load over cellular networks and thus overall file size should be kept small.	Sites are quickly accessed over high-speed networks, which can more easily handle large file sizes.
Lighting	Pages need to be easily visible in outdoor lighting through the use of contrasting colors.	Pages are typically viewed in an office setting, allowing a broader color palette.
Device Tools	Mobile sites often need access to devices such as phone dialing, messaging, mapping, and built-in cameras and video.	Sites rarely have need to access desktop devices.

© 2016 Cengage Learning

Viewing a web page on a mobile device is a fundamentally different experience than viewing the same web page on a desktop computer. As a result, these differences need to be taken into account when designing a website. Figure 5-2 shows the current home page of the Trusted Friends website as it appears on a mobile device.

Figure 5-2   **Trusted Friends home page displayed on a mobile device**

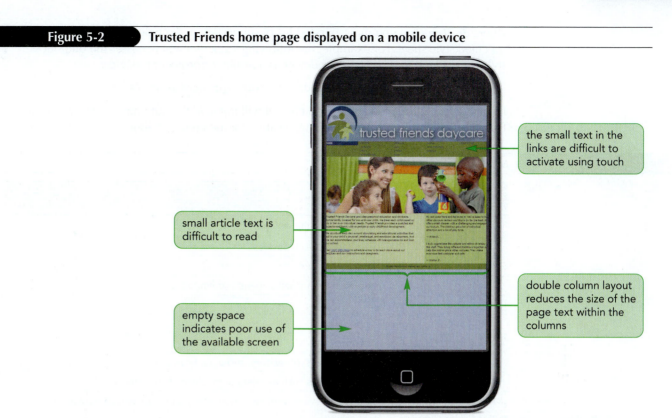

the small text in the links are difficult to activate using touch

small article text is difficult to read

double column layout reduces the size of the page text within the columns

empty space indicates poor use of the available screen

© 2016 Cengage Learning; © Robert Kneschke/Shutterstock.com; BenBois/openclipart

Notice that the mobile device has automatically zoomed out to display the complete page width resulting in text that is difficult to read and small hypertext links that are practically unusable with a touch interface. While the design might be fine for a desktop monitor in landscape orientation, it's clear that it is ill-suited to a mobile device.

What this website requires is a design that is not only specifically tailored to the needs of her mobile users but also is easily revised for tablet and desktop devices. This can be accomplished with responsive design in which the design of the document changes in response to the device rendering the page. An important leader in the development of responsive design is Ethan Marcotte, who identified three primary components of responsive design theory:

TIP

For more information on the development of responsive design, refer to *Responsive Web Design* by Ethan Marcotte (http://alistapart.com/article/responsive-web-design).

- **flexible layout** so that the page layout automatically adjusts to screens of different widths
- **responsive images** that rescale based on the size of the viewing device
- **media queries** that determine the properties of the device rendering the page so that appropriate designs can be delivered to specific devices

In the preceding tutorials, you've seen how to create grid-based fluid layouts and you've used images that scaled based on the width of the browser window and web page. In this session, you'll learn how to work with media queries in order to create a truly responsive website design.

Introducing Media Queries

Media queries are used to associate a style sheet or style rule with a specific device or list of device features. To create a media query within an HTML file, add the following `media` attribute to either the `link` or `style` element in the document head

```
media="devices"
```

where *devices* is a comma-separated list of supported media types associated with a specified style sheet. For example, the following link element accesses the output.css style sheet file, but only when the device is a printer or projection device:

```
<link href="output.css" media="print, projection" />
```

If any other device accesses this web page, it will not load the output.css style sheet file. Figure 5-3 lists other possible media type values for the media attribute.

| Figure 5-3 | Media types |

Media Type	Used For
all	All output devices (the default)
braille	Braille tactile feedback devices
embossed	Paged Braille printers
handheld	Mobile devices with small screens and limited bandwidth
print	Printers
projection	Projectors
screen	Computer screens
speech	Speech and sound synthesizers, and aural browsers
tty	Fixed-width devices such as teletype machines and terminals
tv	Television-type devices with low resolution, color, and limited scrollability

© 2016 Cengage Learning

When no media attribute is used, the style sheet is assumed to apply to all devices accessing the web page.

The @media Rule

Media queries can also be used to associate specific style rules with specific devices by including the following @media rule in a CSS style sheet file

```
@media devices {
    style rules
}
```

where *devices* are supported media types and *style rules* are the style rules associated with those devices. For example, the following style sheet is broken into three sections: an initial style rule that sets the font color of all h1 headings regardless of device, a second section that sets the font size for h1 headings on screen or television devices, and a third section that sets the font size for h1 headings that are printed:

```
h1 {
    color: red;
}

@media screen, tv {
    h1 {font-size: 2em;}
}

@media print {
    h1 {font-size: 16pt;}
}
```

Note that in this style sheet, the font size for screen and television devices is expressed using the relative em unit but the font size for print devices is expressed using points, which is a more appropriate sizing unit for that medium.

Finally, you can specify media devices when importing one style sheet into another by adding the media type to the `@import` rule. Thus, the following CSS rule imports the screen.css file only when a screen or projection device is being used:

```
@import url("screen.css") screen, projection;
```

The initial hope was that media queries could target mobile devices using the `handheld` device type; however, as screen resolutions improved to the point where the cutoff between mobile, tablet, laptop, and desktop was no longer clear, media queries began to be based on what features a device supported and not on what the device was called.

Media Queries and Device Features

To target a device based on its features, you add the feature and its value to the `media` attribute using the syntax:

```
media="devices and|or (feature:value)"
```

where *feature* is the name of a media feature and *value* is the feature's value. The and and or keywords are used to create media queries that involve different devices or different features, or combinations of both.

The `@media` and `@import` rules employ similar syntax:

```
@media devices and|or (feature:value) {
    style rules
}
```

and

```
@import url(url) devices and|or (feature:value);
```

For example, the following media query applies the style rules only for screen devices with a width of 320 pixels.

```
@media screen and (device-width: 320px) {
    style rules
}
```

Figure 5-4 provides a list of the device features supported by HTML and CSS.

| Figure 5-4 | Media features |

Feature	Description
aspect-ratio	The ratio of the width of the display area to its height
color	The number of bits per color component of the output device; if the device does not support color, the value is 0
color-index	The number of colors supported by the output device
device-aspect-ratio	The ratio of the device-width value to the device-height value
device-height	The height of the rendering surface of the output device
device-width	The width of the rendering surface of the output device
height	The height of the display area of the output device
monochrome	The number of bits per pixel in the device's monochrome frame buffer
orientation	The general description of the aspect ratio: equal to portrait when the height of the display area is greater than the width; equal to landscape otherwise
resolution	The resolution of the output device in pixels, expressed in either dpi (dots per inch) or dpcm (dots per centimeter)
width	The width of the display area of the output device

© 2016 Cengage Learning

All of the media features in Figure 5-4, with the exception of `orientation`, also accept `min-` and `max-` prefixes, where `min-` provides a minimum value for the specified feature, and `max-` provides the feature's maximum value. Thus, the following media query applies style rules only for screen devices whose width is at most 700 pixels:

```
@media screen and (max-width: 700px) {
    style rules
}
```

Similarly, the following media query applies style rules only to screens that are at least 400 pixels wide:

```
@media screen and (min-width: 400px) {
    style rules
}
```

You can combine multiple media features using logical operators such as `and`, `not`, and `or`. The following query applies the enclosed styles to all media types but only when the width of the output devices is between 320 and 480 pixels (inclusive):

```
@media all and (min-width: 320px and max-width: 480px) {
    style rules
}
```

Some media features are directed toward devices that do not have a particular property or characteristic. This is done by applying the `not` operator, which negates any features found in the expression. For example, the following query applies only to media devices that are not screen or do not have a maximum width of 480 pixels:

```
@media not screen and (max-width: 480px) {
    style rules
}
```

For some features, you do not have to specify a value but merely indicate the existence of the feature. The following query matches any screen device that also supports color:

```
@media screen and (color) {
    style rules
}
```

Finally, for older browsers that do not support media queries, CSS3 provides the `only` keyword to hide style sheets from those browsers. In the following code, older browsers will interpret `only` as an unsupported device name and so will not apply the enclosed style rules, while newer browsers will recognize the keyword and continue to apply the style rules.

```
@media only screen and (color) {
    style rules
}
```

All current browsers support media queries, but you will still see the `only` keyword used in many website style sheets.

Creating a Media Query

- To create a media query that matches a device in a `link` or `style` element within an HTML file, use the following `media` attribute

  `media="devices and|or (feature:value)"`

  where *devices* is a comma-separated list of media types, *feature* is the name of a media feature, and *value* is the feature's value
- To create a media query, create the following `@media` rule within a CSS style sheet

  ```
  @media devices and|or (feature:value) {
     style rules
  }
  ```

  where *style rules* are the style rules applied for the specified device and feature.
- To import a style sheet based on a media query, apply the following `@import` rule within a CSS style sheet

  `@import url(url) devices and|or (feature:value);`

Applying Media Queries to a Style Sheet

You meet with Marjorie to discuss her plans for the home page redesign. She envisions three designs: one for mobile devices, a different design for tablets, and finally a design for desktop devices based on the current appearance of the site's home page (see Figure 5-5).

Figure 5-5	Trusted Friends home page for different screen widths

© 2016 Cengage Learning; © Robert Kneschke/Shutterstock.com; © dotshock/Shutterstock.com; BenBois/openclipart; JMLevick/openclipart; Molumen/openclipart

The mobile design will be used for screen widths up to 480 pixels, the tablet design will be used for widths ranging from 481 pixels to 768 pixels, and the desktop design will be used for screen widths exceeding 768 pixels. To apply this approach, you'll create a style sheet having the following structure:

```
/* Base Styles */
   style rules

/* Mobile Styles */
@media only screen and (max-width: 480px) {
   style rules
}

/* Tablet Styles */
@media only screen and (min-width: 481px) {
   style rules
}

/* Desktop Styles */
@media only screen and (min-width: 769px) {
   style rules
}
```

Note that this style sheet applies the principle **mobile first** in which the overall page design starts with base styles that apply to all devices followed by style rules specific to mobile devices. Tablet styles are applied when the screen width is 481 pixels or greater and desktop styles build upon the tablet styles when the screen width exceeds 768 pixels. Thus, as your screen width increases, you add on more features or replace features found in smaller devices. In general, with responsive design, it is easier to add new styles through progressive enhancement than to replace styles.

Marjorie has supplied you with the HTML code and initial styles for her website's home page. Open her HTML file now.

To open the site's home page:

1. Use your editor to open the **tf_home_txt.html** and **tf_styles1_txt.css** files from the html05 ▸ tutorial folder. Enter *your name* and *the date* in the comment section of each file and save them as **tf_home.html** and **tf_styles1.css** respectively.

2. Return to the **tf_home.html** file in your editor and, within the document head, create links to the **tf_reset.css** and **tf_styles1.css** style sheet files.

3. Take some time to scroll through the contents of the document to become familiar with its contents and structure and then save your changes to the file, but do not close it.

Next, you'll insert the structure for the responsive design styles in the tf_styles1.css style sheet, adding sections for mobile, tablet, and desktop devices.

To add media queries to a style sheet:

1. Return to the **tf_styles1.css** file in your editor.

2. Marjorie has already inserted the base styles that will apply to all devices at the top of the style sheet file. Take time to review those styles.

3. Scroll to the bottom of the document and add the following code and comments after the New Styles Added Below comment.

```
/* ===============================
   Mobile Styles: 0px to 480px
   ===============================
*/
@media only screen and (max-width: 480px) {

}

/* ===============================
   Tablet Styles: 481px and greater
   ===============================
*/
@media only screen and (min-width: 481px) {

}

/* ===============================
   Desktop Styles: 769px and greater
   ===============================
*/
@media only screen and (min-width: 769px) {

}
```

Figure 5-6 highlights the media queries in the style sheet file.

Figure 5-6   **Creating media queries for different screen widths**

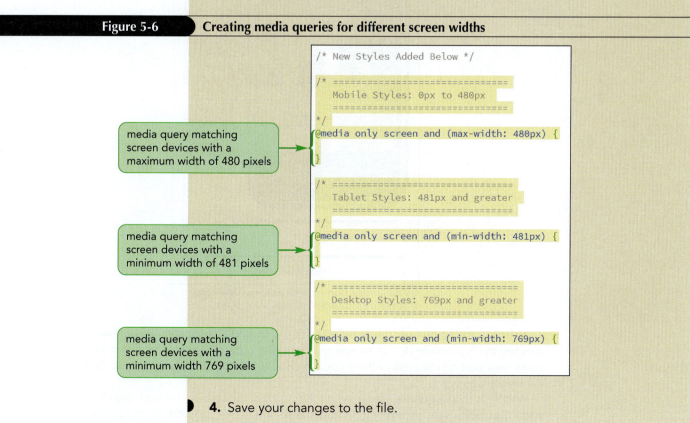

media query matching screen devices with a maximum width of 480 pixels

media query matching screen devices with a minimum width of 481 pixels

media query matching screen devices with a minimum width 769 pixels

4. Save your changes to the file.

The media queries you've written are based on the screen width. However, before you can begin writing styles for each media query, you have to understand how those width values are interpreted by your browser.

Exploring Viewports and Device Width

Web pages are viewed within a window called the viewport. For desktop computers, the viewport is the same as the browser window; however, this is not the case with mobile devices. Mobile devices have two types of viewports: a **visual viewport** displaying the web page content that fits within a mobile screen and a **layout viewport** containing the entire content of the page, some of which may be hidden from the user.

The two viewports exist in order to accommodate websites that have been written with desktop computers in mind. A mobile device will automatically zoom out of a page in order to give users the complete view of the page's contents, but as shown earlier in Figure 5-2, this often results in a view that is too small to be usable. While the user can manually zoom into a page to make it readable within the visual viewport, this is done at the expense of hiding content, as shown in Figure 5-7.

Figure 5-7	Comparing the visual and layout viewports

visual viewport

layout viewport

© 2016 Cengage Learning; © Robert Kneschke/Shutterstock.com;
© dotshock/Shutterstock.com; BenBois/openclipart

Notice in the figure how the home page of the Trusted Friends website has been zoomed in on a mobile device so that only part of the page is displayed within the visual viewport and the rest of the page, which is hidden from the user, extends into the layout viewport.

Widths in media queries are based on the width of the layout viewport, not the visual viewport. Thus, depending on how the page is scaled, a width of 980 pixels might match the physical width of the device as shown in Figure 5-2 or it might extend beyond it as shown in Figure 5-7. In order to correctly base a media query on the physical width of the device, you have to tell the browser that you want the width of the layout viewport matched to the device width by adding the following `meta` element to the HTML file:

```
<meta name="viewport" content="properties" />
```

where *properties* is a comma-separated list of viewport properties and their values, as seen in the example that follows:

```
<meta name="viewport"
  content="width=device-width, initial-scale=1" />
```

In this `meta` element, the `device-width` keyword is used to set the width of the layout viewport to the physical width of the device's screen. For a mobile device, this command sets the width of the layout viewport to the width of the device. The line `initial-scale=1` is added so that the browser doesn't automatically zoom out of the web page to fit the page content within the width of the screen. We want the viewport to match the device width, which is what the above meta element tells the browser to do.

REFERENCE

Configuring the Layout Viewport

- To configure the properties of the layout viewport for use with media queries, add the following `meta` element to the HTML file

  ```
  <meta name="viewport" content="properties" />
  ```

  where *properties* is a comma-separated list of viewport properties and their values.
- To size the layout viewport so that it matches the width of the device without rescaling, use the following viewport `meta` element

  ```
  <meta name="viewport"
    content="width=device-width, initial-scale=1" />
  ```

Add the viewport `meta` element to the tf_home.html file now, setting the width of the layout viewport to match the device width and the initial scale to 1.

To define the visual viewport:

1. Return to the **tf_home.html** file in your editor.

2. Below the `meta` element that defines the character set, insert the following HTML tag:

   ```
   <meta name="viewport"
     content="width=device-width, initial-scale=1" />
   ```

   Figure 5-8 highlights the code for the viewport `meta` element.

Figure 5-8 Setting the properties of the viewport

sets the width of the layout viewport to the width of the device

page does not automatically zoom out when the page is initially opened by the browser

```
<title>Trusted Friends Daycare</title>
<meta charset="utf-8" />
<meta name="viewport" content="width=device-width, initial-scale=1" />
<link href="tf_reset.css" rel="stylesheet" />
<link href="tf_styles1.css" rel="stylesheet" />
</head>
```

3. Save your changes to the file.

4. Open the **tf_home.html** file in your browser. Figure 5-9 shows the initial design of the page.

Figure 5-9 Mobile layout of the Trusted Friends home page

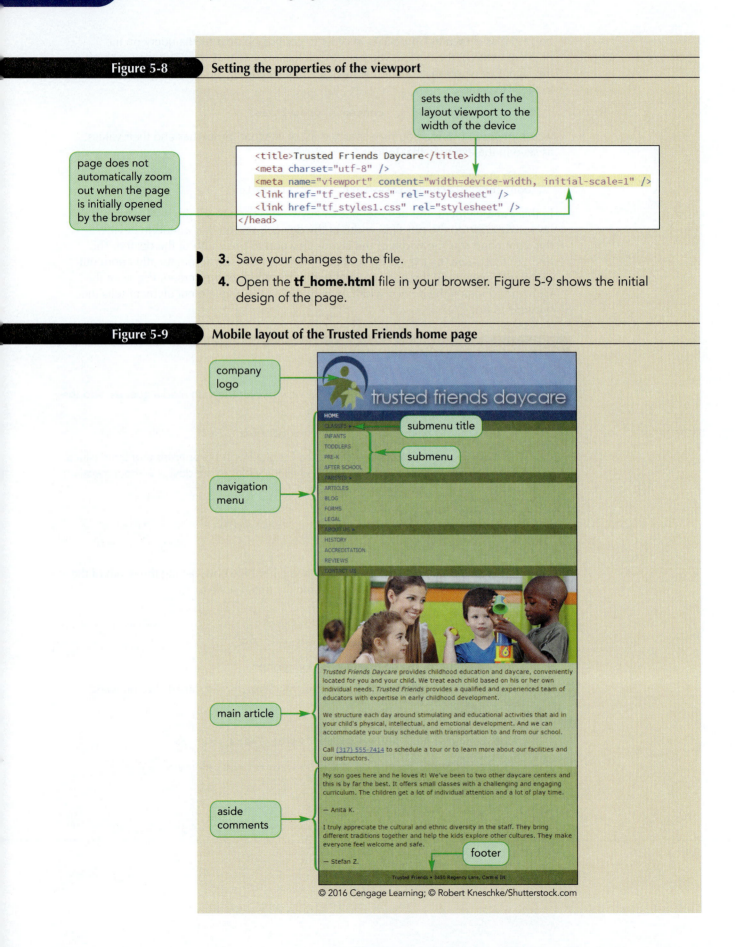

company logo

submenu title

submenu

navigation menu

main article

aside comments

footer

© 2016 Cengage Learning; © Robert Kneschke/Shutterstock.com

Now that you've set up the media queries and configured the viewport, you can work on the design of the home page. You'll start by designing for mobile devices.

INSIGHT

Not All Pixels Are Equal

While pixels are a basic unit of measurement in web design, there are actually two types of pixels to consider as you design a website. One is a **device pixel**, which refers to the actual physical pixel on a screen. The other is a **CSS pixel**, which is the fundamental unit in CSS measurements. The difference between device pixels and CSS pixels is easiest to understand when you zoom into and out of a web page. For example, the following style creates an `aside` element that is 300 CSS pixels wide:

```
aside: {width: 300px;}
```

However, the element is not necessarily 300 device pixels. If the user zooms into the web page, the apparent size of the article increases as measured by device pixels but remains 300 CSS pixels wide, resulting in 1 CSS pixel being represented by several device pixels.

The number of device pixels matched to a single CSS pixel is known as the **device-pixel ratio**. When a page is zoomed at a factor of 2x, the device-pixel ratio is 2, with a single CSS pixel represented by a 2×2 square of device pixels.

One area where the difference between device pixels and CSS pixels becomes important is in the development of websites optimized for displays with high device-pixel ratios. Some mobile devices are capable of displaying images with a device pixel ratio of 3, resulting in free crisp and clear images. Designers can optimize their websites for these devices by creating one set of style sheets for low-resolution displays and another for high-resolution displays. The high-resolution style sheet would load extremely detailed, high-resolution images, while the low-resolution style sheet would load lower resolution images better suited to devices that are limited to smaller device-pixel ratios. For example, the following media query

```
<link href="retina.css" rel="stylesheet"
  media="only screen and (-webkit-min-device-pixel-ratio: 2) " />
```

loads the retina.css style sheet file for high-resolution screen devices that have device-pixel ratios of at least 2. Note that currently the `device-pixel-ratio` feature is a browser-specific extension supported only by WebKit.

Creating a Mobile Design

A mobile website design should reflect how users interact with their mobile devices. Because your users will be working with a small handheld touchscreen device, one key component in your design is to have the most important information up-front and easily accessible, which means your home page on a mobile device needs to be free of unnecessary clutter. Another important principle of designing for mobile devices is that you should limit the choices you offer to your users. Ideally, there should only be a few navigation links on the screen at any one time.

With these principles in mind, consider the current layout of the Trusted Friends home page shown in Figure 5-9. The content is arranged within a single column providing the maximum width for the text and images, but an area of concern for Marjorie is the long list of hypertext links, which forces the user to scroll vertically down the page to view information about the center. Most mobile websites deal with this issue by hiding extensive lists of links in pulldown menus, appearing only in response to a tap of a major heading in the navigation list. You'll use this technique for the Trusted Friends home page.

Creating a Pulldown Menu with CSS

Marjorie has already laid the foundation for creating a pulldown menu in her HTML code. Figure 5-10 shows the code used to mark the contents of the navigation list in the body header.

Figure 5-10   **Submenus in the navigation list**

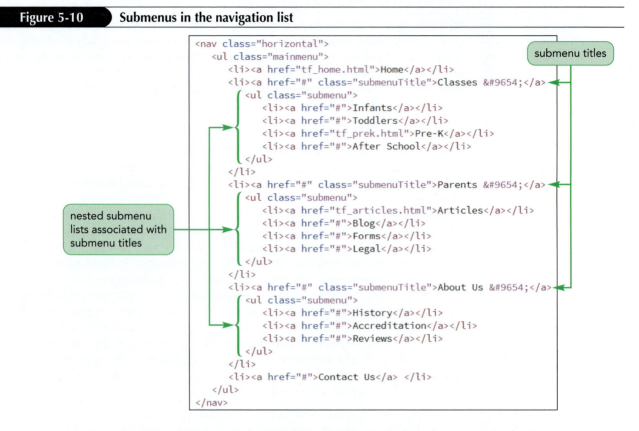

Marjorie has created a navigation bar that includes topical areas named Classes, Parents, and About Us. Within each of these topical areas are nested lists containing links to specific pages on the Trusted Friends website. Marjorie has put each of these nested lists within a class named *submenu*. So, first you'll hide each of these submenus to reduce the length of the navigation list as it is rendered within the user's browser. You'll place this style rule in the section for Base Styles because it will be used by both mobile and tablet devices (but not by desktop devices as you'll see later).

To hide a submenu:

▶ **1.** Return to the **tf_styles1.css** file in your editor.

▶ **2.** Scroll to the Pulldown Menu Styles section and add the following style rule:

```
ul.submenu {
    display: none;
}
```

Figure 5-11 highlights the styles to hide the navigation list submenus.

Figure 5-11   **Hiding the navigation list submenus**

prevents the submenu
unordered lists from
being displayed

```
/* Pulldown Menu Styles */

ul.submenu {
    display: none;
}
```

3. Save your changes to the file and then reload the tf_home.html file in your browser. Verify that the navigation list no longer shows the contents of the submenus but only the Home, Classes, Parents, About Us, and Contact Us links. See Figure 5-12.

Figure 5-12   **Navigation list with hidden submenus**

submenu lists
are hidden

trusted friends daycare

HOME
CLASSES ►
PARENTS ►
ABOUT US ►
CONTACT US

Trusted Friends Daycare provides childhood education and daycare, conveniently located for you and your child. We treat each child based on his or her own

© Robert Kneschke/Shutterstock.com

Next, you want to display a nested submenu only when the user hovers the mouse pointer over its associated submenu title, which for this page are the Classes, Parents, and About Us titles. Because the submenu follows the submenu title in the HTML file (see Figure 5-10), you can use the following selector to select the submenu that is immediately preceded by a hovered submenu title:

```
a.submenuTitle:hover+ul.submenu
```

However, this selector is not enough because you want the submenu to remain visible as the pointer moves away from the title and hovers over the now-visible submenu. So, you need to add `ul.submenu:hover` to the selector:

```
a.submenuTitle:hover+ul.submenu, ul.submenu:hover
```

To make the submenu visible, you change its display property back to `block`, resulting in the following style rule:

```
a.submenuTitle:hover+ul.submenu, ul.submenu:hover {
        display: block;
}
```

You may wonder why you don't use only the `ul.submenu:hover` selector. The reason is that you can't hover over the submenu until it's visible and it won't be visible until you first hover over the submenu title. Add this rule now to the tf_styles1.css style sheet and test it.

To redisplay the navigation submenus:

1. Return to the **tf_styles1.css** file in your editor.

2. Add the following style rule to the Pulldown Menu Styles section:

```
a.submenuTitle:hover+ul.submenu, ul.submenu:hover {
    display: block;
}
```

Figure 5-13 highlights the styles to display the navigation list submenus.

Figure 5-13   **Displaying the hidden submenus**

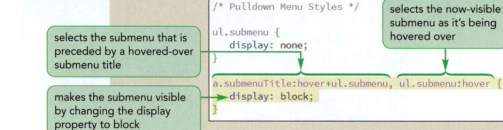

selects the submenu that is preceded by a hovered-over submenu title

selects the now-visible submenu as it's being hovered over

makes the submenu visible by changing the display property to block

```
/* Pulldown Menu Styles */

ul.submenu {
    display: none;
}

a.submenuTitle:hover+ul.submenu, ul.submenu:hover {
    display: block;
}
```

3. Save your changes to the file and then reload the tf_home.html file in your browser. Hover your mouse pointer over each of the submenu titles and verify that the corresponding submenu becomes visible and remains visible as you move the mouse pointer over its contents.

Figure 5-14 shows the revised appearance of the navigation list using the pulldown menus.

Figure 5-14   **Displaying the contents of a pulldown menu**

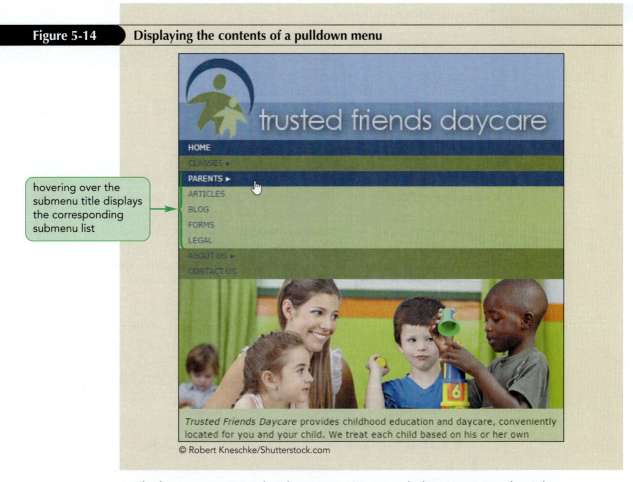

hovering over the submenu title displays the corresponding submenu list

Trusted Friends Daycare provides childhood education and daycare, conveniently located for you and your child. We treat each child based on his or her own

© Robert Kneschke/Shutterstock.com

The hover event is used with mouse pointers on desktop computers but it has a different interpretation when applied to mobile devices. Because almost all mobile devices operate via a touch interface, there is no hovering. A mobile browser will interpret a hover event as a tap event in which the user taps the page object. When the hover event is used to hide an object or display it (as we did with the submenus), mobile browsers employ a double-tap event in which the first tap displays the page object and a second tap, immediately after the first, activates any hypertext links associated with the object. To display the Trusted Friends submenus, the user would tap the submenu title and to hide the submenus the user would tap elsewhere on the page.

To test the hover action, you need to view the Trusted Friends page on a mobile device or a mobile emulator.

Testing your Mobile Website

The best way to test a mobile interface is to view it directly on a mobile device. However, given the large number of mobile devices and device versions, it's usually not practical to do direct testing on all devices. An alternative to having the physical device is to emulate it through a software program or an online testing service. Almost every mobile phone company provides a software development kit or SDK that developers can use to test their programs and websites. Figure 5-15 lists some of the many **mobile device emulators** available on the web at the time of this writing.

| Figure 5-15 | Popular device emulators |

Mobile Emulators	Description
Android SDK	Software development kit for Android developers (*developer.android.com/sdk*)
iOS SDK	Software development kit for iPhone, iPad, and other iOS devices (*developer.apple.com*)
Mobile Phone Emulator	Online emulation for a variety of mobile devices (*www.mobilephoneemulator.com*)
Mobile Test Me	Online emulation for a variety of mobile devices (*mobiletest.me*)
MobiOne Studio	Mobile emulator software for a variety of devices (https://www.genuitec.com/products/mobile/)
Opera Mobile SDK	Developer tools for the Opera Mobile browser (*www.opera.com/developer*)
Windows Phone SDK	Software development kit for developing apps and websites for the Windows Phone (*dev.windows.com/en-us/develop/download-phone-sdk*)

© 2016 Cengage Learning

Browsers are also starting to include device emulators as part of their developer tools. You will examine the device emulator that is supplied with the Google Chrome browser and use it to view the Trusted Friends home page under a device of your choosing. If you don't have access to the Google Chrome browser, review the steps that follow and apply them to the emulator of your choice.

Viewing the Google Chrome device emulator:

1. Return to the **tf_home.html** file in the Google Chrome browser and press **F12** to open the developer tools pane.

2. Click the **device** icon located at the top of the developer pane to display a list of devices in the developer window.

3. Select a device of your choosing from the list of mobile devices in the top-left corner in the developer window. Note that the device's width and height (for example, 400 × 640) are displayed below the device name.

4. Refresh or reload the web page to ensure that the display parameters of your selected device are applied to the rendered page.

   The emulator also allows you to view the effect of changing the orientation of the phone from portrait to landscape.

5. Click the **swap dimensions** button located below the name of the mobile device to switch to landscape orientation. Click the **swap dimensions** button again to switch back to portrait mode.

   Google Chrome's device emulator can also emulate the touch action. The touch point is represented by a semi-transparent circle ●.

6. Move the touch point over Classes, Parents, or About Us and verify that when you click (tap) the touch point on a submenu title the nested submenu contents are displayed.

7. Verify that you when you click elsewhere in the page the submenu contents are hidden.

   Figure 5-16 shows the effect of opening a submenu with the touch emulator.

Figure 5-16	Using the Google Chrome device emulator tool

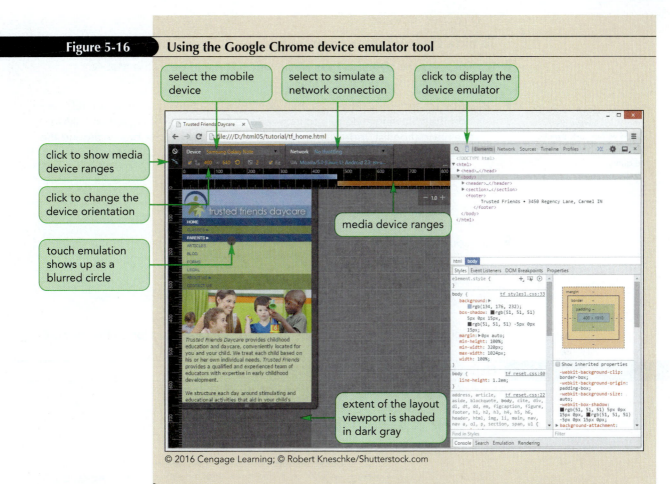

© 2016 Cengage Learning; © Robert Kneschke/Shutterstock.com

8. Continue to explore Google Chrome's device emulators, trying out different combinations of devices and screen orientations. Press **F12** again to close the developer window.

An important aspect of mobile design is optimizing your site's performance under varying network conditions. Thus, in addition to emulating the properties of the mobile device, Google Chrome's device emulator can also emulate network connectivity. You can test the performance of your mobile site under a variety of simulated network connections including WiFi, DSL, 2G, 3G, and 4G mobile connections, as well as offline connections.

Marjorie wants to increase the font size of the links in the navigation list to make them easier to access using touch. She also wants to hide the customer comments that have been placed in the `aside` element (because she doesn't feel this will be of interest to mobile users). Because these changes only apply to the mobile device version of the page, you'll add the style rules within the media query for mobile devices.

To hide the customer comments:

1. Return to the **tf_styles1.css** file in your editor and go to the Mobile Styles section.

The styles rules for a media query must always be placed within curly braces to define the extent of the query.

2. Within the media query for screen devices with a maximum width of 480 pixels, add the following style rule to increase the font size of the hypertext links in the navigation list. Indent the style rule to offset it from the braces around the media query.

```
nav.horizontal a {
    font-size: 1.5em;
    line-height: 2.2em;
}
```

3. Add the following style rule to hide the `aside` element (once again indented from the surrounding media query):

```
aside {
    display: none;
}
```

Figure 5-17 highlights the style rules in the media query for mobile devices.

Figure 5-17   **Hiding the aside element for mobile devices**

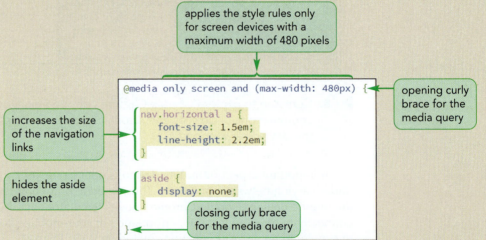

4. Save your changes to the file and then reload the tf_home.html file in your browser. Reduce the width of the browser window to 480 pixels or below (or view the page in your mobile emulator). Verify that the customer comments are no longer displayed on the web page and that the size of the navigation links has been increased.

Figure 5-18 shows the final design of the mobile version.

Figure 5-18   **Final design of the mobile version of the home page**

Now that you've completed the mobile design of the page, you'll start to work on the design for tablet devices.

Creating a Tablet Design

Under the media query you've set up, your design for tablet devices will be applied for screen widths greater than 480 pixels. The pulldown menu you created was part of the base styles, so it is already part of the tablet design; however, with the wider screen, Marjorie would like the submenus displayed horizontally rather than vertically. You can accomplish this by adding a style rule to the tablet media query to float the submenus side-by-side.

To begin writing the tablet design:

1. Return to the **tf_styles1.css** file in your editor and scroll down to the media query for the tablet styles.

2. Within the media query, add the following style to float the five list items, which are direct children of the main menu, side-by-side. Set the width of each list item to 20% of the total width of the main menu.

```
ul.mainmenu > li {
    float: left;
    width: 20%;
}
```

3. Double the widths of the submenus so that they stand out better from the main menu titles by adding the following style rule.

```
ul.submenu {
    width: 200%;
}
```

Figure 5-19 highlights the style rule within the media query for tablet devices.

Figure 5-19   **Formatting the navigation menus for tablet devices**

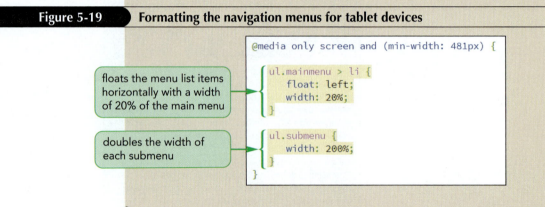

floats the menu list items horizontally with a width of 20% of the main menu

doubles the width of each submenu

```
@media only screen and (min-width: 481px) {

    ul.mainmenu > li {
        float: left;
        width: 20%;
    }

    ul.submenu {
        width: 200%;
    }
}
```

4. Save your changes to the style sheet and then reload the tf_home.html file in your web browser.

5. Increase the width of the browser window beyond 480 pixels to switch from the mobile design to the tablet design. Verify that the submenu titles are now laid out horizontally and that if you hover your mouse pointer over the submenu titles, the contents of the submenu are made visible on the screen. See Figure 5-20.

| Figure 5-20 | Pulldown menus for the tablet layout |

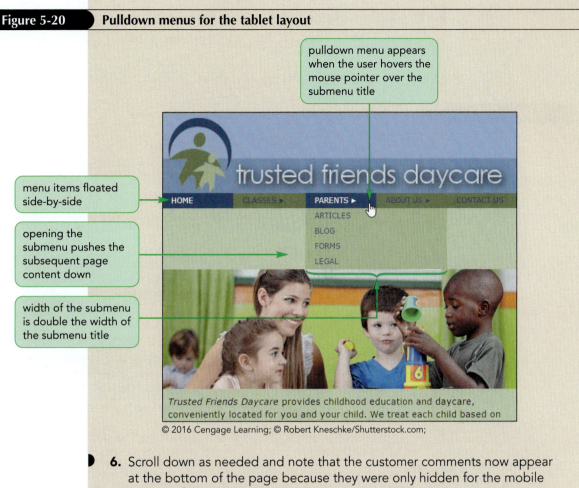

pulldown menu appears when the user hovers the mouse pointer over the submenu title

menu items floated side-by-side

opening the submenu pushes the subsequent page content down

width of the submenu is double the width of the submenu title

© 2016 Cengage Learning; © Robert Kneschke/Shutterstock.com;

▶ **6.** Scroll down as needed and note that the customer comments now appear at the bottom of the page because they were only hidden for the mobile version of this document.

Marjorie notices that opening the submenus pushes the subsequent page content down to make room for the submenu. She prefers the submenus to overlay the page content. You can accomplish this by placing the submenus with absolute positioning. Remember that objects placed with absolute positioning are removed from the document flow and thus, will overlay subsequent page content. To keep the submenus in their current position on the page, you'll make each main list item a container for its submenu by setting its `position` property to `relative`. Thus, each submenu will be placed using absolute positioning with its main list item. You will not need to set the `top` and `left` coordinates for these items because you'll use the default value of 0 for both. Because the submenus will overlay page content, Marjorie suggests you add a drop shadow so, when a submenu is opened, it will stand out more from the page content.

To position the navigation submenus:

▶ **1.** Return to the **tf_styles1.css** style sheet in your editor.

▶ **2.** Locate the style rule for the `ul.mainmenu > li` selector in the Tablet Styles section and add the following style:

```
position: relative;
```

▶ **3.** Add the following style to the `ul.submenu` selector in the Tablet Styles section:

```
box-shadow: rgb(51, 51, 51) 5px 5px 15px;
position: absolute;
```

Figure 5-21 highlights the new styles.

Figure 5-21   **Placing the pulldown menus with absolute positioning**

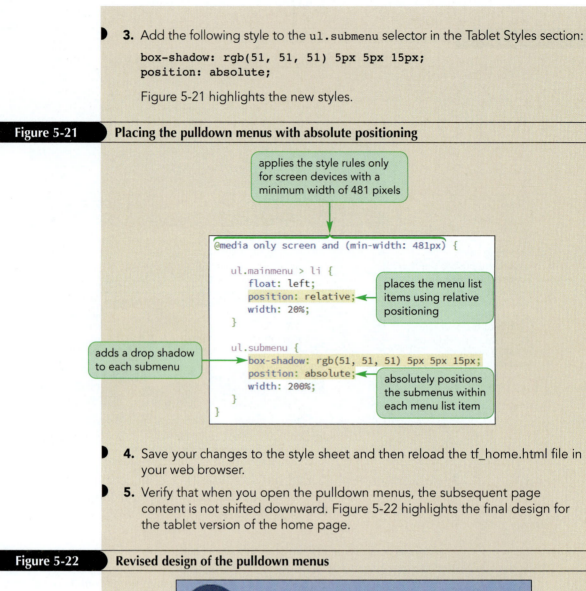

applies the style rules only for screen devices with a minimum width of 481 pixels

```
@media only screen and (min-width: 481px) {

    ul.mainmenu > li {
        float: left;
        position: relative;
        width: 20%;
    }

    ul.submenu {
        box-shadow: rgb(51, 51, 51) 5px 5px 15px;
        position: absolute;
        width: 200%;
    }
}
```

places the menu list items using relative positioning

adds a drop shadow to each submenu

absolutely positions the submenus within each menu list item

▶ **4.** Save your changes to the style sheet and then reload the tf_home.html file in your web browser.

▶ **5.** Verify that when you open the pulldown menus, the subsequent page content is not shifted downward. Figure 5-22 highlights the final design for the tablet version of the home page.

Figure 5-22   **Revised design of the pulldown menus**

page content does not shift when the pulldown menu is opened

© Robert Kneschke/Shutterstock.com

You'll complete your work on the home page by creating the desktop version of the page design.

Creating a Desktop Design

Some of the designs that will be used in the desktop version of the page have already been placed in the Base Styles section of the tf_styles1.css style sheet. For example, the maximum width of the web page has been set to 1024 pixels. For browser windows that exceed that width, the web page will be displayed on a fixed background image of children playing. Other styles are inherited from the style rules for tablet devices. For example, desktop devices will inherit the style rule that floats the navigation submenus alongside each other within a single row. All of which illustrates an important principle in designing for multiple devices: *don't reinvent the wheel*. As much as possible allow your styles to build upon each other as you move to wider and wider screens.

However, there are some styles that you will have to implement only for desktop devices. With the wider screen desktop screens, you don't need to hide the submenus in a pulldown menu system. Instead you can display all of the links from the navigation list. You'll change the submenu background color to transparent so that it blends in with the navigation list and you'll remove the drop shadows you created for the tablet design. The submenus will always be visible, so you'll change their `display` property from none to `block`. Finally, you'll change their position to relative because you no longer want to take the submenus out of the document flow and you'll change their width to 100%. Apply the styles now to modify the appearance of the submenus.

To start working on the desktop design:

▶ 1. Return to the **tf_styles1.css** style sheet in your editor and within the media query for devices with screen widths 769 pixels or greater insert the following style rule to format the appearance of the navigation submenus.

```
ul.submenu {
    background: transparent;
    box-shadow: none;
    display: block;
    position: relative;
    width: 100%;
}
```

▶ 2. The navigation list itself needs to expand so that it contains all of its floated content. Add the following style rule to the media query for desktop devices:

```
nav.horizontal::after {
    clear: both;
    content: "";
    display: table;
}
```

▶ 3. Finally with no hidden submenus, there is no reason to have a submenu title. Add the following style rule to remove the submenu titles:

```
nav.horizontal a.submenuTitle {
    display: none;
}
```

Figure 5-23 highlights the new style rules in the desktop media query.

Figure 5-23 **Adding design styles for the browser background and page body**

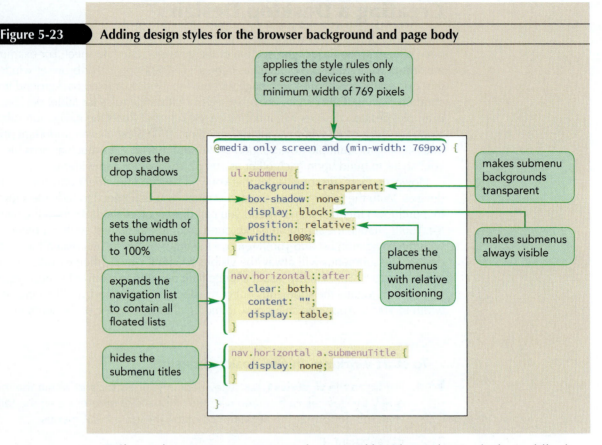

With a wider screen, you want to order to avoid long lines of text, which are difficult to read. Modify the layout of the desktop design so that the main article and the customer comments are floated side-by-side within the same row.

To change the layout of the article and aside elements:

1. Within the media query for desktop devices, add the following style rules to float the `article` and `aside` elements:

```
article {
    float: left;
    margin-right: 5%;
    width: 55%;
}
aside {
    float: left;
    width: 40%;
}
```

Figure 5-24 highlights the final style rules in the desktop media query.

Figure 5-24	Styles for the article and aside elements

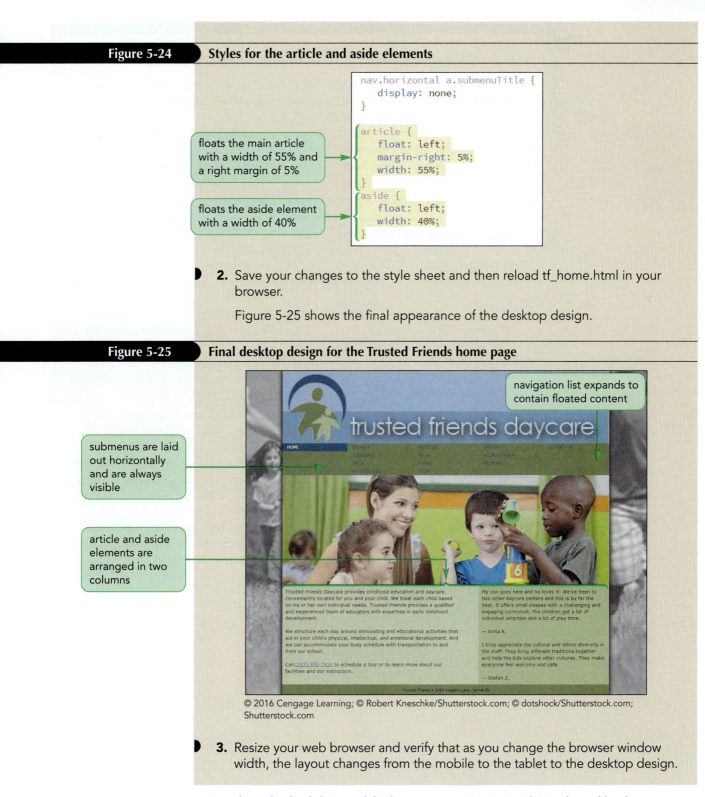

```
nav.horizontal a.submenuTitle {
    display: none;
}

article {
    float: left;
    margin-right: 5%;
    width: 55%;
}
aside {
    float: left;
    width: 40%;
}
```

floats the main article with a width of 55% and a right margin of 5%

floats the aside element with a width of 40%

2. Save your changes to the style sheet and then reload tf_home.html in your browser.

Figure 5-25 shows the final appearance of the desktop design.

Figure 5-25	Final desktop design for the Trusted Friends home page

navigation list expands to contain floated content

submenus are laid out horizontally and are always visible

article and aside elements are arranged in two columns

trusted friends daycare

HOME

Trusted Friends Daycare provides childhood education and daycare, conveniently located for you and your child. We treat each child based on his or her own individual needs. *Trusted Friends* provides a qualified and experienced team of educators with expertise in early childhood development.

We structure each day around stimulating and educational activities that aid in your child's physical, intellectual, and emotional development. And we can accommodate your busy schedule with transportation to and from our school.

Call (317) 555-7414 to schedule a tour or to learn more about our facilities and our instructors.

My son goes here and he loves it! We've been to two other daycare centers and this is by far the best. It offers small classes with a challenging and engaging curriculum. The children get a lot of individual attention and a lot of play time.

— Anita K.

I truly appreciate the cultural and ethnic diversity in the staff. They bring different traditions together and help the kids explore other cultures. They make everyone feel welcome and safe.

— Stefan Z.

Trusted Friends • 3450 Regency Lane, Carmel IN

3. Resize your web browser and verify that as you change the browser window width, the layout changes from the mobile to the tablet to the desktop design.

You show the final design of the home page to Marjorie. She is pleased by the changes you've made and likes that the page's content and layout will automatically adapt to different screen widths.

PROSKILLS

Problem Solving: Optimizing Your Site for the Mobile Web

The mobile browser market is a rapidly evolving and growing field with more new devices and apps introduced each month. Adapting your website for the mobile web is not a luxury, but a necessity.

A good mobile design matches the needs of consumers. Mobile users need quick access to main sources of information without a lot of the extra material often found in the desktop versions of their favorite sites. Here are some things to keep in mind as you create your mobile designs:

- *Keep it simple.* To accommodate the smaller screen sizes and slower connection speeds, scale down each page to a few key items and articles. Users are looking for quick and obvious information from their mobile sites.
- *Resize your images.* Downloading several images can bring a mobile device to a crawl. Reduce the number of images in your mobile design, and use a graphics package to resize the images so they are optimized in quality and sized for a smaller screen.
- *Scroll vertically.* Readers can more easily read your page when they only have to scroll vertically. Limit yourself to one column of information in portrait orientation and two columns in landscape.
- *Make your links accessible.* Clicking a small hypertext link is extremely difficult to do on a mobile device with a touch screen interface. Create hypertext links that are easy to locate and activate.

Above all, test your site on a variety of devices and under different conditions. Mobile devices vary greatly in size, shape, and capability. What works on one device might fail utterly on another. Testing your code on a desktop computer is only the first step; you may also need access to the devices themselves. Even emulators cannot always capture the nuances involved in the performance of an actual mobile device.

You've completed your work on the design of the Trusted Friends home page with a style sheet that seamlessly transitions between mobile, tablet, and desktop devices. In the next session, you'll explore how to use flexible boxes to achieve a responsive design.

Session 5.1 Quick Check

1. What is responsive design?
2. What are the three primary parts of responsive design theory?
3. Provide the code to create a `link` element that loads the talk.css style sheet for aural browsers.
4. Provide the general syntax of a CSS rule that loads style rules for braille devices.
5. Provide the general syntax of a CSS rule that loads style rules for screen devices up to a maximum width of 780 pixels.
6. Provide the code for a `link` element that loads the tablet.css style sheet for screen devices whose width ranges from 480 pixels up to 780 pixels (inclusive).
7. How should you arrange the media queries in your style sheet if you want to support mobile, tablet, and desktop devices?
8. What is the difference between the visual viewport and the layout viewport?
9. Provide the code that sets the width of the layout viewport equal to the width of the device with an initial scale factor of 1.

Session 5.2 Visual Overview:

A **flexbox** contains items whose size automatically expands or contracts to match the dimensions of the box.

To create a flexbox, set the `display` property to flex (or –webkit-flex for older browsers).

To define the orientation of the flexbox and whether items can wrap to a new line, apply the `flex-flow` property.

Use the `flex` property to define the size of the flex items and how they will grow or shrink in response to the changing size of the flexbox.

The **flex-basis** value provides the basis or initial size of the item prior to flexing.

The **flex-grow** value specifies how fast the item grows above its basis size relative to other items in the flexbox.

The **flex-shrink** value specifies how fast the item shrinks below its basis size relative to other items in the flexbox.

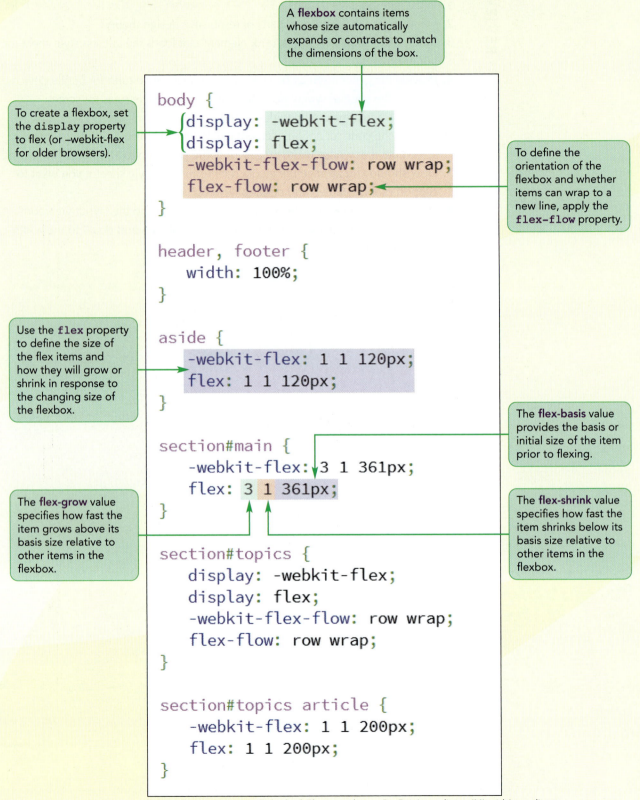

```css
body {
    display: -webkit-flex;
    display: flex;
    -webkit-flex-flow: row wrap;
    flex-flow: row wrap;
}

header, footer {
    width: 100%;
}

aside {
    -webkit-flex: 1 1 120px;
    flex: 1 1 120px;
}

section#main {
    -webkit-flex: 3 1 361px;
    flex: 3 1 361px;
}

section#topics {
    display: -webkit-flex;
    display: flex;
    -webkit-flex-flow: row wrap;
    flex-flow: row wrap;
}

section#topics article {
    -webkit-flex: 1 1 200px;
    flex: 1 1 200px;
}
```

Flexbox Layouts

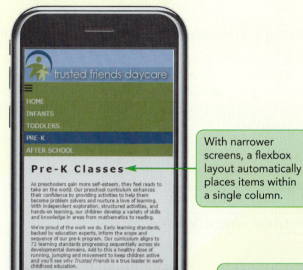

With narrower screens, a flexbox layout automatically places items within a single column.

With wider screens, the items are free to expand, automatically placing themselves into multiple columns.

Introducing Flexible Boxes

So far our layouts have been limited to a grid system involving floating elements contained within a fixed or fluid grid of rows and columns. One of the challenges of this approach under responsive design is that you need to establish a different grid layout for each class of screen size. It would be much easier to have a single specification that automatically adapts itself to the screen width without requiring a new layout design. One way of achieving this is with flexible boxes.

Defining a Flexible Box

A flexible box or flexbox is a box containing items whose sizes can shrink or grow to match the boundaries of the box. Thus, unlike a grid system in which each item has a defined size, flexbox items adapt themselves automatically to the size of their container. This makes flexboxes a useful tool for designing layouts that can adapt to different page sizes.

Items within a flexbox are laid out along a **main axis**, which can point in either the horizontal or vertical direction. Perpendicular to the main axis is the **cross axis**, which is used to define the height or width of each item. Figure 5-26 displays a diagram of two flexboxes with items arranged either horizontally or vertically along the main axis.

Figure 5-26   Horizontal and vertical flexboxes

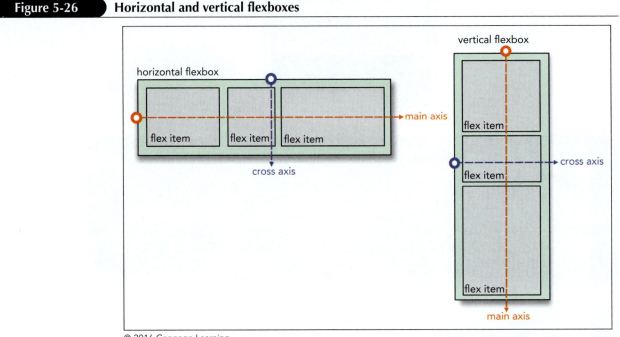

© 2016 Cengage Learning

To define an element as a flexbox, apply either of the following `display` styles

    display: flex;

or

    display: inline-flex;

where a value of `flex` starts the flexbox on a new line (much as a block element starts on a new line) and a value of `inline-flex` keeps the flexbox in-line with its surrounding content.

Cross-Browser Flexboxes

The syntax for flexboxes has gone through major revisions as it has developed from the earliest drafts to the latest specifications. Many older browsers employ a different flexbox syntax, in some cases replacing the word *flex* with *box* or *flexbox*. The complete list of browser extensions that define a flexbox would be entered as:

```
display: -webkit-box;
display: -moz-box;
display: -ms-flexbox;
display: -webkit-flex:
display: flex;
```

To simplify the code in the examples that follow, you will limit your code to the latest WebKit browser extension and the current W3C specification. This will cover the current browsers at the time of this writing. However, if you need to support older browsers, you may have to include a long list of browser extensions for each flex property.

Setting the Flexbox Flow

By default, flexbox items are arranged horizontally starting from the left and moving to the right. To change the orientation of the flexbox, apply the following `flex-direction` property

```
flex-direction: direction;
```

where *direction* is `row` (the default), `column`, `row-reverse`, or `column-reverse`. The `row` option lays out the flex items from left to right, `column` creates a vertical layout starting from the top and moving downward, and the `row-reverse` and `column-reverse` options lay out the items bottom-to-top and right-to-left respectively.

Flex items will all try to fit within a single line, either horizontally or vertically. But if they can't, those items can wrap to a new line as needed by applying the following `flex-wrap` property to the flexbox

```
flex-wrap: type;
```

where *type* is either `nowrap` (the default), `wrap` to wrap the flex items to a new line, or `wrap-reverse` to wrap flex items to a new line starting in the opposite direction from the current line. For example, the following style rules create a flexbox in which the items are arranged in a column starting from the top and going down with any flex items that wrap to the second column starting from the bottom and moving up.

```
display: flex;
flex-direction: column;
flex-wrap: wrap-reverse;
```

Additional items in this flexbox will continue to follow a snake-like curve with the third column starting at the top, moving down, and so forth.

Both the `flex-direction` and `flex-wrap` properties can be combined into the following `flex-flow` style

```
flex-flow: direction wrap;
```

> **TIP**
>
> Some older browsers do not support the `flex-flow` property, so for full cross-browser support, you might use the `flex-direction` and `flex-wrap` properties instead.

where *direction* is the direction of the flex items and *wrap* defines whether the items will be wrapped to a new line when needed. Figure 5-27 shows an example of flexboxes laid out in rows and columns in which the flex items are forced to wrap to a new line. Note that the column-oriented flexbox uses wrap-reverse to start the new column on the bottom rather than the top.

Figure 5-27   Flexbox layouts

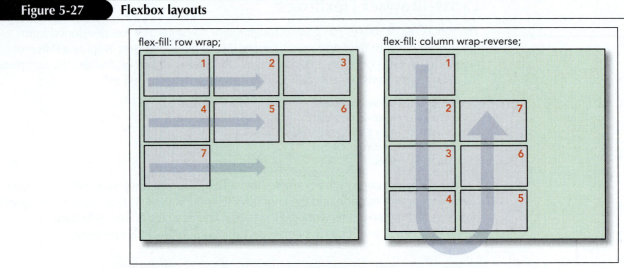

© 2016 Cengage Learning

Defining a Flexbox

- To display an element as a flexbox, apply the `display` style

  `display: flex;`

- To set the orientation of the flexbox, apply the style

  `flex-direction: direction;`

  where `direction` is `row` (the default), `column`, `row-reverse`, or `column-reverse`.
- To define whether or not flex items wrap to a new line, apply the style

  `flex-wrap: type;`

  where `type` is either `nowrap` (the default), `wrap` to wrap flex items to a new line, or `wrap-reverse` to wrap flex items to a new line starting in the opposite direction from the current line.
- To define the flow of items within a flexbox, apply the style

  `flex-flow: direction wrap;`

  where `direction` is the direction of the flex items and `wrap` defines whether the items will be wrapped to a new line when needed.

Marjorie wants you to use flexboxes to design a page she's created describing the pre-k classes offered by Trusted Friends. She has already created the content of the page and several style sheets to format the appearance of the page elements. You'll create a style sheet that lays out the page content drawing from a library of flexbox styles.

To open the pre-k page and style sheet:

1. Use your editor to open the **tf_prek_txt.html** and **tf_flex_txt.css** files from the html05 ▸ tutorial folder. Enter **your name** and **the date** in the comment section of each file and save them as **tf_prek.html** and **tf_flex.css** respectively.

2. Return to the **tf_prek.html** file in your editor and, within the document head, create links to the **tf_reset.css**, **tf_styles2.css**, and **tf_flex.css** style sheets in that order.

> 3. Take some time to scroll through the contents of the document to become familiar with its contents and structure and then save your changes to the file, leaving it open.

> 4. Go to the **tf_flex.css** file in your editor.

Include at least the WebKit browser extension for your flexbox style to ensure compatibility across browsers.

> 5. Go to the Base Flex Styles section and insert the following style rules to display the entire page body as a flexbox oriented horizontally with overflow flex items wrapped to a new row as needed:

```
body {
    display: -webkit-flex;
    display: flex;

    -webkit-flex-flow: row wrap;
    flex-flow: row wrap;
}
```

Figure 5-28 highlights the new flexbox styles in the style sheet.

Figure 5-28   Setting the flex display style

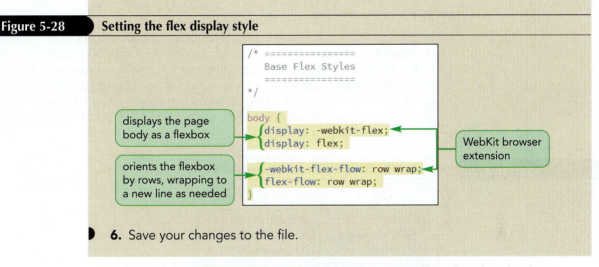

> 6. Save your changes to the file.

Now that you've defined the page body as a flexbox, you'll work with styles that define how items within a flexbox expand and contract to match the flexbox container.

Working with Flex Items

Flex items behave a lot like floated objects though with several advantages, including that you can float them in either the horizontal or vertical direction and that you can change the order in which they are displayed. While the size of a flex item can be fixed using the CSS `width` and `height` properties, they don't have to be. They can also be "flexed" — automatically adapting their size to fill the flexbox. A flex layout is fundamentally different from a grid layout and requires you to think about sizes and layout in a new way.

TIP

Because flexboxes can be aligned horizontally or vertically, the flex-basis property sets either the initial width or the initial height of the flex item depending on the orientation of the flexbox.

Setting the Flex Basis

When items are allowed to "flex" their rendered size is determined by three properties: the basis size, the growth value, and the shrink value. The basis size defines the initial size of the item before the browser attempts to fit it to the flexbox and is set using the following `flex-basis` property

```
flex-basis: size;
```

where *size* is one of the CSS units of measurement, a percentage of the size of the flexbox, or the keyword `auto` (the default), which sets the initial size of the flex item based on its content or the value of its `width` or `height` property. For example, the following style rule sets the initial size of the `aside` element to 200 pixels:

```
aside {
    flex-basis: 200px;
}
```

The `flex-basis` property should not be equated with the `width` and `height` properties used with grid layouts; rather, it serves only as a starting point. The actual rendered size of the `aside` element in this example is not necessarily 200 pixels but will be based on the size of the flexbox, as well as the size of the other items within the flexbox.

Defining the Flex Growth

Once the basis size of the item has been defined, the browser will attempt to expand the item into its flexbox. The rate at which a flex item grows from its basis size is determined by the following `flex-grow` property

```
flex-grow: value;
```

where *value* is a non-negative value that expresses the growth of the flex item relative to the growth of the other items in the flexbox. The default `flex-grow` value is 0, which is equivalent to not allowing the flex item to grow but to remain at its basis size. Different items within a flexbox can have different growth rates and the growth rate largely determines how much of the flexbox is ultimately occupied by each item.

Figure 5-29 shows an example of how changing the size of a flexbox alters the size of the individual flexbox items.

Figure 5-29   **Growing flex items beyond their basis size**

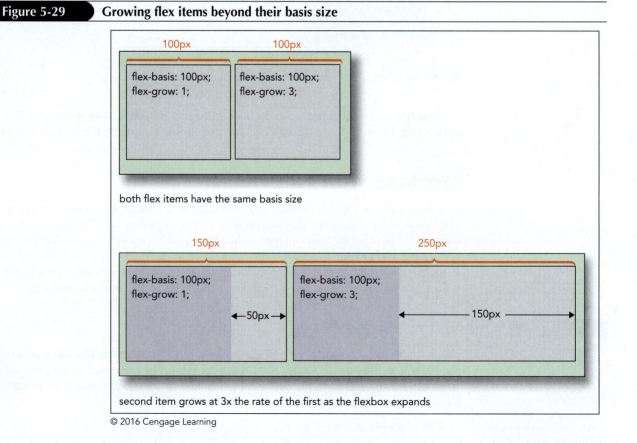

© 2016 Cengage Learning

In the figure, the basis sizes of the two items are 100 pixels each with the growth of the first item set to 1 and the growth of the second item set to 3. The growth values indicate that as the flex items expand to fill the flexbox, item1 will increase 1 pixel for every 3 pixels that item2 increases. Thus, to fill up the remaining 200 pixels of a 400-pixel wide flexbox, 50 pixels will be allotted to the first item and 150 pixels will be allotted to the second item, resulting in final sizes of 150 pixels and 250 pixels respectively. If the width of the flexbox were to increase to 600 pixels, item1 and item2 will divide the extra 400 pixels once again in a ratio of 1 to 3. Item1 will have a total size of 200 pixels (100px + 100px) and item2 will expand to a size of 400 pixels (100px + 300px).

Notice that unlike a grid layout, the relative proportions of the items under a flex layout need not be constant. For the layout shown in Figure 5-29, the two items share the space equally when the flexbox is 200 pixels wide, but at 400 pixels the first item occupies 37.5% of the box while the second item occupies the remaining 62.5%.

TIP

If all items have `flex-grow` set to 1 and an equal flex basis, they will always have an equal size within the flexbox.

To keep a constant ratio between the sizes of the flex items, set their basis sizes to 0 pixels. For example, the following style rules will result in a flexbox in which the first item is always half the size of the second item no matter how wide or tall the flexbox becomes.

```
div#item1 {
    flex-basis: 0px;
    flex-grow: 1;
}
div#item2 {
    flex-basis: 0px;
    flex-grow: 2;
}
```

One of the great advantages of the flexible box layout is that you don't need to know how many items are in the flexbox to keep their relative proportions the same. The following style rule creates a layout for a navigation list in which each list item is assigned an equal size and grows at the same rate.

```
nav  ul {
    display: flex;
}


nav  ul  li {
    flex-basis: 0px;
    flex-grow: 1;
}
```

If there are four items in this navigation list, each will be 25% of the total list size and if at a later date a fifth item is added, those items will then be allotted 20% of the total size. Thus, unlike a grid layout, there is no need to revise the percentages to accommodate new entries in the navigation list; a flexible box layout handles that task automatically.

Note that if the `flex-grow` value is set to 0, the flex item will not expand beyond its basis size, making that basis value the maximum width or height of the item.

Defining the Shrink Rate

What happens when the flexbox size falls below the total space allotted to its flex items? There are two possibilities depending on whether the flexbox is defined to wrap its contents to a new line. If the `flexbox-wrap` property is set to `wrap`, one or more of the flex items will be shifted to a new line and expanded to fill in the available space on that line. Figure 5-30 shows a flexbox layout in which three items each have a basis size of 200 pixels with the same growth value of 1.

Figure 5-30   **Shrinking flex items smaller than their basis size**

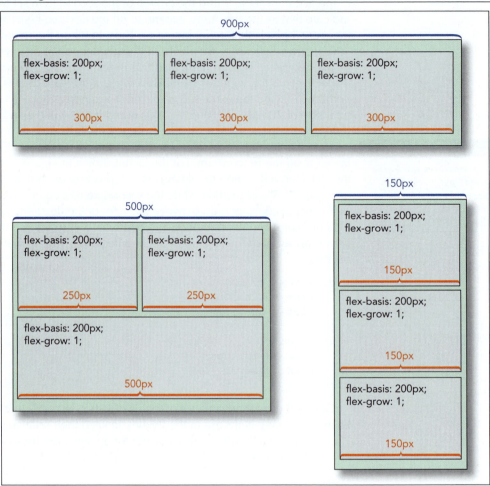

© 2016 Cengage Learning

As shown in the figure, as long as the flexbox is at least 600 pixels wide, the items will equally share a single row. However, once the flexbox size falls below 600 pixels, the three items can no longer share that row and the last item is wrapped to a new row. Once on that new row, it's free to fill up the available space while the first two items equally share the space on the first row. As the flexbox continues to contract, falling below 400 pixels, the first two items can no longer share a row and the second item now wraps to its own row. At this point the three items fill separate rows and as the flexbox continues to shrink, their sizes also shrink.

If the flexbox doesn't wrap to a new line as it is resized, then the flex items will continue to shrink, still sharing the same row or column. The rate at which they shrink below their basis size is given by the following `flex-shrink` property

```
flex-shrink: value;
```

where *value* is a non-negative value that expresses the shrink rate of the flex item relative to the shrinkage of the other items in the flexbox. The default `flex-shrink` value is 1. For example, in the following style rules, item1 and item2 will share the flexbox equally as long as the width of the flexbox is 400 pixels or greater.

```
div {
    display: flex;
    flex-wrap: nowrap;
}
```

```
div #item1 {
    flex-basis: 200px;
    flex-grow: 1;
    flex-shrink: 3;
}
div #item2 {
    flex-basis: 200px;
    flex-grow: 1;
    flex-shrink: 1;

}
```

However, once the flexbox falls below 400 pixels, the two items begin to shrink with item1 losing 3 pixels for every 1 pixel lost by item2. Note that if the `flex-shrink` value is set to 0, then the flex item will not shrink below its basis value, making that basis value the minimum width or height of the item.

The flex Property

All of the size values described above are usually combined into the following `flex` property

```
flex: grow shrink basis;
```

where *grow* defines the growth of the flex item, *shrink* provides its shrink rate, and *basis* sets the item's initial size. The default `flex` value is

```
flex: 0 1 auto;
```

which automatically sets the size of the flex item to match its content or the value of its `width` and `height` property. The flex item will not grow beyond that size but, if necessary, it will shrink as the flexbox contracts.

The `flex` property supports the following keywords:

- `auto`   Use to automatically resize the item from its default size (equivalent to `flex: 1 1 auto;`)
- `initial` The default value (equivalent to `flex: 0 1 auto;`)
- `none`   Use to create an inflexible item that will not grow or shrink (equivalent to `flex: 0 0 auto;`)
- `inherit` Use to inherit the flex values of its parent element

As with other parts of the flex layout model, the `flex` property has gone through several syntax changes on its way to its final specification. To support older browsers, use the browser extensions: `-webkit-box`, `-moz-box`, `-ms-flexbox`, `-webkit-flex`, and `flex` in that order.

Sizing Flex Items

- To set the initial size of a flex item, apply the style

  ```
  flex-basis: size;
  ```

  where *size* is measured in one of the CSS units of measurement or as a percentage of the size of the flexbox or the keyword `auto` (the default).
- To define the rate at which a flex item grows from its basis size, apply the style

  ```
  flex-grow: value;
  ```

  where *value* is a non-negative value that expresses the growth of the flex item relative to the growth of the other items in the flexbox (the default is 0).
- To define the rate at which a flex item shrinks below its basis value, apply

  ```
  flex-shrink: value;
  ```

  where *value* is a non-negative value that expresses the shrink rate of the flex item relative to other items in the flexbox (the default is 0).
- To define the overall resizing of a flex item, apply

  ```
  flex: grow shrink basis;
  ```

  where *grow* defines the growth of the flex item, *shrink* provides its shrink rate, and *basis* sets the item's initial size.

Applying a Flexbox Layout

Now that you've seen how to size items within a flexbox, you can return to the layout for the Pre-K Classes page at Trusted Friends daycare. The `body` element, which you already set up as a flexbox, has four child elements: the page header, an `aside` element describing the daily class schedule, a `section` element describing the classes, and the page footer. Marjorie wants the header and the footer to always occupy a single row at 100% of the width of the page body. For wide screens, she wants the `aside` and `section` elements displayed side-by-side with one-fourth of the width assigned to the `aside` element and three-fourths to the `section` element. For narrow screens she wants the `aside` and `section` elements displayed within a single column. Figure 5-31 displays the flex layout that Marjorie wants you to apply.

Figure 5-31   **Proposed flex layout for the Pre-K page**

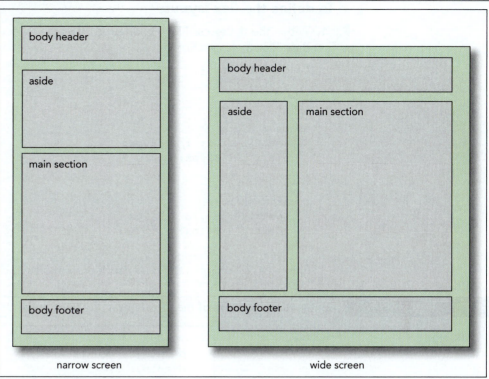

narrow screen   wide screen

© 2016 Cengage Learning

Using the techniques of the first session, this would require media queries with one grid layout for narrow screens and a second grid layout for wide screens. However, you can accomplish the same effect with a single flex layout. First, you set the width of the body header and footer to 100% because they will always occupy their own row:

```
header, footer {
    width: 100%;
}
```

Then, you set the basis size of the `aside` and `section` elements to 120 and 361 pixels respectively. As long as the screen width is 481 pixels or greater, these two elements will be displayed side-by-side; however, once the screen width drops below 481 pixels, the elements will wrap to separate rows as illustrated in the narrow screen image in Figure 5-31. Because you want the main `section` element to grow at a rate three times faster than the `aside` element (in order to maintain the 3:1 ratio in their sizes), you set the `flex-growth` values to 1 and 3 respectively. The flex style rules are

```
aside {
    flex: 1 1 120px;
}

section#main {
    flex: 3 1 361px;
}
```

Note that you choose 481 pixels as the total initial size of the two elements to match the cutoff point in the media query between mobile and tablet/desktop devices. Generally, you want your flex items to follow the media query cutoffs whenever possible. Add these style rules to the tf_flex.css style sheet now.

To define the flex layout:

1. Within the tf_flex.css file in your editor, add the following style rules to the Base Flex Styles section:

```css
header, footer {
    width: 100%;
}

aside {
    -webkit-flex: 1 1 120px;
    flex: 1 1 120px;
}

section#main {
    -webkit-flex: 3 1 361px;
    flex: 3 1 361px;
}
```

Figure 5-32 highlights the newly added style rules to define the flex item sizes.

Figure 5-32   **Set the flex properties of the flex items in the page body**

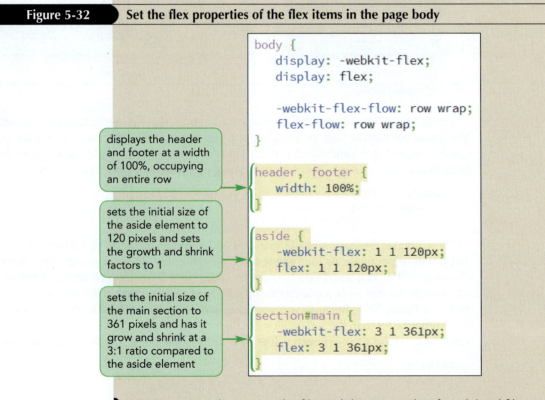

2. Save your changes to the file and then open the tf_prek.html file in your web browser.

3. Change the size of the browser window or use the device emulator tools in your browser to view the page under different screen widths. As shown in Figure 5-33, the layout of the page changes as the screen narrows and widens.

Figure 5-33   **Flex layout under different screen widths**

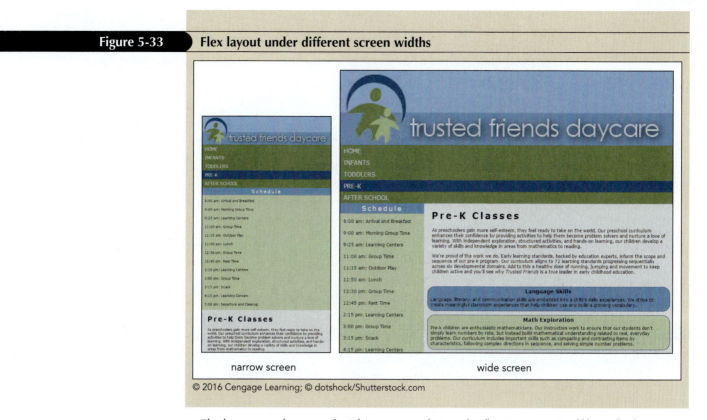

narrow screen   wide screen

© 2016 Cengage Learning; © dotshock/Shutterstock.com

Flexboxes can be nested within one another and a flex item can itself be a flexbox for its child elements. Within the topics section, Marjorie has created six articles describing different features of the center's pre-k curriculum. She wants these articles to share equal space within a row-oriented flexbox, with each article given a basis size of 200 pixels. The style rules are:

```
section#topics {
   display: flex;
   flex-flow: row wrap;
}

section#topics article {
   flex: 1 1 200px;
}
```

Marjorie also wants the items in the navigation list to appear in a row-oriented flexbox for tablet and desktop devices by adding the following style rules to the media query for screen devices whose width exceeds 480 pixels:

```
nav.horizontal ul {
   display: flex;
   flex-flow: row nowrap;
}

nav.horizontal li {
   flex: 1 1 auto;
}
```

The navigation list items will appear in a single row with no wrapping and the width of each item will be determined by the item's content so that longer entries are given more horizontal space. With the growth and shrink values set to 1, each list item will grow and shrink at the same rate, keeping the layout consistent across different screen widths.

Add these style rules now.

To lay out the topic articles and navigation list:

1. Return to the **tf_flex.css** file in your editor and go to the Base Flex Styles section.

2. Add the following style rules to create a flex layout for the page articles.

```css
section#topics {
    display: -webkit-flex;
    display: flex;
    -webkit-flex-flow: row wrap;
    flex-flow: row wrap;
}

section#topics article {
    -webkit-flex: 1 1 200px;
    flex: 1 1 200px;
}
```

Figure 5-34 highlights the style rules for the article topics layout.

Figure 5-34   **Creating a flex layout for articles in the topics section**

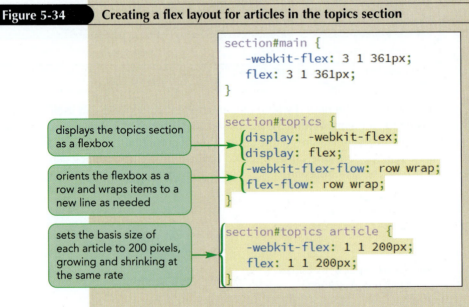

displays the topics section as a flexbox

orients the flexbox as a row and wraps items to a new line as needed

sets the basis size of each article to 200 pixels, growing and shrinking at the same rate

```css
section#main {
    -webkit-flex: 3 1 361px;
    flex: 3 1 361px;
}

section#topics {
    display: -webkit-flex;
    display: flex;
    -webkit-flex-flow: row wrap;
    flex-flow: row wrap;
}

section#topics article {
    -webkit-flex: 1 1 200px;
    flex: 1 1 200px;
}
```

3. Scroll down to the media query for tablet and desktop devices and add the following style rule to create a flex layout for the navigation list. (Indent your code to set it off from the media query braces.)

```css
nav.horizontal ul {
    display: -webkit-flex;
    display: flex;
    -webkit-flex-flow: row nowrap;
    flex-flow: row nowrap;
}

nav.horizontal li {
    -webkit-flex: 1 1 auto;
    flex: 1 1 auto;
}
```

Figure 5-35 highlights the style rules for the navigation list and list items.

Figure 5-35   **Creating a flex layout for the navigation list**

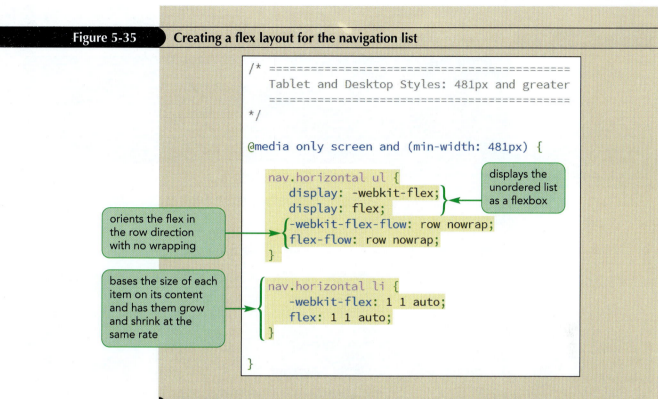

```
/* ============================================
   Tablet and Desktop Styles: 481px and greater
   ============================================
*/

@media only screen and (min-width: 481px) {

   nav.horizontal ul {
      display: -webkit-flex;
      display: flex;
      -webkit-flex-flow: row nowrap;
      flex-flow: row nowrap;
   }

   nav.horizontal li {
      -webkit-flex: 1 1 auto;
      flex: 1 1 auto;
   }

}
```

displays the unordered list as a flexbox

orients the flex in the row direction with no wrapping

bases the size of each item on its content and has them grow and shrink at the same rate

4. Save your changes to the file and reload the **tf_prek.html** file in your web browser.

5. View the page under different screen widths and verify that, for tablet and desktop screen widths, the navigation list entries appear in a single row. Also, verify that the articles in the topics section flex from a single column layout to two or more rows of content. See Figure 5-36.

navigation list appears in a single row for tablet and desktop devices

articles flex in layout from a single column to a 2 × 3 grid, depending on the screen width

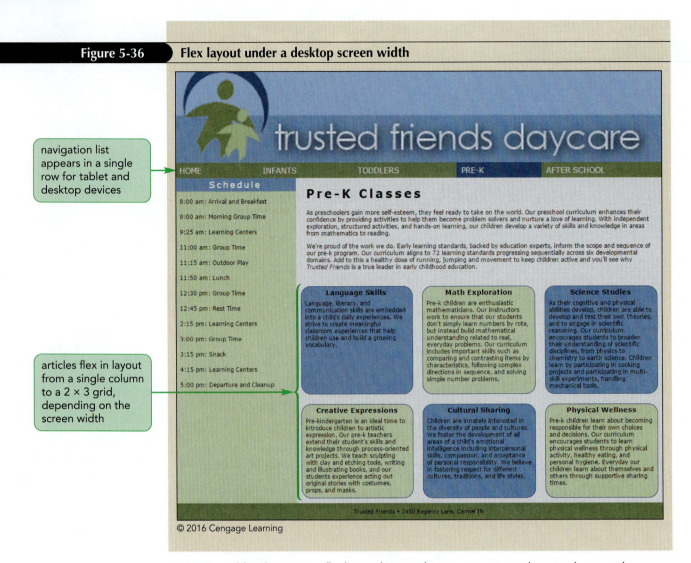

© 2016 Cengage Learning

Marjorie likes how using flexboxes has made it easy to create layouts that match a wide variety of screen sizes. However, she is concerned that under the single column layout used for mobile devices the daily schedule appears first before any description of the classes. She would like the daily schedule to appear at the bottom of the page. She asks if you can modify the layout to achieve this.

Reordering Page Content with Flexboxes

One of the principles of web page design is to, as much as possible, separate the page content from page design. However, a basic feature of any design is the order in which the content is displayed. Short of editing the content of the HTML file, there is not an easy way to change that order.

That at least was true before flexboxes. Under the flexbox model you can place the flex items in any order you choose using the following `order` property

    order: *value*;

where *value* is an integer where items with smaller `order` values are placed before items with larger `order` values. For example, the following style arranges the `div` elements starting first with item2, followed by item3, and ending with item1. This is true regardless of how those `div` elements have been placed in the HTML document.

```
div#item1 {order: 100;}
div#item2 {order: -1;}
div#item3 {order: 5;}
```

TIP

If flex items have the same order value, they are arranged in document order.

Note that order values can be negative. The default order value is 0.

For complete cross-browser support, you can apply the following browser extensions with flex item ordering:

```
-webkit-box-ordinal-group: value;
-moz-box-ordinal-group: value;
-ms-flex-order: value;
-webkit-order: value;
order: value;
```

Most current browsers support the CSS specifications or the latest WebKit browser extension, so you will limit your code to those properties.

REFERENCE

Reordering a Flex Item

- To reorder a flex item, apply the style

  `order: value;`

  where `value` is an integer where items with smaller `order` values are placed before items with larger `order` values.

For mobile devices, Marjorie wants the page header displayed first, followed by the main section, the `aside` element, and ending with the page footer. Add style rules now to the mobile device media query in the tf_flex.css style sheet to reorder the flex items.

To lay out the topic articles and navigation list:

1. Return to the **tf_flex.css** file in your editor and go to the Mobile Devices media query.

2. Add the following style rules, indented to offset them from the braces in the media query:

```
aside {
   -webkit-order: 99;
   order: 99;
}

footer {
   -webkit-order: 100;
   order: 100;
}
```

Note that the other flex items will have a default order value of 0 and thus will be displayed in document order before the `aside` and `footer` elements.

Figure 5-37 highlights the style rules to set the order of the `aside` and `footer` elements.

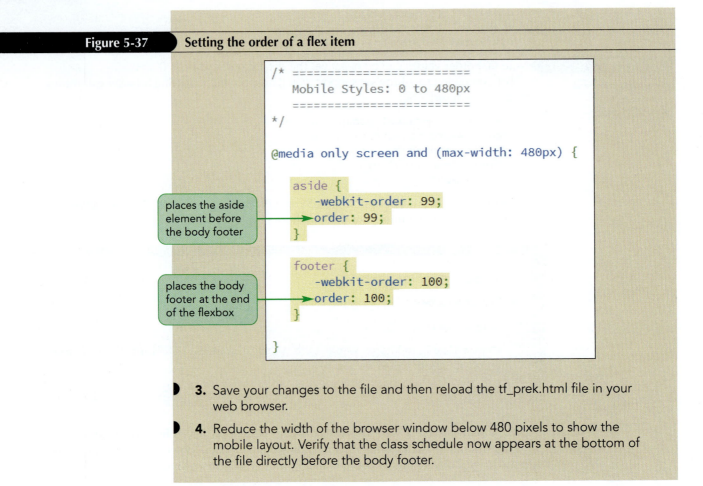

Figure 5-37   Setting the order of a flex item

```
/* ============================
     Mobile Styles: 0 to 480px
   ============================
*/

@media only screen and (max-width: 480px) {

    aside {
        -webkit-order: 99;
        order: 99;
    }

    footer {
        -webkit-order: 100;
        order: 100;
    }

}
```

places the aside element before the body footer → (points to `order: 99;`)

places the body footer at the end of the flexbox → (points to `order: 100;`)

> **3.** Save your changes to the file and then reload the tf_prek.html file in your web browser.

> **4.** Reduce the width of the browser window below 480 pixels to show the mobile layout. Verify that the class schedule now appears at the bottom of the file directly before the body footer.

You've completed the ordering and flex layout of the Pre-K Classes page. You'll conclude your review of flexboxes by examining how flex items can be arranged within the flexbox container.

Exploring Flexbox Layouts

You can control how flex items are laid out using the `justify-content`, `align-items`, and `align-content` properties. You examine each property to see how flexboxes can be used to solve layout problems that have plagued web designers for many years.

Aligning Items along the Main Axis

Recall from Figure 5-26 that flexboxes have two axes: the main axis along which the flex items flow and the cross axis, which is perpendicular to the main axis. By default, flex items are laid down at the start of the main axis. To specify a different placement, apply the following `justify-content` property

```
justify-content: placement;
```

where *placement* is one of the following keywords:

- `flex-start`   Items are positioned at the start of the main axis (the default).
- `flex-end`   Items are positioned at the end of the main axis.
- `center`   Items are centered along the main axis.

- `space-between`   Items are distributed evenly with the first and last items aligned with the start and end of the main axis.
- `space-around`   Items are distributed evenly along the main axis with equal space between them and the ends of the flexbox.

Figure 5-38 shows the impact of different `justify-content` values on a flexbox oriented horizontally.

Figure 5-38   **Values of the justify-content property**

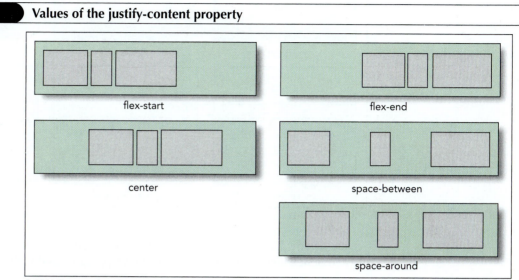

© 2016 Cengage Learning

Remember that, because items can flow in any direction within a flexbox, these diagrams will look different for flexboxes under column orientation or when the content flows from the right to the left. Note that the `justify-content` property has no impact when the items are flexed to fill the entire space. It is only impactful for flex items with fixed sizes that do not fill in the entire flexbox.

Aligning Flex Lines

The `align-content` property is similar to the `justify-content` property except that it arranges multiple lines of content along the flexbox's cross axis. The syntax of the `align-content` property is:

    align-content: value;

where `value` is one of the following keywords:

- `flex-start`   Lines are positioned at the start of the cross axis.
- `flex-end`   Lines are positioned at the end of the cross axis.
- `stretch`   Lines are stretched to fill up the cross axis (the default).
- `center`   Lines are centered along the cross axis.
- `space-between`   Lines are distributed evenly with the first and last lines aligned with the start and end of the cross axis.
- `space-around`   Lines are distributed evenly along the cross axis with equal space between them and the ends of the cross axis.

Figure 5-39 displays the effect of the `align-content` values on three lines of flex items arranged within a flexbox.

Figure 5-39 **Values of the align-content property**

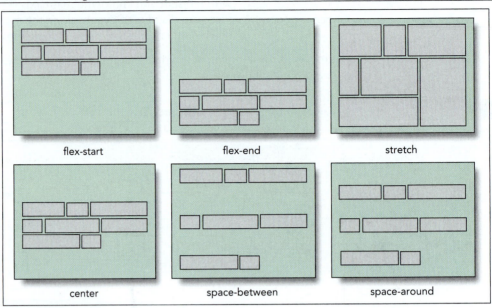

© 2016 Cengage Learning

Note that the `align-content` property only has an impact when there is more than one line of flex items, such as occurs when wrapping is used with the flexbox.

Aligning Items along the Cross Axis

Finally, the `align-items` property aligns each flex item about the cross axis, having the syntax

```
align-items: value;
```

where *value* is one of the following keywords:

- `flex-start` Items are positioned at the start of the cross axis.
- `flex-end` Items are positioned at the end of the cross axis.
- `center` Items are centered along the cross axis.
- `stretch` Items are stretched to fill up the cross axis (the default).
- `baseline` Items are positioned so that the baselines of their content align.

Figure 5-40 displays the effect of the `align-items` values on three flex items placed within a single line.

Figure 5-40	Values of the align-items property

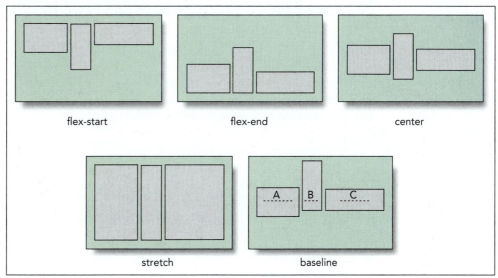

© 2016 Cengage Learning

Note that the `align-items` property is only impactful when there is a single line of flex items. With multiple lines, you use the `align-content` property to layout the flexbox content. To align a single item out of a line of flex items, use the following `align-self` property

```
align-self: value;
```

where `value` is one of the alignment choices supported by the `align-items` property. For example, the following style rule places the footer at the end of the flexbox cross axis, regardless of the placement of the other flex items.

```
footer {
    align-self: flex-end;
}
```

Both the `align-content` and `align-items` properties have a default value of `stretch` so that the flex items are stretched to fill the space along the cross-axis. The effect is that all flex items within a row will share a common height. This can be observed earlier in Figure 5-36 in which all of the article boxes have the same height, regardless of their content. It's difficult to achieve this simple effect in a grid layout unless the height of each item is explicitly defined, but flexboxes do it automatically.

INSIGHT

Solving the Centering Problem with Flexboxes

One of the difficult layout challenges in web design is vertically centering an element within its container. While there are many different fixes and "hacks" to create vertical centering, it has not been easily achieved until flexboxes. By using the `justify-content` and `align-items` properties, you can center an object or group of objects within a flexbox container. For example, the following style rule centers the child elements of the `div` element both horizontally and vertically:

```
div {
    display: flex;
    justify-content: center;
    align-content: center;
}
```

For a single object or a group of items on a single line within a container, use the `align-items` property as follows:

```
div {
    display: flex;
    justify-content: center;
    align-items: center;
}
```

You can also use the `align-self` property to center one of the items in the flexbox, leaving the other items to be placed where you wish.

Creating a Navicon Menu

A common technique for mobile websites is to hide navigation menus but to indicate their presence with a **navicon**, which is a symbol usually represented as three horizontal lines ≡. When the user hovers or touches the icon, the navigation menu is revealed.

Marjorie has supplied you with a navicon image that she wants you to use with the mobile layout of the Pre-K Classes page. Add this image to the Pre-K Classes web page within the navigation list in the body header.

To insert the navicon image:

1. Return to the **tf_prek.html** file in your editor.

2. Directly after the opening `<nav>` tag in the body header, insert the following hypertext link and inline image.

```
<a id="navicon" href="#">
   <img src="tf_navicon.png" alt="" />
</a>
```

Figure 5-41 highlights the code to create the navicon.

| Figure 5-41 | Inserting the navicon |

```
<nav class="horizontal">
   <a id="navicon" href="#"><img src="tf_navicon.png" alt="" /></a>
   <ul>
      <li><a href="tf_home.html">Home</a></li>
      <li><a href="#">Infants</a></li>
      <li><a href="#">Toddlers</a></li>
      <li><a href="#" id="currentPage">Pre-K</a></li>
      <li><a href="#">After School</a></li>
   </ul>
</nav>
```

navicon image

Next, you'll insert the styles to hide and display the contents of the navigation list in a style sheet named tf_navicon.css. You'll apply the same styles for navicon that you used in the last session to hide and display the navigation submenus in the Trusted Friends home page. As with those menus, you'll use the hover pseudo-class to display the navigation list links whenever the user hovers over the navicon, or in the case of mobile devices, touches the navicon. Add these styles now.

To add styles for the navicon image:

1. Within the document head of the tf_prek.html file, add a link to the **tf_navicon.css** style sheet file after the link for the tf_flex.css file. Save your changes to the file.

2. Use your editor to open the **tf_navicon_txt.css** files from the html05 ▸ tutorial folder. Enter *your name* and *the date* in the comment section of the file and save it as **tf_navicon.css**.

3. By default, the navicon will be hidden from the user. Go to the Base Styles section and add the following style rule:

   ```
   a#navicon {
      display: none;
   }
   ```

4. The navicon will be displayed only for mobile devices. Go to the media query for mobile devices and add the following style rule to display the navicon.

   ```
   a#navicon {
      display: block;
   }
   ```

5. When the navicon is displayed, you want the contents of the navigation list to be hidden. Add the following style rule within the mobile device media query:

   ```
   nav.horizontal ul {
      display: none;
   }
   ```

6. Finally, add the following style rule to the mobile device query that displays the contents of the navigation list when the user hovers over the navicon or the contents of the navigation list.

   ```
   a#navicon:hover+ul, nav.horizontal ul:hover {
      display: block;
   }
   ```

Figure 5-42 highlights the style rules for the navicon hypertext link.

Figure 5-42   **Style rules for the navicon image**

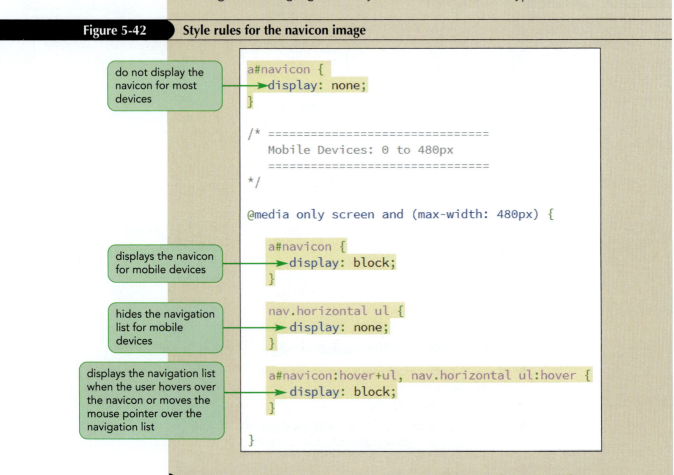

do not display the navicon for most devices

```
a#navicon {
    display: none;
}

/* =================================
   Mobile Devices: 0 to 480px
   =================================
*/

@media only screen and (max-width: 480px) {

    a#navicon {
        display: block;
    }

    nav.horizontal ul {
        display: none;
    }

    a#navicon:hover+ul, nav.horizontal ul:hover {
        display: block;
    }

}
```

displays the navicon for mobile devices

hides the navigation list for mobile devices

displays the navigation list when the user hovers over the navicon or moves the mouse pointer over the navigation list

▶ **7.** Save your changes to the file and then reload the tf_prek.html file in your browser or mobile devices. Resize the viewport as needed to display the mobile layout.

▶ **8.** Verify that as you hover over or touch the navicon, the navigation list appears, as shown in Figure 5-43.

Figure 5-43   **Action of the navicon for mobile devices**

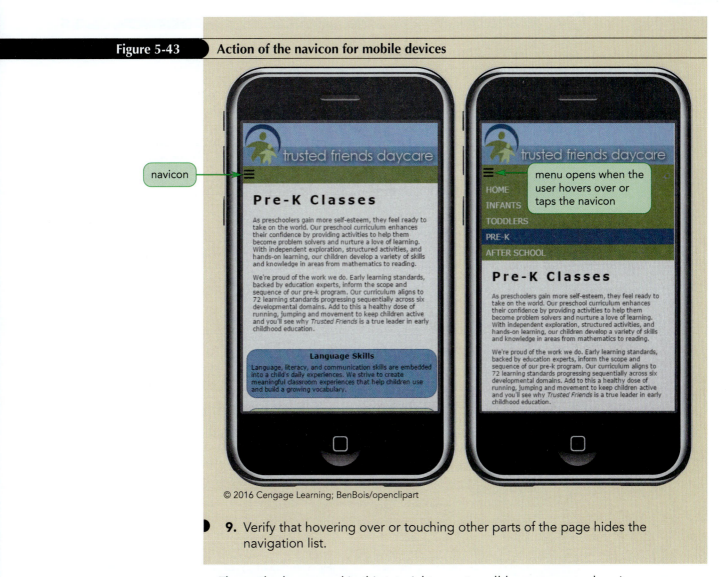

© 2016 Cengage Learning; BenBois/openclipart

> **9.** Verify that hovering over or touching other parts of the page hides the navigation list.

The methods you used in this tutorial to create pulldown menus and navicon menus represent what you can accomplish when limited to CSS3 and the `hover` pseudo-class. As you increase your skill and knowledge of HTML, you'll learn other, more efficient ways of creating mobile navigation menus using program scripts and web frameworks. If you want to explore how to take advantage of these tools, search the web for navicon libraries of pre-written code that can be inserted into your website.

PROSKILLS

Written Communication: Speeding up your Website by Minifying and Compressing

Once your website is working and you are ready to distribute it to the web, you have one task remaining: minifying your code. **Minifying** refers to the process of removing unnecessary characters that are not required for your site to execute properly. For example, the following text in a CSS file contains comments and line returns and blank spaces, which makes the text easy to read but these features are not required and have no impact on how the browser renders the page:

```
/* Tablet Styles */

nav.horizontal > ul > li {
    display: block;
}
```

A minified version of this code removes the comment and the extraneous white-space characters leaving the following compact version:

```
nav.horizontal>ul>li{display:block;}
```

Minifying has several important advantages:

- Minifying reduces the amount of bandwidth required to retrieve the website because the files are smaller.
- The smaller minified files load faster and are faster to process because extraneous code does not need to be parsed by the browser.
- A faster site provides a better user experience.
- Smaller files means less server space required to host the website.
- Search engines, such as Google, evaluate your website based on page load speed and will downgrade sites with bloated code that take too long to load.

There are several free tools available on the web to automate the minification process including CSS Minifier, Compress HTML, HTML Minifier, and CSS Compressor. Also, many HTML editors include built-in minifying tools. Remember, a minified file is still a text file and can be read (though with difficulty) in a text editor.

To further reduce your file sizes, consider compressing your files using utilities like Gzip. A compressed file is no longer in text format and must be uncompressed before it is readable. All modern browsers support Gzip compression for files retrieved from a server. Make sure you know how to properly configure your web server to serve Gzip-compressed file in a readable format to the browser.

The process of minifying your files is irreversible, so make sure you retain the version with the text in a readable format and all of your comments preserved. Most minifying and compression tools will make a backup of your original files.

You've completed your work on the design of the Pre-K Classes page for Trusted Friends Daycare. In the next session, you'll explore other uses of media queries by designing a page for printed output. You may close your files now.

Session 5.2 Quick Check

1. Provide code to display the body header as a flexbox. Include the browser extension for WebKit.
2. Provide a style to display flexbox items in a single line, oriented vertically starting from the bottom and moving up.
3. Provide a style that sets the initial size of a flex item to 250 pixels.
4. Provide a style that sets the growth rate of the flex item to 4.
5. What two things can happen when a flex item drops below its basis size?
6. Provide a style rule that sets the flex size of all `section` elements that are direct children of the page body be equal regardless of the size of the flexbox.
7. What property should be applied to reorder the placement of a flex item?
8. Provide a style to center the flex items along the flexbox's main axis.
9. Provide a style to center the flex items along the flexbox's cross axis.

Session 5.3 Visual Overview:

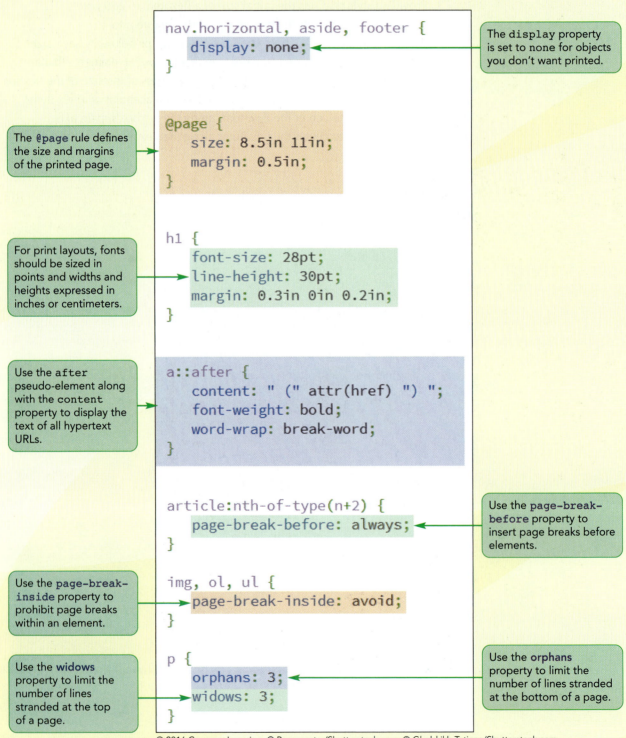

The `display` property is set to none for objects you don't want printed.

The `@page` rule defines the size and margins of the printed page.

For print layouts, fonts should be sized in points and widths and heights expressed in inches or centimeters.

Use the `after` pseudo-element along with the `content` property to display the text of all hypertext URLs.

Use the `page-break-before` property to insert page breaks before elements.

Use the `page-break-inside` property to prohibit page breaks within an element.

Use the `widows` property to limit the number of lines stranded at the top of a page.

Use the `orphans` property to limit the number of lines stranded at the bottom of a page.

```css
nav.horizontal, aside, footer {
    display: none;
}

@page {
    size: 8.5in 11in;
    margin: 0.5in;
}

h1 {
    font-size: 28pt;
    line-height: 30pt;
    margin: 0.3in 0in 0.2in;
}

a::after {
    content: " (" attr(href) ") ";
    font-weight: bold;
    word-wrap: break-word;
}

article:nth-of-type(n+2) {
    page-break-before: always;
}

img, ol, ul {
    page-break-inside: avoid;
}

p {
    orphans: 3;
    widows: 3;
}
```

Print Styles

Page size is set at 8.5 inches by 11 inches with a 0.5 inch margin in portrait orientation.

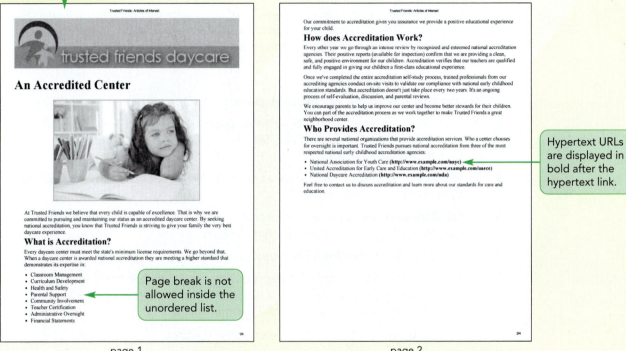

page 1

page 2

Page break is not allowed inside the unordered list.

Hypertext URLs are displayed in bold after the hypertext link.

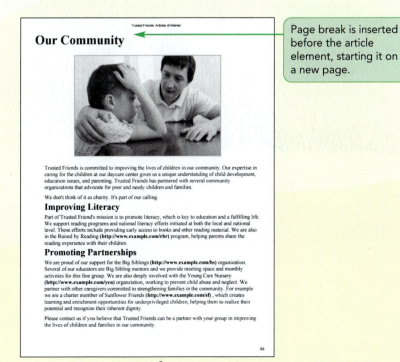

Page break is inserted before the article element, starting it on a new page.

page 3

Designing for Printed Media

So far your media queries have been limited to screens of different widths. In this session you'll explore how to apply media queries to print devices and work with several CSS styles that apply to printed output. To do this you'll create a **print style sheet** that formats the printed version of your web document.

Previewing the Print Version

Marjorie has created a page containing articles of interest for parents at Trusted Friends Daycare. She has already written the page content and the style sheets for mobile, tablet, and desktop devices. Open the articles document now.

To open the Articles of Interest page:

▶ 1. Use your editor to open the **tf_articles_txt.html** file from the html05 ▶ tutorial folder. Enter *your name* and *the date* in the comment section of the file and save it as **tf_articles.html**.

▶ 2. Within the document head, create links to the **tf_reset.css** and **tf_styles3.css** style sheet files in that order.

▶ 3. Scroll through the document to become familiar with its contents and then save your changes to file, but do not close it.

▶ 4. Open the **tf_articles.html** file in your web browser.

▶ 5. Take some time to view the contents of the page under different screen resolutions, noting how Marjorie has used responsive design to create different page layouts based on the screen width.

   Now, you'll examine how Marjorie's page will appear when printed.

▶ 6. Use the Print Preview command within your browser to preview how this page will appear when printed. Figure 5-44 shows a preview of the first two pages of the print version using a black and white printer.

| Figure 5-44 | Print version of the Articles of Interest page |

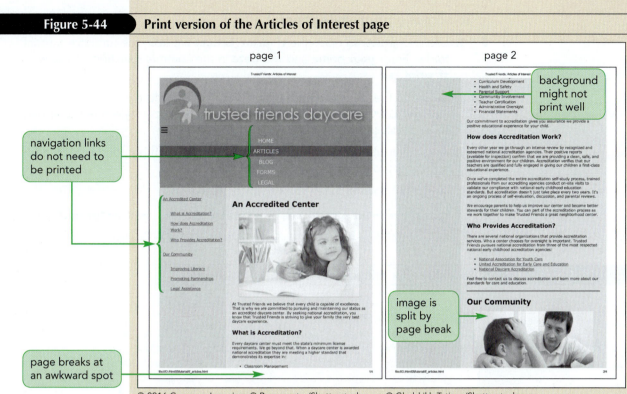

© 2016 Cengage Learning; © Pressmaster/Shutterstock.com; © Gladskikh Tatiana/Shutterstock.com

Trouble? Depending on your browser and printer, your print preview might appear different from the preview shown in Figure 5-44.

Browsers support their own internal style sheet to format the print versions of the web pages they encounter. However, their default styles might not always result in the best printouts. Marjorie points out that the print version of her page has several significant problems:

- The printed version includes two navigation lists, neither of which have a purpose in a printout.
- Page breaks have been placed in awkward places, splitting paragraphs and images in two.
- Background colors, while looking good on a screen, might not print well.

Marjorie would like you to design a custom print style sheet that fixes these problems by removing unnecessary page elements and choosing page breaks more intelligently.

Applying a Media Query for Printed Output

To apply a print style sheet, you use the `media` attribute in your `link` elements to target style sheets to either screen devices or print devices. Modify the tf_articles.html file now to access a new style sheet named tf_print.css into which you include your print styles.

To access a print style sheet:

1. Use your editor to open the **tf_print_txt.css** file from the html05 ▸ tutorial folder. Enter *your name* and *the date* in the comment section and save it as **tf_print.css**.

To avoid mixing screen styles with print styles, identify styles common to both devices with the media type *all*.

2. Return to the **tf_articles.html** file in your editor. Add the attribute **media="all"** to the `link` element for the tf_reset.css style sheet to apply it to all devices.

3. Add the attribute **media="screen"** to the `link` element for the tf_styles3.css style sheet to apply it only to screen devices.

4. Add the following `link` element for print styles:

   `<link href="tf_print.css" rel="stylesheet" media="print" />`

   Figure 5-45 highlights the revised `link` elements in the file.

Figure 5-45   **Style sheets for different devices**

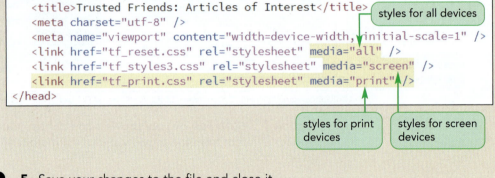

```
<title>Trusted Friends: Articles of Interest</title>
<meta charset="utf-8" />
<meta name="viewport" content="width=device-width, initial-scale=1" />
<link href="tf_reset.css" rel="stylesheet" media="all" />
<link href="tf_styles3.css" rel="stylesheet" media="screen" />
<link href="tf_print.css" rel="stylesheet" media="print" />
</head>
```

styles for all devices

styles for print devices

styles for screen devices

5. Save your changes to the file and close it.

You'll start designing the print version of this page by hiding those page elements that should not be printed, including the navigation list, the `aside` element, and the body footer.

To hide elements in the print version:

1. Return to the **tf_print.css** file in your editor.

2. Go to the Hidden Objects section and add the following style rule:

   ```
   nav.horizontal, aside, footer {
       display: none;
   }
   ```

   Figure 5-46 highlights the style rule to hide page elements.

Figure 5-46 Hiding page elements for printing

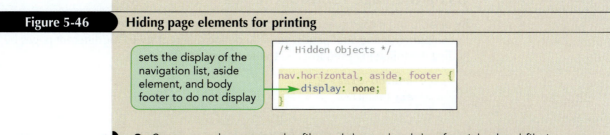

sets the display of the navigation list, aside element, and body footer to do not display

```
/* Hidden Objects */

nav.horizontal, aside, footer {
    display: none;
}
```

3. Save your changes to the file and then reload the tf_articles.html file in your browser and preview the printed output. Verify that the navigation lists, aside elements, and body footer are not displayed in the printed version.

Next, you'll define the page size of the print version of this document.

Working with the @page Rule

In CSS every printed page is defined as a **page box**, composed of two areas: the **page area**, which contains the content of the document, and the **margin area**, which contains the space between the printed content and the edges of the page.

Styles are applied to the page box using the following @page rule

```
@page {
    style rules
}
```

where *styles rules* are the styles applied to the page. The styles are limited to defining the page size and the page margin. For example, the following @page rule sets the size of the page margin to 0.5 inches:

```
@page {
        margin: 0.5in;
}
```

The page box does not support all of the measurement units you've used with the other elements. For example, pages do not support the em or ex measurement units. In general, you should use measurement units that are appropriate to the dimensions of your page, such as inches or centimeters.

Setting the Page Size

Because printed media can vary in size and orientation, the following size property allows web authors to define the dimensions of the printed page:

```
size: width height;
```

TIP

Users can override the page sizes and orientations set in @page rule by changing the options in their print dialog box.

where *width* and *height* are the width and height of the page. Thus to define a page that is 8.5 inches wide by 11 inches tall with a 1-inch margin, you would apply the following style rule:

```
@page {
    size: 8.5in 11in;
    margin: 1in;
}
```

You can replace the width and height values with the keyword auto (to let browsers determine the page dimensions) or inherit (to inherit the page size from the parent element). If a page does not fit into the dimensions specified in the @page rule, browsers will either rotate the page or rescale it to fit within the defined page size.

Using the Page Pseudo-Classes

By default, the @page rule is applied to every page of the printed output. However if the output covers several pages, you can define different styles for different pages by adding the following pseudo-class to the `@page` rule:

```
@page:pseudo-class {
      style rules
}
```

where *pseudo-class* is `first` for the first page of the printout, `left` for the pages that appear on the left in double-sided printouts, or `right` for pages that appear on the right in double-sided printouts. For example, if you are printing on both sides of the paper, you might want to create mirror images of the margins for the left and right pages of the printout. The following styles result in pages in which the inner margin is set to 5 centimeters and the outer margin is set to 2 centimeters:

```
@page:left {margin: 3cm 5cm 3cm 2cm;}
@page:right {margin: 3cm 2cm 3cm 5cm;}
```

Page Names and the Page Property

To define styles for pages other than the first, left, or right, you first must create a page name for those styles as follows

```
@page name {
    style rules
}
```

where *name* is the label given to the page. The following code defines a page style named wideMargins used for pages in which the page margin is set at 10 centimeters on every side:

```
@page wideMargins {
    margin: 10cm;
}
```

Once you define a page name, you can apply it to any element in your document. The content of the element will appear on its own page, with the browser automatically inserting page breaks before and after the element if required. To assign a page name to an element, you use the following `page` property

```
selector {
    page: name;
}
```

where *selector* identifies the element that will be displayed on its own page, and *name* is the name of a previously defined page style. Thus the following style rule causes all block quotes to be displayed on separate page(s) using the styles previously defined as the wideMargins page:

```
blockquote {
    page: wideMargins;
}
```

REFERENCE

Creating and Applying Page Styles

• To define a page box for the printed version of a document, use the CSS rule

```
@page {
    size: width height;
}
```

where *width* and *height* are the width and height of the page.

• To define the page styles for different output pages, use the rule

```
@page:pseudo-class {
    style rules
}
```

where *pseudo-class* is `first` for the first page of the printout, `left` for the pages that appear on the left in double-sided printouts, or `right` for pages that appear on the right in double-sided printouts.

• To create a named page for specific page styles, apply the rule

```
@page name {
    style rules
}
```

where *name* is the label assigned to the page style.

• To apply a named page style, use the rule

```
selector {
    page: name;
}
```

where *selector* identifies the element that will be displayed on its own page, and *name* is the name of a previously defined page style.

You'll use the `@page` rule to define the page size for the printed version of the Articles of Interest document. Marjorie suggests that you set the page size to 8.5 × 11 inches with 0.5-inch margins.

To define the printed page size:

1. Return to the **tf_print.css** file in your editor.

2. Go to the Page Box Styles section and add the following rule:

```
@page {
    size: 8.5in 11in;
    margin: 0.5in;
}
```

Figure 5-47 highlights the rule to set the page size.

Figure 5-47 Setting the page size

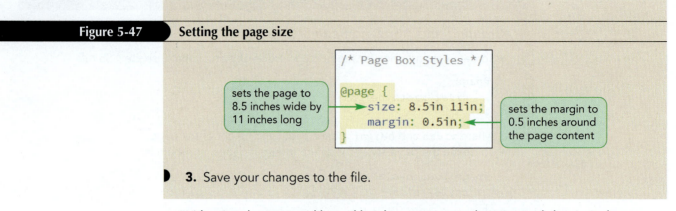

3. Save your changes to the file.

With printed output, widths and heights are measured not in pixels but in inches or centimeters. Font sizes are not measured in pixels but rather in points. With that in mind, create styles to format the sizes of the text and graphics on the page.

To format the printed text:

1. Go to the Typography Styles section and insert the following styles to format the appearance of h1 and h2 headings and paragraphs:

```
h1 {
    font-size: 28pt;
    line-height: 30pt;
    margin: 0.3in 0in 0.2in;
}

h2 {
    font-size: 20pt;
    margin: 0.1in 0in 0.1in 0.3in;
}

p {
    font-size: 12pt;
    margin: 0.1in 0in 0.1in 0.3in;
}
```

2. Within the List Styles section, add the following style rules to format the appearance of unordered lists:

```
ul {
    list-style-type: disc;
    margin-left: 0.5in;
}
```

Figure 5-48 shows the typography and list styles in the print style sheet.

Figure 5-48   **Typographical formats**

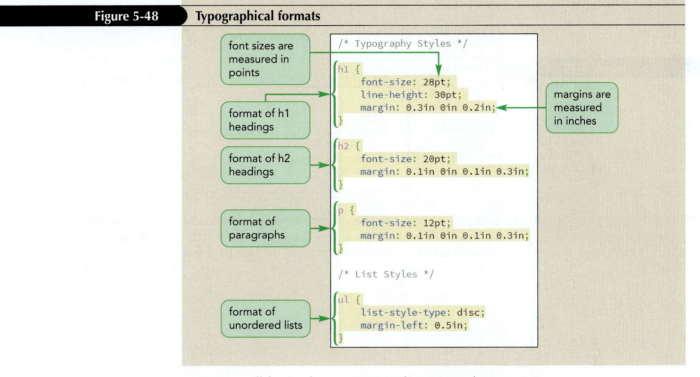

Next, you'll format the appearance of images on the page.

To format the printed images:

1. Within the Image Styles section, add the following style rule to format the appearance of inline images within each `article` element:

```
article img {
    border: 2px solid rgb(191, 191,191);
    display: block;
    margin: 0.25in auto;
    width: 65%;
}
```

Figure 5-49 shows the style rule for inline images on the printed page.

Figure 5-49   **Image formats**

displays all article images with a gray border, with a width of 65% of the page body, and centered horizontally

```
/* Image Styles */

article img {
    border: 2px solid rgb(191, 191, 191);
    display: block;
    margin: 0.25in auto;
    width: 65%;
}
```

2. Save your changes to the style sheet and then reload the tf_articles.html file in your browser and preview the appearance of the printed page. Figure 5-50 shows the appearance of the first page printed using a black and white printer.

Figure 5-50   **Preview of the first printed page**

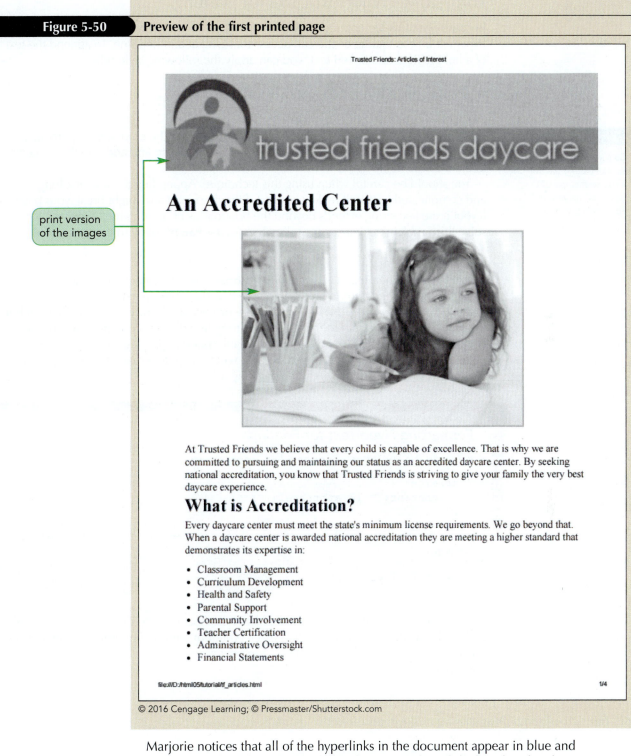

print version of the images

Marjorie notices that all of the hyperlinks in the document appear in blue and underlined as determined by the default browser style. While this identifies the text as a hypertext link, it doesn't provide the reader any information about that link. She asks you to modify the style sheet to fix this problem.

Formatting Hypertext Links for Printing

Because printouts are not interactive, it's more useful for the reader to see the URL of a hypertext link so that he or she can access that URL at another time. To append the text of a link's URL to the linked text, you can apply the following style rule:

```
a::after {
    content: " (" attr(href) ") ";
}
```

This style rule uses the `after` pseudo-element along with the `content` property and the `attr()` function to retrieve the text of the `href` attribute and add it to the contents of the `a` element.

You should be careful when using this technique. Appending the text of a long and complicated URL will make your text difficult to read and might break your page layout if the text string extends beyond the boundaries of its container. One way to solve this problem is to apply the following `word-wrap` property to the URL text:

```
word-wrap: type;
```

where *type* is either `normal` (the default) or `break-word`. A value of `normal` breaks a text string only at common break points such as the white space between words. A value of `break-word` allows long text to be broken at arbitrary points, such as within a word, if that is necessary to make the text string fit within its container. Because a URL has no common break points such as blank spaces, applying the `break-word` option ensures that the text string of the URL will be kept to a manageable length by breaking it as needed to fit within the page layout.

REFERENCE

Formatting Hypertext for Printing

- To add the URL after a hypertext link, apply the style rule:

```
a::after {
    content: " (" attr(href) ") ";
}
```

- To automatically wrap the text of long URLs as needed, add the following style to the link text:

```
word-wrap: break-word;
```

Format the appearance of hypertext links in the document to display each link's URL and to display the hypertext links in a black bold font with no underlining, then use the `word-wrap` property to keep long URLs from extending beyond the boundaries of their container.

To format the hypertext links:

1. Return to the **tf_print.css** file in your editor and go to Hypertext Styles section, inserting the following styles to format the appearance of all hypertext links, appending the URL of each link:

```css
a {
   color: black;
   text-decoration: none;
}

a::after {
   content: " (" attr(href) ") ";
   font-weight: bold;
   word-wrap: break-word;
}
```

Figure 5-51 describes the style rules used to format printed hypertext links.

Figure 5-51   **Formatting printed hypertext links**

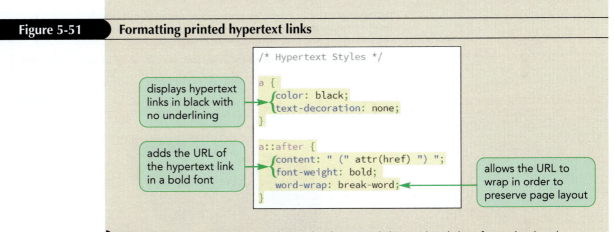

2. Save your changes to the style sheet and then reload the tf_articles.html file in your browser and preview the page printout. Figure 5-52 shows the appearance of the printed hypertext links found on the second page of Marjorie's printout.

Figure 5-52   **Preview of the hypertext links on page 2**

Trusted Friends: Articles of Interest

How does Accreditation Work?

Every other year we go through an intense review by recognized and esteemed national accreditation agencies. Their positive reports (available for inspection) confirm that we are providing a clean, safe, and positive environment for our children. Accreditation verifies that our teachers are qualified and full engaged in giving our children a first-class educational experience.

Once we've completed the entire accreditation self-study process, trained professionals from our accrediting agencies conduct on-site visits to validate our compliance with national early childhood education standards. But accreditation doesn't just take place every two years. It's an ongoing process of self-evaluation, discussion, and parental reviews. We encourage our parents to help us improve our center and become better stewards for their children.

Who Provides Accreditation?

Trusted Friends pursues national accreditation from three of the most respected national early childhood accreditation agencies:

- National Association for Youth Care **(http://www.example.com/nayc)**
- United Accreditation for Early Care and Education **(http://www.example.com/uaece)**
- National Daycare Accreditation **(http://www.example.com/nda)**

Feel free to contact us to discuss accreditation and learn more about our standards for care and education.

URL of each hypertext link

Our Community

Trusted Friends is committed to improving the lives of children in our community. Our expertise in caring for the children at our daycare center gives us a unique understanding of child development, education issues, and parenting. Trusted Friends has partnered with several community organizations that advocate for poor and needy children and families. We don't think of it as charity. It's part of our calling.

2/3

You can search the web for several free scripting tools that give you more options for how your URLs should be printed, including scripts that automatically append all URLs as footnotes at the end of the printed document.

Working with Page Breaks

When a document is sent to a printer, the browser determines the location of the page breaks unless that information is included as part of the print style sheet. To manually insert a page break either directly before or directly after an element, apply the following `page-break-before` or `page-break-after` properties:

```
page-break-before: type;
page-break-after: type;
```

where `type` has the following possible values:

- `always` Use to always place a page break before or after the element
- `avoid` Use to never place a page break
- `left` Use to place a page break where the next page will be a left page
- `right` Use to place a page break where the next page will be a right page
- `auto` Use to allow the printer to determine whether or not to insert a page break
- `inherit` Use to insert the page break style from the parent element

For example, if you want each h1 heading to start on a new page you would apply the following style rule to insert a page break before each heading:

```
h1 {
    page-break-before: always;
}
```

REFERENCE

Adding a Page Break

- To set the page break style directly before an element, apply the property

  ```
  page-break-before: type;
  ```

  where `type` is `always`, `avoid`, `left`, `right`, `auto`, or `inherit`.
- To set the page break style directly after an element, apply

  ```
  page-break-after: type;
  ```

After the first article, Marjorie wants each subsequent article to start on a new page. To select every article after the initial article, use the selector

```
article:nth-of-type(n+2)
```

which selects the second, third, fourth, and so on article elements in the document (see "Exploring the nth-of-type Pseudo-class" in Tutorial 2.) To ensure that each of the selected articles starts on a new page, insert the page break before the article using the following style rule:

```
article:nth-of-type(n+2) {
    page-break-before: always;
}
```

Add this style rule to the print style sheet now.

To print each article on a new page:

1. Go to the Page Break Styles section and insert the following style rule:

   ```
   article:nth-of-type(n+2) {
       page-break-before: always;

   }
   ```

   Figure 5-53 highlights the style rule to insert the article page breaks.

Figure 5-53 Adding page breaks before the document articles

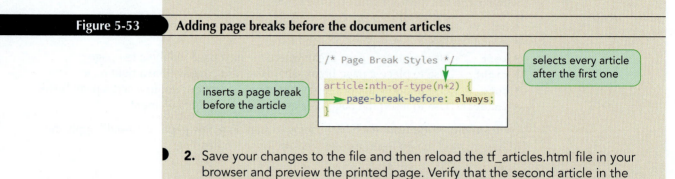

2. Save your changes to the file and then reload the tf_articles.html file in your browser and preview the printed page. Verify that the second article in the document on Community Involvement starts on a new page.

Next, you'll explore how to remove page breaks from the printed version of your web page.

Preventing Page Breaks

You can prevent a page break by using the keyword `avoid` in the `page-break-after` or `page-break-before` properties. For example, the following style rule prevents page breaks from being added after any heading.

```
h1, h2, h3, h4, h5, h6 {
     page-break-after: avoid;
}
```

Unfortunately in actual practice, most current browsers don't reliably support prohibiting page breaks in this fashion. Thus, to prevent page breaks after an element, you will usually have to manually insert a page break before the element so that the element is moved to the top of the next page.

For other print layouts, you will want to prevent page breaks from being placed inside an element. This usually occurs when you have a long string of text that you don't want broken into two pages. You can prevent printers from inserting a page break by using the following `page-break-inside` property

```
page-break-inside: type;
```

where *type* is `auto`, `inherit`, or `avoid`. Thus, to prevent a page break from appearing within any image you can apply the following style rule:

```
img {
    page-break-inside: avoid;
}
```

Unlike the `page-break-before` and `page-break-after` properties, almost all current browsers support the use of the `avoid` keyword for internal page breaks.

Preventing Page Breaks inside an Element

- To prevent a page break from occurring within an element, apply the style:

  ```
  page-break-inside: avoid;
  ```

Marjorie asks you to revise the print style sheet to prevent page breaks from occurring within images, ordered lists, and unordered lists.

To avoid page breaks:

1. Return to the **tf_print.css** file in your editor and go to the Page Break Styles section and insert the following style rule:

   ```
   img, ol, ul {
       page-break-inside: avoid;
   }
   ```

   Figure 5-54 highlights the style rule to avoid page breaks in lists and images.

Figure 5-54   **Avoiding line breaks within lists and images**

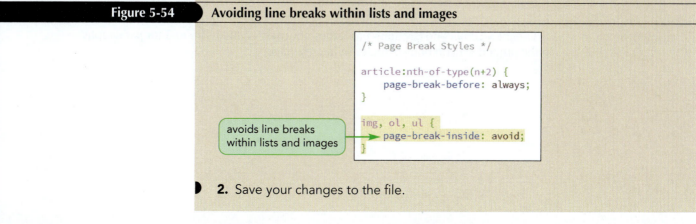

```
/* Page Break Styles */

article:nth-of-type(n+2) {
    page-break-before: always;
}

img, ol, ul {
    page-break-inside: avoid;
}
```

avoids line breaks within lists and images

2. Save your changes to the file.

Note that the `avoid` type does not guarantee that there will never be a page break within the element. If the content of an element exceeds the dimensions of the sheet of paper on which it's being printed, the browser will be forced to insert a page break.

Working with Widows and Orphans

Page breaks within block elements, such as paragraphs, can often leave behind widows and orphans. A widow is a fragment of text left dangling at the top of page, while an orphan is a text fragment left at the bottom of a page. Widows and orphans generally ruin the flow of the page text, making the document difficult to read. To control the size of widows and orphans, CSS supports the following properties:

```
widows: value;
orphans: value;
```

where *value* is the number of lines that must appear within the element before a page break can be inserted by the printer. The default value is 2, which means that a widow or orphan must have at least two lines of text before it can be preceded or followed by a page break.

If you wanted to increase the size of widows and orphans to three lines for the paragraphs in a document, you could apply the style rule

```
p {
    widows: 3;
    orphans: 3;
}
```

and the browser will not insert a page break if fewer than three lines of a paragraph would be stranded at either the top or the bottom of the page.

REFERENCE

Controlling the Size of Widows and Orphans

- To set the minimum size of widows (lines stranded at the top of a page), apply the property

  ```
  widows: value;
  ```

  where *value* is the number of lines that must appear at the top of the page before the page break.
- To set the minimum size of orphans (lines stranded at the bottom of a page), apply the property

  ```
  orphans: value;
  ```

  where *value* is the number of lines that must appear at the bottom of the page before the page break.

Use the `widows` and `orphans` properties now, setting their size to 3 for paragraphs in the printed version of the Articles of Interest page.

To avoid widows and orphans:

1. Within the Page Break Styles section of the tf_print.css file, add the following style rule.

```
p {
    orphans: 3;
    widows: 3;
}
```

Figure 5-55 highlights the style rule for setting the size of widows and orphans.

Figure 5-55 **Setting the size of widows and orphans**

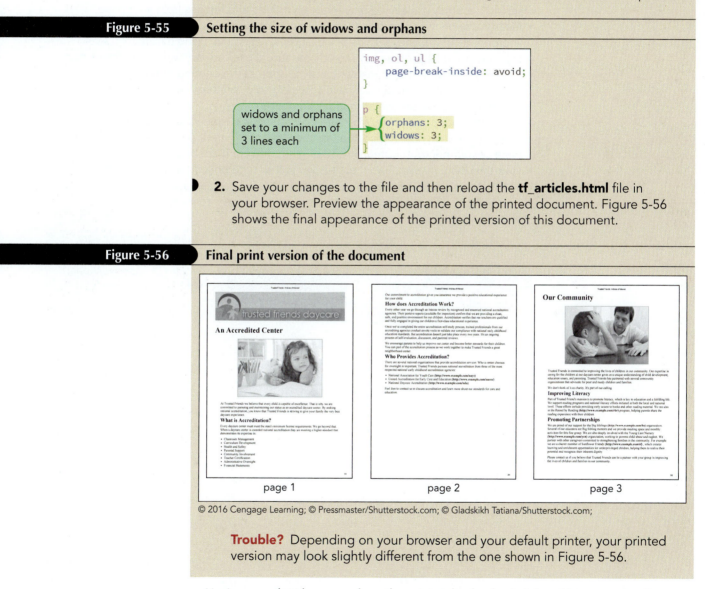

```
img, ol, ul {
    page-break-inside: avoid;
}

p {
    orphans: 3;
    widows: 3;
}
```

widows and orphans set to a minimum of 3 lines each

2. Save your changes to the file and then reload the **tf_articles.html** file in your browser. Preview the appearance of the printed document. Figure 5-56 shows the final appearance of the printed version of this document.

Figure 5-56 **Final print version of the document**

page 1   page 2   page 3

© 2016 Cengage Learning; © Pressmaster/Shutterstock.com; © Gladskikh Tatiana/Shutterstock.com;

Trouble? Depending on your browser and your default printer, your printed version may look slightly different from the one shown in Figure 5-56.

You've completed your work on the print styles for the Articles of Interest page. By modifying the default style sheet, you've created a printout that is easier to read and more useful to the parents and customers of the Trusted Friends Daycare Center.

PROSKILLS

Written Communication: Tips for Effective Printing

One challenge of printing a web page is that what works very well on the screen often fails when transferred to the printed page. For example, some browsers suppress printing background images, so that white text on a dark background, which appears fine on the computer monitor, is unreadable when printed. Following are some tips and guidelines you should keep in mind when designing the printed version of your web page:

- *Remove the clutter.* A printout should contain only information that is of immediate use to the reader. Page elements such as navigation lists, banners, and advertising should be removed, leaving only the main articles and images from your page.
- *Measure for printing.* Use only those measuring units in your style sheet that are appropriate for printing, such as points, inches, centimeters, and millimeters. Avoid expressing widths and heights in pixels because those can vary with printer resolution.
- *Design for white.* Because many browsers suppress the printing of background images and some users do not have access to color printers, create a style sheet that assumes black text on a white background.
- *Avoid absolute positioning.* Absolute positioning is designed for screen output. When printed, an object placed at an absolute position will be displayed on the first page of your printout, potentially making your text unreadable.
- *Give the user a choice.* Some readers will still want to print your web page exactly as it appears on the screen. To accommodate them, you can use one of the many JavaScript tools available on the web that allows readers to switch between your screen and print style sheets.

Finally, a print style sheet is one aspect of web design that works better in theory than in practice. Many browsers provide only partial support for the CSS print styles, so you should always test your designs on a variety of browsers and browser versions. In general, you will have the best results with a basic style sheet rather than one that tries to implement a complicated and involved print layout.

In this tutorial you've learned how to apply different styles to different types of devices and output formats. Marjorie appreciates the work you've done and will continue to rely on your knowledge of media queries, flexible layouts, and print styles as she redesigns the Trusted Friends website. You can close any open files or applications now.

REVIEW

Session 5.3 Quick Check

1. Create a `link` element that loads the myprint.css style sheet file but only for printed output.
2. Create a style rule that sets the size of the page box to 8.5 inches by 11 inches with a 1 inch margin.
3. Create a style rule for right-side pages with a top/bottom margin of 3 centimeters and a left/right margin of 5 centimeters.
4. Create a page style named smallMargins with a margin of 2 centimeters for every side.
5. Apply the smallMargins page style to a `section` element with the id *reviews*.
6. Create a style rule to insert a page break before every `section` element in the document.
7. Create a style rule to stop page breaks from being placed within any header or footer.
8. What style would you apply to allow the browser to wrap long strings of text to a new line whenever needed?
9. Create a style that limits the size of widows and for all `article` elements to 3 lines.

Review Assignments

Data Files needed for the Review Assignments: tf_print2_txt.css, tf_styles4_txt.css, tf_tips_txt.html, 2 CSS files, 4 PNG files

Marjorie meets with you to discuss the redesign of the blog page showing parenting tips. As with the other pages you've worked on, she wants this page to be compatible with mobile devices, tablet and desktop devices, and printers. Marjorie has already written the page content and has done much of the initial design work. She needs you to complete the project by writing media queries for the different display options. Figure 5-57 shows a preview of the mobile design and the desktop design.

Figure 5-57 Parenting Tips page

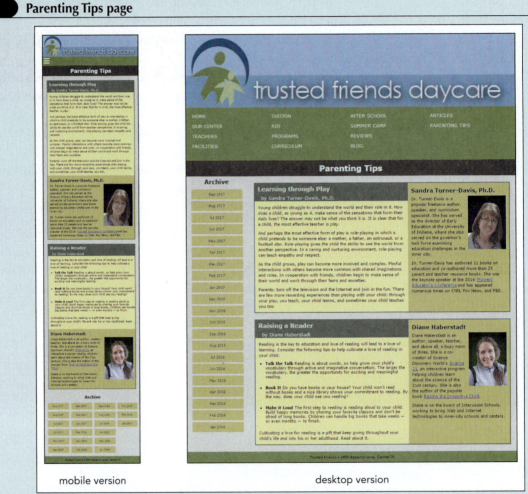

mobile version   desktop version

© 2016 Cengage Learning; © Courtesy Patrick Carey

You'll use several flexboxes to create the layout for these two designs so that the page content automatically rescales as the screen width changes.

Complete the following:

1. Use your HTML editor to open the **tf_tips_txt.html, tf_styles4_txt.css,** and **tf_print2_txt.css** files from the html05 ▸ review folder. Enter *your name* and *the date* in the comment section of each file, and save them as **tf_tips.html, tf_styles4.css,** and **tf_print2.css** respectively.

2. Go to the **tf_tips.html** file in your editor. Add a viewport `meta` tag to the document head to set the width of the layout viewport equal to the width of the device and set the initial scale of the viewport to 1.0.

3. Create links to the following style sheets: a) the tf_base.css file to be used with all devices, b) the tf_styles4.css file to be used with screen devices, and c) the tf_print2.css file to be used for printed output.

4. Take some time to study the contents and structure of the document, paying special attention to the IDs and class names of the elements, and then save your changes.

5. Go to the **tf_styles4.css** file in your editor. Note that Marjorie has placed all of her styles in the tf_designs.css file and imported them into this style sheet. You will not need to edit that style sheet file, but you might want to view it to become familiar with her style rules.

6. Go to the General Flex Styles section. Within this section, you'll create a flexible display layout that varies in response to changing screen widths. Note that when you use the different flex styles be sure you include the latest WebKit browser extension followed by the W3C specification.

7. In the General Flex Styles section create a style rule for the page body that displays the body as a flexbox oriented as a row, wrapping content to a new line as needed.

8. The page content is divided into two `section` elements with IDs of *left* and *right*. The left section does not need as much of the screen width. Create a style rule for the left section that sets its growth and shrink rates to 1 and 8 respectively and sets its basis size to 130 pixels.

9. The right section requires more screen width. Create a style rule for the right section that sets its growth and shrink values to 8 and 1 and sets its basis size to 351 pixels.

10. Next, you'll create a flexbox for the `section` element with class ID of tips that contains an article and a biographical aside, which will be displayed either in two columns or in a single column depending on the screen width. Add a style rule that displays the class of tips section elements as flexboxes in the row direction with wrapping.

11. The articles within each tips section need to occupy more of the screen width. Create a style rule for `article` elements that lays them out as flex items with a growth value of 2, shrink value of 1, and a basis size of 351 pixels.

12. The biographical asides within each tips section need to occupy less screen space. Create a style rule for `aside` elements that lays them out as flex items with a growth value of 1, shrink value of 2, and a basis size of 250 pixels.

13. Finally, the horizontal navigation list at the top of the page will also be treated as a flexbox. Create a style rule for the `ul` element within the horizontal navigation list displaying it as a flexbox in column orientation with wrapping. You do not have to define the sizes of the flex items because the width and height are set in the tf_designs.css style sheet.

14. Go to the Mobile Devices section and create a media query for screen devices with a maximum width of 480 pixels.

15. For mobile devices the vertical list of links to archived parenting tips should be displayed in several columns at the bottom of the page. Within the media query you created in the last step, add the following style rules to

   a. display the `ul` element within the vertical navigation list as a flexbox in column orientation with wrapping. Set the height of the element to 240 pixels.

   b. give the `section` element with an ID of *left* a flex order value of 99 to place it near the bottom of the page.

   c. give the body footer an order value of 100 to put it at the page bottom.

16. Marjorie wants to hide the navigation list at the top of the page when viewed on a mobile device unless the user hovers (or taps) a navicon. Using the technique shown in this tutorial, add the following style rules to set the behavior of the navicon within the media query for mobile devices:

   a. Display the navicon by creating a style rule for the `a#navicon` selector to display it as a block.

   b. Hide the contents of the navigation list by adding a style rule that sets the display of the `ul` element within the horizontal navigation list to `none`.

c. Display the navigation list contents in response to a hover or touch by creating a style rule for the `a#navicon:hover+ul, nav.horizontal ul:hover` selector that sets its display value to `block`.

17. Go to the Tablets and Desktop Devices section. Create a media query for screen devices with a width of at least 481 pixels. Under the wider screens, the contents of the horizontal navigation list at the top of the page should be displayed in several columns. In order to have the list items wrap to a new column, add a style rule to the media query that sets the height of the `ul` element within the horizontal navigation list to 160 pixels.

18. Save your changes to the style sheet and then open the **tf_tips.html** file in your browser or device emulator. Verify that as you change the screen width the layout of the page automatically changes to match the layout designs shown in Figure 5-57.

   Next, you'll create the print styles for the Parenting Tips page. Figure 5-58 shows a preview of the output on a black and white printer.

Figure 5-58   Parenting Tips print version

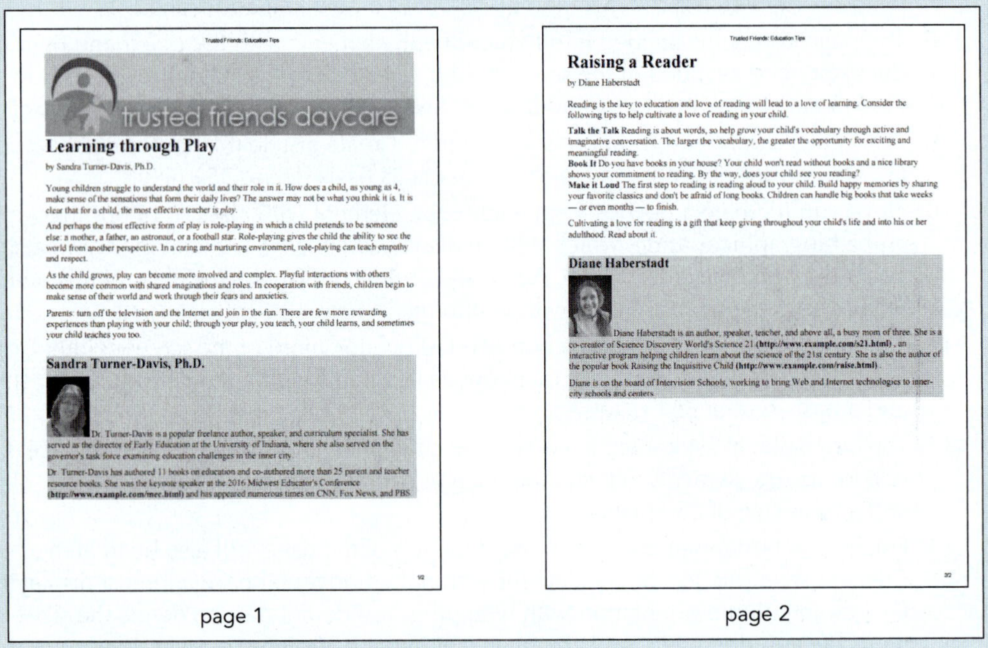

page 1   page 2

© 2016 Cengage Learning; © Courtesy Patrick Carey

19. Go to the **tf_print2.css** file in your editor. Go to the Hidden Objects section and hide the display of the following page elements: all navigation lists, the h1 heading in the body header, the left section element, and the body footer.

20. Go to the Page Box Styles section and set the page size to 8.5 inches by 11 inches with a margin of 0.5 inches.

21. Go the Header Styles section and add a style rule that displays the logo image as a block with a width of 100%.

22. Go to the Typography Styles section and add the following style rules for the text in the printed pages:
   a. For headers within the `article` element, set the bottom margin to 0.2 inches.
   b. For h1 headings within the `article` element, set the font size to 24 points and the line height to 26 points.
   c. For the `aside` element, set the background color to rgb(211, 211, 211) and add a top margin of 0.3 inches.

d. For h1 headings in `aside` elements, set the font size to 18 points and the line height to 20 points.

e. For images within `aside` elements, set the width to 0.8 inches.

f. For paragraphs, set the font size to 12 points with a top and bottom margin of 0.1 inches.

23. Go to the Hypertext Styles section and add style rules to display all hypertext links in black with no underline. Also, insert a style rule that adds the text of the URL after the hypertext link in bold with the `word-wrap` property set to break-word.

24. Go to the Page Break Styles section and add the following style rules to

a. insert page breaks after every `aside` element.

b. never allow a page break within an `ol`, `ul`, or `img` element.

c. set the size of widows and orphans within paragraphs to 3 lines each.

25. Save your changes to the file.

26. Reload the **tf_tips.html** file in your browser and preview its printed version. Verify that your pages resemble those shown in Figure 5-58 (there may be differences depending on your browser and your printer).

Case Problem 1

APPLY

Data Files needed for this Case Problem: gp_cover_txt.html, gp_page1_txt.html, gp_page2_txt.html, gp_page3_txt.html, gp_layout_txt.css, gp_print_txt.css, 2 CSS files, 21 PNG files

Golden Pulps   Devan Ryan manages the website *Golden Pulps*, where he shares tips on collecting and fun stories from the "golden age of comic books"—a period of time covering 1938 through the early 1950s. Devan wants to provide online versions of several classic comic books, which are now in the public domain.

He's scanned the images from the golden age comic book, *America's Greatest Comics 001*, published in March, 1941 by Fawcett Comics and featuring Captain Marvel. He's written the code for the HTML file and wants you to help him develop a layout design that will be compatible with mobile and desktop devices. Figure 5-59 shows a preview of the mobile and desktop version of a page you'll create.

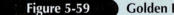

Figure 5-59	Golden Pulps sample page

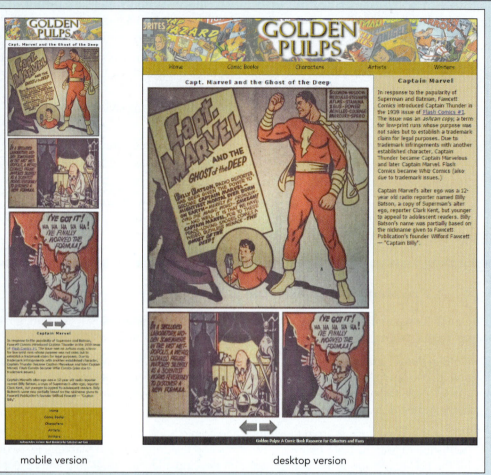

mobile version   desktop version

© 2016 Cengage Learning; © Courtesy Patrick Carey; Source: Comic Book Plus

Complete the following:

1. Using your editor, open the **gp_cover_txt.html, gp_page1_txt.html, gp_page2_txt.html, gp_page3_txt.html, gp_layout_txt.css,** and **gp_print_txt.css** files from the html05 ► case1 folder. Enter *your name* and *the date* in the comment section of each file, and save them as **gp_cover.html, gp_page1.html, gp_page2.html, gp_page3.html, gp_layout.css,** and **gp_print.css** respectively.

2. Go to the **gp_cover.html** file in your editor. Add a viewport `meta` tag to the document head, setting the width of the layout viewport to the device width and setting the initial scale of the viewport to 1.0.

3. Create links to the following style sheets: a) the gp_reset.css file to be used with all devices, b) the gp_layout.css file to be used with screen devices, and c) the gp_print.css file to be used for printed output.

4. Take some time to study the contents and structure of the file. Note each panel from the comic book is stored as a separate inline image with the class name *panel* along with class names of *size1* to *size4* indicating the size of the panel. Size1 is the largest panel down to size4, which is the smallest panel. Close the file, saving your changes.

5. Repeat Steps 2 through 4 for the gp_page1.html, gp_page2.html, and gp_page3.html files.

6. Go to the **gp_layout.css** file in your editor. In this style sheet, you'll create the layout styles for mobile and desktop devices. Note that Devan has used the `@import` rule to import the gp_designs.css file, which contains several graphical and typographical style rules.

7. Go to the Flex Layout Styles section and insert a style rule to display the page body as a flexbox oriented as rows with wrapping. As always, include the latest WebKit browser extension in all of your flex styles.

8. The page body content has two main elements. The `section` element with the ID *sheet* contains the panels from the comic book page. The `article` element contains information about the comic book industry during the Golden Age. Devan wants more of the page width to be given to the comic book sheet. Add a style rule that sets the growth and shrink rate of the sheet section to 3 and 1 respectively and set its basis size to 301 pixels.

9. Less page width will be given to the `article` element. Create a style rule to set its flex growth and shrink values to 1 and 3 respectively and set its basis size to 180 pixels.

10. Go to the Mobile Devices section and create a media query for screen devices with a maximum width of 480 pixels.

11. With mobile devices, Devan wants each comic book panel image to occupy a single row. Create a style rule that sets the width of images belonging to the panel class to 100%.

12. For mobile devices, Devan wants the horizontal navigation links to other pages on the Golden Pulps website to be displayed near the bottom of the page. Within the media query, set the flex order of the horizontal navigation list to 99.

13. Create a style rule to set the flex order of the body footer to 100. (Hint: There are two `footer` elements in the document, use a selector that selects the `footer` element that is a direct child of the `body` element.)

14. Go to the Tablet and Desktop Devices: Greater than 480 pixels section and create a media query that matches screen devices with widths greater than 480 pixels.

15. For tablet and desktop devices, you'll lay out the horizontal navigation list as a single row of links. Within the media query, create a style rule that displays the `ul` element within the horizontal navigation list as a flexbox, oriented in the row direction with no wrapping. Set the height of the element to 40 pixels.

16. For each `li` element within the `ul` element of the horizontal navigation list set their growth, shrink, and basis size values to 1, 1, and `auto` respectively so that each list items grows and shrinks at the same rate.

17. With wider screens, Devan does not want the panels to occupy their own rows as is the case with mobile devices. Instead, within the media query create style rules, define the width of the different classes of comic book panel images as follows:
    a. Set the width of size1 `img` elements to 100%.
    b. Set the width of size2 `img` elements to 60%.
    c. Set the width of size3 `img` elements to 40%.
    d. Set the width of size4 `img` elements to 30%.

18. Save your changes to the file and then open the **gp_cover.html** file in your browser or device emulator. Click the navigation links to view the contents of the cover and first three pages. Verify that with a narrow screen the panels occupy their own rows and with a wider screen the sheets are laid out with several panels per row. Further verify that the horizontal navigation list is placed at the bottom of the page for mobile devices.

19. Devan also wants a print style that displays each comic book sheet on its own page and with none of the navigation links. Go to the **gp_print.css** style sheet in your editor. Add style rules to
    a. hide the `nav`, `footer`, and `article` elements.
    b. set the width of the `section` element with the ID *sheet* to 6 inches. Set the top/bottom margin of that element to 0 inches and the left/right margin to `auto` in order to center it within the printed page.
    c. set the width of size1 images to 5 inches, size2 images to 3 inches, size3 images to 2 inches, and size4 images to 1.5 inches.

20. Save your changes to the file and then reload the contents of the comic book pages in your browser and preview the printed pages. Verify that the printed page displays only the website logo, the name of the comic book, and the comic book panels.

APPLY

Case Problem 2

Data Files needed for this Case Problem: wc_styles_txt.css, 2 CSS files, 18 HTML files, 20 PNG files

Willet Creek   Michael Carpenter is an IT manager at the Willet Creek Resort in Ogden, Utah. You've recently been hired to work on the company's website. Many golfers have asked about mobile-friendly versions of the pages describing the Willet Creek golf course so they can easily view information about each hole on their mobile devices when they're out on the course. Michael would like you to use responsive design to create a mobile-friendly style sheet to be used by the pages describing the golf course holes. A preview of the completed design for one of the holes is shown in Figure 5-60.

Figure 5-60	Willet Creek course website

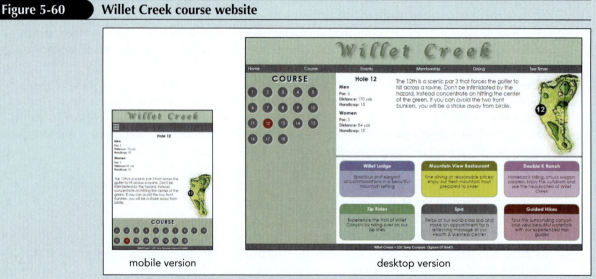

mobile version   desktop version

© 2016 Cengage Learning; © Courtesy Patrick Carey

The work on the HTML code for the 18 pages describing each hole has already been completed for you. Your job will be to write the style sheet that employs the techniques of responsive design.

Complete the following:

1. Using your editor, open the **wc_styles_txt.css** file from the html05 ▶ case2 folder. Enter ***your name*** and ***the date*** in the comment section of the file, and save it as **wc_styles.css**.

2. Open the **wc_hole01.html** file in your editor. For this case problem, you do not need to modify any HTML files, but you should take some time to study the contents and structure of this document (the other 17 HTML files have a similar structure). When you're finished studying the file, you may close it without saving any changes you may have inadvertently made.

3. Return to the **wc_styles.css** file in your editor. Use the @import rule to import the style rules from the wc_designs.css file. Write the rule so that the imported style sheet should only be used with screen devices.

4. You'll layout the golf course pages using a flex layout. Go to the Flex Layout Styles section and create a style rule for the page body that displays the body as a flexbox oriented in the row direction with wrapping. As always, include the WebKit browser extension in all of your flex styles.

5. Two of the child elements of the page body are a navigation list with the ID *hole_list* and an article element containing information about the current hole. Add a style rule that sets the flex growth, shrink, and basis size values of the hole_list navigation list to 1, 3, and 140 pixels.

6. Add a style rule that sets the flex growth, shrink, and basis size values of the article element to 3, 1, and 341 pixels.

7. The `article` element contains statistics and a summary about the current hole. Michael also wants this element to be treated as a flexbox. Add to the style rule for the `article` element styles that display the element as a flexbox oriented in the row direction with wrapping.

8. The two items within the `article` element are a `section` element with the ID *stats* and a `section` element with the ID *summary*. Create a style rule for the stats section that sets its flex growth, shrink, and basis values to 1, 4, and 120 pixels.

9. Create a style rule for the summary section that sets its flex growth, shrink, and basis values to 4, 1, and 361 pixels respectively.

10. The `aside` element contains an advertisement for other services offered by the Willet Creek Resort. Add a style rule that displays this element as a flexbox in row orientation with wrapping.

11. Information about individual services are saved in a `div` element within the `aside` element. Michael wants these `div` elements to be laid out with equal flex sizes. Create a style rule for every `div` element within the `aside` element that sets the flex growth and shrink values to 1 and the basis value to 180 pixels.

12. Next, you'll design the layout for the mobile version of the page. Go to the Mobile Styles section and add a media query for screen devices with a maximum width of 480 pixels.

13. Under the mobile layout, Michael wants the navigation list containing links to the 18 holes on the course to be displayed near the bottom of the page. Create a style rule that sets the flex order of the hole_list navigation list to 99. Create a style rule that sets the flex order of the footer to 100.

14. To reduce clutter, Michael wants the horizontal navigation list at the top of the page to be hidden unless the user taps a navicon. Create this hidden menu system by adding the following style rules to

  a. hide the display of the `ul` element within the horizontal navigation list.

  b. change the `display` property of the `ul` element to `block` if the user hovers over the navicon hypertext link or hovers over the unordered list within the horizontal navigation list. (Hint: Review the hover discussion in session 5.2 as needed.)

15. Michael also wants to hide the `aside` element when the page is viewed on a mobile device. Add a style rule to accomplish this.

16. Next, you'll create the styles that will be used for tablet and desktop devices. Create a media query for all screen devices with a width of at least 481 pixels.

17. Within the media query, create a style rule that hides the display of the navicon.

18. For these wider screens, Michael wants the horizontal navigation list to be laid out within a single row. Create a style rule that changes the display of the `ul` element within the horizontal navigation list to a flexbox that is oriented in the row direction with no wrapping.

19. For every list item in the `ul` element in the horizontal navigation list, set the growth and shrink values to 1 and the basis value to auto so that the list items grow and shrink together on the same row.

20. Save your changes to style sheet and then open the **wc_hole01.html** file in your browser or device emulator. Verify that when you reduce the screen width, the layout automatically changes to a single column layout and the `aside` element is hidden from the user. Further verify that for mobile-sized devices, the navigation links at the top of the page are hidden until the user hovers or touches the navicon.

21. Use the course navigation links on the page to view information on each of the 18 holes on the Willet Creek course. Verify that the layout matches that shown in Figure 5-60 for each page in both mobile and desktop size.

CHALLENGE

Case Problem 3

Data Files needed for this Case Problem: cw_home_txt.html, cw_styles_txt.css, 2 CSS files, 10 PNG files

Cauli-Wood Gallery Sofia Fonte is the manager of the *Cauli-Wood Gallery*, an art gallery and coffee shop located in Sedona, Arizona. She has approached you for help in redesigning the gallery's website to include support for mobile devices and tablets. Your first project will be to redesign the site's home page following the principles of responsive design. A preview of the mobile and desktop versions of the website's home page is shown in Figure 5-61.

Figure 5-61 Cauli-Wood Gallery home page

mobile version   desktop version

Right: © 2016 Cengage Learning; © Tischenko Irina/Shutterstock.com; © re_bekka/Shutterstock.com; © Boyan Dimitrov/ Shutterstock.com; © rubtsov/Shutterstock.com; © Fotocrisis/Shutterstock.com; © Anna Ismagilova/Shutterstock.com; © DeepGreen/Shutterstock.com; Source: Facebook 2015; Source: 2015 Twitter; Left: © 2016 Cengage Learning; © Tischenko Irina/Shutterstock.com; © Courtesy Patrick Carey; © re_bekka/Shutterstock.com; © Anna Ismagilova/ Shutterstock.com; © rubtsov/Shutterstock.com; Source: Facebook 2015; Source: 2015 Twitter

Sofia has already written much of the HTML code and some of the styles to be used in this project. Your job will be to finish the redesign and present her with the final version of the page.

Complete the following:

1. Using your editor, open the **cw_home_txt.html** and **cw_styles_txt.css** files from the html05 ▸ case3 folder. Enter *your name* and *the date* in the comment section of each file, and save them as **cw_home.html** and **cw_styles.css** respectively.

2. Go to the **cw_home.html** file in your editor. Within the document head, insert a `meta` element that sets the browser viewport for use with mobile devices. Also, create links to cw_reset.css and cw_styles.css style sheets. Take some time to study the contents and structure of the document and then close the file saving your changes.

3. Return to the **cw_styles.css** file in your editor. At the top of the file, use the `@import` rule to import the contents of the cw_designs.css file, which contains several style rules that format the appearance of different page elements.

⊕ **Explore** 4. At the bottom of the home page is a navigation list with the id *bottom* containing several `ul` elements. Sofia wants these `ul` elements laid out side-by-side. Create a style rule for the bottom navigation list displaying it as a flexbox row with no wrapping. Set the `justify-content` property so that the flex items are centered along the main axis. Be sure to include the WebKit browser extension in all of your flex styles.

5. Define flex values for `ul` elements within the bottom navigation list so that the width of those elements never exceeds 150 pixels but can shrink below that value.

6. Sofia wants more highly contrasting colors when the page is displayed in a mobile device. Create a media query for mobile screen devices with maximum widths of 480 pixels. Within that media query, insert a style rule that sets the font color of all body text to rgb(211, 211, 211) and sets the body background color to rgb(51, 51, 51).

7. Sofia also wants to reduce the clutter in the mobile version of the home page. Hide the following elements for mobile users: the `aside` element, any `img` element within the `article` element, and the spotlight section element.

8. At the top of the web page is a navigation list with the ID *top*. For mobile devices, display the `ul` element within this navigation list as a flexbox row with wrapping. For each list item within this `ul` element, set the font size to 2.2em. Size the list items by setting their flex values to 1 for the growth and shrink rates and 130 pixels for the basis value.

9. Under the mobile layout, the six list items in the top navigation list should appear as square blocks with different background images. Using the selector `nav#top ul li:nth-of-type(1)` for the first list item, create a style rule that changes the background to the background image cw_image01.png. Center the background image with no tiling and size it so that the entire image is contained within the background.

10. Repeat the previous step for the next five list items using the same general format. Use the cw_image02.png file for background of the second list item, the cw_image03.png file for the third list item background, and so forth.

⊕ **Explore** 11. Sofia has placed hypertext links for the gallery's phone number and e-mail address in a paragraph with the id *links*. For mobile users, she wants these two hypertext links spaced evenly within the paragraph that is displayed below the top navigation list. To format these links, create a style rule that displays the links paragraph as a flexbox row with no wrapping, then add a style that sets the value of the `justify-content` property of the paragraph to `space-around`.

12. She wants the telephone and e-mail links to be prominently displayed on mobile devices. For each `a` element within the links paragraph, apply the following style rule that: a) displays the link text in white on the background color rgb(220, 27, 27), b) sets the border radius around each hypertext to 20 pixels with 10 pixels of padding, and c) removes any underlining from the hypertext links.

13. Next, you'll define the layout for tablet and desktop devices. Create a media query for screen devices whose width is 481 pixels or greater. Within this media query, display the page body as a flexbox in row orientation with wrapping.

14. The page body has four children: the header, the footer, the `article` element, and the `aside` element. The `article` and `aside` elements will share a row with more space given to the `article` element. Set the growth, shrink, and basis values of the `article` element to 2, 1, and 400 pixels. Set those same values for the `aside` element to 1, 2, and 200 pixels.

⊕ **Explore** 15. For tablet and desktop devices, the top navigation list should be displayed as a horizontal row with no wrapping. Enter a style rule to display the top navigation list `ul` as a flexbox with a background color of rgb(51, 51, 51) and a height of 50 pixels. Use the `justify-content` and `align-items` property to center the flex items both horizontally and vertically.

16. Define the flex size of each list item in the top navigation list to have a maximum width of 80 pixels but to shrink at the same rate as the width if the navigation list is reduced.

17. Sofia doesn't want the links paragraph displayed for tablet and desktop devices. Complete the media query for tablet and desktop devices by hiding this paragraph.

18. Save your changes to the style sheet and then open the **cw_home.html** file in your browser or device emulator. Verify that the layout and contents of the page switch between the mobile version and the tablet/desktop version shown in Figure 5-61 as the screen width is increased and decreased.

Case Problem 4

Data Files needed for this Case Problem: jb_home_txt.html, jb_styles_txt.css, 10 PNG files, 1 TXT file

Jersey Buoys   Tony Gallo is the owner of *Jersey Buoys*, a surfing school in Ocean City, New Jersey. Tony has hired you as part of a team that will redesign the school's website, putting more emphasis on supporting mobile devices. Tony wants you to start by redesigning the website's front page. He's supplied you with graphics and sample text. He needs you to write up the HTML code and CSS style sheets.

Complete the following:

1. Using your editor, open the **jb_home_txt.html** and **jb_styles_txt.css** files from the html05 ▸ case4 folder. Enter *your name* and *the date* in the comment section of each file and save them as **jb_home.html** and **jb_styles.css** respectively.

2. Using the content of the jb_info.txt file, create the content and structure of the jb_home.html page. You are free to supplement the material in these text files with additional textual content of your own if appropriate. The case4 folder includes public domain graphics that you may use with your website, but you should feel free to add your own non-copyrighted material appropriate to the case problem. Use the # symbol for the value of the href attribute in your hypertext links because you will be linking to pages that don't actually exist.

3. Be sure to include the viewport meta element so that your page is properly scaled on mobile devices.

4. Link your file to the jb_styles.css style sheet. If you need to create other style sheets for your project, such as a reset style sheet, link to those files as well. Indicate the type of device in your link element.

5. Go to the **jb_styles.css** file in your editor and create the layout and design styles to be used in your page. The design is up to you, but must include the following features:
   - Media queries that match devices of a specific width with a cutoff for mobile devices at 480 pixels in screen width.
   - Layout styles that vary based on the width of the device.
   - A navigation list that is initially hidden from the mobile user but that can be displayed in response to a hover or touch event over a navicon.
   - Telephone and email links that are reformatted to make them easier to use on mobile devices.
   - Tony does not want to display information on surfer slang in the mobile version of this page; exclude those elements in your media query for mobile devices.
   - Flex layouts oriented in either the row or column direction. Be sure to include the WebKit browser extension in all of your flex styles.
   - Flex items that grow and shrink from a defined initial size based on the width of the device screen.
   - Flex items that change their order from the default document order in the HTML file.
   - A flex layout that aligns the flex item content using the justify-content, align-items, align-content, or align-self properties.

6. Include comments in your style sheet to make it easy for other users to interpret.

7. Test your layout and design on a variety of devices, browsers, and screen resolutions to ensure that your sample page is readable under different conditions. If possible verify the behavior of the page on a mobile device or a mobile emulator.

Color Names with Color Values, and HTML Character Entities

Both HTML and XHTML allow you to define colors using either color names or color values. HTML and XHTML support a list of 16 basic color names. Most browsers also support an extended list of color names, which are listed in Table A-1 in this appendix, along with their RGB and hexadecimal values.

Table A-2 in this appendix lists the extended character set for HTML, also known as the ISO Latin-1 Character Set. You can specify characters by name or by numeric value. For example, you can use either ® or ® to specify the registered trademark symbol, ®.

STARTING DATA FILES

There are no starting Data Files needed for this appendix.

Table A-1:
Color names and
corresponding values

Color Name	RGB Value	Hexadecimal Value
aliceblue	(240,248,255)	#F0F8FF
antiquewhite	(250,235,215)	#FAEBD7
aqua	(0,255,255)	#00FFFF
aquamarine	(127,255,212)	#7FFFD4
azure	(240,255,255)	#F0FFFF
beige	(245,245,220)	#F5F5DC
bisque	(255,228,196)	#FFE4C4
black	(0,0,0)	#000000
blanchedalmond	(255,235,205)	#FFEBCD
blue	(0,0,255)	#0000FF
blueviolet	(138,43,226)	#8A2BE2
brown	(165,42,42)	#A52A2A
burlywood	(222,184,135)	#DEB887
cadetblue	(95,158,160)	#5F9EA0
chartreuse	(127,255,0)	#7FFF00
chocolate	(210,105,30)	#D2691E
coral	(255,127,80)	#FF7F50
cornflowerblue	(100,149,237)	#6495ED
cornsilk	(255,248,220)	#FFF8DC
crimson	(220,20,54)	#DC1436
cyan	(0,255,255)	#00FFFF
darkblue	(0,0,139)	#00008B
darkcyan	(0,139,139)	#008B8B
darkgoldenrod	(184,134,11)	#B8860B
darkgray	(169,169,169)	#A9A9A9
darkgreen	(0,100,0)	#006400
darkkhaki	(189,183,107)	#BDB76B
darkmagenta	(139,0,139)	#8B008B
darkolivegreen	(85,107,47)	#556B2F
darkorange	(255,140,0)	#FF8C00
darkorchid	(153,50,204)	#9932CC
darkred	(139,0,0)	#8B0000
darksalmon	(233,150,122)	#E9967A
darkseagreen	(143,188,143)	#8FBC8F
darkslateblue	(72,61,139)	#483D8B
darkslategray	(47,79,79)	#2F4F4F
darkturquoise	(0,206,209)	#00CED1
darkviolet	(148,0,211)	#9400D3
deeppink	(255,20,147)	#FF1493
deepskyblue	(0,191,255)	#00BFFF
dimgray	(105,105,105)	#696969
dodgerblue	(30,144,255)	#1E90FF
firebrick	(178,34,34)	#B22222
floralwhite	(255,250,240)	#FFFAF0
forestgreen	(34,139,34)	#228B22
fuchsia	(255,0,255)	#FF00FF

Color Name	RGB Value	Hexadecimal Value
gainsboro	(220,220,220)	#DCDCDC
ghostwhite	(248,248,255)	#F8F8FF
gold	(255,215,0)	#FFD700
goldenrod	(218,165,32)	#DAA520
gray	(128,128,128)	#808080
green	(0,128,0)	#008000
greenyellow	(173,255,47)	#ADFF2F
honeydew	(240,255,240)	#F0FFF0
hotpink	(255,105,180)	#FF69B4
indianred	(205,92,92)	#CD5C5C
indigo	(75,0,130)	#4B0082
ivory	(255,255,240)	#FFFFF0
khaki	(240,230,140)	#F0E68C
lavender	(230,230,250)	#E6E6FA
lavenderblush	(255,240,245)	#FFF0F5
lawngreen	(124,252,0)	#7CFC00
lemonchiffon	(255,250,205)	#FFFACD
lightblue	(173,216,230)	#ADD8E6
lightcoral	(240,128,128)	#F08080
lightcyan	(224,255,255)	#E0FFFF
lightgoldenrodyellow	(250,250,210)	#FAFAD2
lightgreen	(144,238,144)	#90EE90
lightgrey	(211,211,211)	#D3D3D3
lightpink	(255,182,193)	#FFB6C1
lightsalmon	(255,160,122)	#FFA07A
lightseagreen	(32,178,170)	#20B2AA
lightskyblue	(135,206,250)	#87CEFA
lightslategray	(119,136,153)	#778899
lightsteelblue	(176,196,222)	#B0C4DE
lightyellow	(255,255,224)	#FFFFE0
lime	(0,255,0)	#00FF00
limegreen	(50,205,50)	#32CD32
linen	(250,240,230)	#FAF0E6
magenta	(255,0,255)	#FF00FF
maroon	(128,0,0)	#800000
mediumaquamarine	(102,205,170)	#66CDAA
mediumblue	(0,0,205)	#0000CD
mediumorchid	(186,85,211)	#BA55D3
mediumpurple	(147,112,219)	#9370DB
mediumseagreen	(60,179,113)	#3CB371
mediumslateblue	(123,104,238)	#7B68EE
mediumspringgreen	(0,250,154)	#00FA9A
mediumturquoise	(72,209,204)	#48D1CC
mediumvioletred	(199,21,133)	#C71585
midnightblue	(25,25,112)	#191970
mintcream	(245,255,250)	#F5FFFA
mistyrose	(255,228,225)	#FFE4E1

Color Name	RGB Value	Hexadecimal Value
moccasin	(255,228,181)	#FFE4B5
navajowhite	(255,222,173)	#FFDEAD
navy	(0,0,128)	#000080
oldlace	(253,245,230)	#FDF5E6
olive	(128,128,0)	#808000
olivedrab	(107,142,35)	#6B8E23
orange	(255,165,0)	#FFA500
orangered	(255,69,0)	#FF4500
orchid	(218,112,214)	#DA70D6
palegoldenrod	(238,232,170)	#EEE8AA
palegreen	(152,251,152)	#98FB98
paleturquoise	(175,238,238)	#AFEEEE
palevioletred	(219,112,147)	#DB7093
papayawhip	(255,239,213)	#FFEFD5
peachpuff	(255,218,185)	#FFDAB9
peru	(205,133,63)	#CD853F
pink	(255,192,203)	#FFC0CB
plum	(221,160,221)	#DDA0DD
powderblue	(176,224,230)	#B0E0E6
purple	(128,0,128)	#808080
red	(255,0,0)	#FF0000
rosybrown	(188,143,143)	#BC8F8F
royalblue	(65,105,0)	#4169E1
saddlebrown	(139,69,19)	#8B4513
salmon	(250,128,114)	#FA8072
sandybrown	(244,164,96)	#F4A460
seagreen	(46,139,87)	#2E8B57
seashell	(255,245,238)	#FFF5EE
sienna	(160,82,45)	#A0522D
silver	(192,192,192)	#C0C0C0
skyblue	(135,206,235)	#87CEEB
slateblue	(106,90,205)	#6A5ACD
slategray	(112,128,144)	#708090
snow	(255,250,250)	#FFFAFA
springgreen	(0,255,127)	#00FF7F
steelblue	(70,130,180)	#4682B4
tan	(210,180,140)	#D2B48C
teal	(0,128,128)	#008080
thistle	(216,191,216)	#D8BFD8
tomato	(255,99,71)	#FF6347
turquoise	(64,224,208)	#40E0D0
violet	(238,130,238)	#EE82EE
wheat	(245,222,179)	#F5DEB3
white	(255,255,255)	#FFFFFF
whitesmoke	(245,245,245)	#F5F5F5
yellow	(255,255,0)	#FFFF00
yellowgreen	(154,205,50)	#9ACD32

Table A-2:
HTML character entities

Character	Code	Code Name	Description
	&#09;		Tab
	&#10;		Line feed
	&#32;		Space
!	&#33;		Exclamation mark
"	&#34;	&quot;	Double quotation mark
#	&#35;		Pound sign
$	&#36;		Dollar sign
%	&#37;		Percent sign
&	&#38;	&amp;	Ampersand
'	&#39;		Apostrophe
(	&#40;		Left parenthesis
)	&#41;		Right parenthesis
*	&#42;		Asterisk
+	&#43;		Plus sign
,	&#44;		Comma
-	&#45;		Hyphen
.	&#46;		Period
/	&#47;		Forward slash
0 - 9	0–9		Numbers 0–9
:	&#58;		Colon
;	&#59;		Semicolon
<	&#60;	&lt;	Less than sign
=	&#61;		Equal sign
>	&#62;	&gt;	Greater than sign
?	&#63;		Question mark
@	&#64;		Commercial at sign
A - Z	A–Z		Letters A–Z
[	&#91;		Left square bracket
\	&#92;		Back slash
]	&#93;		Right square bracket
^	&#94;		Caret
_	&#95;		Horizontal bar (underscore)
`	&#96;		Grave accent
a - z	a–z		Letters a–z
{	&#123;		Left curly brace
|	|		Vertical bar
}	&#125;		Right curly brace
~	&#126;		Tilde
,	&#130;		Comma
ƒ	&#131;		Function sign (florin)
"	&#132;		Double quotation mark
…	&#133;		Ellipsis
†	&#134;		Dagger

Character	Code	Code Name	Description
‡	&#135;		Double dagger
^	&#136;		Circumflex
‰	&#137;		Permil
Š	&#138;		Capital S with hacek
‹	&#139;		Left single angle
Œ	&#140;		Capital OE ligature
	–		Unused
'	&#145;		Single beginning quotation mark
'	&#146;		Single ending quotation mark
"	&#147;		Double beginning quotation mark
"	&#148;		Double ending quotation mark
•	&#149;		Bullet
–	&#150;		En dash
—	&#151;		Em dash
~	&#152;		Tilde
™	&#153;	&trade;	Trademark symbol
š	&#154;		Small s with hacek
›	&#155;		Right single angle
œ	&#156;		Lowercase oe ligature
Ÿ	&#159;		Capital Y with umlaut
			Non-breaking space
¡	&#161;	&iexcl;	Inverted exclamation mark
¢	&#162;	&cent;	Cent sign
£	&#163;	&pound;	Pound sterling
¤	&#164;	&curren;	General currency symbol
¥	&#165;	&yen;	Yen sign
¦	&#166;	&brvbar;	Broken vertical bar
§	&#167;	&sect;	Section sign
¨	&#168;	&uml;	Umlaut
©	&#169;	&copy;	Copyright symbol
ª	&#170;	&ordf;	Feminine ordinal
«	&#171;	&laquo;	Left angle quotation mark
¬	&#172;	&not;	Not sign
–	&#173;	&shy;	Soft hyphen
®	&#174;	&reg;	Registered trademark
¯	&#175;	&macr;	Macron
°	&#176;	&deg;	Degree sign
±	&#177;	&plusmn;	Plus/minus symbol
^{2}	&#178;	&sup2;	Superscript ^{2}
^{3}	&#179;	&sup3;	Superscript ^{3}
´	&#180;	&acute;	Acute accent
µ	&#181;	&micro;	Micro sign
¶	&#182;	&para;	Paragraph sign

Character	Code	Code Name	Description
·	&#183;	&middot;	Middle dot
ç	&#184;	&cedil;	Cedilla
¹	&#185;	&sup1;	Superscript 1
º	&#186;	&ordm;	Masculine ordinal
»	&#187;	&raquo;	Right angle quotation mark
¼	&#188;	&frac14;	Fraction one-quarter
½	&#189;	&frac12;	Fraction one-half
¾	&#190;	&frac34;	Fraction three-quarters
¿	&#191;	&iquest;	Inverted question mark
À	&#192;	&Agrave;	Capital A, grave accent
Á	&#193;	&Aacute;	Capital A, acute accent
Â	&#194;	&Acirc;	Capital A, circumflex accent
Ã	&#195;	&Atilde;	Capital A, tilde
Ä	&#196;	&Auml;	Capital A, umlaut
Å	&#197;	&Aring;	Capital A, ring
Æ	&#198;	&Aelig;	Capital AE ligature
Ç	&#199;	&Ccedil;	Capital C, cedilla
È	&#200;	&Egrave;	Capital E, grave accent
É	&#201;	&Eacute;	Capital E, acute accent
Ê	&#202;	&Ecirc;	Capital E, circumflex accent
Ë	&#203;	&Euml;	Capital E, umlaut
Ì	&#204;	&Igrave;	Capital I, grave accent
Í	&#205;	&Iacute;	Capital I, acute accent
Î	&#206;	&Icirc;	Capital I, circumflex accent
Ï	&#207;	&Iuml;	Capital I, umlaut
F	&#208;	&ETH;	Capital ETH, Icelandic
Ñ	&#209;	&Ntilde;	Capital N, tilde
Ò	&#210;	&Ograve;	Capital O, grave accent
Ó	&#211;	&Oacute;	Capital O, acute accent
Ô	&#212;	&Ocirc;	Capital O, circumflex accent
Õ	&#213;	&Otilde;	Capital O, tilde
Ö	&#214;	&Ouml;	Capital O, umlaut
×	&#215;	&times;	Multiplication sign
Ø	&#216;	&Oslash;	Capital O, slash
Ù	&#217;	&Ugrave;	Capital U, grave accent
Ú	&#218;	&Uacute;	Capital U, acute accent
Û	&#219;	&Ucirc;	Capital U, circumflex accent
Ü	&#220;	&Uuml;	Capital U, umlaut
Ý	&#221;	&Yacute;	Capital Y, acute accent
Þ	&#222;	&THORN;	Capital THORN, Icelandic
ß	&#223;	&szlig;	Small sz, ligature
à	&#224;	&agrave;	Small a, grave accent
á	&#225;	&aacute;	Small a, acute accent

Character	Code	Code Name	Description
â	&#226;	&acirc;	Small a, circumflex accent
ã	&#227;	&atilde;	Small a, tilde
ä	&#228;	&auml;	Small a, umlaut
å	&#229;	&aring;	Small a, ring
æ	&#230;	&aelig;	Small ae, ligature
ç	&#231;	&ccedil;	Small c, cedilla
è	&#232;	&egrave;	Small e, grave accent
é	&#233;	&eacute;	Small e, acute accent
ê	&#234;	&ecirc;	Small e, circumflex accent
ë	&#235;	&euml;	Small e, umlaut
ì	&#236;	&igrave;	Small i, grave accent
í	&#237;	&iacute;	Small i, acute accent
î	&#238;	&icirc;	Small i, circumflex accent
ï	&#239;	&iuml;	Small i, umlaut
ð	&#240;	&eth;	Small eth, Icelandic
ñ	&#241;	&ntilde;	Small n, tilde
ò	&#242;	&ograve;	Small o, grave accent
ó	&#243;	&oacute;	Small o, acute accent
ô	&#244;	&ocirc;	Small o, circumflex accent
õ	&#245;	&otilde;	Small o, tilde
ö	&#246;	&ouml;	Small o, umlaut
÷	&#247;	&divide;	Division sign
ø	&#248;	&oslash;	Small o, slash
ù	&#249;	&ugrave;	Small u, grave accent
ú	&#250;	&uacute;	Small u, acute accent
û	&#251;	&ucirc;	Small u, circumflex accent
ü	&#252;	&uuml;	Small u, umlaut
ý	&#253;	&yacute;	Small y, acute accent
þ	&#254;	&thorn;	Small thorn, Icelandic
ÿ	&#255;	&yuml;	Small y, umlaut

HTML Elements and Attributes

This appendix provides descriptions of the major elements and attributes of HTML. The elements and attributes represent the specifications of the W3C; therefore, they might not all be supported by the major browsers. Also, in some cases, an element or attribute is not part of the W3C specifications, but instead is an extension offered by a particular browser. Where this is the case, the element or attribute is listed with the supporting browser indicated in parentheses.

Many elements and attributes have been deprecated by the W3C. Deprecated elements and attributes are supported by most browsers, but their use is discouraged. In addition, some elements and attributes have been marked as *obsolete*. The use of both deprecated and obsolete items is not recommended. However, while deprecated items are in danger of no longer being supported by the browser market, obsolete items will probably still be supported by the browser market for the foreseeable future.

Finally, elements and attributes that are new with HTML5 are indicated by (HTML5) in the text. Note that some of these elements and attributes are not supported by all browsers and browser versions.

The following data types are used throughout this appendix:

- *char* — A single text character
- *char code* — A character encoding
- *color* — An HTML color name or value
- *date* — A date and time in the format: *yyyy-mm-ddThh:mm:ssTIMEZONE*
- *id* — An id value
- *lang* — A language type
- *media* — A media type equal to all, aural, braille, handheld, print, projection, screen, tty, or tv
- *integer* — An integer value
- *mime-type* — A MIME data type, such as "text/html"
- *mime-type list* — A comma-separated list of mime-types
- ***option1**|option2| …* — The value is limited to the specified list of *options*, with the default in **bold**
- *script* — A script or a reference to a script
- *styles* — A list of style declarations
- *text* — A text string
- *text list* — A comma-separated list of text strings
- *url* — The URL for a web page or file
- *value* — A numeric value
- *value list* — A comma-separated list of numeric values

STARTING DATA FILES

There are no starting Data Files needed for this appendix.

General Attributes

Several attributes are common to many page elements. Rather than repeating this information each time it occurs, the following tables summarize these attributes.

Core Attributes

The following attributes apply to all page elements and are supported by most browser versions.

Attribute	Description
class="*text*"	Specifies the class or group to which an element belongs
contenteditable= "*text list*"	Specifies whether the contents of the element are editable (HTML5)
contextmenu="*id*"	Specifies the value of the id attribute on the menu with which to associate the element as a context menu
draggable="true|false"	Specifies whether the element is draggable (HTML5)
dropzone= "copy|move|link"	Specifies what types of content can be dropped on the element and which actions to take with content when it is dropped (HTML5)
hidden="hidden"	Specifies that the element is not yet, or is no longer, relevant and that the element should not be rendered (HTML5)
id="*text*"	Specifies a unique identifier to be associated with the element
spellcheck="true|false"	Specifies whether the element represents an element whose contents are subject to spell checking and grammar checking (HTML5)
style="*styles*"	Defines an inline style for the element
title="*text*"	Provides an advisory title for the element

Language Attributes

The web is designed to be universal and has to be adaptable to languages other than English. Thus, another set of attributes provides language support. This set of attributes is not as widely supported by browsers as the core attributes are. As with the core attributes, they can be applied to most page elements.

Attribute	Description
dir="**ltr**|rtl"	Indicates the text direction as related to the lang attribute; a value of ltr displays text from left to right; a value of rtl displays text from right to left
lang="*lang*"	Identifies the language used in the page where *lang* is the language code name

Form Attributes

The following attributes can be applied to most form elements or to a web form itself, but not to other page elements.

Attribute	Description
accesskey="*char*"	Indicates the keyboard character that can be pressed along with the accelerator key to access a form element
disabled="disabled"	Disables a form field for input
tabindex="*integer*"	Specifies a form element's position in a document's tabbing order

Event Attributes

To make web pages more dynamic, HTML supports event attributes that identify scripts to be run in response to an event occurring within an element. For example, clicking a main heading with a mouse can cause a browser to run a program that hides or expands a table of contents. Each event attribute has the form

```
onevent = "script"
```

where *event* is the name of the event attribute and *script* is the name of the script or command to be run by the browser in response to the occurrence of the event within the element.

Core Events

The core event attributes are part of the specifications for HTML. They apply to almost all page elements.

Attribute	Description
onabort	Loading of the element is aborted by the user. (HTML5)
onclick	The mouse button is clicked.
oncontextmenu	The user requested the context menu for the element. (HTML5)
ondblclick	The mouse button is double-clicked.
onerror	The element failed to load properly. (HTML5)
onkeydown	A key is pressed down.
onkeypress	A key is initially pressed.
onkeyup	A key is released.
onload	The element finishes loading. (HTML5)
onmousedown	The mouse button is pressed down.
onmousemove	The mouse pointer is moved within the element's boundaries.
onmouseout	The mouse pointer is moved out of the element's boundaries.
onmouseover	The mouse pointer hovers over the element.
onmouseup	The mouse button is released.
onmousewheel	The user rotates the mouse wheel.
onreadystatechange	The element and its resources finish loading. (HTML5)
onscroll	The element or document window is being scrolled. (HTML5)
onshow	The user requests that the element be shown as a context menu. (HTML5)
onsuspend	The browser suspends retrieving data. (HTML5)

Document Events

The following list of event attributes applies not to individual elements within the page, but to the entire document as it is displayed within the browser window or frame.

Attribute	Description
onafterprint	The document has finished printing (IE only).
onbeforeprint	The document is about to be printed (IE only).
onload	The page is finished being loaded.
onunload	The page is finished unloading.

Form Events

The following list of event attributes applies to either an entire web form or fields within a form.

Attribute	Description
onblur	The form field has lost the focus.
onchange	The value of the form field has been changed.
onfocus	The form field has received the focus.
onformchange	The user made a change in the value of a form field in the form. (HTML5)
onforminput	The value of a control in the form changes. (HTML5)
oninput	The value of an element changes. (HTML5)
oninvalid	The form field fails to meet validity constraints. (HTML5)
onreset	The form has been reset.
onselect	Text content has been selected in the form field.
onsubmit	The form has been submitted for processing.

Drag and Drop Events

The following list of event attributes applies to all page elements and can be used to respond to the user action of dragging and dropping objects in the web page.

Attribute	Description
ondrag	The user continues to drag the element. (HTML5)
ondragenter	The user ends dragging the element, entering the element into a valid drop target. (HTML5)
ondragleave	The user's drag operation leaves the element. (HTML5)
ondragover	The user continues a drag operation over the element. (HTML5)
ondragstart	The user starts dragging the element. (HTML5)
ondrop	The user completes a drop operation over the element. (HTML5)

Multimedia Events

The following list of event attributes applies to embedded multimedia elements such as audio and video clips and is used to respond to events initiated during the loading or playback of those elements.

Attribute	Description
oncanplay	The browser can resume playback of the video or audio, but determines when the playback will have to stop for further buffering.
oncanplaythrough	The browser can resume playback of the video or audio, and determines the playback can play through without further buffering. (HTML5)
ondurationchange	The DOM duration of the video or audio element changes. (HTML5)
onemptied	The video or audio element returns to the uninitialized state. (HTML5)
onended	The end of the video or audio is reached. (HTML5)
onloadeddata	The video or audio is at the current playback position for the first time. (HTML5)

Attribute	Description
onloadedmetadata	The duration and dimensions of the video or audio element are determined. (HTML5)
onloadstart	The browser begins looking for media data in the video or audio element. (HTML5)
onpause	The video or audio is paused. (HTML5)
onplay	The video or audio playback is initiated. (HTML5)
onplaying	The video or audio playback starts. (HTML5)
onprogress	The browser fetches data for the video or audio. (HTML5)
onratechange	The video or audio data changes. (HTML5)
onseeked	A seek operation on the audio or video element ends. (HTML5)
onseeking	Seeking is initiated on the audio or video. (HTML5)
onstalled	An attempt to retrieve data for the video or audio is not forthcoming. (HTML5)
ontimeupdate	The current playback position of the video or audio element changes. (HTML5)
onvolumechange	The volume of the video or audio element changes. (HTML5)
onwaiting	Playback of the video or audio stops because the next frame is unavailable. (HTML5)

HTML Elements and Attributes

The following table contains an alphabetic listing of the elements and attributes supported by HTML. Some attributes are not listed in this table but instead, they are described in the general attributes tables presented in the previous section of this appendix.

Element/Attribute	Description
`<!-- text -->`	Inserts a comment into the document (comments are not displayed in the rendered page)
`<!doctype>`	Specifies the Document Type Definition for a document
`<a> </a>`	Marks the beginning and end of a link
`charset="text"`	Specifies the character encoding of the linked document (obsolete)
`coords="value list"`	Specifies the coordinates of a hotspot in a client-side image map; the value list depends on the shape of the hotspot: shape="rect" "*left, right, top, bottom*" shape="circle" "*x_center, y_center, radius*" shape="poly" "*x1, y1, x2, y2, x3, y3, …*" (obsolete)
`href="url"`	Specifies the URL of the link
`hreflang="text"`	Specifies the language of the linked document
`name="text"`	Specifies a name for the enclosed text, allowing it to be a link target (obsolete)
`rel="text"`	Specifies the relationship between the current page and the link specified by the href attribute
`rev="text"`	Specifies the reverse relationship between the current page and the link specified by the href attribute (obsolete)
`shape="rect|circle|polygon"`	Specifies the shape of the hotspot (obsolete)
`title="text"`	Specifies the pop-up text for the link
`target="text"`	Specifies the target window or frame for the link
`type="mime-type"`	Specifies the data type of the linked document
`<abbr> </abbr>`	Marks abbreviated text

Element/Attribute	Description
`<acronym> </acronym>`	Marks acronym text (deprecated)
`<address> </address>`	Marks address text
`<applet> </applet>`	Embeds an applet into the browser (deprecated)
`align="align"`	Specifies the alignment of the applet with the surrounding text where *align* is absmiddle, absbottom, baseline, bottom, center, left, middle, right, texttop, or top
`alt="text"`	Specifies alternate text for the applet (deprecated)
`archive="url"`	Specifies the URL of an archive containing classes and other resources to be used with the applet (deprecated)
`code="url"`	Specifies the URL of the applet's code/class (deprecated)
`codebase="url"`	Specifies the URL of all class files for the applet (deprecated)
`datafld="text"`	Specifies the data source that supplies bound data for use with the data source
`datasrc="text"`	Specifies the ID or URL of the applet's data source
`height="integer"`	Specifies the height of the applet in pixels
`hspace="integer"`	Specifies the horizontal space around the applet in pixels (deprecated)
`mayscript="mayscript"`	Permits access to the applet by programs embedded in the document
`name="text"`	Specifies the name assigned to the applet (deprecated)
`object="text"`	Specifies the name of the resource that contains a serialized representation of the applet (deprecated)
`src="url"`	Specifies an external URL reference to the applet
`vspace="integer"`	Specifies the vertical space around the applet in pixels (deprecated)
`width="integer"`	Specifies the width of the applet in pixels (deprecated)
`<area />`	Marks an image map hotspot
`alt="text"`	Specifies alternate text for the hotspot
`coords="value list"`	Specifies the coordinates of the hotspot; the value list depends on the shape of the hotspot: shape="rect" "*left, right, top, bottom*" shape="circle" "*x_center, y_center, radius*" shape="poly" "*x1, y1, x2, y2, x3, y3, …*"
`href="url"`	Specifies the URL of the document to which the hotspot points
`hreflang="lang"`	Language of the hyperlink destination
`media="media"`	The media for which the destination of the hyperlink was designed
`rel="text"`	Specifies the relationship between the current page and the destination of the link
`nohref="nohref"`	Specifies that the hotspot does not point to a link
`shape="rect|circle|polygon"`	Specifies the shape of the hotspot
`target="text"`	Specifies the target window or frame for the link
`<article> </article>`	Structural element marking a page article (HTML5)
`<aside> </aside>`	Structural element marking a sidebar that is tangentially related to the main page content (HTML5)
`<audio> </audio>`	Marks embedded audio content (HTML5)
`autoplay="autoplay"`	Automatically begins playback of the audio stream
`preload="none|metadata|auto"`	Specifies whether to preload data to the browser
`controls="controls"`	Specifies whether to display audio controls

Element/Attribute	Description
loop="loop"	Specifies whether to automatically loop back to the beginning of the audio clip
src="url"	Provides the source of the audio clip
<b> </b>	Marks text offset from its surrounding content without conveying any extra emphasis or importance
<base />	Specifies global reference information for the document
href="url"	Specifies the URL from which all relative links in the document are based
target="text"	Specifies the target window or frame for links in the document
<basefont />	Specifies the font setting for the document text (deprecated)
color="color"	Specifies the text color (deprecated)
face="text list"	Specifies a list of fonts to be applied to the text (deprecated)
size="integer"	Specifies the size of the font range from 1 (smallest) to 7 (largest) (deprecated)
<bdi> </bdi>	Marks text that is isolated from its surroundings for the purposes of bidirectional text formatting (HTML5)
<bdo> </bdo>	Indicates that the enclosed text should be rendered with the direction specified by the dir attribute
<big> </big>	Increases the size of the enclosed text relative to the default font size (deprecated)
<blockquote> </blockquote>	Marks content as quoted from another source
cite="url"	Provides the source URL of the quoted content
<body> </body>	Marks the page content to be rendered by the browser
alink="color"	Specifies the color of activated links in the document (obsolete)
background="url"	Specifies the background image file used for the page (obsolete)
bgcolor="color"	Specifies the background color of the page (obsolete)
link="color"	Specifies the color of unvisited links (obsolete)
marginheight="integer"	Specifies the size of the margin above and below the page (obsolete)
marginwidth="integer"	Specifies the size of the margin to the left and right of the page (obsolete)
text="color"	Specifies the color of page text (obsolete)
vlink="color"	Specifies the color of previously visited links (obsolete)
 	Inserts a line break into the page
clear="none|left|right|all"	Displays the line break only when the specified margin is clear (obsolete)
<button> </button>	Creates a form button
autofocus="autofocus"	Gives the button the focus when the page is loaded (HTML5)
disabled="disabled"	Disables the button
form="text"	Specifies the form to which the button belongs (HTML5)
formaction="url"	Specifies the URL to which the form data is sent (HTML5)
formenctype="mime-type"	Specifies the encoding of the form data before it is sent (HTML5)
formmethod="get|post"	Specifies the HTTP method with which the form data is submitted
formnovalidate="formnovalidate"	Specifies that the form should not be validated during submission (HTML5)
formtarget="text"	Provides a name for the target of the button (HTML5)
name="text"	Provides the name assigned to the form button
type="submit|reset|button"	Specifies the type of form button
value="text"	Provides the value associated with the form button

Element/Attribute	Description
`<canvas> </canvas>`	Marks a resolution-dependent bitmapped region that can be used for dynamic rendering of images, graphs, and games (HTML5)
`height="integer"`	Height of canvas in pixels
`width="integer"`	Width of canvas in pixels
`<caption> </caption>`	Creates a table caption
`align="align"`	Specifies the alignment of the caption where *align* is bottom, center, left, right, or top (deprecated)
`valign="top|bottom"`	Specifies the vertical alignment of the caption
`<center> </center>`	Centers content horizontally on the page (obsolete)
`<cite> </cite>`	Marks citation text
`<code> </code>`	Marks text used for code samples
`<col> </col>`	Defines the settings for a column or group of columns (obsolete)
`align="align"`	Specifies the alignment of the content of the column(s) where *align* is left, right, or center
`char="char"`	Specifies a character in the column used to align column values (obsolete)
`charoff="integer"`	Specifies the offset in pixels from the alignment character specified in the char attribute (obsolete)
`span="integer"`	Specifies the number of columns in the group
`valign="align"`	Specifies the vertical alignment of the content in the column(s) where *align* is top, middle, bottom, or baseline
`width="integer"`	Specifies the width of the column(s) in pixels (obsolete)
`<colgroup> </colgroup>`	Creates a container for a group of columns
`align="align"`	Specifies the alignment of the content of the column group where *align* is left, right, or center (obsolete)
`char="char"`	Specifies a character in the column used to align column group values (obsolete)
`charoff="integer"`	Specifies the offset in pixels from the alignment character specified in the char attribute (obsolete)
`span="integer"`	Specifies the number of columns in the group
`valign="align"`	Specifies the vertical alignment of the content in the column group where *align* is top, middle, bottom, or baseline (obsolete)
`width="integer"`	Specifies the width of the columns in the group in pixels (obsolete)
`<command> </command>`	Defines a command button (HTML5)
`checked="checked"`	Selects the command
`disabled="disabled"`	Disables the command
`icon="url"`	Provides the URL for the image that represents the command
`label="text"`	Specifies the text of the command button
`radiogroup="text"`	Specifies the name of the group of commands toggled when the command itself is toggled
`type="command|radio|checkbox"`	Specifies the type of command button
`<datalist> </datalist>`	Encloses a set of option elements that can act as a dropdown list (HTML5)
`<dd> </dd>`	Marks text as a definition within a definition list

Element/Attribute	Description
`<del> </del>`	Marks text as deleted from the document
`cite="url"`	Provides the URL for the document that has additional information about the deleted text
`datetime="date"`	Specifies the date and time of the text deletion
`<details> </details>`	Represents a form control from which the user can obtain additional information or controls (HTML5)
`open="open"`	Specifies that the contents of the details element should be shown to the user
`<dfn> </dfn>`	Marks the defining instance of a term
`<dir> </dir>`	Contains a directory listing (deprecated)
`compact="compact"`	Permits use of compact rendering, if available (deprecated)
`<div> </div>`	Creates a generic block-level element
`align="left|center right|justify"`	Specifies the horizontal alignment of the content (obsolete)
`datafld="text"`	Indicates the column from a data source that supplies bound data for the block (IE only)
`dataformatas="html |plaintext|text"`	Specifies the format of the data in the data source bound with the the button (IE only)
`datasrc="url"`	Provides the URL or ID of the data source bound with the block (IE only)
`<dl> </dl>`	Encloses a definition list using the dd and dt elements
`compact="compact"`	Permits use of compact rendering, if available (obsolete)
`<dt> </dt>`	Marks a definition term in a definition list
`nowrap="nowrap"`	Specifies whether the content wraps using normal HTML line-wrapping conventions
`<em> </em>`	Marks emphasized text
`<embed> </embed>`	Defines external multimedia content or a plugin (HTML5)
`align="align"`	Specifies the alignment of the object with the surrounding content where *align* is bottom, left, right, or top (obsolete)
`height="integer"`	Specifies the height of the object in pixels
`hspace="integer"`	Specifies the horizontal space around the object in pixels (obsolete)
`name="text"`	Provides the name of the embedded object (obsolete)
`src="url"`	Provides the location of the file containing the object
`type="mime-type"`	Specifies the mime-type of the embedded object
`vspace="integer"`	Specifies the vertical space around the object in pixels (obsolete)
`width="integer"`	Specifies the width of the object in pixels
`<fieldset> </fieldset>`	Places form fields in a common group
`disabled="disabled"`	Disables the fieldset
`form="id"`	The id of the form associated with the fieldset
`name="text"`	The name part of the name/value pair associated with this element
`<figure> </figure>`	A structural element that represents a group of media content that is self-contained along with a caption (HTML5)
`<figcaption> </figcaption>`	Represents the caption of a figure (HTML5)
`<font> </font>`	Formats the enclosed text (deprecated)
`color="color"`	Specifies the color of the enclosed text (deprecated)
`face="text list"`	Specifies the font face(s) of the enclosed text (deprecated)
`size="integer"`	Specifies the size of the enclosed text, with values ranging from 1 (smallest) to 7 (largest); a value of +integer increases the font size relative to the font size specified in the basefont element (deprecated)

Element/Attribute	Description
`<footer> </footer>`	A structural element that represents the footer of a section or page (HTML5)
`<form> </form>`	Encloses the contents of a web form
`accept="mime-type list"`	Lists mime-types that the server processing the form will handle (deprecated)
`accept-charset="char code"`	Specifies the character encoding that the server processing the form will handle
`action="url"`	Provides the URL to which the form values are to be sent
`autocomplete="on|off"`	Enables automatic insertion of information in fields in which the user has previously entered data (HTML5)
`enctype="mime-type"`	Specifies the mime-type of the data to be sent to the server for processing; the default is "application/x-www-form-urlencoded"
`method="get|post"`	Specifies the method of accessing the URL specified in the action attribute
`name="text"`	Specifies the name of the form
`novalidate="novalidate"`	Specifies that the form is not meant to be validated during submission (HTML5)
`target="text"`	Specifies the frame or window in which output from the form should appear
`<frame> </frame>`	Marks a single frame within a set of frames (deprecated)
`bordercolor="color"`	Specifies the color of the frame border
`frameborder="1|0"`	Determines whether the frame border is visible (1) or invisible (0); Netscape also supports values of yes or no
`longdesc="url"`	Provides the URL of a document containing a long description of the frame's contents
`marginheight="integer"`	Specifies the space above and below the frame object and the frame's borders, in pixels
`marginwidth="integer"`	Specifies the space to the left and right of the frame object and the frame's borders, in pixels
`name="text"`	Specifies the name of the frame
`noresize="noresize"`	Prevents users from resizing the frame
`scrolling="auto|yes|no"`	Specifies whether the browser will display a scroll bar with the frame
`src="url"`	Provides the URL of the document to be displayed in the frame
`<frameset> </frameset>`	Creates a collection of frames (deprecated)
`border="integer"`	Specifies the thickness of the frame borders in the frameset in pixels (not part of the W3C specifications, but supported by most browsers)
`bordercolor="color"`	Specifies the color of the frame borders
`cols="value list"`	Arranges the frames in columns with the width of each column expressed either in pixels, as a percentage, or using an asterisk (to allow the browser to choose the width)
`frameborder="1|0"`	Determines whether frame borders are visible (1) or invisible (0); (not part of the W3C specifications, but supported by most browsers)
`framespacing="integer"`	Specifies the amount of space between frames in pixels (IE only)
`rows="value list"`	Arranges the frames in rows with the height of each column expressed either in pixels, as a percentage, or using an asterisk (to allow the browser to choose the height)

Element/Attribute	Description
`<hi> </hi>`	Marks the enclosed text as a heading, where *i* is an integer from 1 (the largest heading) to 6 (the smallest heading)
`align="align"`	Specifies the alignment of the heading text where *align* is left, center, right, or justify (obsolete)
`<head> </head>`	Encloses the document head, containing information about the document
`profile="url"`	Provides the location of metadata about the document
`<header> </header>`	Structural element that represents the header of a section or the page (HTML5)
`<hgroup> </hgroup>`	Structural element that groups content headings (HTML5)
`<hr />`	Draws a horizontal line (rule) in the rendered page
`align="align"`	Specifies the horizontal alignment of the line where *align* is left, center, or right (obsolete)
`color="color"`	Specifies the color of the line (obsolete)
`noshade="noshade"`	Removes 3D shading from the line (obsolete)
`size="integer"`	Specifies the height of the line in pixels or as a percentage of the enclosing element's height (obsolete)
`width="integer"`	Specifies the width of the line in pixels or as a percentage of the enclosing element's width (obsolete)
`<html> </html>`	Encloses the entire content of the HTML document
`manifest="url"`	Provides the address of the document's application cache manifest (HTML5)
`xmlns="text"`	Specifies the namespace prefix for the document
`<i> </i>`	Represents a span of text offset from its surrounding content without conveying any extra importance or emphasis
`<iframe> </iframe>`	Creates an inline frame in the document
`align="align"`	Specifies the horizontal alignment of the frame with the surrounding content where *align* is bottom, left, middle, top, or right (obsolete)
`datafld="text"`	Indicates the column from a data source that supplies bound data for the inline frame (IE only)
`dataformatas="html|plaintext|text"`	Specifies the format of the data in the data source bound with the inline frame (IE only)
`datasrc="url"`	Provides the URL or ID of the data source bound with the inline frame (IE only)
`frameborder="1|0"`	Specifies whether to display a frame border (1) or not (0) (obsolete)
`height="integer"`	Specifies the height of the frame in pixels
`longdesc="url"`	Indicates the document contains a long description of the frame's content (obsolete)
`marginheight="integer"`	Specifies the space above and below the frame object and the frame's borders, in pixels (obsolete)
`marginwidth="integer"`	Specifies the space to the left and right of the frame object and the frame's borders, in pixels (obsolete)
`name="text"`	Specifies the name of the frame
`sandbox="allow-forms|allow-scripts|allow-top-navigation|allow-same-origin"`	Defines restrictions to the frame content (HTML5)
`seamless="seamless"`	Displays the inline frame as part of the document (HTML5)
`scrolling="auto|yes|no"`	Determines whether the browser displays a scroll bar with the frame (obsolete)

Element/Attribute	Description
src="*url*"	Indicates the document displayed within the frame
srcdoc="*text*"	Provides the HTML code shown in the inline frame (HTML5)
width="*integer*"	Specifies the width of the frame in pixels
<img> </img>	Inserts an inline image into the document
align="*align*"	Specifies the alignment of the image with the surrounding content where *align* is left, right, top, text textop, middle, absmiddle, baseline, bottom, absbottom (obsolete)
alt="*text*"	Specifies alternate text to be displayed in place of the image
border="*integer*"	Specifies the width of the image border (obsolete)
datafld="*text*"	Names the column from a data source that supplies bound data for the image (IE only)
dataformatas="html|plaintext|text"	Specifies the format of the data in the data source bound with the image (IE only)
datasrc="*url*"	Provides the URL or ID of the data source bound with the image (IE only)
dynsrc="*url*"	Provides the URL of a video or VRML file (IE and Opera only)
height="*integer*"	Specifies the height of the image in pixels
hspace="*integer*"	Specifies the horizontal space around the image in pixels (deprecated)
ismap="ismap"	Indicates that the image can be used as a server-side image map
longdesc="*url*"	Provides the URL of a document containing a long description of the image (obsolete)
name="*text*"	Specifies the image name (obsolete)
src="*url*"	Specifies the image source file
usemap="*url*"	Provides the location of a client-side image associated with the image (not well-supported when the URL points to an external file)
vspace="*integer*"	Specifies the vertical space around the image in pixels (obsolete)
width="*integer*"	Specifies the width of the image in pixels
<input> </input>	Marks an input field in a web form
align="*align*"	Specifies the alignment of the input field with the surrounding content where *align* is left, right, top, texttop, middle, absmiddle, baseline, bottom, or absbottom (obsolete)
alt="*text*"	Specifies alternate text for image buttons and image input fields
checked="checked"	Specifies that the input check box or input radio button is selected
datafld="*text*"	Indicates the column from a data source that supplies bound data for the input field (IE only)
dataformatas="html|plaintext|text"	Specifies the format of the data in the data source bound with the input field (IE only)
datasrc="*url*"	Provides the URL or ID of the data source bound with the input field (IE only)
disabled="disabled"	Disables the input control
form="*text*"	Specifies the form to which the button belongs (HTML5)
formaction="*url*"	Specifies the URL to which the form data is sent (HTML5)
formenctype="*mime-type*"	Specifies the encoding of the form data before it is sent (HTML5)
formmethod="get|post"	Specifies the HTTP method with which the form data is submitted
formnovalidate="formnovalidate"	Specifies that the form should not be validated during submission (HTML5)

Element/Attribute	Description
`formtarget="text"`	Provides a name for the target of the button (HTML5)
`height="integer"`	Specifies the height of the image input field in pixels (HTML5)
`list="id"`	Specifies the id of a data list associated with the input field (HTML5)
`max="value"`	Specifies the maximum value of the field (HTML5)
`maxlength="integer"`	Specifies the maximum number of characters that can be inserted into a text input field
`min="value"`	Specifies the minimum value of the field (HTML5)
`multiple="multiple"`	Specifies that the user is allowed to specify more than one input value (HTML5)
`name="text"`	Specifies the name of the input field
`pattern="text"`	Specifies the required regular expression pattern of the input field value (HTML5)
`placeholder="text"`	Specifies placeholder text for the input field (HTML5)
`readonly="readonly"`	Prevents the value of the input field from being modified
`size="integer"`	Specifies the number of characters that can be displayed at one time in an input text field
`src="url"`	Indicates the source file of an input image field
`step="any|value"`	Specifies the value granularity of the field value (HTML5)
`type="text"`	Specifies the input type where text is button, checkbox, color, date, datetime, datetime-local, email, file, hidden, image, month, number, password, radio, range, reset, search, submit, tel, text, time, url, or week (HTML5)
`value="text"`	Specifies the default value of the input field
`width="integer"`	Specifies the width of an image input field in pixels (HTML5)
`<ins> </ins>`	Marks inserted text
`cite="url"`	Provides the URL for the document that has additional information about the inserted text
`datetime="date"`	Specifies the date and time of the text insertion
`<kbd> </kbd>`	Marks keyboard-style text
`<keygen> </keygen>`	Defines a generate key within a form (HTML5)
`autofocus="autofocus"`	Specifies that the element is to be given the focus when the form is loaded
`challenge="text"`	Provides the challenge string that is submitted along with the key
`disabled="disabled"`	Disables the element
`form="id"`	Specifies the id of the form associated with the element
`keytype="rsa"`	Specifies the type of key generated
`name="text"`	Specifies the name part of the name/value pair associated with the element
`<label> </label>`	Associates the enclosed content with a form field
`datafld="text"`	Indicates the column from a data source that supplies bound data for the label (IE only)
`dataformatas="html|plaintext|text"`	Specifies the format of the data in the data source bound with the label (IE only)
`datasrc="url"`	Provides the URL or ID of the data source bound with the label (IE only)
`for="text"`	Provides the ID of the field associated with the label
`form="id"`	Specifies the id of the form associated with the label (HTML5)

Element/Attribute	Description
`<legend> </legend>`	Marks the enclosed text as a caption for a field set
`align="bottom|left |top|right"`	Specifies the alignment of the legend with the field set; Internet Explorer also supports the center option (deprecated)
`<li> </li>`	Marks an item in an ordered (ol), unordered (ul), menu (menu), or directory (dir) list
`value="integer"`	Sets the value for the current list item in an ordered list; subsequent list items are numbered from that value
`<link />`	Creates an element in the document head that establishes the relationship between the current document and external documents or objects
`charset="char code"`	Specifies the character encoding of the external document (obsolete)
`href="url"`	Provides the URL of the external document
`hreflang="text"`	Indicates the language of the external document
`media="media"`	Indicates the media in which the external document is presented
`rel="text"`	Specifies the relationship between the current page and the link specified by the href attribute
`rev="text"`	Specifies the reverse relationship between the current page and the link specified by the href attribute (obsolete)
`sizes="any|value"`	Specifies the sizes of icons used for visual media (HTML5)
`target="text"`	Specifies the target window or frame for the link (obsolete)
`type="mime-type"`	Specifies the mime-type of the external document
`<map> </map>`	Creates an element that contains client-side image map hotspots
`name="text"`	Specifies the name of the image map
`<mark> </mark>`	Defines marked text (HTML5)
`<menu> </menu>`	Represents a list of commands
`compact="compact"`	Reduces the space between menu items (obsolete)
`label="text"`	Defines a visible label for the menu (HTML5)
`type="context|list| toolbar"`	Defines which type of list to display
`<meta />`	Creates an element in the document's head section that contains information and special instructions for processing the document
`charset="char code"`	Defines the character encoding for the document (HTML5)
`content="text"`	Provides information associated with the name or http-equiv attributes
`http-equiv="text"`	Provides instructions to the browser to request the server to perform different http operations
`name="text"`	Specifies the type of information specified in the content attribute
`scheme="text"`	Supplies additional information about the scheme used to interpret the content attribute (obsolete)
`<meter> </meter>`	Defines a measurement within a predefined range (HTML5)
`high="value"`	Defines the high value of the range
`low="value"`	Defines the low value of the range
`max="value"`	Defines the maximum value
`min="value"`	Defines the minimum value
`optimum="value"`	Defines the optimum value from the range
`value="value"`	Defines the meter's value
`<nav> </nav>`	Structural element defining a navigation list (HTML5)

Element/Attribute	Description
`<nobr> </nobr>`	Disables line wrapping for the enclosed content (not part of the W3C specifications, but supported by most browsers)
`<noembed> </noembed>`	Encloses alternate content for browsers that do not support the embed element (not part of the W3C specifications, but supported by most browsers)
`<noframe> </noframe>`	Encloses alternate content for browsers that do not support frames (obsolete)
`<noscript> </noscript>`	Encloses alternate content for browsers that do not support client-side scripts
`<object> </object>`	Places an embedded object (image, applet, sound clip, video clip, etc.) into the page
`archive="url"`	Specifies the URL of an archive containing classes and other resources preloaded for use with the object (obsolete)
`align="align"`	Aligns the object with the surrounding content where *align* is absbottom, absmiddle, baseline, bottom, left, middle, right, texttop, or top (obsolete)
`border="integer"`	Specifies the width of the border around the object (obsolete)
`classid="url"`	Provides the URL of the object (obsolete)
`codebase="url"`	Specifies the base path used to resolve relative references within the embedded object (obsolete)
`codetype="mime-type"`	Indicates the mime-type of the embedded object's code (obsolete)
`data="url"`	Provides the URL of the object's data file
`datafld="text"`	Identifies the column from a data source that supplies bound data for the embedded object (IE only)
`dataformatas="html|plaintext|text"`	Specifies the format of the data in the data source bound with the embedded object (IE only)
`datasrc="url"`	Provides the URL or ID of the data source bound with the embedded object (IE only)
`declare="declare"`	Declares the object without embedding it on the page (obsolete)
`form="id"`	Specifies the id of the form associated with the object (HTML5)
`height="integer"`	Specifies the height of the object in pixels
`hspace="integer"`	Specifies the horizontal space around the image in pixels (obsolete)
`name="text"`	Specifies the name of the embedded object
`standby="text"`	Specifies the message displayed by the browser while loading the embedded object (obsolete)
`type="mime-type"`	Indicates the mime-type of the embedded object
`vspace="integer"`	Specifies the vertical space around the embedded object (obsolete)
`width="integer"`	Specifies the width of the object in pixels
`<ol> </ol>`	Contains an ordered list of items
`reversed="reversed"`	Specifies that the list markers are to be displayed in descending order (HTML5)
`start="integer"`	Specifies the starting value in the list
`type="A|a|I|i|1"`	Specifies the bullet type associated with the list items (deprecated)
`<optgroup> </optgroup>`	Contains a group of option elements in a selection field
`disabled="disabled"`	Disables the option group control
`label="text"`	Specifies the label for the option group
`<option> </option>`	Formats an option within a selection field
`disabled="disabled"`	Disables the option control
`label="text"`	Supplies the text label associated with the option
`selected="selected"`	Selects the option by default
`value="text"`	Specifies the value associated with the option

Element/Attribute	Description
`<output> </output>`	Form control representing the result of a calculation (HTML5)
`name="text"`	Specifies the name part of the name/value pair associated with the field
`form="id"`	Specifies the id of the form associated with the field
`for="text list"`	Lists the id references associated with the calculation
`<p> </p>`	Marks the enclosed content as a paragraph
`align="align"`	Horizontally aligns the contents of the paragraph where *align* is left, center, right, or justify (obsolete)
`<param> </param>`	Marks parameter values sent to an object element or an applet element
`name="text"`	Specifies the parameter name
`type="mime-type"`	Specifies the mime-type of the resource indicated by the value attribute (obsolete)
`value="text"`	Specifies the parameter value
`valuetype="data|ref|object"`	Specifies the data type of the value attribute (obsolete)
`<pre> </pre>`	Marks the enclosed text as preformatted text, retaining white space from the document
`<progress> </progress>`	Represents the progress of completion of a task (HTML5)
`value="value"`	Specifies how much of the task has been completed
`max="value"`	Specifies how much work the task requires in total
`<q> </q>`	Marks the enclosed text as a quotation
`cite="url"`	Provides the source URL of the quoted content
`<rp> </rp>`	Used in ruby annotations to define what to show browsers that do not support the ruby element (HTML5)
`<rt> </rt>`	Defines explanation to ruby annotations (HTML5)
`<ruby> </ruby>`	Defines ruby annotations (HTML5)
`<s> </s>`	Marks the enclosed text as strikethrough text
`<samp> </samp>`	Marks the enclosed text as a sequence of literal characters
`<script> </script>`	Encloses client-side scripts within the document; this element can be placed within the head or the body element or it can refer to an external script file
`async="async"`	Specifies that the script should be executed asynchronously as soon as it becomes available (HTML5)
`charset="char code"`	Specifies the character encoding of the script
`defer="defer"`	Defers execution of the script
`language="text"`	Specifies the language of the script (obsolete)
`src="url"`	Provides the URL of an external script file
`type="mime-type"`	Specifies the mime-type of the script
`<section> </section>`	Structural element representing a section of the document (HTML5)
`<select> </select>`	Creates a selection field (drop-down list box) in a web form
`autofocus="autofocus"`	Specifies that the browser should give focus to the selection field as soon as the page loads (HTML5)
`datafld="text"`	Identifies the column from a data source that supplies bound data for the selection field (IE only)

Element/Attribute	Description
dataformatas="html|plaintext|text"	Specifies the format of the data in the data source bound with the selection field (IE only)
datasrc="url"	Provides the URL or ID of the data source bound with the selection field (IE only)
disabled="disabled"	Disables the selection field
form="id"	Provides the id of the form associated with the selection field (HTML5)
multiple="multiple"	Allows multiple sections from the field
name="text"	Specifies the selection field name
size="integer"	Specifies the number of visible items in the selection list
<small> </small>	Represents "final print" or "small print" in legal disclaimers and caveats
<source />	Enables multiple media sources to be specified for audio and video elements (HTML5)
media="media"	Specifies the intended media type of the media source
src="url"	Specifies the location of the media source
type="mime-type"	Specifies the MIME type of the media source
<span> </span>	Creates a generic inline element
datafld="text"	Identifies the column from a data source that supplies bound data for the inline element (IE only)
dataformatas="html|plaintext|text"	Specifies the format of the data in the data source bound with the inline element (IE only)
datasrc="url"	Provides the URL or ID of the data source bound with the inline element (IE only)
<strong> </strong>	Marks the enclosed text as strongly emphasized text
<style> </style>	Encloses global style declarations for the document
media="media"	Indicates the media of the enclosed style definitions
scoped="scoped"	Indicates that the specified style information is meant to apply only to the style element's parent element (HTML5)
type="mime-type"	Specifies the mime-type of the style definitions
****	Marks the enclosed text as subscript text
<summary> </summary>	Defines the header of a detail element (HTML5)
****	Marks the enclosed text as superscript text
<table> </table>	Encloses the contents of a web table
align="align"	Aligns the table with the surrounding content where align is left, center, or right (obsolete)
bgcolor="color"	Specifies the background color of the table (obsolete)
border="integer"	Specifies the width of the table border in pixels (obsolete)
cellpadding="integer"	Specifies the space between the table data and the cell borders in pixels (obsolete)
cellspacing="integer"	Specifies the space between table cells in pixels (obsolete)
datafld="text"	Indicates the column from a data source that supplies bound data for the table (IE only)
dataformatas="html|plaintext|text"	Specifies the format of the data in the data source bound with the table (IE only)

Element/Attribute	Description
`datapagesize="integer"`	Sets the number of records displayed within the table (IE only)
`datasrc="url"`	Provides the URL or ID of the data source bound with the table (IE only)
`frame="frame"`	Specifies the format of the borders around the table where *frame* is above, below, border, box, hsides, lhs, rhs, void, or vside (obsolete)
`rules="rules"`	Specifies the format of the table's internal borders or gridlines where *rules* is all, cols, groups, none, or rows (obsolete)
`summary="text"`	Supplies a text summary of the table's content
`width="integer"`	Specifies the width of the table in pixels (obsolete)
`<tbody> </tbody>`	Encloses the content of the web table body
`align="align"`	Specifies the alignment of the contents in the cells of the table body where *align* is left, center, right, justify, or char (obsolete)
`char="char"`	Specifies the character used for aligning the table body contents when the align attribute is set to "char" (obsolete)
`charoff="integer"`	Specifies the offset in pixels from the alignment character specified in the char attribute (obsolete)
`valign="align"`	Specifies the vertical alignment of the contents in the cells of the table body where *align* is baseline, bottom, middle, or top (obsolete)
`<td> </td>`	Encloses the data of a table cell
`abbr="text"`	Supplies an abbreviated version of the contents of the table cell (obsolete)
`align="align"`	Specifies the horizontal alignment of the table cell data where *align* is left, center, or right (obsolete)
`bgcolor="color"`	Specifies the background color of the table cell (obsolete)
`char="char"`	Specifies the character used for aligning the table cell contents when the align attribute is set to "char" (obsolete)
`charoff="integer"`	Specifies the offset in pixels from the alignment character specified in the char attribute (obsolete)
`colspan="integer"`	Specifies the number of columns the table cell spans
`headers="text"`	Supplies a space-separated list of table headers associated with the table cell
`height="integer"`	Specifies the height of the table cell in pixels (obsolete)
`nowrap="nowrap"`	Disables line-wrapping within the table cell (obsolete)
`rowspan="integer"`	Specifies the number of rows the table cell spans
`scope="col|colgroup|row|rowgroup"`	Specifies the scope of the table for which the cell provides data (obsolete)
`valign="align"`	Specifies the vertical alignment of the contents of the table cell where *align* is top, middle, or bottom (obsolete)
`width="integer"`	Specifies the width of the cell in pixels (obsolete)
`<textarea> </textarea>`	Marks the enclosed text as a text area input box in a web form
`autofocus="autofocus"`	Specifies that the text area is to receive the focus when the page is loaded (HTML5)
`datafld="text"`	Specifies the column from a data source that supplies bound data for the text area box (IE only)
`dataformatas="html|plaintext|text"`	Specifies the format of the data in the data source bound with the text area box (IE only)

Element/Attribute	Description
datasrc="*url*"	Provides the URL or ID of the data source bound with the text area box (IE only)
cols="*integer*"	Specifies the width of the text area box in characters
disable="disable"	Disables the text area field
form="*id*"	Associates the text area with the form identified by *id* (HTML5)
maxlength="*integer*"	Specifies the maximum allowed value length for the text area
name="*text*"	Specifies the name of the text area box
placeholder="*text*"	Provides a short hint intended to aid the user when entering data (HTML5)
readonly="readonly"	Specifies the value of the text area box, cannot be modified
required="required"	Indicates whether the text area is required for validation (HTML5)
rows="*integer*"	Specifies the number of visible rows in the text area box
wrap="**soft**|hard"	Specifies how text is wrapped within the text area box and how that text-wrapping information is sent to the server-side program
<tfoot> </tfoot>	Encloses the content of the web table footer
align="*align*"	Specifies the alignment of the contents in the cells of the table footer where *align* is left, center, right, justify, or char (obsolete)
char="*char*"	Specifies the character used for aligning the table footer contents when the align attribute is set to "char" (obsolete)
charoff="*integer*"	Specifies the offset in pixels from the alignment character specified in the char attribute (obsolete)
valign="*align*"	Specifies the vertical alignment of the contents in the cells of the table footer where *align* is baseline, bottom, middle, or top (obsolete)
<th> </th>	Encloses the data of a table header cell
abbr="*text*"	Supplies an abbreviated version of the contents of the table cell (obsolete)
align="*align*"	Specifies the horizontal alignment of the table cell data where *align* is left, center, or right (obsolete)
axis="*text list*"	Provides a list of table categories that can be mapped to a table hierarchy (obsolete)
bgcolor="*color*"	Specifies the background color of the table cell (obsolete)
char="*char*"	Specifies the character used for aligning the table cell contents when the align attribute is set to "char" (obsolete)
charoff="*integer*"	Specifies the offset in pixels from the alignment character specified in the char attribute (obsolete)
colspan="*integer*"	Specifies the number of columns the table cell spans
headers="*text*"	A space-separated list of table headers associated with the table cell
height="*integer*"	Specifies the height of the table cell in pixels (obsolete)
nowrap="nowrap"	Disables line-wrapping within the table cell (obsolete)
rowspan="*integer*"	Specifies the number of rows the table cell spans
scope="col|colgroup|row|rowgroup"	Specifies the scope of the table for which the cell provides data
valign="*align*"	Specifies the vertical alignment of the contents of the table cell where *align* is top, middle, or bottom (obsolete)
width="*integer*"	Specifies the width of the cell in pixels (obsolete)

Element/Attribute	Description
`<thead> </thead>`	Encloses the content of the web table header
`align="align"`	Specifies the alignment of the contents in the cells of the table header where *align* is left, center, right, justify, or char (obsolete)
`char="char"`	Specifies the character used for aligning the table header contents when the align attribute is set to "char" (obsolete)
`charoff="integer"`	Specifies the offset in pixels from the alignment character specified in the char attribute (obsolete)
`valign="align"`	Specifies the vertical alignment of the contents in the cells of the table header where *align* is baseline, bottom, middle, or top (obsolete)
`<time> </time>`	Represents a date and/or time (HTML5)
`<title> </title>`	Specifies the title of the document, placed in the head section of the document
`<tr> </tr>`	Encloses the content of a row within a web table
`align="align"`	Specifies the horizontal alignment of the data in the row's cells where *align* is left, center, or right (obsolete)
`char="char"`	Specifies the character used for aligning the table row contents when the align attribute is set to "char" (obsolete)
`charoff="integer"`	Specifies the offset in pixels from the alignment character specified in the char attribute (obsolete)
`valign="align"`	Specifies the vertical alignment of the contents of the table row where *align* is baseline, bottom, middle, or top (obsolete)
`<track> </track>`	Enables supplementary media tracks such as subtitles and captions (HTML5)
`default="default"`	Enables the track if the user's preferences do not indicate that another track would be more appropriate
`kind="kind"`	Specifies the kind of track, where *kind* is subtitles, captions, descriptions, chapters, or metadata
`label="text"`	Provides a user-readable title for the track
`src="url"`	Provides the address of the track
`srclang="lang"`	Provides the language of the track
`<tt> </tt>`	Marks the enclosed text as teletype or monospaced text (deprecated)
`<u> </u>`	Marks the enclosed text as underlined text (deprecated)
`<ul> </ul>`	Contains an unordered list of items
`compact="compact"`	Reduces the space between unordered list items (obsolete)
`type="disc|square|circle"`	Specifies the bullet type associated with the list items (obsolete)
`<var> </var>`	Marks the enclosed text as containing a variable name
`<video> </video>`	Defines an embedded video clip (HTML5)
`audio="text"`	Defines the default audio state; currently only "muted" is supported
`autoplay="autoplay"`	Specifies that the video should begin playing automatically when the page is loaded
`controls="controls"`	Instructs the browser to display the video controls
`height="value"`	Provides the height of the video clip in pixels
`loop="loop"`	Instructs the browser to loop the clip back to the beginning
`preload="auto|metadata|none"`	Indicates whether to preload the video clip data
`poster="url"`	Specifies the location of an image file to act as a poster for the video clip
`width="value"`	Provides the width of the video clip in pixels

Element/Attribute	Description
`<wbr />`	Indicates a line-break opportunity (HTML5)
`<xml> </xml>`	Encloses XML content (also referred to as a *data island*) or references an external XML document (IE only)
`ns="url"`	Provides the URL of the XML data island (IE only)
`prefix="text"`	Specifies the namespace prefix of the XML content (IE only)
`src="url"`	Provides the URL of an external XML document (IE only)
`<xmp> </xmp>`	Marks the enclosed text as preformatted text, preserving the white space of the source document; replaced by the pre element (deprecated)

Cascading Styles and Selectors

This appendix describes the selectors, units, and attributes supported by Cascading Style Sheets (CSS). Features from CSS3 are indicated by (CSS). Note that not all CSS3 features are supported by all browsers and all browser versions, so you should always check your code against different browsers and browser versions to ensure that your page is being rendered correctly. Also, many CSS3 styles are still in the draft stage and will undergo continuing revisions and additions. Additional information about CSS can be found at the World Wide Web Consortium website at *www.w3.org*.

STARTING DATA FILES

There are no starting Data Files needed for this appendix.

Selectors

The general form of a style declaration is:

```
selector {attribute1:value1; attribute2:value2; ...}
```

where *selector* is the selection of elements within the document to which the style will be applied; *attribute1*, *attribute2*, and so on are the different style attributes; and *value1*, *value2*, and so on are values associated with those styles. The following table shows some of the different forms that a selector can take.

Selector	Matches
`*`	All elements in the document
`e`	An element, *e*, in the document
`e1, e2, e3, …`	A group of elements, *e1*, *e2*, *e3*, in the document
`e1 e2`	An element, *e2*, nested within the parent element, *e1*
`e1 > e2`	An element, *e2*, that is a child of the parent element, *e1*
`e1+e2`	An element, *e2*, that is adjacent to element, *e1*
`e1.class`	An element, *e1*, belonging to the *class* class
`.class`	Any element belonging to the *class* class
`#id`	An element with the id value *id*
`[att]`	The element contains the *att* attribute
`[att="val"]`	The element's *att* attribute equals "*val*"
`[att~="val"]`	The element's *att* attribute value is a space-separated list of "words," one of which is exactly "*val*"
`[att|="val"]`	The element's *att* attribute value is a hyphen-separated list of "words" beginning with "val"
`[att^="val"]`	The element's *att* attribute begins with "*val*" (CSS3)
`[att$="val"]`	The element's *att* attribute ends with "*val*" (CSS3)
`[att*="val"]`	The element's *att* attribute contains the value "*val*" (CSS3)
`[ns|att]`	References all *att* attributes in the *ns* namespace (CSS3)

Pseudo-Elements and Pseudo-Classes

Pseudo-elements are elements that do not exist in HTML code but whose attributes can be set with CSS. Many pseudo-elements were introduced in CSS2.

Pseudo-Element	Matches
`e::after {content: "text"}`	Text content, *text*, that is inserted at the end of an element, *e*
`e::before {content: "text"}`	Text content, *text*, that is inserted at the beginning of an element, *e*
`e::first-letter`	The first letter in the element *e*
`e::first-line`	The first line in the element *e*
`::selection`	A part of the document that has been highlighted by the user (CSS3)

Pseudo-classes are classes of HTML elements that define the condition or state of the element in the web page. Many pseudo-classes were introduced in CSS2.

Pseudo-Class	Matches
:canvas	The rendering canvas of the document
:first	The first printed page of the document (used only with print styles created with the @print rule)
:last	The last printed page of the document (used only with print styles created with the @print rule)
:left	The left side of a two-sided printout (used only with print styles created with the @print rule)
:right	The right side of a two-sided printout (used only with print styles created with the @print rule)
:root	The root element of the document
e:active	The element, e, that is being activated by the user (usually applies only to hyperlinks)
e:checked	The checkbox or radio button, e, that has been checked (CSS3)
e:disabled	The element, e, that has been disabled in the document (CSS3)
e:empty	The element, e, that has no children
e:enabled	The element, e, that has been enabled in the document (CSS3)
e:first-child	The element, e, which is the first child of its parent element
e:first-node	The first occurrence of the element, e, in the document tree
e:first-of-type	The first element of type e (CSS3)
e:focus	The element, e, that has received the focus of the cursor
e:hover	The mouse pointer is hovering over the element, e
e:lang(text)	Sets the language, text, associated with the element, e
e:last-child	The element, e, that is the last child of its parent element (CSS3)
e:last-of-type	The last element of type e (CSS3)
e:link	The element, e, has not been visited yet by the user (applies only to hyperlinks)
e:not	Negates the selector rule for the element, e, applying the style to all e elements that do not match the selector rules
e:nth-child(n)	Matches n^{th} child of the element, e; n can also be the keywords odd or even (CSS3)
e:nth-last-child(n)	Matches n^{th} child of the element, e, counting up from the last child; n can also be the keywords odd or even (CSS3)
e:nth-of-type(n)	Matches n^{th} element of type e; n can also be the keywords odd or even (CSS3)
e:nth-last-of-type(n)	Matches n^{th} element of type e, counting up from the last child; n can also be the keywords odd or even (CSS3)
e:only-child	Matches element e only if it is the only child of its parent (CSS3)
e:only-of-type	Matches element e only if it is the only element of its type nested within its parent (CSS3)
e:target	Matches an element, e, that's the target of the identifier in the document's URL (CSS3)
e:visited	The element, e, has been already visited by the user (to only the hyperlinks)

@ Rules

CSS supports different "@ rules" designed to run commands within a style sheet. These commands can be used to import other styles, download font definitions, or define the format of printed output.

@ Rule	Description
@charset "*encoding*"	Defines the character set encoding used in the style sheet (this must be the very first line in the style sheet document)
@font-face {*font descriptors*}	Defines custom fonts that are available for automatic download when needed (CSS3)
@import url(*url*) *media*	Imports an external style sheet document into the current style sheet, where *url* is the location of the external stylesheet and *media* is a comma-separated list of media types (optional)
@media *media* {*style declaration*}	Defines the media for the styles in the *style declaration* block, where *media* is a comma-separated list of media types
@namespace *prefix* url(*url*)	Defines the namespace used by selectors in the style sheet, where *prefix* is the local namespace prefix (optional) and *url* is the unique namespace identifier; the @namespace rule must come before all CSS selectors (CSS3)
@page *label pseudo-class* {*styles*}	Defines the properties of a printed page, where *label* is a label given to the page (optional), *pseudo-class* is one of the CSS pseudo-classes designed for printed pages, and *styles* are the styles associated with the page

Miscellaneous Syntax

The following syntax elements do not fit into the previous categories but are useful in constructing CSS style sheets.

Item	Description
style !important	Places high importance on the preceding *style*, overriding the usual rules for inheritance and cascading
/* *comment* */	Attaches a *comment* to the style sheet

Units

Many style attribute values use units of measurement to indicate color, length, angles, time, and frequencies. The following table describes the measuring units used in CSS.

Units	Description
Color	**Units of Color**
`currentColor`	The computed value of the color property (CSS3)
`flavor`	An accent color chosen by the user to customize the user interface of the browser (CSS3)
name	A color name; all browsers recognize 16 base color names: aqua, black, blue, fuchsia, gray, green, lime, maroon, navy, olive, purple, red, silver, teal, white, and yellow
`#`*rrggbb*	A hexadecimal color value, where *rr* is the red value, *gg* is the green value, and *bb* is the blue value
`#`*rgb*	A compressed hexadecimal value, where the *r*, *g*, and *b* values are doubled so that, for example, #A2F = #AA22FF
`hsl(`*hue*`, `*sat*`, `*light*`)`	Color value based on hue, saturation, and lightness, where *hue* is the degree measure on the color wheel ranging from 0° (red) up to 360°, *sat* is the saturation range from 0% to 100%, and *light* is the lightness range from 0% to 100% (CSS3)
`hsla(`*hue*`, `*sat*`, `*light*`, `*alpha*`)`	Semi-transparent color based on the HSL model with *alpha* representing the opacity of the color ranging from 0 (transparent) up to 1 (completely opaque) (CSS3)
`rgb(`*red*`, `*green*`, `*blue*`)`	The decimal color value, where *red* is the red value, *green* is the green value, and *blue* is the blue value
`rgb(`*red*`%, `*green*`%, `*blue*`%)`	The color value percentage, where *red*% is the percent of maximum red, *green*% is the percent of maximum green, and *blue*% is the percent of maximum blue
`rgba(`*red*`, `*green*`, `*blue*`, `*alpha*`)`	Semi-transparent color based on the RGB model with *alpha* representing the opacity of the color ranging from 0 (transparent) up to 1 (completely opaque) (CSS3)
Length	**Units of Length**
`auto`	Keyword that allows the browser to automatically determine the size of the length
`ch`	Width of the "0" glyph found in the font (CSS3)
`em`	A relative unit indicating the width and the height of the capital "M" character for the browser's default font
`ex`	A relative unit indicating the height of the small "x" character for the browser's default font
`px`	A pixel, representing the smallest unit of length on the output device
`in`	An inch
`cm`	A centimeter
`mm`	A millimeter
`pt`	A point, approximately 1/72 inch
`pc`	A pica, approximately 1/12 inch
`%`	A percent of the width or height of the parent element
`rem`	A relative unit basing its size relative to the size in the root (html) element

Units	Description
xx-small	Keyword representing an extremely small font size
x-small	Keyword representing a very small font size
small	Keyword representing a small font size
vw	A percentage of the viewport width
vh	A percentage of the viewport height
vmin	The smaller value between vw and vh
medium	Keyword representing a medium-sized font
large	Keyword representing a large font
x-large	Keyword representing a very large font
xx-large	Keyword representing an extremely large font
Angle	**Units of Angles**
deg	The angle in degrees
grad	The angle in gradients
rad	The angle in radians
turns	Number of complete turns (CSS3)
Time	**Units of Time**
ms	Time in milliseconds
s	Time in seconds
Frequency	**Units of Frequency**
hz	The frequency in hertz
khz	The frequency in kilohertz

Attributes and Values

The following table describes the attributes and values for different types of elements. The attributes are grouped into categories to help you locate the features relevant to your particular design task.

Attribute	Description
Aural	**Styles for Aural Browsers**
cue: url(*url1*) url(*url2*)	Adds a sound to an element: if a single value is present, the sound is played before and after the element; if two values are present, the first is played before and the second is played after
cue-after: url(*url*)	Specifies a sound to be played immediately after an element
cue-before: url(*url*)	Specifies a sound to be played immediately before an element
elevation: *location*	Defines the vertical location of the sound, where *location* is below, level, above, lower, higher, or an angle value
mark: *before after*	Adds a marker to an audio stream (CSS3)
mark-before: *text*	Marks an audio stream with the text *string* (CSS3)
mark-after: *text*	Marks an audio stream afterwards with the text *string* (CSS3)
pause: *time1 time2*	Adds a pause to an element: if a single value is present, the pause occurs before and after the element; if two values are present, the first pause occurs before and the second occurs after
pause-after: *time*	Adds a pause after an element
pause-before: *time*	Adds a pause before an element

Attribute	Description
`phonemes: text`	Specifies the phonetic pronunciation for the audio stream (CSS3)
`pitch: value`	Defines the pitch of a speaking voice, where *value* is x-low, low, medium, high, x-high, or a frequency value
`pitch-range: value`	Defines the pitch range for a speaking voice, where *value* ranges from 0 to 100; a low pitch range results in a monotone voice, whereas a high pitch range sounds very animated
`play-during: url(url) mix repeat type`	Defines a sound to be played behind an element, where *url* is the URL of the sound file; mix overlays the sound file with the sound of the parent element; repeat causes the sound to be repeated, filling up the available time; and *type* is auto to play the sound only once, none to play nothing but the sound file, or inherit
`rest: before after`	Specifies the rest-before and rest-after values for the audio (CSS3)
`rest-before: type`	Specifies a rest to be observed before speaking the content, where *type* is none, x-weak, weak, medium, strong, x-strong, or inherit (CSS3)
`rest-after: type`	Specifies a rest to be observed after speaking the content, where *type* is none, x-weak, weak, medium, strong, x-strong, or inherit (CSS3)
`richness: value`	Specifies the richness of the speaking voice, where *value* ranges from 0 to 100; a low value indicates a softer voice, whereas a high value indicates a brighter voice
`speak: type`	Defines how element content is to be spoken, where *type* is normal (for normal punctuation rules), spell-out (to pronounce one character at a time), none (to suppress the aural rendering), or inherit
`voice-balance: type`	Specifies the voice balance, where *type* is left, center, right, leftwards, rightwards, inherit, or a *number* (CSS3)
`voice-duration: time`	Specifies the duration of the voice (CSS3)
`voice-family: text`	Defines the name of the speaking voice, where *text* is male, female, child, or a text string indicating a specific speaking voice
`voice-rate: type`	Specifies the voice rate, where *type* is x-slow, slow, medium, fast, x-fast, inherit, or a *percentage* (CSS3)
`voice-pitch: type`	Specifies the voice pitch, where *type* is x-low, low, medium, high, x-high, inherit, a *number*, or a *percentage* (CSS3)
`voice-pitch-range: type`	Specifies the voice pitch range, where *type* is x-low, low, medium, high, x-high, inherit, or a *number* (CSS3)
`voice-stress: type`	Specifies the voice stress, where *type* is strong, moderate, none, reduced, or inherit (CSS3)
`voice-volume: type`	Specifies the voice volume, where *type* is silent, x-soft, soft, medium, loud, x-loud, inherit, a *number*, or a *percentage* (CSS3)
Backgrounds	**Styles Applied to an Element's Background**
`background: color url(url) repeat attachment position`	Defines the background of the element, where *color* is a CSS color name or value, *url* is the location of an image file, *repeat* defines how the background image should be repeated, *attachment* defines how the background image should be attached, and *position* defines the position of the background image

Attribute	Description
background: url(url) position size repeat attachment origin clip color	Defines the background of the element, where *url* is the location of the image file, *position* is the position of the image, *size* is the size of the image, *repeat* defines how the image should be repeated, *attachment* defines how the image should be attached, *origin* defines the origin of the image, *clip* defines the location of the clipping box, and *color* defines the background color (CSS3)
background-attachment: *type*	Specifies how the background image is attached, where *type* is inherit, scroll (move the image with the page content), or fixed (fix the image and not scroll)
background-clip: *location*	Specifies the location of the background box, where *location* is border-box, padding-box, content-box, no-clip, a unit of *length*, or a *percentage* (CSS3)
background-color: *color*	Defines the color of the background, where *color* is a CSS color name or value; the keyword "inherit" can be used to inherit the background color of the parent element, or "transparent" can be used to allow the parent element background image to show through
background-image: url(*url*)	Specifies the image file used for the element's background, where *url* is the URL of the image file
background-origin: *box*	Specifies the origin of the background image, where *box* is border-box, padding-box, or content-box (CSS3)
background-position: *x y*	Sets the position of a background image, where *x* is the horizontal location in pixels, as a percentage of the width of the parent element, or the keyword "left", "center", or "right", *y* is the vertical location in pixels, as a percentage of the height and of the parent element, or the keyword "top", "center", or "bottom"
background-repeat: *type*	Defines the method for repeating the background image, where *type* is no-repeat, repeat (to tile the image in both directions), repeat-x (to tile the image in the horizontal direction only), or repeat-y (to tile the image in the vertical direction only)
background-size: *size*	Sets the size of the background image, where *size* is auto, cover, contain, a *length*, or a *percentage* (CSS3)
Block-Level Styles	**Styles Applied to Block-Level Elements**
border: *length style color*	Defines the border style of the element, where *length* is the border width, *style* is the border design, and *color* is the border color
border-bottom: *length style color*	Defines the border style of the bottom edge of the element
border-left: *length style color*	Defines the border style of the left edge of the element
border-right: *length style color*	Defines the border style of the right edge of the element
border-top: *length style color*	Defines the border style of the top edge of the element
border-color: *color*	Defines the color applied to the element's border using a CSS color unit
border-bottom-color: *color*	Defines the color applied to the bottom edge of the element
border-left-color: *color*	Defines the color applied to the left edge of the element
border-right-color: *color*	Defines the color applied to the right edge of the element
border-top-color: *color*	Defines the color applied to the top edge of the element

Attribute	Description
border-image: url(*url*) *size*	Sets an image file for the border, where *url* is the location of the image file and *size* is stretch, repeat, round, none, a *length*, or a *percentage* (CSS3)
border-style: *style*	Specifies the design of the element's border where `style` is dashed, dotted double, groove, inset, none, outset, ridge, or solid
border-style-bottom: *style*	Specifies the design of the element's bottom edge
border-style-left: *style*	Specifies the design of the element's left edge
border-style-right: *style*	Specifies the design of the element's right edge
border-style-top: *style*	Specifies the design of the element's top edge
border-radius: *tr br bl tl*	Specifies the radius of the border corners in pixels, where *tr* is the top-right corner, *br* is the bottom-right corner, *bl* is the bottom-left corner, and *tl* is the top-left corner (CSS3)
border-top-right-radius: *horiz vert*	Specifies the horizontal and vertical radius for the top-right corner (CSS3)
border-bottom-right-radius: *horiz vert*	Specifies the horizontal and vertical radius for the bottom-right corner (CSS3)
border-bottom-left-radius: *horiz vert*	Specifies the horizontal and vertical radius for the bottom-left corner (CSS3)
border-top-left-radius: *horiz vert*	Specifies the horizontal and vertical radius for the top-left corner (CSS3)
border-width: *length*	Defines the width of the element's border, in a unit of measure or using the keyword "thick", "medium", or "thin"
border-width-bottom: *length*	Defines the width of the element's bottom edge
border-width-left: *length*	Defines the width of the element's left edge
border-width-right: *length*	Defines the width of the element's right edge
border-width-top: *length*	Defines the width of the element's top edge
box-shadow: *top right bottom left color*	Adds a box shadow, where *top*, *right*, *bottom*, and *left* set the width of the shadow and *color* sets the shadow color (CSS3)
margin: *top right bottom left*	Defines the size of the margins around the top, right, bottom, and left edges of the element, in one of the CSS units of length
margin-bottom: *length*	Defines the size of the element's bottom margin
margin-left: *length*	Defines the size of the element's left margin
margin-right: *length*	Defines the size of the element's right margin
margin-top: *length*	Defines the size of the element's top margin
padding: *top right bottom left*	Defines the size of the padding space within the top, right, bottom, and left edges of the element, in one of the CSS units of length
padding-bottom: *length*	Defines the size of the element's bottom padding
padding-left: *length*	Defines the size of the element's left padding
padding-right: *length*	Defines the size of the element's right padding
padding-top: *length*	Defines the size of the element's top padding
Browser	**Styles to Affect the Appearance of the Browser**
appearance: *type*	Specifies that an element should be displayed like a standard browser object, where *type* is normal, button, push-button, hyperlink, radio-button, checkbox, pop-up-menu, list-menu, radio-group, checkbox-group, field, or password (CSS3)

Attribute	Description
cursor: *type*	Defines the cursor image used, where *type* is n-resize, ne-resize, e-resize, se-resize, s-resize, sw-resize, w-resize, nw-resize, crosshair, pointer, move, text, wait, help, auto, default, inherit, or a URL pointing to an image file
icon: *value*	Specifies that an element should be styled with with an iconic equivalent, where *value* is auto, a *url*, or inherit (CSS3)
nav-down: *position*	Specifies where to navigate using the arrow-down and arrow-up navigation keys, where *position* is auto, a *target-name*, or an element *id* (CSS3)
nav-index: *value*	Specifies the tabbing order, where *value* is auto, inherit, or a *number* (CSS3)
nav-left: *position*	Specifies where to navigate using the arrow-left and arrow-right navigation keys, where *position* is auto, a *target-name*, or an element *id* (CSS3)
nav-right: *position*	Specifies where to navigate using the arrow-left and arrow-right navigation keys, where *position* is auto, a *target-name*, or an element *id* (CSS3)
nav-up: *position*	Specifies where to navigate using the arrow-down and arrow-up navigation keys, where *position* is auto, a *target-name*, or an element *id* (CSS3)
resize: *type*	Specifies whether an element is resizable and in what direction, where *type* is none, both, horizontal, vertical, or inherit (CSS3)
Column	**Styles for Multi-Column Layouts**
column-count: *value*	Specifies the number of columns, where *value* is the column number or auto (CSS3)
column-fill: *type*	Specifies whether to balance the content of the columns, where *type* is auto or balance (CSS3)
column-gap: *value*	Sets the size of the gap between the columns, where *value* is the width of the gap or auto (CSS3)
column-rule: *width style color*	Adds a dividing line between the columns, where *width*, *style*, and *color* define the style of the line (CSS3)
column-rule-color: *color*	Defines the color of the dividing line (CSS3)
column-rule-style: *style*	Defines the border style of the dividing line (CSS3)
column-rule-width: *width*	Sets the width of the dividing line (CSS3)
columns: *width count*	Sets the width and number of columns in the multi-column layout (CSS3)
column-span: *value*	Sets the element to span across the columns, where *span* is 1 or all (CSS3)
column-width: *value*	Sets the width of the columns (CSS3)
Content	**Styles to Generate Content**
bookmark-label: *value*	Specifies the label of a bookmark, where *value* is content, an *attribute*, or a text *string* (CSS3)
bookmark-level: *value*	Specifies the bookmark level, where *value* is an *integer* or none (CSS3)
bookmark-target: *value*	Specifies the target of a bookmark link, where *value* is self, a *url*, or an *attribute* (CSS3)
border-length: *value*	Describes a way of separating footnotes from other content, where *value* is a *length* or auto (CSS3)
content: *text*	Generates a text string to attach to the content of the element

Attribute	Description
`content: attr(attr)`	Returns the value of the *attr* attribute from the element
`content: close-quote`	Attaches a close quote using the characters specified in the quotes style
`content: counter(text)`	Generates a counter using the text string *text* attached to the content (most often used with list items)
`content: counters(text)`	Generates a string of counters using the comma-separated text string *text* attached to the content (most often used with list items)
`content: no-close-quote`	Prevents the attachment of a close quote to an element
`content: no-open-quote`	Prevents the attachment of an open quote to an element
`content: open-quote`	Attaches an open quote using the characters specified in the quotes style
`content: url(url)`	Attaches the content of an external file indicated in the *url* to the element
`counter-increment: id integer`	Defines the element to be automatically incremented and the amount by which it is to be incremented, where *id* is an identifier of the element and *integer* defines by how much
`counter-reset: id integer`	Defines the element whose counter is to be reset and the amount by which it is to be reset, where *id* is an identifier of the element and *integer* defines by how much
`crop: value`	Allows a replaced element to be a rectangular area of an object instead of the whole object, where *value* is a shape or auto (CSS3)
`hyphenate-after: value`	Specifies the minimum number of characters after the hyphenation character, where *value* is an *integer* or auto (CSS3)
`hyphenate-before: value`	Specifies the minimum number of characters before the hyphenation character, where *value* is an *integer* or auto (CSS3)
`hyphenate-character: string`	Specifies the hyphenation character, *string* (CSS3)
`hyphenate-line: value`	Specifies the maximum number of hyphenated lines, where *value* is an *integer* or no-limit (CSS3)
`hyphenate-resource: url(url)`	Provides an external resource at *url* that defines hyphenation points (CSS3)
`hyphens: type`	Defines the hyphenation property, where *type* is none, manual, or auto (CSS3)
`image-resolution: value`	Defines the image resolution, where *value* is normal, auto, or the dpi of the image (CSS3)
`marks: type`	Defines an editor's mark, where *type* is crop, cross, or none (CSS3)
`quotes: text1 text2`	Defines the text strings for the open quotes (*text1*) and the close quotes (*text2*)
`string-set: values`	Accepts a comma-separated list of named strings, where *values* is the list of text strings (CSS3)
`text-replace: string1 string2`	Replaces *string1* with *string2* in the element content (CSS3)
Display Styles	**Styles that Control the Display of the Element's Content**
`box-sizing: type`	Specifies how the width and height properties should be interpreted for a block element where *type* is content-box, border-box, initial, or inherit (CSS3)
`clip: rect(top, right, bottom, left)`	Defines what portion of the content is displayed, where *top, right, bottom,* and *left* are distances of the top, right, bottom, and left edges from the element's top-left corner; use a value of auto to allow the browser to determine the clipping region

Attribute	Description
display: *type*	Specifies the display type of the element, where *type* is one of the following: block, inline, inline-block, inherit, flex, list-item, none, run-in, table, inline-table, table-caption, table-column, table-cell, table-column-group, table-header-group, table-footer-group, table-row, or table-row-group
flex: *grow shrink basis*	Sets the growth rate, shrink rate, and basis size for items within a flexbox (CSS3)
flex-basis: *length*	Sets the basis size for items within a flex box (CSS3)
flex-direction: *direction*	Sets the direction of items within a flexbox where *direction* is row, row-reverse, column, column-reverse, initial, or inherit (CSS3)
flex-flow: *direction wrap*	Sets the flow of items within a flexbox where *direction* is the flex direction and *wrap* indicates whether items are wrapped to a new line (CSS3)
flex-grow: *value*	Sets the growth rate of a flex item where *value* is a numeric value (CSS3)
flex-shrink: *value*	Sets the shrink rate of a flex item where *value* is a numeric value (CSS3)
flex-wrap: *type*	Sets whether flex items wrap to a new line where *type* is nowrap, wrap, wrap-reverse, initial, or inherit (CSS3)
height: *length*	Specifies the height of the element in one of the CSS units of length
min-height: *length*	Specifies the minimum height of the element
min-width: *length*	Specifies the minimum width of the element
max-height: *length*	Specifies the maximum height of the element
max-width: *length*	Specifies the maximum width of the element
overflow: *type*	Instructs the browser how to handle content that overflows the dimensions of the element, where *type* is auto, inherit, visible, hidden, or scroll
overflow-style: *type*	Specifies the preferred scrolling method for overflow content, where *type* is auto, marquee-line, or marquee-block (CSS3)
overflow-x: *type*	Instructs the browser how to handle content that overflows the element's width, where *type* is auto, inherit, visible, hidden, or scroll (IE only)
overflow-y: *type*	Instructs the browser on how to handle content that overflows the element's height, where *type* is auto, inherit, visible, hidden, or scroll (IE only)
text-overflow: *type*	Instructs the browser on how to handle text overflow, where *type* is clip (to hide the overflow text) or ellipsis (to display the … text string) (IE only)
visibility: *type*	Defines the element's visibility, where *type* is hidden, visible, or inherit
width: *length*	Specifies the width of the element in one of the CSS units of length
Fonts and Text	**Styles that Format the Appearance of Fonts and Text**
color: *color*	Specifies the color of the element's foreground (usually the font color)
direction: *type*	Specifies the direction of the text flow, where *type* equals ltr, rtl, or inherit (CSS3)

Attribute	Description
font: *style variant weight size/line-height family*	Defines the appearance of the font, where *style* is the font's style, *variant* is the font variant, *weight* is the weight of the font, *size* is the size of the font, *line-height* is the height of the lines, and *family* is the font face; the only required attributes are *size* and *family*
font-effect: *type*	Controls the special effect applied to glyphs where *type* is none, emboss, engrave, or outline (CSS3)
font-emphasize: *emphasize position*	Sets the style of the font emphasis and decoration (CSS3)
font-emphasize-position: *position*	Sets the font emphasis position, where *position* is before or after (CSS3)
font-emphasize-style: *style*	Sets the emphasis style, where *style* is none, accent, dot, circle, or disc (CSS3)
font-family: *family*	Specifies the font face used to display text, where *family* is sans-serif, serif, fantasy, monospace, cursive, or the name of an installed font
font-size: *value*	Specifies the size of the font in one of the CSS units of length
font-size-adjust: *value*	Specifies the aspect *value* (which is the ratio of the font size to the font's ex unit height) (CSS3)
font-smooth: *type*	Specifies the type of font smoothing, where *type* is auto, never, always, or a specified size (CSS3)
font-stretch: *type*	Expands or contracts the font, where *type* is narrower, wider, ultra-condensed, extra-condensed, condensed, semi-condensed, normal, semi-expanded, extra-expanded, or ultra-expanded (CSS3)
font-style: *type*	Specifies a style applied to the font, where *type* is normal, italic, or oblique
font-variant: *type*	Specifies a variant of the font, where *type* is inherit, normal, or small-caps
font-weight: *value*	Defines the weight of the font, where *value* is 100, 200, 300, 400, 500, 600, 700, 800, 900, normal, lighter, bolder, or bold
hanging-punctuation: *type*	Determines whether a punctuation mark may be placed outside the text box, where *type* is none, start, end, or end-edge (CSS3)
letter-spacing: *value*	Specifies the space between letters, where *value* is a unit of length or the keyword "normal"
line-height: *value*	Specifies the height of the lines, where *value* is a unit of length or the keyword "normal"
punctuation-trim: *type*	Determines whether or not a full-width punctuation character should be trimmed if it appears at the start or end of a line, where *type* is none, start, end, or adjacent (CSS3)
text-align: *type*	Specifies the horizontal alignment of text within the element, where *type* is inherit, left, right, center, or justify
text-align-last: *type*	Specifies how the last line of a block is aligned for fully justified text, where *type* is start, end, left, right, center, or justify (CSS3)
text-decoration: *type*	Specifies the decoration applied to the text, where *type* is blink, line-through, none, overline, or underline
text-emphasis: *type location*	Specifies the emphasis applied to the text, where *type* is none, accent, dot, circle, or disk and *location* is before or after (CSS3)
text-indent: *length*	Specifies the amount of indentation in the first line of the text, where *length* is a CSS unit of length

Attribute	Description
text-justify: *type*	Specifies the justification method applied to the text, where *type* is auto, inter-word, inter-ideograph, inter-cluster, distribute, kashida, or tibetan (CSS3)
text-outline: *value1 value2*	Specifies a text outline, where *value1* represents the outline thickness and *value2* represents the optional blur radius (CSS3)
text-shadow: *color x y blur*	Applies a shadow effect to the text, where *color* is the color of the shadow, *x* is the horizontal offset in pixels, *y* is the vertical offset in pixels, and *blur* is the size of the blur radius (optional); multiple shadows can be added with shadow effects separated by commas (CSS3)
text-transform: *type*	Defines a transformation applied to the text, where *type* is capitalize, lowercase, none, or uppercase
text-wrap: *type*	Specifies the type of text wrapping, where *type* is normal, unrestricted, none, or suppress (CSS3)
unicode-bibi: *type*	Allows text that flows left-to-right to be mixed with text that flows right-to-left, where *type* is normal, embed, bibi-override, or inherit (CSS3)
vertical-align: *type*	Specifies how to vertically align the text with the surrounding content, where *type* is baseline, middle, top, bottom, text-top, text-bottom, super, sub, or one of the CSS units of length
white-space: *type*	Specifies the handling of white space (blank spaces, tabs, and new lines), where *type* is inherit, normal, pre (to treat the text as preformatted text), or nowrap (to prevent line-wrapping)
white-space-collapse: *type*	Defines how white space inside the element is collapsed, where *type* is preserve, collapse, preserve-breaks, or discard (CSS3)
word-break: *type*	Controls line-breaks within words, where *type* is normal, keep-all, loose, break-strict, or break-all (CSS3)
word-spacing: *length*	Specifies the amount of space between words in the text, where *length* is either a CSS unit of length or the keyword "normal" to use normal word spacing
Layout	**Styles that Define the Layout of Elements**
bottom: *y*	Defines the vertical offset of the element's bottom edge, where *y* is either a CSS unit of length or the keyword "auto" or "inherit"
clear: *type*	Places the element only after the specified margin is clear of floating elements, where *type* is inherit, none, left, right, or both
float: *type*	Floats the element on the specified margin with subsequent content wrapping around the element, where *type* is inherit, none, left, right, or both
float-offset: *horiz vert*	Pushes floated elements in the opposite direction of where they would have been, where *horiz* is the horizontal displacement and *vert* is the vertical displacement (CSS3)
left: *x*	Defines the horizontal offset of the element's left edge, where *x* is either a CSS unit of length or the keyword "auto" or "inherit"
move-to: *type*	Causes the element to be removed from the page flow and reinserted at later point in the document, where *type* is normal, here, or an *id* value (CSS3)
position: *type*	Defines how the element is positioned on the page, where *type* is absolute, relative, fixed, static, and inherit
right: *x*	Defines the horizontal offset of the element's right edge, where *x* is either a CSS unit of length or the keyword "auto" or "inherit"

Attribute	Description
`top: y`	Defines the vertical offset of the element's top edge, where y is a CSS unit of length or the keyword "auto" or "inherit"
`z-index: value`	Defines how overlapping elements are stacked, where *value* is either the stacking number (elements with higher stacking numbers are placed on top) or the keyword "auto" to allow the browser to determine the stacking order
Lists	**Styles that Format Lists**
`list-style: type image position`	Defines the appearance of a list item, where *type* is the marker type, *image* is the URL of the location of an image file used for the marker, and *position* is the position of the marker
`list-style-image: url(url)`	Defines image used for the list marker, where *url* is the location of the image file
`list-style-type: type`	Defines the marker type used in the list, where *type* is disc, circle, square, decimal, decimal-leading-zero, lower-roman, upper-roman, lower-alpha, upper-alpha, or none
`list-style-position: type`	Defines the location of the list marker, where *type* is inside or outside
`marker-offset: length`	Defines the distance between the marker and the enclosing list box, where *length* is either a CSS unit of length or the keyword "auto" or "inherit" (CSS3)
Outlines	**Styles to Create and Format Outlines**
`outline: color style width`	Creates an outline around the element content, where *color* is the color of the outline, *style* is the outline style, and *width* is the width of the outline
`outline-color: color`	Defines the color of the outline
`outline-offset: value`	Offsets the outline from the element border, where *value* is the length of the offset (CSS3)
`outline-style: type`	Defines the style of the outline, where *type* is dashed, dotted, double, groove, inset, none, outset, ridge, solid, or inherit
`outline-width: length`	Defines the width of the outline, where *length* is expressed in a CSS unit of length
Printing	**Styles for Printed Output**
`fit: type`	Indicates how to scale an element to fit on the page, where *type* is fill, hidden, meet, or slice (CSS3)
`fit-position: vertical horizontal`	Sets the position of the element in the page, where *vertical* is top, center, or bottom; *horizontal* is left or right; or either or both positions are auto, a *value*, or a *percentage* (CSS3)
`page: label`	Specifies the page design to apply, where *label* is a page design created with the @page rule
`page-break-after: type`	Defines how to control page breaks after the element, where *type* is avoid (to avoid page breaks), left (to insert a page break until a left page is displayed), right (to insert a page break until a right page is displayed), always (to always insert a page break), auto, or inherit
`page-break-before: type`	Defines how to control page breaks before the element, where *type* is avoid left, always, auto, or inherit
`page-break-inside: type`	Defines how to control page breaks within the element, where *type* is avoid, auto, or inherit
`marks: type`	Defines how to display crop marks, where *type* is crop, cross, none, or inherit

Attribute	Description
size: *width height orientation*	Defines the size of the page, where *width* and *height* are the width and the height of the page and *orientation* is the orientation of the page (portrait or landscape)
orphans: *value*	Defines how to handle orphaned text, where *value* is the number of lines that must appear within the element before a page break is inserted
widows: *value*	Defines how to handle widowed text, where *value* is the number of lines that must appear within the element after a page break is inserted
Special Effects	**Styles to Create Special Visual Effects**
animation: *name duration timing delay iteration direction*	Applies an animation with the specified *duration*, *timing*, *delay*, *iteration*, and *direction* (CSS3)
animation-delay: *time*	Specifies the animation delay *time* in milliseconds (CSS3)
animation-direction: *direction*	Specifies the animation direction, where *direction* is normal or alternate (CSS3)
animation-duration: *time*	Specifies the duration of the animation *time* in milliseconds (CSS3)
animation-iteration-count: *value*	Specifies the number of iterations in the animation (CSS3)
animation-name: *text*	Provides a name for the animation (CSS3)
animation-play-state: *type*	Specifies the playing state of the animation, where *type* is running or paused
animation-timing-function: *function*	Provides the timing function of the animation, where *function* is ease, linear, ease-in, ease-out, ease-in-out, cubic-Bezier, or a *number* (CSS3)
backface-visibility: *visible*	Specifies whether the back side of an element is visible during a transformation, where *visible* is hidden or visible (CSS3)
filter: *type parameters*	Applies transition and filter effects to elements, where *type* is the type of filter and *parameters* are parameter values specific to the filter (IE only)
image-orientation: *angle*	Rotates the image by the specified *angle* (CSS3)
marquee-direction: *direction*	Specifies the direction of a marquee, where *direction* is forward or reverse (CSS3)
marquee-play-count: *value*	Specifies how often to loop through the marquee (CSS3)
marquee-speed: *speed*	Specifies the speed of the marquee, where *speed* is slow, normal, or fast (CSS3)
marquee-style: *type*	Specifies the marquee style, where *type* is scroll, slide, or alternate (CSS3)
opacity: *alpha*	Sets opacity of the element, ranging from 0 (transparent) to 1 (opaque) (CSS3)
perspective: *value*	Applies a perspective transformation to the element, where *value* is the perspective length (CSS3)
perspective-origin: *origin*	Establishes the origin of the perspective property, where *origin* is left, center, right, top, bottom, or a *position* value (CSS3)
rotation: *angle*	Rotates the element by *angle* (CSS3)
rotation-point: *position*	Sets the location of the rotation point for the element (CSS3)
transform: *function*	Applies a 2D or a 3D transformation, where *function* provides the transformation parameters (CSS3)

Attribute	Description
`transform-origin: position`	Establishes the origin of the transformation of an element, where *position* is the position within the element (CSS3)
`transform-style: type`	Defines how nested elements are rendered in 3D space, where *type* is flat or preserve-3d (CSS3)
`transition: property duration timing delay`	Defines a timed transition of an element, where *property*, *duration*, *timing*, and *delay* define the appearance and timing of the transition (CSS3)
`transition-delay: time`	Sets the delay time of the transition in milliseconds (CSS3)
`transition-duration: time`	Sets the duration time of the transition in milliseconds (CSS3)
`transition-property: type`	Defines the name of the CSS property modified by the transition, where *type* is all or none (CSS3)
`transition-timing-function: type`	Sets the timing function of the transition, where *type* is ease, linear, ease-in, ease-out, ease-in-out, cubic-Bezier, or a *number* (CSS3)
Tables	**Styles to Format the Appearance of Tables**
`border-collapse: type`	Determines whether table cell borders are separate or collapsed into a single border, where *type* is separate, collapse, or inherit
`border-spacing: length`	If separate borders are used for table cells, defines the distance between borders, where *length* is a CSS unit of length or inherit
`caption-side: type`	Defines the position of the caption element, where *type* is bottom, left, right, top, or inherit
`empty-cells: type`	If separate borders are used for table cells, defines whether to display borders for empty cells, where *type* is hide, show, or inherit
`table-layout: type`	Defines the algorithm used for the table layout, where *type* is auto (to define the layout once all table cells have been read), fixed (to define the layout after the first table row has been read), or inherit

Making the Web More Accessible

Studies indicate that about 20% of the population has some type of disability. Many of these disabilities do not affect an individual's ability to interact with the web. However, other disabilities can severely affect an individual's ability to participate in the web community. For example, on a news website, a blind user could not see the latest headlines. A deaf user would not be able to hear a news clip embedded in the site's main page. A user with motor disabilities might not be able to move a mouse pointer to activate important links featured on the site's home page.

Disabilities that inhibit an individual's ability to use the web fall into four main categories:

- **Visual disability:** A visual disability can include complete blindness, color-blindness, or an untreatable visual impairment.
- **Hearing disability:** A hearing disability can include complete deafness or the inability to distinguish sounds of certain frequencies.
- **Motor disability:** A motor disability can include the inability to use a mouse, to exhibit fine motor control, or to respond in a timely manner to computer prompts and queries.
- **Cognitive disability:** A cognitive disability can include a learning disability, attention deficit disorder, or the inability to focus on large amounts of information.

While the web includes some significant obstacles to full use by disabled people, it also offers the potential for contact with a great amount of information that is not otherwise cheaply or easily accessible. For example, before the web, in order to read a newspaper, a blind person was constrained by the expense of Braille printouts and audio tapes, as well as the limited availability of sighted people willing to read the news out loud. As a result, blind people would often only be able to read newspapers after the news was no longer new. The web, however, makes news available in an electronic format and in real-time. A blind user can use a browser that converts electronic text into speech, known as a **screen reader**, to read a newspaper website. Combined with the web, screen readers provide access to a broader array of information than was possible through Braille publications alone.

> "The power of the Web is in its universality. Access by everyone regardless of disability is an essential aspect."
>
> — Tim Berners-Lee, W3C Director and inventor of the World Wide Web

STARTING DATA FILES

There are no starting Data Files needed for this appendix.

In addition to screen readers, many other programs and devices—known collectively as **assistive technology** or **adaptive technology**—are available to enable people with different disabilities to use the web. The challenge for the web designer, then, is to create web pages that are accessible to everyone, including (and perhaps especially) to people with disabilities. In addition to being a design challenge, for some designers, web accessibility is the law.

Working with Section 508 Guidelines

In 1973, Congress passed the Rehabilitation Act, which aimed to foster economic independence for people with disabilities. Congress amended the act in 1998 to reflect the latest changes in information technology. Part of the amendment, **Section 508**, requires that any electronic information developed, procured, maintained, or used by the federal government be accessible to people with disabilities. Because the web is one of the main sources of electronic information, Section 508 has had a profound impact on how web pages are designed and how web code is written. Note that the standards apply to federal websites, but not to private sector websites; however, if a site is provided under contract to a federal agency, the website or portion covered by the contract has to comply. Required or not, though, you should follow the Section 508 guidelines not only to make your website more accessible, but also to make your HTML code more consistent and reliable. The Section 508 guidelines are of interest not just to web designers who work for the federal government, but to all web designers.

The Section 508 guidelines encompass a wide range of topics, covering several types of disabilities. The part of Section 508 that impacts web design is sub-section 1194.22, titled

§ 1194.22   **Web-based intranet and internet information and applications.**

Within this section are 15 paragraphs, numbered (a) through (p), which describe how each facet of a website should be designed so as to maximize accessibility. Let's examine each of these paragraphs in detail.

Graphics and Images

The first paragraph in sub-section 1194.22 deals with graphic images. The standard for the use of graphic images is that

§1194.22 (a)   **A text equivalent for every nontext element shall be provided (e.g., via "alt", "longdesc", or in element content).**

In other words, any graphic image that contains page content needs to include a text alternative to make the page accessible to visually impaired people. One of the simplest ways to do this is to use the `alt` attribute with every inline image that displays page content. For example, in Figure D-1, the `alt` attribute provides the text of a graphical logo for users who can't see the graphic.

Figure D-1   Using the alt attribute

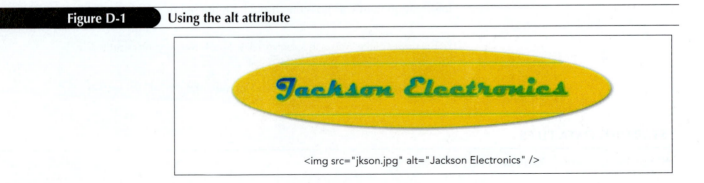

```
<img src="jkson.jpg" alt="Jackson Electronics" />
```

Not every graphic image requires a text alternative. For example, a decorative image such as a bullet does not need a text equivalent. In those cases, you should include the `alt` attribute, but set its value to an empty text string. You should never neglect to include the `alt` attribute. If you are writing XHTML-compliant code, the `alt` attribute is required. In other cases, screen readers and other nonvisual browsers will recite the filename of a graphic image file if no value is specified for the `alt` attribute. Since the filename is usually of no interest to the end-user, this results in needless irritation.

The `alt` attribute is best used for short descriptions that involve five words or fewer. It is less effective for images that require long descriptive text. You can instead link these images to a document containing a more detailed description. One way to do this is with the `longdesc` attribute, which uses the syntax

```
<img src="url" longdesc="url" />
```

where *url* for the `longdesc` attribute points to a document containing a detailed description of the image. Figure D-2 shows an example that uses the `longdesc` attribute to point to a web page containing a detailed description of a sales chart.

Figure D-2   **Using the alt attribute**

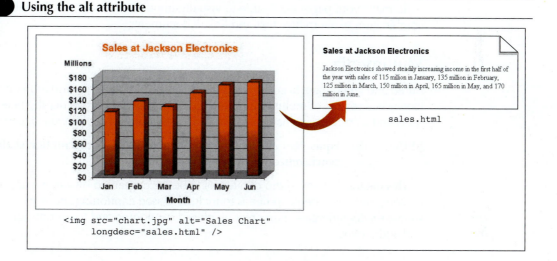

```
<img src="chart.jpg" alt="Sales Chart"
     longdesc="sales.html" />
```

In browsers that support the `longdesc` attribute, the attribute's value is presented as a link to the specified document. However, since many browsers do not yet support this attribute, many web designers currently use a D-link. A **D-link** is an unobtrusive "D" placed next to the image on the page, which is linked to an external document containing a fuller description of the image. Figure D-3 shows how the sales chart data can be presented using a D-link.

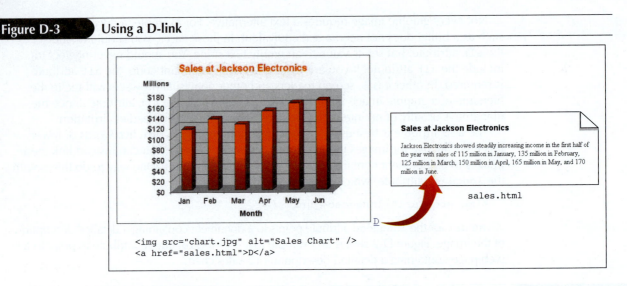

```
<img src="chart.jpg" alt="Sales Chart" />
<a href="sales.html">D</a>
```

To make your pages accessible to visually-impaired users, you will probably use a combination of alternative text and linked documents.

Multimedia

Audio and video have become important ways of conveying information on the web. However, creators of multimedia presentations should also consider the needs of deaf users and users who are hard of hearing. The standard for multimedia accessibility is

§1194.22 (b)   Equivalent alternatives for any multimedia presentation shall be synchronized with the presentation.

This means that any audio clip needs to be accompanied by a transcript of the audio's content, and any video clip needs to include closed captioning. Refer to your multimedia software's documentation on creating closed captioning and transcripts for your video and audio clips.

Color

Color is useful for emphasis and conveying information, but when color becomes an essential part of the site's content, you run the risk of shutting out people who are color blind. For this reason the third Section 508 standard states that

§1194.22 (c)   Web pages shall be designed so that all information conveyed with color is also available without color, for example from context or markup.

About 8% of men and 0.5% of women are afflicted with some type of color blindness. The most serious forms of color blindness are

- **deuteranopia**: an absence of green sensitivity; deuteranopia is one example of red-green color blindness, in which the colors red and green cannot be easily distinguished.
- **protanopia**: an absence of red sensitivity; protanopia is another example of red-green color blindness.
- **tritanopia**: an absence of blue sensitivity; people with tritanopia have much less loss of color sensitivity than other types of color blindness.
- **achromatopsia**: absence of any color sensitivity.

The most common form of serious color blindness is red-green color blindness. Figure D-4 shows how each type of serious color blindness would affect a person's view of a basic color wheel.

Figure D-4	Types of color blindness

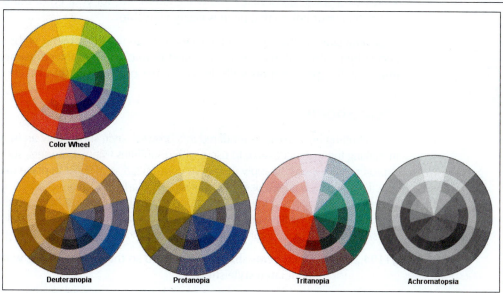

Color combinations that are easily readable for most people may be totally unreadable for users with certain types of color blindness. Figure D-5 demonstrates the accessibility problems that can occur with a graphical logo that contains green text on a red background. For people who have deuteranopia, protanopia, or achromatopsia, the logo is much more difficult to read.

Figure D-5	The effect of color blindness on graphical content

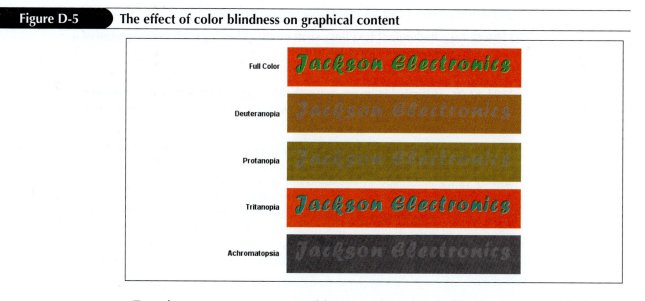

To make your page more accessible to people with color blindness, you can do the following:

- Provide noncolor clues to access your page's content. For example, some web forms indicate required entry fields by displaying the field names in a red font. You can supplement this for color blind users by marking required fields with a red font *and* with an asterisk or other special symbol.
- Avoid explicit references to color. Don't instruct your users to click a red button in a web form when some users are unable to distinguish red from other colors.
- Avoid known areas of color difficulty. Since most color blindness involves red-green color blindness, you should avoid red and green text combinations.

- Use bright colors, which are the easiest for color blind users to distinguish.
- Provide a grayscale or black and white alternative for your color blind users, and be sure that your link to that page is easily viewable.

Several sites on the web include tools you can use to test your website for color blind accessibility. You can also load color palettes into your graphics software to see how your images will appear to users with different types of color blindness.

Style Sheets

By controlling how a page is rendered in a browser, style sheets play an important role in making the web accessible to users with disabilities. Many browsers, such as Internet Explorer, allow a user to apply their own customized style sheet in place of the style sheet specified by a web page's designer. This is particularly useful for visually impaired users who need to display text in extra large fonts with a high contrast between the text and the background color (yellow text on a black background is a common color scheme for such users). In order to make your pages accessible to those users, Section 508 guidelines state that

§1194.22 (d)   Documents shall be organized so they are readable without requiring an associated style sheet.

To test whether your site fulfills this guideline, you should view the site without the style sheet. Some browsers allow you to turn off style sheets; alternately, you can redirect a page to an empty style sheet. You should modify any page that is unreadable without its style sheet to conform with this guideline.

Image Maps

Section 508 provides two standards that pertain to image maps:

§1194.22 (e)   Redundant text links shall be provided for each active region of a server-side image map.

and

§1194.22 (f)   Client-side image maps shall be provided instead of server-side image maps except where the regions cannot be defined with an available geometric shape.

In other words, the *preferred* image map is a client-side image map, unless the map uses a shape that cannot be defined on the client side. Since client-side image maps allow for polygonal shapes, this should not be an issue; however if you must use a server-side image map, you need to provide a text alternative for each of the map's links. Because server-side image maps provide only map coordinates to the server, this text is necessary in order to provide link information that is accessible to blind or visually impaired users. Figure D-6 shows a server-side image map that satisfies the Section 508 guidelines by repeating the graphical links in the image map with text links placed below the image.

Figure D-6   **Making a server-side image map accessible**

Client-side image maps do not have the same limitations as server-side maps because they allow you to specify alternate text for each hotspot within the map. For example, if the image map shown in Figure D-6 were a client-side map, you could make it accessible using the following HTML code:

```
<img src="servermap.jpg" alt="Jackson Electronics"
 usemap="#links" />
<map name="links">
   <area shape="rect" href="home.html" alt="home"
    coords="21,69,123,117" />
   <area shape="rect" href="products.html" alt="products"
    coords="156,69,258,117" />
   <area shape="rect" href="stores.html" alt="stores"
    coords="302,69,404,117" />
   <area shape="rect" href="support.html" alt="support"
    coords="445,69,547,117" />
</map>
```

Screen readers or other nonvisual browsers use the value of the alt attribute within each <area /> tag to give users access to each area. However, because some older browsers cannot work with the alt attribute in this way, you should also include the text alternative used for server-side image maps.

Tables

Tables can present a challenge for disabled users, particularly for those who employ screen readers or other nonvisual browsers. To render a web page, these browsers employ a technique called **linearizing**, which processes web page content using a few general rules:

1. Convert all images to their alternative text.
2. Present the contents of each table one cell at a time, working from left to right across each row before moving down to the next row.
3. If a cell contains a nested table, that table is linearized before proceeding to the next cell.

Figure D-7 shows how a nonvisual browser might linearize a sample table.

table							linearized content
Desktop PCs							Desktop PCs
	Model	**Processor**	**Memory**	**DVD Burner**	**Modem**	**Network Adapter**	Model
	Paragon 2.4	Intel 2.4GHz	256MB	No	Yes	No	Processor
	Paragon 3.7	Intel 3.7GHz	512MB	Yes	Yes	No	Memory
	Paragon 5.9	Intel 5.9GHz	1024MB	Yes	Yes	Yes	DVD Burner

linearized content:

Desktop PCs
Model
Processor
Memory
DVD Burner
Modem
Network Adapter
Paragon 2.4
Intel 2.4GHz
256MB
No
Yes
No
Paragon 3.7
Intel 3.7GHz
512MB
Yes
Yes
No
Paragon 5.9
Intel 5.9GHz
1024MB
Yes
Yes
Yes

One way of dealing with the challenge of linearizing is to structure your tables so that they are easily interpreted even when linearized. However, this is not always possible, especially for tables that have several rows and columns or may contain several levels of nested tables. The Section 508 guidelines for table creation state that

§1194.22 (g)   Row and column headers shall be identified for data tables.

and

§1194.22 (h)   Markup shall be used to associate data cells and header cells for data tables that have two or more logical levels of row or column headers.

To fulfill the 1194.22 (g) guideline, you should use the `<th>` tag for any table cell that contains a row or column header. By default, header text appears in a bold centered font; however, you can override this format using a style sheet. Many nonvisual browsers can search for header cells. Also, as a user moves from cell to cell in a table, these browsers can announce the row and column headers associated with each cell. In this way, using the `<th>` tag can significantly reduce some of the problems associated with linearizing.

You can also use the `scope` attribute to explicitly associate a header with a row, column, row group, or column group. The syntax of the `scope` attribute is

```
<th scope="type"> … </th>
```

where `type` is either `row`, `column`, `rowgroup`, or `colgroup`. Figure D-8 shows how to use the `scope` attribute to associate the headers with the rows and columns of a table.

Figure D-8   Using the scope attribute

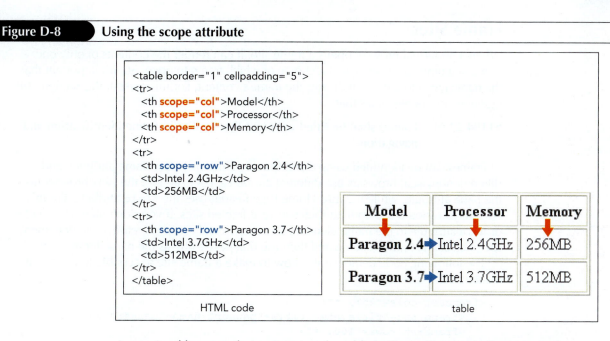

HTML code   table

A nonvisual browser that encounters the table in Figure D-8 can indicate to users which rows and columns are associated with each data cell. For example, the browser could indicate that the cell value "512MB" is associated with the Memory column and the Paragon 3.7 row.

For more explicit references, HTML also supports the `headers` attribute, which specifies the cell or cells that contain header information for a particular cell. The syntax of the `headers` attribute is

```
<td headers="ids"> … </td>
```

where `ids` is a list of id values associated with header cells in the table. Figure D-9 demonstrates how to use the headers attribute.

Figure D-9   Using the headers attribute

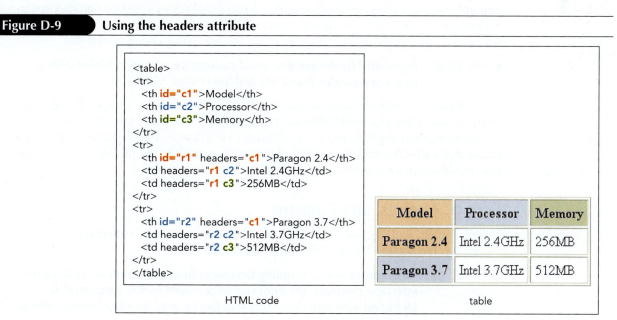

HTML code   table

Note that some older browsers do not support the `scope` and `headers` attributes. For this reason, it can be useful to supplement your tables with `caption` and `summary` attributes in order to provide even more information to blind and visually impaired users.

Frame Sites

When a nonvisual browser opens a frame site, it can render the contents of only one frame at a time. Users are given a choice of which frame to open. So, it's important that the name given to a frame indicates the frame's content. For this reason, the Section 508 guideline for frames states that

§1194.22 (i)   Frames shall be titled with text that facilitates frame identification and navigation.

Frames can be identified using either the title attribute or the name attribute, and different nonvisual browsers use different attributes. For example, the Lynx browser uses the `name` attribute, while the IBM Home Page Reader uses the `title` attribute. For this reason, you should use both attributes in your framed sites. If you don't include a `title` or `name` attribute in the frame element, some nonvisual browsers retrieve the document specified as the frame's source and then use that page's title as the name for the frame.

The following code demonstrates how to make a frame site accessible to users with disabilities.

```
<frameset cols="25%, *">
    <frame src="title.htm" title="banner" name="banner" />
    <frameset rows="100, *">
        <frame src="links.htm" title="links" name="links" />
        <frame src="home.htm" title="documents" name="documents" />
    </frameset>
</frameset>
```

Naturally, you should make sure that any document displayed in a frame follows the Section 508 guidelines.

Animation and Scrolling Text

Animated GIFs, scrolling marquees, and other special features can be sources of irritation for any web user; however, they can cause serious problems for certain users. For example, people with photosensitive epilepsy can experience seizures when exposed to a screen or portion of a screen that flickers or flashes within the range of 2 to 55 flashes per second (2 to 55 Hertz). For this reason, the Section 508 guidelines state that

§1194.22 (j)   Pages shall be designed to avoid causing the screen to flicker with a frequency greater than 2 Hz and lower than 55 Hz.

In addition to problems associated with photosensitive epilepsy, users with cognitive or visual disabilities may find it difficult to read moving text, and most screen readers are unable to read moving text. Therefore, if you decide to use animated elements, you must ensure that each element's flickering and flashing is outside of the prohibited range, and you should not place essential page content within these elements.

Scripts, Applets, and Plug-Ins

Scripts, applets, and plug-ins are widely used to make web pages more dynamic and interesting. The Section 508 guidelines for scripts state that

§1194.22 (l)   When pages utilize scripting languages to display content, or to create interface elements, the information provided by the script shall be identified with functional text that can be read by adaptive technology.

Scripts are used for a wide variety of purposes. The following list describes some of the more popular uses of scripts and how to modify them for accessibility:

- **Pull-down menus**: Many web designers use scripts to save screen space by inserting pull-down menus containing links to other pages in the site. Pull-down menus are usually accessed with a mouse. To assist users who cannot manipulate a mouse, include keyboard shortcuts to all pull-down menus. In addition, the links in a pull-down menu should be repeated elsewhere on the page or on the site in a text format.
- **Image rollovers**: Image rollovers are used to highlight linked elements. However, since image rollovers rely on the ability to use a mouse, pages should be designed so that rollover effects are not essential for navigating a site or for understanding a page's content.
- **Dynamic content**: Scripts can be used to insert new text and page content. Because some browsers designed for users with disabilities have scripting turned off by default, you should either not include any crucial content in dynamic text, or you should provide an alternate method for users with disabilities to access that information.

Applets and plug-ins are programs external to a web page or browser that add special features to a website. The Section 508 guideline for applets and plug-ins is

§1194.22 (m) **When a Web page requires that an applet, plug-in or other application be present on the client system to interpret page content, the page must provide a link to a plug-in or applet that complies with §1994.21(a) through (i).**

This guideline means that any applet or plug-in used with your website must be compliant with sections §1994.21(a) through (i) of the Section 508 accessibility law, which deal with accessibility issues for software applications and operating systems. If the default applet or plug-in does not comply with Section 508, you need to provide a link to a version of that applet or plug-in that does. For example, a web page containing a Real Audio clip should have a link to a source for the necessary player. This places the responsibility on the web page designer to know that a compliant application is available before requiring the clip to work with the page.

Web Forms

The Section 508 standard for web page forms states that

§1194.22 (n) **When electronic forms are designed to be completed on-line, the form shall allow people using assistive technology to access the information, field elements, and functionality required for completion and submission of the form, including all directions and cues.**

This is a general statement that instructs designers to make forms accessible, but it doesn't supply any specific instructions. The following techniques can help you make web forms that comply with Section 508:

- **Push buttons** should always include value attributes. The value attribute contains the text displayed on a button, and is rendered by different types of assistive technology.
- **Image buttons** should always include alternate text that can be rendered by nonvisual browsers.
- **Labels** should be associated with any input box, text area box, option button, checkbox, or selection list. The labels should be placed in close proximity to the input field and should be linked to the field using the label element.
- **Input boxes** and **text area boxes** should, when appropriate, include either default text or a prompt that indicates to the user what text to enter into the input box.
- **Interactive form elements** should be triggered by either the mouse or the keyboard.

The other parts of a web form should comply with other Section 508 standards. For example, if you use a table to lay out the elements of a form, make sure that the form still makes sense when the table is linearized.

Links

It is common for web designers to place links at the top, bottom, and sides of every page in their websites. This is generally a good idea, because those links enable users to move quickly and easily through a site. However, this technique can make it difficult to navigate a page using a screen reader, because screen readers move through a page from the top to bottom, reading each line of text. Users of screen readers may have to wait several minutes before they even get to the main body of a page, and the use of repetitive links forces such users to reread the same links on each page as they move through a site. To address this problem, the Section 508 guidelines state that

§1194.22 (o) A method shall be provided that permits users to skip repetitive navigation links.

One way of complying with this rule is to place a link at the very top of each page that allows users to jump to the page's main content. In order to make the link unobtrusive, it can be attached to a transparent image that is one pixel wide by one pixel high. For example, the following code lets users of screen readers jump to the main content of the page without needing to go through the content navigation links on the page; however, the image itself is invisible to other users and so does not affect the page's layout or appearance.

```
<a href="#main">
    <img src="spacer.gif" height="1" width="1" alt="Skip to main
content" />
</a>

...

<a name="main"> </a>
page content goes here …
```

One advantage to this approach is that a template can be easily written to add this code to each page of the website.

Timed Responses

For security reasons, the login pages of some websites automatically log users out after a period of inactivity, or if users are unable to log in quickly. Because disabilities may prevent some users from being able to complete a login procedure within the prescribed time limit, the Section 508 guidelines state that

§1194.22 (p) When a timed response is required, the user shall be alerted and given sufficient time to indicate that more time is required.

The guideline does not suggest a time interval. To satisfy Section 508, your page should notify users when a process is about to time out and prompt users whether additional time is needed before proceeding.

Providing a Text-Only Equivalent

If you cannot modify a page to match the previous accessibility guidelines, as a last resort you can create a text-only page:

§1194.22 (k)   **A text-only page, with equivalent information or functionality, shall be provided to make a Web site comply with the provisions of this part, when compliance cannot be accomplished in any other way. The content of the text-only pages shall be updated whenever the primary page changes.**

To satisfy this requirement, you should

- provide an easily accessible link to the text-only page.
- make sure that the text-only page satisfies the Section 508 guidelines.
- duplicate the essential content of the original page.
- update the alternate page when you update the original page.

By using the Section 508 guidelines, you can work toward making your website accessible to everyone, regardless of disabilities.

Understanding the Web Accessibility Initiative

In 1999, the World Wide Web Consortium (W3C) developed its own set of guidelines for web accessibility called the **Web Accessibility Initiative (WAI)**. The WAI covers many of the same points as the Section 508 rules, and expands on them to cover basic website design issues. The overall goal of the WAI is to facilitate the creation of websites that are accessible to all, and to encourage designers to implement HTML in a consistent way.

The WAI sets forth 14 guidelines for web designers. Within each guideline is a collection of checkpoints indicating how to apply the guideline to specific features of a website. Each checkpoint is also given a priority score that indicates how important the guideline is for proper web design:

- **Priority 1:** A web content developer **must** satisfy this checkpoint. Otherwise, one or more groups will find it impossible to access information in the document. Satisfying this checkpoint is a basic requirement for some groups to be able to use web documents.
- **Priority 2:** A web content developer **should** satisfy this checkpoint. Otherwise, one or more groups will find it difficult to access information in the document. Satisfying this checkpoint will remove significant barriers to accessing web documents.
- **Priority 3:** A web content developer **may** address this checkpoint. Otherwise, one or more groups will find it somewhat difficult to access information in the document. Satisfying this checkpoint will improve access to web documents.

The following table lists WAI guidelines with each checkpoint and its corresponding priority value. You can learn more about the WAI guidelines and how to implement them by going to the World Wide Web Consortium Web site at *www.w3.org*.

WAI Guidelines	Priority
1. Provide equivalent alternatives to auditory and visual content	
1.1 Provide a text equivalent for every nontext element (e.g., via `alt`, `longdesc`, or in element content). *This includes:* images, graphical representations of text (including symbols), image map regions, animations (e.g., animated GIFs), applets and programmatic objects, ascii art, frames, scripts, images used as list bullets, spacers, graphical buttons, sounds (played with or without user interaction), stand-alone audio files, audio tracks of video, and video.	1
1.2 Provide redundant text links for each active region of a server-side image map.	1
1.3 Until user agents can automatically read aloud the text equivalent of a visual track, provide an auditory description of the important information of the visual track of a multimedia presentation.	1
1.4 For any time-based multimedia presentation (e.g., a movie or animation), synchronize equivalent alternatives (e.g., captions or auditory descriptions of the visual track) with the presentation.	1
1.5 Until user agents render text equivalents for client-side image map links, provide redundant text links for each active region of a client-side image map.	3
2. Don't rely on color alone	
2.1 Ensure that all information conveyed with color is also available without color, for example from context or markup.	1
2.2 Ensure that foreground and background color combinations provide sufficient contrast when viewed by someone having color deficits or when viewed on a black and white screen. [Priority 2 for images, Priority 3 for text].	2
3. Use markup and style sheets and do so properly	
3.1 When an appropriate markup language exists, use markup rather than images to convey information.	2
3.2 Create documents that validate to published formal grammars.	2
3.3 Use style sheets to control layout and presentation.	2
3.4 Use relative rather than absolute units in markup language attribute values and style sheet property values.	2
3.5 Use header elements to convey document structure and use them according to specification.	2
3.6 Mark up lists and list items properly.	2
3.7 Mark up quotations. Do not use quotation markup for formatting effects such as indentation.	2
4. Clarify natural language usage	
4.1 Clearly identify changes in the natural language of a document's text and any text equivalents (e.g., captions).	1
4.2 Specify the expansion of each abbreviation or acronym in a document where it first occurs.	3
4.3 Identify the primary natural language of a document.	3
5. Create tables that transform gracefully	
5.1 For data tables, identify row and column headers.	1
5.2 For data tables that have two or more logical levels of row or column headers, use markup to associate data cells and header cells.	1
5.3 Do not use a table for layout unless the table makes sense when linearized. If a table does not make sense, provide an alternative equivalent (which may be a linearized version).	2
5.4 If a table is used for layout, do not use any structural markup for the purpose of visual formatting.	2

WAI Guidelines	Priority
5.5 Provide summaries for tables.	3
5.6 Provide abbreviations for header labels.	3
6. Ensure that pages featuring new technologies transform gracefully	
6.1 Organize documents so they may be read without style sheets. For example, when an HTML document is rendered without associated style sheets, it must still be possible to read the document.	1
6.2 Ensure that equivalents for dynamic content are updated when the dynamic content changes.	1
6.3 Ensure that pages are usable when scripts, applets, or other programmatic objects are turned off or not supported. If this is not possible, then provide equivalent information on an alternative accessible page.	1
6.4 For scripts and applets, ensure that event handlers are input device-independent.	2
6.5 Ensure that dynamic content is accessible or provide an alternative presentation or page.	2
7. Ensure user control of time-sensitive content changes	
7.1 Until user agents allow users to control flickering, avoid causing the screen to flicker.	1
7.2 Until user agents allow users to control blinking, avoid causing content to blink (i.e., change presentation at a regular rate, such as turning on and off).	2
7.3 Until user agents allow users to freeze moving content, avoid movement in pages.	2
7.4 Until user agents provide the ability to stop the refresh, do not create periodically auto-refreshing pages.	2
7.5 Until user agents provide the ability to stop auto-redirect, do not use markup to redirect pages automatically. Instead, configure the server to perform redirects.	2
8. Ensure direct accessibility of embedded user interfaces	
8.1 Make programmatic elements such as scripts and applets directly accessible or compatible with assistive technologies [Priority 1 if functionality is important and not presented elsewhere, otherwise Priority 2.]	2
9. Design for device-independence	
9.1 Provide client-side image maps instead of server-side image maps except where the regions cannot be defined with an available geometric shape.	1
9.2 Ensure that any element with its own interface can be operated in a device-independent manner.	2
9.3 For scripts, specify logical event handlers rather than device-dependent event handlers.	2
9.4 Create a logical tab order through links, form controls, and objects.	3
9.5 Provide keyboard shortcuts to important links (including those in client-side image maps), form controls, and groups of form controls.	3
10. Use interim solutions	
10.1 Until user agents allow users to turn off spawned windows, do not cause pop-ups or other windows to appear and do not change the current window without informing the user.	2
10.2 Until user agents support explicit associations between labels and form controls, ensure that labels are properly positioned for all form controls with implicitly associated labels.	2
10.3 Until user agents (including assistive technologies) render side-by-side text correctly, provide a linear text alternative (on the current page or some other) for *all* tables that lay out text in parallel, word-wrapped columns.	3
10.4 Until user agents handle empty controls correctly, include default, place-holding characters in edit boxes and text areas.	3
10.5 Until user agents (including assistive technologies) render adjacent links distinctly, include nonlink, printable characters (surrounded by spaces) between adjacent links.	3

WAI Guidelines	Priority
11. Use W3C technologies and guidelines	
11.1 Use W3C technologies when they are available and appropriate for a task and use the latest versions when supported.	2
11.2 Avoid deprecated features of W3C technologies.	2
11.3 Provide information so that users may receive documents according to their preferences (e.g., language, content type, etc.)	3
11.4 If, after best efforts, you cannot create an accessible page, provide a link to an alternative page that uses W3C technologies, is accessible, has equivalent information (or functionality), and is updated as often as the inaccessible (original) page.	1
12. Provide context and orientation information	
12.1 Title each frame to facilitate frame identification and navigation.	1
12.2 Describe the purpose of frames and how frames relate to each other if this is not obvious from frame titles alone.	2
12.3 Divide large blocks of information into more manageable groups where natural and appropriate.	2
12.4 Associate labels explicitly with their controls.	2
13. Provide clear navigation mechanisms	
13.1 Clearly identify the target of each link.	2
13.2 Provide metadata to add semantic information to pages and sites.	2
13.3 Provide information about the general layout of a site (e.g., a site map or table of contents).	2
13.4 Use navigation mechanisms in a consistent manner.	2
13.5 Provide navigation bars to highlight and give access to the navigation mechanism.	3
13.6 Group related links, identify the group (for user agents), and, until user agents do so, provide a way to bypass the group.	3
13.7 If search functions are provided, enable different types of searches for different skill levels and preferences.	3
13.8 Place distinguishing information at the beginning of headings, paragraphs, lists, etc.	3
13.9 Provide information about document collections (i.e., documents comprising multiple pages).	3
13.10 Provide a means to skip over multiline ASCII art.	3
14. Ensure that documents are clear and simple	
14.1 Use the clearest and simplest language appropriate for a site's content.	1
14.2 Supplement text with graphic or auditory presentations where they will facilitate comprehension of the page.	3
14.3 Create a style of presentation that is consistent across pages.	3

Checking Your Web Site for Accessibility

As you develop your website, you should periodically check it for accessibility. In addition to reviewing the Section 508 and WAI guidelines, you can do several things to verify that your site is accessible to everyone:

- Set up your browser to suppress the display of images. Does each page still convey all of the necessary information?
- Set your browser to display pages in extra large fonts and with a different color scheme. Are your pages still readable under these conditions?
- Try to navigate your pages using only your keyboard. Can you access all of the links and form elements?
- Open your page in a screen reader or other nonvisual browser. (The W3C website contains links to several alternative browsers that you can download as freeware or on a short-term trial basis in order to evaluate your site.)
- Use tools that test your site for accessibility. (The WAI pages at the W3C website contain links to a wide variety of tools that report on how well your site complies with the WAI and Section 508 guidelines.)

Following the accessibility guidelines laid out by Section 508 and the WAI will result in a website that is not only more accessible to a wider audience, but whose design is also cleaner, easier to work with, and easier to maintain.

Designing for the Web

Before you begin creating links between your website pages, it's worthwhile to use a technique known as storyboarding to map out exactly how you want the pages to relate to each other. A **storyboard** is a diagram of a website's structure, showing all the pages in the site and indicating how they are linked together. Because websites use a variety of structures, it's important to storyboard your website before you start creating your pages. This helps you determine which structure works best for the type of information your site contains. A well-designed structure ensures that users will be able to navigate the site without getting lost or missing important information.

Every website should begin with a single home page that acts as a focal point for the website. It is usually the first page that users see. From that home page, you add links to other pages in the site, defining the site's overall structure. The websites you commonly encounter as you navigate the web employ several different web structures. You'll examine some of these structures to help you decide how to design your own sites.

Linear Structures

If you wanted to create an online version of a famous play, like Shakespeare's *Hamlet*, one method would be to link the individual scenes of the play in a long chain. Figure E-1 shows the storyboard for this **linear structure**, in which each page is linked with the pages that follow and precede it. Readers navigate this structure by moving forward and backward through the pages, much as they might move forward and backward through the pages of a book.

STARTING DATA FILES

There are no starting Data Files needed for this appendix.

Figure E-1	A linear structure

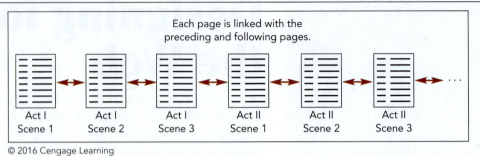

© 2016 Cengage Learning

Linear structures work for websites that are small in size and have a clearly defined order of pages. However, they can be difficult to work with as the chain of pages increases in length. An additional problem is that in a linear structure, you move farther and farther away from the home page as you progress through the site. Because home pages often contain important general information about a site and its author, this is usually not the best design technique.

You can modify this structure to make it easier for users to return immediately to the home page or other main pages. Figure E-2 shows this online play with an **augmented linear structure**, in which each page contains an additional link back to the opening page of each act.

Figure E-2	An augmented linear structure

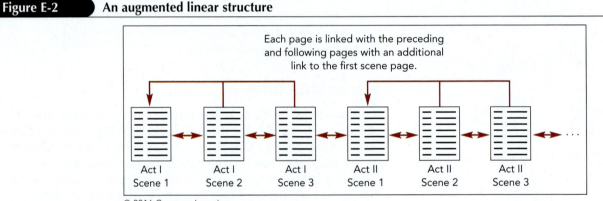

© 2016 Cengage Learning

Hierarchical Structures

Another popular structure is the **hierarchical structure**, in which the home page links to pages dedicated to specific topics. Those pages, in turn, can be linked to even more specific topics. A hierarchical structure allows users to easily move from general to specific and back again. In the case of the online play, you could link an introductory page containing general information about the play to pages that describe each of the play's acts, and within each act you could include links to individual scenes. See Figure E-3.

Figure E-3   **A hierarchical structure**

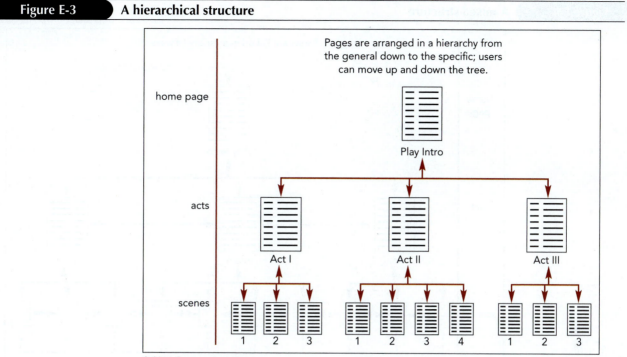

© 2016 Cengage Learning

Mixed Structures

Within this structure, a user could move quickly to a specific scene within the play, bypassing the need to move through each scene that precedes it.

With larger and more complex websites, you often need to use a combination of structures. Figure E-4 shows the online play using a mixture of hierarchical and linear structures. The overall form is hierarchical, as users can move from a general introduction down to individual scenes; however, users can also move through the site in a linear fashion, going from act to act and scene to scene. Finally, each individual scene contains a link to the home page, allowing users to jump to the top of the hierarchy without moving through the different levels.

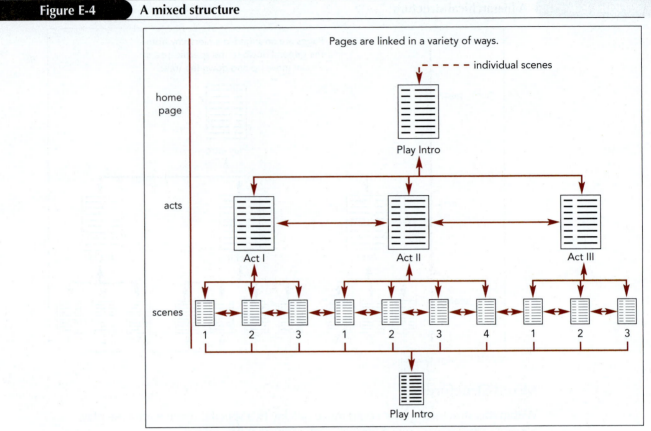

© 2016 Cengage Learning

As these examples show, a little foresight can go a long way toward making your website easier to use. Also keep in mind that search results from a web search engine such as Google or Yahoo! can point users to any page in your website—not just your home page—so users will need to be able to quickly understand what your site contains and how to navigate it. At a minimum, each page should contain a link to the site's home page or to the relevant main topic page. In some cases, you might want to supply your users with a **site index**, which is a page containing an outline of the entire site and its contents. Unstructured websites can be difficult and frustrating to use. Consider the storyboard of the site displayed in Figure E-5.

Figure E-5   **Website with no coherent structure**

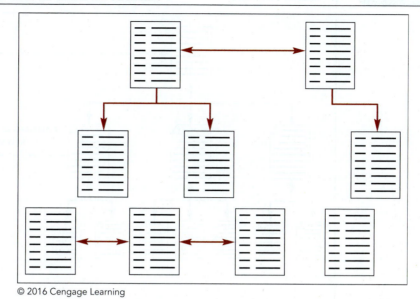

© 2016 Cengage Learning

This confusing structure makes it difficult for users to grasp the site's contents and scope. The user might not even be aware of the presence of some pages because there are no connecting links, and some of the links point in only one direction. The web is a competitive place; studies have shown that users who don't see how to get what they want within the first few seconds often leave a website. How long would a user spend on a site like the one shown in Figure E-5?

Protected Structures

Sections of most commercial websites are often off-limits except to subscribers and registered customers. Storyboarding a protected structure is particularly important to ensure that no unauthorized access to the protected area is allowed in the site design. As shown in Figure E-6, these sites have a password-protected web page that users must go through to get to the off-limits areas.

Figure E-6   **A protected structure**

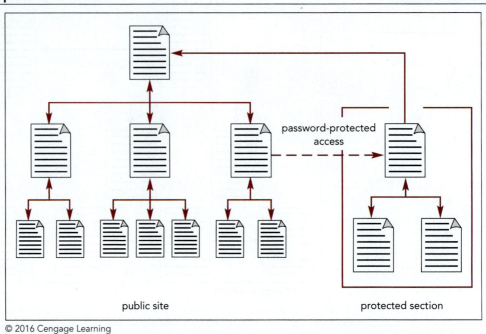

password-protected
access

public site

protected section

© 2016 Cengage Learning

The same website design principles apply to the protected section as the regular, open section of the site. As always, you want to create and maintain detailed storyboards to improve your site's performance and accessibility to all users.

GLOSSARY

`!important` A CSS keyword that forces a particular style to override the default style sheet cascade. HTML 95

`@charset` A rule defining the character encoding used in a style sheet. HTML 84

`@font-face` A rule that defines a web font. HTML 106

`@import` A rule used to import a style sheet file into the current style sheet. HTML 96

`@page` A rule that defines the size and margins of the printed page. HTML 400

`<a>` A tag that marks a hypertext link to an external resource. HTML 46

`<body>` A tag that marks the document body. HTML 2

`<cite>` A tag that marks a citation. HTML 22

`<em>` A tag that marks emphasized text. HTML 22

`<h1>` A tag that marks a major heading. HTML 22

`<head>` A tag that marks the document head within an HTML file. HTML 2

`<html>` A tag that marks the beginning of the HTML document. HTML 2

`<img>` A tag that marks an image using the file specified in the `src` attribute. HTML 22

`<li>` A tag that marks a list item. HTML 46

`<meta>` A tag that marks metadata containing information about the document. HTML 2

`<nav>` A tag that marks a list of hypertext links used for navigation. HTML 46

`<p>` A tag that marks a document paragraph. HTML 22

`<strong>` A tag that marks text of major importance or seriousness. HTML 22

`<title>` A tag that marks the page title, which appears in the browser title bar or browser tab. HTML 2

`<ul>` A tag that marks an unordered list. HTML 46

3D transformation A transformation that involves three spatial axes. HTML 316

A

Absolute path A folder path that starts from the root folder and processes down the entire folder structure. HTML 61

Absolute positioning A layout technique that places an element at specified coordinates within its container element. HTML 224

Absolute unit Units that are fixed in size regardless of the output devices. HTML 121

Accessible Rich Internet Application (ARIA) An HTML standard that assists screen readers in interpreting web page content. HTML 44

`active` A pseudo-class that selects actively-clicked links. HTML 132

Adaptive technology Technology that enables people with disabilities to use the web. HTML D2

`after` A pseudo-element that selects page space directly after the element. HTML 132

American Standard Code for Information Interchange. *See* ASCII (American Standard Code for Information Interchange)

ARIA. *See* Accessible Rich Internet Application (ARIA)

ASCII (American Standard Code for Information Interchange) The character set used for the English alphabet. HTML 33

Assistive technology Technology that enables people with disabilities to use the web. HTML D2

Attribute minimization Element attributes that do not require an attribute value. HTML 11

Augmented linear structure A linear structure in which each page contains an additional link to the opening page of the structure. HTML E2

B

`background` A property that defines all background options, including the use of multiple backgrounds. HTML 258

`background-color` A property that sets the background color. HTML 84

`background-image` A property that applies an image file to the element background. HTML 258

`before` A pseudo-element that selects page space directly before the element. HTML 132

Bitmap image An image format in which the image is comprised of pixels that can be marked with different colors. HTML 264

Border The part of the box model that surrounds the padding space. HTML 139

`border` A property that adds a border around all sides of an element. HTML 258

Border box model A layout model in which the width property refers to the width of the element's content, padding, and border spaces. HTML 191

`border-image` A property that defines an image file to create a graphic border. HTML 258

`border-left` A property that adds a border to the left edge of an element. HTML 258

`border-radius` A property that creates rounded corners with a specified radius. HTML 258

`border-right` A property that adds a border to the right edge of an element. HTML 258

Box model A layout model in which element content is surrounded by padding, border, and margin spaces. HTML 139

`box-shadow` A property that adds a drop shadow to a block element. HTML 286

Browser extension An extension to CSS supported by a specific browser. HTML 90

Browser style A style built into the web browser itself. HTML 87

C

Cascading Style Sheets (CSS) A style sheet language supported by the W3C and used in web page design. HTML 32

Character encoding The process by which the computer converts text into a sequence of bytes and then converts those bytes back into characters. HTML 17

Character entity reference An HTML string that inserts a character based on a defined name. HTML 22

Character set A collection of characters and symbols. HTML 33

Child element An element contained within a parent element. HTML 108

`clear` A property that displays an element only when the left, right, or both floated objects have been cleared. HTML 170

Client A device that receives network information or services. HTML 4

Client-server network A network in which clients access information provided by one or more servers. HTML 4

Client-side image map An image map that is defined within the web page and handled entirely by the web browser. HTML 324

Closing tag The tag that marks the end of the element content. HTML 2

color A property that sets the text color. HTML 84

Color gradient A background in which one color gradually blends into another color. HTML 296

Color value A numeric expression that defines a color. HTML 98

color-stop A parameter of a color gradient that defines the extent of the color. HTML 286

Conditional comment An Internet Explorer extension that encloses content that should only be run by particular versions of Internet Explorer. HTML 20

Container collapse A layout challenge that occurs when an element contains only floated content and thus collapses in height. HTML 195

content A property that inserts content into a page element. HTML 132

Content box model A layout model in which the width property only refers to the width of the element content. HTML 191

content-box A keyword that specifies the background extends only over the element content. HTML 258

Contextual selector A selector that specifies the context under which a particular page element is matched. HTML 108

cover A keyword that specifies that the background image should completely cover the background. HTML 258

Cross axis The flexbox axis that is perpendicular to the main axis. HTML 374

CSS. *See* Cascading Style Sheets (CSS)

CSS at-rule A rule that directs how the browser should interpret and parse the CSS code. HTML 96

CSS pixel A pixel that is the fundamental unit in CSS measurements. HTML 355

CSS3 The third, and most current version, of CSS. HTML 86

Cursive A typeface that mimics handwriting with highly stylized elements and flourishes. HTML 116

D

Deprecated The features and code from earlier HTML versions that have been phased out and are either no longer supported or developed. HTML 6

Descendant element An element that descends from a parent element within the document hierarchy. HTML 108

Description list A list of terms and matching descriptions. HTML 51

Device pixel A pixel that refers to the actual physical pixel on a screen. HTML 355

Device-pixel ratio A measure of the number of device pixels matched to a single CSS pixel. HTML 355

display A property that defines how an element should be laid out. HTML 170

Document body The part of an HTML file containing all of the content that will display in the web page. HTML 2

Document head The part of an HTML file containing information about the document. HTML 2

Document type declaration A processing instruction indicating the markup language used in the document. HTML 2

Domain name The server name portion of a URL. HTML 65

Drop cap A design element in which the initial letter in a body of text drops down into the text body. HTML 218

Dynamic pseudo-class A pseudo-class based on the actions of the user within the element. HTML 148

E

Elastic layout A layout in which all measurements are expressed in em units and based on the default font size. HTML 177

Element attribute The part of an element that provides information to the browser about the purpose of the element or how the element should be handled by the browser. HTML 11

Element tag The fundamental building block of an HTML file, used to mark every document element. HTML 9

Em unit A relative unit of length that expresses a size relative to the font size of the containing element. HTML 106

E-mail harvester An automated program that scans web pages for e-mail addresses. HTML 67

Embedded content Content that is imported from another resource, often nontextual. HTML 36

Embedded element An element containing embedded content such as graphic images, audio soundtracks, video clips, or interactive games. HTML 36

Embedded style A style added to the head of an HTML file. HTML 87

Empty element An element that is either nontextual or contains directives to the browser about how the page should be treated. HTML 9

Ending tag The tag that marks the end of the element content. HTML 9

Extension The top level of a URL, indicating the general audience supported by the web server. HTML 65

External style A style created by the page author and placed into a CSS file and linked to the page. HTML 87

F

Fantasy A highly ornamental typeface used for page decoration. HTML 116

filter A property used to modify an object's color, brightness, contrast, or general purpose. HTML 310

first-of-type A pseudo-class that selects the first element type of the parent element. HTML 132

Fixed grid A grid layout in which the widths of the columns and margins are specified in pixels with fixed positions. HTML 203

Fixed layout A layout in which the size of the page and the page elements are fixed, usually using pixels as the unit of measure. HTML 176

flex A property that defines the size of the flex items and how they will grow or shrink in response to the changing size of the flexbox. HTML 372

flex-basis A property that provides the basis or initial size of the item prior to flexing. HTML 372

flexbox A box that contains items whose sizes automatically expand or contract to match the dimensions of the box. HTML 372

flex-flow A property that defines the orientation of the flexbox and whether items can wrap to a new line. HTML 372

flex-grow A property that specifies how fast the item grows above its basis size relative to other items in the flex box. HTML 372

flex-shrink A property that specifies how fast the item shrinks below its basis size relative to other items in the flex box. HTML 372

float A property that takes an object out of normal document flow and floats it on the left or right margin of its container element. HTML 170

Floating A design technique in which an element is taken out of its default document position and placed along the left or right edge of its parent element. HTML 183

Fluid grid A grid layout in which the widths of the columns and margins are specified in percentages. HTML 203

Fluid layout A layout in which the size of the page elements are set using percentages. HTML 177

Font Definition of the style and appearance of each character in an alphabet. HTML 115

Font stack A list of fonts defined in the font-family property. HTML 115

`font-family` A property that defines a font stack. HTML 106

`font-size` A property that sets the text size. HTML 106

`fr unit` A grid unit that represents a fraction of the available space left on the grid after all other rows and columns have attained their maximum allowable size. HTML 219

Framework A software package that provides a library of tools to design a website. HTML 204

G

Generic font A general description of a font face. HTML 115

GIF. *See* GIF (Graphic Interchange Format)

GIF (Graphic Interchange Format) The oldest bitmap image format, limited to 256 colors, but that also supports transparent colors and animated images. HTML 264

Graphic interchange format. *See* GIF (Graphic Interchange Format)

Grid cell A cell at the intersection of a grid row and grid column. HTML 220

Grid column A column floated within the rows of a grid row. HTML 201

Grid layout A layout that arranges the page within grid rows with grid columns floated inside those rows. HTML 201

Grid row A row found within a grid layout. HTML 201

Grouping element An element that organizes similar content into a distinct group, much like a paragraph groups sentences that share a common theme. HTML 26

H

Hanging indent A layout in which the first line extends to the left of the block. HTML 126

Hexadecimal number A number expressed in the base 16 numbering system. HTML 99

Hierarchical structure A website structure in which the home page links to pages dedicated to specific topics, which are linked to even more specific topics. HTML E2

Host Any network device that is capable of sending and/or receiving data electronically. HTML 4

Hotspot A region within an image that can be linked to a specific URL. HTML 324

`hover` A pseudo-class that selects links that are being hovered over. HTML 132

HSL color value Color defined by its hue, saturation, and lightness values. HTML 84

HTML5 The latest version of HTML, compatible with earlier HTML releases. HTML 5

HTML5 Shiv A script that provides support for HTML5 in older browsers. HTML 39

HTML. *See* HTML (Hypertext Markup Language)

HTML (Hypertext Markup Language) A markup language that supports the tagging of distinct document elements and connecting documents through hypertext links. HTML 5

HTML 4.0 The fourth version of HTML, released in 1999, that provided support for multimedia, online commerce, and interactive scripts. HTML 5

HTML comment A descriptive note added to an HTML file that does not get rendered by a user agent. HTML 2

HTTP. *See* Hypertext Transfer Protocol (HTTP)

Hue The tint of a color, represented by a direction on the color wheel. HTML 99

Hyperlink A link within a hypertext document that can be activated to access a data source. HTML 4

Hypertext A method of organizing information in which data sources are interconnected through a series of hyperlinks that users activate to jump from one data source to another. HTML 4

Hypertext Markup Language. *See* HTML (Hypertext Markup Language)

Hypertext Transfer Protocol (HTTP) The protocol used by devices on the web. HTML 64

I

IANA. *See* Internet Assigned Numbers Authority (IANA)

IDE. *See* IDE (Integrated Development Environment)

IDE (Integrated Development Environment) A software package providing comprehensive coverage of all phases of the HTML development process. HTML 7

Image map Information that specifies the location and URLs associated within each hotspot within an image. HTML 324

Inline element An element in which the content is placed in line with surrounding page content rather than starting on a new line. HTML 29

Inline image An image that is placed, like text-level elements, in line with the surrounding content. HTML 37

Inline style A style added as attributes of an HTML element. HTML 87

`inset` A keyword that places a box shadow inside the element. HTML 286

Interactive element An element that allows for interaction between the user and the embedded object. *Also called* embedded element. HTML 36

Internet A wide area network incorporating an almost uncountable number of networks and hosts across the world. HTML 4

Internet Assigned Numbers Authority (IANA) The registration authority used to register the top levels of every domain name. HTML 65

ISO 8859-1 An extended version of the ASCII character set. HTML 33

J

Joint photographic experts group. *See* JPG (Joint Photographic Experts Group)

JPEG. *See* JPG (Joint Photographic Experts Group)

JPEG (Joint Photographic Experts Group) A bitmap image format that supports a palette of over 16 million colors, as well as file compression. HTML 264

K

Kerning A measure of the space between characters. HTML 106

L

LAN. *See* Local area network (LAN)

`last-of-type` A pseudo-class that selects the last element type of the parent element. HTML 132

Latin-1 An extended version of the ASCII character set. HTML 33

Layout viewport The part of the mobile layout containing the entire page content HTML 352

Leading A measure of the amount of space between lines of text, set using the line-height property. HTML 125

left A property that defines the left coordinates of an element placed using relative, absolute, or fixed positioning. HTML 224

letter-spacing A property that sets the space between letters. HTML 106

Lightness The brightness of a chosen color, ranging from 0% to 100%. HTML 99

Linear structure A website structure in which each page is linked with the pages that follow it and precede it. HTML E1

linear-gradient A property that creates a color gradient proceeding along a straight line. HTML 286

line-height A property that sets the height of a line. HTML 106

link A pseudo-class that selects unvisited links. HTML 132

List marker A symbol displayed alongside a list item. HTML 134

list-style-image A property that inserts an image for the list marker. HTML 132

list-style-type A property that defines the appearance of the list marker. HTML 132

Local area network (LAN) A network confined to a small geographic area, such as within a building or department. HTML 4

Lorem ipsum Nonsensical improper Latin commonly used in page design as filler text. HTML 216

M

mailto A communication scheme used to provide the URL for an e-mail link. HTML 46

Main axis The central axis along which items within a flexbox are laid out. HTML 374

Margin area The page section that contains the space between the printed content and the edges of the page. HTML 405

Margin space The part of the box model that surrounds the element border, extending to the next element. HTML 139

margin-top A property that sets the margin space above the element. HTML 132

Markup-language A language that describes the content and structure of a document by tagging different document elements. HTML 5

max-width A property that defines the maximum width of an element HTML 170

Media query Code used to apply specified style rules to a device based on the device type and the device features. HTML 342

Metadata Content that describes the document or provides information about how the document should be processed by the browser. HTML 15

Minifying The process of removing unnecessary characters from HTML and CSS files in order to increase processing speed. HTML 398

min-width A property that defines the minimum width of an element HTML 170

Mobile device emulator A software program that duplicates the look and feel of a mobile device. HTML 359

Mobile first A design principle by which the overall page design starts with base styles that apply to all devices followed by style rules specific to mobile devices. HTML 350

Modernizr A script that provides support for HTML5 in older browsers. HTML 39

Module A component of CSS3 that focuses on a particular design topic. HTML 86

Monospace A typeface in which each character has the same width, often used to display programming code. HTML 116

N

Navicon A symbol, usually represented as three horizontal lines, used to hide menu items in mobile devices. HTML 394

Navigation list An unordered list of hypertext links placed within the nav element. HTML 55

Nested element An element contained within another element. HTML 9

Nested list A list that is placed inside another list. HTML 50

Network A structure in which information and services are shared among devices known as nodes or hosts. HTML 4

Node A network location that can access and share information and services. HTML 4

no-repeat A keyword that specifies that no tiling should be done with the background image. HTML 258

nth-of-type A pseudo-class that selects the nth element type of the parent element. HTML 132

Numeric character reference An HTML string that inserts a character based on its code value. HTML 22

O

One-sided element tag A tag used for empty elements, containing no closing tag. HTML 9

Opacity A measure of the solidness of a color, ranging from 0 to 1. HTML 100

opacity A property that makes an object semi-transparent. HTML 286

Opening tag The tag that marks the start of the element content. HTML 2

Ordered list A list that is used for items that follow some defined sequential order. HTML 48

orphans A property that limits the number of lines stranded at the bottom of a page. HTML 400

outline A property that draws a line around the selected elements. HTML 200

overflow A property that determines how the browser should handle content that exceeds the space allotted to the element. HTML 224

P

Padding space The part of the box model that extends from the element content to the element border. HTML 139

padding-box A keyword that specifies the background extends through the padding space. HTML 258

Page area The page section that contains the content of the document. HTML 405

Page box The layout definition of the printed page. HTML 405

page-break-before A property that inserts page breaks before elements. HTML 400

page-break-inside A property that prohibits page breaks within an element. HTML 400

Parent element An element that contains one or more child elements. HTML 108

perspective A property and a function used in 3D transformations to measure how rapidly objects appear to recede or approach the viewer. HTML 310

Pixel A single dot on the output device. HTML 122

PNG. *See* PNG (Portable Network Graphic)

PNG (Portable Network Graphic) A bitmap image format designed to replace the GIF format with a palette of a million colors. HTML 264

Portable network graphic. *See* PNG (Portable Network Graphic)

Presentational attribute An attribute that describes how page content should be rendered by the browser. HTML 36

Presentational element An element that describes how page content should be rendered by the browser. HTML 36

Print style sheet A style sheet that formats the printed version of the web document. HTML 402

Progressive enhancement A CSS technique in which styles that conform to older standards are entered first with newer standards placed last. HTML 104

Protocol A set of rules defining how information is passed between two network devices. HTML 64

Pseudo-class A classification of an element based on its current status, position, or use in the document. HTML 145

Pseudo-element An object that exists only in the rendered page. HTML 151

Q

Quirks mode An operating mode in which the browser renders the web page based on styles and practices from the 1990s and early 2000s. HTML 9

quotes A property that defines characters for quotation marks. HTML 132

R

Radial gradient A color gradient proceeding outward from a central point in a series of concentric circles or ellipses. HTML 301

radial-gradient A property that creates a color gradient proceeding outward from a central point. HTML 286

Relative path A folder path expressed relative to the location of the current document. HTML 61

Relative positioning A layout technique that shifts an element from its default position in the document flow. HTML 224

Relative unit A unit that is expressed relative to the size of other objects within the web page or relative to the display properties of the device itself. HTML 121

rem. *See* Root em unit

Reset style sheet A base style sheet that supersedes the browser's default styles, providing a consisting starting point for page design. HTML 172

Responsive design A design principle in which the layout and design of the page changes in response to the device that is rendering the page. HTML 177

RGB color value Color defined by its red, green, and blue components. HTML 84

RGB triplet A color value indicating the red, green, and blue values of a color. HTML 98

Rollover effect An effect in which the page appearance changes as the user hovers the mouse pointer over a hypertext link. HTML 59

Root em unit A relative unit of length that expresses a size relative to the font size of the root element. HTML 122

Root folder The folder at the top of the folder hierarchy, containing all other folders. HTML 60

S

Sans-serif A typeface without any serif ornamentation. HTML 116

Saturation The intensity of a chosen color, ranging from 0% to 100%. HTML 99

Scalable The principle by which text is resized using relative units. HTML 122

Scalable vector image. *See* SVG (Scalable Vector Image)

Script An external program that is run within the browser. HTML 39

Section 508 A section from the 1973 Rehabilitation Act that requires any electronic information to be accessible to people with disabilities. HTML D2

Sectioning element An element used to define major topical areas in the document. HTML 24

Selector CSS code that defines what element or elements are affected by the style rule. HTML 84

Selector pattern A selector that matches only those elements that correspond to the specified pattern. HTML 108

Semantic element An element in which the element name describes the purpose of the element and the type of content it contains. HTML 24

Serif A typeface in which a small ornamentation appears at the tail end of each character. HTML 116

Server A host that provides information or a service to other devices on the network. HTML 4

Server-side image map An image map that relies on a program running on the web server to create and manage the map. HTML 324

Sibling selector A selector that matches elements based on the elements that are adjacent to them in the document hierarchy. HTML 109

Site index A page containing an outline of the entire website structure and its contents. HTML E4

Spam Unsolicited e-mail sent to large numbers of people. HTML 67

Specific font A font that is identified by name. HTML 115

Standards mode An operating mode in which the browser renders the web page in line with the most current HTML specifications. HTML 9

Starting tag The tag that marks the start of the element content. HTML 9

Static positioning A layout technique that places an element where it would have fallen naturally within the flow of the document. HTML 226

Storyboard A diagram of a website's structure, showing all of the pages in the site and how they are linked together. HTML E1

Structural pseudo-class A pseudo-class based on the element's location within the structure of the HTML document. HTML 145

Style CSS code that specifies what aspect of the selector to modify. HTML 84

Style comment Text that provides information about the style sheet. HTML 84

Style inheritance The principle by which style properties are passed from a parent element to its children. HTML 93

Style rule CSS code that sets the display properties of a page element. HTML 84

Style sheet A set of rules defining how page elements are displayed. HTML 32

SVG. *See* SVG (Scalable Vector Image)

SVG (Scalable Vector Image) An XML markup language that can be used to create vector images. HTML 258

Syntax The rules governing how a language should be used and interpreted. HTML 5

T

tel A communication scheme used to provide the URL for a telephone link. HTML 46

text-align A property that defines the horizontal alignment of the content of an element. HTML 106

Text-level element An element within a grouping element that contains strings of the characters or page content. HTML 29

text-shadow A property that adds a drop shadow to a text string. HTML 286

Tiling A process by which a background image is repeated, filling up the background space. HTML 265

top A property that defines the top coordinates of an element placed using relative, absolute, or fixed positioning. HTML 224

Tracking A measure of the amount of space between words, set using the word-spacing property. HTML 125

transform A property used to rotate, rescale, skew, or shift a page object. HTML 310

Typography The art of designing the appearance of characters and letters on a page. HTML 115

U

Unicode The largest character set supporting up to 65,536 symbols that can be used with any of the world's languages. HTML 33

Uniform Resource Locator (URL) A standard address format used to link to a variety of resource documents. HTML 57

Unordered list A list that is used for items that do not follow a defined sequential order. HTML 49

URL. *See* Uniform Resource Locator (URL)

User agent style A style built into the web browser itself. HTML 87

User-defined style A style defined by the user based on settings made in configuring the browser. HTML 87

UTF-8 The most common character encoding in present use. HTML 17

V

Validator A program that tests code to ensure that it contains no syntax errors. HTML 7

Vanishing point An effect of perspective in which parallel lines appear to converge to a point. HTML 317

Vector image An image format in which the lines and curves that comprise the image are based on mathematical functions. HTML 264

Vendor prefix The prefix added to a browser extension. HTML 90

Viewport meta A meta tag used to set the properties of the layout viewport. HTML 342

Viewport unit A relative unit of length that expresses a size relative to the width or height of the browser window. HTML 123

visited A pseudo-class that selects previously-visited links. HTML 132

Visual viewport The part of the mobile layout that displays the web page content that fits within a mobile screen. HTML 352

W

W3C. *See* World Wide Consortium (W3C)

WAN. *See* Wide area network (WAN)

Watermark A translucent graphic that is part of the page content and that displays a message that the content is copyrighted or in draft form or some other message directed toward the reader. HTML 267

Web browser A software program that retrieves and displays web pages. HTML 5

Web font A font in which the font definition is supplied to the browser in an external file. HTML 118

Web Hypertext Application Technology Working Group (WHATWG) A group formed in 2004 to develop HTML5 as a rival version to XHTML 2.0. HTML 5

Web page A document stored by a web server and accessed by a web browser. HTML 5

Web safe font A font that is displayed mostly the same way in all operating systems and on all devices. HTML 116

Web server A server that makes web pages accessible to the network. HTML 5

WHATWG. *See* Web Hypertext Application Technology Working Group (WHATWG)

White-space character An empty or blank character such as a space, tab, or line break. HTML 12

Wide area network (WAN) A network that covers a wide area, such as several buildings or cities. HTML 4

widows A property that limits the number of lines stranded at the top of a page. HTML 400

width A property that defines the width of an element. HTML 170

Wildcard selector A selector that matches all elements. HTML 109

World Wide Consortium (W3C) A group of web designers and programmers that set the standards or specifications for browser manufacturers to follow. HTML 5

World Wide Web (WWW) The totality of interconnected hypertext documents on the Internet. HTML 4

WWW. *See* World Wide Web (WWW)

X

XHTML. *See* XHTML (Extensible Hypertext Markup Language)

XHTML (Extensible Hypertext Markup Language) A version of HTML in which syntax standards are strictly enforced. HTML 5

INDEX